CASTRATION AND CULTURE IN THE MIDDLE AGES

CASTRATION AND CULTURE IN THE MIDDLE AGES

Edited by Larissa Tracy

D. S. Brewer

First published 2013
D. S. Brewer, Cambridge
Paperback edition 2019

ISBN 978 1 84384 351 1 hardback
ISBN 978 1 84384 524 9 paperback

D. S. Brewer is an imprint of Boydell & Brewer Ltd
PO Box 9, Woodbridge, Suffolk IP12 3DF, UK
and of Boydell & Brewer Inc.
668 Mt Hope Avenue, Rochester, NY 14620–2731, USA
website: www.boydellandbrewer.com

A CIP catalogue record for this book is available
from the British Library

Designed and Typeset by Tina Ranft, Woodbridge

Contents

List of Illustrations

List of Contributors

ANTHONY ADAMS is Assistant Professor of English at Colby College, specializing in medieval languages and literatures. He is completing his first book, which examines sacrifice and violence in Middle English literature. He has written on Old English and Carolingian poetry of war, medieval Latin, Thomas Malory, the Middle English Charlemagne romances, Norse sagas, Chaucer, and *Beowulf*, and published (with A.G. Rigg) the first complete English translation and commentary of the ninth-century epic Latin poem *Bella Parisiacae urbis* in the *Journal for Medieval Latin*.

ROLF H. BREMMER JR is Professor of English Philology and, by special appointment, Professor of Frisian at the University of Leiden, the Netherlands. He has published widely in both fields, most recently *An Introduction to Old Frisian: History, Grammar, Reader, Glossary* (2009) and, as co-editor with Kees Dekker, *Practice in Learning: The Transfer of Encyclopaedic Knowledge in the Early Middle Ages* (2010).

JED CHANDLER is in the final year of his PhD at Swansea University, researching gender identity in early romance literature, specifically the passing man, a female-bodied person who presents a male social identity. He is particularly interested in the interactions between the passing man and Merlin, and the antecedents of this episode in late ancient hagiographic literature. His other interests include the Celtic analogues of the Merlin legend and the medieval and contemporary associations of the grail legend with Glastonbury.

ROBERT L.A. CLARK is Associate Professor of French at Kansas State University. He has published broadly on medieval theater, gender issues, illuminated manuscripts, and opera. With Kathleen Ashley, he is co-editor of the volume *Medieval Conduct*.

JACK COLLINS currently lectures for the Department of Religion at the George Washington University in Washington, DC. He earned his PhD from the University of Virginia in 2011. His research interests include early Christian and Jewish apocalyptic literature, with an emphasis on traditions related to the biblical patriarch Enoch. He is currently adapting his dissertation, 'Worthless Mysteries: Forbidden Knowledge, Culture Heroes, and the Enochic Motif of Angelic Instruction', for publication.

CHARLENE M. ESKA is Assistant Professor in the English Department at Virginia Tech. Her research focuses on medieval law codes from the British

Isles, particularly Ireland. She is the author of *Cáin Lánamna: An Old Irish Tract on Marriage and Divorce Law* (2010) and articles dealing with issues in early Irish law, such as slavery, swine values, Sunday laws, and marriage. She is currently editing the medieval Irish legal texts *Recholl Breth*, *Di Thúaslucud Rudrad* and *Anfuigell*.

ELLEN LORRAINE FRIEDRICH is Associate Professor of Modern and Classical Languages at Valdosta State University in Valdosta, Georgia, USA, and Book Review Editor for Romance Literatures for the journal *Arthuriana*. She has published on Bel Acuel and an article on the Diex d'Amors (the God of Love), in the *Romans de la rose* by Guillaume de Lorris. She is also the author of book chapters on the scene at the fountain in the *Chevalier de la charrette* of Chrétien de Troyes, and on the fabliau *Les iiii souhais Saint Martin*. She is presently writing about Lancelot and Tristan in film.

JAY PAUL GATES is Assistant Professor at John Jay College of Criminal Justice-City University of New York. He earned his PhD from the University of Wisconsin-Madison in 2007. His areas of specialization are Anglo-Saxon and Old Norse-Icelandic literature and language and the effects of Anglo-Scandinavian cultural contact, especially as represented in legal rhetoric.

MARY E. LEECH is a Lecturer at the University of Cincinnati. Her work focuses on body metaphor as it is informed by the medieval understanding of medical science. She has published two book chapters, one in *Comic Provocations: Exposing the Corpus of Old French Fabliaux* (ed. Holly A. Crocker, 2006), and another in *The English Loathly Lady Tales: Boundaries, Traditions, Motifs* (ed. Elizabeth Passmore and Susan Carter, 2007). She also has an article on comedic violence in the inaugural issue of LATCH: *A Journal for the Study of the Literary Artifact in Theory, Culture, or History*. She is president of the Société Fableors, a professional society that encourages scholarship on the wide-ranging influences of the fabliaux tradition in literature.

KATHRYN REUSCH is a fourth-year DPhil student at the School of Archaeology, University of Oxford. She received her MSc in Palaeopathology at the University of Durham, in which she investigated through a literature review the social and physical effects of castration. She has presented several papers on castration and archaeology at conferences throughout the UK. Her main areas of interest include bioarchaeology, endocrinology, developmental processes, and funerary archaeology.

KARIN SELLBERG is a postdoctoral teaching fellow in English Literature and part-time lecturer in medical humanities for the medical school at the University of Edinburgh, where she is also Co-Director of the Scottish Universities' International Summer School. She has published extensively on the relationship to history and time in contemporary ideological academic movements, such as new historicism, cultural materialism, queer theory, and feminist theory and conceptions of the body in the work of William Shakespeare, Thomas Dekker, and Thomas Middleton.

SHAUN TOUGHER is Senior Lecturer in Ancient History in the Cardiff School of History, Archaeology and Religion at Cardiff University, where he is also co-director of the Centre for Late Antique Religion and Culture. He specialises in late Roman and Byzantine political and cultural history. His most recent publications include *Julian the Apostate* (2007) and *The Eunuch in Byzantine History and Society* (2008). He is currently completing a study of eunuchs in the Roman Empire.

LARISSA TRACY is Associate Professor of Medieval Literature at Longwood University. She is the author of *Torture and Brutality in Medieval Literature: Negotiations of National Identity* (2012) and *Women of the Gilte Legende: A Selection of Middle English Saints'* Lives (2003). She co-edited (with Jeff Massey), *Heads Will Roll: Decapitation in the Medieval and Early Modern Imagination* (2012). She has published articles on violence, comedy, hagiography, and *Sir Gawain and the Green Knight*. She also co-organizes an annual regional undergraduate research conference in medieval studies.

MARY A. VALANTE is Associate Professor of Medieval History at Appalachian State University. She is the author of *The Vikings in Ireland: Settlement, Trade and Urbanization* (2008), as well as articles on hagiography, charters, and the Vikings in Ireland.

LENA WÅNGGREN is a Research Fellow in English Literature at the University of Edinburgh, where she also teaches. While her main research concerns questions of gender in late nineteenth-century literature and culture, she also works on critical and feminist theory, and the history of medicine. She has published on gender transgression, critical pedagogy, and late nineteenth-century feminism.

Acknowledgements

There are many people to thank in a collection like this, and we are indebted to our families for putting up with us during this process. Special thanks go out to Kelly DeVries, Jeff Massey and Rikk Mulligan for their input and editorial comments on various stages of the project. I am grateful to Asa Simon Mittman, Valeria Finucci, David F. Johnson, Thomas D. Hill, and Bonnie Wheeler for their advice and suggestions, and to Charles Insley for planting the seed. My deepest gratitude goes to Boydell's editorial board and conscientious reader, and to Caroline Palmer for her encouragement and enthusiasm, and for not shying away from such a topic. We are indebted to Rohais Haughton, Anna Robinette and Annie Jackson for their diligence and hard work. Our thanks to *The Journal for the Study of the Literary Artifact in Theory, Culture, or History* for permission to reprint a revised version of Mary E. Leech's article 'The Castrating of the Shrew: The Performance of Masculinity and Masculine Identity in *La dame escolliee*' which appeared in Vol. 1 (2008). We also wish to thank J.C. Neidhardt and the Musée Testut Latarjet D'Anatomie et D'Histoire Naturelle Médicale, Lyon; the British Library, London; and the Museum Boijmans Van Beuningen, Rotterdam for permission to reproduce select images and for the use of rare materials. Reprinted by permission of the publishers and the Trustees of the Loeb Classical Library from STATIUS: VOLUME 1, SILVAE, Loeb Classical Library Volume 206, translated by D.R. Shackleton Bailey, pp. 217, 219, 221, 223, 225, Cambridge, Mass.: Harvard University Press, Copyright © 2003 by the President and Fellows of Harvard College. Loeb Classical Library ® is a registered trademark of the President and Fellows of Harvard College.

This volume would not have been possible without a sabbatical award from Longwood University (Fall 2011).

List of Abbreviations

AB	*Annála as Breifne*, ed. Éamonn De hÓir, *Breifne* 4.13 (1970).
AC	*Annála Connacht. The Annals of Connacht (AD 1224–1544)*, ed. and trans. A. Martin Freeman. Dublin: Dublin Institute for Advanced Studies, 1996.
ACl	*The Annals of Clonmacnoise, being Annals of Ireland from the Earliest Period to AD 1408 Translated into English AD 1627 by Conell Mageoghagan*, ed. Denis Murphy. Dublin: Royal Society of Antiquaries of Ireland, 1896, repr. Felinfach: Llanerch Publishers, 1993.
AFM	*Annals of the Four Masters*, *s.a.* 1247, ed. and trans. John O'Donovan. Dublin: Hodges, Smith, and Co., 1854.
AI	*The Annals of Inisfallen*, ed. and trans. Seán Mac Airt. Dublin: Dublin Institute for Advanced Studies, 1988.
AL	*Ancient Laws of Ireland*, ed. and trans. W. N. Hancock *et al.* Dublin: A Thom, 1865–1901.
ALC	*The Annals of Loch Cé*, ed. and trans. William M. Hennessy. London: Longman and Co., 1871.
AT	*The Annals of Tigernach*, ed. and trans. Whitley Stokes, repr. Felinfach: Llanerch Publishers, 1993.
AU	*Annala Uladh. The Annals of Ulster, otherwise Annala Senait, Annals of Senait: A Chronicle of Irish Affairs from AD 431 to AD 1540*, ed. and trans. W. M. Hennessy and B. Mac Carthy. Dublin: A. Thom, 1887–1901.
AU_2	*The Annals of Ulster (to AD 1131)*, ed. and trans. Seán Mac Airt and Gearóid Mac Niocaill. Dublin: Dublin Institute for Advanced Studies, 1983.
BnF	Bibliothèque nationale de France
CIH	*Corpus Iuris Hibernici*, ed. D. A. Binchy. Dublin: Dublin Institute for Advanced Studies, 1979.
CS	*Chronicum Scottorum: A Chronicle of Irish Affairs from the Earliest Times to AD 1135, with a Supplement Containing the Events from 1141–1150*, ed. and trans. William M. Hennessy, Rolls Series 46. London: Her Majesty's Stationery Office, 1866.
DB	*Domesday Book: A Complete Translation*, ed. Ann Williams and G. H. Martin. London: Penguin, 2002.
EETS, os	Early English Text Society, original series

FA	*Fragmentary Annals of Ireland*, ed. and trans. Joan Newlon Radner. Dublin: Dublin Institute for Advanced Studies, 1978.
GEIL	Fergus Kelly. *A Guide to Early Irish Law*. Early Irish Law Series 3. Dublin: Dublin Institute for Advanced Studies, 1988.
HC	Abelard, *Historia calamitatum*, in *The Letters of Abelard and Heloise*, trans. Betty Radice. London: Penguin Books, 1974
JEGP	*Journal of English and Germanic Philology*
Letter	Personal Letters, in *The Letters of Abelard and Heloise*. Trans. Betty Radice. London: Penguin
LgA	Jacobus de Voragine, *Legenda aurea. The Golden Legend: Readings on the Saints*, trans. William Granger Ryan, vols. 1 and 2. Princeton: Princeton University Press, 1993.
Misc. Ir.	*Miscellaneous Irish Annals (AD 1114–1437)*, ed. and trans. Séamus Ó hInnse. Dublin: Dublin Institute for Advanced Studies, 1947.
MGH SRG	*Monumenta Germaniae Historica Scriptores rerum Germanicarum* 55, ed. Georg Waitz. Hanover, 1884.
PMLA	Publication of the Modern Language Association
SEL	*The South English Legendary, Corpus Christi College Cambridge MS 145 and British Museum MS Harley 2277*, ed. Charlotte d'Evelyn and Anna J.Mill. vol. 1, EETS os 235. Oxford: Oxford University Press, 1956, rpt. 1967; and *The Early South-English Legendary or Lives of Saints, MS Laud 108 in the Bodleian Library*, ed. Carl Horstmann. EETS os 87. Oxford: Oxford University Press, 1887; reprinted 2000.

INTRODUCTION

A History of Calamities: The Culture of Castration

Larissa Tracy

The male body is a paradox – at once strong and resilient, yet fragile and vulnerable, arguably even more vulnerable than the female form which has its generative organs safely tucked up inside. Nations have been founded on the virility and power of the male body, but if that virility is lost, empires can be lost with it. Castration is therefore often a conversational taboo; references to it elicit a cringe, a grimace, a protective stance and yet it has been part of the bodily discourse as long as humans have communicated. In the modern age, castration (surgical or chemical)[1] is punitive, either a legal sentence for unspeakable crimes or a violent, illegitimate action. In an era bombarded by advertisements for Viagra, Cialis, and other 'male enhancement' products, the male genitalia (particularly the penis) are treated as if sacred. Gary Taylor's study, *Castration: An Abbreviated History of Western Manhood*, captures the essence of this dialogue in a foray into all facets of emasculation (including his own vasectomy) and its history from the dawn of time to Tori Amos. Taylor argues that castration calls into question

> the binary categories of human thought – the binaries of Augustine or Claudian or Freud, obviously, but also our own binaries, the binaries that

[1] Chemical castration, the administration of female hormones into the male body through injection with substances like the birth control drug Depo-Provera to dampen sexual urges, is a legal punishment for rape, child molestation, and other sex offenses in at least eight US States. It has been used in other parts of the world including the UK, Australia, Israel, and more recently Argentina and Russia. In 2011, Virginia State Senator Emmett Hanger (Republican) introduced legislation that would require the state to investigate the use of surgical castration to punish sex offenders as a cost-saving measure for state prisons. 'Va. Senator Seeks to Castrate Sex Offenders', *Associated Press*, Jan. 26, 2011, online at http://www.foxnews.com/politics/2011/01/26/va-senator-seeks-castrate-sex-offenders/ (accessed Dec. 9, 2011). Louisiana and Texas currently allow physical castration to be used, and Hanger has lobbied for the use of surgical castration in Virginia since 2006. 'Virginia Lawmaker Proposes Castration for Sex Offenders', Brian Gillie, *The Examiner*, Jan. 26, 2011, online at http://www.examiner.com/strange-news-in-national/virginia-lawmaker-proposes-castration-for-sex-offenders (accessed Dec. 9, 2011).

> organize postmodernist academic discourse. The eunuch confuses not only the categories of 'male' and 'female,' but the categories 'nature' and 'accident,' 'biology' and 'culture,' 'reality' and 'representation,' 'essentialism' and constructionism'.[2]

Modern responses to castration (or its threat) and all the incumbent implications are not so far removed from those of earlier people. Despite the current tendency to view the Middle Ages as a barbaric time beset with violence, in which torture and brutality abounded, medieval people were no more desensitized to physical cruelty than are their modern counterparts.[3] Just as today, for late antique, medieval, and early modern societies castration (like torture and brutality) was often the hallmark of savagery. It was reserved as a punishment for some of the worst offenders – traitors and rapists – and even then it was employed sparingly. Those who castrated others illegally were punished, in some cases by being castrated themselves. Male genitalia were highly valued – as attested by the numerous detailed injury tariffs that could be levied in the event of an unfortunate wounding. Men had to prove the virility of their members (occasionally in court, in front of witnesses) or be prohibited from marrying or entering into ecclesiastical orders. Castration, though sometimes considered more merciful than death, was a means of cutting off rivals or offenders from society – or later, as with the Italian *castrati*, of elevating young men to the heights of stardom and sexual allure. In short, castration meant many things to many societies, each of which placed a certain emphasis on genitalia and its effect on constructions of masculinity.

Recently, there have been specialized studies on castration itself, usually in reference to the position of eunuchs in a particular society. These generally offer localized examinations of castration within a specific context or sweeping

[2] Gary Taylor, *Castration: An Abbreviated History of Western Manhood* (New York and London: Routledge, 2002), p. 175.

[3] Johan Huizinga's image of medieval Europe as a bloody and vicious time, first written in 1919 and translated into English in 1924, is the foundation for many twentieth-century interpretations of the Middle Ages: Johan Huizinga, *The Waning of the Middle Ages* (London: Penguin Books, reprinted 1990). Barbara Tuchman's popular history solidified that view for another generation of readers: Barbara W. Tuchman, *A Distant Mirror: The Calamitous Fourteenth Century* (New York: Ballantine Books, 1978). In the last thirty years, several scholars, notably Edward Peters, have tried to dispel that image and view medieval violence within its historical context. Most recently: Daniel Baraz, *Medieval Cruelty: Changing Perceptions, Late Antiquity to the Early Modern Period* (Ithaca, NY: Cornell University Press, 2003); Mark D. Meyerson, Daniel Thiery, and Oren Falk, eds., *'A Great Effusion of Blood'? Interpreting Medieval Violence* (Toronto: University of Toronto Press, 2004); Albrecht Classen, ed., *Violence in Medieval Courtly Literature: A Casebook* (New York and London: Routledge, 2004); Robert Mills, *Suspended Animation: Pain, Pleasure, and Punishment in Medieval Culture* (London: Reaktion Books, 2005); John H. Langbein, *Torture and the Law of Proof: Europe and England in the Ancien Régime* (Chicago: University of Chicago Press, 2006); and Larissa Tracy, *Torture and Brutality in Medieval Literature: Negotiations of National Identity* (Cambridge: D. S. Brewer, 2012).

studies encompassing two thousand years and a multitude of cultures – a truly 'abbreviated history'. In his detailed and extremely informative article on the history of castration, Mathew S. Kuefler calls for more comparative cultural studies of institutionalized castration, and he argues that there is 'no modern synthesis of castration in Europe in the Middle Ages'.[4] Kuefler's own monograph, *The Manly Eunuch: Masculinity, Gender Ambiguity, and Christian Ideology in Late Antiquity*, which examines these issues from the start of the third century to the middle of the fifth century, lays a firm foundation for pursuing such a study.[5] *Eunuchs in Antiquity and Beyond*, edited by Shaun Tougher, adds another layer to the cross-cultural study of early eunuchs in antiquity, concentrating mainly on Greek evidence across the Persian, Greek, Roman, and Byzantine worlds, but branching out to touch on the history of the court eunuch in China and the influential role of *castrati* in music beyond that of Italian singers of the sixteenth through the nineteenth centuries.[6] However, castration itself – the act, the penalty, the cultural significance – is only part of these very thorough discussions of eunuchs. Taylor's *Castration* wraps all the cultural concerns about castration throughout history into a pithy and engaging discussion of the effect of castration on the male psyche, framing his discussion around early modern texts like Thomas Middleton's *A Game at Chess* (1624). Valeria Finucci's study on castration also focuses on the early modern period, dealing specifically with the gender anxieties surrounding the *castrati*.[7] But there is a gap. Jacqueline Murray writes that despite both the 'dominance of the masculine voice and the phallocentrism of the medieval world view, we know very little about either masculinity or male sexuality in the Middle Ages'.[8] Much has been done since on medieval masculinity, but very little has been done specifically on *medieval* castration, except as it reflects on or carries over the ideas of antiquity into the Renaissance. The need for more specialized study (as gruesome as it may seem) is clearly articulated by Murray who argues that by 'de-universalizing men's voices and analyzing their experience with the methodologies and theoretical perspectives that have done so much to reclaim women's past, new insights are being gained into masculinity

4 Mathew S. Kuefler, 'Castration and Eunuchism in the Middle Ages', in *The Handbook of Medieval Sexuality*, ed. Vern L. Bullough and James A. Brundage (New York: Garland Publishing, 1996), pp. 279–306 at pp. 279, 280.

5 Mathew S. Kuefler, *The Manly Eunuch: Masculinity, Gender Ambiguity, and Christian Ideology in Late Antiquity* (Chicago: University of Chicago Press, 2001).

6 Shaun Tougher, ed., *Eunuchs in Antiquity and Beyond* (London: Classical Press of Wales and Duckworth, 2002).

7 Valeria Finucci, *The Manly Masquerade: Masculinity, Paternity and Castration in the Italian Renaissance* (Durham, NC: Duke University Press, 2003).

8 Jacqueline Murray, 'Hiding Behind the Universal Man: Male Sexuality in the Middle Ages', in *The Handbook of Medieval Sexuality*, ed. Bullough and Brundage, pp. 123–52 at p. 123.

and male sexuality'.[9] But rather than focusing on the theoretical aspects and the psychological analysis that often surrounds it, this collection examines the real, literal act of castration (both testicular and penile) from late antiquity through the early modern period, presenting complex and nuanced discussions of what is often regarded as an offensive, or at least uncomfortable, subject. Throughout history, a variety of social norms and prohibitions have been enacted on the body and the essays in this volume concentrate on the most intimate inscriptions of religious and secular power and their manifestations in chronicles, literature, archaeology, and law. The purpose of this collection is to work from the classic foundations, to fill in gaps in the sweeping studies, and to connect the dots of the more localized discussions in an effort to contribute a comprehensive and cohesive picture of castration in western Europe.

The History of Castration

Castration has been a feature of civilization for more than a thousand years. Tied to notions of identity, masculinity, sexuality, and power, castration has been used as a tool of oppression, slavery, purification, and religious observance. Vern L. Bullough notes that the date of the first appearance of eunuchs 'has been lost to history, but castration of males whether animal or human is an old practice dating from the time when humanity began to herd animals'.[10] Medically speaking, castration can either denote the removal of the testicles or of the entire male genitalia – the visible signs of a man, according to Aristotle. There are three medical possibilities in defining castration: removing or disabling the penis; removing or disabling the testicles; and removing or disabling the entire genitalia.[11] Many studies of castration (medieval and modern) proceed from the premise of Freudian theory and take a psychoanalytical approach which privileges the penis;[12] however, in light of recent research, Murray questions the legitimacy of 'applying this evaluation of the penis to the construction of male sexual identity in the Middle Ages'.[13] Most medieval medical cases of castration involve

[9] Ibid., p. 123.

[10] Vern L. Bullough, 'Eunuchs in History and Society', in *Eunuchs in Antiquity and Beyond*, ed. Tougher, p. 1.

[11] Kuefler, 'Castration and Eunuchism', p. 285.

[12] Karin Sellberg and Lena Wånggren take on the Freudian critics and analyze the effect of reading medieval and early modern castration narratives through a psychoanalytical framework in their conclusion to this volume, 'The Dismemberment of Will: Early Modern Fear of Castration', pp. 295–313.

[13] Murray, 'Hiding Behind the Universal Man', p. 124. According to Murray, 'given the centrality of the penis to male sexual and psychological identity, there is a temptation to evaluate male sexual violence as inherent and transhistorical. This perspective on the meaning of the phallus to masculine sexuality and identity owes much to Sigmund Freud's ideas about the interplay between body and mind, libido and id in the male psyche, a relationship which would not alter significantly across societies' (p. 124).

only the testicles, and concerns regarding their removal had less to do with sexual identity or ability, and more to do with the ability to propagate and sire children. In seventh-century Byzantium, Paulus Aegineta described the different castrative procedures that were widely practiced throughout the Byzantine Empire, despite the danger of bleeding to death and infection.[14] Kuefler writes that 'the opinion of ancient science that castration, despite its risks, could cure or at least alleviate certain ailments also made its way into medieval medicine'.[15] In the thirteenth century, Thomas Aquinas 'justified what had long been medical practice, that castration was a permissible mutilation if used to save the whole person'.[16] Castration was seen as treatment for a variety of related and unrelated diseases: satyriasis, elephantiasis, hernias, hair loss (in extreme cases), leprosy, gout, varicose veins, and epilepsy.[17]

The generation of some of the staple figures of Greek and Roman mythology – Aphrodite/Venus and the Furies (Erinyes) – rests with a violent act of castration perpetrated by a son upon his father, Kronos/Saturn on Uranus/Caelus. In the ancient rite of Cybele, recounted in Ovid's *Metamorphoses*, the goddess's lover Attis castrates himself in a ritual performance. Charles B. Lewis argues this may have been the origin for the May Pole and May festivities, popular throughout medieval Europe, which often featured cross-dressed or sexually ambiguous figures as part of the spectacle. As Lewis points out, Attis emasculated 'was neither man nor woman'; he was a called a 'semi-woman'.[18] Castration was important in religious cults of the Great Goddess, 'worshipped with her son and consort under various titles and names in the syncretic atmosphere of the later Roman Empire'.[19] These rites were problematic for Christian writers who strongly condemned them not only because they were pagan, but also because 'of the sexual practices and blurring of gender distinctions particular to this religion. The condemnation of religious castration was an important part of patristic polemics against pagan religion, and thus found its way into the canon of medieval religious writings.'[20] And yet, Christian theologians resorted to this 'pagan' practice occasionally reconfiguring castration as a form of spiritual purification.

[14] Kuefler, 'Castration and Eunuchism', pp. 285–6. Shaun Tougher examines the works of Paulus Aegineta (Paul of Aegina) in his contribution to this volume, 'The Aesthetics of Castration: The Beauty of Roman Eunuchs', pp. 48–72. See also Robert L.A. Clark, 'Culture Loves a Void: Eunuchry in *De Vetula* and Jean Le Fèvre's *La Vielle*', in this volume, pp. 280–94.

[15] Kuefler, 'Castration and Eunuchism', p. 286.

[16] Ibid., p. 286.

[17] Ibid.

[18] Charles B. Lewis, 'The Part of the Folk in the Making of Folklore', *Folklore* 46.1 (March 1935): 37–75 at pp. 70–1.

[19] Kuefler, 'Castration and Eunuchism', pp. 281–2.

[20] Ibid., p. 282.

Eunuchs and the Ancient World

Eunuchs occupied an ambiguous sexual position in much of the ancient world, and their ability to pass between gendered identities often put them in positions of power. The history of eunuchs in medieval European society stretches back much farther than the beginning of the medieval period, and studies of castration 'must take into consideration the continuities of medieval society with the ancient world'.[21] The production and use of eunuchs in political and domestic spheres was far more common in Byzantium than in Germanic Europe; ancient governments 'depended on eunuchs in their bureaucracies, and literate persons in the Middle Ages could read of them in ancient Greek and Roman histories'.[22] Eunuchs were guardians of the marriage bed, 'qualified for that social function by being disqualified from a biological one'.[23] Some were advisors, many ruled behind the scenes, and several led on the battlefield. Kuefler cites forty-five examples of eunuchs charged with military commands by the Byzantine government, a 'curiously masculine role for a group of men so frequently denigrated as unmanly'.[24] But Byzantine law precluded the use of castration as a punishment for any crime.[25] Kuefler points out that 'continuities with the ancient world in the use of eunuchs are also very much apparent in the Muslim world, and they influenced Christian Europeans whenever and wherever interactions between these two cultures took place'.[26] There was also literary continuity between the ancient and medieval worlds regarding castration: religious texts, including the Bible, provided examples of eunuchs; legal texts, especially after the rediscovery of Roman law in the twelfth century, included castration, and secular literature repeated the accounts of eunuchs found in classical works and incorporated them as a motif in medieval romances.[27]

The *Digest* of Justinian suggests that Roman law was clearly opposed to castration, however common it may have been in later Roman society.[28] In the Roman world, 'notions of sexual difference relied heavily on the absoluteness of the divide between male and female'.[29] Kuefler writes,

> Notions of moral character, of virtue and vice, were directly linked to sexual difference, and social rights were expressed as deriving from masculine superiority and feminine inferiority. Gender ambiguity of any sort was an unsettling proposition, and as much as possible was explained away. The

21 Ibid., p. 280.
22 Ibid., pp. 280, 281.
23 Taylor, *Castration*, p. 33.
24 Kuefler, 'Castration and Eunuchism', p. 281.
25 Ibid., p. 287.
26 Ibid., p. 280.
27 Ibid., p. 280.
28 Ibid., p. 287.
29 Kuefler, *The Manly Eunuch*, p. 19.

> gender ambiguity of the eunuch was not so easily erased, however, and the presence of eunuchs therefore disturbed and challenged those notions of the absolute divide between male and female.[30]

But medieval notions of gender identity could be fluid, and neither male nor female identity was necessarily affected by castration.

Castration, Sexuality, and Masculine Identity

Several influential studies on the nature of medieval masculinity and sexuality have been written in the last twenty years (though most of these only touch on castration),[31] and they all point to the complexity of gender definitions and the fraught relationship between gendered categories. Miri Rubin argues that medieval people 'were worried by contradictions within their bodies and between each other' and challenges the 'boundaries and integrity of bodies in the Middle Ages' in a way that renders any attempt at 'grounding, at claiming determinacy of them, not only impossible, but uninteresting'.[32] Rubin further suggests that medieval gender roles were made in a world which 'possessed very fluid notions of sexuality and of bodily contours. Thus gender is revealed as a complex system, not grounded in biology, but made of attempts to impose upon biological diversity a regulating dichotomy: feminine and masculine.'[33] In her extensive work on castration and masculinity, Murray asserts that 'masculinities reflect patriarchy back on itself. Masculinities naturalize and normalize patriarchy and patriarchy imbues masculinities with the power and privilege that underscore male experience and identity through so much of human history.'[34] Castration both reinforces and threatens masculinity – wielded by foes or political opponents it becomes a means of solidifying power (regardless of how much the recourse to such brutality may destabilize that power). As a mode of

30 Ibid.

31 See Martha A. Brozyna, ed., *Gender and Sexuality in the Middle Ages* (Jefferson, NC: McFarland Publishers, 2005); Conor McCarthy, ed., *Love, Sex and Marriage in the Middle Ages: A Sourcebook* (New York and London: Routledge, 2004); Ruth Mazo Karras, *From Boys to Men: Formations of Masculinity in Late Medieval Europe* (Philadelphia: University of Pennsylvania Press, 2003); Jeffrey Jerome Cohen and Bonnie Wheeler, eds., *Becoming Male in the Middle Ages* (New York: Garland Publishing, 2000); Clare A. Lees, ed., *Medieval Masculinities: Regarding Men in the Middle Ages* (Minneapolis: University of Minnesota Press, 1994); Bullough and Brundage, eds., *Handbook of Medieval Sexuality*; James A. Brundage, *Law, Sex, and Christian Society in Medieval Europe* (Chicago: University of Chicago Press, 1987).

32 Miri Rubin, 'The Person in the Form: Medieval Challenges to Bodily "Order"', in *Framing Medieval Bodies*, ed. Sarah Kay and Miri Rubin (Manchester: Manchester University Press, 1994), pp. 100–22 at p. 100.

33 Ibid., p. 101.

34 Jacqueline Murray, 'Introduction', in *Conflicted Identities and Multiple Masculinities: Men in the Medieval West*, ed. Murray (New York: Garland Publishing, 1999), p. xi.

punishment for rape or treason it acts (potentially or ideally) as a deterrent, trusting that the desire to preserve manhood will outweigh any other felonious desire, or as a *contrapasso* – suffering according to the crime.

Castration is an emasculating practice usually enacted upon men by *other men* – men who either feel threatened or empowered enough to perform an act that masculine sensibilities should decry. Masculine identities were 'constructed, consciously and unconsciously, in oppositional terms'.[35] Few things seem as contradictory as a man desiring – or even being willing – to emasculate another man, whether through fear, anger, vengeance, religious fervor, legal requirement, or accident. And yet men did – perhaps as a means of asserting their own virility. In each of the castration scenarios discussed in this volume, violence is enacted upon a male body (or in rare cases a female body) by other men that results in devastating effects for the entire idea of medieval masculine identity. As Murray notes, medieval society was largely homosocial; however 'tense medieval man's relationship with women might have been, it was male/male relationships that figured most prominently in a male's life'.[36] The act of castration removes men from the male sphere and creates fluid boundaries between masculinity and femininity – it raises questions of whether a castrated man is truly a man, or whether he is female, and if he is now 'female', whether that makes certain activities or identities acceptable.

The practice of castration, which freely 'remade' male sexuality, 'invited questions on what the input of socialization was in making a man a man and whether beliefs in biological determinism were tenable'.[37] In the case of the famous Italian *castrati* of the sixteenth and seventeenth centuries, the testicles were removed before puberty to ensure retention of the angelic quality of a boy's singing voice. *Castrati* appear in Eastern church choirs as early as the fifth century; however, earlier *castrati* were probably not specifically castrated for the choir as they would be later in Italy and Spain.[38] Finucci argues that the *castrato* 'started to be manufactured by surgeons and barbers for the sake of a voice uncannily and studiedly feminine, not in the "decadent" seventeenth century but as early as the middle of the supposedly manly sixteenth century'.[39] Though genitalia 'did not constitute a clear-cut sign of difference, and a sex could always assume the features and functions of the other: a man could, in effect, be constructed'.[40] Jeffrey Jerome Cohen and Bonnie Wheeler argue that biology is not irrelevant, 'but making a boy out of a body born with a penis is a cultural process just as complicated and life-long as "girling" a body declared female on the basis of her

[35] Ibid. p. xi.
[36] Ibid., p. xii.
[37] Finucci, *The Manly Masquerade*, p. 6.
[38] Kuefler, 'Castration and Eunuchism', p. 287.
[39] Finucci, *The Manly Masquerade*, p. 5.
[40] Ibid.

vagina'.[41] But literal castration has physical as well as cultural implications, and medieval perceptions of masculinity (and femininity) were inextricably linked to the biological aspects of sex – the genitalia – and sexual identity.[42] This is not to deny the intersection of feminism, queer theory, and masculinity – in fact, castration often creates such an intersection – but the aim of this volume is to consider *actual* physical acts of castration and genital mutilation in context, and examine what castration meant to medieval societies and their men.

The physical removal of the testicles and/or the penis may, in some cultural contexts, create a 'woman', or have a 'queering' effect; castration ties into homophobic responses to sex, heteronormative concerns of domination, and homosocial fears of violation. As Cohen and Wheeler attest, gender performances 'mark not only private but also cultural constructs of power and powerlessness, and frequently reveal individual and collective anxieties about identity boundaries, about the Other in terms of sex, status, race, and religion'.[43] Castration, as a form of brutality (legitimate and illegitimate), 'others' both the castrated and the castrator. The castrated man becomes something 'else', while those who enact such violence on his body become tyrants, often violating law and social taboo in their cruelty. There is a paradox in ancient, medieval, and early modern constructions and interpretations of castration. Christianity demands bodily purity, which some interpreted as a call for castration – cutting off sexual desire at its root. But as Western culture valued manhood and the masculine ability to procreate, castration (especially self-castration) violated social norms, and castrates were most often viewed as outsiders.

Emasculation and Purification

Castration as a means of purification or of curtailing sexual desires, specifically in the Christian clergy, is enmeshed in interpretations of Matthew 19:12, as many articles in this volume attest:

> All men take not this word, but they to whom it is given. For there are eunuchs, who were born so from their mother's womb: and there are eunuchs, who were made so by men: and there are eunuchs, who have made themselves eunuchs for the kingdom of heaven, he that can take, let him take *it*.[44]

41 Jeffrey Jerome Cohen and Bonnie Wheeler, 'Becoming and Unbecoming', in *Becoming Male in the Middle Ages*, ed. Cohen and Wheeler (New York: Garland Publishing, 2000), pp. vii–xx at p. xix.

42 Murray, 'Introduction', p. xv.

43 Cohen and Wheeler, 'Becoming and Unbecoming', p. xiii.

44 Douay-Rheims version of the Holy Bible, with commentary by Bishop Richard Challoner (1749–52) (Rockford, IL: Tan Books and Publishers, 1971, photographic reproduction of 1899 edition). Bishop Challoner's commentary clarifies that this sentiment is *not* to be taken literally.

This passage was read literally by several early Christian theologians, most famously, Origen (*c.* AD 185–254), whose autocastration is recounted by Eusebius of Caesarea (*c.* AD 260–before 341) in his *Ecclesiastical History* as 'Origen's Daring Deed'.[45] Eusebius qualifies the account with his own commentary that 'a deed was done by him which evidenced an immature and youthful mind, but at the same time gave the highest proof of faith and continence'.[46] Origen paid a surgeon to make him a eunuch and thus more acceptable as a teacher of women and (presumably) to quell any lustful thoughts he might harbor. His reputation grew *after* his castration, and he was elevated in the Church hierarchy. But Origen's example was not to be followed, however earnest or sincere. The First Council of Nicaea (AD 325) suspended priests and denied promotion to clerics who took it upon themselves to quench their sexual desires through castration; only men who had been surgically castrated for medical reasons, or were the victims of violence, could retain their ecclesiastical position.[47]

Many Eastern Christian writers in the early Middle Ages regarded eunuchs as dangerous because of the potential sexual attraction for other men, and they were considered licentious and without virtue.[48] Kuefler writes that eunuchs, 'despite their maleness, were often portrayed as the equivalent of women in early medieval writings, and the stereotypes of their character are virtually the same as those of women: carnal, voluptuous, wanton, irrational, fickle, manipulative, deceitful',[49] though Tougher points out that some men were made eunuchs specifically to preserve their youthful beauty.[50] Others saw self-castration as the ultimate sacrifice, a noble act that 'allowed eunuchs to serve God without worrying about accusations of sexual misconduct'.[51] Yet that was part of the appeal: despite the 'extremity, illegality and moral condemnation of castration, it continued to have an inescapable lure, both metaphorically and literally, perhaps because it provided certainty in the face of unreliable and weak flesh,

45 Jack Collins examines the original Latin text of Eusebius' account, in conjunction with the Greek texts of Matthew and the Hebrew texts of the rabbinic tradition later in this volume. See 'Appropriation and Development of Castration as Symbol and Practice in Early Christianity', pp. 73–86.

46 Eusebius Pamphili, Bishop of Caesarea, *Church History from AD 1–324, Life of Constantine the Great, Oration in Praise of Constantine*, in *A Select Library of Nicene and Post-Nicene Fathers of the Christian Church,* second series, vol. 1, ed. Philip Schaff and Henry Wace (Grand Rapids, MI: W. B. Eerdmans, second printing 1961), p. 254; excerpted in Brozyna, *Gender and Sexuality in the Middle Ages*, p. 79.

47 Jacqueline Murray, 'Mystical Castration: Some Reflections on Peter Abelard, Hugh of Lincoln and Sexual Control', in *Conflicted Identities*, ed. Murray, pp. 73–91 at p. 74.

48 Ruth Mazo Karras, *Sexuality in Medieval Europe: Doing unto Others* (New York and London: Routledge, 2005), p. 39.

49 Kuefler, 'Castration and Eunuchism', p. 291.

50 Tougher, 'The Aesthetics of Castration', pp. 48–72.

51 Karras, *Sexuality in Medieval Europe*, pp. 39–40.

as well as incontrovertible evidence with which to silence accusations of impropriety'.[52] However, autocastration was (in one sense) an easy way out because spiritual salvation came from overcoming sexual temptation through sheer force of will. Ruth Mazo Karras points out that castrating oneself 'physically took a one-time great act of will, but, once it was done, there was no further struggle against temptation, whereas castrating oneself metaphorically was a constant battle. (In fact castration after puberty may eradicate neither desire nor the ability to have an erection, but medieval people believed that it did.)'[53]

Virginity, Castration, Circumcision and the Body of Christ

Castration figures prominently in early Christian discussions on the nature of virginity and the inherent sinfulness of human flesh. There is a shift in Christian attitudes towards castration in relation to rabbinic discussions that focused not on questions of stamping out sexual desire, but on the ability to procreate, as Jack Collins argues.[54] Medieval Jewish tradition had its own legends of men divinely castrated by angels, but in general it was prohibited by ancient regulations and the Mishnah forbids eunuchs from entering Jewish congregations.[55] The Talmud delineates three different types of eunuchs: 'castrated men, men who were wounded in the genitals, and men with disorders preventing their genitals from developing at puberty'.[56] Circumcision, required by Jewish tradition, often ties into castration anxieties. The practice was opposed by Christian authors partly because of its perceived relationship to castration, 'since Roman and medieval texts tend to regard it as a sort of half castration'.[57] Abelard (rather ironically) condemns circumcision as a practice that makes Jewish men less sexually attractive to women, and would require the artificial 'awakening of mutual love'.[58] Some early Christians (like Origen) also saw circumcision, 'not always disapprovingly, as occasioning a loss of virile sexual energy'.[59] Circumcision, like castration, was a paradox for Christian theologians because Christ was circumcised: 'From Christ himself came the notion that a man could inhabit one physical body yet signify another abstract, powerful corpus.'[60]

52 Murray, 'Mystical Castration', p. 75.
53 Karras, *Sexuality in Medieval Europe*, p. 39.
54 Collins, 'Appropriation and Development', p. 75.
55 Kuefler, 'Castration and Eunuchism', pp. 283, 284.
56 Ibid., p. 284.
57 Ibid.
58 Steven F. Kruger, 'Becoming Christian, Becoming Male', in *Becoming Male in the Middle Ages*, ed. Cohen and Wheeler, pp. 21–41 at p. 23.
59 Ibid., p. 22.
60 D. Vance Smith, 'Body Doubles: Producing the Masculine Corpus', in *Becoming Male in the Middle Ages*, ed. Cohen and Wheeler, pp. 3–19 at p. 3.

The corporeality of Christ was highly contested – a debate that led to the codification of transubstantiation by the Fourth Lateran Council in 1215 – a question tied to physical relics (including Christ's foreskin, which was preserved after the Circumcision) that marked Christ as biologically *male*. Murray points out that the body was central to the 'most sustained, systematic, and articulate discussions of medieval sexuality', founded in the theological discourse initiated by the patristic fathers which 'developed throughout the whole of the Middle Ages and even up to today'.[61] Ambrose and Jerome both saw the body as a point of weakness that had to be strictly controlled,[62] but they did not advocate literal castration. Augustine of Hippo, who only embraced chastity later in his life, mitigated the condemnation of human sexuality somewhat but still saw some aspects of it as problematic.[63] As Murray asserts, 'it is not surprising to find that a series of competing and conflicting beliefs and behaviors pertaining to male sexuality could and did coexist in medieval society'.[64] More and more, Christian authors condemned castration, much as the First Council of Nicaea did, as the practice of barbarians. Guibert of Nogent, in his *Gesta Dei per Francos* (*Deeds of God through the Franks*), reports that the Greek emperor commanded each family in his realm to make one daughter a prostitute and one son a eunuch, a practice which he condemns because castration 'enervated and devirilized not just the individual but the nation'.[65] Guibert argues that the castration edict brought the enemy down upon the Greeks and led to their defeat because castrating the sons rendered them 'weak and effeminate, no longer fit for military service. Even worse, they were cut off from producing progeny for the future, who might have been looked for as aid against their enemies.'[66] It is the loss of virility, the inability to produce heirs, to repopulate depleted communities after famine, plague, and disease, that drives many of the medieval laws prohibiting or sanctioning castration.

Abelard's Calamitous History

One of the most famous (or infamous) episodes of medieval extra-judicial brutality and barbarism is, of course, the castration of Peter Abelard (1079–1142). Bound up in the intrigue of twelfth-century religious politics, the affair and later marriage of Abelard and Heloise (*c.* 1101–64), and her uncle Fulbert's unsanctioned punishment of Abelard's transgressions, captivated

[61] Murray, 'Hiding Behind the Universal Man', p. 125.

[62] Ibid.

[63] Ibid., p. 126.

[64] Ibid., p. 129.

[65] Kruger, 'Becoming Christian, Becoming Male', p. 22. See also Guibert of Nogent, *The Deeds of God through the Franks*, trans. Robert Levine (Woodbridge: Boydell Press, 1997), p. 38.

[66] Guibert of Nogent, *The Deeds of God through the Franks*, p. 38.

contemporary audiences and enthralled others throughout the Middle Ages. Abelard's castration 'is presented as a violation of an overpowered victim, not as just punishment for Abelard's own act of perceived violation'.[67] Abelard may have engaged in fornication but nothing justified this particularly heinous form of vigilante justice meted out by Heloise's uncle.[68] The servants who carried out Fulbert's revenge were subjected to the same punishment they inflicted upon Abelard, in addition to blinding.[69] The unlawful castration of Abelard, and his autobiographical account *Historia calamitatum* (*History of Calamities*), disguised as *Ad amicum suum consolatoria* (*A Letter of Consolation to a Friend*) (*c.* 1132), create a framework for discussing the taboo of male (and occasionally female) genital mutilation – its reception, inception, legal boundaries, ancient origins, and early modern legacies.[70] *Historia calamitatum* is 'a skilled, dense, complex, and aggressive confession of a life and of a life's work designed to engage the sympathies of the reader – and not just the reader's sympathy'.[71] It is within Abelard's calamitous history that we ground our study on the culture of castration from late antiquity through the sixteenth century.[72] Abelard is the

67 Martin Irvine, 'Abelard and (Re)writing the Male Body: Castration, Identity, and Remasculinization', in *Becoming Male in the Middle Ages*, ed. Cohen and Wheeler, pp. 87–106 at p. 96, also cited in Tracy, *Torture and Brutality*, p. 195.

68 Tracy, *Torture and Brutality*, p. 208.

69 Abelard, *Historia calamitatum*, in Betty Radice, ed., *The Letters of Abelard and Heloise* (London: Penguin Books, 1974), p. 75. Matthew Paris relates a similar tale in which Godfrey de Millers, a knight of Norfolk, was seized in the house of John Brito where he had gone with the intent of sleeping with John's daughter. He was caught in a trap, hung upside down by his feet from the beams, castrated, and then thrown out of the house half-dead: 'However, in this case, it was decided that this "punishment squad" had exceeded the bounds of acceptable reaction, and all of those involved were prosecuted and convicted': Trevor Dean, *Crime in Medieval Europe* (Edinburgh: Pearson Education, 2001), p. 138.

70 Irvine explains that this title has been ascribed to the text by modern editors, and the correct title is *Letter of Consolation to a Friend*: 'Abelard and (Re)writing the Male Body', p. 87. But since that is the title most familiar to modern audiences, we use it consistently throughout the volume.

71 Bonnie Wheeler, 'Origenary Fantasties: Abelard's Castration and Confession', in *Becoming Male in the Middle Ages*, ed. Cohen and Wheeler, pp. 107–28 at p. 109.

72 Yves Ferroul makes a compelling argument that medieval people understood 'castration' only as the removal of the testicles, and 'emasculation' as removal of the penis. In this vein he argues that Abelard was clearly only castrated and would have been able to perform sexually and thus remain married to Heloise. 'Abelard's Blissful Castration', in *Becoming Male in the Middle Ages*, ed. Cohen and Wheeler, pp. 129–49, p. 135. But since Abelard compares himself to Origen, and uses his castration as a justification for ministering to the Paraclete and continuing to instruct women, he seems to imply that he is no longer capable of intercourse. Murray agrees with Ferroul's assessment and suggests that why Abelard did not stay married to Heloise 'has much to tell us about how Abelard understood his sexual nature, both before and after he was castrated by Fulbert's hit men' ('Mystical Castration', pp. 76–7). However, as is most common in modern discourse, we use these terms interchangeably.

touchstone for many medieval discussions about castration, especially because his injury was publicly debated not only during his lifetime, but long after. It served as an enduring example of human frailty and sexual temptation in theological debates, it was held up as a romantic tragedy, it informed humorous criticism of ecclesiastical philanderers in the fabliaux, and it exposed fractures in legal structures that permitted castration in certain circumstances but decried it in others.

Castration is a physical paradox, not in theoretical terms, but in historical, contextual, and literary terms. Abelard embodies this paradox – he was castrated because of his desire to embody everything, to be everything, to have everything. He was a master theologian and teacher who wanted to retain his intellectual status while engaging in a sexual and emotional relationship with Heloise. He married her when she became pregnant (though she resisted the marriage), but did not want to jeopardize his scholarly reputation by making their union public. His refusal to acknowledge the legitimacy of his wife and child leads to the illegitimate punishment ordered by Fulbert. In *Historia calamitatum* he describes the injury that was done to him one night as he slept 'peacefully in an inner room' of his lodgings. The perpetrators proceed like thieves, bribing one of his servants to let them in. He writes that they 'took cruel vengeance on me of such appalling barbarity as to shock the whole world; they cut off the parts of my body whereby I had committed the wrong of which they complained'.[73] The crime is widely known by morning, as 'the whole city' gathered in front of his house – a 'scene of horror and amazement, mingled with lamentations, cries and groans which exasperated and distressed' him (*HC*: 75). He suffers more from 'their sympathy than from the pain of [his] wound, and felt the misery of [his] mutilation less than [his] shame and humiliation' (*HC*: 75). Once he is emasculated, Abelard again attempts to retain both his intellectual status and his relationship with Heloise, but in different terms. Sexual gratification is replaced by intellectual stimulation and a rhetorical construction of castration, reaffirming not only Abelard's masculine identity but also his victimization.[74] Abelard positions his castration in rhetorical terms, constructing from the violent correction of his body a figure of intellectual

[73] Peter Abelard, *Historia calamitatum* (*HC*), p. 75. Hereafter, page numbers in this edition are given in parentheses in the text.

[74] In reference to the ambiguous sexuality of Chaucer's Pardoner, who is often thought of as a castrated man, a cross-dressing woman, or the homosexual paramour of the Summoner, Rita Copeland examines how 'scientific or disciplinary classification in antiquity and the Middle Ages constitutes one domain or category of the body, and how notions of violent physical correction or "discipline" to be enacted on the human body are transferred metaphorically to the realm of intellectual disciplines'. She argues that gender and sexuality are part of 'the political text of rhetoric's institutional history'. 'The Pardoner's Body and the Disciplining of Rhetoric', in *Framing Medieval Bodies*, ed. Kay and Rubin, pp. 138–59 at p. 138.

contrition and martyrdom. As Cohen and Wheeler write, 'sundering sexuality from gender, Abelard constructs masculinity as intellectual performance and (in a brilliant inversion of expectation) he *essentializes* his gender, not his bodily sexuality'.[75]

Abelard centers his grief not on his emasculation, but on the harm to his reputation and position as a scholar, the very things he sought to preserve by keeping his marriage to Heloise a secret. He writes,

> All sorts of thoughts filled my mind – how brightly my reputation had shone, and now how easily in an evil moment it had been dimmed or rather completely blotted out; how just a judgment of God had struck me in the parts of the body with which I had sinned, and how just a reprisal had been taken by the very man I had myself betrayed. I thought how my rivals would exult over my fitting punishment, how this bitter blow would bring lasting grief and misery to my friends and parents, and how fast the news of this unheard-of disgrace would spread over the whole world. (*HC*: 75–6)

He attempts to set himself up as an intellectual and physical martyr, appropriating the terminology of hagiography in his account of his calamities. Unlike the martyred saints, he tells his own tale, spinning the narrative to his own ends: to explain both his arrogance and his continued contact with Heloise and the sisters of the Paraclete, and to elicit sympathy for his continued troubles and the condemnation of his scholarly work (which he portrays as even worse than his physical wound). He writes: 'I wept much more for the injury done to my reputation than for the damage to my body, for that I had brought upon myself through my own fault, but this open violence had come upon me only because of the purity of my intentions and love of our Faith which had compelled me to write' (*HC*: 84–5). Through his castration – the violent removal of his vile members – Abelard constructs his wounding as a necessary evil for achieving salvation, if not sanctity. His acceptance of it as such, and his acceptance of all his trials and tribulations, verify his holiness. For Abelard, 'castration became a positive act of divine grace that freed him from the sexual demands of his imperfect male body and ensured his ability to lead henceforth a holy life'.[76]

But Heloise rejects his construction of martyrdom, as she does his assumption of divine (purifying) punishment, and calls this act a crime, even more insidious because it was done *after* they were married and were living chaste, contemplative lives apart: 'The punishment you suffered would have been proper vengeance for men caught in open adultery. But what others

75 Cohen and Wheeler, 'Becoming and Unbecoming', p. xv.

76 Jacqueline Murray, '"The law of sin that is in my members": The Problem of Male Embodiment', in *Gender and Holiness: Men, Women and Saints in Late Medieval Europe*, ed. Samantha J. E. Riches and Sarah Salih (London and New York: Routledge, 2002), pp. 9–22 at p. 18.

deserve for adultery came upon you through a marriage which you believed had made amends for all previous wrongdoing' (*Letter 3*: 130).[77] She takes responsibility for being part of the cause of his castration, but she also urges him to stop thinking that he deserved this. She sees a temporal crime, not divine grace. Abelard tells Heloise to 'accept patiently what mercifully befell us. This is a father's rod, not a persecutor's sword' (*Letter 4*: 153). Much as saints defy their tormentors in medieval hagiography by constructing their continued and excessive punishment as a gift from God that allows them to achieve salvation faster, Abelard argues with Heloise that he too has been spiritually healed through his physical wound. He writes:

> The father strikes to correct, and to forestall the enemy who strikes to kill. By a wound he prevents death, he does not deal it; he thrusts in the steel to cut out disease. He wounds the body, and heals the soul; he makes to live what he should have destroyed, cuts out impurity to leave what is pure. He punishes once so that he need not punish forever. (*Letter 4*: 153)

He speaks of the crown of martyrdom that is reserved for her by his sacrifice and by the suffering it continues to cause her; the many 'greater sufferings of the heart through the continual prompting of the flesh of your own youth he has reserved for a martyr's crown' (*Letter 4*: 154). This crown can only be achieved by continually striving against temptations, but he laments that 'no crown is waiting for me, because no cause for striving remains. The matter for strife is lacking in him from whom the thorn of desire is pulled out' (*Letter 4*: 154). In asking Heloise and the nuns to pray for him, to intercede on his behalf as handmaidens of Christ, he constructs *her* in the image of female hagiography – not a virgin martyr, but a repentant sinner whose voice should be heard.

But while he seems to deny himself the possibility of a martyr's crown, he shapes his account in *Historia calamitatum* in hagiographical terms, comparing

77 Whether castration was actually an acceptable punishment for adultery is somewhat uncertain. French customary law states that any party who causes the loss of blood or visible bruising, and is proved guilty by witnesses, is culpable for 60 *sous* in damages to the judge and 15 *sous* to the plaintiff, and is responsible for the cost of the plaintiff's lost days of work and having the wound healed (*Customs of the Orléans District* 2:24): *The Etablissements de Saint Louis: Thirteenth-Century Law Texts from Tours, Orléans, and Paris*, trans. F. R. P. Akehurst (Philadelphia: University of Pennsylvania Press, 1996), p. 144. This particular statute gives townsmen and commoners equal status in paying remuneration for serious, but not-life-threatening, wounds unless amputation is involved: 'But [the judge] must look at where the blood came from, and if there is a serious wound [*plaie mortiex*], he must pay the fine mentioned above, according to the practice of the Orléans district; for townsmen and commoners pay no more than sixty sous as a fine, whatever offense they have committed, except larceny, or rape, or murder, or treachery [*traïson*]; or unless there is some loss of limb, such as foot or hand, nose or ear, or eye, according to the provisions of the charter, as it is stated above'(2:24). Even though castration is not mentioned, it must have fallen under the provisions for graver bodily crimes like amputation (Tracy, *Torture and Brutality*, pp. 223–4 and n. 113).

himself as the 'flea with the lion, the ant with the elephant', and complaining that his rivals persecuted him 'with the same cruelty as the heretics in the past did St Athanasius' (*HC*: 93). His foes are so relentless that he considers exile: 'I was continuously harassed by these anxieties and as a last resort had thought of taking refuge with Christ among Christ's enemies' (*HC*: 94). Abelard envisions himself driven into the wild like many Latin saints, pursued by enemies, not only those who tormented his body, but those who ripped apart his words and his work at the Council of Soissons (1121). He accuses God, 'constantly repeating the lament of St Antony', who faced temptation in the desert and remained steadfast (*HC*: 84). He fears public derision as a monstrous spectacle and is concerned that his injury will prevent him from serving in his vocation, remembering that 'according to the cruel letter of the Law, a eunuch is such an abomination to the Lord that men made eunuchs by the amputation or mutilation of their members are forbidden to enter a church as if they were stinking and unclean' (*HC*: 76). Throughout his career, Abelard clearly 'advanced a performative model of masculinity: a man is he who acts like a man, using superior intellect, the power of dialectic, and written discourse as the ultimate tools of masculine power and self-definition'.[78] Like the virgin martyrs who use words as their weapons against their pagan persecutors, through his intellect, Latinity, and rhetoric, Abelard was able to overcome the social liabilities, popular ridicule, and marginalization that accompanied his very public mutilation.[79]

So much of Abelard's identity is tied to the consequences of castration – who he is as a man, a scholar, as Heloise's husband, teacher, and the father of their child. He uses theological rhetoric to condemn his punishment and to suggest that it was deserved, that he is better off for it and that he is a hapless victim who has withstood these torments for the greater glory of God. Jacqueline Murray aptly asserts that as Abelard 'mulled over the events of his life, he came to see the hand of God in his mutilation. His evaluation of his own castration evolved from an act of punishment, to one of human vengeance, to a divine punishment, until he finally saw it as an expression of divine grace that elevated him above his own human imperfection.'[80] The violence of Abelard's castration and its rehearsal in his written works, the public sphere, theological conversations in his lifetime, and its literary legacy long after his death had a profound effect on medieval responses to castration.

Martin Irvine contends that 'contemporary castration narratives and the letters of his enemies reveal that Abelard's social identity was thus marked by the stigma of the feminized eunuch'.[81] Fulco, Prior of Deuil, parodied Abelard's consolation epistle in 1118 (addressing it to him directly), turning the public

78 Irvine, 'Abelard and (Re)writing the Male Body', p. 102.
79 Murray, 'Mystical Castration', p. 76.
80 Ibid., p. 77.
81 Ibid., p. 94.

response to Abelard's castration into a 'mock-heroic satire with close affinities to fabliau'.[82] While many of Abelard's critics reveled in his punishment (even though it was contrary to law), others decried its savagery. It may have had an unfortunate effect on the behavior of the community of nuns at Watton, Yorkshire, who appear to have used Abelard's punishment as an exemplar. According to St Aelred of Rievaulx, in the mid-twelfth century the sisters chose to punish the sexual indiscretions of a young nun who became pregnant by beating her and forcing her to castrate her lover 'with her own hands'.[83] But by the thirteenth century Abelard and Heloise had achieved mythic status.[84] The resonance of Abelard's castration and its implications for medieval audiences cannot be underestimated. He was remembered by later authors as a victim of vigilante brutality.[85] In her *Book of the City of Ladies* (*c.* 1405), Christine de Pizan (1365–*c.* 1434) attacks Abelard's suppression of Heloise while still condemning his punishment and its cruelty. Jean de Meun's continuation of the *Romans de la rose* (*c.* 1275) 'both extends twelfth-century discourse on sexuality and charts the popular reception of Abelard in the thirteenth century'.[86] In the course of the narrative, which 'reveals a fascination with castration and dismemberment',[87] Jean inserts various exempla dealing with the castration of Uranus and Origen as well as that of Abelard. Jean complains bitterly in Abelard's defense, and condemns the entire practice of castration:

> Anyone who castrates [*escoille*] a worthy man does him very great shame and injury. … It is a great sin to castrate a man. Anyone who castrates a man robs him not just of his testicles [*la coille*], nor of his sweetheart whom he holds very dear and whose fair face he will never see, nor of his wife, for these are the least; he robs him especially of the boldness in human ways that should exist in valiant men.[88]

[82] Irvine, 'Abelard and (Re)writing the Male Body', p. 92, also cited in Tracy, *Torture and Brutality*, p. 208.

[83] Sarah Salih provides a detailed account of this event, its implications for monastic virginity, and the dangers of obligating children into religious life before they have or even understand the idea of a vocation. Unlike Heloise who was delighted with the prospect of bearing Abelard's child, gave birth, but then gave the child to be raised by his sister, this nun had a dream in which her child was taken away and she awoke to find all the signs of her pregnancy gone – though infanticide was suspected: Sarah Salih, *Versions of Virginity in Late Medieval England* (Cambridge: D. S. Brewer, 2001), pp. 152–65.

[84] Constant J. Mews, ed., *The Lost Love Letters of Heloise and Abelard: Perceptions of Dialogue in Twelfth-Century France*, 2nd edn (New York: Palgrave Macmillan, 2008), p. 42.

[85] Ibid., p. 90, also cited in Tracy, *Torture and Brutality*, p. 208.

[86] Irvine, 'Abelard and (Re)writing the Male Body,' p. 90.

[87] Ibid. See Ellen Lorraine Friedrich, 'Insinuating Indeterminate Gender: A Castration Motif in Guillaume de Lorris's *Romans de la rose*', in this volume, pp. 255–79.

[88] Jean de Meun, *Roman de la Rose*, trans. Charles Dahlberg, *The Romance of the Rose* (Princeton, NJ: Princeton University Press, 1971); lines 20007–44, pp. 329–30; quoted in Irvine, 'Abelard and (Re)writing the Male Body', p. 90, also cited in Tracy, *Torture and Brutality*, p. 208.

Abelard engages in a discourse of cultural anxieties by detailing these unfortunate events himself. He manipulates audience perception of brutality by refocusing the castration narrative, first accepting some of the blame for his actions but then centering the true blame firmly upon Fulbert's men (not Fulbert himself) for acting outside the law. Abelard resigns himself to this justice, while at the same time decrying its brutality and excess in his simple acknowledgment of his own guilt. We thus understand and relate to the frailty of man and are horrified at the events that unfolded.

Castration as Punishment

The use of castration as punishment for legal offenses, and the resort to it by parties interested in vengeance rather than justice, continued to trouble the discourse of physical purity and its ecclesiastical prohibition, both of which were bound up in questions of masculine, and in some cases national, identity. While dismemberment (including castration) and capital punishment do figure in medieval jurisprudence to varying degrees, they were generally reserved for the gravest offenses and served as part of the spectacle of punishment – they were designed to horrify, to cow, to deter.[89] Caroline Walker Bynum points to chronicle accounts of dismemberment in capital cases which make it clear 'both that it was reserved for only the most repulsive crimes and that the populace was expected to be able to read the nature of the offense from the precise way in which the criminal's body was cut apart and the pieces displayed'.[90] Mitchell B. Merback argues that medieval punitive justice was deeply rooted in a 'magico-religious conception of the world', a framework which allowed for its 'smooth functioning as an assertion of political power and a tactic of social control'.[91] The rituals of punitive justice were intensely visual, and were 'played out in public and before the collective gaze, the drama of state-sponsored death was a form of *spectacle*'.[92]

The execution of William Wallace in 1305 for treason in his guerilla enter-

89 William Ian Miller describes the very real effect of punitive spectacle, and rejects the psychoanalytic tendency to read all forms of mutilation as castration: 'Consider the horror motif of severed hands, ears, heads, gouged eyes. These do not strike me as so many stand-ins for castration. Castration is merely a particular instance of severability that has been fetishized in psychoanalysis and the literary theoretical enterprises that draw on it. Severability is unnerving no matter what part is being detached … [P]art of death's horror is that it too is a severance of body and soul and then, via putrefaction, of the body's integrity.' *Anatomy of Disgust* (Cambridge, MA: Harvard University Press, 1997), p. 27.

90 Caroline Walker Bynum, *Fragmentation and Redemption: Essays on Gender and the Human Body in Medieval Religion* (New York: Zone Books, 1992), pp. 272, 276.

91 Mitchell B. Merback, *The Thief, the Cross and the Wheel: Pain and the Spectacle of Punishment in Medieval and Renaissance Europe* (London: Reaktion Books, 1999), p. 18.

92 Ibid., p. 18.

prise against English rule in Scotland embodied this spectacle of punishment that included castration. Timothy S. Jones describes the 'gut-churning' execution as 'the most spectacular denouncement of an outlaw in medieval England'.[93] Wallace was hanged until partially strangled, taken down, emasculated, eviscerated, and finally beheaded. The corpse was then quartered, his head placed on a pike on London Bridge, and the four sections of his body sent 'to four towns in Scotland as warning against rebellion'.[94] The castration of convicted traitors reinforces the genetic claim of the monarch to the throne. Royal inheritance is based on masculine propagation and those who trespass against that royal lineage must be wiped out. Literal emasculation becomes a symbolic neutering of an opposing line, cut off to insure no further rebellion or revenge. Castration as a punishment for miscegenation (either religious or ethnic) serves a similar purpose: 'Penetration symbolizes power. For men of one group to have sex with women of another is an assertion of power over the entire group.'[95] The aim is, therefore, to remove the penetrative power of one's enemies, even *post mortem*. As Klaus van Eickels aptly points out, 'Unmanning was considered an appropriate punishment for treason because its connotations were not necessarily sexual. A nobleman's genitals were signifiers of his gender and being male was a prerequisite for the warrior status he claimed.'[96] According to Irvine, 'narratives of emasculating mutilation abound in accounts of the crusades, local wars, and revenge in the twelfth and thirteenth centuries', reflecting social anxieties about this practice and its effect on the construction of French masculinity.[97] After his defeat and death at the battle of Evesham in 1265, the body of Simon de Montfort, Earl of Leicester, the Anglo-French noble who opposed Henry III, was mutilated. His testicles and his head were presented to the wife of Roger de Mortimer, one of the king's supporters.[98] In 1326, for supposedly corrupting King Edward II and turning his affections away from his wife (among other crimes), Edward's favorite Hugh Despenser

[93] Timothy S. Jones, *Outlawry in Medieval Literature* (New York: Palgrave Macmillan, 2010), p. 48.

[94] Ibid., p. 48.

[95] Karras, *Sexuality in Medieval Europe*, p. 25. According to Irvine, canon law also prescribed castration for a Christian European found guilty of adultery with a Saracen woman, and that other castration narratives 'indicate that genital mutilation was often used against clerics and monks for sexual crimes': 'Abelard and (Re)writing the Male Body', p. 88. But evidence in the French customary laws suggests it was not a widespread practice.

[96] Klaus van Eickels, 'Gendered Violence: Castration and Blinding as Punishment for Treason in Normandy and Anglo-Norman England', in *Violence, Vulnerability and Embodiment: Gender and History*, ed. Shani D'Cruze and Anupama Rao (Oxford: Blackwell, 2005), pp. 94–108 at p. 103.

[97] Irvine, 'Abelard and (Re)writing the Male Body', p. 88.

[98] J.R. Maddicott, *Simon de Montfort* (Cambridge: Cambridge University Press, 1996), p. 344.

was subjected to a traitor's death similar to that of William Wallace.[99] Michel Foucault asserts that execution is 'a ceremonial by which a momentarily injured sovereignty is reconstituted'.[100] But castration adds another dimension to execution, revealing the sovereign fear of procreative opposition. Execution in these instances is not enough, and the 'injured sovereignty' resorts to mutilation as a further attempt to reaffirm what Elaine Scarry calls the 'wholly illusory but, to the torturers and the regime they represent, wholly convincing spectacle of power'.[101] Castration resists the goals of torture or execution as exercises of dominance and power because it subverts accepted social ideas against genital mutilation, exemplified by its absence in the most brutal torture narratives and customary laws of the period and its presence in Abelard's construction of sympathy.[102] The desire to use castration as a way of stamping out foes undermines notions of inherited right and suggests a deeper instability within power structures. Like torture, castration is a weapon employed by the weak: those whose hold on power is tenuous or questionable. Ultimately, of course, the mutilation of William Wallace did not quell the rebellious spirit of Scotland, and if nothing else, the added injury of their leader being castrated may well have galvanized the Scottish nobles into further rebellion against Edward I, culminating in the Battle of Bannockburn in 1314 and resulting in England's defeat.

Otherwise, castration seems to have been ordained as punishment only to a limited degree in medieval Europe. As several articles in this volume argue, legal references to it in annals and law codes do not necessarily indicate widespread practice. French customary law does not mention castration, but 'the customs deal with the interesting exceptions rather than the mainstream law.

[99] According to Jean Froissart in his *Chronicles*, though not in other sources, public castration is exactly the punishment visited upon Hugh Despenser, Edward II's favourite. Jean Froissart, *Chronicles*, BnF Fr 2643, fol. 11. The graphic illumination of Hugh Despenser being publicly disemboweled and castrated takes up a quarter of the left-hand column. The following transcription is mine: 'Quant it fut / ainsi loye on lui coupa tout / prennerement le vit & les / couillons pour tant quil / estoit heretique & sodomite/ … Et pour ce auoit / le roy dechassee la royne de / lui & par son ennorteniet / Quant le vit & les couil / lons furent de lui coupez on / les getta ou feu pour adroit / Et après lui fut le aieur / coupe hor[es] du ventres et gette/ ou feu pour tant q'[i]l estoit / [fol.11v] faubo & traytre de cuer et que/ par traytre conseil & enortement le roy.' Lee Patterson, however, cautions against taking Froissart entirely at his word. He points out that in later medieval England castration as a punishment for any kind of crime is 'very rare, if not entirely absent', and that while Froissart reports the castration of Hugh Despenser, 'this is no more historically verifiable than the claim that Edward was himself killed by having a hot poker inserted in his anus': 'Chaucer's Pardoner on the Couch: Psyche and Clio in Medieval Literary Studies', *Speculum* 76.3 (July 2001): 638–80 at p. 659.

[100] Michel Foucault, *Discipline and Punish: The Birth of the Prison*, trans. Alan Sheridan (New York: Vintage, 1979), p. 48.

[101] Elaine Scarry, *The Body in Pain: The Making and Unmaking of the World* (Oxford: Oxford University Press, 1985), p. 27.

[102] Tracy, *Torture and Brutality*, p. 222.

Everybody knew about the laws or customs that governed common or everyday situations, so it was not necessary to write them down.'[103] The customs of Toulouse include an illustration of a public castration for a sexual crime,[104] and the castration of priests who engage in adultery features in two Old French fabliaux, *De Connebert* and *Du Prestre crucefié*. However, it does not seem to have been a legally prescribed punishment for adultery. Irvine notes the existence of 'revenge narratives where men are castrated by other men offended by discovered sexual intercourse, usually consensual, with a kinswoman'.[105] He further points out that castration was 'a recognized punishment for adultery in some regions, though the courts sought to control the application of the penalty'.[106] The cultural anxieties about bodily mutilation inherent in castration suggest that public opinion was not uniform on the application of these cruelties, and the representation of these acts and their analogues in fabliaux and other literary genres are not merely a mimetic display of contemporary practice, but rather a systematic condemnation of continuing them.[107]

There are only two sources that record the use of castration as punishment for political crimes outside the Norman world (Normandy and later Anglo-Norman England in particular), according to van Eickels.[108] He writes that in 'Carolingian and post-Carolingian Europe, castrating an enemy was considered an atrocity only likely to occur on the borders of Latin Christianity'.[109] The Anglo-Saxons considered the maiming of aristocrats a 'barbarian cruelty', and castration remained a punishment for sexual offenses alone – but only rarely, as Jay Gates points out.[110] According to van Eickels, castration and blinding as punishment for treason were brought to Normandy by Scandinavian settlers in the tenth century, who then brought the practice to England in 1066 during the Norman Conquest, where it remained on the books until the thirteenth century.[111] Secular tribunals throughout Europe offered a choice of penalties for rape, including the death penalty, exile, forfeiture of property, fines,

[103] Akehurst, *The Etablissements de Saint Louis*, p. xxxvi.

[104] Dean, *Crime in Medieval Europe*, p. 138.

[105] Irvine, 'Abelard and (Re)writing the Male Body', p. 88.

[106] Ibid.

[107] Tracy, *Torture and Brutality*, p. 208.

[108] van Eickels, 'Gendered Violence', p. 99. Emily Zack Tabuteau counters this image of the Normans and argues that they do not deserve their reputation for 'punitive rigor and harshness'. She writes that the 'surviving evidence indicates that punishments not only were relatively lenient but were often not rigorously enforced': 'Punishments in Eleventh-Century Normandy', in *Conflict in Medieval Europe: Changing Perspectives on Society and Culture*, ed. Warren C. Brown and Piotr Górecki (Aldershot: Ashgate, 2003), pp. 131–49 at p. 133.

[109] van Eickels, 'Gendered Violence', p. 98.

[110] Jay Paul Gates, 'The *Fulmannod* Society: Social Valuing of the (Male) Legal Subject', in this volume pp. 131–48.

[111] van Eickels, 'Gendered Violence', pp. 100–1.

compensation for the victim or her family, imprisonment, flogging, or mutilation and 'castration was an obvious favorite, although by the end of the thirteenth century it had begun to fade out of fashion'.[112]

This is the case in England as well. Compared to the Anglo-Norman and Tudor periods, penal brutality was uncommon in England in the later Middle Ages and despite the references in thirteenth-century legal treatises to castration and blinding for rape or felonious wounding, in practice they had probably ceased to be used by the turn of the fourteenth century.[113] Corinne Saunders traces the fluctuation in English penalties regarding rape, and posits that the punishment diminished in severity as the status of women declined in society and the crime of rape was relegated to one of trespass.[114] In fact, there is evidence that castration and blinding were only applied on one known occasion – in 1222 – before the law changed the penalty to two years' imprisonment and a fine in 1275.[115] Possibly because of population decline, authorities recognized the need to propagate and so limited the application of castration as punishment, especially for sexual crimes. According to Charles F. Briggs, in England between 1300 and 1500 'roughly one quarter of families in the upper nobility became extinct in the male line every twenty-five years'.[116] But in certain communities, stemming population growth was part of the point of castration. In Iceland, beggars were castrated to limit their offspring, and in Norway castration was a punishment for bestiality, but its use was prohibited in all other cases.[117] Castration by various ingenious means (like hanging by the testicles) was also prescribed as a punishment for sodomy and sexual deviance, especially in the second half of the thirteenth century, which 'witnessed a sharp growth of legislation about homosexual relationships', including increased associations of homosexuality with heresy.[118] However, the mortality of the nobility, which led to a rising merchant class, fed fears about infertility and succession, and perhaps explains heightened anxieties about castration evident in the later Middle Ages. England's fraught relationship with interrogatory torture, and a popular interest in distancing thirteenth-century

[112] Brundage, *Law, Sex, and Christian Society*, p. 471.

[113] John Bellamy, *Crime and Public Order in England in the Later Middle Ages* (London: Routledge and Kegan Paul, 1973), p. 181. Barbara A. Hanawalt notes that it 'seems not to have been practiced frequently': *'Of Good and Ill Repute': Gender and Social Control in Medieval England* (Oxford: Oxford University Press, 1998), p. 126.

[114] Corinne Saunders, *Rape and Ravishment in the Literature of Medieval England* (Cambridge: D. S. Brewer, 2001), pp. 49–67.

[115] Dean, *Crime in Medieval Europe*, p. 83.

[116] Charles F. Briggs, *The Body Broken: Medieval Europe 1300–1520* (London and New York: Routledge, 2011), p. 49.

[117] Jenny Jochens, *Women in Old Norse Society* (Ithaca, NY: Cornell University Press, 1995), p. 66.

[118] Brundage, *Law, Sex, and Christian Society*, pp. 472–3.

English society from its recent Norman ancestors in favor of more distant Anglo-Saxon ones,[119] also explains the decline of castration, a barbaric tool that threatened the stability and longevity of the masculine elite.

The accounts of castration in this collection construct a contextual portrait of how that act shaped social images or conceptions of masculinity, femininity, and gender, revealing how medieval and early modern people responded to and reacted against physical threats that jeopardized carefully crafted social constructions of gender identity. This collection explores this grave subject and its implications for cultural *mores* and custom in western Europe and seeks to demystify and demythologize castration. The articles in this volume include archaeological studies of modern eunuchs, historical accounts of castration in the Norse slave trade, and legal accounts concerning castration and genital wounding in Anglo-Saxon England, Frisia, medieval Ireland, and Wales. Several pieces focus on literary examples of castration as punishment or comedy (as in the Old French fabliaux), as well as the prohibition against genital mutilation in hagiography. Finally, the concluding essay interrogates early modern anxieties about punitive castration enacted on the Elizabethan stage, rejecting the psychoanalytic lens. The essays progress from very concrete, tangible evidence of modern castration in archeological research (an untapped area of study) to the medieval legal incidents of and prohibitions against castration, the more interpretative accounts of actual castration as a literary motif, and finally to the persistence of medieval attitudes towards castration in early modern plays juxtaposed against medical texts.

The essays are arranged according to their primary focus, beginning with the ground-breaking archaeological research of Kathryn Reusch, who examines physical evidence found in modern Romanian castrate burials as the first step in establishing how the physical difference of eunuchs reflected on their cultural status. The first section is concerned with the body of eunuchs, what remains to be found, and how they were idealized and fetishized in certain communities. From this modern archaeological perspective, the essays proceed chronologically from late antiquity to the sixteenth century. Because the study of late antique and medieval castration is enmeshed in spiritual concerns about the body and both religious practice and prohibition, the volume focuses next on the situation of castration within religious discourse. From the adoration of eunuchs in ancient Rome explored by Tougher, the essays turn to Judaism and early Christianity including the implications of Origen's self-castration, and then to Abelard's effect on accounts of brutality in medieval hagiography. The next set of essays charts the legal requirements and ramifications of castration and genital wounding across medieval Europe and finally the benefits

[119] Tracy, *Torture and Brutality*, pp. 132–90.

of it in the Viking slave trade. The essays on historical accounts give way to chapters focused on literary depictions that analyze castration as both comedy and tragedy in a variety of texts, closing with a final word on how the early modern era perceived castration in its own time.

In the first essay, Reusch examines the physical effects of prepubertal castration on skeletons that may make it possible to locate castrates in the archaeological record. She reviews recent studies on the physical remains of modern castrates, as well as social, historical, and gender studies of castrates and castration. Next, Tougher uses a variety of late antique evidence gleaned from histories, biographies, poems, panegyrics, invectives, medical texts, legal texts, and ecclesiastical texts, as well as material evidence, to explore how Roman society valued eunuchs, the beauty that young castrated boys were said to possess, and the part their presence played in Roman politics. The Roman adoration of eunuchs was problematic for early Christian societies that saw castration as both a physical mutilation and a necessary spiritual mortification. Collins compares the practices and prohibitions of castration within Jewish and Christian polemics and argues that castration imagery continued to play an important role in Christian self-definition, whether to differentiate the Jesus movement from the mundane concerns of other Jews, to defend against outside criticism, to symbolize ideal behavior, or to denounce perceived heresy. The collision of Greco-Roman ideals of manhood and fear of emasculation vying with the Christian insistence on celibacy created an uncertain environment for men of the era.

Abelard, whose iteration of his castration creates the framework for this volume, struggled with Christianity's contradictory polemic and attempted to fashion himself as a martyr purified by his injury. His account left its mark on subsequent castration narratives, and influenced the categorization of castration as an acceptable mode of holy endurance. Despite the exceptionally graphic depiction of torture in medieval English hagiography, castration is a forbidden form of torture or punishment in hagiography. I juxtapose Abelard's rhetorical construction of his castration as a form of martyrdom against the relatively rare scenes of castration in Middle English hagiography, explaining that even though the thirteenth-century *South English Legendary* contains some of the most brutal expositions of judicial torture that negotiate anxieties about national identity, social boundaries of 'acceptable' violence expected in a genre like hagiography do not go as far as castration and female genital mutilation.

But castration (and other forms of genital wounding) certainly played a part in medieval law, even if it did not appear much in hagiography. Rolf Bremmer addresses a number of problems in the *Lex Frisionum*, a Latin Carolingian capitulary dated to *c.* 800, and later vernacular texts, including the unusual occurrence of castration as a punishment in an ecclesiastical legal text and the gendered distinction between male and female genital mutilation. Anglo-Saxon injury tariffs included payments for all manner of wounds. Gates examines the social valuing of an individual and why the structure of Anglo-Saxon laws suddenly shifts from a head-to-toe order to finish with a seemingly spasmodic series of injuries to genitals, arm, shoulder, hand, rib, eye, shoulder, shin, sinews, and tendons. Irish and Welsh annals record accounts of genital injury as punishment, and Charlene Eska compares Irish annal accounts and legal texts to laws imposed on societies by the Norman invasion, and argues that while insular societies regarded groin wounds similarly to those on the continent, in many ways the punishment of castration was a colonial invention. The Norse slave trade offers an intriguing venue for castration. Mary Valante examines the evidence of young boys and men, captured in Viking raids, castrated and sold into service in the Greek and Arab world. Monks, literate in the international languages of the day (like Latin and Greek) made some of the most valuable eunuchs in the slave economy.

The historical incidence of castration in the Norse world is also articulated in Old Norse/Icelandic literary sources. In northern literature, which has a tradition of using the rhetoric of castration as an insult for enemies, castration is part of the humiliation of unmanliness. The shame of it is an important theme in Scandinavian sagas, but it was not necessarily widespread in practice outside of slavery.[120] Anthony Adams looks at the vengeful castration of family blood feuds in *Sturlunga saga* and focuses on affective qualities of its very real occurrence in literary and historical texts. While eunuchs were prized for their learning and held in high esteem in some regions for their feminine demeanor, the same did not apply to women who behaved like men. If a woman assumes a 'masculine' identity, is castration an apt punishment for her, to return her to her female state? Mary Leech investigates this conundrum, questioning the comedy in fabliaux accounts of castration, with particular emphasis on the 'gelding' of the shrewish mother-in-law in *La dame escolliee*. Leech interrogates the appropriation of masculinity in this shrew-taming tale and suggests that the mother-in-law is not the only one gelded at the end.

Literary castration, implied in thigh wounds inflicted with withering effect, could also construct a form of virginity necessary in chivalric pursuits – an unmanning that produced unparalleled purity. Jed Chandler applies questions of sexual ambiguity to the seemingly neutered gender of the Grail knights, wounded in the groin as a means of purifying them and codifying their virginity to make them worthy of fulfilling their quest. But there is a fraught relationship between castration and courtliness. In his continuation of the *Romans de la rose*, Jean de Meun vehemently defends castrated men (specifically Abelard) and many critics have commented that the castration motif is Jean's addition to the text. In her essay, Ellen Friedrich argues that the theme

[120] Kuefler, 'Castration and Eunuchism', p. 291.

of castration is present in Guillaume de Lorris's section of the *Rose* as well, embodied in a marginal image of a beaver castrating himself, and that Jean continues it in his defense of masculinity. She also examines the homoerotics within the text that are partly articulated in this theme of castration. Robert Clark uses the sterile eunuch as a focal point for a discussion of Jean Le Fèvre's *La Vieille, ou les dernières amours d'Ovide* (before 1376) and Jean's source, the thirteenth-century Pseudo-Ovidian Latin poem *De Vetula*, commonly attributed to Richard de Fournival, arguing that the sterile eunuch is fertile grounds for cultural considerations. He engages with the clever wordplay of these authors, investigating the 'grammatical monstrosity of eunuchry'. The volume concludes with a synopsis of early modern castration motifs – literary, theatrical, and medical; how they have been read in theoretical terms and what they actually meant to Renaissance audiences. Fears of castration and gender ambiguity are major tenets of the early modern stage. Karin Sellberg and Lena Wånggren contextualize the fears of actual castration in William Shakespeare's *Titus Andronicus* and *Antony and Cleopatra* against fears of virtual effeminacy and the tangible threat castration posed in early modern society.

This 'history of calamities' investigates castration's role in shaping cultural attitudes towards masculinity, femininity, and national identities. This work covers several historical dimensions of castration from the eunuchs of antiquity to laws and customs regulating castration as punishment in the Middle Ages through the early modern period. It is the first extended study to examine castration in the context of ancient, medieval, and early modern cultures together, analyzing social taboos regarding the body in the framework of modern anxieties about gender, torture, punishment, and identity. As much as society (medieval and modern) may be horrified by accounts of castration, as much as it may threaten constructions of masculinity (and at times femininity) in both past and present, as illegitimate as it may have become in legal terms, there is still a morbid fascination with it. In 1993, America was horrified and yet morbidly intrigued when news broke of Lorena Bobbitt's castration of her husband in retaliation for spousal rape and ongoing domestic abuse (of which he was later acquitted), and the disposal of the severed penis in a field.[121] Bobbitt's violence against her husband seemed to strike at the very core of American masculinity – masculinity that has been perceived by some to be under attack over the last generation. Taylor argues that 'this is a specter that has haunted men for centuries: the fear that manhood will become, or has already become, obsolete, superfluous, ridiculous, at best quaint, at worst

[121] Lorena Bobbitt was found not guilty in 1994 by reason of insanity, caused by post-traumatic stress brought on by the emotionally abusive relationship with her husband, though he was also acquitted in 1994 of actually raping her.

disgusting'.[122] When Mel Gibson rewrote the story of William Wallace for his 1996 film *Braveheart*, he emphasized the virile masculinity of the Scottish rebel, even going so far as having Wallace supplant the effeminate Prince Edward and (inaccurately) impregnate Princess Isabella.[123] The final punishment, designed to strike at the very heart of that sexual and genetic usurpation, made audiences (male and female) cringe as their imaginations filled in the visual gaps of that final scene. Today we are fascinated and yet appalled at the thought or even the concept of castration, a sentiment that seems to have been shared by numerous facets of society across a span of centuries.

[122] Taylor, *Castration*, p. 9.

[123] Laurie Finke and Martin B. Shichtman, *Cinematic Illusions: The Middle Ages on Film* (Baltimore: Johns Hopkins University Press, 2009).

CHAPTER 1

Raised Voices: The Archaeology of Castration[1]

Kathryn Reusch

Castration is a topic that both repels and interests, provoking profound feelings of horror and intrigue. Castrates have filled many roles: musician, singer, clergyman, historian, inventor, warrior, general, and advisor. The modern world has been shaped greatly by the influence of castrates, but most people have little to no concept of a castrate's life, especially when the common belief is that in the modern period all forms of castration have disappeared.[2] Castrates tend to be the butt of humorous anecdotes, the victims of vicious invective, and the focus of righteous indignation and pity.[3] Modern popular

1 My thanks to Dr. Shaun Tougher and Professor Richard Wassersug for reading and commenting on this chapter in its early stages.

2 It is unclear whether the *hijiras* of India still practise castration, but these are not the only instances of modern castration. Leslie F. Roberts and her colleagues have compiled evidence of individuals who wish to be castrated to such a degree that they sometimes attempt to castrate themselves or visit 'underground cutters' who will perform the operation for them. See Leslie F. Roberts *et al.*, 'A Passion for Castration: Characterizing Men who Are Fascinated with Castration, but Have not Been Castrated', *Journal of Sexual Medicine* 5.7 (2008): 1669–80 at p. 1674; Thomas W. Johnson *et al.*, 'Desire for Castration Is not a Body Integrity Identity Disorder (BIID): A Response', *Journal of Sexual Medicine* 7.2, part 1 (2010): 853–5 at p. 855. There are also chemically castrated individuals who are either undergoing medical treatment or are convicted rapists. See Gary Taylor, *Castration: An Abbreviated History of Western Manhood* (New York and London: Routledge, 2002); Nikolaus Heim and Carolyn J. Hursch, 'Castration for Sex Offenders: Treatment or Punishment? A Review and Critique of Recent European Literature', *Archives of Sexual Behavior* 8.3 (1979): 281–304; Michael William Aucoin and Richard Joel Wassersug, 'The Sexuality and Social Performance of Androgen-Deprived (Castrated) Men throughout History: Implications for Modern Day Cancer Patients', *Social Science and Medicine* (1982) 63.12 (2006): 3162–73; Ross E. Gray *et al.*, 'The Experiences of Men Receiving Androgen Deprivation Treatment for Prostate Cancer: A Qualitative Study', *Canadian Journal of Urology* 12.4 (2005): 2755–63.

3 As in the running joke about eunuchs in the *Pirates of the Caribbean* films, the furious diatribes written from the Greek and Roman periods up to and including the modern era, and the reactions of early modern European writers referring to *castrati* singers and eunuchs in the Ottoman and Chinese empires.

depictions of castrates and castration often attempt to present them humorously, thereby nullifying the horror of castration. However, as the articles in this volume attest, modern scholars are developing an interest in the factual experiences of castration and the information these facts can provide about the past. Castration can shed light on past mores, thought, and culture and is being studied by a diverse range of academic disciplines, such as gender, history, medicine, and music,[4] but one field which has yet to undertake a study of castration is archaeology.

Archaeology has much to offer the study of castration. History shows that numerous castrates existed at varying times and in widely diverse areas of the world; archaeology may substantiate their existence and numbers, confirming historical accounts and elucidating further the cultures in which they existed. As no written records of many cultural traditions exist, the study of castrates' physical remains provides a foundation for filling in gaps in this knowledge. The archaeological investigation of castration is currently under way through the examination of castrates' skeletons historical, social, and cultural affiliations, material culture, and burial practices, creating a picture of castrate treatment in life and in death, but there are many challenges facing its application.

To avoid the cultural associations attached to the terms eunuch[5] (most

4 Gender: Elizabeth James, ed., *Women, Men and Eunuchs: Gender in Byzantium* (New York and London: Routledge, 1997); Mathew S. Kuefler, *The Manly Eunuch: Masculinity, Gender Ambiguity, and Christian Ideology in Late Antiquity* (Chicago: University of Chicago Press, 2001); Serena Nanda, '*Hijras*: An Alternative Sex and Gender Role in India', in *Third Sex, Third Gender: Beyond Sexual Dimorphism in Culture and History*, ed. Gilbert Herdt (New York: Zone Books, 1994), pp. 373–417; Kathryn M. Ringrose, *The Perfect Servant: Eunuchs and the Social Construction of Gender in Byzantium* (Chicago: University of Chicago Press, 2003). Historical: Mary M. Anderson, *Hidden Power: The Palace Eunuchs of Imperial China* (Buffalo, NY: Prometheus Books, 1990); Jane Hathaway, *Beshir Agha* (Oxford: Oneworld, 2005); Zia Jaffrey, *The Invisibles: A Tale of the Eunuchs of India* (New York: Pantheon Books, 1996); Shaun Tougher, ed., *Eunuchs in Antiquity and Beyond* (London: Classical Press of Wales and Duckworth, 2002). Musical: Nicholas Clapton, *Moreschi: The Last Castrato* (London: Haus, 2004); Laura E. DeMarco, 'The Fact of the *Castrato* and the Myth of the Countertenor', *Musical Quarterly* 86.1 (2002): 174–85; Giuseppe Gerbino, 'The Quest for the Soprano Voice: *Castrati* in Renaissance Italy', *Studi Musicali* 33 (2004): 303–57; Elisabeth Krimmer, '"Eviva Il Coltello?" The *Castrato* Singer in Eighteenth-Century German Literature and Culture', *PMLA* 120.5 (2005): 1543–59; Anthony Milner, 'The Sacred Capons', *Musical Times* 114.1561 (1973): 250–2; Neil Moran, 'Byzantine *Castrati*', *Plainsong and Medieval Music* 11.2 (2002): 99–112; Todd P. Olson, '"Long Live the Knife": Andrea Sacchi's Portrait of Marcantonio Pasqualini', *Art History* 27.5 (2004): 697–722.

5 *Oxford English Dictionary* (Eunuch) 'Forms: [ME eunuchus], ME enuke, 15–16 eunuche, 15– eunuch. Etymology: < Latin *eunūch-us*, < Greek *εὐνοῦχος*, < *εὐνή* bed + *-οχ-* ablaut-stem of *ἔχειν* to keep; the literal sense is thus a bedchamber guard or attendant. n. a. (a) A castrated person of the male sex; also, such a person employed as a harem attendant, or in Oriental courts and under the Roman emperors, charged with important affairs of state. Also *fig.* (freq. preceded by a descriptive adj.). (b) In the LXX. and the Vulgate the Greek *εὐνοῦχος*, Latin *eunūchus*, following the corresponding Hebrew *sārīs*, sometimes

commonly seen as guardians of women and harems) and *castrato*[6] (the church and opera singers of the early modern period), all castrated individuals will be referred to as castrates.[7] The word *liminal*, as applied to castrates and defined in the *Concise Oxford Dictionary of Archaeology*, refers to a social group distanced from a main group of individuals in a society and a stage of cultural progression, often a 'rite of passage'.[8] Castration, in a sense, is a 'rite of passage' in that it is a transformative process. It takes a boy or a man, excludes them from their main social or cultural group, puts them in a liminal position (which lasts at least for the duration of the castration and possibly for the rest of the castrate's life, depending on how their society viewed castrates), and then reincorporates them into the social sphere, but *not in the same cultural or social group from which they had been removed*. In some respects, the process of castration 'freezes' individuals into a liminal position – boy cannot become man, man cannot rejoin the male fraternity – which may have led to the formation of the specific, liminal, often gendered, social group of castrates. This liminality, and how a castrate's social or cultural group perceives it, is one of the most useful tools for the archaeology of castrates, as it may have contributed to special or unique social practices

designate palace officials who were not "eunuchs", *e.g.* Potiphar (Genesis xxxix. 1, where AV has "officer"). Hence the English word has occasionally been similarly used in discussions of passages in which the meaning of the word is disputed. b. A male singer, castrated in boyhood, so as to retain an alto or soprano voice. c. Used as *adj.*: Emasculated. *Rare*).' http://www.oed.com/viewdictionaryentry/Entry/64995.

6 *Oxford English Dictionary* (Castrato): 'Forms: Pl. castrati. Etymology: Italian; past participle of *castrare* used substantively, < Latin *castrāre* to castrate. n. A male singer castrated in boyhood so as to retain a soprano or alto voice.' http://www.oed.com/viewdictionaryentry/Entry/28620.

7 *Oxford English Dictionary* (Castrate): 'Etymology: < Latin *castrāt-* participial stem of *castrāre* to castrate, prune, expurgate, deprive of vigour, etc. v. 1. a. *trans.* To remove the testicles of; to geld, emasculate. 3. a. *transf.* and *fig.* To deprive of vigour, force, or vitality; to mortify. b. To mutilate, "cut down". *Obs.* Etymology: < Latin *castrāt-us* past participle of *castrāre* A. *adj.* Castrated. *Obs.* exc. in *Bot.* B. *n.* A castrated man, a eunuch. *arch.* (= French *castrat*, Italian *castrato*).mortify. b. To mutilate, 'cut down'. *Obs.* Etymology: < Latin *castrāt-us* past participle of *castrāre* A. *adj.* Castrated. *Obs.* exc. in *Bot.* B. *n.* A castrated man, a eunuch. *arch.* (= French *castrat*, Italian *castrato*), http://www.oed.com/view/Entry/28616).

8 'Liminal: *[Th]* A state of being on the edge or margins of society, applied archaeologically in three interrelated ways. Physical liminality may be seen in terms of a place or activity being detached from the centre of things (e.g. a cemetery placed on the boundary of a territory) in a "liminal zone". Social liminality may be seen in terms of subcultures who are distanced from those who see themselves as the mainstream (e.g. peripatetic workers who join a community for a while but then move on). Cultural liminality refers to a stage in the progression through a "rite of passage" such as birth, initiation, marriage, or death, which often follows a tripartite structure involving separation, liminality, and reincorporation.' *The Concise Oxford Dictionary of Archaeology*, ed, Timothy Darvill. Oxford Reference Online (Oxford: Oxford University Press, 2008), http://www.oxfordreference.com/views/ENTRY.html?subview=Main&entry=t102.e4833 (accessed September 23, 2011).

by or for castrates in both daily life and burial, allowing castrates to be distinguished in the archaeological record.

Castrates existed in large numbers in societies across the ancient world throughout many periods of history. They were present in the imperial systems of the Roman,[9] Persian,[10] Chinese,[11] Vietnamese,[12] Korean,[13] Byzantine,[14] and Ottoman Empires,[15] the Islamic caliphates,[16] the early Christian Church,[17] a sect of Christianity from the late eighteenth century to the modern day,[18] religious sects in India,[19] and choirs and opera troupes of early modern Europe.[20] Most of the cultures in western Europe from the fall of the Roman Empire to

9 Keith Hopkins, *Conquerors and Slaves* (Cambridge: Cambridge University Press, 1978), pp. 172–96; Orlando Patterson, 'The Ultimate Slave', in *Slavery and Social Death: A Comparative Study* (Cambridge, MA: Harvard University Press, 1982), pp. 299–333.

10 Piotr O. Scholz, *Eunuchs and* Castrati: *A Cultural History* (Princeton, NJ: Markus Wiener Publishers, 2001), pp. 81–2; Lloyd Llewellyn-Jones, 'Eunuchs and the Royal Harem in Achaemenid Persia (599–331 BC)', in *Eunuchs in Antiquity and Beyond*, ed. Tougher, pp. 19–49 at p. 21.

11 Jennifer W. Jay, 'Another Side of Chinese Eunuch History: Castration, Marriage, Adoption, and Burial', *Canadian Journal of History/Annales canadiennes d'histoire* 28.3 (1993): 459–78; p. 460; Taisuke Mitamura, *Chinese Eunuchs: The Structure of Intimate Politics* (Rutland, VT: C. E. Tuttle, 1970), p. 100; Scholz, *Eunuchs and* Castrati, p. 129.

12 Jay, 'Another Side of Chinese Eunuch History', p. 462.

13 Ibid.

14 Kuefler, *The Manly Eunuch*, pp. 64–7; Ringrose, *The Perfect Servant*, pp. 128–41; Scholz, *Eunuchs and* Castrati, p. 81; Shaun Tougher, 'Byzantine Eunuchs: An Overview, with Special Reference to Their Creation and Origin', in *Women, Men, and Eunuchs: Gender in Byzantium*, ed. Liz James (New York and London: Routledge, 1997), pp. 168–84; Shaun Tougher, *The Eunuch in Byzantine History and Society* (London and New York: Routledge, 2008), pp. 54–67.

15 Ronald Segal, *Islam's Black Slaves: The Other Black Diaspora* (New York: Farrar, Straus and Giroux, 2001), p. 109; Scholz, *Eunuchs and* Castrati, p. 188.

16 David Ayalon, *Outsiders in the Lands of Islam: Mamluks, Mongols, and Eunuchs* (London: Variorum, 1988), pp. 67–124; David Ayalon, *Eunuchs, Caliphs and Sultans: A Study in Power Relationships* (Jerusalem: Magnes Press, The Hebrew University, 1999), p. 13. Shaun Elizabeth Marmon, *Eunuchs and Sacred Boundaries in Islamic Society* (Oxford: Oxford University Press, 1995), pp. 31–54; Scholz, *Eunuchs and* Castrati, pp. 193–234; Segal, *Islam's Black Slaves*, pp. 23–34; Patterson, 'The Ultimate Slave', p. 299.

17 Scholz, *Eunuchs and* Castrati, pp. 159–92.

18 Eugène Pittard, *La castration chez l'homme et les modifications morphologiques qu'elle entraîne. Recherches sur les adeptes d'une secte d'eunuques mystiques: Les Skoptzy* (Paris: Masson, 1934); Jean D. Wilson and Claus Roehrborn, 'Long-Term Consequences of Castration in Men: Lessons from the Skoptzy and the Eunuchs of the Chinese and Ottoman Courts', *Journal of Clinical Endocrinology and Metabolism* 84.12 (1999): 4324–31.

19 Vern L. Bullough, 'Eunuchs in History and Society', in *Eunuchs in Antiquity and Beyond*, ed. Tougher, pp. 1–17 at p. 2; J. B. Mukherjee, 'Castration – A Means of Induction into the *Hijirah* Group of the Eunuch Community in India', *American Journal of Forensic Medicine and Pathology* 1.1 (1980): 61–5; Laurence W. Preston, 'A Right to Exist: Eunuchs and the State in Nineteenth-Century India', *Modern Asian Studies* 21.2 (1987): 371–87.

20 Bullough, 'Eunuchs in History and Society', pp. 8–9; Gerbino, 'The Quest for the Soprano Voice'; John S. Jenkins, 'The Voice of the *Castrato*', *Lancet* 351.9119 (1998): 1877–80 at pp. 1878–9; Milner, 'The Sacred Capons'; John Rosselli, 'The *Castrati* as a Professional Group and a Social Phenomenon, 1550–1850', *Acta Musicologica* 60.2 (1988): 143–79; Scholz, *Eunuchs and* Castrati, pp. 271–90.

the rise of the *castrati* did not practice castration on a large or consistent scale, mostly using it as an extreme punishment for sexual or social disobedience. As the majority of those castrated in these cultures were adults and were often the only castrates in their immediate area, they cannot currently be studied archaeologically. The social and religious impact of several accounts of castration in the Western late antique, early medieval, and medieval periods is the focus of other essays here.[21] Interestingly, castration appears not to have occurred in the New World,[22] though more archaeological work may alter this presumption. The gender perceptions of and social allowances for castrates varied considerably in each of these cultures, even in those that used castrates for similar purposes. These differences will provide important and interesting information about the cultures in which these castrates lived, especially as they may be reflected not only in the historical records, but also in the material culture.

Castrates were generally perceived as feminine, submissive, and weak, both physically and morally,[23] despite the large number of warrior castrates.[24]

21 In Western Europe, most accounts of castration stop at the castration itself and exclude any mention of the after-effects. Men like Peter Abelard, whose castration was widely known in the medieval period thanks in large part to his own account in the *Historia Calamitatum*, were rare. For a full account of Abelard's castration in this volume, see Larissa Tracy, '"Al defouleden is holie bodi": Castration, the Sexualization of Torture, and Anxieties of Identity in the *South English Legendary*', pp. 87–107 and Introduction. Medieval law texts in Ireland, Frisia, and England (both Anglo-Saxon and Anglo-Norman) refer only to the monetary cost of castration or crimes for which it could be used as a punishment; they infrequently deal with the social aftermath except in a man's ability to procreate. See Rolf H. Bremmer Jr, 'The Children He Never Had; The Husband She Never Served: Castration and Genital Mutilation in Medieval Frisian Law', pp. 108–30; Jay Paul Gates, 'The *Fulmannod* Society: Social Valuing of the (Male) Legal Subject', pp. 131–48; and Charlene M. Eska, '"Imbrued in their owne bloud": Castration in Early Welsh and Irish Sources' pp. 149–73 in this volume. Castration had humiliating effects in Norse culture, but in ancient Rome eunuchs were venerated for their beauty and often elevated because of it. See Anthony Adams, '"He took a stone away": Castration and Cruelty in the Old Norse *Sturlunga saga*', pp. 188–209 and Shaun Tougher, 'The Aesthetics of Castration: The Beauty of Roman Eunuchs', pp. 48–72, in this volume.

22 There is one anecdote from the conquistador period in which a ship ran aground in the Caribbean. When the natives rowed out to the ship to rescue the sailors, they apparently took the sailors captive, castrated them, then fattened them to be eaten. The veracity of the story is unclear. Pietro Martyr d'Anghiera, *De orbe novo: Petri Martyris Anglerii decades octo, diligenti temporum observatione et utilissimis annotationibus illustratae, suoque nitori restitutae, labore et industria*, ed. Richard Hakluyt (Paris: G. Auvray, 1587), Second Decade, Book VI.

23 Kathryn M. Ringrose, 'Passing the Test of Sanctity: Denial of Sexuality and Involuntary Castration', in *Desire and Denial in Byzantium*, ed. Liz James (Aldershot: Ashgate, 1999), pp. 124–125; Nadia Maria El-Cheikh, 'Servants at the Gate: Eunuchs at the Court of al-Muqtadir', *Journal of the Economic and Social History of the Orient* 48.2 (2005): 234–52, p. 245; Marmon, *Eunuchs and Sacred Boundaries*, pp. 40, 63.

24 Aucoin and Wassersug, 'The Sexuality and Social Performance of Androgen-Deprived (Castrated) Men Throughout History'; Lawrence Herbert Fauber, *Narses, Hammer of the Goths: The Life and Times of Narses the Eunuch* (New York: St Martin's Press, 1990); Xie Zhu, *Zheng He* (Beijing: Sheng huo, du shu, xin zhi san lian shu dian, 1956).

Throughout the duration of the Byzantine Empire, when castrates were likely perceived not as boys but not as men,[25] and marriage was intended only for reproduction, castrates could adopt heirs but not marry.[26] Gender appears always to have been more fluid in China,[27] where castrates were referred to in male terms and were allowed to adopt children and to marry.[28] In both of these cultures, marriage and adoption would have had huge effects on the disposition of property, as a castrate with heirs would do his best to ensure that any wealth and power he had accrued would remain with his adoptive family rather than return to the crown or the state. For the Skoptsy, an offshoot sect of Christianity which began in Russia in the eighteenth century, spread to Romania due to persecution, and likely ended in AD 1959, members voluntarily underwent castration in order to preserve their chastity, removing the external, 'dirty' signifiers of sex and creating pure, sexless, and genderless beings.[29] For the *hijiras*, an Indian sect devoted to a mother goddess, castration creates a powerful being which is at the same time neither male nor female and *both* male and female.[30] These differences would seem to widely separate these two religious sects, but both groups tended to live fairly humble lives, the *hijiras* normally begging and existing on land grants, and the Skoptsy living as drivers of horse-drawn taxis and farmers.[31]

The wide-ranging geographical, temporal, and cultural use of castrates suggests that there is the potential for much archaeological evidence, but that potential has not yet been recognized. Clues may come from daily items such as personal care objects, adornments, or insignia, or from funerary contexts such as burial methods, grave goods, or epitaphs. Perhaps the best evidence for castration in the archaeological record is the skeletons of the castrates themselves, as they provide evidence of castrates' life histories – the records of their health and diet. These allow a picture of the treatment of castrates in a particular society to be developed. Therefore, if castrates are to be explored

25 Roger Freitas, 'The Eroticism of Emasculation: Confronting the Baroque Body of the *Castrato*', *Journal of Musicology* 20.2 (2003): 196–249 at pp. 203–4; Catriona MacLeod, 'The "Third Sex" in an Age of Difference: Androgyny and Homosexuality in Winckelmann, Friedrich Schlegel, and Kleist', in *Outing Goethe and His Age*, ed. Alice A. Kuzniar (Stanford, CA: Stanford University Press, 1996), pp. 194–214 at pp. 200–2; Kathryn M. Ringrose, 'Living in the Shadows: Eunuchs and Gender in Byzantium', in *Third Sex, Third Gender*, ed. Herdt, pp. 85–110 at pp. 87–90.

26 Shaun Tougher, 'Images of Effeminate Men: The Case of the Byzantine Eunuchs', in *Masculinity in Medieval Europe*, ed. Dawn M. Hadley (London: Longman, 1999), pp. 89–100 at p. 99.

27 Martin W. Huang, *Negotiating Masculinities in Late Imperial China* (Honolulu: University of Hawai'i Press, 2006), pp. 4, 91.

28 Jay, 'Another Side of Chinese Eunuch History'.

29 Pittard, *La castration chez l'homme*, pp. 68–114.

30 Nanda, '*Hijras*', p. 373.

31 Pittard, *La castration chez l'homme*; Preston, 'A Right to Exist'.

archaeologically, castration itself and its effects on the bodies of those castrated must first be understood.

While the historical record provides some of the detail surrounding the lives and social roles of castrates, it must be remembered that it is the physical state of these individuals that makes them so remarkable. All too often, that physicality is ignored, except as a passing remark in a social or historical study. However, the investigation of the physical aspects of castration, especially those which affect the bodies of castrates, may help to uncover new and interesting areas of study. The different methods of castration have been discussed in depth in both the introduction and elsewhere,[32] and will only be summarized here. Castration can be effected in one of two ways: the removal of only the testicles and the scrotum (partial castration)[33] or the total removal of the testes, scrotum, and penis (complete castration).[34] Other methods include crushing the testes or severing the spermatic cords.[35] Most modern works that refer to the physical act of complete castration quote G. Carter Stent's account of castration in China.[36] This method differs from the Nubian[37] method of castration by washing the wound in antiseptic solutions and bandaging it before letting the patient heal over several days. However, by the time Stent recorded this method, castration in China was a specialized skill handed down through family lineages, leading to fewer fatalities and better healing.[38] The Skoptsy would either remove the testes and scrotum (called the Lesser Seal) or the testes, scrotum, and penis (called the Greater Seal). It was considered most holy to undergo the Greater Seal, but a man could work his way up to it by first undergoing the Lesser Seal, with a later removal of the penis.[39] While only the

32 Bullough, 'Eunuchs in History and Society', pp. 1–5; Jay, 'Another Side of Chinese Eunuch History', p. 464; Wilson and Roehrborn, 'Long-Term Consequences of Castration in Men'; Chieh Ping Wu and Fang-Liu Gu, 'The Prostate in Eunuchs', *EORTC Genitourinary Group Monograph* 10 (1991): 249–55.

33 Jenkins, 'The Voice of the *Castrato*'; Scholz, *Eunuchs and* Castrati, p. 14.

34 Jay, 'Another Side of Chinese Eunuch History', p. 464.

35 Rosselli, 'The *Castrati* as a Professional Group', p. 151.

36 Carter G. Stent, 'Chinese Eunuchs', *Journal of the North China Branch of the Royal Asiatic Society*, new series 11 (1876): 143–84.

37 This method was used in Nubia in the early modern period to supply castrates to the Ottoman court and normally involved removing the penis, testicles, and scrotum in one slice, followed by cauterization of the wound with a hot poker or burial in hot sand to the waist for several days without food or water. After several days, the boy would be unearthed, bandaged, and nursed, and complete healing would take three months. Due to the lack of hygienic conditions, up to three-quarters of the boys who underwent this procedure died. Peter Tompkins, *The Eunuch and the Virgin: A Study of Curious Customs* (New York: C. N. Potter, 1962), pp. 12, 75.

38 Wilson and Roehrborn, 'Long-Term Consequences of Castration in Men', pp. 4325–6; Wu and Gu, 'The Prostate in Eunuchs', pp. 250–1.

39 Wilson and Roehrborn, 'Long-Term Consequences of Castration in Men', p. 4325.

surgical removal of the testes falls within the modern definition of castration,[40] the removal of the penis was considered part of the process in many cultures and the physical changes to the skeleton are similar no matter the method of testicular ablation. Moreover, the method of ablation is invisible archaeologically, therefore it is prudent to refer to all individuals who display these skeletal characteristics as castrates.

Most studies of castrates have focused on the soft tissue changes to the body, as they are the most immediately noticeable and important for a living individual.[41] However, castration before puberty also affects the skeleton as it develops,[42] and it is these changes to the skeleton that are most important archaeologically, as most human remains recovered are skeletons not mummies. The lack of testosterone caused by the removal of the testes makes the bones develop similarly to a female's in that castrates do not attain as much bone mass as an intact male. Testosterone promotes an increase in bone mass, while oestrogen, which a small amount of testosterone becomes,[43] ends bone growth. Thus, a castrate who lacks enough testosterone to build heavy, robust bones and enough oestrogen to stop bone growth in the late teens, develops elongated, normally gracile, long bones, a phenomenon which sometimes produces extreme height and body disproportions.[44] The pelvis and skull, which develop sexually dimorphic characteristics during puberty due to oestrogen and testosterone, are also affected. They do not develop 'female' characteristics, but they do not follow the typical course of male development

[40] *Oxford English Dictionary* (Castration): 'Etymology: < French *castration*, or < Latin *castrātiōn-em*, n. of action < *castrāre* to castrate. The action of castrating, in various senses. 1. a. The removing of the testicles, gelding. 3. Mutilation, "cutting down". *Obs.*' http://www.oed.com/view/Entry/28618?redirectedFrom=castration&print.

[41] Soft tissue changes include soft, smooth skin, fat deposits over the hips, thighs, and buttocks, a child-like, high voice due to the shortness of the vocal chords, lack of body hair, and the growth of some pubic hair, following a female shape. Freitas, 'The Eroticism of Emasculation', p. 226.

[42] Castration after puberty will also affect the skeleton but not to the same extent as prepubertal castration. J.T. Eng, Q. Zhang, and H. Zhu, 'Skeletal Effects of Castration on Two Eunuchs of Ming China', *Anthropological Science* 118 (2010): 2–5; Wilson and Roehrborn, 'Long-Term Consequences of Castration in Men', p. 4328.

[43] Anne M. Kenny and Lawrence G. Raisz, 'Androgens and Bone', in *Androgens in Health and Disease*, ed. Carrie J. Bagatelle and William J. Bremner (Totowa, NJ: Humana Press, 2003), pp. 221–32 at pp. 223–5.

[44] Melvin M. Grumbach and Richard J. Auchus, 'Estrogen: Consequences and Implications of Human Mutations in Synthesis and Action', *Journal of Clinical Endocrinology and Metabolism* 84.12 (1999): 4679–83; Olaf Hiort, 'Androgens and Puberty', *Best Practice and Research Clinical Endocrinology and Metabolism* 16.1 (March 2002): 31–41 at p. 32; Dirk Vanderschueren, Steven Boonen, and Roger Bouillon, 'Action of Androgens versus Estrogens in Male Skeletal Homeostasis', *Bone* 23.5 (1998): 392–3; Stephen J. Winters and Barbara J. Clark, 'Testosterone Synthesis, Transport and Metabolism', in *Androgens in Health and Disease*, ed. Bagatelle and Bremner, pp. 3–22 at pp. 16–17.

either.[45] The bones of the face, which grow the most during puberty,[46] develop more slowly in castrates due to a lack of oestrogen, and so a castrate's craniofacial area retains what is described as a small, child-like appearance.[47] The lack of development of the midface region in castrates can distort the appearance of a castrate's skull, making the mandible appear heavier and the nose deep-set over a protruding maxilla (Figure 1.1). The pelvis develops the typical male shapes in the sciatic notch and the subpubic angle (Figure 1.2),[48] but the wings of the ilia flare outwards.

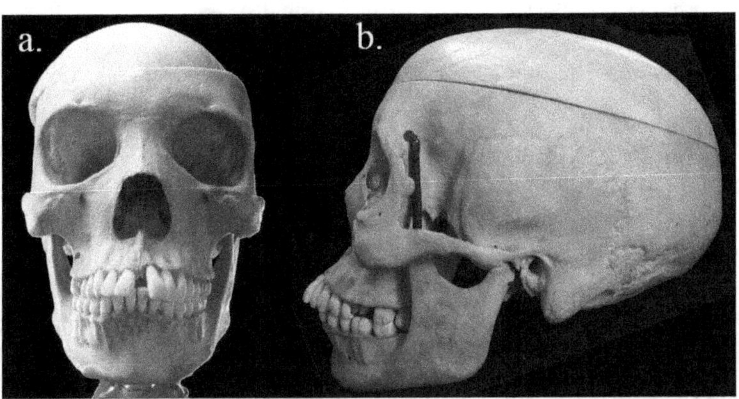

FIGURE 1.1 Skull of a castrate, demonstrating the small craniofacial area (a) and heavy mandible (b). Photo by Kathryn Reusch, printed with permission of Musée Testut Latarjet d'Anatomie et d'Histoire Naturelle Médicale, Lyon.

45 Louis-Charles Lortet, 'Allongement des membres infèrieurs du à la castration', *Archives d'Anthropologie Criminelle* 64 (1896): 361–4 at p. 363; Julius Tandler and Siegfried Grosz, 'Über den Einfluss der Kastration auf den Organismus I. Beschreibung eines Eunuchen Skeletes', *Archiv für Entwicklungsmechanik der Organismen* 27 (1909): 35–45 at pp. 44, 49, 56–7, 59, 61.

46 Donald H. Enlow and Seong Bang, 'Growth and Remodeling of the Human Maxilla', *American Journal of Orthodontics* 51.6 (1965): 459–62; Johannes Lang, *Clinical Anatomy of the Nose, Nasal Cavity, and Paranasal Sinuses*, trans. Philip M. Stell (New York: Thieme-Stratton Corp, 1989), pp. 31–85; Marion M. Maresh, 'Paranasal Sinuses from Birth to Late Adolescence: I. Size of the Paranasal Sinuses as Observed in Routine Posteroanterior Roentgenograms', *American Journal of Diseases of Children* 60.1 (1940): 64–71; Gert-Horst Schumacher, 'Principles of Skeletal Growth', in *Fundamentals of Craniofacial Growth*, ed. Andrew D. Dixon (New York: CRC Press, 1997), pp. 1–21 at pp. 11–14, 19; Gerhard K. Wolf, Wolfgang Anderhuber, and Frank Kuhn, 'Development of the Paranasal Sinuses in Children: Implications for Paranasal Sinus Surgery', *Annals of Otology, Rhinology and Laryngology* 102 (1993): 705–11.

47 Freitas, 'The Eroticism of Emasculation', pp. 214, 218; Tandler and Grosz, 'Über den Einfluss der Kastration auf den Organismus I', p. 44.

48 Maria Giovanna Belcastro *et al.*, 'Hyperostosis Frontalis Interna (HFI) and Castration: The Case of the Famous Singer Farinelli (1705–1782)', *Journal of Anatomy* 219.5 (2011): 633–4; Eng, Zhang, and Zhu, 'Skeletal Effects of Castration', pp. 5–6; Lortet, 'Allongement des membres', p. 363; Tandler and Grosz, 'Über den Einfluss der Kastration auf den Organismus I', pp. 48–50.

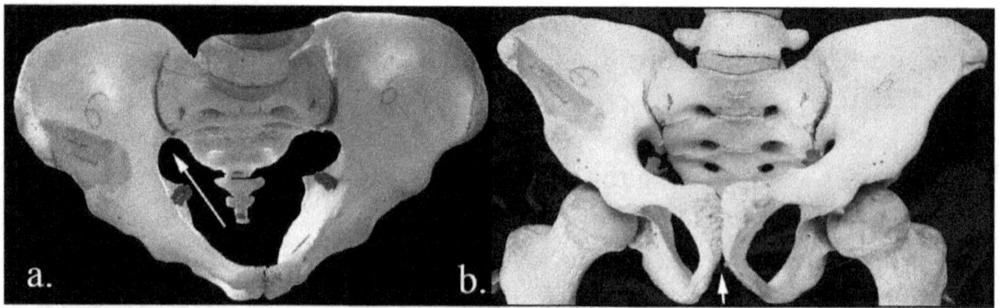

FIGURE 1.2 Castrate pelvis, displaying the unusual shape of the ilia and a typically male sciatic notch (a) and subpubic angle (b). Photo by Kathryn Reusch, printed with permission of Musée Testut Latarjet d'Anatomie et d'Histoire Naturelle Médicale, Lyon.

Due to the obvious physical effects of castration, castrates' skeletons should be very apparent in a cemetery containing a mixture of non-castrate and castrate burials, yet few skeletons of castrates have been reported. There are several possible reasons for this. Potentially the skeletons do not survive the burial environment; castration can cause early-onset osteopenia, leading to osteoporosis, which makes skeletons more fragile.[49] Castrates may also have been too poor to afford burial in a cemetery, or the proper trappings for burial, including coffins, which make survival of the remains more likely. There may also have been specific cemeteries or areas within a cemetery set aside for castrates, and as entire cemeteries are rarely excavated, these remains may not be discovered. The most basic problem that can affect their detection is that it is difficult to identify castrates during excavation through visual analysis. Most of the height and body proportion differences that marked castrates in their daily lives become unnoticeable in a burial context. Castrate skeletons laid supine do not appear any more disproportionate than normal skeletons, and if burial involved a position other than supine (such as crouched, flexed, or disarticulated) or involved multiple inhumations, it would be next to impossible to detect castrates in the ground. Detection must then come in the laboratory when the skeletons are recorded for age, sex, and stature.[50]

At the end of the nineteenth century, Louis C. E. Lortet brought a eunuch's remains to Lyon from Cairo and published several papers on the skeleton, discussing its characteristics and the common presence of castrates in Cairo at the time.[51] In the first decade of the twentieth century, Julius Tandler and Siegfried Grosz (Austrian medical doctors) examined the remains of a castrate who had

49 Wilson and Roehrborn, 'Long-Term Consequences of Castration in Men', pp. 4328–30.

50 Megan Brickley and Jacqueline I. McKinley, eds., 'Guidelines to the Standards for Recording Human Remains' (Institute of Field Archaeologists Paper No. 7, 2004); Jane E. Buikstra and Douglas H. Ubelaker, *Standards for Data Collection from Human Skeletal Remains: Proceedings of a Seminar at the Field Museum of Natural History*, ed. Jane E. Buikstra (Fayetteville: Arkansas Archeological Survey, 1994).

51 Lortet, 'Allongement des membres'.

died in Vienna[52] and carried out studies on a group of five Skoptsy men in Bucharest in order to further their understanding of the hormonal processes driving the changes seen in castrate skeletons.[53] Walter Koch examined and radiographed thirteen Skoptsy men in Romania during World War I, focusing mainly on the characteristics of their skulls.[54] At the same time, Ferdinand Wagenseil (a German doctor) was examining eleven Ottoman eunuchs, taking radiographs and anthropometric measurements, and reporting enlarged pituitaries and thinned cranial bones in two castrates.[55] The last groups of castrates to be studied and measured anthropologically were a group of Skoptsy who had emigrated to a small village on the Black Sea coast in Romania (by Pittard) and a group of Chinese eunuchs in Beijing (by Wagenseil) in the 1930s.[56] Pittard carried out typical anthropometric studies of the Skoptsy, noting that they were taller than their uncastrated peers and that they had disproportionate limb to torso lengths.[57] Wagenseil's study involved measuring and classifying the eunuchs into groups based on body shape and physical characteristics, and grouped measurements according to these categories, averaging each group's results.[58]

In the eighty years since the last medical investigation into castration, both medical and anthropological techniques have developed which allow for greater knowledge and understanding of the effects of castration. Doctors today know more about endocrinology and have better imaging techniques, allowing them to trace the development of the skeleton and other internal organs and determine which parts of the body are being affected by hormonal imbalance at specific points in the developmental process.[59] Physical anthropology techniques have also improved over the years, with the introduction of standards for the recording of skeletons, giving researchers a common ground in landmarks and acceptable tools, so that examinations may be repeated and verified.[60]

52 Tandler and Grosz, 'Über den Einfluss der Kastration auf den Organismus I'.

53 Julius Tandler and Siegfried Grosz, 'Über den Einfluss der Kastration auf den Organismus II. Die Skopzen', *Archiv für Entwicklungsmechanik der Organismen* 28 (1910): 236–53.

54 Walter Koch, 'Über die russisch-rumänische Kastratensekte der Skopzen', *Veroffentlichungen Kreigs Konstitutionspathologie* 7 (1921): 1–39.

55 Ferdinand Wagenseil, 'Beiträge zur Kenntnis der Kastrationsfolgen und des Eunchoidismus beim Mann', *Zeitschrift für Morphologie und Anthropologie* 26.2 (1927): 264–304.

56 Pittard, *La castration chez l'homme*; Ferdinand Wagenseil, 'Chinesische Eunuchen. (Zugleich ein Beitrag zur Kenntnis der Kastrationsfolgen und der rassialen und körperbaulichen Bedeutung der anthropologischen Merkmale)', *Zeitschrift für Morphologie und Anthropologie* 32.3 (1933): 415–468.

57 Pittard, *La castration chez l'homme*, pp. 132–136.

58 Wagenseil, 'Chinesische Eunuchen'.

59 Stephen Plymate, 'Hypogonadism in Men: An Overview', in *Androgens in Health and Disease*, ed. Bagatelle and Bremner, pp. 45–76; Kenny and Raisz, 'Androgens and Bone'; Winters and Clark, 'Testosterone Synthesis, Transport and Metabolism'.

60 Brickley and McKinley, 'Guidelines to the Standards for Recording Human Remains'; Buikstra and Ubelaker, *Standards for Data Collection*.

The improvement in imaging techniques has also benefited physical anthropologists, allowing them to examine previously difficult or complicated subjects such as mummies and complete but pathological bones. Individuals with specific physical and pathological skeletal characteristics are most likely to have been castrated or intersex individuals. Standardized recording of skeletal traits and improved imaging and osteological techniques will allow these individuals to be identified more readily within larger skeletal populations.

Castrates were studied in the late 1800s and early 1900s in an effort to better understand hormones and their effects on the body and its development.[61] This led to further investigations of hormones and the studies in the second half of the twentieth century of those individuals with androgen-insensitivity syndrome and primary hypogonadism.[62] These investigations expanded into the field of endocrinology, which has helped doctors better understand the effects of too

[61] Ernst Alterthum, 'Folgezustände nach Castration', *Beiträge zur Geburtshülfe und Gynäkologie* 2 (1899): 13; Philipp Becker, *Der männliche Castrat mit besonderer Berücksichtigung seines Knochensystems* (Freiburg im Breisgau: Kuttruff, 1898); Philipp Becker, 'Über das Knochensystem eines Castraten', *Archiv für Anatomie und Physiologie [anat. Abth.]* 1 and 2 (1899): 83; Frédéric-Guillaume Bergmann, *Origine, signification et histoire de la castration, de l'eunuchisme et de la circoncision* (Palermo: L. Pedone Lauriel, 1883); Alexander Ecker, *Zur Kenntniss des Körperbaues schwarzer Eunuchen: Ein Beitrag zur Ethnographie Afrika's* (Frankfurt am Main, 1865); Charles-Emile Félix, *Recherches sur l'excision des organes génitaux externes chez l'homme* (Lyon: L. Duc et F. Demaison, 1883); Gaetano Fichera, 'Sur l'hypertrophie de la glande pituitaire consecutive a la castration', *Archives Italiennes de Biologie* 43 (1905): 405–26; Hugo Lüthje, 'Über die Castration und ihre Folgen', *Archiv für experimentelle Pathologie und Pharmakologie* 48.3 (1902): 184–222; Jean-Jacques Matignon, 'La castration industrielle en Chine', *Gazette hebdomadaire des sciences médicales de Bordeaux* 17 (1896): 403; Richard Millant, *Castration criminelle et maniaque (étude historique et médico-légale)* (Paris: Jules Rousset, 1902); Eugen Pelikan, *Gerichtlich-medicinische Untersuchungen über das Skopzenthum in Russland*, with historical notes by E. Pelikan, trans. from Russian into German by N. Iwanoff (Giessen: J. Ricker, 1876); Ludwig Prochownick, *Beiträge zur Castrationsfrage: nach einem am 6. April 1886 im ärztlichen Vereine zu Hamburg gehaltenen Vortrage* (Leipzig: A. Th. Engelhardt, 1886); Conrad Rieger, *Die Castration in rechtlicher, socialer und vitaler Hinsicht.* (Jena: Fischer, 1900); Jules Rouyer, 'Des eunuques', *Gazette Médicale de Paris* 14 (1859): 601–2, 606, 609; Hugo Sellheim, 'Castration und Knochenwachsthum', *Beiträge zur Geburtshülfe und Gynäkologie* 2 (1899); Fr. N. Schulz and O. Falk, 'Phosphorsäureausscheidung nach Castration', *Zeitschrift für Physiologische Chemie* 27.3 (1899): 250–254; Tandler and Grosz, 'Über den Einfluss der Kastration auf den Organismus I'; Tandler and Grosz, 'Über den Einfluss der Kastration auf den Organismus II'; Julius Tandler and Siegfried Grosz, 'Über den Einfluss der Kastration auf den Organismus III. Die Eunuchoide', *Archiv für Entwicklungsmechanik der Organismen* 29 (1910): 290–324; G. Tournès, *La liberté par l'humanité. Les eunuques en Égypte. Extrait des notes sur l'Égypte (inédit)* (Geneva: Vaney, 1869).

[62] Robert P. Kelch *et al.*, 'Estradiol and Testosterone Secretion by Human, Simian, and Canine Testes, in Males with Hypogonadism and in Male Pseudohermaphrodites with the Feminizing Testes Syndrome', *Journal of Clinical Investigation* 51.4 (1972): 824–30; William A. Marshall, *Human Growth and Its Disorders* (London and New York: Academic Press, 1977); Richard L. Weinstein *et al.*, 'Secretion of Unconjugated Androgens and Estrogens by the Normal and Abnormal Human Testis Before and After Human Chorionic Gonadotropin', *Journal of Clinical Investigation* 53.1 (1974): 1–6.

much or too little testosterone, growth hormone, and the reasons that bodies react and develop in the manner that they do.[63] There has been a long hiatus in the study of castrates' physical bodies[64] but this is changing. A report on the physical remains of two eunuchs exhumed in China has recently been published,[65] and an Italian team based at the universities of Bologna and Pisa has been working on the exhumed remains of the famous castrate Farinelli.[66] However, both of these studies are case reports on only one or two individuals. To better understand both the widespread and the specific changes to the skeleton as affected by human variation, including ancestry, cemetery-wide examinations of castrates must be undertaken, a project which is currently under way.

There is some evidence from animal bone studies that long bone disproportion within a skeletal population will indicate the presence of castrates, but this method has only been consistently utilized in sheep.[67] This work is being expanded to more mammalian species, in the hopes that long bone disproportion will indicate castrates in all mammals, creating a simple and fast method for checking for castrates in a skeletal population. If this can be accomplished, it will be relatively easy to identify the majority of castrates in a cemetery population, allowing them to be studied and a better understanding of castrate skeletal variation to be gained. This will give a better understanding of what changes are unilaterally intrinsic to castration and which are modified by external factors such as diet, ancestry, and health.

Castrates, in a similar manner to any other group of people throughout history, have left traces in the archaeological record, traces which may allow a deeper interrogation not only of castrates and their lives, but of the societies which employed them. These traces may be ephemeral, such as written records and organic materials; controversial, such as the purported castration clamps discovered in England, Switzerland, and Germany;[68] or as large and permanent

[63] Hiort, 'Androgens and Puberty'; Kenny and Raisz, 'Androgens and Bone'; Plymate, 'Hypogonadism in Men'; Constantine A. Stratakis *et al.*, 'The Aromatase Excess Syndrome Is Associated with Feminization of Both Sexes and Autosomal Dominant Transmission of Aberrant P450 Aromatase Gene Transcription', *Journal of Clinical Endocrinology and Metabolism* 83.4 (1998): 1348–57; Vanderschueren *et al.* 'Action of Androgens versus Estrogens'; Winters and Clark, 'Testosterone Synthesis, Transport and Metabolism.'

[64] Pittard, *La castration chez l'homme*; Tandler and Grosz, 'Über den Einfluss der Kastration auf den Organismus I'.

[65] Eng *et al.*, 'Skeletal Effects of Castration'.

[66] Belcastro *et al.*, 'Hyperostosis Frontalis Interna (HFI) and Castration'.

[67] Simon J. M. Davis, 'The Effect of Castration and Age on the Development of the Shetland Sheep Skeleton and a Metric Comparison between Bones of Males, Females and Castrates', *Journal of Archaeological Science* 27.5 (May 2000): 382–6.

[68] Alfred G. Francis, 'On a Romano-British Castration Clamp Used in the Rights of Cybele', *Proceedings of the Royal Society of Medicine* 19 (1926): 95–110; Stijn Heeren, 'New Views on the Forfex of Virilis the Veterinarian: Shears, Emasculator or Twitch?', *Journal of Archaeology in the Low Countries* 1 (2009): 87–95; Alfons Kolling, 'Römische Kastrierzangen', *Archäologisches Korrespondensblatt* 3 (1973): 353–7.

as a monastery or stone memorial.[69] Little to nothing is known about most castrates' daily lives. Most historical sources which discuss castrates tend to describe their character (greedy, corrupt, cowardly, venal individuals who were only loyal as long as they received excess compensation for their efforts and who could bring down entire kingdoms)[70] rather than the routine of day-to-day living. A list of positions castrates could hold in the bureaucracy of the Byzantine Empire[71] gives some idea of the responsibilities given to this group of men, as do the nineteenth- and early twentieth-century reports of Chinese and Ottoman eunuchs written by Westerners,[72] but these sources are frustratingly silent on the more mundane aspects of daily life. We hear about the vast fortunes some castrates accumulated and the luxurious houses they then filled with treasures, such as those of the Ming eunuch Feng Pao[73] or the Byzantine master of the palace eunuchs Euphratas,[74] but this was only a tiny fraction of the castrate population. We have little idea what life was like for those castrates who never made fortunes and who spent their lives in low-level positions with little or no real reward.

Most sources that hint at daily life for castrates tend to focus on small, specific areas or time periods or are anthropological studies of isolated groups of individuals. For example, the Skoptsy have received a lot of attention as a group of castrated individuals,[75] but their circumstances do not really reflect the conditions of castrates in an imperial system. However, they may more closely reflect the lives of unsuccessful *castrati*[76] during the sixteenth through

69 Moran, 'Byzantine *Castrati*', p. 105.

70 Such as Charles D'Ancillon, *Eunuchism Display'd. Describing All the Different Sorts of Eunuchs; ... Written by a Person of Honour*, trans. Robert Samber (London: E. Curll, 1718), pp. 94–9; Procopius, *The Secret History: with Related Texts*, trans. Anthony Kaldellis (Indianapolis: Hackett Publishing Company, 2010), pp. 19, 69, 71.

71 Rodolphe Guilland, 'Les eunuques dans l'empire byzantin: Étude de titulature et de prosopographie byzantines', *Études Byzantines* 1 (1943): 197–238.

72 Edmund Andrews, 'The Oriental Eunuchs', *JAMA: Journal of the American Medical Association* 30.4 (January 22, 1898): 173–7; Lortet, 'Allongement des membres', p. 361; Gustav Nachtigal, *Sahara and Sudan: Wadai and Darfur*, trans. Allan G. B. Fisher and Humphrey J. Fisher (Berkeley: University of California Press, 1975), pp. 46, 121, 175–7; Stent, 'Chinese Eunuchs', pp. 4–5; Rupprecht von Bayern, *Reiseerinnerungen aus dem südosten Europas und dem Orient* (Munich: Kösel & Pustet, 1923).

73 Ray Huang, *1587, A Year of No Significance: The Ming Dynasty in Decline* (New Haven, CT: Yale University Press, 1981), pp. 34–5.

74 Procopius, *The Secret History*, p. 126.

75 Laura Engelstein, *Castration and the Heavenly Kingdom: A Russian Folktale* (Ithaca, NY: Cornell University Press, 1999); Pelikan, *Gerichtlich-medicinische Untersuchungen*; Pittard, *La castration chez l'homme*; Tandler and Grosz, 'Über den Einfluss der Kastration auf den Organismus II'.

76 'Unsuccessful' castrate singers could be those individuals who did not manage to secure either a place in a church choir or an opera role or those who lost their voice at puberty and could not sing. These individuals often became teachers, government officials, or clerks. See Naomi Adele André, *Voicing Gender:* Castrati, *Travesti, and the Second Woman*

twentieth centuries AD, who more than likely would have lived modest lives integrated into a larger, mostly uncastrated, community. *Hijiras*, a group of castrates living in colonial and modern India, have also received a lot of anthropological attention,[77] but are religious castrates, and therefore may not be the best correlates for the majority of historical castrates, most of whom tended to serve in imperial institutions. The accounts of Ottoman and Chinese eunuchs provide interesting glimpses into the lives of imperial castrates, but most accounts, even and especially that of Sun Yaoting,[78] the last eunuch of China, came at the very end of imperial dynastic control in their areas, which may colour the accounts and their accuracy, making it difficult to take them as models of the daily life of imperial castrates throughout Ottoman and Chinese history.

Perhaps one of the most important times in a castrate's life, the castration itself, may also produce the best archaeological evidence. Bronze objects, which may be castration clamps from the Roman period, have been recovered from several northern European rivers.[79] It is unclear whether the objects were used as castration clamps or as a veterinary tool called a twitch, which is placed around a horse's lip to calm and control it.[80] While there is still debate over the actual use of these items, they may provide an interesting glimpse of the castration process in the Roman period. If they are clamps, they would be indicative of the medical knowledge of the time, and the understanding that the process could be dangerous, that the wound needed to clot in order to heal, and therefore needed to be stitched quickly and efficiently.[81] These clamps

in Early Nineteenth-century Italian Opera (Bloomington: Indiana University Press, 2006), p. 37; Patrick Barbier, *The World of the* Castrati*: The History of an Extraordinary Operatic Phenomenon*, new edn (London: Souvenir Press, 1998), p. 15; John Potter, 'The Tenor–*Castrato* Connection, 1760–1860', *Early Music* 35.1 (2007), p. 99; Rosselli, 'The *Castrati* as a Professional Group', pp. 151–3, 161, 165–6, 169–73, 176.

77 Anuja Agrawal, 'Gendered Bodies: The Case of the "Third Gender" in India', *Contributions to Indian Sociology* 31.2 (1997): 273–97; Mukherjee, 'Castration'; Nanda, '*Hijras*'; Serena Nanda, *Neither Man Nor Woman: The Hijras of India* (Belmont, CA: Wadsworth, 1999); Preston, 'A Right to Exist'.

78 Yinghua Jia, *The Last Eunuch of China: The Life of Sun Yaoting*, trans. Sun Haichan (Beijing: China Intercontinental Press, 2008).

79 Francis, 'On a Romano-British Castration Clamp'; Heeren, 'New Views on the Forfex of Virilis the Veterinarian'; Kolling, 'Römische Kastrierzangen'.

80 Heeren, 'New Views on the Forfex of Virilis the Veterinarian', pp. 88–9.

81 As shown by the drastically different survival rates in China, where the majority of castrates survived the process due to rapid staunching of the wound and clean bandaging, and Nubia, where large numbers of the boys castrated died, mostly due to unsanitary healing practices such as burial in river mud. See Stent, 'Chinese Eunuchs', pp. 170–1; Wu and Gu, 'The Prostate in Eunuchs', p. 250; Andrews, 'The Oriental Eunuchs', p. 176; A. Hickmet and Félix Régnault, 'Les eunuques de Constantinople', *Bulletins de la Société d'anthropologie de Paris* 2.1 (1901): 234–40 at p. 234; and John O. Hunwick and Eve Troutt Powell, *The African Diaspora in the Mediterranean Lands of Islam* (Princeton, NJ: Markus Wiener Publishers, 2002), pp. 100–1.

would hold the penis out of the way of the blade and secure the skin (which has a tendency to roll up on itself), and the spermatic cords and vessels, which would retract into the body, allowing for the fast treatment of the wound.[82] It is also possible that certain cultures, especially those in which castration was performed for ritual purposes, utilized specific tools to castrate individuals. Special knives or sharp implements may have been employed, and certain rites may have been performed with the removed parts. In the *hijira* castration ritual, the removed penis and scrotum are buried underneath a tree.[83] The excised penis and scrotum of Chinese eunuchs were kept preserved in jars of alcohol, as a eunuch had to present them every time he was promoted, to prove he had been castrated.[84] These jars were then buried with the eunuch, so that they could be complete men again in the afterlife. This means that in both India and China, finding the buried remains of eunuchs' genitals is possible, which (while grisly sounding), would provide interesting information about the history of the practices surrounding castration in these cultures and the material culture used to carry them out.

As most historical records worldwide are chiefly concerned with elites and governmental administration, and castration artefacts will only have affected a castrate once in their lives, most information about the daily life of castrates will have to come from the archaeological record. In societies such as China and the Ottoman Empire, where most castrates' lives centred on the ruler, many of the palaces and institutional buildings have survived to the modern period, making studies of servants' living quarters and remaining artefacts possible. However, for the majority of castrates, the places they once lived and the items they once used are likely mixed in with the artefacts left by the rest of their society. Few settlements are abandoned wholesale, and items are passed down, thrown away, recycled, or otherwise destroyed before ever being deposited. As an additional complicating factor, many complex societies tend to use mass-produced items for most of their daily activities. Therefore, to confidently identify an object as belonging to a castrate, it must be inscribed with the name of a known castrate, be found with a castrate's possessions or burial, or be an item that would only be useful to a castrate.

Most likely the physical items in castrates' daily lives would not have differed greatly from those of their non-castrated contemporaries, but they do appear to have differed greatly based upon a castrate's culture, wealth, duties, and reasons for castration. As in most hierarchical societies, those positioned in closest proximity to the head of power benefited the most financially and mate-

[82] Francis, 'On a Romano-British Castration Clamp', pp. 97–8.

[83] Roberta Gilchrist, *Gender and Archaeology: Contesting the Past* (London and New York: Routledge, 1999), p. 59; Nanda, '*Hijras*', p. 384.

[84] Stent, 'Chinese Eunuchs', pp. 172–3

rially. A Chinese castrate serving an emperor or empress would have been favourably positioned within court life and presumably would have used daily items such as gold and silver plates and utensils, fine cloth for clothing, and jewellery and other adornments of a far finer quality than a castrate who worked in the imperial kitchens and never saw a member of the royal family. The same holds true for any castrate in an imperial system. For castrates involved in religious systems, such as the *hijira* and Skoptsy, where asceticism is the ideal and where the majority of members tend to be from poorer classes, it is likely that the material culture of daily life would have consisted of plain, sturdy, not especially fancy items with one or two more elaborate items for special occasions.

Ostensibly, castrates lived the same way as any other member of their social class in their society. Thus, the burial environment will perhaps produce the most evidence about them, especially as this is one area in which historical sources are all but silent. This information could be derived from a mixture of studies of funerary and burial customs and osteology. By identifying and then studying prepubertal castrates, we will begin to gain an understanding of the funerary practices for castrates within a society. This can then be applied to postpubertal castrates, giving us a larger data set from which to draw conclusions and allowing us to learn more about their social lives.

Little is known about how or where castrates were buried, whether there were special funerary rituals prescribed for them, or if they were buried in the same manner as other individuals in their society. Some of these questions will be answered by a castrate's place in society. A rich castrate will have a different funeral from a poor one, but what of their extended social groups? Did castrates form networks that allowed them to protect and prepare themselves for burial? Did they have families (both birth and adopted) who would take care of a funeral for them? There do seem to be trends in burial practices, from the little that can be gleaned from modern archaeological studies. Castrates in south and east Asia and Africa appear to have been buried in discrete cemeteries set aside just for them, perhaps because of their place in society (the majority of them having been involved in some form of institutionalized eunuchism).[85] In Europe and north-west Asia (or at least those parts of north-west Asia containing Russia and the Byzantine Empire), castrates appear to have been buried with the rest of the population.[86] These instances are spread across a wide geographical area and temporal scale, which may make this an inaccurate observation, given how little data there is about castrate burial. However, it is

85 Jay, 'Another Side of Chinese Eunuch History', p. 476.

86 Belcastro *et al.*, 'Hyperostosis Frontalis Interna (HFI) and Castration', p. 633; Lucian, *The Syrian Goddess: Being a Translation of Lucian's 'De Dea Syria': with a Life of Lucian*, trans. Herbert A. Strong (London: Constable, 1913), p. 85.

worth considering whether there is a connection between burial practices in these areas and overall perception and use of castrates, with those areas which engaged in institutionalized eunuchism burying eunuchs in cadres and those cultures in which castration was a more individual act burying the individual with the rest of society.

Castrate burial customs seem to vary between cultures and time periods within these larger geographic areas, given current knowledge of castrate burial practices. In sixteenth- through twentieth-century AD Europe, the castrated singers of the Catholic Church and opera stage may have been buried in church cemeteries with the rest of the population, as Farinelli was,[87] whereas a fourth-century BC text recommended that Chinese eunuchs have a frugal funeral at night with few or no mourners.[88] Lucian, a rhetorician in the second century AD, describes the burial of the Galli priests of Cybele, a process which appears to have consisted of the body being carried to the cemetery, covered in stones, and the exclusion of the priests from the temple for a week, which he says differs from the normal Roman funerary ritual without describing in what manner.[89] These three anecdotes are the only knowledge we have of castrate burials, and of them, one is a proscribed rite, which may not have been followed all that closely, one is an extremely vague anecdote, and the last is a single individual who was independently wealthy and able to provide for his chosen burial method. Unfortunately, too little is known about the standard burial practices of most cultures or about castrate burial itself to determine at this time how castrate burial might have adhered to or differed from societal norms.

Beyond the type and location of burial, grave goods may also indicate castrate status. It is unclear if castrates would have had specific burial goods, but there is the possibility that certain items necessary to castrates in life may have entered the burial environment. It is possible that the jars used to hold the severed genitals of Chinese eunuchs (if not their contents) have survived burial and could indicate castrate graves. If complete removal of the testes, scrotum, and penis occurs, there is a strong possibility that the urethral opening will heal shut, which quickly proves fatal. This was often avoided by inserting some form of hollow tube or plug into the urethral opening.[90] If this plug or tube was made of material that was not considered valuable enough to remove before burial, it might still exist in the burial environment. If such plugs were found, they would not only help to identify castrate burials, but

87 Belcastro *et al.*, 'Hyperostosis Frontalis Interna (HFI) and Castration', p. 633.

88 Hsun-tžu, *Xunzi: A Translation and Study of the Complete Works*, trans. John Knoblock (Stanford CA: Stanford University Press, 1988), pp. 63–4.

89 Lucian, *The Syrian Goddess*, p. 85.

90 Jay, 'Another Side of Chinese Eunuch History', p. 464; Wilson and Roehrborn, 'Long-Term Consequences of Castration in Men', pp. 4325–7.

also identify the type of castrate, which would provide more information about the use of castrates in that particular society and about the medical knowledge of the time.

There is great potential for the use of archaeology to study castration. The physical traces of castrates can add to the knowledge passed down through historical sources, allowing for better and more complete pictures of social, cultural, and gender roles in the past. The examination of the physical remains of castrates can tell us about their diets, health, treatment in life, treatment in death, and social groups, showing whether the myths which have accompanied castrates through history have any basis in fact. Better understanding of each cultural group of castrates will allow us to draw better conclusions about what is common to all castrates, and what is contributed by the unique cultural and social settings encountered by each group. This will in turn create a better picture of castrates both within their specific societies and as one of the most important and long-lasting human phenomena.

CHAPTER 2

The Aesthetics of Castration: The Beauty of Roman Eunuchs

Shaun Tougher

For Romans, castration was a fact of life. Influenced by the Hellenistic East, the Roman Empire began to consume castrated slaves – eunuchs – from at least the first century BC.[1] A rare account of the operation of castration is provided by a late antique source, the medical encyclopaedia of Paul of Aegina (himself a doctor) composed in the seventh century AD.[2] In his *Epitome of Medicine*, Paul describes two methods of castration, one by compression and the other by excision. He writes:

> compression is performed thus: children, still of a tender age, are placed in a vessel of hot water, and then when the bodily parts are softened in the bath, the testicles are to be squeezed with the fingers until they disappear, and, being dissolved can no longer be felt. The method by excision is as follows: let the person to be made a eunuch be placed upon a bench, and the scrotum with the testicles grasped by the fingers of the left hand, and stretched; two straight incisions are then to be made with a scalpel, one in each testicle; and when the testicles start up they are to be dissected around and cut out, having merely left the very thin bond of connexion [*sic*] between the vessels in their natural state.[3]

Under the Roman emperors castrated favourites, such as Sporus under Nero (AD 54–68) and Earinus under Domitian (AD 81–96), became infamous and celebrated. Indeed eunuchs remained a desirable commodity into the later

1 For eunuchs in the Roman empire see, for instance, Peter Guyot, *Eunuchen als Sklaven und Freigelassene in der griechisch-römischen Antike* (Stuttgart: Klett-Cotta, 1980), pp. 121–9, and Shaun Tougher, *The Roman* Castrati*: Eunuchs of the Roman Empire* (forthcoming).

2 Paul of Aegina, *Epitome of Medicine* 6.68, trans. Francis Adams, *The Seven Books of Paulus Aegineta*, vol. 2 (London: The Sydenham Society, 1846), pp. 379–80.

3 Adams, *The Seven Books of Paulus Aegineta*, pp. 379–80. In Roman and Byzantine society eunuchs generally retained their penises, unlike in Chinese society, for instance.

Roman Empire, when they became an institutional feature of the imperial court, serving primarily in the capacity of chamberlains (*cubicularii*), a development often associated with the emperor Diocletian (AD 284–305).[4] The eunuchs employed by the later Roman imperial court were typically products of the slave trade, and thus of non-Roman extraction. Roman imperial legislation declared that the only acceptable source of eunuchs was barbarians, and the first-century Roman emperor Domitian was celebrated for having outlawed castration within the empire.[5] Of the later Roman court eunuchs whose origins are known several hailed from Armenia, such as Eutropius, the grand chamberlain of Arcadius (AD 395–408).[6] By the reign of Justinian I (AD 527–65), according to the historian Procopius, most of the eunuchs found at the imperial court in Constantinople were from Abasgia, on the eastern shore of the Black Sea.[7] It was not just the foreignness of the Abasgian boys which made them suitable for castration; their physical appearance was also a consideration. Observing that it was the two Abasgian kings themselves who castrated their subjects, Procopius asserts that they 'used to take such boys of this nation as they noted having comely features and fine bodies [*ἀγαθούς τε τὴν ὄψιν καὶ τὸ σῶμα καλοὺς*], and dragging them away from their parents without the least hesitation they would make them eunuchs and sell them at high prices to any persons in Roman territory who wished to buy them' (Procopius, *Wars* 8.3.15).[8] He continues that the fathers of such boys would also be killed so that they would not seek to avenge their children, and concludes 'the physical beauty [*εὐμορφία*] of their sons was resulting in their destruction; for the poor wretches were being destroyed through the misfortune of fatal comeliness [*θανάσιμον ... εὐπρέπειαν*] in their children' (*Wars* 8.3.16–17).[9] Thus Procopius raises the question of the aesthetics of castration – the selection of candidates

4 For the court eunuchs of the later Roman empire, see Keith Hopkins, *Conquerors and Slaves* (Cambridge: Cambridge University Press, 1978), pp. 172–96; Guyot, *Eunuchen als Sklaven und Freigelassene*, pp. 130–76; and Shaun Tougher, *The Eunuch in Byzantine History and Society* (London and New York: Routledge, 2008), pp. 36–53. For the important office of grand chamberlain (*praepositus sacri cubiculi*), which brought with it power and status, see for instance James E. Dunlap, 'The Office of Grand Chamberlain in the Later Roman and Byzantine Empires', in *Two Studies in Later Roman and Byzantine Administration*, ed. Arthur E. R. Boak and James E. Dunlap (New York and London: Macmillan, 1924) 161–324; and Helga Scholten, *Der Eunuch in Kaisernähe: zur politischen und sozialen Bedeutung des* praepositus sacri cubiculi *im 4. und 5. Jahrhundert n. Chr.* (Frankfurt and New York: Peter Lang, 1995).

5 See for instance Suetonius, *Domitian* 7.1, and Ammianus Marcellinus 18.4.5.

6 Claudian, *Against Eutropius* 1.45–9.

7 Procopius, *Wars* 8.3.17, trans. H. B. Dewing, *Procopius of Caesarea*, History of the Wars, vol. 5 (London: Heinemann, 1928). Hereafter, citations to this work will be given in parentheses in the text.

8 Trans. Dewing, p. 79

9 Trans. Dewing, p. 81.

for eunuchization on the grounds of their physical attractiveness. This indicates that consumers of eunuchs sought the quality of beauty in castrated boys, and that castration was understood as a method of preserving youthful beauty.

Another late antique source, the famous author and ascetic Jerome, indicates that buyers of eunuchs were motivated by aesthetic considerations, for he wrote to one of his correspondents (Demetrias, an elite Roman woman) advising her that she should select her eunuch personnel on the grounds of their good morals, not their good looks.[10] Beauty (and sex) also surface in Claudian's account of the early career of the famous grand chamberlain Eutropius; Claudian asserts that the eunuch was the lover of a certain Ptolemy, but eventually the latter 'longo lassatus paelicis usu' (tired of Eutropius' long service to his lusts) and dispensed with his services, at which the eunuch lamented his fate, comparing himself to a widow and exclaiming 'cum forma dilapsus amor; defloruit oris gratia' ['Love perishes with my beauty; the roses of my cheeks are faded] (*Against Eutropius* 1.61–77).[11] Claudian also emphasizes the youthful beauty and sexual allure of eunuchs when he observes that 'the Parthians employed the knife to stop the growth of the first down [*lanuginis*] of manhood and forced their boys, kept boys by artifice, to serve their lusts by thus lengthening the years of youthful charm [*diu puerili flore*]' (Claudian, *Against Eutropius* 1.342–5).[12] Also telling is that the late antique poet Prudentius assumes that the beautiful boy Antinous, the famous lover of the emperor Hadrian (AD 117–38), was a eunuch.[13] Thus a number of late antique sources indicate that eunuchs could be thought beautiful and desirable. It comes as some surprise, then, to read in two books published in the first decade of this century concerned with the earlier Roman imperial period – and both commenting on the case of Earinus, the eunuch of the emperor Domitian – that 'the eunuch was a constant figure of physical and moral repugnance in Roman society',[14] and that in Rome 'eunuchs are not normally praised with the same palette as pretty boys', but are usually presented in negative terms 'as hideously made-up and flabby, deformed even', and that if they are considered in sexual terms 'it is usually as objects of derision and disgust rather than as

10 Jerome, *Letters* 130.13. See also Mathew S. Kuefler, *The Manly Eunuch: Masculinity, Gender Ambiguity, and Christian Ideology in Late Antiquity* (Chicago: University of Chicago Press, 2001), p. 246.

11 Trans. Maurice Platnauer, *Claudian*, vol. 1 (London and Cambridge, MA: Heinemann and Harvard University Press, 1963), pp. 143-5. For Claudian's invectives on Eutropius see Jacqueline Long, *Claudian's* In Eutropium*: Or, How, When, and Why to Slander a Eunuch* (Chapel Hill: University of North Carolina Press, 1996).

12 Trans. Platnauer, p. 165.

13 See Caroline Vout, *Power and Eroticism in Imperial Rome* (Cambridge: Cambridge University Press, 2007), p. 139.

14 Carole E. Newlands, *Statius'* Silvae *and the Poetics of Empire* (Cambridge: Cambridge University Press, 2002), p. 106.

objects of desire'.[15] These assertions might suggest that there had been a shift in the appreciation of the physical appearance of eunuchs by the time of the later Roman Empire. However, closer examination reveals that such assertions are in fact flawed and misleading, for they depend primarily on views of a very particular set of eunuchs, the Galli, the self-castrating devotees of the mother goddess Magna Mater (the Great Mother, also known as Cybele).[16] Roman sources which discuss slave eunuchs do typically characterize them as beautiful and desirable, as far back as the second century BC and the first mention of eunuchs in Roman literature in Terence's play *The Eunuch*. In Roman society there persisted a long-established view that eunuchs were physically attractive and sexually desirable, a view that should not be minimized if the Roman attitude towards eunuchs is to be properly understood.

Apart from the use of eunuchs at the imperial court in the later Roman Empire there is one other major reason for the association of eunuchs with Rome, and this is the role of eunuch devotees in the cult of the Magna Mater.[17] The cult of this goddess was introduced to Rome from the Greek East in 204 BC, in the context of the Romans' ongoing conflict with Hannibal and the Carthaginians. The goddess was also known as the Idaean Mother for her association with Mount Idaea near Troy, and she had a major shrine at Pessinus in Phrygia. The story (as recorded by the historian Livy at the end of the first century BC) runs that the Sibylline books foretold that if a foreign enemy invaded Italy he could be expelled and conquered 'if the Idaean Mother should be brought from Pessinus to Rome'.[18] Thus the senate despatched a delegation to Attalus I (241–197 BC), the king of Pergamum, to seek his assistance with the transferral of the goddess to Rome. The delegation received further divine support for their mission on the journey when they visited the oracle at Delphi in Greece. The goddess was duly despatched to Rome by ship.

15 Vout, *Power and Eroticism*, p. 198.

16 Auto-castration is the primary point of contention for early Christians as well, particularly after the very publicized act of Origen, discussed by Jack Collins in this volume: 'Appropriation and Development of Castration as Symbol and Practice in Early Christianity', pp. 73–86.

17 For the Magna Mater and her eunuchs see Mary Beard, 'The Roman and the Foreign: The Cult of the "Great Mother" in Imperial Rome', in *Shamanism, History, and the State*, ed. Nicholas Thomas and Caroline Humphrey (Ann Arbor: University of Michigan Press, 1994) 164–90; Robert Turcan, *The Cults of the Roman Empire*, trans. Antonia Nevill (Oxford: Blackwell, 1996), pp. 28–74; Lynn E. Roller, *In Search of God the Mother: The Cult of Anatolian Cybele* (Berkeley and Los Angeles: University of California Press, 1999), esp. pp. 263–325; and Hugh Bowden, *Mystery Cults in the Ancient World* (London: Thames & Hudson, 2010), esp. pp. 93–104.

18 Livy's account of the introduction of the cult of the Great Mother to Rome is found at 29.10.4–11.8 and 29.14.5–14, trans. Frank Gardner Moore, *Livy*, vol. 8 (London and Cambridge, MA: Heinemann and Harvard University Press, 1949), pp. 245–9 and 259–63.

She reached the imperial city via the port of Ostia, and was installed on the Palatine in the temple of Victory, before being given her own temple there, which was dedicated in 191 BC. The Megalesia, a festival celebrated every April, was also established in her honour, in which participated her eunuch devotees, usually known as the Galli (often referred to as priests of the goddess, but now thought to be general adherents of the cult). These Galli are depicted as expressing their devotion to the goddess by castrating themselves, and it is thought that at least some of them did take this step even if it is obviously difficult to be certain. It is the existence of these Galli that contributed to the rather lurid and hostile image of eunuchs that existed at times in Roman society. As Mary Beard has remarked, the Galli, '[w]ith their flowing hair, extravagant jewelry, and long yellow silken robes', 'stalk the pages of Roman literature as mad, frenzied, foreign eunuchs'.[19] The dress and appearance of the Galli is portrayed as very distinctive, as is their behaviour. They wore their hair long, dressed in non-Roman attire, begged for alms, played frenzied music, and injured their bodies. In Roman literature Galli are depicted as large, effeminate and ineffectual, unattractive and unappealing, as in the works of the famous Roman satirists Juvenal and Martial, both active in the first century AD. In his sixth satire (on Roman women as wives) Juvenal addresses the superstitious nature of women, describing how a eunuch of the Great Mother warns a woman of impending trouble 'unless she purifies herself with a hundred eggs and presents him with her old russet-coloured dresses' (alluding to the feminine attire of the Galli).[20] Juvenal introduces the eunuch as alarming and unattractive:

> Look! In comes the troupe of frenzied Bellona and the Mother of the Gods, along with an enormous eunuch [*ingens semivir*], a face his perverted [*obsceno*] sidekick must revere. A long time ago now he picked up a shard and cut off his soft [*mollia*] genitals. The noisy band [*rauca cohors*] and the common drums [*tympana*] fall quiet in his presence and his cheeks are clothed in the Phrygian cap. (Juvenal, *Satire* 6.511–16).[21]

Martial touches on eunuchs several times in his *Epigrams*, referring to their size, softness, and effeminacy. He describes a certain Dindymus as 'Spadone cum sis eviratior fluxo, et concubine mollior Celaenaeo, quem sectus ululat Matris entheae Gallus' [more emasculate than a flabby eunuch, more womanish than the catamite of Celaenae [Attis, the mortal consort of the Mother Goddess, and a self-castrate], whose name the [gelded] priest of the mad Mother howls]

[19] Beard, 'The Roman and the Foreign', pp. 164 and 174.

[20] Juvenal, *Satire* 6.518–19, trans. Susanna Morton Braund, *Juvenal and Persius* (Cambridge, MA: Harvard University Press, 2004), p. 283. Hereafter, citations to this work will be given in parentheses in the text.

[21] Ibid.

(*Epigrams* 5.41.1–3).[22] The softness of Attis is also mentioned when he is compared unfavourably with a beautiful boy called Cestus, to whom Martial declares 'te Cybele molli mallet habere Phryge' [Cybele would rather have had you than her womanish Phrygian] (*Epigrams* 8.46.4).[23] The identification of eunuchs with women is emphasized again in the short epigram which declares that 'Numa saw Thelys the eunuch [*spadonem*] in a gown [*toga*] and said he was a convicted adulteress [*moecham*]' (Martial, *Epigrams* 10.52).[24] The eunuch (whose name Thelys means 'female' in Greek) is being equated with women, for women convicted of adultery had to dress in a toga like prostitutes. In another epigram Martial depicts a eunuch as a very unsatisfactory sexual partner for a woman, since he is not a man:

> Eunuch [*spado*] Dindymus and an old man harass Aegle in common, and the girl lies dry in the middle of the bed. Lack of strength makes the one, length of years the other useless for the job; so each labours in fruitless desire. She begs in supplication for herself and the two unfortunates, Cytherea [Venus], that you make one of them young and the other a man [*virum*]. (Martial, *Epigrams* 11.81)[25]

The gender identity of eunuchs was already a matter for discussion in Rome by the first century BC. The poet Catullus, who was active in the middle of that century, takes Attis as his subject.[26] Famously, once he has castrated himself in Phrygia, Attis becomes a she; Catullus changes the male pronoun to the female pronoun.[27] Catullus writes:

> [G]oaded by raging madness, bewildered in mind, he cast down from him with sharp flint-stone the burden of his members. So when she felt her limbs to have lost their manhood, still with fresh blood dabbling the face of the ground, swiftly with snowy hands she seized the light timbrel, your timbrel, Cybele, thy mysteries, Mother, and shaking with soft fingers the hollow oxhide thus began she to sing to her companions tremulously.[28]

Not only has Attis become feminized, but he has also become a leader of the

22 Trans. D.R. Shackleton Bailey, *Martial,* Epigrams, 3 vols (Cambridge, MA: Harvard University Press, 1993), vol. 1, p. 365. Note that there is a typographical error in Shackleton Bailey's translation, for it reads 'gilded' rather than 'gelded'. Note also that he translates 'Gallus' as 'priest'.

23 Ibid., vol. 2, pp. 195–7.

24 Ibid., vol. 2, p. 375.

25 Ibid., vol. 3, p. 69.

26 Catullus 63.

27 For comment see Marilyn B. Skinner, '*Ego Mulier*: The Construction of Male Sexuality in Catullus', *Helios* 20 (1993): 107–30.

28 Catullus 63.4–11, trans. F. W. Cornish, *Catullus* (London and Cambridge, MA: Heinemann and Harvard University Press, 1962), p. 91. Hereafter, citations to this work will be given in parentheses in the text.

Galli, exhorting them to follow him into the Phrygian forests of Cybele, 'where the noise of cymbals sounds, where timbrels re-echo, where the Phrygian flute-player blows a deep note on his curved reed, where the Maenads ivy-crowned toss their heads violently, where with shrill yells they shake the holy emblems' (Catullus 63.21–4).[29] Interestingly, when his frenzy has passed Attis reflects on what he has done, and laments his former life and his status as a beautiful youth:

> 'I, shall I from my own home be borne far away into these forests? from my country, my possessions, my friends, my parents, shall I be absent? absent from the market, the wrestling-place, the racecourse, the playground [*foro*, *palaestra*, *stadio et guminasiis*]? unhappy, ah unhappy heart, again, again must thou complain. For what form of human figure is there which I had not? I, to be a woman – I who was a stripling [*adolescens*], I a youth [*ephebus*], I a boy [*puer*], I was the flower [*flos*] of the playground, I was once the glory [*decus*] of the palaestra [*olei*]: mine were the crowded doorways, mine the warm thresholds, mine the flowery garlands to deck my house when I was to leave my chamber at sunrise. I, shall I now be called – what? a handmaid of the gods, a ministress of Cybele?' (Catullus 63.58–68).[30]

Attis is no longer a beautiful boy, but a feminine servant of the Great Mother. In fact, in this case, castration renders the subject not just feminine but female, transforming a male youth into a woman. His identity as a beautiful boy has been overridden. This was one way in Roman culture to understand the nature of eunuchs.

An alternative view was to understand Galli and eunuchs as neither male nor female but essentially as a 'third gender', as is seen in Valerius Maximus' *Memorable Doings and Sayings*. This text is dedicated to the emperor Tiberius (AD 14–37), but the salient episode is from the early first century BC, when Mamercus Aemilius Lepidus was consul (77 BC). In a chapter concerning rescinded wills, Valerius Maximus records:

> And now, how weighty the judgment of Consul Mamercus Aemilius Lepidus! A certain Genucius, a eunuch priest ['a Gallus'] of the Great Mother, had obtained an order from City Praetor Cn. Orestes restoring to him the property of Naevius Anus, of which he had received possession from the Praetor himself according to the will. Surdinus, whose freedman had made Genucius his heir, appealed to Mamercus, who cancelled the Praetor's ruling, saying that Genucius, whose genital parts had been amputated by his own choice, should not be reckoned among either men or women [*amputatis sua ipsius sponte genitalius corporis partibus neque virorum neque mulierum numero haberi debere*].

[29] Ibid., p. 93.
[30] Ibid., p. 95.

> A judgment appropriate to a Mamercus, appropriate to a Leader of the Senate; it provided that magistrates' tribunals should not be defiled by Genucius' obscene presence and tainted voice [*obscena Genucii praesentia inquinataque voce*] under the pretext of seeking justice.[31]

Thus the Gallus Genucius was categorized as neither male nor female to invalidate the bequest made to him by the freedman of Surdinus. The Roman distaste for such eunuchs is palpable; they fear defilement though his mere presence and voice.

The repulsion that the Romans could feel for Galli can appear puzzling, for these self-castrates are often closely associated with the figure of Attis, the beautiful youthful consort of the Great Mother. The connections between the Great Mother and Attis, and Attis and the Galli, are addressed (for instance) in Ovid's *Fasti*, a poem on the Roman calendar dating to the early first century AD. The poem includes reflection on the April festival of the goddess, in which the muse Erato answers the poet's questions about aspects of the cult.[32] Narrating the story of Attis and the goddess, Erato reveals that Attis was a 'facie spectabilis' (good-looking) Phrygian boy who shares a 'casto … amore' (chaste passion) with the Great Mother. He promises to always be a boy and guard her temple, and that if he breaks his oath the love for which he did so will be his last. However, he falls in love with the nymph Sargaritis, which brings down the goddess's revenge. She damages the tree of the Naiad (who thus dies) and Attis goes mad, fleeing to the top of Mount Dindymus. There he swears that the Furies are upon him, and he 'mangled … his body with a sharp stone, and trailed his long hair in the filthy dust; and his cry was, "I have deserved it! With my blood I pay the penalty that is my due. Ah, perish the parts that were my ruin"'; then he rid himself of his genitals 'and of a sudden was bereft of every sign of manhood [*viri*]' (Ovid, *Fasti* 4.237–42).[33] Amongst the questions Ovid poses to Erato about the cult (Why does the goddess delight in a perpetual din? Why do lions submit to her? Why does she wear a turreted crown? Where did she come from? Was she always in Rome? Why does she collect money in small coins? Why do people invite others to so many feasts and banquets at the time of her festival? Why is the Megalesia the first games of the year in Rome? Why are herbs offered to her?) is why do the Galli castrate themselves (as well as why are they called Galli?) Erato's response is that the Galli are imitating Attis: '"His madness [*furor*] set an example, and still his unmanly minsters [*mollesque ministri*] cut their vile members [*vilia membra*] while they toss their hair"'

[31] Valerius Maximus, *Memorable Doings and Sayings* 7.7.6, trans. D. R. Shackleton Bailey, 2 vols (Cambridge, MA: Harvard University Press, 2000), vol. 2, pp. 177–9.

[32] Ovid, *Fasti* 4.179–372. trans. J. G. Frazer, *Ovid's* Fasti (London and Cambridge, MA: Heinemann and Harvard University Press, 1967).

[33] Ibid., p. 207.

(Ovid, *Fasti* 4.243–4).[34] The very name of the Galli emphasizes the madness of their (and Attis') act, for it is derived from a Phrygian river, the Gallus, 'a river of mad water ... Who drinks of it goes mad' (Ovid, *Fasti* 4.363–6).[35] Thus, although Attis was a beautiful Phrygian boy, by self-castration he surrenders his maleness (as already seen in Catullus and Martial), and the Galli by imitating him become soft and unmanly too. Ovid also emphasizes their frenzied and unmanly qualities. Addressing the nature of the festival he writes:

> Eunuchs [*semimares*] will march and thump their hollow drums, and cymbals clashed on cymbals will give out their tinkling noises: seated on the unmanly necks of her attendants [*molli comitum cervice*], the goddess herself will be borne with howls through the streets in the city's midst. (Ovid, *Fasti* 4.183–6)[36]

Further, when Erato describes the castrated attendants of the goddess in her account of the arrival of the Magna Mater in Rome she observes that as the goddess was brought into the city '[t]he attendants howled [*exululant comites*], the mad flute blew, and hands unmanly [*molles ... manus*] beat the leathern drums' (Ovid, *Fasti* 4.341–2).[37]

Thus the Galli play a key role in establishing a negative perception of eunuchs in Rome as wild, feminized, unattractive beings. However, a contrasting example – a eunuch praised for his beauty – is provided by Earinus, famous for his association with the emperor Domitian. Earinus was celebrated by the contemporary poets Statius and Martial. Statius' *Silvae*, a collection of occasional poetry, contains a 106-line poem commemorating the dedication of Earinus' hair at the temple of Asclepius in Pergamum, a poem apparently commissioned by the eunuch himself and published in AD 93.[38] Martial features Earinus in six of his epigrams (all part of Book 9) which appeared in AD 94.[39] Apart from a reference to Earinus in the epitome of the third-century history of Cassius Dio,[40] these are the only sources that exist about Earinus, and as Christer Henriksén observes, 'Martial does not make any substantial addition to our knowledge of Earinus'.[41] Thus Statius' *The Hair of Flavius*

[34] Ibid.

[35] Ibid., p. 215.

[36] Ibid., p. 203.

[37] Ibid., p. 213.

[38] Statius, *Silvae* 3.4. The fact that Earinus commissioned the poem is revealed in the dedication of Book 3, lines 17–21: 'Earinus, our Germanicus' freedman, knows how long I put off his request, when he asked me to dedicate in verse the hair that he was sending to Pergamene Asclepius along with a jewelled box and mirror', trans. D. R. Shackleton Bailey, *Statius,* Silvae (Cambridge, MA: Harvard University Press, 2003), p. 175.

[39] Martial, *Epigrams* 9.11, 12, 13, 16, 17, and 36.

[40] Cassius Dio, *Roman History* 67.2.3.

[41] Christer Henriksén, 'Earinus: An Imperial Eunuch in the Light of the Poems of Martial and Statius', *Mnemosyne* 50 (1997): 281–94 at p. 282.

Earinus is the crucial source for Earinus' life and career, and it warrants providing a full translation (by Shackleton Bailey):[42]

> Go, locks, and speed, I pray, across a favouring sea, go, lying softly on the garlanded gold, go! Gentle Cytherea shall give you fair voyage and calm the south winds. Perhaps she will take you from the perilous craft and lead you over the waters in her own shell.
>
> Accept, son of Phoebus, the lauded tresses that Caesar's lad presents to you; accept them gladly and show them to your unshorn father. Let him compare them how they shine, and long think they are from his brother Lyaeus. Perhaps he in turn will sever the beauty of his own unfailing hair and place it for you enclosed in other gold.
>
> Pergamus, more fortunate by far than pine-clad Ida, though Ida pride herself on the cloud of a holy rape – for surely she gave the High Ones him [Ganymede] at whom Juno ever looks askance, recoiling from his hand and refusing the nectar: but you have the gods' favour, specially commended by your fair nurseling. You sent to Latium a servant whom Ausonian Jupiter [Domitian] and Roman Juno [Domitia Longina] alike regard with kindly brow, both approving; and not without the will of the gods is the lord of the earth so well pleased.
>
> 'Tis said that as golden Venus was driving her soft swans on her way from Eryx' height to the Idalian groves, she entered the Pergamene dwelling where the gentle god [Asclepius] is present to aid the sick, their greatest helper, staying the hastening Fates and brooding over his health-giving serpent. She sees a boy, shining with star of peerless beauty, as he plays before the altar of the very god. Deceived at first for a little while by the sudden apparition, she fancies him one of her many sons; but he had no bow and no shades springing from his radiant shoulders. She wonders at his boyish grace, gazing at his face and hair, and 'Shall you go,' she says, 'to the Ausonian towers neglected of Venus? Shall you bear a mean dwelling and common yoke of servitude? Far be it! I shall give this beauty the master it deserves. Come now with me, boy, come! I shall fly you through the stars in my winged chariot to the leader, a gift of gifts. No common bondage shall await you: you are destined to

42 Shackleton Bailey, *Statius*, pp. 217–25.

serve dignity in the Palace [*Palatino*]. Nothing so sweet in all the world have I seen or given birth to, I own it. The boys of Latmos [Endymion] and Sangaris [Attis] shall freely yield to you, and he that a vain image in a fountain and a barren love consumed [Narcissus]. The cerulean Naiad would have preferred you [to Hylas] and seized your urn in a stronger grip to drag you down. Boy, you are beyond them all; more beautiful he only to whom you shall be given.'

So saying, she lifts him by her side through the light air and tells him to take a seat in the swan-drawn car. In a trice, there are the Latian Hills and the home of ancient Evander, that Germanicus [Domitian], renowned father of the world, adorns with new masonry and levels with the topmost stars. Then it becomes the goddess' closer care how best to arrange his locks, what dress is meet to kindle his rosy countenance, what gold is worthiest on his fingers, what on his neck. Well she knew the leader's celestial eyes; she herself had joined the marriage torches and given him his bride with bounteous hand. So she decks the hair, so drapes him with Tyrian raiment, gives him beams of her own fire. Former favourites retire, the flocks of servitors; he bears first cups to the great leader, weighty murrhine and crystal, with a hand more fair. New grace enhances the wine.

Boy dear to the High Ones, chosen to sip first the reverenced nectar and touch so often that mighty hand, the hand the Getae seek to know, and Persians, Armenians, Indians to touch! O born under a lucky star, greatly have the gods favoured you. Once too your country's god himself left lofty Pergamus to cross the sea, lest the first down mar your shining cheeks and darken your beauty's joys. None other was entrusted with the power to soften the boy, but with silent skill Phoebus' son [Asclepius] gently bade this body leave its sex [*de sexu transire*], not shocked by any gash. Yet Cytherea is gnawed by worry, fearing the boy might suffer. Not yet had the leader's noble clemency begun to keep male children intact from birth. Now 'tis forbidden to mollify sex [*frangere sexum*] and change manhood; rejoicing Nature sees only those she created. No more under an evil law do slave mothers fear to bear the burden of sons.

You too, had you been born later, would now be a young man, with shaded cheeks and limbs full-grown, stronger. More gifts than one you would have sent rejoicing to

> Phoebus' shrine: as it is, let only the tress sail to your native shores. The Paphian used to steep it in plenteous perfume, a kindly Grace used to comb it. The severed lock of purple Nisus will yield to it, and that which proud Achilles was keeping for Sperchius. When first it was decreed to crop your snow-white brow and unveil your gleaming shoulders, the tender winged ones with their Paphian mother run up and make ready your tresses and place a silken robe over your breast. Then they cut the lock with linked arrows and place it on gold and gems. Mother Cytherea herself catches it as it falls and anoints it once again with her secret essences. Then spoke a boy from the throng who had chanced to carry in upturned hands the mirror resplendent with jewelled gold: 'Let us give this too. No gift will be more welcome to his native temple; it will be more potent [*potentius*] than the gold itself. Only do you fix a look therein and leave your face there forever.' So he spoke and shut in the mirror, catching the likeness.
>
> But the peerless boy, stretching his hands to the stars: 'In return for these gifts, gentlest guardian of mankind, may you long wish, if I have so deserved, to renew our lord's youth and preserve him for the world. The stars ask this with me, and the waters and the lands. Let him, I pray, pass through Ilian and Pylian years both, rejoicing that his own home and the Tarpeian temple grow old along with himself.'
>
> So he spoke, and Pergamus wondered that the altars shook.

From the poem it appears that Earinus hails from Pergamum, and as a boy came to Rome as a slave and ended up in the imperial household, where he became a favourite of the emperor Domitian; in the poem he is Domitian's cupbearer. The poem indicates that only after coming to Rome was Earinus castrated, a transformation which is presented as taking place before the emperor's anti-castration edict was issued. The occasion which led to the writing of the poem was the cutting of Earinus' hair (which echoes his castration), which was dedicated to Asclepius at his temple in Pergamum, the hair being despatched with a jewelled box and a mirror. How much further the poem can be pushed to reveal facts is a moot point,[43] but it certainly emphasizes

[43] See the effort of Henriksén, 'Earinus', but note the comments of Vout, *Power and Eroticism*, p. 205, n. 8. For an interesting discussion of the poem see also John Garthwaite, 'Statius, *Silvae* 3.4: On the Fate of Earinus', *Aufstieg und Niedergang der römischen Welt* II.32.1 (1984): 111–24.

the idea of the physical attractiveness of eunuchs. The poem conjures up an intoxicating image of the alluring and sensuous beauty of Earinus. This is conveyed in particular by Venus' own reaction on first seeing the boy, 'egregiae praeclarum sidere formae' [shining with star of peerless beauty] (*Silvae* 3.4.26–7) in front of the altar of Asclepius. Initially she mistakes him for one of her own sons, a cupid, and considers that she has never seen anything so sweet (*dulce*) and that he surpasses a clutch of youths celebrated for their beauty: Endymion, Attis, Narcissus, and Hylas.[44] She declares that such is Earinus' beauty that he is worthy of serving the emperor himself, who alone is more beautiful than the boy.[45] Other comparisons emphasize the physical appeal of Earinus, revealing that eunuchs were appreciated for their youthful beauty, which the texts on the Galli tend to obscure. Earinus' hair is compared to that of Apollo and his brother Lyaeus (Bacchus), of Nisus and of Achilles. Most emphatic of all is the comparison of Earinus with Ganymede, the beautiful Phrygian boy whom Jupiter abducted to be his cupbearer and catamite on Olympus.[46] The allusion to Ganymede points to the physical nature of the relationship between Domitian and Earinus, or at least the presence of sexual desire in the relationship, revealing that the physical attractiveness of eunuchs could elicit physical arousal, as does the patronage of the boy by Venus herself, the goddess of love. Thus Earinus is compared to ideals of youthful male beauty and is found exceptional. Interestingly, his castration itself is presented as a means of securing eternal youthful beauty for him, suggesting that one of the motivations for castration of boys was to prolong the physical attractiveness of youth. Asclepius performs the operation (without leaving a wound on the body) 'ne prima genas lanugo nitentes carperet et pulchrae fuscaret gaudia formae' [lest the first down mar your shining cheeks and darken your beauty's joys] (*Silvae* 3.4.65–6). The poem alludes to the fact that it is only his head hair that Earinus can dedicate; his castration means that he will not be able to grow a beard and dedicate the clippings from his first shave, such a crucial ritual in the transition from youth to manhood.[47] It may be that Statius is lamenting the fact that because of his castration Earinus will never become a man, but at the same time his poem serves to preserve a snapshot of the eunuch at the peak of his youthful beauty, just like the reflection of Earinus caught in the mirror that was dedicated to Asclepius.

44 Statius, *Silvae* 3.4.29–30, 39–44.

45 Ibid. 3.4.34–5, 44–5.

46 Ibid. 3.4.12–15, 60–2. Note that it is emphasized that Domitian and his wife are the earthly Jupiter and Juno: *Silvae* 3.4.18. For Jupiter and Ganymede see Craig A. Williams, *Roman Homosexuality*, 2nd edn (New York: Oxford University Press, 2010), esp. pp. 59–64. Williams describes Ganymede as 'an archetype of the agelessly beautiful young man literally swept off his feet by an older male lover' (p. 60).

47 Statius, *Silvae* 3.4.78–81.

There are also indications that (like the Galli) Earinus has become feminized. The castration is referred to as a softening (*mollire*) of the boy, whose body leaves its sex (*corpus de sexu transire*).[48] When Earinus is having his hair cut his brow is described as 'snow-white', and he is draped in a 'silken robe' (*Serica … pallia*),[49] images which are suggestive of femaleness, as is his dedication of the mirror and the box.[50] There is a feminine aspect to Earinus even before his castration, however, for Venus is depicted preparing the boy for Domitian as if he were a bride for the emperor, which also recalls the divine gift of Pandora to man.[51] This may simply be the inevitable consequence of presenting a younger passive male partner of an older active adult male, but the example of Ganymede and Zeus was also to hand and deployed by Statius. Perhaps then Earinus' destiny to become a eunuch has already shaped the perception and presentation of him prior to his castration, endowing him with a feminine aspect, but one that conveys and enhances his beauty too. Nevertheless, in general Statius presents Earinus in a sensuous manner as a beautiful and desirable eternal youth, and it is thus entirely appropriate that at the end of the poem the eunuch prays for Domitian to have his youth renewed (*renovare iuventa*).[52]

Martial also dwells on the beauty and allure of Earinus in his epigrams on the eunuch (though unlike Statius he never makes explicit that Earinus is a eunuch). Three of these also deal with the dedication of hair (9.16, 17, and 36), but the other three concern Earinus' name itself (9.11, 12, and 13), which derives from the Greek word for one of the four seasons – spring. The poet exploits the sweet and sensuous associations of that time of year in order to celebrate such qualities of Earinus. Martial writes:

> Name born together with violets and roses, by
> which is named the best part of the year, which has
> the flavour of Hybla and Attic flowers [honey] and the
> fragrance of the proud bird's [the phoenix] nest: name sweeter
> than blessed nectar …
> … that noble,
> soft [*molle*], and dainty [*delicatum*] name I wished to put into polished verse.
>
> (Martial, *Epigrams* 9.11./1–5, 10–11).[53]

48 Ibid. 3.4.68, 70–1. It is noted that Domitian's anti-castration law means that it is now 'forbidden to mollify sex and change manhood' (*frangere sexum atque hominem mutare nefas*): *Silvae* 3.4.74–5.

49 Ibid. 3.4.86, 89–90.

50 See also Vout, *Power and Eroticism*, p. 183. Perhaps the image in the mirror also recalls Narcissus again.

51 Statius, *Silvae* 3.4.50–6.

52 Ibid. 3.4.101.

53 Trans. Shackleton Bailey, vol. 2, pp. 241–3.

Martial also refers to Earinus' name as announcing the 'teneri … tempora' (tender season).[54] The beauty of Earinus is asserted directly too. He possesses 'iuvenale decus' (youthful loveliness),[55] and the mirror (which is 'beauty's counsellor' – *Consilium formae*)[56] keeps safe his 'felix facies' (blooming countenance).[57] The cut locks of his hair are themselves sweet (*dulcisque capillos*).[58] Martial also adopts other strategies used by Statius to convey the beauty of Earinus, perhaps suggesting that there were standard ways in Roman culture to communicate the physical attractiveness of eunuchs. Earinus is associated with Venus, who inscribes the boy's name.[59] Once again the eunuch is brought into the company of other famous and beautiful boys, in this case just Attis and Ganymede. Martial asserts that 'Cybele's boy and he who mixes the Thunderer's cups' would rather be called by the name of Earinus (Martial, *Epigrams* 9.11.6–7).[60] He claims that Pergamum would not prefer the hair of Ganymede to that of Domitian's favourite.[61] Ganymede even takes centre stage in one of the epigrams about Earinus:

> The Phrygian boy, famed joy of the other Jupiter,
> had seen the Ausonian page [*ministrum*] with his hair newly
> shorn: 'What your Caesar (look!) has allowed his
> young man [*ephebo*], please allow yours, greatest of rulers,'
> said he. 'Already the first down [*lanugo*] lies hidden by my
> long locks; already your Juno laughs at me and calls
> me a man [*virum*].' To him said the Heavenly Father:
> 'Sweetest [*dulcissime*] boy, not I but the case itself denies you
> what you ask. My Caesar has a thousand pages [*mille ministros*] like
> yourself; the vast palace has scarcely room for so
> many star-like youths [*sidereos … mares*]. But if shorn hair gives you a
> manly look [*vultus…viriles*], whom else shall I have to mix the nectar?'
>
> (Martial, *Epigrams* 9.36)[62]

In contrast to Statius, then, Martial does raise the prospect of Earinus maturing (signified by the cutting of his hair), something Ganymede was unable to do because without his long hair he would no longer have been an appropriate person to serve as Jupiter's cupbearer. Nevertheless, it emerges

[54] Martial, *Epigrams* 9.12 (13).1, ibid., vol. 2, p. 243.
[55] Ibid. 9.17.7, ibid., vol. 2, p. 247.
[56] Ibid. 9.16.1, ibid., vol. 2, p. 245.
[57] Ibid. 9.17.6, ibid., vol. 2, p. 247.
[58] Ibid. 9.16.1, ibid., vol. 2, p. 245.
[59] Ibid. 9.12 (13).4, and see also *Epigrams* 9.11.9.
[60] Trans. Shackleton Bailey, vol. 2, p. 243.
[61] Martial, *Epigrams* 9.16.6.
[62] Trans. Shackleton Bailey, vol. 2, p. 263.

clearly from both Statius and Martial that Earinus was considered beautiful in the way that male youths were deemed beautiful as 'pretty boys'. However, both Caroline Vout and Carole Newlands see the praise of a eunuch's beauty as unusual, and thus suggest that the presentation of Earinus as a pretty boy is an exception to the rule.[63] They clearly see the hostile and mocking attitudes expressed by Romans towards Galli as the norm, but their assumptions are questionable; there are other indications that eunuchs were thought beautiful, and the case of the Galli should be treated separately as a very particular category of eunuch. The Galli were distinct from the slave eunuchs utilized in Roman society, for the devotees of the Magna Mater embraced self-castration voluntarily, when they had already attained physical maturity. For Romans this was horrifying as it amounted to a conscious decision to freely renounce one's masculinity and potency, so vital for male identity in Roman society. This affected how the Galli were presented by Roman authors. In contrast, eunuch slaves were castrated against their will, before reaching puberty, so could be appreciated and lauded for their physical beauty which was associated with that of both male youths and women. Earinus is certainly not an exception, indicating that in Roman society some eunuchs were valued for their attractiveness and desirability. This had a long history in Roman thought and reveals that there was a positive appreciation of eunuchs well before the later Roman period.

Other sources certainly suggest that Romans deemed eunuchs beautiful and desirable. Although late and condensed, the comments of Cassius Dio about Earinus imply a more general appreciation of eunuchs. Cassius Dio (or rather his epitomator) reports that Domitian issued his anti-castration edict to spite the memory of his brother Titus (AD 78–81), who had had an especial enthusiasm for eunuchs. The imperial biographer Suetonius, writing in the reign of Hadrian, also refers to Titus' penchant for eunuchs, observing that he kept 'exoletorum et spadonum greges' [troupes of catamites and eunuchs] (*Titus* 7).[64] Another relevant imperial eunuch favourite is Sporus, who is particularly associated with the emperor Nero.[65] A key source for this eunuch (and the one usually cited, though there are others) is Suetonius. He first mentions Sporus in his biography of Nero when addressing the sexual activities of the emperor in general. He relates that the emperor had the boy Sporus castrated and 'in muliebrem naturam transfigurare conatus' [attempted to transform him into a woman] (*Nero* 28).[66] Nero married him 'with dowry and bridal veil and all due ceremony' after which he took him home (escorted by

63 See also Newlands, *Poetics of Empire*, p. 109.

64 Trans. Catherine Edwards, *Suetonius,* Lives of the Caesars (Oxford: Oxford University Press, 2000), p. 276.

65 Sporus is also discussed by Vout, *Power and Eroticism*, pp. 136–66.

66 Trans. Edwards, p. 209.

a large crowd of people), where he treated him as his wife. It is clear that this event happened in Greece (which Nero toured in AD 66–7), for Suetonius adds that Sporus (dressed as an empress and transported in a litter) accompanied Nero 'around the meeting places and markets of Greece and later, at Rome, around the Sigillaria', the emperor occasionally kissing the eunuch; such treatment of Sporus has been labelled 'demasculization' by Craig Williams, who comments that the 'public flaunting' of the wifely eunuch 'may well have been perceived as a significant threat to masculine privilege'.[67] The subsequent episodes featuring Sporus relate to the fall and suicide of Nero. One of the portents foretelling the emperor's end was the eunuch's gift on New Year's Day (while Nero was taking the auspices) of a ring engraved with the rape of Proserpina, who had been abducted by Pluto, the god of the underworld.[68] When the emperor fled Rome for the villa of his freedman Phaon, Sporus was one of the four attendants who accompanied him.[69] As Nero contemplated suicide in the villa he exhorted Sporus to lament and to wail.[70] Sporus also features several times in the condensed version of the history of Cassius Dio; in fact he is mentioned more times than in any other source, which led Charles Murison to remark that 'Dio seems to have a slightly morbid interest in the eunuch Sporus'.[71] Notably Cassius Dio mentions an aspect of the eunuch's story, seen as critical by Caroline Vout but which is not spelt out by Suetonius – Sporus physically resembled Nero's dead wife, Poppaea Sabina, who died in AD 65.[72] Thus the castration of Sporus is presented as the result of the emperor pining for his deceased partner and attempting to bring her back to life.[73]

Again Nero is said to have married the eunuch, and it is noted that the Romans (and others) celebrated the wedding publicly. It is recorded that the wedding occurred in Greece and Tigellinus (the praetorian prefect of Nero) gave the 'bride' away.[74] In their celebration of the marriage the Greeks are said to have uttered 'all the customary good wishes, even to the extent of praying

67 Williams, *Roman Homosexuality*, p. 286. The Sigillaria was a fair at which gifts for Saturnalia were sold.

68 Suetonius, *Nero* 46.2.

69 Ibid. 48.

70 Ibid. 49.3.

71 Charles Leslie Murison, *Rebellion and Reconstruction: Galba to Domitian. An Historical Commentary on Cassius Dio's* Roman History *Books 64–67 (AD 68–96)* (Atlanta, GA: Scholars Press, 1999), p. 57. Edward Champlin remarks that compared to the account of Suetonius about Nero's relationship with Sporus: 'For once, Dio's narrative is superior'. *Nero* (Cambridge, MA: The Belknap Press of Harvard University Press, 2003), p. 145.

72 Note also that Plutarch, *Galba* 9, asserts that after Nero's death Nymphidius (his praetorian prefect who had imperial aspirations) took possession of Sporus (having sent for him while Nero's body was still burning on the pyre), and treated him like his consort and called him Poppaea.

73 Cassius Dio, *Roman History* 62.28.

74 Ibid. 62.13.

that legitimate children might be born to them', though presumably such acquiescence may simply have been the result of pandering to the imperial whims.[75] The fact that Nero married Sporus in Greece is given as another reason why the emperor called the eunuch Sabina, for it was also in Greece that he had married the real Sabina. Once again Nero is said to have treated Sporus as his wife, his 'lady and empress and mistress'. Apparently, a certain Calvia Crispinilla (a socially distinguished woman) was charged with the care of the eunuch, as well as his wardrobe.[76] In addition, Cassius Dio is interested in what happened to Sporus after the death of Nero, and records that the emperor Vitellius (AD 69) planned (as part of gladiatorial contests he was organizing) to have Sporus put on stage 'in the rôle of a maiden being ravished', but the eunuch 'would not endure the shame and committed suicide'.[77] Sporus thus provides another example of a high-profile eunuch from the early Roman Empire, one who owed his prominence to imperial favour. He was clearly valued for his looks, though in his case the degree of his feminization was extreme.

From the diverse information that exists about Sporus it appears that he was a Greek slave at the court of Nero, and the emperor was motivated to castrate the beautiful boy by his appearance, as was the case for Earinus. However, it appears that Sporus was valued not so much for his attractions as a pretty boy but for his feminine beauty since he was treated and dressed like a wife and empress of Nero. Sporus thus takes on the aspect of a transvestite, or even a transsexual, transformed from a boy into a woman, more akin to Catullus' Attis than Statius' Earinus, but still valued for his physical appearance. A late antique source, Sextus Aurelius Victor's *The Caesars* (a brief history of the rulers of Rome from Augustus to Constantius II, published in 360), declares that Nero 'spadone, quem quondam exsectum formare in mulierem tentaverat' [had once tried to make [Sporus] into a woman by surgery] (*The Caesars* 5.16).[78] But some critics have questioned whether desire is of any relevance to the emperor's castration of Sporus. Edward Champlin observes that Nero's love was for the dead Sabina, not Sporus himself, and wonders how the eunuch felt about his master.[79] David Woods has even suggested that there was a political motive for the castration of Sporus (the emperor believed that he was of imperial blood and thus a potential rival), and thus Nero's actions were

[75] Trans. Ernest Cary, *Dio's* Roman History, vol. 8 (London and Cambridge, MA: Heinemann and Harvard University Press, 1925), p. 159.

[76] Cassius Dio, *Roman History* 62.12.3–4.

[77] Ibid. 64.10.1, trans. Cary, p. 237. Champlin, *Nero*, pp. 147 and 309, n. 5, argues that the specific case of the rape of Persephone/Proserpina is meant.

[78] Trans. H. W. Bird, *Aurelius Victor:* De Caesaribus (Liverpool: Liverpool University Press, 1994), p. 8.

[79] Champlin, *Nero*, esp. p. 147.

designed to neutralize and humiliate Sporus.[80] Yet, whatever the true nature of the relationship, it is clear that contemporaries did read it in terms of love and desire, as is particularly evident in one of the orations of Dio Chrysostom.

Dio was a Greek from Prusa who lived from the middle of the first century to the early second century AD. He studied and worked in Rome, though he found himself exiled by the emperor Domitian. He comes to the subject of Sporus (tellingly enough) in a discourse *On Beauty*.[81] It seems that Dio wrote this oration during Domitian's reign, for he observes that everyone wishes Nero was still alive (implying that the present emperor is worse).[82] In the discourse Dio proposes that masculine beauty is dying out and becoming unappreciated (which he regrets), while feminine beauty is increasingly appreciated, an attitude he associates with Eastern culture. He observes that the Persians thought feminine beauty superior to masculine beauty, witness their making eunuchs of beautiful males, motivated by lust (*εὐνούχος ἐποίουν τοὺς καλοὺς ... διὰ τὸ μόνον τὰ ἀφροδίσια ἐννοεῖν*).[83] This brings him to Nero and Sporus. He declares 'we all know how in our time that [Nero] not only castrated the youth whom he loved [*τὸν ἐρώμενον*], but also changed his name for a woman's [that of Poppaea Sabina]', and that the eunuch 'actually wore his hair parted, young women attended him whenever he went for a walk, he wore women's clothes, and was forced to do everything else a woman does in the same way'.[84] He adds that Nero even offered to reward with honours and money anyone who managed to make Sporus a woman.[85] Thus Dio Chrysostom indicates that Sporus was originally a youthful lover of Nero, but was deliberately feminized through castration, and by name, dress, and behaviour. Nevertheless this left scope for beauty, a feminine beauty which he presents as being increasingly appreciated, displacing traditional masculine beauty.

The Roman advocate and rhetorician Quintilian advances a similar thesis in his *Training in Oratory* (*Institutio Oratoria*), which also dates to the reign of Domitian. When discussing legal speeches he asserts that declamations (rhetorical speeches) are now designed purely to give pleasure rather than being a genuine form of sparring. He remarks:

> declaimers are guilty of exactly the same offence as slave-dealers who castrate boys in order to increase the attractions of their beauty [*formae puerorum virilitate excisa lenocinantur*]. For just as the slave-dealer regards

[80] David Woods, 'Nero and Sporus', *Latomus* 68 (2009): 73–82.

[81] Dio Chrysostom, *Oration* 21.6–9. It is odd that Vout, *Power and Eroticism*, does not utilize this oration, though Champlin, *Nero*, does.

[82] Dio, *Oration* 21.10.

[83] Ibid. 21.4.

[84] Ibid. 21.6, trans. J. W. Cohoon, *Dio Chrysostom*, vol. 2 (London and Cambridge, MA: Heinemann and Harvard University Press, 1939), pp. 277–9.

[85] On this point see Champlin, *Nero*, pp. 146 and 309, n. 3.

> strength and muscle, and above all, the beard and other natural characteristics of manhood as blemishes, and softens down all that would be sturdy if allowed to grow, on the ground that it is harsh and hard, even so we conceal the manly form of eloquence and power of speaking closely and forcibly by giving it a delicate complexion [*tenera* … *cute*] of style and, so long as what we say is smooth and polished, are absolutely indifferent as to whether our words have any power or no.[86]

However, Quintilian is no fan of this fashion. He adds:

> But I take Nature for my guide and regard any man whatsoever as fairer to view than a eunuch, nor can I believe that Providence is ever so indifferent to what itself has created as to allow weakness to be an excellence, nor again can I think that the knife can render beautiful that which, if produced in the natural course of birth, would be regarded as a monster. A false resemblance to the female sex may in itself delight lust [*Libidinem*], if it will, but depravity of morals will never acquire such ascendancy as to succeed in giving real value to that which it has succeeded in giving a high price … When the masters of sculpture and painting desired to carve or paint forms of ideal beauty [*corpora* … *speciosissima*], they never fell into the error of taking some Bagoas or Megabyzus as models, but rightly selected the well-known Doryphorus, equally adapted either for the fields of war or for the wrestling school [*palaestrae*], and other warlike and athletic youths as types of physical beauty. Shall we then, who are endeavouring to mould the ideal orator, equip eloquence not with weapons but with timbrels [*tympana*]?[87]

Thus Quintilian expresses very similar ideas to the Greek Dio Chrysostom, perhaps suggesting that there had been a change in cultural attitude towards beauty in the early empire, possibly associated with the increasing use of eunuch slaves in Roman society. Tellingly, Quintilian alludes to the Galli in his rejection of the beauty of eunuchs, referring to timbrels so associated with them, and citing the figure of Megabyzus, the name for a eunuch priest of the goddess Artemis in Ephesus.[88] The other eunuch he mentions, Bagoas, is

[86] Quintilian, *Training in Oratory* 5.12.17–18, trans. H. E. Butler, *The* Institutio Oratoria *of Quintilian*, vol. 2 (Cambridge, MA and London: Harvard University Press and Heinemann, 1960), pp. 307–9.

[87] Ibid. 5.12.19–21, trans. Butler, p. 309.

[88] E.g. Strabo, *Geography* 14.1.23, and Pliny the Elder, *Natural History* 35.36.93 and 35.40.131–2. For the Megabyzoi see James O. Smith, 'The High Priests of the Temple of Artemis in Ephesus', in *Cybele, Attis and Related Cults*, ed. Eugene N. Lane (Leiden: Brill, 1996) 323–35. Note that Smith thinks it unlikely that Quintilian is referring to a eunuch priest when he uses the name Megabyzus, and perhaps has in mind some other famous eunuch by that name (p. 325). Smith also doubts whether the Megabyzoi were eunuchs (or that there was a priesthood by this name).

extremely relevant for this is likely to be the Bagoas who was reputed to be the eunuch lover of Alexander the Great (336–323 BC), king of Macedon and lord of Asia, and made famous in the twentieth century by the second novel in the Alexander trilogy of Mary Renault, *The Persian Boy*.[89] In her study of *Power and Eroticism in Imperial Rome*, Vout refers only in passing to the story of Alexander and Bagoas, relegating the pair to a footnote without even naming the eunuch.[90] Her justification for doing so is that this case is distinct from the issue of Roman sexual attitudes to eunuchs because it is in a Macedonian context. However, there was resonance for Romans in the story of Alexander and his eunuch. Probably in the first century AD (most likely either in the reign of Claudius or that of Vespasian) Quintus Curtius Rufus wrote a Latin history of the famous Macedonian monarch (indeed, the only life of Alexander in Latin) that depicts him as a ruler who becomes corrupted and sinks into tyranny.[91] There is no doubt that the history is meant to speak to a Roman audience about imperial rule, and the role of the eunuch informs this subject. Not only is Bagoas presented as a physically desirable sexual partner of Alexander but he also uses his intimacy with the king to bring about the destruction of the satrap Orxines, who snubbed the eunuch. But it is the issue of beauty that is of concern here, and Curtius certainly dwells on the sexual attractiveness of Bagoas. He describes him as 'specie singulari spado atque in ipso flore pueritate' [an exceptionally good-looking eunuch in the very flower of his youth] (*History of Alexander* 6.5.23), and notes that the Persian king Darius III (336–330 BC) had had a sexual relationship with him too. He emphasizes that it is the eunuch's sexual hold over Alexander which gives him his power, asserting for instance that he would slander Orxines while he was having sex with Alexander.[92] Curtius is in fact one of the key sources for Bagoas, suggesting a Roman interest in the figure of the eunuch. The Greek biographer Plutarch, who died early in the reign of Hadrian, also mentions the relationship between Bagoas and Alexander in his biography of the Macedonian king.[93] Describing an incident when Alexander attended singing and dancing contests in which his favourite Bagoas was awarded the prize, he reports that the eunuch

[89] Mary Renault, *The Persian Boy* (London: Longman, 1972). For exploration of her depiction of the beautiful Bagoas see for instance Shaun Tougher, 'The Renault Bagoas: The Treatment of Alexander the Great's Eunuch in Mary Renault's *The Persian Boy*', *New Voices in Classical Reception Studies* 3 (2008), pp. 77–89.

[90] Vout, *Power and Eroticism*, p. 211, n. 104.

[91] For Quintus Curtius Rufus and his history of Alexander see for instance Elizabeth Baynham, *Alexander the Great: The Unique History of Quintus Curtius* (Ann Arbor: University of Michigan Press, 1998). For Alexander in the Roman world generally see Diana Spencer, *The Roman Alexander: Reading a Cultural Myth* (Exeter: University of Exeter Press, 2002).

[92] Quintus Curtius Rufus, *History of Alexander* 10.1.29.

[93] Plutarch, *Alexander* 67.3–4.

then came and sat beside the king; the Macedonians applauded and urged Alexander to kiss the winner, which he did while embracing him.[94] This is reminiscent of Suetonius' assertion that Nero kissed Sporus in public, and thus readers may have associated Sporus with Bagoas, suggesting that it is important to bring the figure of Bagoas into discussions of Roman eunuchs. A consideration of Bagoas supports the case for arguing that Romans did find eunuchs physically attractive.

That Romans did consider eunuchs attractive and desirable is testified to by another author from the late first century and early second century AD, the historian Tacitus. In his (incomplete) *Annals*, a history of the Roman empire from Tiberius to Nero dating to the end of his life, Tacitus mentions the eunuch Lygdus, who served in the household of Drusus, the son of Tiberius (AD 14–37). Tacitus remarks that the eunuch's 'aetate atque forma carus domino' [years and looks had won him the affection of his master] (*Annals* 4.10), and reports the rumour that Tiberius' praetorian prefect Sejanus corrupted the eunuch sexually in order to have him poison Drusus.[95] The desirability of eunuchs in the early imperial period is also indicated by Pliny the Elder in his *Natural History*, which again touches on the figure of Sejanus. He records that after the fall of the praetorian prefect one of his eunuchs (Paezon) was bought by Clutorius Priscus for 50,000,000 sesterces, a payment for lust, not beauty, in this case (*quam libidinis, non formae*).[96]

However, the idea of the beautiful and desirable youthful eunuch survives in a Roman source as early as the middle of the second century BC – the earliest extant source in Roman literature to use the term 'eunuch'. This is Terence's comedy, *The Eunuch*.[97] The play was written and performed for the Megalesian games in 161 BC, and was adapted from a (lost) Greek play of the same name by the Athenian Menander, a leading figure in New Comedy who was active in the late fourth and early third centuries BC. The play, set in Hellenistic Athens, pivots around the conceit of a young Athenian gentleman (Chaerea, the younger brother of Phaedria) gaining access to the house of Thais (a non-Athenian courtesan, and lover of Phaedria) by disguising himself as a eunuch (called Dorus, whom Phaedria had given to Thais as a gift) in order to seduce Pamphila (a young girl who has been taken into Thais' household as a slave, gifted to her by another lover, the soldier Thraso). The play has much to say about the roles that eunuch slaves played, as well as the contemporary percep-

94 Bagoas also surfaces in Plutarch's *How to Tell a Flatterer from a Friend* 24, where his influence with Alexander is asserted.

95 Trans. John Jackson, *Tacitus*, vol. 3 (London and Cambridge, MA: Heinemann and Harvard University Press, 1951), p. 21.

96 Pliny the Elder, *Natural History* 7.39.

97 On Terence see John Barsby, *Terence*, vol. 1 (Cambridge, MA: Harvard University Press, 2001), esp. pp. 1–6.

tions of eunuchs, including ideas about their appearance and attractiveness. The proposition that Chaerea substitute himself for Dorus is first made by Parmeno, a slave in the household of Chaerea's father. Parmeno remarks to Chaerea "'forma et aetas ipsast facile ut pro eunucho probes"' ['you're so young and good-looking, you could easily pass as a eunuch'] (*The Eunuch* 375).[98] When Parmeno presents Chaerea in the guise of the eunuch to Thais, he declares 'Here's the eunuch for you. With the looks of a gentleman and in the bloom of youth [*quam aetate integra*]!'.[99] Thais exclaims that 'Dorus' is indeed handsome (*honestust*), and Thraso, who is also present, is obviously moved by desire, for he implies that he would like to fuck the eunuch even when sober.[100] Of course, the joke is that in reality, they are both admiring Chaerea, but the fact remains that eunuchs could be imagined as youthful, beautiful, and desirable. It might be argued that these remarks say more about Greek attitudes than Roman ones, given the Greek source of Terence and the Greek setting of the play. However, these concepts clearly did enter Roman thought, and the popularity of Terence's play (it was performed twice in the same day and set a financial record in terms of how much he was paid for it) suggests that Romans were receptive to these ideas anyway.[101] If this is the case it indicates that the Roman view of eunuchs as attractive and desirable is much older and more prevalent than one might otherwise guess, and it shows that the idealization of Earinus as a beautiful youth is not an exception.

It has become clear, then, that Earinus is not a unique eunuch; in Roman literature eunuchs could indeed be depicted as beautiful and attractive, as archetypal pretty boys. It is evident that in the Roman Empire such ideas stretch at least as far back as the second century BC, and continue into the later Roman Empire and beyond.[102] At the same time, there were Roman views of eunuchs that were derogatory and hostile, but it is essential not to confuse different types of eunuchs in the Roman Empire. Vout and Newlands obviously base their assertions of what constituted the typical Roman attitude to eunuchs primarily on texts reacting to the Galli, but these eunuchs are quite distinct from the castrated slave boys who fed the Roman markets. The Galli were religious devotees of a Mother Goddess, who dressed and acted in distinct ways for particular reasons. Further, the Galli chose to castrate themselves, and presumably usually took this decision when they had already

98 Trans. Barsby, p. 355.

99 Terence, *The Eunuch* 472–3, trans. Barsby, p. 367.

100 Ibid. 474 and 479. See also the comment of Thais' maid Pythias: Terence, *The Eunuch* 681–2.

101 For the popularity and financial success of the play see Barsby, *Terence*, p. 307.

102 For the beauty attributed to eunuchs in the Byzantine empire see Myrto Hatzaki, *Beauty and the Male Body in Byzantium: Perceptions and Representations in Art and Text* (Basingstoke: Palgrave Macmillan, 2009), esp. pp. 94–6.

passed puberty. The Roman abhorrence of self-castration, the voluntary renunciation of masculinity that was so central to Roman male identity, must be appreciated, for it informs the revulsion Romans could feel for the Galli. Depictions of the Galli emphasize their feminization and effeminacy, which can apply to other eunuchs too, but could be presented in these other cases as contributing to their quality of beauty, just as it could in cases of boys prized for delicacy and youthfulness. It is vital to appreciate that different views of eunuchs could co-exist in Roman society, and it is essential to be sensitive to the reasons for this in order to understand Roman culture fully. However, the beauty of eunuchs could be ephemeral. Eutropius was eventually cast off by his lover Ptolemy, and Claudian goes on to present an horrific image of the eunuch in old age:

> And now his skin had grown loose with age; his face, more wrinkled than a raisin, had fallen in by reason of the lines in his cheeks. Less deep the furrows cloven in the cornfield by the plough, the folds wrought in sails by the wind. Loathsome grubs ate away his head and bare patches appeared amid his hair. It was as though clumps of dry barren corn dotted a sun-parched field, or as if a swallow were dying in winter sitting on a branch, moulting in the frosty weather … When his pallor and fleshless bones had roused feelings of revulsion in his masters' hearts, and his foul complexion and lean body offended all who came in contact with him, scaring children, disgusting those that sat at meat, disgracing his fellow-slaves, or terrifying with an evil omen those that met him … then at last they thrust him from their houses like a troublesome corpse or an ill-omened ghost.[103]

This recalls, perhaps, the eventual fate of Oscar Wilde's Dorian Gray. Interestingly, this contrast between the beautiful young eunuch and the repellent old eunuch is also exploited in Terence's *The Eunuch*. Chaerea poses as an attractive youthful eunuch, but this is at odds with descriptions of the real Dorus. Parmeno refers to Dorus disparagingly as 'decrepito hoc eunucho' [this decrepit eunuch] (*The Eunuch* 231),[104] and Chaerea calls him 'illum, obsecro, inhonestum hominem … senem mulierem' [a repulsive fellow and a woman of [an old] man] (*The Eunuch* 356–7).[105] When Pythias reports that 'Dorus' has made off after the rape, Phaedria comments 'I'd be very surprised if the useless creature [*ille … ignavos*] has got too far.'[106] When the real Dorus is brought before Pythias she is perplexed, and declares 'Oh! There's no comparison between them. The other one was good-looking, a handsome

[103] Claudian, *Against Eutropius* 1.110–31, trans. Platnauer, pp. 146–9.
[104] Trans. Barsby, p. 337.
[105] Ibid., p. 353.
[106] Terence, *The Eunuch* 661–2, trans. Barsby, p. 389.

fellow … This one is a shrivelled, lethargic, senile old man with the colour of a weasel [*hic est vietus vetus veternosus senex colore mustelino*].[107] Thus, despite the appreciation they could have of the beauty of eunuchs, Romans were under no illusion that castration was a guarantee of eternal youth. As Jupiter observed, Ganymede had advantages over Earinus.

[107] Ibid. 681–9, trans. Barsby, p. 391. This description of the shrivelled fossil of a eunuch has elicited much comment, especially for its reference to a weasel. The late antique grammarian Aelius Donatus, who wrote a commentary on Terence in the fourth century AD, remarked that Terence had here misunderstood the Greek of Menander, who had described the eunuch rather as 'a spotted lizard of an old man', alluding to the freckled skin of eunuchs: see for instance A. J. Brothers, *Terence,* The Eunuch (Warminster: Aris & Philips Ltd, 2000), p. 191.

CHAPTER 3

Appropriation and Development of Castration as Symbol and Practice in Early Christianity

Jack Collins

When Peter Abelard (1079–1142) was castrated by the order of his wife's uncle, he turned to the example of Origen of Alexandria, a third-century Church father who purportedly castrated himself in a fit of religious zeal. Abelard argued that his own castration made him a more appropriate teacher for nuns, because it alleviated his sexual tensions and temptations. While scholars continue to debate the accuracy of the traditional account of Origen's self-castration, Abelard's understanding of that tradition reflects an ongoing tension within Christianity regarding the role of sexuality in Christian life. This tension is evident in the ways early Christian perceptions of castration changed in response to the shifting locus of sexual anxiety in Christian communities. The 'eunuchs for the sake of the kingdom of heaven' of Matthew 19:12 probably represent celibate, childless men, reflecting the Matthean community's desire to reconcile the commandment to be fruitful with an apocalyptic skepticism about the value of marriage and reproduction. Such a reading is supported by rabbinic discussions of castration, in which the primary concern is the eunuch's inability to produce offspring. But with the decline of eschatological expectation, this characteristically Jewish exegesis was replaced in the gentile Church by readings focused on earthly sexual immorality, intended both to condemn illicit sexual practices within the Church and to defend the Church from accusations of such practices from the outside.

Emerging as it did from the intersection of Jewish traditions and Greco-Roman culture, the early Church struggled to reconcile the strong condemnation of castration in the Hebrew Bible with the development of Christian asceticism, not to mention the ubiquitous (if ambiguous) presence of eunuchs in the gentile world outlined by Shaun Tougher.[1] The first reference to

[1] See Shaun Tougher, 'The Aesthetics of Castration: The Beauty of Roman Eunuchs', in this volume, pp. 48–72.

castration in Christian literature – and indeed the *Ursprung* of all early Christian discourse on the topic – occurs in the original Greek of the Gospel of Matthew (*c.* AD 70).

> δὲ εἶπεν αὐτοῖς· οὐ πάντες χωροῦσιν τὸν λόγον [τοῦτον] ἀλλ' οἷς δέδοται. εἰσὶν γὰρ εὐνοῦχοι οἵτινες ἐκ κοιλίας μητρὸς ἐγεννήθησαν οὕτως, καὶ εἰσὶν εὐνοῦχοι οἵτινες εὐνουχίσθησαν ὑπὸ τῶν ἀνθρώπων, καὶ εἰσὶν εὐνοῦχοι οἵτινες εὐνούχισαν ἑαυτοὺς διὰ τὴν βασιλείαν τῶν οὐρανῶν. ὁ δυνάμενος χωρεῖν χωρείτω.
>
> But he said to them, 'Not everyone can accept this teaching, but only those to whom it is given. For there are eunuchs who have been so from birth, and there are eunuchs who have been made eunuchs by others, and there are eunuchs who have made themselves eunuchs for the sake of the kingdom of heaven. Let anyone accept this who can.' (Matthew 19:11–12)[2]

This passage has proved a stumbling block from the earliest days of the Church because, if read literally, it advocates a level of sexual asceticism far beyond even the deeply skeptical views of marriage expressed by Paul (1 Corinthians 7:1–9). The most common exegetical strategy has been to read it hyperbolically, much like the commands to sever other offending appendages in Matthew 5:29–30.[3] But there is more going on in this passage than simple hyperbole. The logion comes in response to the disciples' conclusion that it is better not to marry than to risk divorce (Matthew 19:10), and Jesus prefaces it with a warning that the teaching could only be accepted by a select few. This seems an unlikely caveat for a general admonition.

A hyperbolic reading does not explain why Jesus draws a distinction between two classes of involuntary eunuchs (congenital and manmade), on the one hand, and those who castrate (εὐνούχισαν, lit. 'eunuchize') themselves 'for the sake of the kingdom of heaven', on the other. This third classification – invoking as it does the central motif of the Matthean kerygma – is particularly puzzling to modern scholars, many of whom have drawn a connection to the Galli, the priests of the syncretic cult of Magna Dea/Cybele, who were reputed to castrate themselves as an act of ritual devotion.[4] But these speculations largely ignore the biblical context of the saying, and fail to fully apprehend its specifically Jewish, specifically apocalyptic origins.

2 Greek New Testament from Barbara Aland *et al.*, eds. *Novum Testamentum Graece*, 4th edn (Stuttgart: United Bible Societies, 1993) throughout. Translations from *The Holy Bible: New Revised Standard Version* (Nashville: Thomas Nelson Publishers, 1989).

3 Mathew S. Kuefler, *The Manly Eunuch: Masculinity, Gender Ambiguity, and Christian Ideology in Late Antiquity* (Chicago: University of Chicago Press, 2001), pp. 259–60.

4 Ibid., pp. 246–54. In this volume, Tougher fully explores the role of the Galli and the Roman sources for eunuchs. See 'The Aesthetics of Castration', pp. 48–72.

Whatever the original source of the saying (which is unique to Matthew),[5] the received text of Matthew clearly places it within a larger discussion of marriage and divorce. More specifically, it comes after Jesus makes a declaration forbidding divorce under most circumstances, in direct contradiction of established Jewish law which allowed a man to divorce his wife if 'he finds something objectionable about her' (Deuteronomy 24:1–3).[6] Jesus challenges the very foundation of the law, stating that Moses was making concessions to the hard-heartedness of the Jews, not dictating God's true will (Matthew 19:8). It stands to reason that the author of Matthew understood the pronouncement regarding eunuchs as a challenge to some aspect of the established order as well, calling into question the basic Jewish understanding that marriage and sexuality are inextricable from reproduction.

Reading Matthew 19 in dialogue with other Jewish sources relating to castration and eunuchs – specifically the rabbinic legal debates and commentary collected in the Mishnah and Talmud – further clarifies the nature of Jesus' challenge. By the time of the redaction of the Palestinian Talmud and Tosefta (*c.* AD 400), the Jewish attitude toward castration of any sort was categorically negative. One rabbinic opinion even includes a prohibition of castration – both of men and of animals – among the seven so-called Noachide Commandments applicable to the entire human race.

More to the point, there is one discussion, attributed to rabbis of the first-century AD (*Mishnah Yevamot* 8:4–6 || *Bavli Yevamot* 79b), that seems to express much the same distinction made by Jesus between congenital eunuchs (Heb. סריס המה , *saris ḥammah*, lit. 'eunuch of the sun') and those castrated by humans (Heb. סריס אדם , *saris 'adam*, lit. 'eunuch of man'):[7]

> אמר רבי עקיבה, אני אפרש: סריס אדם חולץ וחולצין לאשתו, שהייתה לו שעת הכושר; וסריס חמה לא חולץ ולא חולצין לאשתו, שלא הייתה לו שעת הכושר. רבי אליעזר אומר, לא כי, אלא סריס חמה חולץ וחולצין לאשתו, שיש לו רפואה; וסריס אדם לא חולץ ולא חולצין לאשתו, מפני שאין לו רפואה.

5 The logion is considered of probable authenticity both by the Jesus Seminar and by Ulrich Luz; see Robert Walter Funk and Roy W. Hoover, eds., *The Five Gospels: The Search for the Authentic Words of Jesus* (New York: Macmillan, 1993), pp. 221–2; Ulrich Luz, *Matthew: A Commentary*, trans. Wilhelm C. Linss (Minneapolis: Augsburg, 1989), pp. 500–1.

6 Matthew 19:6–9. In this case, Jesus makes an exception for 'unchastity' (Matthew 12:9), but parallel passages (Mark 10:11–12) do not.

7 The redaction of Talmudic material covers many centuries, of course, and the dates of these traditions are notoriously difficult to fix, so even sayings attributed to first-century rabbis cannot be taken as *prima facie* evidence of prevailing Jewish standards in Jesus' time. The Mishnaic material, at least, can be safely dated to the third century or earlier, however, and so the priorities expressed in these writings are useful insofar as they derive from the same general cultural context as the Jesus movement.

> Said R. Aqiba, 'I shall explain. A eunuch castrated by man performs the rite of *halisah*, and they perform the rite of *halisah* with his wife, because there was a time in which he was valid [as a husband]. A eunuch by nature does not perform the rite of *halisah*, and they do not perform the rite of *halisah* with his wife, because there was never a time in which he was valid.' R. Eliezer says, 'Not so, but: A eunuch by nature performs the rite of *halisah*, and they perform the rite of *halisah* with his wife, because he may be healed. A eunuch castrated by man does not perform the rite of *halisah*, and they do not perform the rite of *halisah* with his wife because he may never be healed.' (*m. Yev.* 8:4)[8]

This indicates that Jesus was adapting existing Jewish rhetoric regarding castration to his own ends – rhetoric that would have been familiar to his Jewish audience. If the two familiar categories of eunuch are distinguished by their inability to father children, then Jesus probably intended for that quality to be assumed in his third category.

Indeed, rabbinic discussions of eunuchs are most often directly related to questions of procreation. The topic of the passage quoted above is Levirate marriage, a custom whose very purpose is to insure the survival of the line of men who die childless.[9] The question of Levirate obligation depends upon whether a *saris* can legitimately enter a marriage. Where the rabbis disagree on the legal standing of the two types of *saris*, the disagreement hinges upon whether the rabbi believes it is possible to cure a *saris ḥammah*, and thus render him capable of procreation. Likewise, *Bavli Shabbat* 110b speaks of castration – specifically medical treatments that lead to impotence or sterility – entirely in terms of the ability of the eunuch to produce children. The Mishnah defines the characteristics of a *saris* in direct parallel to those used to identify an *'aylonit* (איילונית) – an infertile woman (*Mishnah Niddah* 5:9). Likewise, rabbinic discussions of Leviticus 21:20 – which forbids one with crushed testicles from serving as a priest – are couched in terms of the continuation of the priestly lineage (*b. Yev.* 75a–76b). To be castrated, in the rabbinic viewpoint, is to be rendered incapable of procreation, and thus incapable of fulfilling the first commandment given by God to Adam and Eve (Genesis 1:28).[10]

[8] Isadore Epstein, ed. *Tractate Yebamoth* (Hebrew–English edition of the Babylonian Talmud, vol. 10; London: Soncino Press, 1984). Trans. Jacob Neusner, *The Mishnah: A New Translation* (New Haven, CT: Yale University Press, 1988), pp. 355–6.

[9] Levirate marriage is the legal requirement that a man marry his brother's widow if the brother dies without fathering children, as a way of symbolically continuing the dead brother's line (Deuteronomy 25:5–6). The *halisah* mentioned in the quote is a ritual by which the widow and her husband's brother can nullify this legal requirement.

[10] In later medieval laws, there is also a particular emphasis on the ability to procreate in regulating compensation for a groin wound or castration. For a discussion for laws in Frisia, Ireland and Wales, and Anglo-Saxon England, see Rolf H. Bremmer Jr, 'The Children He Never Had; The Husband She Never Served: Castration and Genital

The close relationship in the rabbinic mind between eunuchs and questions of reproduction is further evident in two Talmudic terms that do not refer to eunuchs *per se*, but to other individuals falling outside binary definitions of sex and gender, akin to the idea of a 'third gender' explored in several articles in this collection.[11] These terms are *tumtum* (טומטום) and *androgynos* (אנדרוגינוס); the latter is a simple Aramaization of the Greek term. Both terms refer to those of ambiguous biological sex – intersexed persons, in modern parlance – with the former word generally understood as a person born without clearly visible sexual organs, and the latter possessing the organs of both sexes. In keeping with rabbinic interest in unlikely cases relating to marginal legal status, these two classifications allowed the rabbis to explore the foundations of legal distinctions between genders by blurring those distinctions. Curiously, *tumtum* is used in reference to Abraham and Sarah in their elderly, childless state, before the miraculous birth of Isaac: 'אמר רבי אמי, אברהם ושרה טומטמין היו.' [Rabbi Ammi said, Abraham and Sarah were *tumtumin*] (*b. Yev.* 64a).[12] It seems unlikely that this characterization is meant to be taken literally – Abraham does successfully father Ishmael by Hagar without divine intervention.[13] Instead, it appears *tumtum* is used symbolically for childlessness, as if the two were identical in the minds of the rabbis.[14] Indeed, this association between eunuchs and the childless is reinforced by the fact that as *b. Yev.* 83b states that some (but not all) *tumtumin* are also *sarisim ḥammah*.

It is thus likely that Jesus' Pharisaic interlocutors in Matthew 19 shared their rabbinic successors' strong association between sexuality and procreation, and conversely, between castration and the absence of offspring. The teachings of Jesus (at least as they are portrayed by Matthew) thus not only undermine the prevailing interpretation of the law, they also undermine the Jewish understanding of the very purpose of marriage. Jesus says nothing of procreation in his polemic against divorce, instead focusing only on the marital union itself. And when the disciples interpret this to imply that it is better not to marry, Jesus does not rebuke them, but instead uses the 'eunuchs for the sake of the kingdom' to illustrate that only some are capable of such a sacrifice. While Jesus

Mutilation in Medieval Frisian Law', pp. 108–30; Charlene M. Eska, '"Imbrued in their owne bloud": Castration in Early Welsh and Irish Sources', pp. 149–73; and Jay Paul Gates, 'The *Fulmannod* Society: Social Valuing of the (Male) Legal Subject', pp. 131–40 in this volume.

11 See Tougher, 'The Aesthetics of Castration', pp. 54–5; and Jed Chandler, 'Eunuchs of the Grail', pp. 231, 253 in this volume.

12 Translation mine.

13 In its Talmudic context, the statement is used to explain why Abraham did not follow the Mishnah's requirement (*Mishnah Yevamot* 6:6) that a man take another wife if his first wife fails to produce a child after ten years.

14 *Bavli Yevamot* 83b does speak of a class of *tumtumin* who are capable of fatherhood once their genitals are freed from a membrane by surgery, but this only reinforces the link between the condition of the *tumtum* and infertility.

avoids commanding his followers to be celibate, he opens the possibility of celibacy as a legitimate, even preferable path for the righteous, something unthinkable within mainstream Judaism.

The sentiment that sexual renunciation is, while desirable, beyond the capacity of most is closely echoed by Paul's words in his first letter to the Corinthians:

> καλὸν ἀνθρώπῳ γυναικὸς μὴ ἅπτεσθαι διὰ δὲ τὰς πορνείας ἕκαστος τὴν ἑαυτοῦ γυναῖκα ἐχέτω καὶ ἑκάστη τὸν ἴδιον ἄνδρα ἐχέτω. τῇ γυναικὶ ὁ ἀνὴρ τὴν ὀφειλὴν ἀποδιδότω, ὁμοίως δὲ καὶ ἡ γυνὴ τῷ ἀνδρί. … θέλω δὲ πάντας ἀνθρώπους εἶναι ὡς καὶ ἐμαυτόν· ἀλλὰ ἕκαστος ἴδιον ἔχει χάρισμα ἐκ θεοῦ, ὁ μὲν οὕτως, ὁ δὲ οὕτως. Λέγω δὲ τοῖς ἀγάμοις καὶ ταῖς χήραις, καλὸν αὐτοῖς ἐὰν μείνωσιν ὡς κἀγώ· εἰ δὲ οὐκ ἐγκρατεύονται, γαμησάτωσαν, κρεῖττον γάρ ἐστιν γαμῆσαι ἢ πυροῦσθαι.
>
> 'It is well for a man not to touch a woman.' But because of cases of sexual immorality, each man should have his own wife and each woman her own husband. The husband should give to his wife her conjugal rights, and likewise the wife to her husband … I wish that all were as I myself am. But each has a particular gift from God, one having one kind and another a different kind. To the unmarried and the widows I say that it is well for them to remain unmarried as I am. But if they are not practicing self-control, they should marry. For it is better to marry than to be aflame with passion. (1 Corinthians 7:1–3, 7–9)

Paul's acceptance of marriage (and marital sex) seems grudging at best. He clearly considers celibacy the preferable path, but recognizes that not all share his 'particular gift', just as Matthew's gospel recognizes that only a few will make themselves 'eunuchs'.

The perception of marriage and celibacy in Matthew and Paul reflects the overarching apocalyptic eschatology permeating the early Church, which led believers to question the value of all aspects of their current existence. The anticipation of an imminent end of the world precipitated a radical shift in the priorities of Jesus' followers, over against both mainstream Jews and Hellenistic gentiles. Jesus' seemingly hyperbolic pronouncements that people should abandon their families (Luke 14:26) their livelihoods (Matthew 4:18–20), and their possessions (Matthew 19:21–2), are quite consistent with the dualistic, apocalyptic rejection of this world in favor of the coming Kingdom. Matthew Keufler observes that Matthew 19:11–12 'echoes a passage from the Biblical book of Isaiah in which the requirements of marriage would no longer be paramount in the future kingdom of Israel'.[15]

In a world approaching its end, procreation becomes unnecessary for the

[15] Viz. Isa. 56:3–5; Kuefler, *Manly Eunuch*, p. 258.

continuation of the species, so marital relations – in stark contrast to the rabbinic view – only function to curb the lusts of those not gifted with the capacity for celibacy. The Essenes, also steeped in Jewish apocalyptic thought, are similarly reported to have renounced marriage, at least according to external reports from their contemporaries.[16] Such celibates, by cutting themselves off from reproduction, become eunuchs from a Jewish perspective. Gary Taylor even sees the subsequent verses of Matthew ('Let the little children come to me …') as an acknowledgment of the necessity of adoption in celibate sects.[17] Thus Matthew's gospel inverts the Jewish perception of eunuchs as reproductive dead-ends, and turns childlessness into a sign of faith in the nearness of the Kingdom of Heaven.

This level of imminent eschatological expectation necessarily waned as the decades passed, and the growth of Christianity as a primarily gentile institution brought about changes in the Church's understanding of manhood and castration. In a world whose end could not be surely anticipated, the necessity of some degree of procreation ceased to be a matter of debate within the Christian proto-orthodoxy (although it was questioned by other Christian groups). Instead, castration – as both a symbol and practice – came to be applied to other points of sexual anxiety within the Christian world.

One such focus was apologetic, specifically to defend Christians from accusations of sexual impropriety. Because of its integration of both male and female members, and indeed its 'love feasts' and proclamation that there is 'no male or female' in Christ (Galatians 3:28), the early Church was commonly subject to allegations of sexual licentiousness.[18] It also became a point of divergence for Christian and non-Christian communities, as circumcision would in later Christian discourse. For instance, the late second-century apologist Athenagoras contrasts Christians living 'in the state of an eunuch' with the pagans' indulgence of 'every kind of vile pleasure'.[19] Symbolic castration, therefore, functioned as a powerful rhetorical device for stressing Christian sexual continence as a defining characteristic over against the wider Greco-Roman culture.

These early sources generally eschewed a literal reading of Matthew 19, not only for theological and hermeneutical reasons, but also out of skepticism

16 Josephus, *De bello Iudaico* 2.120–1, ed. Benedikt Niese (Berlin: Weidmann; 1895), but cf. 2.160–1; Pliny the Elder, *Naturalis Historia* 5.15, ed. Karl F. T. Mayhoff (Leipzig: Teubner, 1906).

17 Gary Taylor, *Castration: An Abbreviated History of Western Manhood* (New York and London: Routledge, 2002), p. 196.

18 Minucius Felix, *Octavius* 9.1–7, ed. B. Kytzler (Leipzig: Teubner, 1992), preserves an exaggerated version of these accusations as a straw man. Cf. Origen 6.27, *Contra Celsem*, ed. C. de la Rue *et al.* (Berlin: Haude and Spencer, 1845).

19 *Legatio* 33–34, in Alexander Roberts and James Donaldson, eds., *The Ante-Nicene Fathers* (Peabody, MA: Hendrickson, 1995), 2:146–7, hereafter cited as *ANF*.

towards the physical and spiritual efficacy of castration as a shield against sexual sin.[20] Clement of Alexandria (AD 132–217) observes:

> εὐνοῦχοι πολλοὶ καὶ οὗτοι μαστροποί, τῷ ἀξιοπίστῳ τοῦ μὴ δύνασθαι φιληδεῖν τοῖς εἰς ἡδονὰς ἐθέλουσιν ῥᾳθυμεῖν ἀνυπόπτως διακονούμενοι. Εὐνοῦχος δὲ ἀληθὴς οὐχ ὁ μὴ δυνάμενος, ἀλλ' ὁ μὴ βουλόμενος φιληδεῖν.
>
> Many are eunuchs; and these panderers serve without suspicion those that wish to be free to enjoy their pleasures, because of the belief that they are unable to indulge in lust. But a true eunuch is not one who is unable, but one who is unwilling, to indulge in pleasure. (*Paedegogus* III, 4.26.221)[21]

So for Clement, the *act* of castration is meaningless, while the *idea* of castration, of being *like* a eunuch for the sake of the Kingdom of Heaven, remained a powerful symbol. This is in keeping with Clement's broader theme of distinguishing between the plain and spiritual meanings of scripture, or, indeed with Paul's distinction between circumcision of the flesh and the 'true' circumcision of the spirit (Romans 2:24–9).[22] Castration of the flesh then is (at best) an imperfect type to the antitype of spiritual castration, viz. celibacy. At worst, castration becomes a form of false piety, which can ape the appearance of 'true' Christianity, but lacks its spiritual foundation.

Most of the references to *literal* eunuchs in the second- and third-century proto-orthodox sources come in polemics, either against pagan practices (notably the aforementioned Galli),[23] or against those of 'heretical' Christian groups like the Marcionites and various so-called Gnostics. More fiercely dualistic even than apocalyptic Judaism, these groups 'tended to denigrate the body as the nagging link between the human soul and the evils they believed inherent in the material world'.[24] Escape from this corruption was not to be found in a coming eschatological event, but rather through some sort of spir-

[20] A common theme in late antique discourse about eunuchs is the fact (known to anyone who has owned a neutered dog) that castration (or specifically orchidectomy) does *not* necessarily render one incapable of intercourse or bereft of desire. Just as a *hymen intacta* was understood to be a potentially *false* signifier of a woman's chastity, the removal of the testes was understood to have the potential to free a man from the inconvenient sequellae of sexual congress (i.e., impregnation), without actually insuring purity of thought or action. See Kuefler, *Manly Eunuch*, pp. 96–102; Peter Brown, *The Body and Society: Men, Women, and Sexual Renunciation in Early Christianity* (New York: Columbia University Press, 1988), p. 19.

[21] Clement of Alexandria, *Paedogogus*, ed. Otto Stählin (Leipzig: J. C. Hinrichs, 1905). Trans. Roberts and Donaldson, *ANF* 2:278.

[22] See Kuefler, *Manly Eunuch*, p. 264.

[23] E.g., Tertullian, *Ad nationones* 1.20.4; 2.7.16, ed. August Reifferscheid and Georg Wissowa (Vienna: F. Tempsky, 1890); Minucius Felix, *Octavius* 21; Lactantius, *Divinae institutiones* 1.21, ed. Samuel Brandt and Georg Laubmann (Vienna: F. Tempsky, 1890).

[24] Daniel F. Caner, 'The Practice and Prohibition of Self-Castration in Early Christianity', *Vigiliae Christianae* 51.4 (November 1997): 395–415 at p. 404.

itual transcendence. It is unsurprising that many of these groups are said to have rejected sexuality, marriage, and reproduction far more radically than their proto-orthodox contemporaries.

One such sect, the Encartites, held 'that Christ did not consider it possible to conquer death as long as women gave birth'.[25] The reports of Clement detail several other heterodox Christian teachings, such as those of Julius Cassian and Valentinus, which are ambiguous on the subject of castration, but seem to imply the obsolescence of genital organs for the saved.[26] In derision of the Marcionite sanction against marriage, Tertullian (*c.* AD 160–220) writes, 'Iam et bestiis illius barbariei importunior Marcion. Quis enim tam castrator carnis castor quam qui nuptias abstulit? Quuis tam comesor mus Ponticus quam qui evangelia corrosit?' [Marcion is more savage than even the beasts of that barbarous region. For what beaver was ever a greater emasculator than he who has abolished the nuptial bond?] (*Adversus Marcionem* 1.1).[27] Tertullian likewise ridiculed the Galli as 'tertio sexu: illud aptius de viro et femina viris et feminis iunctum' [a third race in sex, and, made up as it is of male and female in one, it is more fitted to men and women [for offices of lust]] (*Ad nat.* 1.20.4).[28] Yet elsewhere, Tertullian still praises the idea of living *like* a eunuch, lauding *voluntarii spadones* 'voluntary eunuchs' who renounce sexual relations within a marriage (*Ad uxorem* 6.2). In his later, Montanist writings, he goes so far as to call Jesus *spado* 'a eunuch', and describes Paul as *castratus* 'castrated' (*De monogamia* 3). As Walter Stevenson notes, 'Tertullian is not using his terms very consistently'.[29] Rather, he appears to invoke castration imagery in whatever manner best suits his particular argument, implying that the associations with such imagery were far from fixed in Tertullian's cultural context.

While Tertullian's application of castration language runs the gamut of conventional proto-orthodox approaches, from condemning it in the literal sense to praising it in the figurative, there are a few exceptional examples in Christian discourse where literal castration was used for the same apologetic ends as metaphoric castration. Justin Martyr thus reports (writing *c.* AD 150) of a young Christian who sought castration in order to demonstrate Christian sexual purity:

25 Piotr O. Scholz, *Eunuchs and* Castrati*: A Cultural History* (Princeton, NJ: Markus Wiener Publishers, 2001), p. 165.

26 Walter Stevenson, 'Eunuchs and Early Christianity', in *Eunuchs in Antiquity and Beyond*, ed. Shaun Tougher (London: Classical Press of Wales and Duckworth, 2002), pp. 127–8.

27 Tertullian, *Adversus Marcionem*, ed. Emile Kroymann (Vienna: F. Tempsky, 1906), trans. *ANF* 3:272. For the legendary self-castration of beavers, see Ellen Lorraine Friedrich's chapter 'Insinuating Indeterminate Gender: A Castration Motif in Guillaume de Lorris's *Romans de la rose*' in this volume, pp. 255–79.

28 Trans. *ANF* 3:127. See Kuefler, *Manly Eunuch*, p. 249.

29 Stevenson, 'Eunuchs and Early Christianity', p. 126.

> καὶ ἤδη τις τῶν ἡμετέρων,ὑπὲρ τοῦ πεῖσαι ὑμᾶς ὅτι οὐκ ἔστιν ἡμῖν μυστήριον ἡ ἀνέδην μίξις, βιβλίδιον ἀνέδωκεν ἐν Ἀλεξανδρείᾳ Φήλικι ἡγεμονεύοντι ἀξιῶν ἐπιτρέψαι ἰατρῷ τοὺς διδύμους αὐτοῦ ἀφελεῖν·ἄνευ γὰρ τῆς τοῦ ἡγεμόνος ἐπιτροπῆς τοῦτο πράττειν ἀπειρῆσθαι οἱ ἐκεῖ ἰατροὶ ἔλεγον. καὶ μηδ' ὅλως βουληθέντος Φήλικος ὑπογράψαι, ἐφ' ἑαυτοῦ μείνας ὁ νεανίσκος ἠρκέσθη τῇ ἑαυτοῦ καὶ τῶν ὁμογνωμόνων συνειδήσει.
>
> And that you may understand that promiscuous intercourse is not one of our mysteries, one of our number a short time ago presented to Felix the governor in Alexandria a petition, craving that permission might be given to a surgeon to make him an eunuch. For the surgeons there said that they were forbidden to do this without the permission of the governor. And when Felix absolutely refused to sign such a permission, the youth remained single, and was satisfied with his own approving conscience, and the approval of those who thought as he did. (*Apology* 1.29)[30]

While this youth's petition ultimately failed, and he chose instead to live a life of voluntary chastity, Justin does not express the sort of disapprobation seen in Clement or Origen. For Justin, it appears that at least the desire for castration could function as a positive sign of Christian chastity. This model, however, is frowned upon in later hagiographical texts – such as the thirteenth-century Middle English *South English Legendary* examined by Larissa Tracy in this volume – in miraculous accounts of self-castration and suicide. In those cases, while the castrate is returned to life, he is not returned to virility – his members are not restored.[31]

Perhaps the most notorious case of early Christian self-castration also seems to fall into this category of apologetic demonstration, at least according to the Church historian Eusebius (AD 263–339). Writing more than a century after the fact, Eusebius reports that in a youthful fit of religious zeal, Origen of Alexandria (AD 184–253) chose to castrate himself in response to a literal reading of Matthew 19 (*Historia ecclesiastica* 6.8.1–3).

> Ἐν τούτῳ δὲ τῆς κατηχήσεως ἐπὶ τῆς Ἀλεξανδρείας τοὔργον ἐπιτελοῦντι τῷ Ὠριγένει πρᾶγμά τι πέπρακται φρενὸς μὲν ἀτελοῦς καὶ νεανικῆς, πίστεώς γε μὴν ὁμοῦ καὶ σωφροσύνης μέγιστον δεῖγμα περιέχον. τὸ γάρ· εἰσὶν εὐνοῦχοι οἵτινες εὐνούχισαν ἑαυτοὺς διὰ τὴν βασιλείαν τῶν οὐρανῶν ἁπλούστερον καὶ νεα νικώτερον ἐκλαβών, ὁμοῦ μὲν σωτήριον φωνὴν ἀποπληροῦν οἰόμενος, ὁμοῦ δὲ καὶ διὰ τὸ νέον τὴν ἡλικίαν ὄντα μὴ ἀνδράσι μόνον, καὶ γυναιξὶ δὲ τὰ θεῖα προσομιλεῖν, ὡς ἂν πᾶσαν τὴν παρὰ τοῖς ἀπίστοις αἰσχρᾶς διαβολῆς ὑπόνοιαν ἀποκλείσειεν, τὴν σωτήριον

30 E. J. Goodspeed, ed., *Die ältesten Apologeten* (Göttingen: Vandenhoeck & Ruprecht, 1915); trans. *ANF* 1:172.

31 Larissa Tracy, '"Al defouleden is holie bodi": Castration, the Sexualization of Torture, and Anxieties of Identity in the *South English Legendary*', pp. 87–107 in this volume.

> φωνὴν ἔργοις ἐπιτελέσαι ὡρμήθη, τοὺς πολλοὺς τῶν ἀμφ' αὐτὸν γνωρίμων διαλαθεῖν φροντίσας. οὐκ ἦν δὲ ἄρα δυνατὸν αὐτῷ καίπερ βουλομένῳ τοσοῦτον ἔργον ἐπικρύψασθαι. γνοὺς δῆτα ὕστερον ὁ Δημήτριος, ἅτε τῆς αὐτόθι παροικίας προεστώς, εὖ μάλα μὲν αὐτὸν ἀποθαυμάζει τοῦ τολμήματος, τὴν δέ γε προθυμίαν καὶ τὸ γνήσιον αὐτοῦ νῦν μᾶλλον ἔχεσθαι αὐτὸν τοῦ τῆς κατηχήσεως ἔργου παρορμᾷ.
>
> At this time while Origen was conducting catechetical instruction at Alexandria, a deed was done by him which evidenced an immature and youthful mind, but at the same time gave the highest proof of faith and continence. For he took the words, 'There are eunuchs who have made themselves eunuchs for the kingdom of heaven's sake', in too literal and extreme a sense. And in order to fulfill the Saviour's word, and at the same time to take away from the unbelievers all opportunity for scandal, – for, although young, he met for the study of divine things with women as well as men, – he carried out in action the word of the Saviour. He thought that this would not be known by many of his acquaintances. But it was impossible for him, though desiring to do so, to keep such an action secret. When Demetrius, who presided over that parish, at last learned of this, he admired greatly the daring nature of the act, and as he perceived his zeal and the genuineness of his faith, he immediately exhorted him to courage, and urged him the more to continue his work of catechetical instruction. (*Historia ecclesiastica* 6.8.1–3)[32]

The veracity of this report has been debated for centuries; the most thorough evaluation of the evidence, by Markschies, fails to come to a firm conclusion beyond the fact that castration may have been practiced among some Christians of Origen's era.[33] Regardless, Eusebius explicitly imparts an apologetic motivation to Origen's 'daring deed', saying it was done 'to take away from the unbelievers all opportunity for scandal', scandal potentially aroused by the fact that 'he met for the study of divine things with women as well as men' (*Historia ecclesiastica* 6.8.2).[34] In Origen's (purported) case, his position of catechetical teacher to both men and women placed him under suspicion that could be alleviated by his castration.[35] For Eusebius, at least, castration

[32] G. Bardy, *Eusèbe de Césarée. Histoire ecclésiastique* (Paris: Éditions du Cerf, 1955). Trans. from Eusebius Pamphili, Bishop of Caesarea, *Church History from* AD *1–324, Life of Constantine the Great, Oration in Praise of Constantine*, in *A Select Library of Nicene and Post-Nicene Fathers of the Christian Church,* second series, vol. 1, ed. Philip Schaff and Henry Wace (Grand Rapids, MI: W. B. Eerdmans, second printing 1961), p. 254; Hereafter cited as *NPNF*$_2$.

[33] Christoph Markschies, 'Kastration und Magenprobleme? Einige neue Blicke auf das asketische Leben des Origenes', in *Origenes und sein Erbe: Gesammelte Studien* (Berlin: Walter de Gruyter, 2007), pp. 15–34.

[34] *NPNF*$_2$ 1:254.

[35] Abelard evokes Origen to plead his case as a teacher of women, arguing that though his castration was involuntary, he is now a more appropriate instructor for the Paraclete.

could function as an antidote (albeit excessive) to external perceptions of sexual immorality.

With the exception of Justin Martyr's testimony, the anxiety over the sexual temptations inherent in Christian mixed-sex congregations seems more at home within Eusebius' fourth-century milieu than in Origen's own. The writings of Basil of Ancyra, the canons of the early councils, Palladius of Galatia, and Eusebius himself all reflect a concern for such appearances, especially with regard to male Christian leaders mingling (and in some cases cohabiting) with female virgins.[36] It is possible, therefore, that Eusebius, seizing upon an unfounded rumor, projected the concerns of his own time onto Origen to address the matter obliquely.

And it is in the fourth century that the most concrete condemnations of the Christian practice of self-castration occur, most notably by the Council of Nicea (AD 325), which declared:

> Εἴ τις ἐν νόσῳ ὑπὸ ἰατρῶν ἐχειρουργήθη, ἢ ὑπὸ βαρβάρων ἐξετμήθη, οὗτος μενέτω ἐν τῷ κλήρῳ. Εἰ δέ τις ὑγιαίνων ἑαυτὸν ἐξέτεμε, τοῦτον καὶ ἐν τῷ κλήρῳ ἐξεταζόμενον, πεπαῦσθαι προσήκει· καὶ ἐκ τοῦ δεῦρο, μηδένα τῶν τοιούτων χρῆναι προάγεσθαι. Ὥσπερ δὲ τοῦτο πρόδηλον, ὅτι περὶ τῶν ἐπιτηδευόντων τὸ πρᾶγμα, καὶ τολμώντων ἑαυτοὺς ἐκτέμνειν εἴρηται· οὕτως, εἴ τινες ὑπὸ βαρβάρων, ἢ δεσποτῶν εὐνουχίσθησαν, εὑρίσκοιντο δὲ ἄλλως ἄξιοι, τοὺς τοιούτους εἰς κλῆρον προσίεται ὁ κανών.
>
> If someone enjoying good health has castrated himself, this matter is to be investigated, and his belonging to the clerical estate is to be at an end, and in the future such persons must never be brought forward. But since it is clear that this applies to those who do such a thing intentionally and who dare to castrate themselves, it follows, then in regard to those who have been made eunuchs by barbarians or by their masters, that the canon admits such men as these, be they found worthy, into the clerical estate.[37]

The necessity of a prohibition of self-made eunuchs in the clergy carries with it a clear implication that such persons were numerous enough to be considered a problem, as Scholz rightly notes.[38] For example, Athanasius cited the case of an Arian presbyter from Antioch:

> Λεόντιος ὁ ἀπόκοπος, ὃν οὐδὲ ὡς λαικὸν κοινωνεῖν ἐχρῆν, διότι ἑαυτὸν

[36] Caner, 'Practice and Prohibition', pp. 409–12.

[37] Nicene Canon 1, from 'Concilium Nicaenum I – Canones (Altera Lectio)', Documenta Catholica Omnia, online at http://www.documentacatholicaomnia.eu/03d/0325-0325,_Concilium_Nicaenum_I,_Canones_(Altera_Lectio),_GR.pdf, accessed September 19, 2012. Trans. from W. A. Jurgens, trans., *The Faith of the Early Fathers* (Collegeville MN: The Liturgical Press, 1970), p. 282, quoted in Scholz, *Eunuchs and* Castrati, p. 171.

[38] Scholz, *Eunuchs and* Castrati, p. 171.

> ἀπέκοψεν ὑπὲρ τοῦ μετ' ἐξουσίας λοιπὸν κοιμᾶσθαι μετὰ Εὐστολίου τινός, γυναικὸς μὲν δι' αὐτόν, λεγομένης δὲ παρθένου.
>
> The eunuch Leontius, who ought not to remain in communion even as a layman, because he mutilated himself that he might henceforward be at liberty to sleep with one Eustolium, who is a wife as far as he is concerned, but is called a virgin. (*Historia Arianorum* 28)[39]

Not long after this, Epiphanius of Salamis wrote a polemic against the Valensians, an order of castrated desert ascetics (*Panarion* 2.1).[40] The polemics against castration in this period rarely make reference to the (mis)interpretation of Matthew 19. Instead, they characterize the practice as misguided, ineffective, or depraved.[41] Based on this testimony, it seems likely that, rather than existing as an ongoing, fringe practice from the earliest days of Christianity, self-castration emerged at some point in the third century as a response to sexual anxieties within the Christian community and became enough of an issue in the fourth century to be formally condemned by the emerging orthodoxy.

These later forays into literal self-castration notwithstanding, while most early Christian sources used castration imagery to signify the same thing – voluntary chastity – it cannot be assumed that this voluntary chastity itself had the same significance for all. For the Jewish audience of the logion in Matthew 19, celibacy was synonymous with childlessness, and by extension, with a transformation into a new, eschatological existence where the existing values (including marriage and procreation) no longer applied. But for later Christians, the meaning of chastity had less to do with rejecting the values of this world than it did with redirecting them towards new ends. Tertullian, for instance, speaks of chastity primarily within the confines of the marriage bond, a concession perhaps to the entrenched social structures of Roman society.[42] With regard to Origen's own interpretation of Matthew 19, far from endorsing the extreme asceticism he was later reputed to have practiced, it appears to be designed, according to Stevenson, 'to mould a Christianity that is not repulsive to non-Christians'.[43] Kuefler argues that by the fourth century, the 'spiritual eunuch', the man who chooses sexual continence by will, subverted the Greco-Roman ideal of manliness much as Matthew's 'eunuch for the sake of the Kingdom' (the man who forsakes fatherhood) did for the Jewish. The almost militant rhetoric of Jerome and Ambrose in praise of male chastity takes the

39 H. G. Opitz, *Athanasius Werke* (Berlin: De Gruyter, 1940). Trans. *NPNF*$_2$ 4:279.

40 See Stevenson, 'Eunuchs and Early Christianity', p. 129.

41 Caner, 'Practice and Prohibition', pp. 406–7.

42 Kuefler, *Manly Eunuch*, pp. 267–8.

43 Stevenson, 'Eunuchs and Early Christianity', pp. 134–6.

manliest qualities of *virtus* and *enkrateia*, and attaches them to the *least* manly figure in the ancient social lexicon, while equating lack of self-control with physical weakness and *literal* emasculation.[44] But where Matthew rejects the entire value of marriage and procreation within the new, eschatological Kingdom, these later Christian authors *redefine* the prevailing understanding of manliness while retaining manliness as a cultural value.

The many functions served in early Christian discourse by symbols, language, and practice related to castration and eunuchs reveal a complex interplay between Jewish foundations, scriptural exegesis, identity formation, and the structures and values of Greco-Roman society. The same images, the same practices, often serve opposite purposes depending on the context, even within the works of a single author. A figurative eunuch could be a paragon of self-control, or a heretic who defies God's design. And literal eunuchs could be lascivious pagan priests or paragons of self-sacrifice in the name of faith. But the eunuch in early Christian discourse always seems to appear at the soft spots in Christian self-perception, be it differentiating themselves from pagans, defending themselves against allegations of immorality, or developing a new model of strength from a position of weakness.

[44] See Ambrose, *De viduis* 13.75–7.

CHAPTER 4

'Al defouleden is holie bodi' *Castration, the Sexualization of Torture, and Anxieties of Identity in the* South English Legendary[1]

Larissa Tracy

Castration is a frequent feature of early Christian debates on the purity of the body, but it remained a difficult issue in the pursuit of sanctity, particularly in accounts of male saints and martyrs. As Jacqueline Murray writes, 'the whole problem of the body was perceived to be located in the male genitals. Once they were removed, it was believed that the problem of lack of control of the flesh would simply disappear.'[2] As a result of such (well-intentioned) logic, self-castration was practiced among some early Christian theologians, most notably Origen (*c*. AD 185–254) and Ignatius of Constantinople (AD 799–877); however it was condemned by the First Council of Nicaea (AD 325) as an excessive misinterpretation of the biblical verse Matthew 19:12 which ends with the exhortation 'there are eunuchs, who have made themselves eunuchs for the kingdom of heaven, he that can take, let him take *it*'.[3] Peter Abelard, in the

1 I touch on the relative lack of genital mutilation in hagiography in ch. 1 of *Torture and Brutality in Medieval Literature: Negotiations of National Identity* (Cambridge: D. S. Brewer, 2012); in my effort to flesh out that discussion I have synthesized some components from that chapter in this essay. My original material from that work is cited where used, and I have cited some of the same secondary sources.

2 Jacqueline Murray, '"The law of sin that is in my members": The Problem of Male Embodiment', in *Gender and Holiness: Men, Women and Saints in Late Medieval Europe*, ed. Samantha J. E. Riches and Sarah Salih (London and New York: Routledge, 2002), pp. 9–22 at p. 17

3 Douay-Rheims version of the Holy Bible, with commentary by Bishop Richard Challoner (1749–52) (Rockford, IL: Tan Books and Publishers, 1971, photographic reproduction of 1899 edition). In this volume, Jack Collins fully addresses the implications of Origen's action. See 'Appropriation and Development of Castration as Symbol and Practice in Early Christianity', pp. 78–86.

twelfth-century account of his own castration (*Historia calamitatum*), lauds Origen as a model (albeit excessive) for sexual restraint but constructs his own forced, punitive mutilation as a form of martyrdom, a necessary trial to achieve spiritual purity. Martin Irvine suggests that Abelard 'will be able to imitate the exemplary self-castrator, Origen, and other saints and martyrs who rejoiced to be without genitals'.[4] However, there are relatively few instances of castration in hagiographical narratives; most occur as part of a miracle performed by the saint. Even in the thirteenth century *South English Legendary* (*SEL*), which contains some of the most graphic and most brutal depictions of torture in hagiography, that line is not crossed. Despite the gruesome nature of its narratives, the *SEL* condemns castration and sexual mutilation as taboo, especially when self-inflicted, because such wounding diminishes the sanctity of the inviolate body and contradicts the societal constructions of masculinity embedded in the resistance to torture. As a result, the *SEL* rejects castration – like that of Abelard – as an excessive brutality that endangers the holy masculine ideal and disrupts English notions of national identity.

In *Historia calamitatum* and his letters to his wife Heloise, Abelard portrays himself as a vainglorious and foolish young man, castrated (justly) on the order of Heloise's uncle Fulbert for his own sexual weakness, who has come to see his mutilation as a divine test and form of martyrdom without ever relinquishing the rhetoric of victimization. He compares himself to Origen, whom he accuses of having an 'ill-formed zeal' for God and charges with homicide for his self-mutilation (*Letter 4*: 149).[5] Abelard places Origen's autocastration in the context of popular castration miracles, suggesting that some believe Origen acted either 'at the suggestion of the devil or in grave error' (*Letter 4*: 149) like the young men in prior narratives. But Abelard deems himself fortunate: 'in my case, through God's compassion, it was done by another's hand. I do not incur blame, I escape it. I deserve death and gain life' (*Letter 4*: 149). Bonnie Wheeler notes that Abelard's narrative is 'notoriously evasive' in claiming that his castration was appropriate, 'yet he finds it acceptable for his castrators to be punished'[6] – but only those who actually carried it out. He seems satisfied that only Fulbert's servants were castrated and blinded for inflicting his injury and not Fulbert himself. Their punishment is either that

4 Martin Irvine, 'Abelard and (Re)writing the Male Body: Castration, Identity, and Remasculinization', in *Becoming Male in the Middle Ages*, ed. Jeffrey Jerome Cohen and Bonnie Wheeler (New York: Garland Publishing, 2000), pp. 87–106 at p. 93.

5 Peter Abelard, *Letter 4*, in *The Letters of Abelard and Heloise*, ed. and trans. Betty Radice (London: Penguin Books, 1974), p. 75. Hereafter, text and page numbers in this edition are given in parentheses.

6 Bonnie Wheeler, 'Origenary Fantasties: Abelard's Castration and Confession', in *Becoming Male in the Middle Ages*, ed. Jeffrey Jerome Cohen and Bonnie Wheeler (New York: Garland Publishing, 2000) 107–28, p. 112.

of traitors (since that was one of the options for that crime), or simply the most appropriate considering their illegitimate punishment of Abelard.

The effect of such a brutal action enacted on a prominent figure had serious implications for medieval ideas of justice, law, torture, and punishment.[7] Abelard's very public castration – public in the sense that it was part of literary and religious dialogue in his lifetime and in subsequent centuries – may have actually triggered the response against such brutality in the Old French fabliaux[8] and influenced other texts that engage in discourses on castration like the thirteenth-century Latin *De Vetula* and its fourteenth-century French translation, Jean Le Fèvre's *La Vieille*.[9] But in the centuries that followed, and in the vast corpus of hagiography (both Latin and vernacular), castration seems to have been rejected, particularly in the *SEL*, as one of the litany of torments to which select male saints were subjected en route to achieving martyrdom. This may partly be because of the influence of Abelard's work and the impact his literary construction of castration had on religious discourse and medieval ideas of masculinity. In the *SEL*, castration is not a component of martyrdom because it violates the purity of the body and undermines the masculinity of the saints who serve a specifically English agenda.

In the course of enduring heinous tortures inflicted by illegitimate, barbarian authority, male saints are rarely (if ever) castrated. Although a select few male saints in the *SEL* are stripped naked and have their flesh ripped from their bodies (even to the bone), castration is largely absent from these narratives. Similarly, while female saints are subjected to a litany of tortures in their martyrdom accounts, those torments rarely amount to genital mutilation; in fact, female saints are – almost without exception – protected from rape or sexualized torture (except for mastectomies)[10] because in order to achieve

7 Tracy, *Torture and Brutality*, p. 211.

8 See Mary E. Leech, 'The Castrating of the Shrew: The Performance of Masculinity and Masculine Identity in *La dame escolliee*', pp. 210–28, in this volume.

9 See Robert L. A. Clark, 'Culture Loves a Void: Eunuchry in *De Vetula* and Jean Le Fèvre's *La Vieille*', in this volume, pp. 280–94.

10 Several female saints are subjected to breast ripping including Lucy, Agatha, Agnes, and Christina and a few are threatened with rape and despoilment. Beth Crachiolo contends that the nakedness of the female body is part of the virgin martyr legend, that 'women martyrs are routinely deprived of their clothes just before they are tortured', which functions as a facet of the torture and humiliation to which these women are subjected. 'Female and Male Martyrs in the *South English Legendary*', in '*A Great Effusion of Blood*'?: *Interpreting Medieval Violence*, ed. Mark D. Meyerson, Daniel Thiery, and Oren Falk (Toronto: University of Toronto Press, 2004) pp. 147–63 at p. 158. However, in most instances when the judges attempt to strip the martyr they are unsuccessful; either the clothes cling fast, the woman's hair grows to cover her body, or she is shrouded in divine light which blinds the pagan witnesses or strikes them down. The purity of the virgin martyr must remain intact, her virginity *and* her modesty. Many artistic renderings of these legends depict the martyrs in various states of undress that lends to the visual aspects of the torture, but it is rarely a component of the narrative legends except in the

sainthood they must remain intact as virgins, and any genital mutilation that might border on sexual violation could threaten their purity.

The image of brutalized and tortured saints was a common one in the Middle Ages, thanks in large part to Jacobus de Voragine's thirteenth-century *Legenda aurea* (*LgA*) (1255–66)[11] which collected hundreds of *vitae* into one Latin volume. The mutilated and torn bodies of saints were visible to the average lay person on altars, in paintings, stonework, and stained glass, and their stories were, 'retold with gusto'; in the retelling, 'horrors became more horrible, even as triumph over pain, decay and fragmentation became more impressive and more improbable.'[12] For medieval audiences, 'the relationship between the body and holiness was tense, indeed, fraught, as they sought to reconcile the inherent goodness of the body, as exemplified in the doctrines of the Incarnation and the Resurrection of the Body, with the antimaterialist critique proffered by dualism.'[13] Nowhere is this relationship more fraught than in the *SEL*, singular in its brutality, 'which by far exceeds what we find in both the *Legenda aurea* and in most contemporary vernacular legends.'[14] But there were limits to the level of brutality even in those narratives that capture the most horrific physical punishments conceived by mankind. The vernacular *SEL* negotiates anxieties of national identity in the torture of male and female saints. By not including castration as one of the many horrific torments inflicted on his saints, the author rejects this extreme form of punishment that was only a tenet of English law because it was imported by Norman invaders.

South English Legendary. For further information on visual aspects of torture in medieval art, see Robert Mills, *Suspended Animation: Pain, Pleasure, and Punishment in Medieval Culture* (London: Reaktion Books, 2005). Karen Winstead has also edited and translated a selection of virgin martyr legends from various English collections. See *Chaste Passions: Medieval English Virgin Martyr Legends*, ed. Karen Winstead (Ithaca, NY: Cornell University Press, 2000).

11 The *LgA*, of which some one thousand manuscripts survive, was translated into French (*Legende doreé*, 1380–1480), and Middle English (the *Gilte Legende*, *c.* 1438), and later printed by William Caxton as *The Golden Legend* (1483). Genevieve Hasenohr records the popularity of the *LgA* and its French vernacular translation the *Legende doreé* in northern France, in 'Religious Reading amongst the Laity in France in the Fifteenth Century', in *Heresy and Literacy, 1000–1530*, ed. Peter Biller and Anne Hudson (Cambridge: Cambridge University Press, 1994), pp. 205–21. The *Legenda aurea* has been translated and edited by both William Granger Ryan and Christopher Stace. See Jacobus de Voragine, *The Golden Legend: Readings on the Saints,* trans. and ed. William Granger Ryan, 2 vols. (Princeton, NJ: Princeton University Press, 1993); and *The Golden Legend,* ed. Christopher Stace with an introduction by Richard Hamer (London: Penguin Books, 1998).

12 Caroline Walker Bynum, *Fragmentation and Redemption: Essays on Gender and the Human Body in Medieval Religion* (New York: Zone Books, 1992), p. 269.

13 Murray, '"The law of sin that is in my members"', p. 9.

14 Karen Winstead, *Virgin Martyrs: Legends of Sainthood in Late Medieval England* (Ithaca, NY: Cornell University Press, 1997), p. 73.

In doing so, the *SEL* author establishes a clear idea of bodily sanctity that, while not contingent on the body's wholeness, must retain its sexual integrity.

The Middle English *SEL* (1270–80) evolved independently from continental hagiography; it was assembled in the southwest Midlands during the second half of the thirteenth century and was revised and supplemented around 1380–90.[15] There are more than sixty extant *SEL* manuscripts, and its adaptation of Latin material is marked by a specific attention to native English saints' lives, making it one of the best-represented works in Middle English, next to *Prick of Conscience*, the *Canterbury Tales*, and *Piers Plowman*.[16] These native legends relate the history of the English Church from a time 'when Christianity was first brought to England by St Augustine [of Kent] up to the thirteenth century when the *SEL* was composed'.[17] The *SEL* collection is unique in its concentration on the lives of English saints as well as more standard continental ones, particularly in the oldest extant manuscript Bodleian Library, Oxford, Laud Misc. MS 108, which also contains romances adapted from French sources into Middle English. As Kimberly K. Bell writes, 'the *SEL* shows a vested interest in creating an overarching image of England that possesses a singular type of holiness, a sanctity that is political and distinctively English'.[18] The *SEL* engages with its contemporary English audience by providing extensive details of local placenames, laws, death duties, the situation of the poor, the rights of the Church versus the state, historical conflicts, particularly between the Old English and the Danes, as well as accounts of Old English kingdoms.[19] In these highly localized accounts, the unique brutality of judicial torture in the *SEL* takes on an additional, and decidedly national, agenda because interrogatory torture was largely illegal in England throughout the Middle Ages and many English texts reject its use as the practice of a barbarian

15 Tracy, *Torture and Brutality*, p. 35. The torture of male and female saints in *SEL* is featured in ch. 1, pp. 31–69.

16 Winstead, *Virgin Martyrs*, pp. 71–2.

17 Renee Hamelinck, 'St Kenhelm and the Legends of the *South English Legendary*', in *Companion to Early Middle English Literature*, ed. N.H.G.E. Veldhoen and H. Aertsen (Amsterdam: VU University Press, 1995), pp. 19–28 at p. 19.

18 Kimberly K. Bell, '"Holie mannes liues": England and Its Saints in Oxford, Bodleian Library, MS Laud Misc. 108's *King Horn* and *South English Legendary*', in *the Texts and Contexts of Oxford, Bodleian Library, MS Laud Misc. 108: The Shaping of English Vernacular Narrative*, ed. Kimberly K. Bell and Julie Nelson Couch (Leiden: Brill, 2011), pp. 251–74 at p. 254.

19 Klaus P. Jankofsky, 'National Characteristics in the Portrayal of English Saints in the *South English Legendary*', in *Images of Sainthood in Medieval Europe*, ed. Renate Blumenfeld-Kosinski and Timea Szell (Ithaca, NY: Cornell University Press, 1991), pp. 81–93 at p. 84. Also see Jill Frederick, 'The *South English Legendary*: Anglo-Saxon Saints and National Identity', in *Literary Appropriations of the Anglo-Saxons from the Thirteenth to the Twentieth Century*, ed. Donald Scragg and Carole Weinberg (Cambridge: Cambridge University Press, 2000), pp. 57–73.

'Other'.[20] In most hagiography the pagan authority functions as a sovereign (judge and witness), but also as a 'symbol of anti-Christian forces, of heresy, of sadistic voyeurism, of government gone bad'.[21] To an English audience the tormentors are even *more* barbarous, even *more* alien, but they have a particular resonance within the political contests of thirteenth-century England.[22] While the *SEL* author made the political decision to write in English, the wicked judges use phrases like 'bel ami', 'beu frere' and 'beu sire', mimicking the aristocracy whose primary court language was still French.[23] Robert Mills writes that the 'use of such language places the tormentors within an Anglo-Norman milieu and hints at another context for the [*SEL*'s] circulation'.[24] The excessive brutality of the Latin saints' lives thus becomes a critique of perceived continental influence, especially in relation to emasculation. As noted previously, castration was a feature of Anglo-Norman law, imported with the Conquest of 1066. It is possible that the author and compilers of the *SEL* deliberately rejected castration as a hagiographical motif in order to distance thirteenth-century England from its ruling class (descended as most of it was from invading Normans), instead aligning it with Anglo-Saxon England. The absence of castration among the catalog of vicious tortures so gruesomely depicted throughout the *SEL* implies that not even barbarian tyrants would resort to measures that rob male saints of their masculine identity.

In the *SEL*, the English *vitae* are 'grounded in the specificity of English history'.[25] Those specifically English narratives often express anti-Norman (or anti-Danish) sentiments and encode their male saints with a virile voice of opposition and resistance. *Saint Wulfstan*'s account of the Battle of Hastings, for example, is a potent rejection of the Norman Conquest and its leaders.[26] William is described as the 'Bastard' who 'þouȝte to winne Enguelond: þoruȝ strencþe and tricherie' and 'destruyde and nam al þat he fond: and þat folk sore aferde' (*SEL* 20:64–8).[27] The narrator complains bitterly that when William is made king, 'al enguelond bi-sette, / Ase he wolde, with straunge men' (*SEL* 20: 101–2), emphasizing the foreignness of the Normans as he relates the Arthurian-style

20 Tracy, *Torture and Brutality*, pp. 35, 132–90.

21 Martha Easton, 'Pain, Torture and Death in the Huntington Library *Legenda aurea*', in *Gender and Holiness: Men, Women and Saints in Late Medieval Europe*, ed. Riches and Salih, pp. 49–64 at p. 56.

22 Tracy, *Torture and Brutality*, p. 35.

23 Robert Mills, 'Violence, Community and the Materialisation of Belief', in *A Companion to Middle English Hagiography*, ed. Sarah Salih (Cambridge: D. S. Brewer, 2006), pp. 87–103 at p. 100.

24 Ibid., p. 100.

25 Bell, '"Holie mannes liues"', p. 255.

26 Jankofsky, 'National Characteristics', p. 85.

27 *The Life of Saint Wulfstan*, in *The Early South-English Legendary or Lives of Saints, MS Laud 108 in the Bodleian Library*, ed. Carl Horstmann, EETS, os 87 (Oxford: Oxford University Press, 1887; reprinted 2000), pp. 70–7.

miracle of Wulfstan pulling his crozier from a stone in Edward the Confessor's tomb (*SEL* 20: 139–88). Such sentiment is echoed by several thirteenth-century authors including Robert of Gloucester and Matthew Paris, who felt their country was being overrun by outsiders. Robert of Gloucester specifically reminds the audience of his metrical chronicle that their country has an 'English past which predates recent Norman-usurped history, and which is, into the bargain, a past enshrining values of good, and Godly, governance which has, unhappily for the people, been corrupted'.[28] Robert's anxieties about foreigners are directed against the people whom he describes as the French, 'particularly because of the preferment given to them over the English; the increase in their numbers is attributed by him solely to the royal family'.[29] King John (1199–1216), his son Henry III (1216–72), his grandson Edward I (1272–1307), and great-grandson Edward II (1307–27) found themselves in difficulty in the thirteenth and fourteenth centuries as questions of national identity based on cultural inheritance and right to rule came to the fore.[30] Robert of Gloucester's chronicle narrates contemporary disturbances like the barons' rebellion, which essentially ended with the battle of Evesham (1265), and further woes that were to be expected under Henry's reign if it did not return to the 'gode olde law' of the Anglo-Saxon past.[31] The battle of Evesham, and the *post-mortem* mutilation of the rebel leader Simon de Montfort, whose severed head and testicles were sent as a trophy to Lady Mortimer, the wife of Lord Roger Mortimer (one the king's supporters), were a particular mark of this perceived 'Norman' brutality.

The legend of St Dominic in MS Laud 108 incorporates a complimentary statement about Simon de Montfort's father, 'a thinly veiled allusion to the son himself'.[32] The younger de Montfort was a popular hero who epitomized resistance to monarchical power and was venerated 'as a saint-like figure' after his death at Evesham and so the sympathetic reference in certain versions of the *SEL* 'is in keeping with the anti-Norman sentiments expressed elsewhere in the collection, since it points towards tensions between the monarchy and

28 Sarah Mitchell, 'Kings, Constitution and Crisis: "Robert of Gloucester" and the Anglo-Saxon Remedy', in *Literary Appropriations of the Anglo-Saxons*, ed. Scragg and Weinberg, pp. 39–56 at p. 43. Mitchell explains that the 'Robert of Gloucester' chronicle is extant in two recensions containing the same material until 1135, at which point they divide, the first (longer) recension goes up to 1271; the second recension provides a lengthy account of Stephen's reign and ends with a brief account of the accession of Edward I in 1272. The chronicle can be dated to the late thirteenth/early fourteenth century, the earliest surviving manuscript of which is London, British Library, Cotton Caligula A.xi, dated on palaeographical grounds to 1300–30 (p. 39, n. 3). Cited in Tracy, *Torture and Brutality*, pp. 134–5.

29 Mitchell, 'Kings, Constitution and Crisis', pp. 43–4.

30 Tracy, *Torture and Brutality*, p. 135.

31 Mitchell, 'Kings, Constitution and Crisis', p. 41.

32 Mills, 'Violence, Community and the Materialisation of Belief', p. 101.

high nobility, characterized as foreign, and the broad ranks of English baronage'.[33] His castration, designed as a deterrent to other potential rebels, stripped him of the symbols of masculine virility, adding to the indignity of his death which left a smoldering resentment among his supporters. Portrayed as a martyr, Simon embodies the enduring suffering of the English people under Normanized rule. The *SEL* develops an idea of Englishness that is 'not limited to and does not depend on dynasty: by turning to the saintly past of England before the Norman Conquest, it imagines an English Christian identity that bypasses the crisis in dynastic authority and lineage'.[34] Bell writes that the *SEL* re-envisions the nation of England in its concentration on vernacular English saints' lives, constructing 'a sense of English self-identity, one that is sanctified, holy, and singular',[35] and ultimately masculine.

The native *vitae* thus recount the 'historical' brutality of invaders and usurpers but avoid more popular accounts of miracles that include literal castration as a motif. For example, William of Malmesbury's twelfth-century *Vita Wulfstani* (translated from Old English into Latin) recounts the miracle of Thomas Elderfield. Castrated for injuring another man, Thomas protests his innocence (while local teens kick his amputated testicles and eyes about); he then appeals to the saint who restores him to health.[36] It is possible that the Latin version exaggerates the details of the castration and blinding, making it public so that the miracle seems trustworthy,[37] but the text states that castration and blinding are merciful, a reprieve from the standard punishment of hanging. Klaus van Eickels cites this episode as evidence that twelfth- and thirteenth-century hagiographical texts 'show how the sentence was executed in public', further arguing that 'it is hardly conceivable that the author of a saint's life would depict an almost contemporary miracle in a way that departed far from the common practice familiar to his audience'.[38] In contrast, Mills argues that these spectacular punishments, specifically in artistic renderings, do not reflect 'realism', because that would assume that medieval viewers witnessed comparable scenes in real life when they usually did not.[39] The episode in the *Vita Wulfstani* seems to be a unique reference to castration in English hagiography. It is not in the *SEL* version of Wulfstan's *vita*, despite the inclusion of other

33 Ibid.

34 Catherine Sanock, *Her Life Historical: Exemplarity and Female Saints' Lives in Late Medieval England* (Philadelphia: University of Pennsylvania Press, 2007), p. 84.

35 Bell, '"Holie mannes liues"', p. 260.

36 William of Malmesbury, *Vita Wulfstani*, ed. R. R. Darlington (London: Royal Historical Society, 1928): pp. 168–75 at p. 171. Cited in Klaus van Eickels, 'Gendered Violence: Castration and Blinding as Punishment for Treason in Normandy and Anglo-Norman England', in *Violence, Vulnerability and Embodiment: Gender and History*, ed. Shani D'Cruze and Anupama Rao (Oxford: Blackwell, 2005), pp. 94–108 at p. 101.

37 van Eickels, 'Gendered Violence', p. 101.

38 Ibid.

39 Mills, *Suspended Animation*, p. 121.

healing miracles performed by the saint. Two Latin versions of the *vita* of Thomas Becket (by William of Canterbury and Benedict of Peterborough) also relate a restorative miracle where the saint heals a man sentenced to castration and blinding for breaking and entering, but it is not repeated in the *SEL* version of Thomas's life.[40] Castration and blinding were legal punishments largely introduced to England by the Normans, and while there are Anglo-Saxon references to castration as punishment (as Jay Paul Gates explains in this volume),[41] it seems to have been a foreign practice before 1066. In fact, castration as a legally sanctioned punishment had faded in northern Europe by the thirteenth century.[42] And while castration and blinding were a punishment for rape *before* the reign of Edward I (1239–1307), according to the *Mirror of Justices* (1285–90), in later medieval England castration as a punishment for *any* crime was extremely rare.[43] The omission of this specific miracle from the Middle English *Wulfstan* suggests that either the author is reflecting a change in English practice, or he is distancing his Anglo-Saxon patriot from the brutality of the Norman invaders and Becket from the perceived tyranny of Angevin kings.

Castration as punishment for a crime (specifically treason) was a hallmark of Norman changes to existing Anglo-Saxon law. William I brought a specifically Scandinavian flavor of justice to England when he invaded. As Corinne Saunders writes, 'loss of member and blinding are generally presented in the

40 William of Canterbury, *Miracula sancti Thomae Cantuariensis,* in *Materials for the History of Thomas Becket, Archbishop of Canterbury*, vol. 1, ed. James Craigie Robertson. Rolls Series 67 (London: Longmans, 1875), pp. 156–8; and Benedict of Peterborough, *Miracula sancti Thomae Cantuariensis*, in *Materials for the History of Thomas Becket,* vol. 2, ed. Robertson (London: Longmans, 1876), pp. 173–82 at p. 177 (cited in van Eickels, 'Gendered Violence', p. 101). The *SEL* version in MS Laud 108 is quite long and gives extraordinary detail about facets of Thomas's life. The author chastises Henry II and his sons, particularly John, who is described as having usurped the throne from his nephew Arthur. *St Thomas of Canterbury*, in *The Early South-English Legendary or Lives of Saints, MS Laud 108 in the Bodleian Library*, ed. Carl Horstmann, EETS, os 87 (Oxford: Oxford University Press, 1887; reprinted 2000), pp. 106–77. Ironically, John was urged by his advisors to have Arthur blinded and castrated, rendering him unfit to rule (van Eickels, 'Gendered Violence', p. 100). Another account of Becket's life relates that Geoffrey of Anjou (father of Henry II) ordered the bishop of Séez and several of his clerics to be castrated for electing a bishop without his approval (van Eickels, 'Gendered Violence', p. 102); and while the account exists in several versions it is possible that the repeated used of castration for political purposes by the Angevin house and its forebears may function more as a motif designed to paint Henry II and his people (enemies of Becket) as the most cruel and wicked tyrants, rather than accurately depicting actual practice. Hagiography was often constructed as political and religious propaganda.

41 Even then, it is only mentioned as punishment for a slave who rapes another slave and is only able to make compensation through his castration. Gates, 'The *Fulmannod* Society', p. 133 and Eska, '"Imbrued in their owne bloud"', p. 155.

42 Peter Browe, *Zur Geschichte der Entmannung: Eine religions- und rechtsgeschichtliche Studie* (Breslau: Müller & Seiffert, 1936).

43 Lee Patterson, 'Chaucer's Pardoner on the Couch: Psyche and Clio in Medieval Literary Studies', *Speculum* 76.3 (July 2001): 638–80 at p. 659.

Leis Willelme as punishments most acceptable to William I'.[44] Van Eickels argues that castration, virtually unknown in France, Germany, and Anglo-Saxon England, was 'frequently employed in the Scandinavian north' where it was used to eliminate rivals who could not be killed because they were family.[45] He further suggests that the Scandinavians who settled Normandy in the tenth century brought that legal practice with them: 'Unlike other features, it survived the process of cultural and linguistic assimilation, which otherwise integrated them into post-Carolingian France within only three generations.'[46] He cites evidence of Anglo-Norman and French chroniclers who recount 'a considerable number of cases' in which William I's sons (William II and Henry I) have noblemen and other political rivals castrated and blinded for conspiring against them.[47] Most notably, Henry I ordered the castration of all the financiers in England in 1125 for debasing the currency.[48] However, frequent references to castration in chronicles do not necessarily mean it was as common in practice. In this volume, Charlene Eska gives a detailed analysis of the commonality of the practice and the effect the Norman laws regarding castration had on societies they invaded, specifically Wales and Ireland. Van Eickels points out that 'maiming or execution was almost never inflicted upon members of the higher nobility' in Anglo-Angevin England.[49] But the threat of death or mutilation seemed sufficient cause for English barons opposing the king to seek safe haven in the French court as 'the spheres of English and French rule overlapped on the continent'.[50]

The bodily sufferings of saints depicted in hagiography and in art were reminiscent of those inflicted on accused criminals.[51] Castration may have been taboo in hagiography as a genre because the authors did not want to align their saints with the criminals against whom the sentence was historically applied – actual criminals convicted under law rather than holy innocents persecuted in a pagan farce. The introduction of castration into English law by the Normans may have been too reminiscent of castration rituals attributed to pagan practice in the eyes of English hagiographers. The Normans could have been recast as barbarians for employing such measures. But even the pagan persecutors in these texts do not resort to castration, regardless of how much they may

44 Corinne Saunders, *Rape and Ravishment in the Literature of Medieval England* (Cambridge: D. S. Brewer, 2001), p. 49.

45 van Eickels, 'Gendered Violence', p. 100. See Anthony Adams, '"He took a stone away": Castration and Cruelty in the Old Norse *Sturlunga saga*' in this volume, pp. 188–209 for a fuller discussion on castration in Scandinavian tradition.

46 van Eickels, 'Gendered Violence', p. 100.

47 Ibid.

48 He also had their right hands cut off – the Anglo-Saxon punishment – in an attempt to synthesize the two legal traditions (ibid.).

49 Ibid., p. 101.

50 Ibid.

51 Easton, 'Pain, Torture and Death', p. 55.

mutilate the body of a male saint for imagined crimes. In this context, the *SEL* serves a specifically English, rather than Anglo-Norman, purpose. Of course, this 'English' purpose was complicated by the diversity of a thirteenth-century England populated by Anglo-Scandinavians of Danish descent, those of Anglo-Saxon ancestry, Anglo-Normans in the ruling class torn between French and English identities while also claiming descent from the Danes of Normandy, and the Welsh, Scots, and Cornish.[52] As Diane Speed explains, 'the creative literature of the latter part of the thirteenth century, as England ceased to function as a colony in the control of an alien aristocracy, may specifically be said to mark the clear emergence of English literature as the text of the nation'.[53]

Other texts of the *SEL* reflect not only the tensions of national identity inscribed in omitting castration miracles of English saints, but the anxieties of self-castration for spiritual purification enmeshed in the ecclesiastical discourse of chastity and virginity. Anke Bernau cites an episode from the life of St Paul Hermit where Paul witnesses the torture of a Christian man who is tied down to a bed and fondled by a prostitute; as the man is moved to lechery, he fights the sexual urges by biting off a piece of his tongue and spitting it at her – a metaphorical castration.[54] Mastering his unruly flesh this way highlights some of the underlying attitudes to male sanctity.[55] Male saints were venerated partly for their self-control, for the ability to overcome the weaknesses of their bodies and remain steadfast. Despite the self-control embodied by physical acts like that of biting off the tongue to curb desire, castration, especially autocastration (whatever the motive), is threatening because it violates the purity and sanctity of the masculine body. In the *SEL vita* of St James, James restores a young pilgrim to life who has been tricked by the devil into castrating himself and committing suicide. However, James does not restore the severed organ: 'His menbres, þat he carf of: euer-eft he dude misse, / Bote a luytel wise ȝware-þoruȝ he miȝhte: ȝwane he wolde pisse' (15: 380–1).[56] The young man must live with a dire and foolish action that renders him physically 'female' – he must now squat to piss.

The same miracle is told by Guibert of Nogent,[57] and is a central feature of

52 Tracy, *Torture and Brutality*, pp. 136–7.

53 Diane Speed, 'The Construction of the Nation in Medieval English Romance', in *Readings in Medieval English Romance*, ed. Carol M. Meale (Cambridge: D. S. Brewer, 1994), pp. 135–57 at p. 139.

54 Anke Bernau, 'Gender and Sexuality', in *A Companion to Middle English Hagiography*, ed. Salih, pp. 104–21 at p. 115.

55 Ibid.

56 All *SEL* quotations from *Saint James the Great* are in *The Early South-English Legendary*, ed. Horstmann, pp. 33–45.

57 Irvine, 'Abelard and (Re)writing the Male Body', p. 88. In his autobiographical memoirs *De vita sua*, Guibert relates 'castration anxiety nightmares' as well as war stories with graphic accounts of genital mutilation like that Thomas of Coucy who would hang his enemies up by their testicles and penises until they ripped free (p. 88).

the Spanish legend of Santiago de Compostela.[58] In that legend, the pilgrim is convinced to castrate himself by a devil in the likeness of St James, which suggests that hagiographers see castration as the work (or at least by-product) of devilish temptation rather than as a legitimate means of spiritual purification. The sinner can only be induced to castrate himself if he believes St James urges it, but he is woefully led astray because a true saint would never sanction such an act. In short, castration was not a substitute for self-control.[59] This episode also reinforces the Christian prohibition against self-castration suggesting that 'radical self-mutilation was not necessarily an acceptable method of bodily sublimation for ordinary Christians'[60] – or extraordinary ones, for that matter. Where female saints are often lauded for their 'masculine' defiance of torture, both Guibert and the *SEL* author suggest that this kind of self-mutilation is feminizing and degrading. According to Murray, the consequence was that

> cushioned among the many assertions of masculine superiority, especially with regard to the control of the flesh, there are also faint echoes of men's dis-ease with their own bodies and the chasm that separated their own lived experience of a male body from the ideal of chastity and bodily control that was established as an essential aspect for salvation.[61]

Castrating a male saint would destabilize the sanctity of the masculine body, but also remove the male saint from a gendered (if not sexualized) existence.

Most male saints (with a few notable exceptions such as George and Laurence) are not actually tortured or interrogated but are simply executed in particularly gruesome ways – horrific and slow ends, pure exercises in judicial brutality rather than systematic and repetitive cycles of torments and ordeals. Torture is unnecessary for a man to achieve sanctity.[62] Individual forms of punishment inflicted on male saints do not seem as spectacular as the litany of torments inflicted on the bodies of female saints. Beth Crachiolo argues that this is because there is no spectacle of torture for male saints, only female ones; torture in the *vita* of a male martyr is an event in which he is involved, while torture in the *vita* of a female saint is a spectacle she must endure.[63] Crachiolo

[58] Ryan D. Giles, 'The Miracle of Gerald the Pilgrim: Hagiographic Visions of Castration in the *Liber Sancti Jacobi* and *Milagros de Nuestra Senora*', *Neophilologus* 94 (2010): 439–50.

[59] Jacqueline Murray, 'Mystical Castration: Some Reflections on Peter Abelard, Hugh of Lincoln and Sexual Control', in *Conflicted Identities and Multiple Masculinities: Men in the Medieval West* (New York: Garland Publishing, 1999), pp. 73–91, p. 74.

[60] Mills, 'Violence, Community and the Materialisation of Belief', p. 102.

[61] Murray, '"The law of sin that is in my members"', p. 12.

[62] Though there are certainly female saints like Paula and Elizabeth of Hungary whose piety is enough to insure sanctity without being subjected to torture, virgin martyrs are the most common female saints.

[63] Crachiolo, 'Female and Male Martyrs', pp. 152, 153.

further argues that there are two concerns in the life of a male saint: how the saint deals with torture and who he is outside of the torture, neither of which specifically focuses on the body.[64] Male martyrs have identities unconnected with their bodily suffering – archdeacon, deacon, bishop, knight, abbot – that shift focus away from the tortured male bodies.[65] But in the *SEL*, the torture of male saints is as much a spectacle as that of the female saints because in these narratives the gender boundaries are often blurred and frustrated. There is no 'gendered' torture for male saints, because they do not have physical markers that can be removed without excising the defining feature of their gender. Many of the male saints suffer as a form of *imitatio Christi*, which involves a physical mortification of the flesh that, by the twelfth century, had been physically defined as male. Many religious debates emphasized the 'humanation' of God, of which 'enfleshing' Christ and 'the full range of his members', was a significant part.[66] As Caroline Walker Bynum points out, 'growing out of a twelfth-century concern for imitating the human Christ, the theme of humanation was present in a wide variety of saints' lives and devotional texts of the thirteenth and fourteenth centuries'.[67]

The *SEL* version of St Laurence's martyrdom emphasizes his courage and steadfastness as he is stretched out on the gridiron, placed over burning coals and turned with fire forks, but it also makes the point that he *suffers*:[68]

> Þe tormentores stoden al-a-boute: and bleowen þat fuyr wel faste;
> with Irene pikes huy pulten him: and schouen In faste a-boue.
> Louerd, muche was þe pyne: þat he soffrede for þi loue!
> Þat fuyr bi-neoþe rostede him: al quic mid flesch and blode,
> And þe Irene pikes in is flesch: ful bitterliche huy wode.
>
> (*SEL* 157–61)

Significantly, his genitalia are never mentioned. Nothing that is done to him marks him as 'male'; he is not tortured according to his gender – his masculine body is not the central focus of his sanctity. Laurence curses his tormentors for their brutality:

> 'þov wrechche,' seide þis holie man: 'mi wille hath euere i-beo
> For-to come to þis murie solas: þat ich here nouþe i-seo.

64 Ibid., p. 151.

65 Ibid., p. 156.

66 Bynum, *Fragmentation and Redemption*, p. 90.

67 Ibid.

68 This is a departure from female hagiography and certain iconographic representations where saints specifically do not feel pain, and often taunt the tormentors to do their worst. As Winstead notes, 'Despite their graphic representation of torture and dismemberment, however, late medieval artists rarely suggest that the saints suffer. In this respect, the iconography of martyrdom differs from the iconography of the Passion which was so profoundly concerned with Christ's agony' (*Virgin Martyrs*, p. 88).

Wel mo tormenz þane here beoth: to þe beoth i-mad al-ȝare
In þe pine of helle: ȝwane ich schal to þe Ioye of heue ne fare.'
(*SEL* 108–11)[69]

In contrast, the narrative of St George hinges on an accusation of treason. Dacian brands him a 'traytour' and orders him to be punished as one:

he liet him hangi up an heiȝ: In one-manere rode
And þare-to him binde faste al naked: with ropes strongue and guode.
With kene Owles þer-under: þe tormentores stode
And to-drowen is holie lymes: þat faste huy ronne on blode;
Al huy to-teren is te[n]dre flesch: þe peces fullen to grounde.
(43:31–5)[70]

It is possible in the course of this brutal dismemberment – when the flesh is torn off his body until it falls on the ground – that he is also castrated, but the author makes no specific reference to his genitalia. The narrative certainly does not lack detail. He is covered with burning oil, brought down and scourged 'and wounde op-on oþur made – / to þe bare bon þe scourgene comen' (43:39–40), salt is rubbed into the wounds 'and sethþe with a clout of here' (43:42). The author interjects, bemoaning his suffering: 'louerd, muche was þe pine þat he hadde' (43:43). George is cast into prison to sit out the night in pain; unlike his female contemporaries, he is not miraculously healed but 'he lai al þe longue niȝt: to oþur wo þat he hadde' (43:49). A brass wheel of swords is then constructed 'þat þe swerdes scholden is bodi to-rende: and to-drawe al-so' (43:56) but the wheel bursts by God's will so 'þat þis holie man: harmless þarof he was' (43:59). Next Dacian makes a brass furnace, fills it with molten lead, and tosses George in. Here, George's response parallels that of female saints like Christina who act as though boiling metal is nothing but a bath:

þare-Inne he sat wel softe a-doun: ase þei him noþing nere,
And leonede to þe brerde stille: ase þei he a-slepe were;
he lai ase þei he in reste were: for-to þat led atþe laste
was al in-to þe colde i-turnd: þat boylede er so faste.
(43:67–70)

Despite the brutality of the first set of punishments (and his evident pain), George appears unharmed by the later ones much like the female saints whose tender bodies remain miraculously unscathed, or are healed over and over until the killing blow. Finally, frustrated in his efforts to hurt the saintly George,

69 All *SEL* quotations from *Saint Laurence* are in *The Early South-English Legendary*, ed. Horstmann, pp. 340–5.

70 All *SEL* quotations from *Saint George* are in *The Early South-English Legendary*, ed. Horstmann, pp. 294–6.

Dacian orders his men to 'drowen him þoruȝ-ovt al þe toun: for-to huy with-oute come, / [& þat] huy smitten of his heued: with-oute þe toun atþe laste, / And is bodi þare in sum foul place: to wilde bestes it caste' (43:78–80). After George prays for his feast day to be observed in April, and for those who venerate him to be protected, his wish is granted by a heavenly voice and he is beheaded.

George's martyrdom is very much like a plethora of virgin martyr legends and in resisting the torture inflicted on his body he takes on many aspects of the female saint – especially in the emphasis on his virginity. But his tortured body is naked, whereas most female saints cannot be stripped, no matter how hard their tormentors try. According to Martha Easton, a naked martyr 'particularly one who is depicted with ambiguous, androgynous physical gender, suggests a rebirth into a state of grace in which gender is transcended'.[71] Mills suggests that the life of St George masks 'a voyeuristic, erotic subtext' that places comparable emphasis on the 'penetrative exploration of the male martyr's tender, naked flesh' as similar texts do with female saints like Margaret.[72] Gender affects sanctity and sanctity affects gender: 'Sainthood often works by breaking with normal social values, and gendered identity may be amongst these: constructing one's gender identity differently may be a marker of holiness.'[73] Samantha J. E. Riches provides an eloquent and detailed discussion of St George's various narratives and the variety of punishments to which he is subjected (including dismemberment, boiling, sawing in half), arguing that he was a 'borrower *par excellence*' and his story appropriates many of the torture methods found in female hagiography in an effort to focus on his status as a virgin.[74] In fact, several of the torments to which he is subjected appear in the lives of other male and female saints.[75] The legends of female virgin martyrs are 'both stories of Christian faith and tales of sexual denial and frustration, with an emphasis on sexuality and physicality that is less common in the lives of male martyrs'.[76] Easton cites the example of St Hippolytus who is stripped naked in an effort to humiliate and shame him,

71 Easton, 'Pain, Torture and Death', p. 53. She is referring specifically to the illuminated images in the Huntington *Legenda aurea* in which 'a fine line between the legs functions as a generic stand-in for the genitalia of both sexes'.

72 Robert Mills, '"Whatever You Do Is a Delight to Me": Masculinity, Masochism, and Queer Play in Representations of Male Martyrdom', *Exemplaria* 13.1 (2001): 1–37 at p. 8.

73 Riches and Salih, *Gender and Holiness*, pp. 1–8 at p. 5, cited in Tracy, *Torture and Brutality*, p. 62.

74 Samantha J. E. Riches, 'St George as a Male Virgin Martyr', in *Gender and Holiness*, ed. Riches and Salih, pp. 65–85 at pp. 68–9, 71.

75 Ibid., p. 71. Riches points out that George's legend borrows the torment of the wheel from St Katherine, but that he is less fortunate because for her, the wheel falls apart before she can be tortured on it. It is worth noting that in the *SEL*, the wheel bursts as well, aligning George even more firmly with the female virgin martyr.

76 Easton, 'Pain, Torture and Death', p. 59

which he resists, arguing that he is clothed in heavenly bliss. Frustrated, Decius orders him clothed again, but more richly.[77] In the *SEL* version, Hippolytus remains naked while with 'scourges and with staues al-so: huy beoten him ase huy weren wode, And al defouleden is holie bodi: þat is limes ronnen a-blode' (*SEL* 67: 37–8). His holy body is defiled, drenched in blood, and *then* he is clothed in rich raiment. The emperor appeals to his manhood, his masculine identity as a knight in order to get him to worship the idols: 'bi-þench þe wuch a man þou art: and ʒwuch a knyʒht þou hast i-beo, / Noble and hende, ase þou ʒuyt schalt: ʒif þou wolt þe bi-seo; / bi-þench þe-of þat þou hast i-haued: of þi noble dignete' (67: 49–51). In denying the emperor, however, Hippolytus does not deny his masculinity. He pronounces that he has become a new kind of knight, with new battles to fight: 'Godes knyʒht of heouene ich am: and al mi wille so is / Þat ich in his batayle be: sone i-martred, i-wis' (*SEL* 67:54–6). In response, the emperor tortures and beheads all the Christian men of Hippolytus' household, and finally has him tied to the tails of wild colts and dragged to his death through a briar patch, much like George is dragged before being beheaded.

Castration, besides being part of the discourse on bodily purity, was also seen as a feature of pagan barbarity. Early Christian writers, without exception, condemned the depravity of pagan religions by citing their castration rituals, like that of Cybele and Attis.[78] Lactantius, Tertullian, and Prudentius all criticized the gender ambiguity that resulted from castration and Prudentius, in particular, viewed the castration of pagan priests as proof of pagan violence.[79] He went so far as to have the Christian martyr Romanus criticize pagan castration in defense of martyrdom.[80] Prudentius saw a sharp contrast between 'the manly self-sacrifice of the Christian martyrs as soldiers of Christ and the unmanly sacrifice of the eunuch priests'.[81] The *SEL* rejects the dialogue about spiritual, mystical, or literal castration altogether and although certain male saints are subjected to physical harm, their manhood remains intact. Mills argues that female saints' lives produce their own disruptive effects in the context of torture, because while male martyrs might be 'divested of certain signifiers of earthly masculinity' during their torture, 'the battles that female virgin martyrs undergo to protect their chastity potentially associate them with privileges that, in late medieval culture, were normally gendered male: speaking eloquently, for instance, or thumping demonic entities with

77 Ibid.

78 Mathew S. Kuefler, *The Manly Eunuch: Masculinity, Gender Ambiguity, and Christian Ideology in Late Antiquity* (Chicago: University of Chicago Press, 2001), p. 249.

79 Ibid. See also Shaun Tougher, 'The Aesthetics of Castration: The Beauty of Roman Eunuchs', in this volume, pp. 48–72.

80 Kuefler, *The Manly Eunuch*, p. 250.

81 Ibid..

hammers'.[82] While their bodies are threatened, ripped, and torn, the only gendered marker of their torture is the removal of their breasts, and while this may be seen as extreme sexualized violence the saint 'simultaneously remains inviolate and sexually pure', conveying an 'essential and ubiquitous hagiographic paradox: the juxtaposition of violence and virginal impermeability'.[83] As Salih points out, 'the virgins are most passionate when they are apparently most vulnerable, as they suffer torture and death', but it is important that 'rape is never really an option in these legends'.[84] While there is no sexual rape, the version of St Margaret's life in the *SEL* is a notable exception to the standard mastectomy motif because her womb is ripped out and her 'deorne limes hi totere' (*SEL* 1:296).[85] But Salih argues that Margaret's body resists being seen pornographically or even anatomically, as the 'narrative does not see filth when the virgins are torn open. It sees wounds and blood, but not unmediated, and not for long.'[86]

Some critics have seen the physical torture of young female bodies as a deliberate attempt on the part of hagiographers to either objectify the bodies of female saints or to titillate themselves by reproducing images of disarticulated and mutilated bodies.[87] In general, 'the images of the tortures of virgin martyrs are often conceived in such a way that their punishments become forms of sexual molestation. They are stripped and displayed, their breasts are grabbed and mutilated, their bellies are penetrated with phallic swords.'[88] But more than a few male martyrs undergo the same kind of 'prurient "body-ripping" and phallic penetration'.[89] Torture is a standard motif for saints: the purer the virgin, the more innocent the body, and thus the greater the effect of

82 Mills, *Suspended Animation*, p. 173. Mills sees male saints as being 'visually de-phallicized' by being decapitated, disembowelled, and flayed; and female saints such as Barbara and Agatha as purportedly 'de-sexed' by having their breasts removed (p. 173). However phallocentric the image of disembowellment or decapitation may seem to modern critics, medieval audiences would not necessarily have read the torture of male saints as sexualized in any way, except in the rare cases of castration; and female genital mutilation was equally rare, the sexualization of torture for female saints is generally enacted in the mastectomies. But in either case, the saints' transcendence of physical abuse elevates them from the corporeal world and lowers their persecutors.

83 Mills, *Suspended Animation*, p. 117.

84 Sarah Salih, *Versions of Virginity in Late Medieval England* (Cambridge: D. S. Brewer, 2001), pp. 73, 89.

85 *Saint Margaret*, in *The South English Legendary Corpus Christi College Cambridge MS 145 and British Museum MS Harley 2277*, ed. Charlotte d'Evelyn and Anna J.Mill, vol. 1, EETS, os 235 (Oxford: Oxford University Press, 1956, rpt. 1967), p. 126.

86 Salih, *Versions of Virginity*, p. 93.

87 Tracy, *Torture and Brutality*, p. 55.

88 Easton, 'Pain, Torture and Death', p. 57.

89 Mills, '"Whatever You Do Is a Delight to Me"', p. 7. Acts of castration evoke fears of homosexuality in the heterosexual paradigm, which is why Abelard takes such pains to inscribe his heterosexual relationship with Heloise, even though he has forsaken it.

ripping it to shreds.[90] To some extent the physical violation of the saint is a necessary component of his or her sacrifice. Without the apparent objectification of the victim of torture, there can be no response to the brutality of the torture; torture objectifies both the saints and the tormentor.[91] The saint is sanctified, the tormentor is demonized and the use of torture resonates with the audience as a tool of the barbarian Other.[92] For audiences of the *SEL* who could comfortably situate judicial torture outside the practice of their realm, relocating acts of castration would be more difficult. In England, where castration remained on the law books as a punishment for treason until the fourteenth century,[93] it was not the tool of foreigners or distant barbarians, but of English jurisprudence that should have been more equitable and less brutal. More importantly, in both the punishment of treason and rape, castration was designed to remove the propagating ability of the offender; emasculation was not about limiting the ability to have sex (necessarily) but about removing the capacity for siring children – the defining feature of medieval masculinity.

Male saints who were constructed as chaste and virginal (even if they were not *actually* virgins) retain that masculine capability as part of their defiance against foreign tyranny. Salih argues that male virginity potentially involves 'regendering' because clerics are forbidden both marriage and fighting, 'the marks of secular masculinity', but for male saints, sexual status is rarely the 'locus of their sanctity'.[94] For female saints, defiance rests in their vocal resistance to authority – which generally begins when an authority covets the body of the female saint and attempts to woo or force her into marriage. For many of the female saints, their religion is secondary to their desire to retain their virginity; Christianity is their primary defense for not wanting to submit to the cruel and wanton desires of a pagan judge or prince. Their beliefs protect

90 Tracy, *Torture and Brutality*, p. 55. There have been several valuable studies on female saints and the male gaze, as well as the construction of female saints by male authors. See Anne Clark Bartlett, *Male Authors, Female Readers: Representations and Subjectivity in Middle English Devotional Literature* (Ithaca, NY: Cornell University Press, 1995); Catherine M. Mooney, ed., *Gendered Voices: Medieval Saints and Their Interpreters* (Philadelphia: University of Pennsylvania Press, 1999); Salih, *Versions of Virginity*; Winstead, *Virgin Martyrs*; and Jocelyn Wogan-Browne, *Saints' Lives and Women's Literary Culture c. 1150–1300: Virginity and Its Authorisations* (Oxford: Oxford University Press, 2001).

91 Tracy, *Torture and Brutality*, p. 56.

92 Ibid.

93 Castration remained the punishment of record in England for rape until 1275. In 1234, 'orders were given for the proclamation of regulations regarding the supervision of hundred courts (in line with the revisions of Magna Carta that year) and in 1248, it was decreed that the right to castrate another man as a punishment for fornication was to be restricted to a husband in the case of his wife's adulterer': Anthony Musson, *Medieval Law in Context: The Growth of Legal Consciousness from Magna Carta to the Peasants' Revolt* (Manchester: Manchester University Press, 2001), p. 225.

94 Salih, *Versions of Virginity*, p. 17.

them from illicit pursuit and, through martyrdom, women could 'leave behind their culturally constructed gender roles'.[95] Karen Winstead writes that virgin martyr legends did not 'simply embody tensions about changing gender roles and relation' but often show the disintegration of other traditional power relations, such as lordship and the patriarchal structure of authority.[96] As such, their bodies become the parchment upon which the discourse of female virginity is written – the more they endure in defense of their bodies, the more their bodies are torn, healed, and torn again, the more successful they are in defying that authority.

The sexual difference of both male and female saints resides in the social construction of their gender based, in part, on the preservation of their genitalia. Crachiolo asserts that the gendered difference of the violence in the *SEL* depends on the degree to which the narratives focus on the body itself.[97] In the narratives of female virgin martyrs, rape is the area of unease because the texts are not 'prepared to contemplate the hymen regenerating itself as the other wounds do, however theoretically possible this might be'.[98] Salih writes that however much the martyr legends 'proclaim virginity's imperviousness, they are unwilling to put it to the test, or to challenge the fantasy of the intact hymen'.[99] With male saints, the penis and the testicles become the comparable area of unease. Even though there are castration miracles in which a pious male saint heals (although often without restoring the offending member) the self-mutilated or wrongly castrated man, the body of the male saint itself must remain genitally intact. Salih understands the torture scenes as a 'virginity test' that simultaneously produces and displays the virgin body; they are enacted before an audience 'because gender is a cultural construction which must be read'.[100] Male holiness 'can be a kind of default position, due to male dominance of the Church, but it may also demand a radical break from the secular norms of masculinity'.[101] In the cultural construction of masculinity, the holy male body must retain that which the society signifies as male.

So much of the construction of male saints in the *SEL* rests in their specifically masculine identity. They are less ambiguous or androgynous than saints in the *Legenda aurea* or the Middle English *Gilte Legende*; they are marked out as male in the display of their masculine bodies and in the construction of their chivalric identity. Riches suggests that when George is divested of his armor (as depicted in various visual and written accounts of his torture) 'he has relin-

95 Easton, 'Pain, Torture and Death', p. 51.
96 Winstead, *Virgin Martyrs*, p. 109.
97 Crachiolo, 'Female and Male Martyrs', p. 151.
98 Salih, *Versions of Virginity*, p. 90.
99 Ibid.
100 Ibid., p. 96.
101 Riches and Salih, *Gender and Holiness*, p. 5.

quished his masculine, heroic role and adopted the demasculinised status of the tortured martyr'.[102] But in the *SEL*, regardless of being stripped and beaten, he is still St George, patron saint of England, who was most often depicted as a splendid vision of 'nobility, chivalry and masculinity'.[103] His masculine courage is equivalent to that ascribed to female saints who are rendered 'masculine' in their defiance of tyranny because women were believed to be frailer, their weakness as women something to overcome. This is the dilemma in hagiography – if female saints are 'masculine' in their resistance to torture, and male saints are 'feminized' by being tortured, then social gender constructions are subverted in either case, regardless of gender. The idea of the instability of the body 'meshes nicely with the theory of social construction, even as it troubles those with faith-based concerns about the complex relationship between embodiment, morality and holiness'.[104] Riches clarifies that George is not feminized, but demasculinized, removed out of the masculine gender and into a third, 'indeterminate, perhaps virginal, gender' and not made a pseudo-female.[105] But the 'third gender' also applied to eunuchs as well as male virgins, as Jed Chandler points out in reference to the potentially neutered Grail knights.[106] And eunuchs were regarded with suspicion, even rejected by society, hence Abelard's fears post-castration.

The gender ambiguity of eunuchs (since early Christian centuries) sparked an animosity toward them and the unmanliness that they represented.[107] That categorization would be troublesome for many medieval audiences who valued valorized masculinity (in men or women) in hagiographic accounts of torture and brutality. While male chastity was certainly a concern of medieval audiences (as the debate over Origen's autocastration, the ruling of the First Council of Nicaea, and Abelard's wounding reveal) it had to be constructed without voluntary harm to the male body. Jerome voiced his concern about the integrity of the human body, and argued that the genitals must be present in heaven so that the victory over sexual desire inspired by them can continue for all eternity; in attacking the Origenist Rufinus (AD 401) he explicitly states that 'amputation of members in the resurrection would mean we would all come to equality of condition; the virgin would then be equal to the prostitute'.[108] Thus, male saints must achieve their martyrdom with their genitalia intact or be incomplete at the Last Judgment. The emphasis on masculine chastity in those committed to

[102] Riches, 'St George as a Male Virgin Martyr', p. 75.
[103] Ibid., p. 68.
[104] Murray, '"The law of sin that is in my members"', p. 9.
[105] Riches, 'St George as a Male Virgin Martyr', p. 75.
[106] Jed Chandler, 'Eunuchs of the Grail', in this volume, pp. 231, 253.
[107] Kuefler, *The Manly Eunuch*, p. 257.
[108] Caroline Walker Bynum, *The Resurrection of the Body in Western Christianity, 200–1336* (New York: Columbia University Press, 1995), p. 91.

a holy (if violent) cause was solidified by the crusades which produced a new brand of knight, the *miles Christi* (like the Templars) who embodied the masculine traits of chivalry while remaining chaste. Bernard of Clairvaux praised them as a 'manly brotherhood, spurning the effeminate trappings of wordly knights' that included silks, curls, and rich clothing.[109] This is the image of George and Hippolytus offered in the *SEL* in conjunction with an English rejection of torture and brutality as foreign practices. In order to maintain the demeanor of masculine triumph, in order for the stripping and torture of these male saints to avoid the categorization of the tortured body as 'female', they cannot be castrated. As Katherine J. Lewis explains, these saints, and the men and women who read and wrote about them, 'lived within settings which did assign specific meanings (social, cultural, ideological and other) to male and female and to being man or woman'.[110] While sexual activity and everything tied to it (from sexual prowess to fathering children) are an important part of manliness in medieval culture, the struggle against the enemy inherent in one's own sexual desire (for men or women) was manly too.[111] The gendered aspects of hagiography, while often fluid for women, do not extend to the male members.[112] Because the 'possession of a gendering attribute mediates the gender of the holder, the loss of such an attribute can also signify gender'.[113] The emasculation of male saints would render them 'female' and would denigrate the sacrifice of the male saint – they would become the weakened, feminized eunuchs that the Church (and much of male Christendom) reviled: an identity against which Abelard struggled. And for male saints like George (an emblem of national English identity), castration – like that perpetuated by the ruling Normans of the thirteenth century – was unacceptable.

[109] Jo Ann McNamara, 'The *Herrenfrage*: The Restructuring of the Gender System, 1050–1150', in *Medieval Masculinities: Regarding Men in the Middle Ages*, ed. Clare A. Lees (Minneapolis: University of Minnesota Press, 1994), pp. 3–29 at p. 17.

[110] Katherine J. Lewis, 'Gender and Sanctity in the Middle Ages', in *Gendering the Middle Ages*, ed. Pauline Stafford and Anneke B. Mulder-Bakker (Oxford: Blackwell, 2001), pp. 205–14 at p. 209.

[111] Ruth Mazo Karras, *Sexuality in Medieval Europe: Doing unto Others* (New York and London: Routledge, 2005), p. 42.

[112] However, in the fifteenth-century Stamford cycle of stained glass (*c.* 1450) in the chancel of St George's Church, Stamford, Lincolnshire, recorded in the seventeenth-century *Book of Monuments*, George is tortured by being sawn in half with millstones around each ankle. As Riches points out, he is wearing a loincloth out of modesty, but 'the fact that he is being sawn in half from the bottom up strongly implies injury to the genitalia' ('St George as a Male Virgin Martyr', pp. 72–3). This potentially sexualized scene seems to be unique to the Stamford cycle.

[113] Ibid., p. 73.

CHAPTER 5

The Children He Never Had; The Husband She Never Served: Castration and Genital Mutilation in Medieval Frisian Law

Rolf H. Bremmer Jr

For most of the Middle Ages, the Frisians were a people who saw their lives dominated by violence.[1] At least, this is the impression gained by studying their laws. Stretched out along the North Sea coast of present-day Netherlands and Germany, their homeland was threatened by land-hungry powers from without and by feuding from within. The first detailed view of the Frisians' legal traditions is the result of foreign occupation. In the second half of the eighth century, the Franks had gradually managed to expand their territory to the north at the expense of the Frisians, culminating in their complete subjection by Charlemagne, around AD 785. As he had done for other conquered peoples in his empire, Charlemagne required the Frisians to record their laws in writing. The result of this policy is the *Lex Frisionum*, which, in all likelihood, was presented at the Diet of Aachen in 802 where the laws of the recently subdued Saxons and Thuringians were also formulated and imposed.[2] The *Lex Frisionum* is counted among the *Leges barbarorum*, the early medieval laws drafted in Latin by or for the various Germanic peoples.[3] Yet, the name of this Frisian legal record

1 I would like to thank my brother Jan for his helpful suggestions, Anne Popkema and Mike Ruijsenaars for casting their expert eyes over a draft version of this paper, and Dirk Jan Henstra for sharing with me his expertise in monetary matters.

2 Heiner Lück, 'Der wilde Osten: Fränkische Herrschaftsstrukturen im Geltungsbereich der *Lex Saxonum* und *Lex Turingorum* um 800', in *Von den* leges barbarorum *bis zum* ius barbarum *des Nationalsozialismus: Festschrift für Hermann Nehlsen zum 70. Geburtstag*, ed. Thomas Gutmann, Hans-Georg Hermann, Joachim Rückert, Mathias Schmoeckel, and Harald Siems (Cologne: Böhlau, 2007), pp. 118–31 at p. 118. On monetary grounds, the origin of the text of the *Lex Frisionum* has been dated to the period 785–793/794; see Dirk Jan Henstra, 'Het probleem van de geldbedragen in de *Lex Frisionum*', in *'Fon jelde': Opstellen van D. J. Henstra over middeleeuws Frisia*, ed. Anne T. Popkema (Groningen: Barkhuis, 2010), pp. 47–70 at p. 69.

3 Lisi Oliver, *The Body Legal in Barbarian Law* (Toronto: University of Toronto Press, 2011), pp. 8–10, and the literature quoted there, esp. Patrick Wormald, 'The *Leges Barbarorum*: Law and Ethnicity in the Medieval West', in Regna *and* Gentes: *The*

is somewhat of a misnomer, coined as it was by the first editor of the text, the Basel scholar-printer Joannes Herold in 1557. Unfortunately, the manuscript on which he based his edition has since disappeared, so that we cannot confirm the correctness of Herold's title. As it is, the *Lex Frisionum* was never given the status of a law; rather, the text presents a survey of disparate rules and regulations, including quite a few duplications and contradictions, from which a more or less coherent law had to be made up. This final editorial phase did not materialize, however, and the code as it now exists would have hardly been suitable for use in court. The major part of it consists of a long list of compensations to be paid for injuries, both physical and social (including castration), inflicted on others, similar to such enumerations found in, for example, Anglo-Saxon legal sources.[4] In addition, the *Lex* also contains rules for regulating the new social life of the recently converted Frisians, such as curbing Sunday labor and restricting the degrees within which marriage was permissible. Following the main text is a considerable list of *Additiones*, compiled by the wise men (*sapientes*) Saxmund and Wlemar. In view of its provisional nature, then, it is unlikely that the *Lex Frisionum* was ever put into effect.[5]

In the later Middle Ages (*c.* 1250–1500), when it had *de facto* slipped away from imperial power, Frisia consisted of a loose confederacy of autonomous lands that were ruled not by a feudal nobility as elsewhere in Europe (with the exception of Switzerland), but by free allodial landowners. For this period, there is a considerable corpus of extant legal texts, by far the majority of which have survived in the vernacular.[6] Again, as in the *Lex Frisionum*, long lists of wounds and injuries with their compensations – called 'registers' or 'tariff lists' – make up a conspicuous part of the vernacular legal tradition. Because of the absence of feudal officials (dukes, counts) who had elsewhere appropriated the monopoly on violence, feuding was often resorted to in Frisia when the balance of justice had been disturbed.[7] These registers, therefore, were used as an aid

Relationship between Late Antique and Early Medieval Peoples and Kingdoms in the Transformation of the Roman World, ed. Hans-Werner Goetz, Jörg Jarnut, and Walter Pohl (Leiden and Boston: Brill, 2003), pp. 21–53.

4 Jay Paul Gates examines Old English injury tariffs in his article in this volume, 'The *Fulmannod* Society: Social Valuing of the (Male) Legal Subject', pp. 131–48.

5 An exhaustive and exemplary introduction is given by Harald Siems, *Studien zur* Lex Frisionum (Ebelsbach: Rolf Gremer, 1980); also see Ruth Schmidt-Wiegand, '*Lex Frisionum*', in *Reallexikon der germanischen Altertumskunde*, 2nd edn, ed. Heinrich Beck *et al.*, vol. 18 (Berlin: Walter De Gruyter, 2001), pp. 318–20; Nikolaas E. Algra, 'The *Lex Frisionum*: The Beginnings of a Legalized Life', in *The Law's Beginnings*, ed. Ferdinand J. M. Feldbrugge (Leiden: Brill, 2003), pp. 77–92.

6 Cf. my *Introduction to Old Frisian. History, Grammar, Reader, Glossary* (Amsterdam and Philadelphia: John Benjamins, 2009; corrected repr. 2011), ch. 1.

7 Paul N. Noomen, 'De Friese vetemaatschappij: sociale structuur en machtsbases', in *Fryslân, staat en macht 1450–1650*, ed. Johan Frieswijk, Arend H. Huussen Jr, and Y. B. Kuiper (Hilversum: Verloren, 1999), pp. 43–64.

in establishing what damage had been done to life and limb, often elaborated in minute detail, and what compensations had to be paid by the offender to the aggrieved party in order to become reconciled, to restore the injured honor, and to re-establish social harmony.[8] The Frisian genre of injury lists has for a long time been neglected by scholars, even though they figure (sometimes prominently) in every legal miscellany. This disregard can be accounted for, perhaps, by the terse style in which these tariff lists are composed, the sometimes rather boring enumerations of body parts, the possible wounds that could have been inflicted, and the complexity of monetary systems – often a mixture of amounts from different periods and in different values, as a result of continuous copying – in which the amounts due are calculated. However, a recent study by Han Nijdam has demonstrated how the Frisian compensation registers can be turned into a welcome source of historical, cultural, and anthropological information.[9]

When it comes to castration in the laws, distinction should be made between castration as a form of punishment and emasculation as the result of injury.[10] The two forms of mutilation are indeed included in the Frisian laws, both in the *Lex Frisionum* and in the vernacular laws. Castration as a punishment is rare, essentially because corporal punishments were on the whole alien to the Frisian legal system in which practically all offenses could either be compensated by money or denied by oath. Understandably, therefore, much more attention is given in the laws to genital injuries and their compensations than to castration as a punishment. In what comes next, castration as a punishment will be discussed first, to be followed by an analysis of the genital injuries as they are recorded in the tariff lists.

In the *Leges barbarorum*, castration is not uncommonly mentioned as a punishment, usually in connection with sexual misdemeanors, especially rape. For example, in the Frankish *Lex Salica* castration is mandated for the man who rapes a virgin in such a violent way that she dies; the *Lex Ribuaria*, the code for the Ripuarian Franks who lived around Cologne, prescribes castration for violating a slave girl.[11] In both cases, however, the rapist is a slave – an unfree man. Still, in both cases he can save his testicles by paying compensation if he has the money or if his owner is willing to pay for him. On the other hand, in

8 Cf. Oliver, *The Body Legal*, p. 10.

9 Han Nijdam, *Lichaam, eer en recht in middeleeuws Friesland. Een studie naar de Oudfriese boeteregisters* (Hilversum: Verloren, 2008); cf. Ernst Schubert, 'Vom Wergeld zur Strafe: die übersehene Bedeutung der friesischen Rechtsquellen zur Interpretation eines epochalen mittelalterlichen Wandels', in *Tota Frisia in Teilansichten: Hajo van Lengen zum 65. Geburtstag*, ed. Heinrich Schmidt, Wolfgang Schwarz, and Martin Tielke (Aurich: Ostfriesische Landschaft, 2005), pp. 97–120.

10 Annette Niederhellmann, *Arzt und Heilkunde in den frühmittelalterlichen Leges* (Berlin and New York: Walter De Gruyter, 1983), ch. 4 'Kastration', esp. pp. 142–3.

11 Susan Tuchel, *Kastration im Mittelalter* (Düsseldorf: Droste, 1998), pp. 77–8.

Gothic Spain, the *Lex Visigothorum* also demanded castration for 'those who lie with males, or consent to participate passively in such act'; Jews and Christians who had newly been circumcised or had circumcised somebody else were threatened with the same punishment.[12] All such cases are examples of a mirror punishment, by which the part of the criminal's body with which the crime was committed is punished, a principle that is related to the familiar concept of Mosaic law 'an eye for an eye, a tooth for a tooth', the so-called *lex talionis*. However, castration is also sometimes demanded for criminals who have committed a crime that did not involve the usage of their 'tools'. For instance, according to the *Lex Salica*, a slave who has stolen something worth 40 *denarii* can be punished with either castration or with a fine of 6 *solidi*. In such a case, there is question neither of a mirror punishment nor of retaliation.[13]

There is only one instance of a regulation in the *Lex Frisionum* that stipulates castration, but its special character has attracted considerable scholarly attention because it concerns the execution of someone who has robbed a pagan shrine:[14]

> Hoc trans Laubachum. De honore templorum. Qui fanum effregerit, et ibi aliquid de sacris tulerit, ducitur ad mare, et in sabulo, quod accessus maris operire solet, finduntur aures eius, et castratur, et immolatur diis quorum templa violavit.
>
> This [applies to the region] across the River Lauwers. Concerning the honor of temples. Whoever has broken into a pagan shrine and has carried away from there any of the sacred objects, he shall be taken to the sea, and on the sand that will be covered by the tide, his ears will be cut off, and he will be castrated and sacrificed to the gods whose temples he has dishonored.

This narrative ordinance, the very last of the wise man Wlemar's additions to the *Lex*, invites further analysis. First of all, the region for which this rule is in force is recorded as being east of the Lauwers, the river that later marked the border between West and East Frisia. The latter region had only recently been introduced to Christianity through evangelizing efforts, especially those of the York-trained Frisian Liudger (742–804; first bishop of Münster) and the Northumbrian missionary Willehad (*c.* 740–89; first bishop of Bremen). Certainly, at the time when the *Lex* was drafted, there would have been plenty

12 Niederhellmann, *Arzt und Heilkunde*, pp. 143–5; Louis Crompton, *Homosexuality and Civilization* (Cambridge, MA: Harvard University Press, 2003), p. 152.

13 Tuchel, *Kastration im Mittelalter*, pp. 77–8; cf. K. Berdolt, 'Kastration', in *Reallexikon des germanischen Altertums*, vol. 16 (2000), pp. 326–7.

14 *Lex Frisionum*, ed. Karl August Eckhardt and Albrecht Eckhardt (Hanover: Hahn, 1982), p. 102: Tit. XI §1 (Latin text with German translation).

of first-hand knowledge about all kinds of aspects of the pagan life in Frisia beyond the Lauwers. It is therefore very probable that before their conversion the Frisians would have dealt with temple robbers in the way described in the *Lex*: after the robber had been caught and sentenced (stages in the procedure which are silently passed over), he was led, in all likelihood in a procession, to the sea. The place of execution is clearly located outside the community, a common place for such activities. The Israelites, for example, executed their criminals 'outside the camp'; accordingly, Jesus was crucified 'outside the gates'.[15] In Frisia, quite understandably in view of its maritime location, the execution is staged on the shore, notably on the part that is washed by the tide – now dry, now flooded – thus marking the unstable boundary in the dichotomy of land and sea: neither here nor there.[16] Once this ambivalent space had been entered, there was no way back for the victim. On this stretch of no-man's land, he was deprived of his extremities, ears first.

Cutting off ears is not otherwise recorded as a punishment in Frisian laws. In classical times, however, this act of bodily mutilation was much practiced in the Near East and from there it gradually spread to the west, usually together with the disfigurement of the nose, in order to make the victims so hideous to look at that they could no longer function normally in society: losing their ears and noses this way implied losing their honor.[17] In this special

15 Richard W. Johnson, *Going Outside the Camp: The Sociological Function of the Levitical Critique in the Epistle to the Hebrews* (Sheffield: Sheffield Academic Press, 2001), pp. 74–5. For Ancient Greece, e.g., see Jan N. Bremmer, 'Myth and Ritual in Greek Human Sacrifice: Lykaon, Polyxena and the Case of the Rhodian Criminal', in *The Strange World of Human Sacrifice*, ed. J. N. Bremmer (Leuven: Peeters, 2007), pp. 55–80 at p. 57.

16 In later Frisian law, certain criminals (thieves) are sometimes to be executed *wtor dike* 'outside the dike'. See Wybren Jan Buma and Wilhelm Ebel, *Westerlauwerssches Recht I. Jus municipale Frisonum*, 2 vols (Göttingen: Vandenhoeck & Ruprecht, 1977), XVI.8 ('Von Königssatzung'). At least six instances are known of gallows erected on the seaward side of the dike. See Johannes A. Mol, 'Gallows in Late Medieval Frisia', in *Advances in Old Frisian Philology*, ed. Rolf H. Bremmer Jr, Stephen Laker, and Oebele Vries (Amsterdam and New York: Rodopi, 2007), pp. 263–99 at p. 281.

17 Robert Rollinger, 'Extreme Gewalt und Strafgericht. Ktesias und Herodot als Zeugnisse für den Achaimenidenhof', in *Der Achämenidenhof*, ed. Bruno Jacobs and Robert Rollinger (Wiesbaden: Harrassowitz, 2010), pp. 559–666. For Rome: Amy Richlin, 'Invective against Women in Roman Satire', in *Latin Verse Satire: An Anthology and Critical Reader*, ed. Paul Allen Miller (New York and London: Routledge, 2005), pp. 377–89 at p. 382 and n. 19; *Handwörterbuch zur deutschen Rechtsgeschichte*, ed. Adalbert Erler and Eckehard Kaufmann, 5 vols (Berlin: Schmidt, 1971–98), I, *s.v.* Ehrenstrafe (W. Brückner). Late medieval Europe: Valentin Groebner, 'Das Gesicht wahren: Abgeschnittene Nasen, abgeschnittene Ehre in der spätmittelalterlichen Stadt', in *Verletzte Ehre: Ehrkonflikte in Gesellschaften des Mittelalters und der frühen Neuzeit*, ed. Klaus Schreiner and Gerd Schwerhoff (Cologne: Böhlau, 1995), pp. 361–80. For the motivations underlying punitive mutilation see Wolfgang Schild, 'Der gequählte und entehrte Körper. Spekulative Vorbemerkungen zu einer noch zu schreibenden Geschichte des Strafrechts', in *Gepeinigt, begehrt, vergessen. Symbolik und Sozialbezug des Körpers im späteren Mittelalter und in der frühen Neuzeit*, ed. Klaus Schreiner and Norbert Schnitzler (Munich: Wilhelm Fink, 1992), pp. 147–68.

case, though, there was no question of a possible return to society; the forceful removal of his ears rather marked a first step in the physical demolition of the robber's body. After his ears had been cut off, the next step was the removal of his genitals, not as a punishment for offensively using them but as a dehumanizing act, turning him into a person of undeterminable sex – neither man nor woman – reflecting the undeterminable spot he was standing on: neither land nor sea. Finally, having thus been taken to pieces, he was 'sacrificed to the gods whose temples he had violated'. No further details are given of the sacrifice, but we may assume, in view of the location, that he was drowned.[18] To which gods the sacrifice was intended remains a mystery. Of course, speculations abound and one of these gods might have been Fosite, an otherwise unknown Germanic god whose name and maritime sanctuary are mentioned in Alcuin's *Life of St Willibrord*.[19]

The greatest problem scholars have had with this rule in the *Lex Frisionum* is how to interpret an obvious remnant of a pagan practice in which a criminal is sacrificed to the gods (plural!) within the context of a set of law codes that clearly bears a monotheistic Christian stamp. However, the robbing of pagan temples in a time of religious transition can perhaps be accounted for: confiscating pagan sanctuaries, especially their valuables, seems to have been profitable and the spoils were divided between the king and the missionary according to an allocation formula.[20] Robbery of pagan sanctuaries thus implied a defiance of the highest authorities. But it is difficult to explain the sacrifice to the (pagan) gods as a tolerable reality. Perhaps, the measure presents an example of how pagans dealt with violators of sanctuaries, thus silently urging Christians likewise to show no mercy on thieves who rob churches; curiously, the *Lex Frisionum* contains no measures for church robbery. All in all, however, a satisfactory solution to this problem has not yet been found.[21]

The other instance in which castration plays a part is found in the Old West Frisian *Sendriocht*, a collection of instructions for ecclesiastical jurisdiction (*send* = 'synod'), the surviving version of which seems to have received its definitive form in the thirteenth century. However, in view of the unlimited application of ordeals and duels, judicial instruments that were banned from

18 In later medieval Frisian law, drowning in the North Sea is recorded as a punishment for traitors; see Wybren Jan Buma and Wilhelm Ebel, *Das Emsiger Recht* (Göttingen: Vandenhoeck & Ruprecht, 1967), A VIII.26 ('Vermischtes').

19 As suggested, e.g., by Ruth Schmidt-Wiegand, 'Spuren paganer Religiosität in den frühmittelalterlichen Leges', in *Iconologia Sacra: Mythos, Bildkunst und Dichtung in der Religions- und Sozialgeschichte Alteuropas*, ed. Hagen Keller and Nikolaus Staubach (Berlin and New York: Walter De Gruyter, 1994), pp. 249–62 at pp. 255–56.

20 Siems, *Lex Frisionum*, p. 343.

21 Ibid. 350; B. Maier, 'Gotteslästerung', in *Reallexikon des germanischen Altertums*, vol. 12 (2001), pp. 483–85 at p. 484.

ecclesiastical lawcourt procedures by the Fourth Lateran Council of 1215,[22] parts of this code must be older. The reference to baptizing pagans also points to a date before the thirteenth century. In other words, the *Sendriocht* is a collection of stipulations that was regularly updated and added to. Among its ordinances is the following:[23]

> *Fan wildinghum dera schettena.* Hweer soe en man Godes ewa ende Godes riocht ende Octauianus riocht ende Moyses ewa britzen haet ende al der wralde, dat hi scetten wildath haet, soe aegh him di riochter tre kerren ti delane, als hi en eetmel alomme liuwet haet mey twam heldem spanned ende hi dis alles biechte wert, dat hi dyn kerre habbe, her hi zijn machta weer zijn lyf ofsnide ende sine sonda bettrie, soe dat ma anne kulc dele, deer alle dat quick jn moege ende dat ma him al benida brenge, iefta dyn tredda kerre, dat ma alle dat heer gaedrie of dera schettena sterten ende meckie deerof en beynd ende byndene deermey ende bernene.

> *About sexual abuse of cattle.* Whenever a man has broken God's law and God's rules and Octavian's rules and Moses's law and [the law] of all the world, [namely] that he has abused cattle,[24] then the judge must sentence him to choosing between three options, after he has remained tied with two fetters for a full twenty-four hours and has been convicted of all this, so that he has the choice either to cut off his genitals from his body and amend his sins, or that a pit is dug big enough to put all the cattle in and that he is put bottommost, or the third choice, that all the hair of the cows' tails is gathered and a fetter is made of it and he is bound with it and burnt.

No decree in the corpus of Frisian laws formulates a breach of law so forcefully and indignantly. No fewer than five authorities are adduced here to express how utterly abject the author considered the act of sexual intercourse with animals. *Godes ewa* is natural law, which, since Gratian compiled his *Decretals* in the twelfth century, was commonly equated with divine law;[25] *Godes riucht* refers to canon law;[26] the 'right' of Octavian (i.e. Emperor Augustus) means the *Lex Julia* (i.e. Roman Law),[27] while Moses' law, of course, comprises the laws

[22] In the eighteenth canon, known as the 'Judgements of Blood', see James Q. Whitman, *The Origins of Reasonable Doubt: Theological Roots of the Criminal Trial* (New Haven, CT: Yale University Press, 2008), pp. 48 and 126.

[23] Buma *et al.*, *Westerlauwersches Recht I*, IX.46 ('Das Sendrecht').

[24] The stem of the noun *weldighum* and the verb *wildath* is the same as in German *vergewaltigen* 'to rape'.

[25] Gratian, *The Treatise on Laws: (Decretum DD. 1–20)*, trans. Augustine Thompson, with *The Ordinary Gloss*, trans. James Gordley, and an introduction by Katherine Christensen (Washington, DC: The Catholic University of America Press, 1993), pp. xxi–xxvii.

[26] *Deutsches Rechtswörterbuch*, s.v. Gottesrecht II; online at http://drw-www.adw.uni-heidelberg.de/drw/, accessed October 20, 2011.

[27] Crompton, *Homosexuality and Civilization*, p. 197.

of the Old Dispensation. To ensure that no legislative authority was possibly omitted, the author clinches the matter with an appeal to everybody's sense of justice wherever in the world they are.

The vehemence with which the author formulates his indignation is an indication of the time when it was codified, viz. the thirteenth century. Bestiality was not considered to be a crime by the ancient Romans nor is it listed as such in the *Leges barbarorum*. In the early medieval Irish *Cummean Penitential*,[28] having sex with animals was treated rather mildly, on the same level as masturbation, as if the act of bestiality were a form of solosex:[29] the perpetrator had to do penance for a year. But there were also mitigating circumstances: If a man living on his own had had sex with an animal, the penance was downsized to three times forty days. No word is said about the animal.[30] The penitentials suggest that the act was approached with increasingly more severity in ecclesiastical circles from the seventh century onwards,[31] partly inspired by Mosaic Law which forcibly condemned sex with animals, for men and women alike, because it was a 'confusion' (AV, Leviticus 18:23), i.e. sex with animals transgressed the boundary between human and non-human[32] (Exodus 22:19; Leviticus 18:23; 20:15–6; Deuteronomy 27:21; the perpetrator was either cursed or sentenced to death, the animal killed).

Gradually, as in Mosaic Law, the animal involved was no longer seen as irrelevant in the deed, but was considered to be a participant that needed to be killed and destroyed to prevent it from reminding people afterwards of the horrible sin in which it had been involved.[33] Twelfth- and thirteenth-century schoolmen dealt extensively with the sin of bestiality in their *summae*. The Franciscan Alexander of Hales (*c.* 1185–1245) called it 'the most grievous kind of unnatural sex crime',[34] while his fellow-countryman Thomas of Chobham (*c.* 1160–1233/6) in his *Summa confessorum* categorized bestiality as the most heinous of all sins against nature.[35] Of the four kinds of unnatural vice (those

28 Charlene M. Eska gives a full account of Irish and Welsh laws regarding castration and genital injury in her essay in this volume, '"Imbrued in their owne bloud": Castration in Early Welsh and Irish Sources', pp. 149–73.

29 Joyce E. Salisbury, *The Beast Within: Animals in the Middle Ages*, 2nd edn (Abingdon: Routledge, 2011), p. 72.

30 Joyce E. Salisbury, 'Bestiality in the Middle Ages', in *Sex in the Middle Ages. A Book of Essays*, ed. J. E. Salisbury (New York: Garland, 1991), pp. 173–86 at pp. 177–8.

31 Rob Meens, *Het tripartite boeteboek: overlevering en betekenis van vroegmiddeleeuwse biechtvoorschriften* (Hilversum: Verloren, 1994), p. 561.

32 The Council of Ancyra in 314 marked the boundary as one between rational and irrational, cf. Salisbury, *The Beast Within*, p. 70.

33 Ibid. pp. 73–4.

34 James A. Brundage, *Law, Sex, and Christian Society in Medieval Europe* (Chicago: University of Chicago Press, 1987), p. 473.

35 Piers Beirne, *Confronting Animal Abuse: Law, Criminology, and Human–Animal Relationships* (Lanham, MD: Rowman & Littlefield, 2009), p. 105.

not aimed at procreation), Thomas Aquinas (1225–75) ranked bestiality first in his *Summa theologica*, before homosexuality, intercourse in any other than the proper way (i.e. the 'missionary position'), and masturbation. Thomas's censure, more than that of Alexander of Hales and Thomas of Chobham, highly influenced subsequent legislators,[36] and it is against this background that the ecclesiastical jurist who drafted this Frisian regulation, most likely no earlier than the middle of the thirteenth century, must be viewed.[37] Finally, it should be noted that, unlike in the proscription of animal sex in Leviticus 18 and 20, the deed is here imagined to be a male affair only.

Next, the *Sendriocht* regulation introduces the judge, without any further indication of who he is and how the court session has to proceed.[38] On the other hand, two detailed conditions are given to insure that the procedure cannot be frustrated by a capricious accusation. The suspect has to remain in custody for the full cycle of a day and a night, apparently in order to prevent any over-hasty actions. Moreover, the detailed stipulation of tying him with precisely two – not one or three – fetters is probably intended to express the care with which his custody is to be executed.[39] In other words, there is to be no abuse or torture before his execution. Finally, full evidence must have been put forward to make certain that the suspect has not been falsely accused. Once it is clear that the authorities in charge have complied with these prescriptions and the suspect has admitted his guilt, the judge comes to a verdict that leaves the choice of punishment to the perpetrator.

Presenting the convict with alternative measures is not uncommon in Frisian law, the simplest choice being that between paying the compensation and swearing innocence, or, alternatively, between paying and, if the defendant

36 Anthony Musson, *Boundaries of the Law: Geography, Gender and Jurisdiction in Medieval and Early Modern Europe* (Aldershot: Ashgate, 2005), pp. 106–7; Etienne Gilson, *The Christian Philosophy of St Thomas Aquinas*, trans. Edward Bullough (Salem, NH: Ayer, 1983), p. 298.

37 In Sweden and Norway, bestiality also became an ecclesiastical and legal concern from the late twelfth century onwards. At best, the Scandinavian perpetrator of the 'sin against nature' was sent on a pilgrimage to Jerusalem, at worst he was castrated and outlawed; the animal was driven out to sea and drowned. See Anne Irene Riisøy, *Sexuality, Law and Legal Practice and the Reformation in Norway* (Leiden: Brill, 2009), pp. 47–8; Kari Ellen Gade, 'Homosexuality and Rape of Males in Old Norse Law and Literature', *Scandinavian Studies* 58 (1986): 124–41 at pp. 127–9.

38 The text uses *riochtere*, the generic word for 'judge', whereas elsewhere in the *Sendriocht* it is usually the bishop or dean who functions as judge in the ecclesiastical court. On the whole, clerics could not be involved in the spilling of blood, including branding, mutilation, or execution; see note 22 above and James A. Brundage, *Medieval Canon Law* (London: Longman, 1994), p. 92.

39 On the proclivity of Frisian legal discourse for concrete details, see Daniel P. O'Donnell, 'The Spirit and the Letter: Literary Embellishment in Old Frisian Legal Texts', in *Approaches to Old Frisian Philology*, ed. Rolf H. Bremmer Jr, Thomas S. B. Johnston, and Oebele Vries (Amsterdam and Atlanta, GA: Rodopi, 1998), pp. 245–56.

refused to swear an oath of innocence, being subjected to an ordeal. But not infrequently, the choice is between three punishments. Perhaps the best-known example is provided by the legend of Charlemagne and the Twelve *Asegas*. After he had occupied Frisia, so the narrative tells, Charlemagne ordered the *asegas* (highest legal experts) to choose new laws for the Frisians. When they prove to be unable and reluctant to do this, Charlemagne offers them the choice between decapitation, serfdom, or being cast adrift at sea in a rudderless boat, without rope and rigging.[40] Another example: When a woman has been accused of adultery and her husband does not exonerate her by oath, he may choose between having her scourged or decapitated by the sword under which she passed when she got married,[41] or he can take her back (but then he runs the risk of being the subject of neighborhood gossip). A last example: If one of two spouses, who have no children, happens to kill the other with a stick or a pole or a sharp weapon and is convicted of murder, the guilty one is offered the choice between being burnt, having a stick driven through their heart from the front so that it comes out at the back, or being blinded followed by exile and doing penance for their sins. Usually, therefore, when a choice is given in such cases, there is at least one with a touch of mercy that gives the convict a possibility to emerge from the process with their life intact, if not their body and their honor.[42] In the present case, too, the convict is presented with an opportunity to escape alive, for the choice is one between castration, interment, or burning. As for the last two options, the choice seems to be that between the devil and the deep blue sea.

Being buried alive as a punishment for bestiality is also found in the thirteenth-century English legal treatise *Fleta*, 'provided that they [*sc.* homosexuals and those that commit bestiality] be taken in the act and convicted by law and open testimony', but it does not include the burial of the animal(s), as in the Frisian case.[43] However, burying the animal involved in the sex act is in line with Mosaic Law which stipulates that it be killed (Leviticus 20:15). The case in the *Sendriocht* prescribes the perpetrator to be buried *al benida* 'completely beneath', as far away removed from the face of the earth as is possible and, with the cows on top of him, visually carrying the heavy burden of his lust objects on his shoulders. Burning, too, implies destruction and erasure of the criminal's

40 The last punishment being a case of exposure (German 'Aussetzung'), see Karl von Amira, *Die germanischen Todesstrafen. Untersuchungen zur Rechts- und Religionsgeschichte*, (Munich: Bayerische Akademie der Wissenschaften, 1922), pp. 144–7.

41 Cf. H. R. Ellis Davidson, 'The Sword at the Wedding', *Folkore* 71 (1960): 1–18 at pp. 2–3.

42 The three examples can be found in Buma *et al.*, *Westerlauwerssches Recht I*, IV.3 ('Die Sage von König Karl und Redbad'), IX.50 ('Das Sendrecht'), and XVIII.9 ('Das Rudolfsbuch'), respectively. See also Rudolf His, *Das Strafrecht der Friesen* (Leipzig: Dieters'che Verlagbuchhandlung, 1901), pp. 169–70.

43 Allen J. Frantzen, *Before the Closet: Same-sex from* Beowulf *to* Angels in America (Chicago: University of Chicago Press, 2000), p. 255.

body. Burning as a punitive measure for unnatural sex (as it was defined then) is found elsewhere in the Frisian laws, in an enumeration without context of the various crimes that merit capital punishment: 'Thene kattere barnma jefta siuth ma, jd est eum qui peccat contra naturam' [The homosexual, that is he who sins against nature, should be burnt or boiled].[44] Burning a man convicted of unnatural sex is also encountered elsewhere in northwestern Europe,[45] but remarkable to the Frisian case is that before ascending the stake, the culprit must be bound with a fetter made of all the hair collected from the tails of the cows involved.[46] In agricultural societies like that of medieval Frisia, no part of a butchered animal was considered useless; indeed, cow hair was not uncommonly used in the medieval period for making threads and cords, but cow-hair ropes are rarely, if ever, recorded.[47] Its application here is therefore not an instance of how cow hair was employed, but rather a visual and symbolic expression of how the convict was sinfully tied to the cow: if he behaved like a beast, the rope was made to fit the crime. Whether the cows were burnt along with their abuser is not mentioned, but they would certainly have been killed. Perhaps, as an alternative to incineration, their meat was thrown to the dogs, as was stipulated for such cases, for example, by the *Poenitentiale Parisiense compositum*, a late eleventh-century penitential composed in northern France.[48]

Only the first of the three options given by the judge shows some degree of mercy to the convict, to the extent that he is allowed to live on albeit with the loss of his manhood. If castration as a punishment in later medieval Frisian law is unique, what makes this case even more special is that the act of severing the genitals from his body is left to the convict himself. Autocastration as such was not unknown, and was practiced in antiquity in the pagan Syrian cult of the goddess Atargatis, as well as in certain ascetic circles in the early Christian

[44] Wybren Jan Buma and Wilhelm Ebel, *Das Fivelgoer Recht* (Göttingen: Vandenhoeck & Ruprecht, 1972), XVI.24. The word *kattere* derives from 'Cathar', a religious group that flourished in the twelfth and thirteenth centuries, whose members were often accused of homosexual activities; hence, the verb *ketzern* 'to have anal intercourse' was coined in Middle High German. See Birgitte Spreitzer, *Die stumme Sünde: Homosexualität im Mittelalter* (Göppingen: Kümmerle, 1988), pp. 57–8.

[45] Rudolf His, *Das Strafrecht des deutschen Mittelalters.* II: *Die einzelnen Verbrechen* (Weimar: Hermann Böhlaus, 1935), pp. 166–8; for burning the animal lover; von Amira, *Die germanischen Todesstrafen*, p. 197, conjectures Roman influence by way of Frankish legal practice.

[46] The phrases 'all dat quick' [all the cattle] and 'alle dat heer … dera schettena sterten' [all the hair … of the cows' tails] suggest that the culprit had subjected more than one cow to his lusts; alternatively, the man's entire stable was executed to make sure that no cow stayed alive that might possibly have been abused; cf. note 33 above.

[47] I thank Professor Gale Owen-Crocker for this information; see also Elizabeth Coatsworth and Gale R. Owen-Crocker, *Medieval Textiles of the British Isles 450–1100* (Oxford: Archaeopress, 2007).

[48] Meens, *Het tripartite boeteboek*, p. 499, no. 88.

church.[49] The church father Origen is the famous example, reputedly castrating himself in answer to Christ's words that 'there are eunuchs who have made themselves eunuchs for the kingdom of heaven' (Matthew 19:12, Douay-Rheims).[50] From the early fourth century onwards, however, successive councils condemned this voluntary, drastic practice as counter to God's purpose for the body and successfully eradicated it.[51] Forcing the perpetrator of the unnatural sex act to perform the equally unnatural act of castration upon himself brings out the disgust which the Frisian ecclesiastical authorities must have felt. What is left for the man afterwards, if he chooses this option (Figure 5.1), is to do penance for the terrible sin that he will be vividly reminded of every time he urinates, and in all likelihood more often than that.

Having discussed castration as a punitive measure, attention will now be directed to cases of genital mutilation in the Frisian registers of compensation, beginning with the man. It is fair to assume that the male members of society would have more often been involved in and exposed to violent encounters than the females, so it comes as no surprise that the registers indeed pay attention to injuries inflicted upon the genitals as early as the *Lex Frisionum*. 'Si veretrum quis alium absciderit, weregildum suum componat' [If anyone should have cut off somebody else's penis, he must compensate with the man's *wergild*.] The implication of this rule is that the full *wergild* had to be paid, because the man could no longer be considered a man. Cutting off one testicle was rated at half a *wergild*, for two testicles the full *wergild* had to be paid. However, if a testicle was hanging out of the scrotum and could be successfully restored to its original position, the compensation amounted to that of a particular wound, in addition to 6 *solidi* (= 72 pennies) to be paid (presumably) to the doctor.[52] These provisions are as far as the *Lex Frisionum* goes concerning male genital injuries.

The later, vernacular Frisian laws, especially the registers of compensations, are richer and more detailed on this matter. For these tariff lists, a distinction should be made between the supra-regional *General Register of Compensations*,

49 Atargatis: Jan N. Bremmer, *Greek Religion and Culture, the Bible and the Ancient Near East* (Leiden and Boston: Brill, 2008), pp. 288–9. Early Christianity: Robert Muth, 'Kastration', in *Reallexikon für Antike und Christentum. Sachwörterbuch zur Auseinandersetzung des Christentums mit der antiken Welt*, ed. Georg Schöllgen *et al.*, vol. 20 (Stuttgart: Anton Hierschemann, 2004), cols. 285–342.

50 For a critical analysis of Origen's case, see Christoph Markschies, *Origenes und sein Erbe: Gesammelte Studien* (Berlin: Walter De Gruyter, 2007), ch. 2 'Kastration und Magenprobleme? Eine neue Blicke auf das asketischen Leben des Origenes'.

51 Tuchel, *Kastration im Mittelalter*, ch. IV: 'Kastration in Kirchenrecht und Kirchengeschichte'. In this volume, Jack Collins compares early Christian condemnations of autocastration with prohibitions of Jewish law in his article 'Appropriation and Development of Castration as Symbol and Practice in Early Christianity', pp. 73–86.

52 Eckhardt and Eckhardt, *Lex Frisionum*, Tit. XXII.57–9 ('De dolg'); cf. Niederhellmann, *Arzt und Heilkunde*, p. 148.

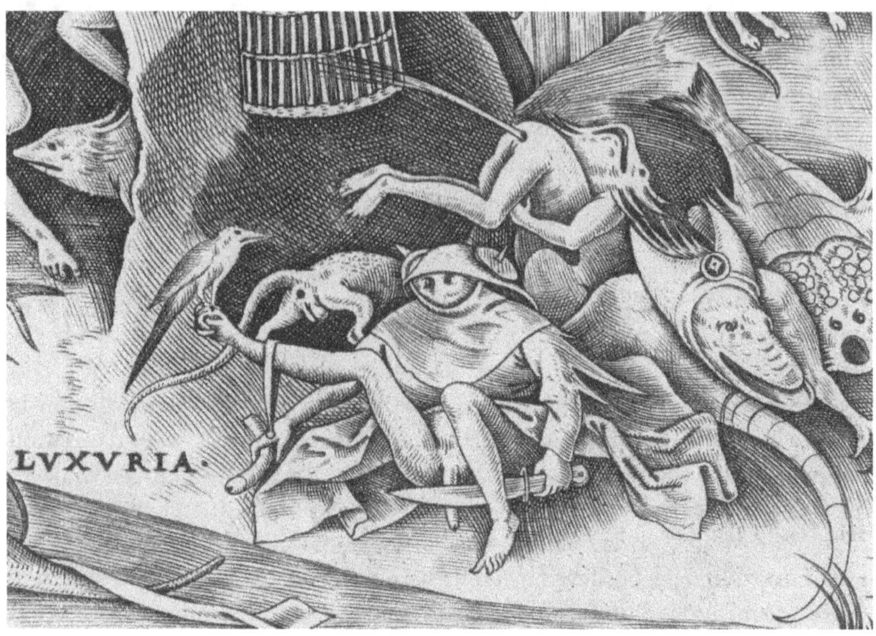

FIGURE 5.1 Pieter Breugel the Elder (c.1520/25–9 September 1569), published by Hieronymus Cock (c. 1510–3 October 1570). Copper engraving by Pieter van der Heyden (c.1530–after March 1572): 'The Seven Deadly Sins: Luxuria [Lust]' (1558, detail): monstrous man cutting off his own penis. Museum Boijmans Van Beuningen, Rotterdam. Photo provided by Studio Buitenhof, The Hague.

redactions of which are found in all the major Frisian legal miscellanies from east of the river Lauwers, and the regional registers, which are usually considered to be somewhat later than the *General Register*, partly because they borrow from it.[53] Remarkably, no attention is paid to male genital injuries in the *General Register*, but this absence of attention is amply compensated for by the concern that appears in regional lists, especially in those that circulated west of the Lauwers. Trouble may start when a man is grabbed by his genitals and is treated 'dishonorably' (*quadelicke*). In this case, he must be compensated for this misdeed with 20 pennies, whereas when the same is done 'in anger' (*bi ira mode*) the payment is 28 pennies; it is even worse if he is dealt a blow on his testicles (*scalsleeck*), for then the bill is 4 shillings (= 48 pennies). The summit seems to be when a man raises a complaint of having been grabbed by his genitals so violently that he pisses blood afterwards; in such a case the compensation rockets to 26 shillings (= 312 pennies) or, alternatively, the

53 Nijdam, *Lichaam, eer en recht*, pp. 85–8, 94–5.

defendant is allowed to swear six oaths of innocence.[54] All of these injuries seem to have been inflicted by bare hands. But what if knives are pulled?

If someone's testicles are cut off, the law says that the loss is to be compensated with 6 pounds for the right one and 5½ for the left.[55] Elsewhere, removing somebody's testicles completely – technically, in such a way that they have become *gersfallich* 'having fallen on the grass' – is rated at 11 pounds. However, if it appears afterwards that the disabled man has begotten children nonetheless, he must return the money and do penance for the oath that he wrongfully swore when he claimed to have lost his fertility.[56] A penis cut off, quite understandably, requires a higher recompense than does each of the testicles: 8 pounds.[57] In the latter case, there is a similar restriction concerning the payment of the money as for the testicles. If a man has been compensated for the loss of his penis, but is afterwards caught *eth wiuem* 'with a woman',[58] in the act presumably, 'so ne ach hi nene bote vmbe thet [vn]manslike, vmbe thene pinth offesney*n*' [he has no right to the compensation for the inhuman deed, (viz.) for the penis (that is) cut off].[59] Fraud in these serious matters does not pay.

Occasionally, the registers expand on an injury and provide further information on why a simple compensation might not be the last step in the process of reconciliation. This is the case, for example, when an arrow has wrought havoc in a man's crotch:[60]

> Hweer so en man wr sine machte scetten werth, truch sine machte, truch thet fel, thio bote is ij ensa, hit en sie thet hi ferra spreka vvolla; so mei hi habbe thre sinekerff. Thio aersta hath thio stiapsine. Thio ander hath thio wieldsine. Thio thredda thio fruchtsine. Ther moth hi fan bitigia thria vnnameda morth, tha ach ma allerlick to betane also dyore soe en manslachta iefta xij-sum to onswerne.

> Whenever a man is shot on his genitals, [or] through his genitals, through the skin, the compensation is two ounces, unless he wants to pursue a further complaint; then he can claim [compensation for] three 'sinew cuts'.

54 Buma *et al.*, *Westerlauwerssches Recht*, respectively, XXI.92–93 ('Die Busstaxen von Wymbritseradeel') and XXVIII.243–44 ('Busstaxen von Wonseradeel und die Fünf Diele').

55 E.g., Buma *et al.*, *Westerlauwerssches Recht*, XXIII.118 ('Busstaxen von Ferweradeel and Dongeradeel'). On the distinction between left and right, see below.

56 Ibid. XXI.88 ('Busstaxen von Wymbritseradeel').

57 Ibid. XXIII.119.

58 Actually, *eth wiuem* is plural, 'with women', suggesting that the formerly injured man was involved in a sex act with more than one woman. More likely, though, we are dealing here with a type of the 'generalizing' or 'generic' plural, cf. Bruce Mitchell, *Old English Syntax*, 2 vols (Oxford: Clarendon Press, 1985), I.§75.

59 Buma *et al.*, *Westerlauwerssches Recht*, XXIX.123 ('Busstaxen von Leeuwarderadeel'); MS manslicke; offesneyth; cf. the redaction of this regulation in XXIII.119 ('Busstaxen von Ferweradeel und Dongeradeel').

60 Buma *et al.*, *Westerlauwerssches Recht*, XXVIII. 239 ('Interregionale Busstaxen').

> The first is called the 'steep sinew', the second is called the 'wield sinew', the third the 'fruit sinew'. On account of this [i.e. these three injuries], he is allowed to claim three unborn children; these must each be compensated as high as [in the case of] manslaughter, or [the defendant] must swear to innocence with eleven oath helpers.

The – imagined – situation is as follows: a man is shot through his genitals, but no circumstances are given to explain how, when, or where this occurred. Apparently, such information is irrelevant; what matters is the compensation for the injury, which is set at one pound. However, if the victim suspects that the injury has impaired the proper workings of his genitals, he has the right to appeal and demand a more specified retribution, because the finer fabrics of his reproductive organs have been damaged, notably three 'sinews'. The interpretation of the *stiapsine*, the *wieldsine*, and the *fruchtsine* has proven difficult. The first elements of these three compounds, it is true, are quite lucid: *stiap* is cognate with English 'steep', *wield* (also found as *wald*) is related to English 'to wield' ('control') and *frucht* (from Latin *fructus*) means 'fruit'. The second element, *sine* is cognate with English 'sinew', but covers a wider range of meanings than just that; it also includes 'nerve, tendon, muscle', that is any cordlike body part that is not a vein, artery, or gut. So much for the linguistic side of these words.

A greater interpretative difficulty lies in the anatomical parts to which the 'sinews' refer. Willem van Helten, a giant in Old Frisian lexicology, confessed more than a century ago: 'Was mit diesen drei sehnen gemeint ist, habe ich bis jetzt nicht ermitteln können' [I have until now been unable to find out what is meant with these three sinews].[61] Wybren Jan Buma and Wilhem Ebel in their dual-language edition translated these three terms into German as *Hochsehne* 'high sinew', *Rückennerv* 'dorsal nerve', and *Zeugungsnerv* 'generative nerve', respectively, translations that do not really bring us much further.[62] Elsewhere, Buma glossed the same words with *Schwellkörper* 'corpus cavernosum', *Rückennerv* 'dorsal nerve',[63] and *Fortpflanzungssehne*, *Samenleiter* 'generative sinew, vas deferens', thus forcing modern anatomical concepts onto the medieval Frisian text.[64] Hofmann and Popkema, in their recent dictionary of

[61] Willem L. van Helten, 'Zur Lexicologie und Grammatik des Altwestfriesischen', *Beiträge zur Geschichte der deutschen Sprache und Literatur* 19 (1894): 345–440 at p. 365, n. 1.

[62] Buma *et al.*, *Westerlauwerssches Recht*, XXVIII.239 ('Interregionale Busstaxen'). The translation 'Zeugungsnerv' was coined by Karl von Richthofen, *Altfriesisches Wörterbuch* (Berlin: Dieter'sche Buchhandlung, 1840), s.v. *fruchtsine*; it is a nonce-word not included in any of the major German dictionaries that I consulted.

[63] Buma arrives at the translation of 'dorsal nerve', in all likelihood by equating it with Old Frisian *wald(e)waxe* and *waldandsine* 'spinal nerve, *spina dorsi*'.

[64] Wybren Jan Buma, *Vollständiges Wörterbuch zum westerlauwerschen Jus Municipale Frisonum* (Leeuwarden: Fryske Akademy, 1996), s.vv.; cf. Nijdam, *Lichaam, eer en recht*, p. 276, who follows, and expands on, Buma.

Old Frisian, have steered away from precision and give *eine Sehne am Penis* 'a sinew on the penis' and *Sehne am Zeugungsglied* 'sinew on the generative member' for *stiapsine* and *fruchtsine*, respectively, while, like Buma, they take *wieldsine* to be a variant of *waldandsine* 'Rückennerv, Rückenmuskulatur' [dorsal nerve, dorsal musculature].[65] However, it takes quite some imagination to envisage an arrow or some other missile that comes down from above cut not only through specific parts of the penis but also through the dorsal nerve. Therefore it is preferable to interpret *wieldsine* as a part of the penis and not of the spine. Clearly, scholars of Old Frisian have struggled with the interpretation of these three 'sinews', most probably because they did not realize that medieval ideas of the anatomy of the male genitals differ considerably from modern ones, based as the latter are on experimental dissection. For a proper understanding, therefore, the opinions of contemporary authorities on the anatomy of the penis are important to consider.

On the whole, the penis was afforded little attention in the classical anatomical treatises, nor was it, for that matter, discussed in any great detail in the Arab-influenced works that were produced in the medical school of Salerno. According to Constantinus the African (1017–87), author of the *Pantegni* – the first comprehensive medieval anatomical treatise that brought fame to the Salernitan school – the penis is a *cauda nervorum* (tail of nerves), which is 'concave so that with the arrival of appetite it is filled with air and becomes erect. Lateral muscles on both sides prevent it from bending, so that the sperm is ejaculated directly into the vulva.'[66] According to this description, the penis is hollow and consists of a duct through which the sperm flows and two muscles, one on either side of the penis. The *Anatomia vivorum* (Anatomy of the Living), written in Paris in the first half of the thirteenth century,[67] expands on Constantinus' description and explains that the penis 'has two ducts, one for the sperm from the testicles and the other for the urine from the bladder which join at the neck of the penis. It also has two pairs of muscles [*lacerti*], one which governs the length and extension of the erection and the other which keeps it straight.'[68] The Frisian classification of the three 'sinews' must have been inspired by knowledge derived from such medical treatises, the *stiapsine* referring to the muscle that

[65] Dietrich Hofmann and Anne T. Popkema, *Altfriesisches Handwörterbuch* (Heidelberg: Universitätsverlag Winter, 2008), s.vv.

[66] Constantinus, *De genecia* (On genecology), p. 323. For the Latin text, see Monica H. Green, 'The *De genecia* Attributed to Constantinus the African', *Speculum* 62 (1987): 299–323 at p. 323 'De uirga' (On the penis).

[67] George W. Corner, *Anatomical Texts of the Earlier Middle Ages. A Study in the Transmission of Culture, with a Revised Latin Text of* Anatomia Cophonis *and Translations of Four Texts* (Washington, DC: Carnegie Institution, 1927), p. 36; cf. Plinio Prioreschi, *A History of Medicine*, vol. 5: *Medieval Medicine* (Omaha, NE: Horatius Press, 2003), p. 343.

[68] Corner, *Anatomical Texts*, p. 24. Cf. John W. Baldwin, *The Language of Sex: Five Voices from Northern France around 1200* (Chicago: University of Chicago Press, 1994), p. 91.

takes care of the erection, while the *wieldsine* reflects the one that keeps the penis straight. The *fruchtsine*, then, must be identified with the duct that guides the sperm from the testicles to the neck of the penis. If this interpretation is right, the absence of the urine duct from the Frisian regulation needs to be accounted for. There are two possible explanations for this. First of all, a tripartite division tallies with the three children the injured man will never have; secondly, the inability to create offspring is a much more serious handicap than having difficulty discharging urine and therefore the focus of this particular regulation is directed here on a man's fertility.[69]

Finally, the injured man can claim a compensation for each of the three children that he has not been able to generate. The regulation refers to the children as 'unnamed murders', a term that is occasionally used in Frisian laws to refer to children who die an unnatural death (usually through abortion) before they have even been given a name and, with it, an identity.[70] The amount of the compensation required in this law text for each of the three children that were never born equals that to be paid for manslaughter – a full *wergild*. *Wergild* has to be paid, because the victim's masculine capacity to generate life has been lost.

As mentioned above, cutting off the right testicle was more expensive in terms of compensation than doing the same to the left one. In general, such a valuation concurs with places in the tariff lists where other symmetrical body parts are involved, such as eyes and hands.[71] Because the majority of mankind is right-handed, the use of the right hand and the right eye was more important than that of their left counterparts. Where no such functional difference seems relevant, for example, with respect to a woman's breasts, no difference is made in the amount to be compensated for their violent loss.[72] Nevertheless, there may be an additional reason for this difference in valuation: the opinion expressed both in classical and contemporary medical treatises was that the right testicle, sometimes in combination with the right side of the uterus, was responsible for the birth of a boy, while girls were associated with the left.[73] In

[69] Elsewhere, injury leading to a man's incontinence is set at a compensation of a third wergild, see Buma and Ebel, *Das Emsiger Recht*, A VI.2 ('Allgemeine Busstaxen'). The stipulation is the second entry in the Emsigo redaction of the *General Register of Compensations*, which would seem to contradict my remark on p. 120 that this register does not pay attention to injuries in the male genitals. However, the stipulation was inserted (by scribal error?) from the Emsigo regional register, see Nijdam, *Lichaam, eer en recht*, p. 420.

[70] Cf. Marianne Elsakkers, '*Her anda neylar*: An Intriguing Criterion for Abortion in Old Frisian Law', *Scientiarum Historia* 30 (2004): 107–54 at pp. 113–14.

[71] As pointed out by Nijdam, *Lichaam, eer en recht*, pp. 276–77.

[72] See p. 128 below.

[73] See, e.g., Joan Cadden, *Meanings of Sex Difference in the Middle Ages: Medicine, Science, and Culture* (Cambridge: Cambridge University Press, 1993), pp. 35, 62–3, 93.

the archaic, male-oriented society of medieval Frisia, sons would generally have been preferred over daughters. It is the more remarkable, in the light not only of the prevailing importance of right as opposed to left in the valuation of body parts, but also of medical knowledge as it was current then, to read the following passage from the Emsigo tariffs:[74]

> Huersa hir en mon thruch sine mechte vndad werth, thet hi nauuet tia ni mughe: nioghen merck to bote fora tha nioghen bern ther hi tia machte. Het hi ac bern etein, sa nime ma hit ofta berena and retze hit tha vneberena. Het hi thene winstera prelleng bihalden and thene farra urleren, thach mey hi bern tia. Neth hi thene winstera nauuet, thach hi thene ferra hebbe, sa is hi thes thochtalas.
>
> Whenever a man is wounded here [in Emsigo] through his genitals, so that he can no longer create offspring: nine marks as a compensation for the nine children that he might have begotten. However, if he has [already] begotten children, then it [i.e. part of the compensation] must be taken from the born [children] and be given to the unborn [children]. If he has retained the left testicle and lost the right one, yet he can beget children. Does he not have the left one [any longer], though he [still] has the right one, then he is unable to beget because of that.

Again, paramount in a man's life is his offspring who are to continue his bloodline and eventually to inherit and defend the ancestral manor. In this specific case, a man is imagined to bring forth a maximum number of nine children and this number determines the compensation for the wound that has disabled his generative faculties: 9 marks for the man who has not yet become a father.[75] On the other hand, the compensation is to be decreased by 1 mark for each child born to him before he became sexually impaired. Presumably, up to here the regulation deals with the loss of the penis. But what if the penis is still there and he has lost one of his testicles? The text continues to communicate emphatically, first by phrasing this positively and then negatively, how a man's fertility is lodged in his left testicle and not in his right one. Such a claim is not in line with what we have seen earlier, namely that the right testicle was valued more highly than the left one, even though the difference was relatively small (6 pounds against 5½). Apparently, both testicles were commonly assumed to play an active part in the procreative process. Nijdam has observed in connection with this passage that the authors of the registers

[74] Buma and Ebel, *Das Emsiger Recht*, A VII.91–94 ('Emsiger Busstaxen').

[75] One mark is equal to 12 shillings, so 9 marks is 5 pounds and 8 shillings. The *Hunsigo Register of Compensations* likewise stipulates 9 *wergilds* for a man who has become infertile as a result of genital mutilation. See Wybren Jan Buma and Wilhelm Ebel, *Das Hunsigoer Recht* (Göttingen: Vandenhoeck & Ruprecht, 1967), VII.29 ('Hunsigoer Busstaxen I').

were rather ignorant of the more detailed aspects of the male reproductive organs,[76] and from a modern point of view this is true, of course. Rather than judging from modern superior medical knowledge, however, there is contemporary evidence to show that the author of the *Emsigo Register* was not alone in his opinion.

In medieval Ireland, too, a curious preference is attested for the left testicle over the right one, according to the tract *Bretha Éitgid* (Judgements of Inadvertance). In this legal text, violent removal of the penis must be compensated not only with a full body-price (the counterpart of the Frisian *wergild*), but also a full honor-price and restitution. The height of the compensation is indicative of the importance of the loss of the male member. Following upon the penis, the text deals with the testicles – *na hairne toile* (glands of desire), as they are quite charmingly called – and declares that loss of the left testicle requires a full injury payment, *is uaithi ata in geinemain* 'because the progeny is from it'. As in the Frisian text, the reason for the full amount being due is emphatically explained. Compensation for loss of the right testicle, on the other hand, was set at the value of the injury and did not require a full body-price.[77] So how must we explain this Hiberno-Frisian parallel of attributing the power of generation to the left testicle rather than to the right one, a notion that runs counter to all the major medical treatises from antiquity to the close of the Middle Ages? After all, it was established medical knowledge that the right testicle produces boys and the left one girls. Familiarity in Frisia with vernacular Irish texts need not be assumed, nor is it likely that Irish legal experts consulted Frisian registers of compensation. In both countries, knowledge of the mainstream medical literature is apparent,[78] but evidently, when it comes to the testicles, preference is sometimes given to other, perhaps older, traditions. In view of the prevailing positive connotations with right (*dexter*) and negative associations with left (*sinister*), autogenesis of the notion of the superiority of the left testicle seems unlikely. Until new evidence turns up that points in another direction, it seems, therefore, that the notion of the exclusive procreative function for the left testicle only stems from a tradition that is very ancient and not yet influenced by Mediterranean medical knowledge.

Men were more likely to contract injuries than women, if only because feuding expeditions were staged by men. This generalization does not imply

76 Nijdam, *Lichaam, eer en recht*, p. 276.

77 See Brónagh Ní Chonaill, 'Impotence, Disclosure and Outcome: Some Medieval Irish Legal Comment', 17–18, online at http://www.arts.gla.ac.uk/scottishstudies/earticles/LegalConcern.pdf (accessed September 2011). Eska also discusses this passage in her article in this volume, '"Imbrued in their owne bloud"', pp. 167–8.

78 For Frisia, Galen and Hippocrates are referred to several times in the thirteenth-century chronicle of Bloemhof Abbey, while Vindicianus's treatise on gynecology, or a derivative thereof, must also have been around; see Nijdam, *Lichaam, eer en recht*, p. 216, n. 164, and Elsakkers, '*Her anda neylar*', p. 124, respectively.

that women never resorted to violence, only that they were not expected to do so and if they did, the stakes were high: 'Hversar en wiff annen mon onfiucht anda hine sla blaw iefta blodich, and hi hine bewerth and hir deth dath ieftha dolg, sa heth hiu hire froulika bota wrlern anda is thiu bota lic aien like dethem' [If a woman attacks a man and beats him black or bloody, and he defends himself and kills her or inflicts her a wound, then she has lost her woman's compensation and the compensation [for both] is equally high for equal injuries].[79] In other words, women who started a fight ran the risk of losing the additional half of a compensation that was assigned to women compared to the compensation for a similar wound inflicted on a man.[80] On the whole, women led a far less public life than men and their daily activities were basically confined to the manor, and are therefore far less frequently represented in the compensation tariffs. Rather than the consequence of fighting, female genital injuries and mutilations appear to be the result mainly of sexual assaults that may begin with inappropriate touching and end with outright rape.[81] The early medieval *Lex Frisionum* only provides for lasciviously touching either a free-woman's breasts or her genitals, the latter requiring a compensation that was twice as high as fondling her bosom.[82]

As with punishments doled out to men, the later, vernacular laws likewise show more variety than the *Lex Frisionum* in the judicial directions concerning women. Infringing upon a woman's physical integrity, and at the same time her honor and that of the men with whom she was immediately associated, most often started with indecent touching. For this misdeed the Frisians had coined the term *bas(e)feng*, (evil-minded grabbing) (cf. German *böse* 'malicious, wicked'); it referred to acts against women only. *Basefeng*, according to the Emsigo tariffs, was envisaged to begin by groping her outside her clothes (compensation: 3 shillings) and next, by putting a hand inside (9 shillings). The offense was taxed even higher (1 mark = 12 shillings) if the woman was pregnant or having her monthly period ('hire stilnesse').[83] Perhaps to facilitate grabbing, a man might cut a woman's clothes, so that her nakedness was exposed: 21 pennies for cutting her upper dress, 4 pennies for her inner dress and 7 pennies for her chemise.[84] Denuding is never mentioned in the Frisian legal sources as an offense against men, but for women the act was seen as

79 Buma and Ebel, *Das Emsiger Recht*, C II.7 ('Ergänzungen'). On the usage of alliterative pairs ('blaw ieftha blodich', 'dath ieftha doch'), so typical for Frisian legal discourse, see most recently Rolf H. Bremmer Jr, 'Dealing Dooms: Alliteration in the Old Frisian Laws', in *Alliteration in Culture*, ed. Jonathan Roper (Basingstoke: Palgrave Macmillan, 2011), pp. 74–92.

80 See, e.g., Buma and Ebel, *Das Emsiger Recht*, C I.189 ('Emsiger Busstaxen').

81 Rape itself will not be discussed here, as it falls outside the scope of this contribution.

82 Eckhardt and Eckhardt, *Lex Frisionum*, Tit. XXII.89–90 ('De dolg').

83 Buma and Ebel, *Das Emsiger Recht*, A VII.99–100 ('Emsiger Busstaxen').

84 Ibid. A VII.103.

inflicting shame. According to the Hunsigo tariffs, the least form of denudation was when 'hire clathar uperauad send and hire skeme blicht' [when her clothes have been pulled up and her shame becomes visible].[85] It should be noted that such terms as *skeme* and *skonde*, 'shame', to denote the genitals, like *basefeng*, are used in the laws only with reference to women. Denuding and grabbing may be shameful for the woman who has to undergo these expressions of lasciviousness, at the same time these deeds affect her father or husband under whose tutelage she was customarily placed. Physical harm followed denudation when a nipple was cut off (11 shillings = 132 pennies) or worse still, one of her breasts (a third of her *wergild*, regardless of whether it was the left or the right breast; two-thirds of her *wergild* for both breasts off). These compensations had to make up not only for her bodily disfigurement but also for losing the life-sustaining function of nursing a child.[86] The registers do not leave it at that, for they also provide for sexual mutilation: rending a woman's genitals ('Enre frowa hire macht torent'), required 15 shillings (= 180 pennies) for recompense, which is nothing compared to a third *wergild*, the compensation paid to a woman who, as a result of this mutilation, was unable to keep in her urine any longer ('hire mese nawit behalda ne muge').[87] This amount implies that genital mutilation leading to a woman's incontinence was rated just as highly as violently depriving her of a breast. Maltreating her genitals in such a way that they are bleeding made the perpetrator liable to pay a compensation of 3 pounds and 3 shillings.[88]

A stock ingredient of the registers in use west of the Lauwers is the following:[89]

> Fan der cuntta bote: thria ensa and vj pund, thet is sex sneza grata and fyf grate. Jef hio also dulghet werth, thet hio tha herum nath tho tancke thyania ne mey, thet wite hio selua mith here selua onbringhe.
>
> About the compensation for [mutilation of] the cunt: three ounces and six pounds, that is six score stoters and five stoters. If she gets so wounded that she cannot serve the lords [i.e. her husband] satisfactorily, she may herself swear to this.

At first sight, this regulation would seem to suggest that establishing the right amount of money for an injured vulva is more important than the injury itself or indeed the victimized woman, for an older currency is recalculated, because

85 Buma and Ebel, *Das Hunsigoer Recht*, VII.88 ('Hunsigoer Busstaxen I).
86 Buma and Ebel, *Das Emsiger Recht*, A VII.106 ('Emsiger Busstaxen').
87 Ibid. VII.96–7.
88 Buma and Ebel, *Das Hunsigoer Recht*, VII.30 ('Hunsigoer Busstaxen I').
89 Buma *et al.*, *Westerlauwerssches Recht*, XXIV.64 ('Busstaxen des südwestfriesischen Küstengebietes').

of continuous inflation in the later Middle Ages, into a more modern one: 3 ounces (= 60 pennies) plus 6 pounds (= 1,440 pennies) is said to be (more or less) equal to 125 stoters (= 1,500 pennies). The size of the amount of compensation and the care with which it is calculated, however, demonstrate the seriousness of the deed. Once the pecuniary arithmetic has been settled, the focus is directed to the woman who (not entirely surprisingly) fears that because of the gravity of her injury she will from now on be unfit for sexual intercourse – almost as if she had been castrated – and hence runs the danger of being excluded from a normal future as wife. The social perspective is completely male-oriented, for the sexual act is seen as one in which a woman performs a service for *tha heran*, literally 'the lords'. The plural is idiomatic here,[90] but the use of the word 'lord' is not otherwise found in the context of compensation tariffs and underscores a woman's inferior position with respect to her future husband.

Ultimately, then, castration in the medieval Frisian laws is a punitive measure that was rarely exercised. The cases in which emasculation was stipulated apparently called for drastic action: Robbing of a pagan sanctuary in the Carolingian *Lex Frisionum* (*c.* 800) and committing an act of bestiality in the thirteenth-century vernacular *Sendriocht*. Both stipulations are carefully couched in narrative scripts that outline the ritual procedures accompanying the execution. Furthermore, the extensive corpus of compensation tariffs allows us to catch glimpses of how Frisian law imagined all kinds of injuries that could be inflicted to the genitals, ranging from those that would heal in time to serious ones that led to permanent incapacity or infertility. Noteworthy are the differences in the way mutilations are positioned for men and women. For men, injuries are envisaged that on the whole result from fighting, whether with bare hands or armed. Judging by the height of the compensations, a man's greatest concern appears to lie in the loss of penis and/or testicles.[91] For women, genital mutilation is rarely conceived of as the result of fighting, and if this is the case, the woman is to blame and loses her right to an increased compensation. Overall, her genital injuries are envisaged to originate in situations where she is the object of male sexual harassment, expressed by the specialized term *basefeng* 'evil-minded grabbing a woman'. Attempts at denudation are mentioned only with respect to women and, significantly, only the female

[90] See note 58, above.

[91] Perhaps, this concern explains the greater variety of Old Frisian words for the male genitals in comparison to those for the female ones. The generic term for the genitals of both males and females is *macht/mecht*, also plural *machte/mechte* (cognate with MoE 'might'). The penis is called either *pint* (cf. MoE *pintle*) or *tilinge* (derived from *tilia* 'to obtain, cultivate', cf. MoE *to till*), while a testicle is designated by *pralling/prelling* (obscure etymology, confined to Frisian), *hotha* (cf. MoG *Hoden*), or *skal* (cf. MoE *shell*). The vulva is called *cunta* (cf. MoE *cunt*); no further details of the female genitals are mentioned by name.

sexual organs are euphemistically, albeit with a value-loaded twist, referred to as 'shame' (*skeme, skonde*). Moreover, whereas the law enumerates the children a genitally mutilated man might have fathered, no such concern is expressed with respect to women who had befallen the same fate. Finally, the possibility that genitally mutilated women might not be able to 'serve the lords satisfactorily' finds no counterpart in mutilated men being worried about their inability to have sex to the gratification of their wives. Clearly, the anonymous laws, rooted in a centuries-long tradition, were composed by males (first orally and later in writing), applied by males, and, on the whole, addressed to males. Whatever genital wounds were inflicted on women were rephrased in terms and conditions that were basically subservient to the most important male interests in medieval Frisia: offspring and honor.

CHAPTER 6

The Fulmannod *Society: Social Valuing of the (Male) Legal Subject*

Jay Paul Gates

A volume of essays taking up the theme of castration invites an exploration of the relationship between the biological and the social, the private and the public. Indeed, the 'private parts', those which are kept hidden, are by their very nature not private but social: they can only perform their biological, generative function with another person. A focus not just on the body, but on the male generative organ, raises a number of questions about the human, sexed body and the interpretation of the social role of the biological body: what is its value, how should it be used, who may act on it, what does its presence or absence signify, and what does it indicate about an individual's social function? Taking the male member by itself provides an opportunity for a *pars pro toto* response to a long-standing conundrum in social theory: 'Is the person merely a collection of roles or is the person the organizing principle which integrates and orchestrates given social roles?'[1] Evidence from the Anglo-Saxon period indicates that the body was valued for the functions it could perform. The individual gave a means for recognizing a collection of functions; but the evidence depicts the individual primarily in terms of how a larger social matrix incorporated, and therefore valued, him rather than the individual holding inherent value. However, there is no single social matrix for the Anglo-Saxon period, but a changing vision of social order, how the individual fit into it, and the part the individual played in maintaining it.

Miri Rubin has suggested that an approach emphasizing synecdoche focuses on 'the body as it was lived and experienced, *in parts*, rather than as whole'.[2]

1 Bryan S. Turner, *The Body and Society: Explorations in Social Theory*, 2nd edn (London: Sage, 1996), p. 29. Cf. Roy Porter, 'History of the Body Reconsidered', in *New Perspectives on Historical Writing*, ed. Peter Burke, 2nd edn (University Park: Pennsylvania State University Press, 2001), pp. 233–60.

2 Miri Rubin, 'The Person in the Form: Medieval Challenges to Bodily Order', in *Framing Medieval Bodies*, ed. Sarah Kay and Miri Rubin (Manchester: Manchester University Press, 1994), pp. 100–22 at p. 101.

That is, considering just one part of the body and how it was conceived of and experienced can give perspective on how a whole person lived and was perceived. The Anglo-Saxon understanding of the body and its social roles, particularly their understanding of the body legal, suggests that the individual body was under constant inspection and interpretation[3] (at least as much as the modern body), but at no point did they lose sight of the social functions the body performed. Rather, the individual held a social role and the individual body was valued according to its social functions. Texts treating violent action on the male genitals indicate what was valued – not simply bodily integrity, but integrity of function, integrity of the value attributed to the body – and who benefited from that integrity.

In short, there is no evidence that castration was a particular concern for the Anglo-Saxons nor that they experienced any particular castration anxieties, as was the case in subsequent eras.[4] The only mention of castration as punish-

3 A number of important studies concerning the body and inspection have been written. Katherine O'Brien O'Keeffe has examined corporal punishment and ordeal in Anglo-Saxon England and argues for the importance of the legibility of the body. 'Body and Law in Late Anglo-Saxon England', *Anglo-Saxon England* 27 (1998): 209–32. Responding to O'Brien O'Keeffe's article, Mary P. Richards examines the early laws' injury tariffs and argues that the wounded body conveyed both the evidence of a crime and a means to a restitution, connecting individual and community stability. 'The Body as Text in Early Anglo-Saxon Law', in *Naked Before God: Uncovering the Body in Anglo-Saxon England*, ed. Benjamin C. Withers and Jonathan Wilcox (Morgantown: West Virginia University Press, 2003), pp. 97–115 at pp. 105–6. Andrew Rabin develops these ideas and argues for the focus of Wulfstan's laws on the knowable self. In particular, he argues that it provides a means of ordering social relations as well as a model for structuring the legal subject – as law organizes society in response to external pressures, the individual must internalize the legal text so that the ordered psychology of the legal subject parallels the ordered community of which he is a part. 'The Wolf's Testimony to the English: Law and the Witness in the *Sermo Lupi ad Anglos*', *JEGP* 105 (2006): 388–414. Most recently, Lisi Oliver has addressed the body in barbarian law and provides the process and procedure of law as well as an analysis of how the marked body is interpreted by the law. *The Body Legal in Barbarian Law* (Toronto: University of Toronto Press, 2011); especially relevant to this discussion are chs 2 and 3.

4 Castration was imposed as a symbolic punishment for treason in England as early as the post-Conquest period. Klaus van Eickels, 'Gendered Violence: Castration and Blinding as Punishment for Treason in Normandy and Anglo-Norman England', in *Violence, Vulnerability, and Embodiment: Gender and History*, ed. Shani D'Cruze and Anupama Rao (Oxford: Blackwell, 2005), pp. 94–108. For an alternate reading of Anglo-Saxon castration anxiety as part of a larger set of anxieties about bodily destruction, see John M. Hill, 'The Sacrificial Synecdoche of Hands, Heads, and Arms in Anglo-Saxon Heroic Story', in *Naked Before God: Uncovering the Body in Anglo-Saxon England*, ed. Benjamin C. Withers and Jonathan Wilcox (Morgantown: West Virginia University Press, 2003), pp. 116–37. Hill, drawing on Melanie Klein's Freudian reading of anxiety about body destruction, applies it to the 'fiercely righteous body, that of the super-ego hero', which defies such anxieties in heroic action and 'has a sense of momentary omnipotence to it – the feeling that not only can one not be castrated (beheaded, cut asunder, killed) but in fact one is invulnerable during the particular action in question' (p. 121).

ment in the laws is for a slave who rapes another slave and is only able to make compensation through his castration – the *lex talionis* still applies to a slave because he lacks property with which to pay compensation. However, examining the texts that address violent action on the male genitals does offer insight into the ever-elusive Anglo-Saxon view of sex as well as their understanding of manhood. Note, 'manhood' rather than 'masculinity', because the evidence suggests that a man was defined more in relation to his contribution to the society as a whole than in his gendered performance.[5] The physical body was a collection of tools useful in the performance of what a person contributed. Thus arms and legs were as useful to a thegn in fighting as to a churl in digging, and genitals were for procreation. If, as Paul Hyams has suggested, the fundamental goal of assigning monetary values to bodies – in the form of *wergild* or injury tariffs – was to maintain a secure and stable society,[6] tracing secular references to the genitals, especially violent action on the penis and testicles,[7] shows a shifting valuation of the male in Anglo-Saxon society according to developing ideas about the *vita activa*, which in Anglo-Saxon England is a life concerned with sustaining and protecting bodies, including the spiritual body of the Church, and of how to achieve security and stability. In particular, there is a shift from the emphasis on kinship ties and the value of a man's status (rank – e.g. thegn or churl – honor, physical integrity, and ability to reproduce that status) *within the family* to an emphasis

5 Although the focus of this chapter is necessarily on males, the Old English *mann* indicated, according to Bosworth and Toller's *Anglo-Saxon Dictionary*, 'a human being of either sex'. Certainly a woman (*wifmann*) performed particular social roles that were valued and that defined her personhood as much as a man's. However, as has been noted, women were often perceived as existing on the fringe of free status. Ruth Mazo Karras, 'Desire, Descendants, and Dominance: Slavery, the Exchange of Women, and Masculine Power', in *The Work of Work: Servitude, Slavery, and Labor in Medieval England*, ed. Allen J. Frantzen and Douglas Moffat (Glasgow: Cruithne Press, 1994), p. 17; Elizabeth Stevens Girsch, 'Metaphorical Usage, Sexual Exploitation, and Divergence in the Old English Terminology for Male and Female Slaves', in *The Work of Work*, ed. Frantzen and Moffat, pp. 30–54 at pp. 44–5. Yet the importance of masculinity to the Anglo-Saxons should not be ignored. Discussions concerning masculinity in the early medieval north such as Preben Meulengracht Sørensen's *The Unmanly Man: Concepts of Sexual Defamation in Early Northern Society* (Odense: Odense University Press, 1983) suggest that there was concern with the performance and maintenance of masculinity. However, the discussion here suggests that in Anglo-Saxon England such masculinity was simply not reliant on the penis.

6 Paul R. Hyams, *Rancor and Reconciliation in Medieval England* (Ithaca, NY: Cornell University Press, 2003), pp. 3–4.

7 The vocabulary in the texts discussed here is not entirely clear about what it is referring to. For instance, the term *lendenbræde* is used to refer to male genitals in Alfred's laws. This may very well refer to the testicles, as Lisi Oliver takes it to mean (my thanks to Dr. Oliver for allowing me to see an unpublished draft of an article on genital wounds in Æthelberht's laws). However, it is not clear to me that the texts here distinguish the parts of the genitals – penis, scrotum, testicles.

on all men of all free ranks as equally necessary and valuable to the society.[8] Peace and social order in relation to the *vita activa* were presented as bound up with manhood throughout the Anglo-Saxon period and, finally, were only achievable by what King Alfred, in the translation of Boethius's *Consolation of Philosophy*, refers to as a *fulmannod* (fully manned) society.[9] Yet to get to the *fulmannod* society of Alfred's vision required a significant shift of perspective on social order, the social relationships of individuals, and the obligations of a man.

Nearly two decades ago, Caroline Walker Bynum noted that too great an emphasis in studies on the body had been placed on sexuality and gender at the expense of consideration of topics like work and death.[10] In the intervening years, scholars have attempted to redress this, but have not adequately brought the sexed male body together with its social value. There have been worthwhile considerations of sexuality and gender, but these have generally focused on women, not men, and on religious texts and contexts which dramatize 'a struggle for power between a threatening world, which is destructive and sexual, and an embracing spirituality, which is asexual'.[11] There have been considerations of labor, death, disability, and materiality, but not of their relation to sex.[12] Matters of genealogy and succession have been treated, but largely with focuses on heroic literature, politics, and propaganda, and rarely with a consideration of children or sex, even though it is only in recent history

8 On the social status of slaves and the work they performed, see Girsch, 'Metaphorical Usage, Sexual Exploitation', pp. 30–54.

9 Malcolm Godden and Susan Irvine, eds. *The Old English Boethius: An Edition of the Old English Versions of Boethius's* De Consolatione Philosophiae, 2 vols (Oxford: Oxford University Press, 2009), vol. 2, B 17, p. 26.

10 Caroline Walker Bynum, 'Why All the Fuss about the Body? A Medievalist's Perspective', *Critical Inquiry* 22 (1995): 1–33 at p. 33.

11 Hugh Magennis, 'No Sex Please, We're Anglo-Saxons: Attitudes to Sexuality in Old English Prose and Poetry', *Leeds Studies in English* 26 (1995): 1–27 at p. 3; Clare A. Lees, 'Engendering Religious Desire: Sex, Knowledge, and Christian Identity in Anglo-Saxon England', *Journal of Mediaeval and Early Modern Studies* 27 (1997): 17–45; Jocelyn Wogan-Browne, 'Chaste Bodies: Frames and Experiences', in *Framing Medieval Bodies*, ed. Kay and Rubin, pp. 24–42; Karen Biddick, 'Genders, Bodies, Borders: Technologies of the Visible', *Speculum* 68 (1993): 389–418.

12 Caroline Walker Bynum, *Christian Materiality: An Essay on Religion in Late Medieval Europe* (New York: Zone Books, 2011); Christina Lee, 'Body Talks: Disease and Disability in Anglo-Saxon England', in *Anglo-Saxon Traces*, ed. Jane Roberts and Leslie Webster (Tempe: Arizona Center for Medieval and Renaissance Studies, 2011), pp. 145–64; Withers and Wilcox, ed., *Naked Before God*; Kay and Rubin, ed., *Framing Medieval Bodies*; Frantzen and Moffat, ed., *The Work of Work*. Exceptions to this are two essays in *The Work of Work*: Karras, 'Desire, Descendants, and Dominance', pp. 16–29, and Girsch, 'Metaphorical Usage, Sexual Exploitation', pp. 30–54. However, both of these essays are concerned with the sexual exploitation of unfree people, especially women, and, therefore, offer only a very limited understanding of the larger perception of the sexed male body in the *vita activa* of Anglo-Saxon England.

that children have been perceived as valuable in their own right or as distinct from the sex act.[13] This essay attempts to fill this gap by drawing the lay, male, sexed body and work in Anglo-Saxon England into dialogue in order to consider how the Anglo-Saxons understood the function and value of the sexed male body, and the development of their understanding, because no person exists outside a matrix of social contexts.

There is, as has been widely noted, very little reference to sex or the sexed body in the vernacular Old English corpus and what exists falls roughly into three categories: religious, practical, and secular.[14] The religious texts are not particularly reliable evidence for how the Anglo-Saxons thought about sex and the body. Those religious texts that do address sex (especially the male genitals) show an anxiety about it and a desire to control it.[15] Hagiographical texts show saintly figures binding up their loins[16] and homiletic and pastoral texts are interested in the regulation of sexual interactions, especially on Church holidays.[17] Perhaps most famous among these appears in Archbishop Wulfstan's *Sermo Lupi ad Anglos*, in which he condemns the practice of men who 'sceotað togædere and ane cwenan gemænum ceape bicgað gemæne, and wið þa ane fylþe adreogað, an æfter anum, and ælc æfter oðrum, hundum geliccast, þe for fylþe ne scrifað' [group together and buy one woman in common, and with her practice filth, one after another, and each after the other, most like dogs who do not care about filth].[18] However, none of the religious texts offers useful evidence about the lay understanding of sex or the body, not even Wulfstan's graphic example which, given the goals of the genre,

13 Michael D. C. Drout, 'Blood and Deeds: The Inheritance Systems in *Beowulf*, *Studies in Philology* 104 (2007): 199–226; Frederick M. Biggs, 'The Politics of Succession in *Beowulf* and Anglo-Saxon England', *Speculum* 80 (2005): 709–41; Pauline Stafford, 'Succession and Inheritance: A Gendered Perspective on Alfred's Family History', in *Alfred the Great: Papers from the Eleventh-Centenary Conferences*, ed. Timothy Reuter (Aldershot: Ashgate, 2003), pp. 251–64; Richard J. Schrader, 'Succession and Glory in *Beowulf*, *JEGP* 90 (1991): 491–504; Sally Crawford, *Childhood in Anglo-Saxon England* (Stroud: Sutton, 1999); Mathew S. Kuefler, '"A Wryed Existence": Attitudes toward Children in Anglo-Saxon England', *Journal of Social History* 24 (1991): 823–34.

14 This essay will only address the written. On visual depictions of sex and sexed bodies, see Catherine E. Karkov, 'Exiles from the Kingdom: The Naked and the Damned in Anglo-Saxon Art', in *Naked Before God*, ed. Withers and Wilcox, pp. 181–220.

15 Magennis, 'No Sex Please, We're Anglo-Saxons', p. 7.

16 A search of the *Dictionary of Old English Corpus* online for *lenden*, the most basic of term for loins, produces twenty results relating to the religious category, most of which refer to binding up one's loins. Larissa Tracy discusses the relative absence of castration among the litany of tortures doled out to martyrs in English hagiography, '"Al defouleden is holie bodi": Castration, the Sexualization of Torture, and Anxieties of Identity in the *South English Legendary*', in this volume, pp. 87–107.

17 Magennis, 'No Sex Please, We're Anglo-Saxons', p. 15.

18 Dorothy Whitelock, ed., *Sermo Lupi ad Anglos* (Exeter: University of Exeter Press, 1977), lines 88–91.

cannot be comfortably accepted as representative or even commonplace.[19] Practical medical texts make the greatest number of references to the genitals in terms of healing sore or wounded genitals, but with little suggestion of how injuries were received and with little to guide interpretation of the Anglo-Saxon understanding of the sexed body.[20] Rather, the most evidence for violent action on the genitals appears in a seemingly ill-fitting pair of secular vernacular genres – riddles and laws. However, when read against one another, they provide the best evidence of the Anglo-Saxons' broad concerns with the sexed body and offer a common method for considering the developing understanding of the role of the male member, and thus of a man, in the *vita activa*.[21]

The riddles and the laws both direct their audiences' attention beyond the matter at hand and encourage them to reflect on the familiar social world. A handful of suggestive riddles are contained in the tenth-century Exeter Book, possibly the earliest extant collection of vernacular poetry from Anglo-Saxon England.[22] These appear to refer to the penis, but redirect the right-thinking respondent to familiar, non-bodily, objects such as an onion, a key, and bread dough,[23] all of which receive rough treatment at the hands of another. In the

19 Perhaps an intermediary genre dealing with sex could be penitential literature. Although fundamentally religious and Latinate, the ostensible intent of penitentials was to guide confessors. However, as John T. McNeill and Helena M. Gamer note, much of what appears in the Anglo-Saxon penitential texts is drawn from early Christian models and is, therefore, not reliable as evidence for Anglo-Saxon practice. *Medieval Handbooks of Penance* (New York: Columbia University Press, 1990), p. 180. However, see Pierre J. Payer, *Sex and the Penitentials: The Development of a Sexual Code, 550–1150* (Toronto: University of Toronto Press, 1984).

20 *The Dictionary of Old English Corpus* online lists thirty-nine references to *lenden* in medical texts, but it is difficult to generalize about these because *lenden* is also used to refer to the kidneys.

21 This essay will not treat sexuality and the unfree because slaves were not able to act within the *vita activa*. However, it is worth briefly noting that the laws do concern themselves with the consequences of sex with slaves and the status of the offspring of such encounters. Karras, 'Desire, Descendants, and Dominance', pp. 16–29.

22 The most recent editor has dated it *c.* 965–75. *The Exeter Anthology of Old English Poetry*, ed. Bernard J. Muir, 2nd edn, 2 vols (Exeter: University of Exeter Press, 2000), p. I:1. Although the extant riddles post-date the laws, the way they work in their treatment of the body offers insight into the laws' approach to it.

23 Respectively, riddles 25, 44, and 45 in *The Exeter Anthology*, ed. Muir, pp. I:303 and 319. Many commentators and editors have noted several *double-entendre* riddles besides these. Reinhard Gleissner discusses as employing some degree of *double entendre* the following riddles: 11 (cup or beaker of wine), 12 (ox, leather), 20 (sword), 30a (tree or wood in various forms), 37 (bellows), 44 (key), 45 (bread dough), 54 (churn), 61 (helmet), 62 (poker, boring tool), 63 (beaker), 75 (piss), 76 (oyster, horn), and 91 (beech tree and book, battering ram). *Die 'zweideutigen' altenglischen Rätsel des Exeter Book in ihrem zeitgenössischen Kontext* (Frankfurt: P. Lang, 1984) (proposed responses are taken from *The Exeter Anthology*, ed. Muir, II:655–63 and 735–39). Others have been added to this list by various scholars. For example: Mercedes Salvador, 'The Key to the Body: Unlocking Riddles 42–46', in *Naked Before God*, ed. Withers and Wilcox, pp. 60–96; Sarah L. Higley,

laws of King Æthelberht of Kent (r. *c.* 587x590–616x618)[24] and of King Alfred of Wessex (r. 871–99)[25] the lists of injury tariffs lay out the prices for kinds and degrees of wounds, including wounds to the genitals. It is striking that the language and imagery of the riddles are violent – grabbing, grasping, striking, piercing – and overlap with the laws' concerns with bodily harm:

> on þæt banlease bryd grapode,
> hygewlonc hondum.
>
> the proud woman grasped that boneless thing in her hand. (Riddle 45)[26]

> Gif feaxfang geweorð, L sceatta to bote.
>
> For seizing by the hair, 50 sceattas as compensation. (Æthelberht 33)[27]

> heo on mec gripeð,
> ræseð mec on reodne, reafað min heafod,
> fegeð mec on fæsten.
>
> she grips me, violently reddens me, deprives me of my head, binds me in fastness. (Riddle 25)[28]

'The Wanton Hand: Reading and Reaching into Grammars and Bodies in Old English Riddle 12', in *Naked Before God*, ed. Withers and Wilcox, pp. 29–59. Patrick J. Murphy, *Unriddling the Exeter Riddles* (University Park: Pennsylvania State University Press, 2011) provides a particularly compelling analysis of the sex riddles.

24 In this dating format, 'x' indicates 'between possible dates'. Æthelberht's exact dates are difficult to ascertain. Those supplied here are from Lisi Oliver, *The Beginnings of English Law* (Toronto: University of Toronto Press, 2002), pp. 1–14. The traditional dating is 560x590–616: Michael Lapidge *et al.*, eds., *The Blackwell Encyclopaedia of Anglo-Saxon England* (Oxford: Blackwell, 1999). However, skeptical of some of the evidence, especially the possible fifty-six-year reign, Oliver has challenged this and provided a more reasonable chronology. Æthelberht's laws are extant only in the twelfth-century *Textus Roffensis*.

25 Alfred issued his *Domboc*, with the laws of Ine (r. 688–726) appended to it, in the late 880s or early 890s. The earliest extant copy is in Corpus Christi College, Cambridge (CCCC) MS 173. Liebermann dates this to *c.* 925. For a full discussion of the manuscript context and history, see Patrick Wormald, *The Making of English Law: King Alfred to the Twelfth Century.* Vol. I: *Legislation and Its Limits* (Oxford: Blackwell, 2001), pp. 264–85. All references to Alfred's laws cite CCCC 173.

26 On female violence see Carole Hough, 'Two Kentish Laws Concerning Women: A New Reading of Æthelberht 73 and 74', *Anglia* 119 (2001): 554–78. Unless otherwise noted, all translations are my own.

27 The law numbers are editorial. Citations to Æthelberht's laws are taken from Oliver, *Beginnings of English Law.* Alfred's laws are taken from Felix Liebermann, *Die Gesetze der Angelsachsen: Text und Übersetzung*, vol. 1 (Halle: Max Niemeyer, 1903). On hair-pulling, see Oliver, *The Body Legal*, pp. 108–9. In particular, she notes that laws against hair-pulling, which we perhaps associate more with women who appear on *Jerry Springer*, are bound up with the barbarian custom of men wearing long hair and probably have two main intentions: 'they regulate against a deliberate affront in which the hair is jeeringly (and probably publicly) pulled, and they also fine the person who makes the first physical attack in a fight.'

28 On the insult of binding, see Oliver, *The Body Legal*, p. 170. While *reodne* simply indicates the color red, Bosworth and Toller's *Anglo-Saxon Dictionary* defines *reodan* 'to redden,

Wrætlice hongað bi weres þeo,
frean under sceate. Foran is þyrel.

A wondrous thing hangs by a man's thigh, under its lord's cloak. It is pierced through in front. (Riddle 44)

Gif man gekyndelice lim awyrdeþ, þrym leudgeldum hine man forgelde.
Gif he þurhstinð, VI scill gebete.
Gif man inbestinð, VI scill gebete.

If a person[29] destroys the generative member, he must pay three times the *wergild.*
If he pierces it through, compensate with 6 shillings.
If he partially pierces it, compensate with 6 shillings. (Æthelberht 64–64.2)

Gif sio lendenbræde bið forslegen, þær sceal LX scill. to bote.
Gif hio bið onbestungen, geselle XV scill. to bote.
Gif hio bið ðurhðyrel, ðonne sceal ðær XXX scill. to bote.

If the loins are violently struck,[30] pay 60 shillings as compensation; if they are pierced, give 15 shillings as compensation; if they are pierced through, then pay 30 shillings as compensation. (Alfred 67–67.2)

Through the language of violently abused genitals, the riddles and the laws alike evoke questions about the purpose and value of the organ.[31] Most importantly, both riddles and laws assume a social interaction with the penis. Someone (female) acts on it in riddles 25 and 45; in riddle 44 a man lifts his cloak with the intention of using the object publicly;[32] and the laws inherently address an injury inflicted by another. Thus the 'private part' is only ever

stain with blood' (I) and 'to redden a person by causing blood to flow from a wound, to wound, kill' (II). Such an understanding is certainly promoted by the surrounding verbs *ræsan*, meaning 'to move against violently, attack' (II), and the verb *reafian.*

29 The repetition of *man* (person) in the law is suggestive of anyone, male or female, injuring a man's genitals.

30 *The Dictionary of Old English* notes that *forslean* can carry the meanings 'to strike, smite, beat' (1), 'to injure (someone/something) by striking' (1.a), 'to break, wound (a part of the body) with a blow; to cut through (the neck) with a stroke' (1.a.i). F. L. Attenborough translates it as 'maimed', but this seems too strong given the following degrees of wound: *The Laws of the Earliest English Kings* (Cambridge: Cambridge University Press, 1922; rpt Clark, NJ: The Lawbook Exchange, 2006).

31 In riddles 25 and 45, it is precisely the figure of the female agent and the contradiction of the imagery of violence in the feminine, domestic, space that must be resolved and that suggests the object as a penis. Similarly, the language of anxiety over injury pervades the law, and is most clearly expressed in the injury tariffs.

32 'þonne se esne his agen hrægl / ofer cneo hefeð, wile þæt cuþe hol / mid his hangellan heafde gretan / þæt he efenlang ær oft gefylde' [when the man lifts his cloak above the knee, he intends to greet with the head of that hanging thing that well-known hole of matching length which he has often filled before].

presented in relation to others, and in this, the audiences of both riddles and laws are invited to examine it.[33]

However, riddles perform the 'double task of revealing and concealing',[34] and the 'correct' answers to the riddles redirect an audience's attention and thought process away from the male sex organs. Nonetheless, as has been widely recognized, 'it is in part through posing and solving riddles that people test the conceptual boundaries of their world, rendering abstract relations concrete and endowing common things with sentience'.[35] Patrick Murphy has suggested that riddles are not even so much about reaching a correct solution, but about understanding an underlying metaphor.[36] In particular, in those he groups simply as the 'sex riddles' he sees a concern with the body in service.[37] Although the penis disappears from view with the presentation of the desired response, the penis as a social object has been established and it has been associated with common and useful objects. Although the language of the riddles is violent, Magennis suggests that sexuality is presented in the riddles as quotidian and non-threatening.[38]

> *Double-entendre* riddles teasingly introduce the indecorous into a decorous literary form, in such a way as to implicate the audience in the indelicacy: the riddler can always claim that the correct answer to the riddle is an innocent one, despite the unseemly conclusion to which the audience is inclined to leap. Such riddles accept the principle that sex is not a proper subject for them to deal with – otherwise there would be no need for *double entendre* – but they deal with it anyway. Their attitude is one of good-humoured impudence rather than of hostility to sexuality; and they also proceed on the assumption that the audience accepts that sex is an interesting subject.[39]

Similarly, the laws dealing with injury tariffs redirect from simple compensation for an injury to other, supra-bodily, concerns. As Suzanne Lewis notes, 'we never encounter the body unmediated by the meanings that cultures, including our own as well as medieval, give to it';[40] and focusing this point, Stefan Jurasinski suggests that 'Anglo-Saxon injury tariffs offer scholarship

33 On examination of the body, Richards, 'The Body as Text in Early Anglo-Saxon Law.'

34 Marie Nelson, 'The Rhetoric of the Exeter Book Riddles', *Speculum* 49 (1974): 421–40 at p. 424.

35 John D. Niles, *Old English Enigmatic Poems and the Play of the Texts* (Turnhout: Brepols, 2006), p. 54.

36 Murphy, *Unriddling the Exeter Riddles*, p. 23.

37 Ibid., p. 182.

38 Magennis, 'No Sex Please, We're Anglo-Saxons', p. 18.

39 Ibid., pp. 16–17.

40 Suzanne Lewis, 'Medieval Bodies Then and Now: Negotiating Problems of Ambivalence and Paradox', in *Naked Before God*, ed. Withers and Wilcox, pp. 15–28 at p. 15.

striking indices of how meaning and value were accorded to bodies'.[41] In addition to composition – the putting back together of the broken or injured body through compensation – the law codes of Æthelberht and Alfred, each in its own fashion, direct the audience to consider the function of the body in the larger, integrated social web, not simply as it is valued by the injured man. In this, the laws present a body social and indicate what is valued about any given (male) body and by whom.[42]

The laws of the Kentish Æthelberht contain schedules of injury tariffs addressing a range of wounds and degrees of severity, running in a roughly head-to-toe order. As mentioned above, composition laws are fundamentally about the maintenance of peace in the society and so analysis of them provides a sense of their underlying assumptions about social order and the role of the individual in the *vita activa*. As William Miller points out, 'the English word *peace*, coming via Latin *pax* from *pacare*, derives from the idea of paying'.[43] Thus composition is not only about making whole the individual through compensation, but about making whole the society in order to maintain peace. However, standing out from all of the values attributed to injuries in the laws of Æthelberht is the compensation to be paid for injury to the genitals, which hints that the social order was conceived according to family groups. Rather than a simple *bot* (compensatory fine), as in the other injury tariffs, Æthelberht 64 requires the payment of three-fold *wergild* for the destruction of the generative member:

> Gif man gekyndelice lim awyrdeþ,[44] þrym leudgeldum hine man forgelde.
> Gif he þurhstinð, VI sciłł gebete.
> Gif man inbestinð, VI sciłł gebete.
>
> If a person destroys the generative member, he must pay three times the *wergild*.
> If he pierces it through, compensate with 6 shillings.
> If he partially pierces it, compensate with 6 shillings.

Æthelberht 64 suggests that a man receives compensation not just for the injury, as is clearly the case in all the other injury tariffs, but for the loss of his ability

[41] Stefan Jurasinski, 'Germanism, Slapping and the Cultural Contexts of Æthelberht's Code: A Reconsideration of Chapters 56–58', *Haskins Society Journal* 18 (2006): 51–71 at p. 52.

[42] For similar arguments regarding injury tariffs and laws in Frisia and in Ireland and Wales see in this volume Rolf H. Bremmer Jr, 'The Children He Never Had; The Husband She Never Served: Castration and Genital Mutilation in Medieval Frisian Law', pp. 108–30 and Charlene M. Eska, '"Imbruded in their owne bloud": Castration in Early Welsh and Irish Sources', pp. 149–73.

[43] William Ian Miller, *Eye for an Eye* (Cambridge: Cambridge University Press, 2006), p. 15.

[44] Although *awyrdan* can mean both 'injure' and 'destroy', it seems unlikely in this case that any wound is intended, but rather that impairment of function is.

to procreate.[45] Defining the member (*lim*) that is injured as *gekyndelice* implies that what is valued so highly is its function, not the wound *per se*.[46] This is further suggested by the subsequent *bot* fines of a mere 6 shillings, which do compensate the wound.[47] Moreover, Æthelberht's laws distinguish elsewhere between damage and function, as in the case of injury to an ear, which is valued differently depending on whether or not the hearing is impaired.[48] Yet none of those laws establishing compensation for function comes anywhere near the three-fold *wergild* owed for destruction of the generative member. However, this should not be interpreted as some kind of castration anxiety or compensation for lost masculine identity. Rather, it is indicative of a compensation for a man's ability to reproduce his social function (a thegn producing future thegns, a churl future churls) and thus contribute to the security of the larger society. However, payment valued according to *wergild* rather than *bot* indicates the imagined social structure. *Bot* was paid to the victim; *wergild* was paid to the family. In this, the social structure is represented as one of families and the social value of the individual is couched within his value to the family; manhood is tied to the security of the family and its continuation.

Others have posited that Æthelberht 64 applies such a high price for a wound to the penis because of the shame it would incur. Acknowledging the proposal that it might compensate the harm to function, Mary Richards states, 'we should not overlook, however, the factors of shame and embarrassment such a wound might involve and the possibility, therefore, of compensatory damages beyond those for other catastrophic injuries'.[49] Miller goes further, claiming that the penis here takes on symbolic value and that 'fetishization is clearly needed to explain the hyperevaluation of *one* part as three times greater than the whole'.[50] Certainly Miller raises the issue of reproductive ability, pointing to a law in the Frankish *Lex Salica* that requires three-fold *wergild* for killing a fertile woman, but only a single *wergild* for one beyond her fertile years,[51] but he emphasizes the symbolic quality. Although possible, such speculations do not seem to be supported by any hard evidence. There is no primary-source evidence in the Anglo-Saxon laws to indicate that there was a

45 Oliver, *Beginnings of English Law*, p. 99.

46 Interestingly, this could theoretically refer to an injury to a man or a woman. Bosworth and Toller's *Anglo-Saxon Dictionary* identifies *gecyndlim* as 'a birth-limb, womb; vulva'. However, the context of the injury tariffs suggests that the interest is injury to the male member.

47 Oliver suggests that these are referring to wounds to the scrotum rather than the penis itself: *Beginnings of English Law*, p. 99.

48 Æthelberht 39–42. Oliver, *Beginnings of English Law*, p. 100.

49 Richards, 'The Body as Text in Early Anglo-Saxon Law', p. 105.

50 Miller, *Eye for an Eye*, pp. 125–8.

51 Cf. Marianne Elsakkers, 'Inflicting Serious Bodily Harm: The Visigothic *Antiquae* on Violence and Abortion', *Legal History Review* 71 (2003): 55–63 at p. 62.

particular shame to being unable to procreate.[52] Without question, the laws compensate shame in that they value visible wounds more highly than those covered by clothing or hair.[53] However, a wound to the genitals, an area usually kept covered, would presumably be no more shameful than any other wound.[54] Rather, it is the value of future lives that is being compensated in the three-fold *wergild*. Rolf Bremmer finds similar compensations for genital wounding in the *Lex Frisionum* and the later, vernacular Frisian laws.[55] There is literary evidence from *Beowulf* that matters of succession and inheritance were important, at least for the nobility,[56] and the very constructedness of West-Saxon genealogical material in the *Anglo-Saxon Chronicle* and Asser's *Vita Ælfredi* reinforces such a conclusion in practice. More broadly, children in Anglo-Saxon society must have been an important resource, valued for their labor as well as for the care they would likely provide aged parents.[57] Consequently, although shame and embarrassment for a genital wound or for the subsequent inability to procreate may have been factors, there seems to be a more practical logic involved in the extraordinary compensation paid for the destruction of the generative member.

There is one final piece of evidence that procreative function is being compensated in Æthelberht 64. Despite rank-based *wergild*, compensation for injuries did not change according to rank,[58] except, Stanley Rubin notes, in the case of Æthelberht 64.[59] He then offers a reasonable speculation about the reason for this exception:

> It seems probable that this variable compensation could well stem from the Anglo-Saxons' strict view of their personal status reasserting itself even within an 'egalitarian' tariff of payments. It would have been uppermost in their minds that the loss of virility and fertility would always constitute a far more serious genealogical handicap for a member of the noble class whose chances of parenthood might consequently be put in grave jeopardy. The resulting absence of descendants and risk of severing family lineage could be sufficient for royal agreement to be given for this rare variant in compensation law.[60]

[52] In personal correspondence, Dr. Lisi Oliver has indicated that she also knows of no such evidence for particular shame attaching to infertility.

[53] On compensation for shame, see Oliver, *The Body Legal*, ch. 6.

[54] This would change during the Anglo-Norman period when castration and blinding were explicitly established as symbolic punishments for treason in place of execution: van Eickels, 'Gendered Violence', pp. 94–108.

[55] Bremmer, 'The Children He Never Had', pp. 109–10.

[56] See infra. n. 12.

[57] Oliver, *The Body Legal*, p. 135.

[58] Stanley Rubin, 'The *Bot*, or Composition in Anglo-Saxon Law: A Reassessment', *Legal History* 17 (1996): 144–54 at p. 146; Richards, 'The Body as Text in Early Anglo-Saxon Law', p. 101.

[59] Rubin, 'The *Bot*, or Composition in Anglo-Saxon Law', pp. 150–1.

[60] Ibid., p. 151.

Moreover, since *wergild* is rank-based, the compensation paid is dependent on the rank of the injured man. In this, the law recognizes rank in the case of injury only in terms of the man's social function, that is, his ability to reproduce within the family. While the injury tariffs generally indicate how to make whole the individual, however he came by his injury, the exceptional Æthelberht 64 redirects the understanding of all the tariffs. They are not concerned simply with a wounded body, but with a body that does work in the society and is therefore valued according to that work. Thus while a thegn's ability to fight and a churl's to farm might be equally valued in the composition laws, the thegn's function (evident in the distinction of *wergild*) and his ability to reproduce that function for the society were deemed far more valuable than the churl's. It is the family unit that must be made whole in order to maintain peace and social order.

The imagined social order shifts from family as the defining social unit in Æthelberht's laws to the individual in relation to the king in Alfred's. This must be an active revision of his model since Alfred says in the prologue to his laws that he drew on Æthelberht's in compiling the *Domboc* (Alfred Prologue 49.9), likely as a rhetorical consolidation of royal power.[61] Alfred's laws, like those of Æthelberht, redirect the attention of the audience from the simple compensation for an injury to the social function of the individual, but Alfred's laws accomplish this through an intriguing structural shift. Unlike Æthelberht, Alfred does not compensate so highly for the lost future generation, but his injury tariffs do value all (male) members of the society equally, indicating a significant development in the overall logic of the laws, which becomes evident when read through the larger intellectual projects of his reign, particularly the translations of Gregory's *Pastoral Care* and Boethius' *Consolation of Philosophy*.

Taking up the kingship as he did in the midst of massive Viking incursions at the end of the ninth century, Alfred's conception of the *vita activa* is fundamentally about supporting the security of the society. He was focused on re-establishing order and to this end he addressed himself to educational and legal reform. The two great products of Alfred's reign are the translations of Latin material[62] and his law code. Although the translations and the law are usually discussed separately,[63] it is far from clear that Alfred perceived them as having unrelated functions. He referred to the translated texts as 'suma bec, ða þe

[61] On assertion of royal ideology through law, see Andrew Rabin, 'Old English *Forespeca* and the Role of the Advocate in Anglo-Saxon Law', *Mediaeval Studies* 69 (2007): 232–54 at pp. 232–3.

[62] The question of what Alfred actually produced has long been debated. The simplest suggestion concerning authorship of the works produced during his reign is that Alfred took part as a member of a team, and probably not the most learned member. Allen Frantzen, 'The Form and Function of the Preface in the Poetry and Prose of Alfred's Reign', in *Alfred the Great*, ed. Reuter, pp. 121–36 at p. 128; idem, *King Alfred* (Boston: Twayne, 1986), p. 1.

[63] An important exception to this is Frantzen, *King Alfred*.

nidbeðyrfesta sien eallum monnum to witanne' [some books which are most needful for all men to know],[64] and Allen Frantzen stresses that 'Alfred translated and encouraged translating not only because he hoped to create an educated clergy and nobility for the good of his nation, but also because he loved learning and literature'.[65] Moreover, Patrick Wormald has discussed the literary quality of Alfred's *Domboc* and several later Anglo-Saxon law codes that drew on it and he concludes that the laws had a more ideological, less utilitarian purpose.[66] Both the translations and the law seem to work, if not together, at least in the same vein, to reconceive what made the society secure. The logic of the shift from Æthelberht's model of three-fold *wergild* compensation to a flat tariff for injury to a man's ability to procreate is indicative of this, pointing to the social matrix no longer being individual to family, but individual to king, with a realignment of individual obligation.

In his texts, Alfred grapples with both social and individual order and how one is supported by means of the other. At the level of the society, Alfred's translation of Boethius's *Consolation of Philosophy* provides the first extant use of the idea of the 'three orders' of society:[67]

> Tola ic wilnolde þeah and andweorces to þam weorce þe me beboden was to wyrcanne; þæt was þæt ic unfracodlice and gerisenlice mihte steoran and reccan þone anweald þe me befæst wæs. Hwæt þu wast þæt nan mon ne mæg nænne cræft cyþan ne nænne anweald reccan ne stioran butan tolum and andweorce. Þæt bið ælces cræftes andweorc þæt mon þone cræft buton wyrcan ne mæg. Þæt bið þonne cyninges andweorc and his tol mid to ricsianne þæt he hæbbe his land fulmannod. He sceal habban gebedmen and fyrdmen and weorcmen. Hwæt þu wast þætte butan þisum tolum nan cyning his cræft ne mæg cyðan. Þæt is eac his andweorc þæt he habban sceal to þam tolum þam þrim geferscipum biwiste.[68]

[64] *King Alfred's West-Saxon Version of Gregory's Pastoral Care*, ed. Henry Sweet, 2 vols (London: Oxford University Press, 1871–72; rpt 1958), p. 6.

[65] Frantzen, *King Alfred*, p. 6.

[66] Wormald, *The Making of English Law*, p. 264; Patrick Wormald, '*Lex Scripta* and *Verbum Regis*: Legislation and Germanic Kingship, from Euric to Cnut', in *Early Medieval Kingship*, ed. P. H. Sawyer and I.N. Wood (Leeds: University of Leeds, 1977), pp. 105–38.

[67] Timothy E. Powell, 'The "Three Orders" of Society in Anglo-Saxon England', *Anglo-Saxon England* 23 (1994): 103–32 at p. 103. It has been suggested that, although the author of the preface to the Old English *Consolation* claims Alfred as its translator, the text may have been produced after Alfred's death. The earliest extant manuscript is dated *c.* 950, and Godden and Irvine suggest a composition date between 890 and 930: Godden and Irvine, *Old English Boethius* I, pp. 140–6; Malcolm Godden, 'Did King Alfred Write Anything?' *Medium Aevum* 76 (2007): 1–23 at pp. 15–17. However, the text may be understood as a product of Alfred's translation program, whether or not it was produced after his death. I would like to thank Dr Nicole Marafioti for bringing this point to my attention.

[68] *The Old English Boethius*, ed. Godden and Irvine, vol. 1, B 17, p. 277.

> I sought tools and material for the work that I was commanded to carry out; that was so that I could safely and fittingly steer and direct the power that was entrusted to me. Truly you know that no-one can show any skill, or exercise or control any power, without tools and material. The material of any skill is that without which one cannot exercise that skill. Then the material for a king and his tools for ruling with are that he has his land fully manned. He must have prayer-men and army-men and work-men. You know that without these tools no king can show his skill. His material is also that he must have for these tools sustenance for the three communities.[69]

As Timothy Powell interprets this, the kingdom is supported by a (male) population comprised of three interdependent, non-hierarchical groups. He stresses, 'the basis of the model is differentiation rather than stratification'.[70] The *gebedmen* fulfill the role of the *vita contemplativa*; the latter two participate in the *vita activa*. The non-hierarchical division of labor is interesting in itself because this was a hierarchical society, but it becomes fully meaningful as a change in practical social value when read in conjunction with Alfred's revision of Æthelberht's model. As Alfred's *Consolation of Philosophy* highlights social order and the necessities of royal government, his laws insist on the individual man's role in maintaining social order. The foundation of Alfred's law is the social individual: 'Æt ærestan we lærað, þæt mæst ðearf is, þæt æghwelc mon his að and his wed wærlice healdan' [First we instruct what is of greatest necessity, that each man carefully hold his oath and his pledge] (Alfred 1). The individual is thus defined under the law in relation to the society, not to the family. And although he is an individual, he only has meaning in relation to the social whole. Consequently, this appears to be a part of an effort to consolidate royal power through individual obligation.

Like Æthelberht's laws, a man's value (his *wergild*) is set according to the status he holds.[71] However, Alfred's laws are far more literarily elaborated than Æthelberht's,[72] and their structure indicates a shift in the legal conception of the value of the individual body. Alfred 44–77 are the schedules of injury tariffs.

69 The translation is Godden and Irvine's. *The Old English Boethius*, ed. Godden and Irvine, vol. 2, B 17, p. 26.

70 Powell, 'The "Three Orders"', p. 104.

71 In seventh-century Kent, a nobleman (*eorl*) carried a *wergild* of 300 Kentish shillings, a churl 100. In Alfred's time a nobleman carried a *wergild* of 1,200 shillings, a churl of 200. There was, at one point, a class of *gesithas* who carried a *wergild* of 600 shillings, but this may have disappeared by Alfred's day: Dorothy Whitelock, *The Beginnings of English Society* (London: Penguin, 1954), pp. 83–4.

72 On the careful rhetorical shaping of Alfred's laws, especially the prologue, there are two excellent studies: Frantzen, 'The Form and Function of the Preface in the Poetry and Prose of Alfred's Reign' and Michael Treschow, 'The Prologue to Alfred's Law Code: Instruction in the Spirit of Mercy', *Florilegium* 13 (1994): 79–110.

Like Æthelberht's, the schedules of injury tariffs do not vary the cost for a wound according to rank, but Alfred's laws do not make an exception concerning compensation for loss of procreative function either. As with Æthelberht's laws, these run roughly head to toe until, at Alfred 65, the structure of the laws suddenly shifts to finish with a seemingly spasmodic series of injuries to genitals, arm, shoulder, hand, rib, eye, shoulder, shin, sinews, and tendons. Stranger than the sudden structural disruption is that several of the final twelve laws are redundant, having been covered in some way in the previous injury tariffs. Indeed, there are two laws treating wounds to the genitals in this list and they are themselves divided by a tariff for injury to the arm. What these laws do, however, is drive the understanding of the value of the body social. As Wormald comments in relation to the structure of Alfred's laws, they develop according to logical connections; 'continuity was preserved, even if the overall result was that the code went round in circles'.[73] In fact, the two laws regarding genital wounds and the law on the arm provide a kind of logic through which to understand the injury tariffs as a whole and the structurally fragmented list in particular. The apparent structural disruption invites interpretation as the riddles do in revealing and concealing and suggest a common logic is applied to all of the injuries in this list.[74]

The break in the head-to-toe order disrupts the otherwise clear logical progression of the *Domboc* and invites interpretation:

> [65] Gif mon sie on þa herðan to ðam swiðe wund, þæt he ne mæge bearn gestrienan, gebete him ðæt mid LXXX scill.
>
> If a man is so badly wounded in the testicles that he cannot beget children, compensate him for that with 80 shillings.
>
> [66] Gif men sie se earm mid honda mid ealle ofacorfen beforan elmbogan, gebete ðæt mid LXXX scill.
> [66.1] Æghwelcere wunde beforan feaxe and beforan sliefan and beneoðan cneowe sio bot bið twysceatte mare.
>
> If the arm of a man be cut off at the elbow, complete with the hand, compensate it with 80 shillings.
> Each wound before the hair and before the sleeve and beneath the knee should be compensated with two sceattas more.
>
> [67] Gif sio lendenbræde bið forslegen, þær sceal LX scill. to bote.
> [67.1] Gif hio bið onbestungen, geselle XV scill. to bote.
> [67.2] Gif hio bið ðurhðyrel, ðonne sceal ðær XXX scill. to bote

[73] Wormald, *The Making of English Law*, p. 270.
[74] Nelson, 'The Rhetoric of the Exeter Book Riddles', p. 424.

> If the loins are violently struck, pay 60 shillings as compensation; if they are pierced, give 15 shillings as compensation; if they are pierced through, then pay 30 shillings as compensation.

Alfred 65 clearly addresses the loss of function. There is a further implication of loss of function with the odd qualifier in Alfred 66 that the compensation is for an arm cut off at the elbow *complete with the hand*. Presumably, if the hand had already been lost, the loss of the forearm alone would be worth far less. Of particular note is that the *bot* for these injuries is equal. The only other injuries worth as much are a shin struck off at the knee, 80 shillings (Alfred 72), and the damage of tendons in the neck, so that the victim loses control of his head, 100 shillings (Alfred 77). The logic connecting these laws suggests that the concern is for the work that the individual is able to contribute to the society. However, Alfred 65 significantly lowers the compensation to be paid for a wound that deprives a man of his ability to procreate from the three-fold *wergild* in Æthelberht 64. In fact, it is hardly more expensive than a straightforward wound to the genitals in Alfred 67, expensive though that is. In this shift from Æthelberht 64, Alfred's injury tariffs seem to agree with the social framework laid out in his *Consolation of Philosophy*. Each of the three categories of men is necessary to the society and the work each does is equally necessary. Injuries that deprive a man of the bodily tools that allow him to contribute are thus compensated equally. Moreover, it is not difficult to see that the penis, the hand, and the foot would be of equal value to a thegn or a churl. What then stands out in the logic of Alfred's injury tariffs, highlighted by the logic that binds the final set, is the revaluation of the individual body that understands all men as equally important in their contributions to the Anglo-Saxon society. Manhood, in both the body legal and the oath-bound man, is elaborated in relationship to the labor he provides to the king, no longer simply to the family.

Analyzing the laws through the riddles offers a new way of conceiving of the laws. If the riddles are intended to drive thought processes and the development of logical connections, and if Wormald's claim that the laws are primarily ideological documents is accurate, then it is reasonable to think of the riddles and the laws working in similar ways. Thus it is important to focus on the exception of Æthelberht 64 and the logic that appears to drive the structural shift in Alfred's list of injury tariffs. The texts discussed here (riddles and laws alike) all present the male procreative organ as an object that is fundamentally social in its purpose. However, the value attributed to the injured genitals indicates how the society values the body social. In the change from Æthelberht's to Alfred's laws there is significant development: the status of a person was differentiated from the contribution the individual made to the society. This is a reflection on the social value of the individual and how the laws attempt to deal not with the (male) individual himself – which is adequately addressed by the earlier composition laws – but with the work he can do within the society, how he is productive. Manhood, then, under the law, is not about which tool a man uses – penis, sword, or shovel – but what he can contribute to the maintenance of the society, workforce, and work. The body is a collection of tools, but a whole man makes use of them to maintain the wholeness of society.

Reading through references to violence against the genitals in the Exeter Book riddles and the laws of Æthelberht and Alfred provides evidence for how the Anglo-Saxons viewed the embodied and sexed individual, which provides an answer to the social theory question that started this: 'Is the person merely a collection of roles or is the person the organizing principle which integrates and orchestrates given social roles?'[75] Like the penis to the body, the individual only held a value for what he contributed in social relations. For the riddles, there are both practical (procreative) and pleasurable relationships between man and woman, object and individual; for Æthelberht, the individual contributes to the larger society through his role within his family; for Alfred, the man is of value in his relationship as an individual capable of contributing to what the king requires.

The secular Old English texts which address violent action on the male genitals, considering the understanding of the male member, point to the shifting relationship of the individual to society in Anglo-Saxon England. Reading the laws through the model of the riddles' redirecting an audience's focus by revealing and concealing points up the laws' own way of suggesting an imagined social structure, how an individual fits into it, and how manhood is defined in relation to it. There is a shift from a fragmented, family-, and feud-oriented imagined social structure to one based on the relationship of individual to king. And in this, the society can only be successful if *fulmannod*,[76] with all its members valued equally.

[75] Turner, *Body and Society*, p. 29.
[76] Godden and Irvine, ed., *The Old English Boethius*, vol. 2, B 17, p. 26.

CHAPTER 7

'Imbrued in their owne bloud': Castration in Early Welsh and Irish Sources

Charlene M. Eska

In his 1587 *Chronicles*, Raphael Holinshed describes the following events surrounding the aftermath of the Battle of Bryn Glas in June of 1402:

> [Y]et neither the crueltie of Tomyris nor yet of Fuluia is comparable to this of the Welshwomen; which is worthie to be recorded to the shame of a sex pretending to the title of weake vessels, and yet raging with such force of fiercenesse and barbarisme. For the dead bodies of the Englishmen, being aboue a thousand lieng vpun the ground imbrued in their owne bloud, was a sight [a man would thinke] greeuous to looke vpon, and so farre from exciting and stirring vp affections of crueltie; that it should rather haue mooued the beholders to commiseration and mercie: yet did the women of Wales cut off their priuities, and put one part thereof into the mouthes of euerie dead man, in such sort that the cullions hoong downe to their chins; and not so contented, they did cut off their noses and thrust them into their tailes as they laie on the ground mangled and defaced.[1]

The author assures his readers that these deeds were done in open sight and recorded in history, thus justifying his need to relate the events in his mother tongue so that all his countrymen will know (Holinshed 2:528). Holinshed continues what is in all actuality nothing but anti-Welsh propaganda, despite it being recorded in contemporary sources such as the *Annales Ricardi Secundi et Henrici Quarti*:

1 Raphael Holinshed, *The Chronicles of England, Scotland and Ireland* (London: John Harison, George Bishop, Rafe Newberie, Henrie Denham, and Thomas Woodcocke, 1587), 2:528. Translations are my own unless otherwise noted. I should like to thank Katharine Olson for valuable discussion on medieval Welsh historical sources. I should also like to thank Robin Chapman Stacey for reading a draft of this paper and making many valuable suggestions for improvements. Any oversights are, of course, my own. Hereafter, references are given in parenthesis.

> Ibique perpetratum est facinus, a sæculis inauditum: nam foeminæ Wallencium, post conflictum, accesserant ad corpora peremptorum, et, abscindentes membra genitalia, in ore cujuslibet posuerunt membrum pudendum, inter dentes testiculis dependentibus, supra mentum; et nasos abscissos presserunt in culis eorundem.[2]
>
> In that place was performed a deed unheard of by people: namely the Welsh women, after the fight, approached the dead bodies, and, having cut off the genitals, they placed the shameful member in the mouth of each [dead man], between the teeth with the testicles hanging down above the chin; and the torn off noses they pressed into their anuses.

Holinshed's gruesome description of the mutilation of the bodies of the dead Englishmen was, furthermore, the source of Westmorland's speech to King Henry in Shakespeare's *I Henry IV*:

> My liege, this haste was hot in question,
> And many limits of the charge set down
> But yesternight, when all athwart there came
> A post from Wales, loaden with heavy news,
> Whose worst was that the noble Mortimer,
> Leading the men of Herefordshire to fight
> Against the irregular and wild Glyndŵr,
> Was by the rude hands of that Welshman taken,
> A thousand of his people butchered,
> Upon whose dead corpse' there was such misuse,
> Such beastly shameless transformation,
> By those Welshwomen done as may not be
> Without much shame retold or spoken of.[3]

Shakespeare's play thus immortalizes a lie, but raises the question: to what extent was castration a form of punishment during the Middle Ages in the British Isles? The evidence from medieval Wales answers this question to some extent and suggests that the Welsh (and probably the Irish) borrow from the Normans a means of dealing with political enemies. Significantly, what seems not to have been borrowed was the cultural stigma attached to castration; for

[2] 'Annales Ricardi Secundi et Henrici Quarti', in *Johannis de Trokelowe et Anon Chronica et Annales*, ed. H. T. Riley, Rolls Series (London: Longmans, Green, Reader, and Dyer, 1866), p. 341; and R. R. Davies, *The Revolt of Owain Glyn Dŵr* (Oxford: Oxford University Press, 1995), p. 157.

[3] William Shakespeare, *I Henry IV*, in *The Norton Shakespeare*, gen. ed. Stephen Greenblatt (New York: W. W. Norton & Company, 1997) p. 1158, 1.1.35–46 and n. 5. I should like to thank Ernest W. Sullivan II for pointing me towards this reference. See also Richard Hosley, ed. *Shakespeare's Holinshed* (New York: G. P. Putnam's Sons, 1968), pp. 98–108.

the Irish and the Welsh, castration was an effective means of eliminating future rivals and avoiding the taint of being a kin-slayer.[4]

The medieval Welsh laws, like those of the Anglo-Saxons and Irish, are based on a system of compensation. They are, however, later in date than the earliest Anglo-Saxon and Irish codes, only being attested from the thirteenth century. That being said, early and late features of the codes can be detected. There are different versions of the Welsh laws; the main ones are *Llyfr Cyfnerth*, *Llyfr Iorwerth*, the Latin redactions (A, B, C, D, and E), and *Llyfr Blegywryd*, which is largely a Welsh translation of Latin D. Other redactions, i.e., *Llyfr Colan* (which is a reworking of *Llyfr Iorwerth*), Latin C, and *Llyfr Cynog*, do not survive in any manuscript in a complete copy. *Llyfr Cyfnerth*, *Llyfr Iorwerth*, and *Llyfr Blegywryd* survive in multiple manuscripts, and, especially with *Llyfr Cyfnerth* and *Llyfr Iorwerth*, there can be a great deal of variation in the texts from one manuscript to another.[5]

The 'laws of women' are of particular significance because there are clear indications of English influence in the laws regarding rape, including castration as punishment in certain circumstances.[6] According to the *Llyfr Iorweth* version of the law (§50), if a man rapes a woman, he pays a fine to the king and her lord. If she was a virgin, she is paid a series of very expensive fines, and if she was married, her husband's insult-price is augmented by half and paid to him.[7] The *Llyfr Cyfnerth* version is different in that manuscripts *U*,[8] *W*,[9] and *X*[10] all contain additional material not found in *V*,[11] *Mk*,[12] and *Z*,[13] specifically, the material that corresponds to *U* §73/19–21.[14] *Llyfr Cyfnerth Mk* §73/14–15a lists

4 Lizabeth Johnson, 'Mutilation as Cultural Commerce and Criticism: The Transmission, Practice, and Meaning of Castration and Blinding in Medieval Wales', *Istoria* 1 (2008):1–23 at pp. 14, 17.

5 T. M. Charles-Edwards, *The Welsh Laws* (Cardiff: University of Wales Press, 1989), pp. 20–1.

6 For a discussion of some of the outside influences on Welsh law, see Morfydd E. Owen, 'The *Excerpta de Libris Romanorum et Francorum* and *Cyfraith Hywel*', in *Tair Colofn Cyfraith, The Three Columns of Law in Medieval Wales: Homicide, Theft and Fire*, ed. T. M. Charles-Edwards and Paul Russell (Bangor: Welsh Legal History Society, 2005), pp. 171–95. I should like to thank Robin Chapman Stacey for valuable assistance on this topic.

7 'The "Iorwerth" Text', ed. and trans. T. M. Charles-Edwards in *The Welsh Law of Women*, ed. Dafydd Jenkins and Morfydd E. Owen (Cardiff: University of Wales Press, 1980), pp. 161–79.

8 National Library of Wales, MS Peniarth 37.

9 British Library, MS Cotton Cleopatra A.XIV.

10 British Library, MS Cotton Cleopatra B. V.

11 British Library, MS Harleian 4353.

12 Bodorgan MS, the property of Sir George Meyrick.

13 National Library of Wales, MS Peniarth 259.

14 Dafydd Jenkins, 'The "Cyfnerth" Text', in *The Welsh Law of Women*, pp. 132–45 at p. 134. Transcriptions of Welsh often use '6' for 'w' which reflects the form of the letter found in the manuscripts. I have followed the editorial convention of my primary sources.

a series of fines paid to the woman and her lord for her rape, which is similar in structure and content to that found in *Llyfr Iorwerth*:

> 14 Y neb a dycco treis ar wreic, talet y hamobyr y'r argl6yd a'e dir6y, a'e dilysta6t a'e heg6edi a'e sarhaet a tal idi hitheu. 15 Or g6atta g6r treissa6 g6reic, ac os kadarnha y wreic yn y herbyn, kymeret hi y gala y g6r yn y lla6 asseu, a'r creir yn y lla6 deheu, a thyget ry d6yn treis ohona6 ef erni hi a'r gala honno, ac uelly ny chyll hi dim o'e ia6n. 15a Y neb a wato tries, rodet l6 deg wyr a deu vgeint heb gaeth a heb alltut.

> 14 He who rapes a woman, let him pay her amobr to the lord and her dirwy; and her dilystod and agweddi and sarhead he pays to her. 15 If a man denies raping a woman and the woman confirms it against him, let her take the man's penis in her left hand the relic in her right hand, and let her swear that she was raped by him with that penis, and so she will lose none of her right. 15a He who denies rape, let him give the oath of fifty men without a slave and without an alien.[15]

Llyfr Cyfnerth U §73/19–21 states that if a man does not deny the charge of rape, he must pay the woman a series of fines and he must pay the king a silver rod.[16] If he cannot pay these fines, his testicles are to be removed. If he raped two women, each woman receives one of the testicles:

> 19 Od ymda gwreic e hunan, a dyuot g6r idi a'e threissa6, os diwat a wna yr g6r roddet l6 deng wyr a deugeint, a thri ohonunt yn diofreda6c, o uarchogaeth a lliein, a gwreic. 20 Ony myn diwat, talet y'r wreic y gwada6l, a'e dilysta6t, a dir6y a gwialen aryant y'r brenh*in* yn y wed y dylyo. 21 Ony eill y g6r y thalu dyker y d6y geill.

> 19 If a woman travels alone, and a man comes to her and rapes her, if the man denies let him give the oath of fifty men, three of them being under vows against horsemanship and linen and women. 20 If he does not wish to deny, let him pay the woman her gwaddol and her dilystod, and a dirwy and a silver rod to the king in the manner which is right. 21 If the man cannot pay let his two testicles be taken.[17]

In the Latin versions of the Welsh laws, there is a similar situation. Latin C

[15] Jenkins, 'The "Cyfnerth" Text', pp. 138–9. *Amobr, dilystod, agweddi, sarhead, dirvvy*, and *gwaddol* refer to specific kinds of payment depending on the victim's sexual status.

[16] The length of the rod is given in other texts as being as tall as the king's head while he is sitting. See Paul Russell, *Welsh Law in Medieval Anglesey: British Library Harleian MS 1796 (Latin C)* (Cambridge: Seminar Cyfraith Hywel, 2011), pp. xxxix–xli.

[17] Jenkins, 'The "Cyfnerth" Text', pp. 142–3. Although castration is not found in the main text of manuscript *Z*, it is found in the 'tail'. As with the other references to castration, it appears as the final clause of the section; *Llawysgrif Pomffred: An Edition and Study of Peniarth MS 259B*, ed. and trans. Sara Elin Roberts (Leiden: Brill, 2011), pp. 23–6, and #1331.

does not contain laws dealing with rape,[18] but the other Latin texts do. Latin B[19] and Latin E[20] both have a final clause added onto the end of the section that the other texts do not, listing castration as the punishment for rape if the offender cannot pay the appropriate fines. Latin A[21] and Latin D[22] make no mention of castration. *Llyfr Blegywryd* likewise does not include castration as a punishment;[23] the text specifically states that castration is *not* the punishment for rape in the law of Hywel Dda, implying that this practice has been borrowed: 'Nyt oes yg kyfreith Hywel Da yspadu gwr yr treissaw gwraic' [In the law of Hywel Dda, there is no castrating of a man for the rape of a woman] (63.31–2). The very fact that the redactor of the tract felt the need to state this fact is revealing in and of itself. It demonstrates a knowledge of the legal practices of other cultures and implies that in some areas of Wales castration had been making inroads as a valid legal punishment for rape.

In her edition and translation of Cyfnerth manuscript Z, Sara Elin Roberts discusses English influences found in the 'tail' of the manuscript. Her wording, however, is ambiguous as to whether she believes that these influences are pre- or post-1282:

> Much of the other material in the tail of Z also appears to be post-1282, and there are elements which point to influence from England: the possible reference to dueling, the references to losing a limb as a punishment for theft, and castrating a man for rape are not found in Welsh law. This suggests greater English influence in Wales after the conquest of 1282, or perhaps a Marcher origin for some of the texts in Z if not for the manuscript itself.[24]

As demonstrated by the material from Latin B (which exists in a mid-thirteenth-

18 Latin C is the earliest of the Latin texts, dating to between 1226 and *c.* 1240. See Russell, *Welsh Law in Medieval Anglesey*, p. xliii.

19 Hywel D. Emanuel, ed., *The Latin Texts of the Welsh Laws* (Cardiff: University of Wales Press, 1967), p. 224.17–26 (hereafter *LTWL*). The manuscript dates to the middle of the thirteenth century. See Charles-Edwards, *The Welsh Laws*, p. 102; and Daniel Huws, *Medieval Welsh Manuscripts* (Aberystwyth: University of Wales Press and The National Library of Wales, 2000), pp. 58–9.

20 *LTWL*, p. 473.8–15. Cambridge, Corpus Christi College MS 454, which contains the law code, dates to the first half of the fifteenth century. See Charles-Edwards, *The Welsh Laws*, p. 102.

21 *LTWL*, p. 144.29–37; and Ian F. Fletcher, trans., *Latin A Redaction of the Law of Hywel* (Aberystwyth: Centre for Advanced Welsh and Celtic Studies, University of Wales, 1986). The manuscript dates to the mid-thirteenth century. See Charles-Edwards, *The Welsh Laws*, pp. 34–6, and 102, and references therein.

22 *LTWL*, 338.10–14. The manuscript dates to *c.* 1300. See Huws, *Medieval Welsh Manuscripts*, p. 58.

23 *Llyfr Blegywryd*, ed. Stephen J. Williams and J. Enoch Powell, 2nd edn (Cardiff: University of Wales Press, 1961), 43.31–41.1; and *The Laws of Hywel Dda (The Book of Blegywryd)*, trans. Melville Richards (Liverpool: Liverpool University Press, 1954).

24 Roberts, *Llawysgrif Pomffred*, pp. 21–2.

century manuscript), i.e., that castration was a punishment for rape, there was definite influence from English law before 1282. Thus, the later English influence Roberts sees in *Z* need not necessarily be post-1282; for example, the Welsh word *edling* (heir-apparent) was borrowed from Anglo-Saxon *ætheling*.[25] The influence did not only go in one direction. Robin Chapman Stacey has pointed out that §33 of the laws of Alfred contains an example of the 'God-suretyship' (*godborges*) found in Welsh law (*briduw*) and suggests that there is a strong possibility that this concept was borrowed from Welsh law.[26]

The earliest Anglo-Saxon law code, the laws of Æthelberht, makes no mention of castration as a punishment.[27] Like the early Welsh law codes, the usual punishment for rape in the Anglo-Saxon laws was to pay compensation to the victim's kin, e.g., Æthelberht §10.[28]

> 10. Gif a man wið cyninges mægdenam geligeþ, L scillenga gebete.
> 11. Gif hio grindende þeowa sio, XXV scillenga gebete.
>
> 10. If a man lies with the king's maiden, let him pay 50 shillings.
> 11. If she should be a 'grinding' slave, let him pay 25 shillings.[29]

Julie Coleman has noticed the difference in the fine structure between the law as stated in Æthelberht §10 and that as stated in Alfred §11; in Æthelberht, fines are paid to a woman's legal guardian, while in Alfred they are paid to the woman herself according to her social and moral standing.[30] The law is rather different, though, if the situation involves the rape of a slave:

25 *The Law of Hywel Dda: Law Texts from Medieval Wales*, ed. and trans. Dafydd Jenkins (Llandysul: Gomer Press, 1986), pp. 222–3.

26 Robin Chapman Stacey, *The Road to Judgment: From Custom to Court in Medieval Ireland and Wales* (Philadelphia: University of Pennsylvania Press, 1994), pp. 208–9.

27 Jay Paul Gates gives a detailed analysis of castration and genital injuries (and their relative absence) in Anglo-Saxon injury tariffs in his article in this volume, 'The *Fulmannod* Society: Social Valuing of the (Male) Legal Subject', pp. 131–48.

28 *Die Gesetze der Angelsachsen*, ed. and trans. F. Liebermann (Halle: M. Niemeyer, 1898–1912), 1:3; and Lisi Oliver, *The Beginnings of English Law* (Toronto: University of Toronto Press, 2002), p. 64; §10 in *Die Gesetze der Angelsachsen* corresponds to Oliver's §16.

29 Text and translation from Oliver, *The Beginning of English Law*, pp. 64 and 65. I have retained the section numbering found in *Die Gesetze der Angelsachsen*.

30 Julie Coleman, 'Rape in Anglo-Saxon England', in *Violence and Society in the Early Medieval West*, ed. Guy Halsall (Woodbridge: Boydell Press, 1998), pp. 193–204 at p. 198. Carole Hough, 'Alfred's *Domboc* and the Language of Rape: A Reconsideration of Alfred ch.11', *Medium Ævum* 66 (1997): 1–27. Hough notes that this 'constitutes the earliest explicit reference in the extant Anglo-Saxon laws to a woman's right to receive compensation for offenses against herself' (p. 5). See also Shari Horner, 'The Language of Rape in Old English Literature and Law: Views from the Anglo-Saxon(ist)s', in *Sex and Sexuality in Anglo-Saxon England*, ed. Carol Braun Pasternack and Lisa M. C. Weston (Tempe: Arizona Center for Medieval and Renaissance Studies, 2004), pp. 149–81; and Sir Frederick Pollock and Frederic William Maitland, *The History of English Law before the Time of Edward I*, 2nd edn (Cambridge: Cambridge University Press, 1898: Liberty Fund repr. 2009), pp. 513–15.

25. Gif mon ceorles mennen to nedhæmde geðreatað mid V scill. gebete þam ceorle, LX scill. to wito.
    1. Gif ðeowmon þeowne to nedhæmde genede, bete mid his eowende.[31]

25. If anyone rapes a ceorl's slave-woman, he is to pay 5 shillings compensation to the ceorl, and 60 shillings' fine.
    1. If a slave rapes a slave-woman, he is to pay by suffering castration.[32]

The penalties change and become much more severe in the eleventh- or twelfth-century *Leis Willelme*,[33] but Carole Hough has noted the direct parallel between this section of the law code and the passage in Alfred §11:[34]

18. Cil ki purgist femme a force, forfeit ad les menbres.
    1. Ki abat femme a terre pur fere lui force, la munte al seinur X solo.
    2. S'il la purgist, forfeit est de membres.[35]

18. If anyone assaults a woman he shall suffer castration as a penalty.
    1. If anyone throws a woman to the ground in order to offer violence to her, the compensation to her lord for breach of his *mund* shall be 10 shillings.
    2. If he assaults her, he shall suffer castration.[36]

The mid-thirteenth-century legal writer Henry de Bracton notes that in former times the punishment for rape was loss of life,[37] but that, in his own time, the punishment for the rape of a virgin was blinding and castration.[38] However, in Ruth Kittel's examination of thirteenth-century rape cases, she found that not only was the guilty party usually only charged a relatively small fine, but also that (out of all those convicted), not a single one was castrated,

[31] *Die Gesetze der Angelsachsen*, 1:62 and 64.

[32] Dorothy Whitelock, M. Brett, and C. N. L. Brooke, eds, *Councils and Synods with Other Documents Relating to the English Church*, vol. 1: *AD 871–1204*, part 1, *871–1066* (Oxford: Clarendon Press, 1981), p. 31. See also David A. E. Pelteret, *Slavery in Early Medieval England: From the Reign of Alfred until the Twelfth Century* (Woodbridge: Boydell Press, 1995), pp. 81–9.

[33] Liebermann, *Die Gesetze der Angelsachsen*, 1:492 dates the text to between 1090 and 1135; see also Patrick Wormald, *The Making of English Law: King Alfred to the Twelfth Century* (Oxford: Blackwell, 1999), pp. 407–409.

[34] Hough, 'Alfred's *Domboc* and the Language of Rape', pp. 19–20.

[35] *Die Gesetze der Angelsachsen*, 1:504.

[36] A. J. Robertson, *The Laws of the Kings of England from Edmond to Henry I* (Cambridge: Cambridge University Press, 1925), pp. 262–263. Castration is also mentioned as the punishment for rape in the *Anglo-Saxon Chronicle*; see Dorothy Whitelock, trans. *The Anglo-Saxon Chronicle* (New Brunswick, NJ: Rutgers University Press, 1961), *s.a.* 1087.

[37] Henry de Bracton, *De Legibus et Consuetudinibus Angliæ*, ed. George E. Woodbine (New Haven, CT: Yale University Press, 1915–1942); Bracton, *On the Laws and Customs of England*, trans. Samuel E. Thorne (Cambridge, MA: Harvard University Press, 1968), fol. 148.

[38] Bracton, *On the Laws and Customs of England*, fol. 147.

thus highlighting the difference between the laws as stated and the legal reality of the time.[39]

Although compiled more than a generation after the Conquest, the so-called *Leis Willelme* (Laws of William the Conqueror)[40] state that the death penalty in England is to be abolished and replaced with blinding and castration:

> 10. Interdico etiam, ne quis occidatur aut suspendatur pro aliqua cupla, sed eruantur oculi et testiculi abscidantur; et hoc praeceptum non sit uiolatum super forisfacturam meam plenam.[41]
>
> 10. I also forbid that anyone shall be slain or hanged for any fault, but let his eyes be put out and let him be castrated. And this command shall not be violated under pain of a fine in full to me.[42]

It is easy to dismiss this text for a variety of reasons, not least of which is, as Klaus van Eickels has noted, that capital punishment was still being practiced after 1066.[43] Furthermore, physical mutilation was already in the pre-Conquest legal system, as Jay Gates explains in his chapter in this volume.[44] Thus, at the time this text was written, capital punishment and mutilation were both facets of the legal system. Article 10 is, however, culturally relevant. Van Eickels has explored the history of blinding and castration as a means of eliminating political enemies in Anglo-Norman England. He traces this punishment back to medieval Scandinavia, where (as in Ireland) there were cultural taboos surrounding the killing of members of one's kin-group, bearing in mind that most of the free families were related to each other. Van Eickels further argues that this practice of castrating and blinding enemies rather than killing them

39 Ruth Kittel, 'Rape in Thirteenth-Century England: A Study of the Common-Law Courts', in *Women and the Law*, ed. D. Kelly Weisberg, vol. 2 (Cambridge, MA: Schenkman Publishing Co., 1982), pp. 101–15 at pp. 108–10.

40 This text is fraught with difficulties surrounding its correct title, manuscript tradition, and origins. For an overview, see Wormald, *The Making of English Law*, pp. 402–4. Not only does this text share the same manuscript tradition as *Instituta Cnuti*, but the *Instituta Cnuti* clearly influenced the text. Without doubt the *Instituti Cnuti* are based on I and II Cnut; see Wormald, *The Making of English Law*, p. 404; and Lieberman, *Die Gesetze der Angelsachsen*, 3:277–9. In this volume, see Larissa Tracy, '"Al defouleden is holie bodi": Castration, the Sexualization of Torture, and Anxieties of Identity in the *South English Legendary*', pp. 87–107.

41 *Die Gesetze der Angelsachsen*, 1:488.

42 David C. Douglas and George W. Greenway, eds., *English Historical Documents 1042–1189*, 2nd edn (London: Eyre & Spottiswoode, 1968), p. 400.

43 Klaus van Eickels, 'Gendered Violence: Castration and Blinding as Punishment for Treason in Normandy and Anglo-Norman England', *Gender and History* 16 (2004): 588–602 at p. 589; see also John Earle, ed., *Two of the Saxon Chronicles Parallel* (Oxford: Clarendon Press, 1865), p. 253, *s.a.* 1124; trans. in Whitelock, *The Anglo-Saxon Chronicle*, p. 191.

44 Gates, 'The *Fulmannod* Society'.

was brought from Scandinavia to Normandy with the early settlers in the tenth century.[45] The practice continued as part of Norman culture and was brought to England with the Conquest.[46] The Anglo-Saxon codes already had elements of this practice in place, thus making the addition of judicial blinding and castration to the legal system seem more of a point on a continuum rather than a wholesale new practice.[47] For example, the pre-Conquest law code Cnut II §30.4–5 lists several forms of mutilation, including scalping, blinding, removal of the ears, nose, hands, upper lip, and feet, as the punishment for various crimes, so the later addition of another form of mutilation, i.e. castration, would not be entirely new to the legal system.[48] Just as changes in the Anglo-Saxon legal system can be seen as the result of contact and conquest, the same can be said of the Welsh laws.

In many ways, the Welsh annals present a similar picture to that found in the Irish annals[49] in that there are references therein to politically motivated blindings and castrations. For example, in the year 1130,[50] Meredudd ap Bleddyn had Llywelyn ab Owain castrated and blinded. In that same year, Madog ap Llywarch was slain by Meurig, his first cousin. The following year,

45 In this volume, Anthony Adams discusses the application of castration as a punishment in Norse sources in his article '"He took a stone away": Castration and Cruelty in the Old Norse *Sturlunga saga*', pp. 188–209. Although van Eickels's argument is persuasive and no doubt correct, there is some concern regarding whether the practice was truly as common as he would lead us to believe.

46 van Eickels, 'Gendered Violence', pp. 593–4. See also John Gillingham, 'Killing and Mutilating Political Enemies in the British Isles from the Late Twelfth to the Early Fourteenth Century: A Comparative Study', in *Britain and Ireland 900–1300*, ed. Brendan Smith (Cambridge: Cambridge University Press, 1999), pp. 114–34.

47 This practice would continue for many years. Cf. the account in the *Anglo-Saxon Chronicle s.a.* 1125 of Henry ordering all the moneyers in England not only to be castrated, but also to lose their right hands: Whitelock, *The Anglo-Saxon Chronicle*, p. 191.

48 Cf. also the account of Gowine 'mutilating' the companions of Alfred: Whitlock, *The Anglo-Saxon Chronicle*, *s.a.* 1036.

49 For discussions of the Welsh annals and their relationship to each other and the Irish annals, see John Edward Lloyd, 'The Welsh Chronicles', *Proceedings of the British Academy* 14 (1928): 369–91; Thomas Jones, 'Historical Writing in Medieval Welsh', *Scottish Studies* 12 (1968): 15–27; Kathleen Hughes, 'The Welsh Latin Chronicles: *Annales Cambriae* and Related Texts', *Proceedings of the British Academy* 59 (1973): 233–58; Brynley Roberts, 'Geoffrey of Monmouth and Welsh Historical Tradition', *Nottingham Medieval Studies* 20 (1976): 29–40; Kathleen Hughes, *Celtic Britain in the Early Middle Ages*, ed. David Dumville (Woodbridge: Boydell Press, 1980); Caroline Brett, 'The Prefaces of Two Late Thirteenth-Century Welsh Latin Chronicles', *Bulletin of the Board of Celtic Studies* 35 (1988): 63–73; J. Beverley Smith, *The Sense of History in Medieval Wales* (Aberystwyth: University College of Wales, 1991); Julian Harrison, 'A Note on Gerald of Wales and *Annales Cambriae*', *Welsh History Review* 17 (1994): 252–255; David N. Dumville, *Annales Cambriae, AD 682–954: Texts A–C in Parallel* (Cambridge: Department of Anglo-Saxon, Norse and Celtic, 2002), pp. v–xv; and Erik Grigg, '"Mole Rain" and Other Natural Phenomena in the Welsh Annals: Can *Mirabilia* Unravel the Textual History of the *Annales Cambriae*?', *Welsh History Review* 24.4 (2009): 1–40.

50 This is the earliest year in which there is record of castration in the Welsh sources.

Meurig was blinded and castrated in revenge for Madog's death.[51] The Welsh annals do record incidents of politically motivated blindings, e.g., in the Red Book of Hergest version of the *Brut* for the year 1113. Lizabeth Johnson notes that all the incidents of castration post-date the Norman Conquest, which strongly suggests that the practice was borrowed from the Normans. She uses the work of van Eickels as her starting point and expands the area of inquiry to medieval Wales, pointing out the cultural differences between Welsh and Norman attitudes towards castration. For the Welsh, a castrated man could not reproduce and as such could not produce a political rival. For the Normans, castration carried the stigma of effeminacy. This stigma and the gendered language surrounding castration are lacking in the Welsh sources.[52] The introduction of castration as a punishment into the Welsh law codes most likely also post-dates the Norman Conquest. There are far fewer references to mutilation in general in the Welsh sources than the Irish sources (discussed below), but there is still the possibility (as with the Irish sources) that not all incidents of castration were recorded as such. Taking into account the situation in Wales, it may not be a coincidence that all of the recorded accounts of castration in the Irish annals also post-date the 1169 Norman invasion of Ireland.

Understandably, the Welsh annals are concerned not only with events in Wales, but also with those involving their English neighbors. For example, both the Peniarth 20 and Red Book of Hergest versions of the *Brut* record for the year 1004 the politically motivated blinding of the Anglo-Saxons Wulfheah and Ufegeat.[53] The annals also mention the blinding and possible castration of Henry II's Welsh hostages in 1165. When the Welsh broke the peace they had sworn to Henry II, he launched a campaign against them. After being defeated by bad weather in the Berwyn Mountains, Henry decided to return to England. Furious at the loss of his own men, resources, and time, he took his anger out on his Welsh hostages: he had the men blinded and possibly castrated, and he had the ears and noses of the female hostages cut off.[54]

[51] *Brut y Tywysogyon: Peniarth MS. 20*, ed. Thomas Jones (Cardiff: University of Wales Press, 1941); *Brut y Tywysogyon: Peniarth MS. 20*, trans. Thomas Jones (Cardiff: University of Wales Press, 1952); *Brut y Tywysogyon: Red Book of Hergest Version*, ed. and trans. Thomas Jones (Cardiff: University of Wales Press, 1955); *Brenhinedd y Saesson*, ed. and trans. Thomas Jones (Cardiff: University of Wales Press, 1971); and *Annales Cambriae*, ed. John Williams ab Ithel (London: Longman, Green, Longman, and Roberts, 1860). The Peniarth 20 and Red Book of Hergest versions of the *Brut* contain incidents of castration for the years 1130, 1131, and 1175. The *Annales Cambriae* has accounts of castration for the years 1130, 1131, and 1166, and the *Brenhinedd y Saesson* for the years 1130 and 1131.

[52] Johnson, 'Mutilation as Cultural Commerce and Criticism', pp. 15–20. See also Frederick Suppe, 'The Cultural Significance of Decapitation in High Medieval Wales and the Marches', *Bulletin of the Board of Celtic Studies* 36 (1989): 146–60.

[53] Elizabeth Boyle, 'A Welsh Record of an Anglo-Saxon Political Mutilation', *Anglo-Saxon England* 35 (2006): 245–9.

[54] Both versions of the *Brut* provide an account of Henry's campaign. The blinding of his

Although castration might not figure in the reality presented by the law codes, it is a political reality in the Irish annals.[55] The probable driving force behind so many of the mutilations recorded in the annals is the widespread early belief that a ruler had to be without physical blemish.[56] Part and parcel with this belief is the fact that rulers were expected to be effective military leaders. Thus, if a potential ruler blinds his brother, his brother is no longer eligible for kingship, and a rival is thus eliminated. Furthermore, by mutilating a kinsman, the mutilator is not guilty of the crime of *fingal* 'kin-slaying'.[57] Kin-slaying not only violates the kin-based structure of early Irish society, but it poses legal problems in terms of compensation. The victim's family would normally be paid compensation for their loss, but with kin-slaying, the same group that would receive payment is also the group that would be responsible for contributing to the payment. Thus, it is not possible for kin-slaying to be compensated, nor could the killing be avenged without the avengers themselves being guilty of *fingal*.

There are exceptions to these general statements. Katharine Simms has remarked that there are a number of chiefs in the later years of the annals described with epithets such as *An Cammhuinéalach* 'the wry-necked' Ó Baoighill[58] and Conn *Bacach* 'the lame' Ó Néill.[59] When Brian Bóroimhe's son, Donnchadh, lost his right hand in an attack in 1019, he continued to rule for at least another forty years.[60] Although Irish legal Heptad 13 lists *fingal* as one

male hostages is mentioned, but not castration. The *Annales Cambriae s.a.* 1166 mentions both the blinding and castration. *Chronica de Mailros* refers to the mutilation of the female hostages: *Chronica de Mailros*, ed. Joseph Stevenson (Edinburgh: Bannatyne Club, 1835), p. 79. See also Paul Latimer, 'Henry II's Campaign against the Welsh in 1165', *Welsh Historical Review* 14.4 (1989): 523–52; and Johnson, 'Mutilation as Cultural Commerce and Criticism', pp. 9–10. Van Eickels argues that cutting off the nose of the women was a form of symbolic castration.

55 For an overview of the Irish annals and how they relate to each other, see Katharine Simms, *Medieval Gaelic Sources* (Dublin: Four Courts Press, 2009), pp. 19–38.

56 D. A. Binchy, *Celtic and Anglo-Saxon Kingship* (Oxford: Oxford University Press, 1970), p. 10; Katharine Simms, *From Kings to Warlords* (Woodbridge: Boydell Press, 1987), p. 50.

57 Fergus Kelly, *A Guide to Early Irish Law* (Dublin: Dublin Institute for Advanced Studies, 1988), pp. 127–128 (hereafter *GEIL*). See also Thomas Charles-Edwards, *Early Irish and Welsh Kinship* (Oxford: Oxford University Press, 1993), pp. 119–21.

58 *Annals of the Four Masters*, ed. and trans. John O'Donovan (Dublin: Hodges, Smith, and Co., 1854), *s.a.* 1247 (hereafter *AFM)*.

59 Ibid., *s.a.* 1559.

60 Simms, *From Kings to Warlords*, p. 50. The event is recorded in a number of the annals: *The Annals of Tigernach*, ed. and trans. Whitley Stokes (Felinfach: Llanerch Publishers, 1993), *s.a.* 1018/1019 (hereafter *AT*); *The Annals of Inisfallen*, ed. and trans. Seán Mac Airt (Dublin: Dublin Institute for Advanced Studies, 1988), *s.a.* 1019 (hereafter *AI*); *The Annals of Loch Cé*, ed. and trans. William M. Hennessy (London: Longman and Co., 1871), *s.a.* 1019 (hereafter *ALC*); *The Annals of Ulster (to AD 1131)*, ed. and trans. Seán Mac Airt and Gearóid Mac Niocaill (Dublin: Dublin Institute for Advanced Studies, 1983), *s.a.* 1019 (hereafter *AU*$_2$); and *AFM*, *s.a.* 1018.

of the actions that would cause a king to lose his honor-price,[61] the annals record accounts of kings who gained their thrones by slaying their own kinsmen. For example, the *Annals of Ulster s.a.* 864 (= 865) record the death of Tadc son of Diarmait, king of the Uí Cheinnselaig, by his own kinsmen. For the year 875 (= 876), the same annal records the death of Tadc's killer, his brother Cairpre, who reigned as king of the Uí Cheinnselaig until he himself became the victim of *fingal*.[62]

Despite the unambiguous references to blinding and castration of various personages, Simms has noted with regard to castration that 'there is reason to suppose that this operation is often concealed beneath the annalists' euphemisms of *dalladh* "blinding" and *scathadh* "lopping off"'.[63] As potential candidates for such concealment, she lists the *Annals of Connacht s.a.* 1224.3 (where blinding is given as the punishment for raping a woman), 1244.2 (where Tadc, son of Aed Mac Cathail Chrobdeirg, was *do dalladh* 'blinded' and *do spochad* 'castrated'; in this case the text is explicit), and 1272.4 (which lists the death of the same Tadc from 1244.2; this entry mentions the fact that he was blinded, but says nothing of his castration).[64] Simms includes the *Annals of Ulster s.a.* 1490 (which records the *scathadh* of Tadhg, son of Toirdelbach, son of Philip Mag Uidhir, at the hands of his own kinsmen; 'maimed' is the translation given in the text), 1496 (the same fate befell Eogan at the hands of his

61 *Corpus Iuris Hibernici*, ed. D. A. Binchy (Dublin: Dublin Institute for Advanced Studies, 1979), 14.34 and 15.1–4, at 15.4 (hereafter *CIH*). The text from *CIH* reads: '[A]tait.UII. rig LĀ na dligh dire na logh enech: rig istoing cach recht cina daim *techtai*, ar ni eitech do neoch ma daim *techtai* cia isto; ri ithis gait ⁊ brait; ri feall*as for* einech; ri foluing air no aire; ri feartar cath; ri gaibis cu oc imthecht aenar can a mancaine techta; ri dogne fingal.' [There are seven kings according to Irish law who are not entitled to compensation or honor-price: a king who refuses each lawful person apart from his proper retinue, for it is not refusal [of hospitality] by someone if [he refuses] a proper retinue, though he refuses; a king who eats [food acquired by] theft and robbery; a king who betrays [those under his] protection; a king who tolerates satire or satirizing; a king who is defeated in battle; a king who takes a dog [and] sets off alone without his proper attendants; a king who commits kin-slaying.] There is also a translation of this Heptad in *Ancient Laws of Ireland*, ed. and trans. W. N. Hancock *et al.* (Dublin: A Thom, 1865–1901), 5:172 (hereafter *AL*). The editorial method and translations found in *AL* are widely known to be problematic. In early Irish law, refusing a guest hospitality was considered a crime, although there were limits on a host's obligations. According to this Heptad, a king is obliged to provide hospitality to every lawful person, but not the person's retinue. Although being defeated in battle is considered grounds for a king to lose his honor-price (and thus his kingship), there are no records in the annals of this taking place. See *GEIL*, p. 19. Not only was it considered dishonorable for a king to be without his attendants (except during times of heavy agricultural labor), but it also meant that any woman with an illegitimate child could claim it was the king's. On satire and kingship, see Roisin McLaughlin, *Early Irish Satire* (Dublin: Dublin Institute for Advanced Studies, 2008), pp. 3–4.

62 *AU*$_2$ *s.a.* 864 and 875; this example of *fingal* is discussed in *GEIL*, p. 128, n. 20.

63 Simms, *From Kings to Warlords*, p. 50, n. 71.

64 *Annála Connacht. The Annals of Connacht (AD 1224–1544)*, ed. and trans. A. Martin Freeman (Dublin: Dublin Institute for Advanced Studies, 1996) (hereafter *AC*).

two brothers, Conn the Red and Feidhlimidh), 1503 (records the same injury being done to Donchadh by Domnall, son of O'Domnaill, such that Donchadh died of his injury), and 1504 (when Tadhg Ua hOgain was hanged along with his two sons and an unnamed third man was mutilated).[65] John O'Donovan discusses further evidence of editorial censorship (for lack of a better word) regarding an entry in *The Annals of the Four Masters s.a.* 1244. This entry refers to the same Tadc mentioned in the *Annals of Connacht s.a.* 1244 above, except the text in *The Annals of the Four Masters* has 'Tadhg mac Aodha mic Cathail Croibhdheirg do dhalladh ⁊ do chrochadh,' which the editor translates as 'Teige, the son of Hugh, son of Cathal Crovderg, was blinded and hanged.' O'Donovan notes that 'Charles O'Conor writes *inter lineas* "do spochadh, *potius; vide infra*"'. He also notes that the Dublin copy of the *Annals of Ulster* has *do dalladh ⁊ do sbochadh*, which the old translator of the annals had rendered 'Teige O'Conner blinded and maimed by Coconaght O'Rely' (*AFM* 3:309). Even more recent editors are guilty of leaving out material of this nature. Simms notes that the editor of the *Annals of Clonmacnoise*, Denis Murphy,

> arbitrarily omits parts of the text that were available in the manuscript the editor used, because he considered them unedifying for the general public, for example a passage in which the Vikings are said to have practiced the custom of ius primae noctis, by which the lord claims the right to sleep with every bride on her wedding night, or an implausible tale involving the post-mortem castration of the high-king Niall Glúndub.[66]

At times, editorial 'prudishness' (to quote Whitley Stokes) can be particularly misleading. For example, he notes that Mac Carthy, the translator of the third volume of the *Annals of Ulster s.a.* 1498, rendered 'Ocus tri hordlaighe do bhuain do bhod Emain Moirtla, idon, athair Tomais Mortla, d'orcar do gunna andsa cumusg cetna sin ⁊ tuilledh ar fichid do chlainn do breith dho 'n-a dhiaigh sin' as 'And Edmond Mortel namely, father of Thomas Mortel, was partially mutilated by shot of gun in that same encounter and more than a score of children were born to him after that' when the first clause should read 'three inches were struck off E. M.'s penis'.[67]

Despite these euphemistically worded accounts, there are some entries in the annals that leave no doubt that castration is what is meant. Not all of the

[65] *Annala Uladh. The Annals of Ulster, otherwise Annala Senait, Annals of Senait; A Chronicle of Irish Affairs from* AD *431 to* AD *1540*, ed. and trans. W. M. Hennessy and B. Mac Carthy (Dublin: A. Thom, 1887–1901) (hereafter *AU*).

[66] Simms, *Medieval Gaelic Sources*, p. 27; *The Annals of Clonmacnoise, being Annals of Ireland from the earliest period to* AD *1408 translated into English* AD *1627 by Conell Mageoghagan*, ed. Denis Murphy (Dublin: Royal Society of Antiquaries of Ireland, 1896, repr. Felinfach, 1993) (hereafter *ACl*); and Sarah Sanderlin, 'The Manuscripts of the Annals of Clonmacnoise', *Proceedings of the Royal Irish Academy* 82C (1982): 111–23.

[67] Whitley Stokes, 'The Annals of Ulster', *Revue celtique* 18 (1897): 74–8 at p. 85.

Irish annals contain accounts of castration; for example, the *Annals of Tigernach* does not, although it does contain accounts of other politically motivated mutilations such as blinding.[68] (See Table 7.1 for castrations by annal and year.) In comparison to the number of blindings recorded in the annals, the difference in terms of sheer numbers is striking. (See Table 7.2 for the number of blindings by annal and year.) There is a shift from mutilating to killing starting in the fifteenth century and continuing through the early seventeenth.[69] The number of blindings decreases dramatically, replaced with accounts of beheading, burning, and hanging instead, perhaps indicating a shift away from more 'traditional' methods of eliminating political enemies and the adoption of practices more in line with those of the post-Conquest rulers.[70] Considering Simms's observations and the examples discussed above, the high incidence of recorded blindings most likely masks a number of castrations as well, thus the annals most likely underreport the number of politically motivated castrations, and perhaps incidents of castration in retaliation for rape, making it very difficult to determine how widespread castration was in reality.

It is significant that all of the unambiguous accounts of castration take place after the Norman invasion. Like the Welsh, the Irish seem to have borrowed the practice, but not the Norman social stigma associated with it. An account given for the year 1250 demonstrates this view:

> The cause of the coming of the Burkes to take possession of lands in Tir Amhalgaidh. At one time when the Barretts had supremacy over Tir Amhalgaidh [as we have said], they sent their steward, who was called Sgornach *bhuidh bhearrtha*, to exact rents from the Lynotts. The Lynotts killed this steward, and cast his body into a well called Tobar na Sgornaighe, near Garranard, to the west of the castle of Carns in Tir Amhalgaidh. When the Barretts had received intelligence of this, they assembled their armed forces and attacked the Lynotts, and subdued them. And the Barretts gave the Lynotts their choice of *two modes of punishment*, namely, to have their men either blinded or emasculated; and the Lynotts, by advice of some of the elders among them, took the choice of being blinded, because blind men could propagate their species, whereas emasculated men could not. The Barretts then thrust needles into the eyes of the Lynotts, and accordingly as each man of them was blinded, they compelled him to cross over

[68] Blindings occur for the following years: 999, 1020, 1036, 1037, 1039, 1041, 1069, 1098, 1114, 1136, 1138, 1153, 1156, 1158, 1166, 1168, 1175, and 1177; see Table 7.2. It should be noted that it is not uncommon for an annal to list the death of a person as a result of their injuries. For example, *s.a.* 1036, Donnchad Mac Dunlaing was blinded and died as a result.

[69] This is not to imply that there are no accounts of murders by various means before the fifteenth century; there are a number of such accounts.

[70] E.g., *AFM s.a.* 1452, 1474, 1478, 1496, 1504, 1505, 1552, 1557, 1582, 1583, 1584, 1586, 1589, 1590, 1591, 1595, 1599, 1600, 1601, 1602, 1611, and 1615.

> the stepping-stones of Clochan na n-dall, near Carns, to see if more or less of sight remained with them, and if any of them crossed the Clochan without stumbling he was taken back and re-blinded![71]

By way of contrast with medieval Wales and Anglo-Saxon England, the canonical texts of the early Irish law codes (as opposed to the annals) were compiled within a fairly narrow period of time, *c.* AD 650–800, based on linguistic evidence. Most of the surviving law codes (in varying states of completeness) are found in manuscripts that date to the fourteenth through sixteenth centuries.[72] Many of the texts were glossed and commented upon by generations of Irish legal scholars, and, as a result of such activity, the volume of material surrounding any given text can be quite substantial. Members of the hereditary Irish legal families produced many of the surviving manuscripts, often in collaboration with each other.[73] Despite the continuous copying and recopying of the texts and accompanying glosses and commentary, the scribes and glossators on the whole tended not to make substantive changes to the texts themselves, thus preserving linguistically (and sometimes legally) stratified texts covering a range of close to a thousand years.[74] Like their Anglo-Saxon counterparts examined by Gates in this volume, the secular Irish law tracts are written in the vernacular; most of the early Germanic law codes on the continent, discussed by Rolf Bremmer, are written in Latin, so this seems to be a purely Insular phenomenon, at least in the early Middle Ages. Although the Icelandic laws codified in *Grágás* are in the vernacular, they were committed to writing

TABLE 7.1. *Castrations by annal and year*[1]

AC	*AU*	*ALC*	*AFM*
1194	1194		
1244	1243	1244	1244
1321		1321	
		1496[2]	

Notes
1 It should be noted that the dating systems between the annals do not always accord with each other.
2 The text has *scathad* (maiming).

[71] John O'Donovan, ed. and trans., *The Genealogies, Tribes, and Customs of Hy-Fiachrach: Commonly Called O'Dowda's Country* (Dublin: The Irish Archaeological Society, 1844), pp. 335 and 337 (for the translation).

[72] *GEIL*, p. 1; Rudolf Thurneysen, 'Die Bürgschaft im irischen Recht', *Forschungen und Fortschritte* 4. 18 (1928): 183.

[73] *GEIL*, pp. 250–63.

[74] One does, however, tend to find a mix of orthographic practices from various periods of the language; see Fergus Kelly, 'Texts and Transmissions: The Law-Texts', in *Ireland and Europe in the Early Middle Ages: Texts and Transmission / Irland und Europa im früheren Mittelalter: Texte und Überlieferung*, ed. Próinséas Ní Chatháin and Michael Richter (Dublin: Four Courts Press, 2002), pp. 230–42 at p. 231.

TABLE 7.2. *Blindings by annal and year*[1]

AU_2	*AU*	*AC*	*AI*	*ALC*	*AFM*	*ACl*	*AB*[2]	*AT*	*Misc. Ir.*[3]
863									
918									
925									
			956						
						977			
						993			
996									
					999			999	
1009									
1010									
					1017				
1018			1018						
					1019				
1020								1020	
			1023						
1027					1027				
					1029				
1031									
					1032				
1036					1036			1036	
1037					1037	1037		1037	
					1039				
					1041			1041	
1044					1044				
			1051	1051					
					1067				
						1069		1069	
			1072						
			1092						
1093				1093					
					1094				
								1098	
					1103				
					1113				
								1114	
					1136			1136	
								1138	
					1139				
					1141				
					1150				
					1153			1153	1153[4]
					1154				

TABLE 7.2. *Blindings by annal and year*[1] *continued*

AU_2	*AU*	*AC*	*AI*	*ALC*	*AFM*	*ACl*	*AB*[2]	*AT*	*Misc. Ir.*[3]
					1156			1156	
					1158	1158		1158	
	1166				1166			1166	
					1167				
			1168		1168			1168	1168[5]
					1169				1169[6]
								1175	
				1177				1177	
			1181						
	1185								
				1187					
				1193					
			1194						
					1207				
				1208					
			1211						1211[7]
					1224				
			1233						1233
		1234							
		1236		1236					
									1243[8]
				1246					
		1250		1250	1250[9]				
		1251		1251		1251			
		1254		1254	1254				
	1257	1257		1257	1257		1257		
				1259	1259				
				1265	1265	1265			
				1266	1266				
		1272		1272					
	1296			1296	1296				
					1310				
	1321				1321	1321			
					1399				
		1411			1411				
	1444								
					1473				
	1496								

See following page for notes to TABLE 7.2.

Notes to TABLE 7.2.

1 No attempt has been made to correlate events, only years. The annals list many other ways with which political threats were dealt, including drowning (*AT s.a.* 738), hanging (*AC s.a.* 1228), beheading (AU_2 *s.a.* 890), starving (*AI s.a.* 824), suffocating (*ALC s.a.* 1059), poisoning (*ACl s.a.* 781), and strangling (*AT s.a.* 741). The table is meant to be representative rather than strictly exhaustive. Some years contain accounts of more than one person being blinded, e.g., *AT s.a.* 1177 lists that Cuilén Húa Cuileoin was blinded by the son of Mac Carthaigh in revenge for the killing of his son, Cormac, and Murchad, son of Ruadri, was blinded for his misdeeds.
2 *Annála as Breifne*, ed. Éamonn De hÓir, *Breifne* 4.13 (1970): 59–86.
3 *Miscellaneous Irish Annals (AD 1114–1437)*, ed. and trans. Séamus Ó hInnse (Dublin: Dublin Institute for Advanced Studies, 1947). Hereafter *Misc. Ir.*
4 From Mac Carthaigh's Book in *Misc. Ir.*
5 Ibid.
6 Ibid.
7 Ibid.
8 From *Rawlinson B.488* in *Misc. Ir.* This entry refers to the same Tadc discussed above, except his castration is not mentioned.
9 O'Donovan (3:340, n. h) notes that this event is recorded in greater detail in *The Genealogies, Tribes, and Customs of Hy-Fiachrach: Commonly Called O'Dowda's Country*, pp. 335 and 337 (for the translation).

AD 1117–18,[75] which is much later than the earliest Anglo-Saxon and Irish codes. The earliest Anglo-Saxon code, that of Æthelberht, dates to *c.* AD 602–3.[76] In recent years, there has been a great deal of debate amongst scholars regarding the amount of Christian influence found in the early Irish secular codes. Part of this debate deals with the issue of who wrote Irish law for whom. Although there was definitely a certain amount of cooperation between lay and ecclesiastical scholars, it is difficult to say with any confidence at this time whether the laws were originally committed to writing in a purely 'secular' or purely 'ecclesiastical' environment.[77]

Early Irish society was largely agricultural and status based. Every freeman born into a community possessed a *lóg n-enech* (honor-price), which was based on his status within the community, similar to the Germanic *wergild*. A woman's honor-price was calculated at half of whichever man was legally responsible for her, usually her father before she married and her husband afterwards; the unfree did not have an honor-price except in certain circumstances.[78] The honor-price was the amount paid to a person or his/her kin for

[75] *Laws of Early Iceland: Grágás*, eds. and trans. Andrew Dennis, Peter Foote, and Richard Perkins (Winnipeg: University of Manitoba Press), pp. 4–5.
[76] *Die Gesetze der Angelsachsen*, 3:2–3.
[77] An even-handed summary of this debate can be found in Robin Chapman Stacey, *Dark Speech: The Performance of Law in Early Ireland* (Philadelphia: University of Philadelphia Press, 2007), pp. 57–9.
[78] Such a circumstance would be when a crime was committed against the wife of a slave. If a bondman has a free wife, he is entitled to compensation for any type of crime committed against her. If his wife is also a slave, he is only entitled to compensation for sexual crimes

various crimes committed against him/her. The amounts given in the law tract *Críth Gablach* (Branched Purchase [?]) lists the value of a female calf as the honor-price of the low-status freeman and the value of seven female slaves as the honor-price of a king.[79] In early Irish society, it was also possible to lose one's honor-price. For example, Heptad 15 lists the seven categories of women who lose their honor-price as follows: a woman who steals; a woman who satirizes others; a traitor; a woman who gives false testimony; a woman of loose morals; a woman who inflicts wounds; and a woman who refuses hospitality to guests.[80] Each person was also assigned an *éraic* (body-fine), which was a fixed penalty in cases of homicide; the amount was fixed at seven *cumals*[81] for each person, regardless of status.[82]

In a section of the law tract *Bretha Éitgid* (Judgments of Inadvertence), there is a system of fines which details the injury done to various parts of the body and the fines associated with each.[83] This catalog of fines includes injury to the male member and testicles:

> Masi a uidi*m* rob*en*eth asi*n* dui*ne*, lancoirp*dire* ⁊ lanen*eclann* ⁊ ai*thgin* co*m*lan do intibh. Na hairne toile ⁊ in toilfheith, cidbe dib b*en*tar as [ar][84] tús, is an*n* ata in coirp*dire* co*m*lan, ⁊ coirp*dire* fo tr*um*a na *cneid*e isi*n*ni b*entar* de fo dheoigh. Masí a uirghi cle robenadh as ar tus, is la*n*coirp*dire* uair is uaithi at*a* in gei*nemain*. Ma uirghi dhes, is coirp*dire* fo tr*um*a na cn*eide*. Dai*ne* dia fhoghnat si*n* ⁊ dogni clan*nugud* doibh. Ma dai*ne* dona foghnat ⁊ na denat clan*nugud* doib, am*ail* at*a* senior diblidhe *nó* fer graidh, ni fuil doib intibh *acht* coirp*dire* fo tr*um*a na cn*eide*.[85]

committed against her; her owner receives compensation for other crimes. In early Irish society, a crime committed against a woman was considered also to be a crime committed against her male guardian. These provisions are laid out in a law code on the *fuidir* 'semi-freeman'. The passage in question can be found in *CIH*, 1:248.22–5. See also *Fuidir*-tract, ed. and trans. Rudolf Thurneysen, 'Irische Recht'. II. Zu den unteren Ständen in Irland.: *Abhandlungen der preussischen Akademie der Wissenschaften, Philosophisch-historische*, Jahrgang 1931, nr. 2. (Berlin: Verlag der Akademie der Wissenschaften), pp. 60–87 at pp. 60–83. For an English translation, see *AL*, 5:515. See also Liam Breatnach, *A Companion to the Corpus Iuris Hibernici* (Dublin: Dublin Institute for Advanced Studies, 2005), p. 294; *GEIL*, p. 11; Charles-Edwards, *Early Irish and Welsh Kinship*, pp. 307–36. For slavery in the early Irish laws, see *GEIL*, pp. 95–8; and Charlene M. Eska, 'Women and Slavery in the Early Irish Laws', *Studia Celtica Fennica* 8 (2011): 29–39.

79 *Críth Gablach*, ed. D. A. Binchy (Dublin: Stationery Office, 1941), lines 24 and 450.

80 *CIH* 15.10–24; *GEIL*, p. 349; and *AL*, 5:177.

81 The word *cumal* means 'female slave', but it is commonly used in the law codes as a unit of value.

82 For an overview of the currency systems used in the law codes, see Fergus Kelly, *Early Irish Farming* (Dublin: Dublin Institute for Advanced Studies, 1998), pp. 587–99.

83 See Breatnach, *Companion*, pp. 176–82. No complete copy of the text survives, but sizable fragments are found scattered across several manuscripts. The edition in *AL* 3:82–547 and appendix at 3:550–61 is under the erroneous title *Lebor Aicle* 'Book of Acaill'.

84 Emendation suggested by Binchy, *CIH*, 1623, n.f.

85 The text is taken from *CIH*, 1623.22–9.

> If it is his penis that was cut off, [he will receive] full body-fine and full honor-price and complete compensation for it. The glands of desire[86] and the penis, whichever of them is cut off first, there is complete body-fine [as compensation for it], and body-fine according to the severity of the wound of the one which is struck from him last. If his left testicle was cut off first, it is full body-fine because the generative power is from it. If the right testicle, it is body-fine according to the severity of the wound. [This is the case for] a person to whom they are a use and who begets children by them. If [it is the case that it regards] a person to whom they are not a use and who does not beget children by them, as is [the case with] an elderly decrepit man or cleric, they do not receive anything for them [i.e., the wounded members], but body-fine according to the severity of the wound.[87]

The Irish of the text is unambiguous, referring explicitly to complete loss of the penis and/or testicles. The legal commentators draw a distinction regarding the amount of compensation owed to different sorts of people. The virile man capable of siring children is owed his full body-fine, honor-price, and complete compensation for the loss of his member. If he loses both his penis and his testicles, he is entitled to complete body-fine for whichever is lost first, and compensation according to the degree of severity of the wound for whichever was lost second. There is some question as to why the left testicle is assigned a greater amount of compensation than the right. The editors of the *Dictionary of the Irish Language* list *semen virile* as one of the meanings of *genemain*,[88] thus suggesting that the higher compensation is based on where it was believed that potent semen originated. As Bremmer explains, in Frisia and elsewhere on the continent the *right* testicle was considered more valuable than the left, noting, however, that there is one exception to the general rule for which he uses the Irish source as comparative material.[89] Bronagh Ní Chonaill points out that the assigned values are counter to the medical belief in the Middle Ages that the left testicle produced female children and the right one produced males.[90] Those for whom the loss of their genitalia would perhaps be considered a lesser

[86] The 'glands of desire' refer to the testicles. Rolf H. Bremmer Jr cites the Irish text as well, in 'The Children He Never Had; The Husband She Never Served: Castration and Genital Mutilation in Medieval Frisian Law', in this volume, 108–30 at p. 126.

[87] There is also a translation in *AL*, 3:355. For a discussion of impotence in early Irish law, see Brónagh Ní Chonaill, 'Impotence, Disclosure and Outcome: Some Medieval Irish Legal Comment', online at http://www.arts.gla.ac.uk/scottishstudies/earticles/LegalConcern.pdf, accessed October 18, 2011. See also Ruth Mazo Karras, *Sexuality in Medieval Europe* (New York and London: Routledge, 2005), pp. 70–5.

[88] *Dictionary of the Irish Language*, gen.ed. E. G. Quin, compact edition (Dublin: Royal Irish Academy, 1990), *s.v. genemain.*

[89] Bremmer 'The Children He Never Had', pp. 124–5. Bremmer compares the references to castration and genital wounding in *Bretha Éitgid* to Frisian law texts (p. 126).

[90] Ní Chonaill, 'Impotence, Disclosure and Outcome', p. 17.

hardship are those either too old for procreation or those who have vowed not to beget children (i.e., those in holy orders), are assigned a comparatively smaller amount of compensation based solely on the severity of the wound.[91] The commentary presents a system of compensation based on practicality. For those to whom the loss of their member and testicles would diminish their procreative capabilities (and thus their potential desirability as a marriage partner), higher compensation was owed.

Prior to the twelfth century, a prominent feature of all the European law codes was 'the institution of fixed monetary sanctions payable by the kin of the wrongdoer to the kin of the victim'.[92] Starting in the twelfth and thirteenth centuries as a result of the renewed study of Roman law on the continent, these early legal systems shift to more punitive than compensatory systems, i.e., instead of the threat of pecuniary damages, one had to contend with the threat of capital punishment or bodily mutilation.[93] Medieval Ireland was no

[91] A very disturbing account of self-mutilation is associated with St Mo Ling († 697), founder of the monastery of St Mullins. The account is preserved only in the mid-twelfth-century *Book of Leinster* and can be summarized as follows: St Mo Ling had an evil neighbor named Grác, whose wife was named Crón. Grác sent his wife to Mo Ling to seduce him, but when she uncovered her private parts, Mo Ling (to resist temptation) took the awl he had in his hand and pierced it through his member with such force that the awl penetrated the vessel in which he sat. He thereupon cursed Crón, saying that she would be gang raped until her own member was distorted. On her way home, she was set upon by a group of twelve robbers and became pregnant as a result. She later bore a son, and Grác (ever the bad neighbor) suggested she name Mo Ling as the father. However, the scheme did not go as planned and Grác was killed by Mo Ling's kinsmen; Crón was left with her son.

Aside from the tale's ferocity and overall misogyny, the eye-for-an-eye type of biblical justice is rendered in specifically gendered terms. Just as Mo Ling has to endure physical mutilation of his male member to avoid sexual temptation, so must Crón endure the violation of her person and the resulting disfigurement of her own genitalia as punishment for tempting the holy man. *Oxford Dictionary of National Biography*, *s.v.* Mo Ling, online at http://www.oxforddnb.com.ezproxy.lib.vt.edu:8080/view/article/7007?docPos=1, accessed October 18, 2011.

The editor, Vernam Hull, suggests that the vessel might be a bathtub: 'Two Anecdotes Concerning St Moling', *Zeitschrift für celtische Philologie* 18 (1930): 90–9 at p. 93, n. 3. The text reads *'Maith, a banscel'*, *or se-seom*, *'ro·riastrat droch-dóine do gabol combat saíthech ídt'* ['Very well, O woman', he said, 'wicked men shall distort your member until they have had enough of you']: ibid., pp. 92–4, p. 93 for translation. Self-mutilation to avoid sexual temptation, in this case, probably owes much to the story of Origen. The account of Origen castrating himself is given in Eusebius, *The Ecclesiastical History*, trans. J. E. L. Oulton (Cambridge, MA: Harvard University Press, 1932), 2:29. See also Karras, *Sexuality in Medieval Europe*, 30–7, and in this volume, Jack Collins, 'Appropriation and Development of Castration as Symbol and Practice in Early Christianity', pp. 73–86, and Tracy, '"Al defouleden is holie bodi"'.

[92] Harold J. Berman, *Law and Revolution: The Formation of the Western Legal Tradition* (Cambridge, MA: Harvard University Press, 1983), p. 55. It should be noted that although numerous societies have this feature in common, the details of each legal system differ.

[93] Ibid.

exception, and the law codes and legal commentary frequently provide systematic and very detailed descriptions of the fines payable for a variety of offenses. In fact, the secular codes assign a fine for every crime; nowhere do they assign any form of corporal punishment. If a person has committed a crime and neither he nor his family can pay the amount owed to the victim or his kin, the wrongdoer can become the property of the victim or his kin. Once the wrongdoer is the victim's property, he is free to do whatever he likes with him, including killing, mutilating, or selling into slavery; there is a legal principle quoted in several law texts which states 'do not kill a condemned person until he is yours'.[94] It is also possible for the wrongdoer (the legal term for the person in this position is *cimbid* [captive]) to be saved from whatever fate the victim has in store for him. This is possible when someone else pays the victim the money owed.[95] The law tract *Críth Gablach* recommends that every king have amongst his bodyguard a person he has saved from captivity.[96]

This is not to say that corporal punishment does not find its way into the early Irish legal corpus; it does, but not in the secular law codes. Adomnán of Iona's 697 promulgated law code *Cáin Adomnáin* (also known by its Latin title *Lex Innocentium*) states that the punishment for killing a woman is twofold: first the murderer has his right hand and left foot cut off, then he is killed, and on top of that, his kin pays seven *cumal*s and the price of seven years' penance.[97] If the murderer is well enough off, he has the option of paying for fourteen years of penance and fourteen *cumal*s instead of being mutilated and killed.[98] Considering that everyone's *éraic* is set at seven *cumal*s, this is double the fine payable under secular law. Another ecclesiastical text which adopts a more punitive scheme of punishments is Irish Canon IV (*Canones Hibernensis*). In §1, hanging or paying a fine worth the value of seven female slaves is the

94 Translation in *GEIL*, p. 216; see further pp. 13, 97–8, and 215–16. The legal principle reads: *ní gonae cimbid manip lat*; e.g., *CIH* 328.7 (*Bretha Éitgid* 'Judgments of Inadvertence').

95 In Adomnán's *Vita Sancti Columbae* is the story of Librán. Librán had killed a man and been taken as a captive by the victim's kin. The text states that he was 'held in chains, as one condemned' until a wealthy relative paid the amount due, thus rescuing him from his captivity; Adomnán, *Vita Sancti Columbae*, in *Adomnán's Life of Columba*, ed. and trans. Alan Orr Anderson and Marjorie Ogilvie Anderson, 2nd edn (Oxford: Oxford University Press, 1991), 87a–92b; *GEIL*, pp. 97 and 215. The text dates to the late seventh century.

96 *GEIL*, p. 97; *CIH*, 570.14; and *Críth Gablach*, l. 579.

97 'Penance' here refers to the fine payable to the church for which the original penance has been commuted; see also *Bretha Crólige*, ed. D. A. Binchy, *Ériu* 12 (1934–38), pp. 1–77, at §4 and note on p. 57.

98 The purpose of Adomnán's law was to protect women, children, and clerics from acts of warfare and general violence. It should be noted that the Columban federation of monasteries received payment from the wrongdoer too. A translation of the text can be found in Máirín Ní Dhonnchadha, 'The Law of Adomnán: A Translation', in *Adomnán at Birr, AD 697*, ed. Thomas O'Loughlin (Dublin: Four Courts Press, 2001), pp. 53–68, §33.

punishment for shedding the blood of a bishop, monastic superior, or scribe, provided that a drop of the blood falls to the ground. If, however, a drop of blood does not fall to the ground and the victim does not require a dressing, the assailant's hand should be cut off, or he should pay a fine that is worth half the value of seven female slaves (§4). If the blood of a presbyter is shed so that it falls on the ground and a dressing is required, the assailant's hand is cut off, or he pays a fine worth half the value of seven female slaves (§7).[99] The Irish laws dealing with rape share similarities with those of Wales and Anglo-Saxon England, but have some marked differences as well. Irish law recognized two forms of rape, that done by physical violence (*forcor*) and that done by stealth (*sleth*), such as sleeping with a woman who has passed out from intoxication. In both situations, the penalty due was a portion of the *éraic*. If the victim was a primary wife, girl of marriageable age, or virgin nun who did not renounce her veil, the full *éraic* was paid. Secondary wives were only entitled to half the *éraic*. In addition, the rapist had to pay the honor-price of the victim's legal guardian.[100] Monetary compensation for rape was still the norm during the period following the Norman invasion of 1169. For example, in Gillian Kenny's discussion of violence against women, she recounts the 1310 case in Dublin of the abduction and rape of eleven-year-old Eva, the daughter of William de Londoun. The rapist, Richard Tyrel of Castleknock, did not deny the charges against him and was imprisoned at the request of Richard de Burgh, earl of Ulster, and his son, John. A settlement was reached whereby Tyrel agreed to pay Eva 100 marks as compensation. He further arranged for her to be married to Thomas Skybas, and he made an additional financial settlement on Eva. According to the source, Eva was satisfied with these arrangements, and Tyrel was then pardoned.[101]

In 1307, there is a record of an incident involving a husband castrating his wife's lover.[102] According to the records, the parties involved were John Don, a wine merchant from Youghal, his wife Basilia, and her lover Stephen O'Regan. Shortly after John and Basilia married, he went abroad on a business trip.

[99] 'Canones Hibernensis IV', in *The Irish Penitentials*, ed. and trans. Ludwig Bieler (Dublin: Dublin Institute for Advanced Studies, 1975), pp. 170–1. See also *GEIL*, pp. 217 and 221.

[100] *GEIL*, pp. 134–5; *Cáin Lánamna*, ed. and trans. Charlene M. Eska, in *Cáin Lánamna: An Old Irish Tract on Marriage and Divorce Law* (Leiden: Brill, 2010), pp. 282–5, §37; Lisi Oliver, 'Forced and Unforced Rape in Early Irish Law', *Proceedings of the Harvard Celtic Colloquium* 13 (1993): 93–105; Lisa M. Bitel, *Land of Women: Tales of Sex and Gender from Early Ireland* (Ithaca, NY: Cornell University Press, 1996), pp. 72–3, 223–7; and Christina Harrington, *Women in a Celtic Church: Ireland 450–1150* (Oxford: Oxford University Press, 2002), pp. 144, 146 and 153. For an overview of the different types of marriages recognized under Irish law, see Eska, *Cáin Lánamna*, pp. 13–18.

[101] Gillian Kenny, *Anglo-Irish and Gaelic Women in Ireland c. 1170–1540* (Dublin: Four Courts Press, 2007), pp. 42–3 and references therein.

[102] The case was heard in Cork in May of that year.

During his absence, Stephen began an affair with Basilia. Upon John's return, the neighbors informed him of the affair, and John warned Stephen to stay away from his house. When John left on another business trip, Stephen came to the house and slept with Basilia again. John was informed of the events which took place in his absence and came up with a ruse whereby he could catch Stephen in the act. The ruse involved an elaborate plan with the keeper of the tavern attached to his house. John told his wife he would be away for another trip, but in reality the tavern-keeper was to spy on Stephen and Basilia. When Basilia went to her bedroom, Stephen and the tavern-keeper followed her. Stephen and Basilia tried to buy the tavern-keeper's secrecy, but the tavern-keeper double-crossed them and informed John and the armed men waiting with him where he could find Basilia and Stephen.[103] In the end, Stephen was caught by John's armed men trying to escape; they promptly bound him and castrated him. Stephen won a case of assault against John and his associates (he was awarded £20); John avoided prison by a payment of 5 marks, and later won a counterclaim against Stephen for compensation for damage done to goods in his house and was awarded £2.[104] Despite having evidence of his wife's adultery, the courts clearly frowned on John and his associates taking the law into their own hands. The records have nothing to say about what Basilia thought of all this.

Despite the difficulties of determining how closely theory follows practice in regard to medieval law codes, or any legal system for that matter, changes in the written legal and annalistic sources can be tracked. The earliest layer of the Welsh law codes was similar to the Irish and early Anglo-Saxon codes in that there is no mention of castration. The Anglo-Saxon codes (as they progress through time) list increasingly harsh physical punishments for some types of crime, including castration as punishment for a slave raping another slave. After the Norman Conquest, there is an increase found in annalistic sources of accounts of physical mutilation as a means of dealing with enemies; there is the strong possibility that the increase in this practice was due to

[103] The Old French fabliaux include similar quasi-farcical episodes, at least three of which end in castration or mock castration. In this volume, Mary E. Leech examines castration as a comic motif: 'The Castrating of the Shrew: The Performance of Masculinity and Masculine Identity in *La dame escolliee*', pp. 210–28.

[104] The case of John Don and Basilia is summarized and discussed in Art Cosgrove, 'Marriage in Medieval Ireland', in *Marriage in Ireland*, ed. Art Cosgrove (Dublin: College Press, Ltd., 1985)pp. 25–50 at pp. 36–7. In the early Irish law codes, adultery was considered grounds for divorce, and there were financial penalties levied against the adulterous party, but castration was not a legal option. Unlike canon law, the Irish law codes recognized a variety of valid reasons for divorce, including adultery, spreading false rumors about one's spouse, sorcery, impotence, homosexuality, sterility, and inducing an abortion. The law also had the equivalent of the no-fault divorce. See *GEIL*, pp. 73–5; and Eska, *Cáin Lánamna*, pp. 14–16.

cultural practices that came with the Normans, but mutilation was already part of the law codes (e.g., Cnut II) before the Normans invaded.[105] Some later Welsh codes, even pre-1282, do add castration as a punishment for rape. The Welsh annals contain few accounts of castration, but they are all post-1066. With all of the annalistic sources, there is the strong possibility that many instances of political and judicial castration were either not recorded due to the sensitive nature of the subject matter or were euphemistically expressed by referring to 'blinding' or 'mutilating'. It may just be a fact of more accurate and/or contemporary record-keeping, but it is striking that most of the political mutilations cluster in the twelfth and thirteenth centuries, providing further evidence that the practice was introduced by the Normans. Castration is not found within the corpus of secular Irish legal texts, but it is found in the annals starting in the late twelfth century as a means of eliminating political enemies without acquiring the stigma of being a murderer, strongly suggesting Norman influence. Despite the differences in all three legal systems, Welsh, Anglo-Saxon, and Irish society all adopted judicial and/or political practices associated with the Normans, attesting to just how profound legal and cultural changes can be in situations where multiple cultures coexist as a result of contact and conquest.

[105] Cf. also the account of Gowine 'mutilating' the companions of Alfred: Whitlock, *The Anglo-Saxon Chronicle*, *s.a.* 1036.

CHAPTER 8

Castrating Monks: Vikings, Slave Trade, and the Value of Eunuchs

Mary A. Valante

'I asked a group of them about the process of castration, and I learned that the Romaeans castrate their youngsters intended for dedication to the church … When the Muslims raid, they attack the churches and take the youngsters away from them', says the tenth-century geographer, al-Muqaddasi. He describes Arab raids that deliberately targeted Greek churches and monasteries during his own time, a time when the Greeks castrated some young boys to keep them as singers in the Church, and a time when the Arab world wanted eunuchs.[1] The demand for slaves, including talented and literate non-Muslim eunuchs, was enormous across the Islamic world at the time of the early Abbasid caliphate (mid-eighth to the late tenth century). Judging by the actions described in al-Muqaddasi's geography, the captives did not even need to be literate in Arabic in order to be useful. This demand generated a ripple effect that spread throughout Abbasid territories, throughout the Mediterranean basin and also into eastern and western Europe. Scholars are just starting to acknowledge the large-scale influence of this long-distance slave trade on the start of the Viking Age in northwestern Europe, the same eighth through eleventh centuries. Indeed, some still deny the importance of the economics of the slave trade when it comes to Viking raiding activities.[2] But women were often targeted during Viking raids, as potential mothers and wives in Iceland and Scandinavia, or as high-value trade objects to be exchanged as far away as Byzantium and the Abbasid Empire.[3] Men, too, were kidnapped by Viking raiders active in both western and eastern Europe and sold as slaves. As with

1 al-Muqaddasi, *The Best Divisions for Knowledge of the Regions: A Translation of Ahsan Al-Taqasim Fi Ma'Rifat Al-Aqalim*, trans. Basil Anthony Collins (Ithaca, NY: Center for Muslim Contribution to Civilization, 1995), p. 216.

2 See David Wyatt, *Slaves and Warriors in Medieval Britain and Ireland, 800–1200* (Leiden: Brill, 2009), pp. 3–5.

3 Mary A. Valante, *The Vikings in Ireland* (Dublin: Four Courts Press, 2009), pp. 88–90.

female captives, some of course were sold to Scandinavia and Iceland where they worked fields, tended animals, and otherwise helped with farmwork. Others were traded further afield. But most men did not carry the added value that young, 'exotic' European women did in the slave trade. Most men were valued for their strong backs, which meant that transporting them over very long distances when local men were available was not usually economically feasible. However, boys and young teens could be very valuable as slaves in the Greek and Arab worlds, especially if they were young enough to castrate, even more so if they were educated and literate. In other words, the Arab worlds required exactly the sort of young men who lived in medieval monasteries. Scandinavian raiders traded some of their captives along routes that ended in Venice, the major hub for buying young males from all over and then selling them on as eunuchs to Jewish, Byzantine, and Islamic traders.[4] So while north-western Europe was certainly not the source for anywhere near the majority of the slaves flowing into the Islamic world, it was the source for some. Monasteries were targets of Viking attacks for more than their undefended moveable wealth and potential general-use slave population; the Vikings also targeted them to capture literate young males who could be turned into eunuchs and sold off to the east.

Ruth Mazo Karras's work, *Slavery and Society in Medieval Scandinavia*, is the most important work analyzing the uses and origins of slaves in Scandinavian lands during the Viking Age. Most significantly, she argues that there was (at best) a modest economic profit at the time in actually owning slaves; instead, she demonstrates that the primary benefit was enhanced social status.[5] As she points out, in the ninth and tenth centuries, Viking-Age slaves could work in a household caring for animals, in the fields, performing any combination of tasks; very rarely, women might be concubines, though it was less wasteful to simply use *any* slave sexually rather than to keep one purely for sexual exploitation.[6] Karras does not address the sudden beginning of the Viking raids at the close of the eighth century, nor the fate of the many people from north-western Europe captured by Vikings raiders, because neither of these issues are the focus of her research. More recently Michael McCormick has helped answer those questions by showing that two major changes regarding the slave trade took place in western Europe just at the start of the ninth century.[7] He argues that slavery became an 'export business' from western Europe for the first time, and that Slavic lands became the main source for exporting slaves to Byzantium

4 Michael McCormick, *Origins of the European Economy: Communications and Commerce AD 300–900* (Cambridge: Cambridge University Press, 2001), p. 764.

5 Ruth Mazo Karras, *Slavery and Society in Medieval Scandinavia* (New Haven, CT: Yale University Press, 1998).

6 Ibid., pp. 73–94.

7 McCormick, *Origins of the European Economy*, pp. 738–40.

and the Abbasid caliphate, though lands farther west (from Ireland to Anglo-Saxon England to Frankia) were also sources of slaves for the new international markets.[8] In contrast, David Wyatt (in *Slaves and Warriors in Medieval Britain and Ireland*) is highly critical of scholarship connecting the Viking raids on the British Isles with the economic importance of the long-distance slave trade.[9] Instead, Wyatt argues that early medieval European slavery was a social institution only. But when Wyatt criticizes Dáibhí Ó Cróinín and others for making a distinction between the economics of slave-owning and the vitality of the slave trade during the early Viking Age,[10] he gets it wrong.[11] Owning slaves in northwestern Europe during the Viking Age was very much a social institution, where the benefit to the owner had more to do with enhanced social status than with economic gain. The slave trade, though, was an economic institution.

Throughout northwestern Europe, primary sources show that the social benefits of slave-ownership (as well as some lesser economic ones) were much the same in societies throughout the region. Slave-owning was ubiquitous, despite Anglo-Saxon Bishop Wulfstan's early and eloquent opposition to Christians selling fellow Christians abroad. But even Wulfstan, with his famous sympathy for the plight of slaves, saw nothing inherently immoral about the practice.[12] The institution of slavery thrived, even in Wulfstan's England. According to the *Domesday Book* from eleventh-century England, slave-owning was omnipresent, even though many small landowners only had one or two slaves. As just one example, the small village of Tollington, held by one Ranulf from King William, included two smallholders, one cottager, and one slave.[13]

Slaves came from a variety of sources; there were varying degrees of enslavement and slavery was not always permanent. There was a slave class, and children of slaves were generally born slaves.[14] People could find themselves enslaved due to dire economic circumstances.[15] Slaves could be freed, though they were never equal with freeborn citizens; however, the children of freedmen were born entirely free. Later medieval Icelandic law even makes the distinction between children born to a woman freed while pregnant and the same woman's children conceived and born after she was freed – the former had a lower status

8 Ibid., pp. 738–54 and 611.

9 Wyatt, *Slaves and Warriors*.

10 Dáibhí Ó Cróinín, *Early Medieval Ireland: 400–1200* (New York: Longman, 1995), p. 258.

11 Wyatt, *Slaves and Warriors*, pp. 3–5.

12 David Pelteret, *Slavery in Early Medieval England: From the Reign of Alfred until the Twelfth Century* (Woodbridge: Boydell Press, 1995), pp. 90–2.

13 *Domesday Book: A Complete Translation* (DB), ed. Ann Williams and G. H. Martin (London: Penguin, 2002). DB 11, fol. 130b.

14 Fergus Kelly, *Guide to Early Irish Law* (Dublin: Dublin Institute for Advanced Studies, 1988), pp. 112–13.

15 Ibid., p. 95.

than their siblings.[16] Warfare was a constant source of new slaves. The Irish *Cogadh Gaedhil re Gallaib* describes an occasions when Irish warriors stole girls, women, and young men from the Viking town of Limerick: 'Tuccait aningena mini maccactda etrochta echramla, a hócmna blathi brecsrola, ocus a maccaimi mer morglana' [They carried away their soft, youthful, bright, matchless girls; their blooming silk-clad young women; and their active, large, and well-formed boys].[17] Thus across northwestern Europe in the early Middle Ages, slaves were taken, born, and freed for a variety of reasons and in a variety of circumstances.

The work slaves did was much the same across northern Europe as well. According to the *Cogadh*, after king Brian Boru defeated and sacked Viking Dublin: 'ocus ni moba ni re mna ní dornd im meli bron, no funi bargini, no nigi a hétaig, acht gall no gaillrech danenam' [nor did a woman deign to put her hands to the grinding of a quern, or to knead a cake, or to wash her clothes, but had a foreign man or foreign woman to work for them] (116–17). Fergus Kelly, in *Early Irish Farming*, describes slaves herding animals, cutting firewood, milking, and churning and (as in the *Cogadh*) kneading bread and grinding grain with a quern.[18] In general, slaves in northwestern Europe helped out with basic farm and housework.

In Scandinavian lands, the homelands of the Vikings as well as regions they settled, a very similar picture emerges. There was a class of people born slaves.[19] Slaves could also be captured in raids and in warfare.[20] When Iceland was first settled men greatly outnumbered women, so females brought in as slaves and children born to them might well find themselves freed.[21] But that practice did not last, and within a century or so, anyone born a slave in Iceland was likely to stay a slave. In addition to enhancing an owner's social status, owning slaves within Viking territories did provide some minor economic benefits. Women's workloads around the house and men's around the farm were lightened by the work of the slaves, just as in Ireland, as described in the *Cogadh*.[22] The labor of slaves and servants left the high-status women free to actually manage the household and men free to oversee their lands. For some free women, slave labor gave them enough time to do finer versions of the same work the slaves

16 Kristen Hastrup, *Culture and History in Medieval Iceland: An Anthropological Analysis of Structure and Change* (Oxford: Oxford University Press, 1985), pp. 114–15.

17 *Cogadh Gaedhel re Gallaib*, ed. and trans. James H. Todd, Rolls Series 48 (London: Her Majesty's Stationery Office, 1867), pp. 78–81. Hereafter page numbers are given in parentheses in the text.

18 Kelly, *Early Irish Farming*, pp. 438–9.

19 *Rígsþula*, trans. R. I. Page in *Chronicles of the Vikings, Records, Memorials and Myths* (London: British Museum Press), pp. 150–1.

20 Judith Jesch, *Women in the Viking Age* (Woodbridge: Boydell Press, 1991), pp. 87–8.

21 Jenny Jochens, *Women in Old Norse Society* (Ithaca, NY: Cornell University Press, 1998), pp. 86–7.

22 Karras, *Slavery and Society*, pp. 69–70.

were doing. Thus women organized the meals, kept track of stores, and oversaw the preparations for feasts.[23] The slaves and servants in the meanwhile did the actual cleaning, cooking, and serving for the evening. In western Europe, however, castration was not part of slavery.

In Byzantium and in the caliphate, eunuchs were a specialized commodity. But while castration did exist in western Europe, it was mostly unrelated to slavery and had nothing to do with creating a slave class of eunuchs. Curiously, castration in western Europe almost inevitably went hand and hand with blinding, as several articles in this volume attest.[24] In many cases, castration of free men was meant to push someone forcibly out of a potential line of succession, as in the case of the descendants of Gruffudd ap Cynan. His two sons went to war, and in 1130, Maredudd castrated and blinded his nephew in order to bolster his own claims to succession.[25] Castrating and blinding an enemy was more rarely used to punish rebellion;[26] blinding was clearly punishment but using castration to ensure someone could not father future claims to a title or position was equally important in a world where feuds could last over generations. In Scotland, for example, a bishop called Wimund laid claim to his ancestral lands as a secular rule and rebelled against the Scottish king David I. His blinding and castration by the king ensured that he was not only punished, but that he would father no heirs who might rebel using the same claims.[27] According to Klaus van Eickels, under Norman monarchs, the dual penalty of castration and blinding increased as a punishment against traitors.[28] However, there is some debate over the frequency with which some of these punishments were actually inflicted.[29]

[23] Jochens, *Women in Old Norse Society*, pp. 126–30.

[24] See, in this volume: Rolf H. Bremmer Jr, 'The Children He Never Had; The Husband She Never Served: Castration and Genital Mutilation in Medieval Frisian Law', pp. 108–30; Charlene M. Eska, '"Imbrued in their owne bloud": Castration in Early Welsh and Irish Sources', pp. 149–73 and Jay Paul Gates, 'The *Fulmannod* Society: Social Valuing of the (Male) Legal Subject', pp. 131–48.

[25] *Brut y Tywysogyon*: *Peniarth MS. 20*, ed. Thomas Jones (Cardiff: University of Wales Press, 1941); *Brut y Tywysogyon*: *Peniarth MS. 20*, trans. Thomas Jones (Cardiff: University of Wales Press, 1952); *Brut y Tywysogyon*: *Red Book of Hergest Version*, ed. and trans. Thomas Jones (Cardiff: University of Wales Press, 1955); see as well Eska, '"Imbrued in their owne bloud"', in this volume, pp. 158–9 for a more detailed treatment of this incident and others like it.

[26] See Larissa Tracy, '"Al defouleden is holie bodi": Castration, the Sexualization of Torture, and Anxieties of Identity the *South English Legendary*', in this volume, pp. 87–107.

[27] William of Newburgh, *The History of English Affairs: Book I*, trans. P. G. Walsh and M. J. Kennedy (Warminster: Aris & Phillips, 1988), pp. 106–7.

[28] Klaus van Eickels, 'Gendered Violence: Castration and Blinding as Punishment for Treason in Normandy and Anglo-Norman England', *Gender and History* 16.3 (November 2004): 599–602.

[29] Emily Zack Tabuteau, 'Punishments in Eleventh-Century Normandy', in *Conflict in Medieval Europe: Changing Perspectives on Society and Culture*, ed. Warren C. Brown and Piotr Górecki (Aldershot: Ashgate, 2003), pp. 131–49.

Regardless of its role in punishing traitors or criminals, castration in western Europe had nothing to do with slavery and certainly not with the creation of eunuch slaves. In a rare example of circumstances under which a slave might be castrated, the Anglo-Saxon laws of Alfred the Great provide that a male slave who raped a female one should be castrated.[30] But the act of castration here was purely punitive. It should also be noted that, as with those cases involving succession, there was clearly an attempt on the part of male slave-holders to control the procreation of slaves via castration; since female slaves were always available sexually to their owners, and at times their owner's friends, in most cases, only upper-status men should be able to impregnate slave women.[31] Thus there was no specific demand for eunuch slaves in western Europe. In the east, however, there was a booming market for eunuch slaves, and the Viking raiders who helped supply this human commodity often sent their captives to sites where they could be castrated in preparation for sale.

In general, long-distance trade in the pre-modern world consisted of either bulk necessities or luxury goods. In this case, slaves (a high-value luxury good) were traded long-distance across the great Northern Arc of the Viking Age, which stretched from northern Europe through Scandinavia and south through what is Russia, from which goods could easily move on to Venice, Byzantium, and the Abbasid caliphate.[32] For the Vikings, and thus for captives from northwestern Europe, the northern trade routes were most important. Scandinavian trade centers stretched eastwards from Hedeby in Denmark and Birka in Sweden to Staraya Ladoga in northern Russia before the end of the eighth century. This traffic continued into the ninth century as Scandinavians founded more trade centers at Kaupang in southwestern Norway and Novgorod, farther south than Staraya Ladoga, and Kiev, farther south still and closer to Byzantium. Dublin and other northwestern European Viking settlements were established as gateways through which captives were traded northwards.[33] The *Laxdeala Saga* provides a well-known example that encapsulates this trade, in which a Rus merchant, 'Gilli inn gerzki', attends a fair in the Brenn Isles in Sweden selling female slaves from northwestern Europe, along with his other wares: 'Þá lypti Gilli tjaldinu, ok sá Hskuldr, at tólf konur sátu fyrir innan tjaldit' [Gilli lifted it up [a curtain], and Hoskuld could now see there were twelve women sitting behind it].[34]

30 Oliver J. Thatcher, trans., *The Library of Original Sources*, vol. 4: *The Early Medieval World* (Milwaukee: University Research Extension Co., 1901), pp. 211–39 at p. 219. See also Gates, 'The *Fulmannod* Society', p. 133.

31 Wyatt, *Slaves and Warriors*, p. 10.

32 McCormick, *Origins of the European Economy*, pp. 562–4.

33 Valante, *The Vikings in Ireland*, p. 59.

34 Einar ól Sveonsson (ed), *Laxdæla Saga: Halldórs Þættir Snorrasonor Stúfs Þáttr* Íslenzk Fornrit 5 (Reykjavik: Hid Islenzka Fornritafelag, 1934), pp. 22–4 at p. 23. See also Magnus Magnusson and Hermann Pálsson (trans.), *Laxdæla Saga* (New York: Penguin, 1995), pp. 63–5 at p. 64.

Certain types of slaves, including educated males young enough to be castrated, were worth far more when traded along these routes than when brought home to Scandinavian farms. Viking raiders provided this valuable commodity in part through their attacks on monasteries, feeding the growing desire (rather than need) for educated and castrated slaves. The castration houses in Venice were the main source for eunuchs for the caliphate, though Verdun and the Andalusian region of Spain may also have produced large numbers of eunuchs.[35] The majority of boys and young men who were castrated in Venice were clearly Slavs[36] – Paul the Deacon in the eighth century describes 'innumerable troops of captives', from Germanic and Slavic lands being sold southwards.[37] A treaty between Venice and Charlemagne's grandson, Lothar, stated that Venice would not sell Lothar's people (the Franks) to Muslims, which meant that Slavs would have to do. According to the ninth-century Arabic *Book of Routes and Kingdoms*, Jewish merchants transported eunuchs from western Europe to Constantinople and various sites in the Islamic world.[38]

But there is still a question whether any monks were *actually* castrated and sold to the caliphate. A tenth-century biography of St Naum describes a group of some 200 churchmen, captured by Vikings from Slavic territories, being sold to the slave markets at Venice.[39] McCormick cites a number of examples of Byzantine and Slavic youths, captured from monasteries and later sold as eunuchs to the Arab world. According to the *Vita Rimberti*, one nun was rescued from being sold as a slave into the Arab world when she was overheard singing psalms.[40] Methodius, the ninth-century apostle to the Slavs, describes churchmen captured by raiders and sold to Venice.[41] So, religious *were* being captured and *were* being sold through centers where castration was being practiced regularly, and records exist of large numbers of young men being sold specifically as eunuchs, suggesting that some slaves may have been taken for precisely that purpose – feeding the eastern market for young, educated castrates.

In northwestern Europe, monasteries were the most frequent targets of Viking raids, where people as well as valuables were stolen. For example, 'Orggain Lughmaidh di Loch Echdach o genntibh qui episcopos & praespiteros

[35] Olivia Remie Constable, *Trade and Traders in Muslim Spain: The Commercial Realignment of the Iberian Penninsula, 900–1500* (Cambridge: Cambridge University Press, 1996), pp. 96–7.

[36] McCormick, *Origins of the Europen Economy*, p. 761.

[37] Paul the Deacon, *History of the Lombards*, trans William Dudley Foulke (Philadelphia: University of Pennsylvania Press, 1974), p. 2; *Historia Langobardorum*, ed. Ludwig Bethmann and Georg Waitz (Hanover: Hahnian, 1878), I.1.

[38] McCormick, *Origins of the European Economy*, pp. 688–93, 764.

[39] Ibid., p. 766, see as well p. 249 for a list of people, some from western Europe, known by name who were sold into slavery in the Islamic world in the eighth and ninth centuries.

[40] *Vita Rimberti*, ed. Georg Waitz (Hanover: Hahnian, 1884), pp. 95–6.

[41] McCormick, *Origins of the European Economy*, p. 766.

& sapientes captiuos duxerunt & alios mortificauerunt' [Louth was plundered by the heathens from Loch Neagh and they led away captive bishops and priests and scholars, and put others to death] (*AU* 840.1).[42] In AD 842 alone, six Irish monasteries were plundered for captives. In AD 869, 'Orccain Airdd Macha o Amhlaim coro loscadh cona derthaigibh; .x.c. etir brith & mharbad & slat mor chena' [Armagh was plundered by Olaf and burned with its oratories. Ten hundred were carried off or killed, and great rapine also committed] (*AU* 869.6).[43] Bishops and abbots and other men of name and rank could always hope to be ransomed, but for the majority of captives, such hopes must have been nearly non-existent. Anyone young enough to be castrated (and already literate and educated) might have found his way to the castration houses in Venice. That young boys lived at monasteries and were taught to read and write is clear. The tenth-century Rule from the Céli Dé reform movement in Ireland states that 'It is the duty of every one in Orders with whom these boys study to correct and chastise them and to press them to take ecclesiastical Orders forthwith, because they are being bred up for the Church and for God with a view to receiving Orders'.[44] One monk from Byzantine territories in Italy was sent by his bishop to North Africa to redeem other monks caught in raids.[45] The traffic in monastic slaves is well documented, especially as demand increased outside of Europe.

Some of those captured during Viking raids remained in northwestern Europe and became slaves in the old-fashioned sense, fulfilling the social need to own slaves and yet not serving a particularly significant economic function. Other captives, though, faced a far different fate and entered the long-distance slave trade. Goods including silver from Baghdad and silk from Byzantium traveled to Europe, while western and eastern Europe exported slaves in exchange for these luxury goods.[46] Captives from northwestern Europe traveled primarily across the great Northern Arc, north along the Irish Sea into Scandinavia; some then continued southwards via Rus territory, processed at the trade centers of Novgorod and Kiev.

42 *The Annals of Ulster (to AD 1131)*, ed. and trans. Seán Mac Airt and Gearóid Mac Niocaill (Dublin: Dublin Institute for Advanced Studies, 1983). Hereafter, references to this text, by year, are given in parentheses in the text.

43 The same entry can be found in the *Chronicum Scottorum*, *s.a.* 869 (CS869.2) and the *Fragmentary Annals of Ireland*, *s.a.* 869 (FA869.374). See *Chronicum Scottorum: A Chronicle of Irish Affairs From the Earliest Times to AD 1135, with a Supplement Containing the Events From 1141–1150*, ed. and trans. William M. Hennessy, Rolls Series 46 (London: Her Majesty's Stationery Office, 1866); *Fragmentary Annals of Ireland*, ed. and trans. Joan Newlon Radner (Dublin: Dublin Institute for Advanced Studies, 1978).

44 'Rule of the Céli Dé', ed. and trans. Edward Gwynn, in *The Rule of Tallaght*, Hermathena 44, second supplemental volume (Dublin: Hodges, Figgis, 1927), pp. 64–89 at pp. 84–5.

45 McCormick, *Origins of the European Economy*, p. 515.

46 Valante, *The Vikings in Ireland*, pp. 58–9, 86–90, 128–31.

Other western Europeans were carried into Muslim lands via a southern route. As McCormick demonstrates, trade from Frankia to Muslim lands was very important from the Carolingian period onwards, and Jewish merchants were especially important in facilitating this trade. A Jewish slave merchant (Abraham from Saragossa) was granted legal protections by Louis the Pious (AD 813–40), as long as he did not sell enslaved Christians to non-Christians. Louis the Pious similarly protected other Jewish slave merchants, in particular those operating out of Lyons. The ninth-century Arabic writer, Ibn Khurradadhbih, produced a *Book of Routes and Kingdoms*, describing trade routes taken by Jewish merchants who traded slaves from western Europe (especially Spain, Frankia, and Italy) to eastern Mediterranean sites like Constantinople, Egypt, and Antioch and on to Baghdad.[47] One ninth-century pilgrim named Bernard stated that in a single day he watched two ships laden with human cargo leaving Taranto in southern Italy for Egypt.[48] This southern route, dominated by Jewish merchants, was a major pathway by which captive western Europeans were transported to Muslim lands.

At first glance, slave-ownership among the Christian Byzantine Greeks looked much the same as in early medieval northwestern Europe, which might make a demand for slaves from Europe seem unnecessary. Traditionally, most slaves worked on farms, as demonstrated in the *Farmer's Law* (a collection of Byzantine legislation concerning agriculture passed and compiled in the seventh and eighth centuries): 'If a man's slave often steals beasts at night, or often drives away flocks, his master shall make good what is lost on the ground that he knew his slave's guilt, but let the slave himself be hanged.'[49] Slaves could be born into slavery or captured, but also slaves could be freed. Greeks were sometimes captured in raids and sold as slaves. However, the Byzantine Greeks were in the process of moving away from having slaves perform most heavy farm labor during the Viking Age, but it took time.[50] In the ninth century, Constantine the Philosopher (better known as Cyril) and Methodius were early missionaries into Slavic territories in an effort to convert the Turkic Khazar Khan on the Volga. They failed to convince him to convert to Orthodox Christianity and instead the Khan converted to Judaism. But Cyril and Methodius did return home to Constantinople with 200 Greeks whom they had freed from slavery during their mission. In a future mission they traveled to Moravia to establish a bishopric, and then they moved on to Rome via

47 McCormick, *Origins of the European Economy*, pp. 675–6, 688–93.

48 Bernard, *Itinerarium*, ed. Titus Tobler and August Molinier, *Itinera hierosolymitana et descriptiones terrae sanctae bellis sacris anteriora* 1.2 (Geneva: Fick, 1880), p. 311.

49 Walter Ashburner, 'The Farmer's Law (Continued)', *Journal of Hellenic Studies* 32 (1912): 68–95 at p. 91.

50 Robert Sabatino Lopez, 'The Dollar of the Middle Ages', *Journal of Economic History* 11.3 (1951): 209–34 at pp. 223–4.

Pannonia and Venice, freeing Christian slaves wherever they traveled, thus providing the best witnesses to the fates of captured and enslaved Greeks of the period.[51] But, as in northwestern Europe, castration was simply not a part of slavery in rural areas.

Within the Byzantine Empire, however, among the many categories of slaves, eunuchs represented a unique subset – largely in urban areas.[52] Only young males could be castrated somewhat safely, and given the roles they played, education was highly desirable as well. As Shaun Tougher points out, from the reign of Diocletian (AD 284–305) onwards, eunuchs were increasingly important in the courts of Eastern Roman emperors. By the ninth century many important functions at the imperial court were filled only by eunuchs, including personal guards, wardrobers, and the head of security. Eunuchs could hold other offices in the palace as well, in fact only three court offices were reserved for non-eunuchs, while at least ten were reserved for eunuchs alone.[53]

Eunuchs were popular slaves among the urban elite of Byzantium, far beyond the imperial palace.[54] They could act as guards for children and women, or as message-carriers for women since they had more freedom to travel than the women who owned them. Within the palace, they were guards, oversaw the rest of the servants, managed the emperor's schedule, and were trained as professionals, including as barbers and doctors. Their tasks ranged from singing to overseeing ceremonies; they were the staff most loyal to the emperor and each member of the royal family.[55] Some were military commanders.[56] Within the Eastern Church, eunuchs were singers, monks, priests, and even patriarchs, though these eunuchs could not have been slaves.[57] And the more well-placed eunuchs had more eunuchs on staff. Not all eunuchs were successful, however, and those who never became part of wealthy households could still be found around the city as entertainers and even prostitutes in lower neighborhoods.[58]

The Byzantine Empire had both a demand for and a supply of eunuchs, fed partly by trade with northern Europeans, including Vikings. Until and

51 McCormick, *Origins of the European Economy*, pp. 188–90.

52 Of course, Western Christianity (unlike Eastern Orthodox Byzantium) prohibited castration, despite the ascetic allure. See Jack Collins, 'Appropriation and Development of Castration as Symbol and Practice in Early Christianity', in this volume, pp. 73–86.

53 Shaun F. Tougher, 'Byzantine Eunuchs: An Overview, with Special Reference to their Creation and Origin', in *Men, Women and Eunuchs: Gender in Byzantium* ed. Liz James (New York and London: Routledge, 1997), pp. 168–84 at pp. 168, 171–2.

54 McCormick, *Origins of the European Economy*, p. 533.

55 Kathryn M. Ringrose, *The Perfect Servant: Eunuchs and the Construction of Gender in Byzantium* (Chicago: University of Chicago Press, 2003), pp. 1–2.

56 Ibid., pp. 130–1.

57 McCormick, *Origins of the European Economy*, p. 533.

58 Ringrose, *The Perfect Servant*, pp. 1–2.

including the fifth century, no citizen eunuchs could be sold – but some were.[59] In the sixth century, Procopius stated that most eunuchs serving the emperor were not Romans.[60] Some eunuchs were Roman-born, though their status as free or slave remains unclear.[61] By the time of the Viking Age, some Persian, Arab, and Armenian eunuchs from Byzantium were known by name, and these non-Byzantine eunuchs were all sold and bought as slaves.[62] By the tenth century, even very wealthy and ambitious families might have one of their own sons castrated at a young age, a practice so well-known that Guibert of Nogent wrote about and condemned it.[63] And by the eleventh century, most Byzantine eunuchs came from free families within Byzantium.[64] The most famous example of this is the eleventh-century Basil Lekapenos, the illegitimate son of the emperor Romanos I. Castrating him had the dual effect of removing him completely from the line of succession while allowing him to remain at the palace in increasingly important roles. In fact, he survived at the palace even after his father was deposed. He became a general, and by the time he died he had even acted as regent for an underage ruler.[65]

So while eunuchs were imported, particularly from farther east (Persia), or received by emperors as gifts, evidence from Byzantium suggests that physicians performed the operation on an *ad hoc* basis, and that not all survived. Most eunuchs were castrated as children, some (more rarely) in puberty.[66] The Byzantine Empire even exported eunuchs to the caliphate: 'From the Byzantine's country [we import]: gold- and silverware, dinars of pure gold, medicinal plants, gold-woven textiles, *abrūn* [?], silk brocade, spirited horses, female slaves, rare copperware, unpickable locks, lyres, hydraulic engineers, agrarian experts, marble workers and eunuchs.'[67] Byzantine eunuchs were also sometimes the deliberate target of Arab raiders. Even so, only the Christian West was very much in the business of creating eunuchs on a large scale for export.

By way of contrast, the institution of slavery in the Muslim world was dramatically different than in northwestern Europe or the rural areas of

59 Tougher, 'Byzantine Eunuchs', p. 177.

60 Procopius, *History of the Wars*, vol. 5: *Books 7.36–8: Gothic War*, trans. H.B. Dewing (London: Hutchinson, 1928), viii.3.17.

61 Tougher, 'Byzantine Eunuchs', p. 178.

62 Ibid.

63 Guibert of Nogent, *The Deeds of God through the Franks*, trans. Robert Levine (Woodbridge: Boydell Press, 1997), p. 38. See Larissa Tracy, 'Introduction', in this volume, p. 12.

64 Tougher, 'Byzantine Eunuchs', p. 90.

65 Ringrose, *The Perfect Servant*, pp. 130–1; Tougher, 'Byzantine Eunuchs', p. 178.

66 Tougher, 'Byzantine Eunuchs', pp. 175–7; Paul of Aegina, *Surgery*, ch. 46, in *Paulus Aegineta*, ed. J. L. Heiberg, 2 vols. (Leipzig: Teubner, 1921–24). Cf. Shaun Tougher, 'The Beauty of Roman Eunuchs', in this volume, pp. 48–9.

67 al Djahiz, *A Clear Look*, trans in McCormick, *Origins of the European Economy*, p. 591; David Ayalon, *Eunuchs, Caliphs and Sultans: A Study in Power Relationships* (Jerusalem: The Magnes Press, 1999), pp. 106–7.

Byzantium. From the eighth century onwards, great changes were afoot in the east. The Abbasid dynasty rose to seize control of the Islamic Empire in AD 750, remaining on the throne until 1258, though their direct power began to wane after the mid-tenth century. Remnants of the previous ruling dynasty (the Umayyad) fled westwards and seized control of Muslim Spain and parts of North Africa. While not all regions of the Islamic world were under Abbasid control, socially and culturally the area remained connected. Among the many social changes that took place under the early Abbasid was a massive shift in the ways that slaves were utilized, and the resulting continuing demand for huge numbers of slaves, many of whom were castrated. Slavery under the Abbasid was certainly a social construct, but slaves played many more roles than in western or eastern Europe. Slaves were builders, especially of the great city of Bagdhad. Slaves were agricultural workers; in Iraq the Zanj slaves worked on large-scale plantations. Slaves were soldiers, an institution that eventually led to the Mamluks of Egypt. Slaves were concubines in the harems of the wealthy and those with more modest wealth seeking to increase their social status.[68] Exotic women were very popular as slave-concubines.[69] The harems of the wealthy across the Islamic world were filled with people. Concubines themselves were bought, and yet more enslaved women served them.[70] Caliphs freed and married slave women who had no family ties that could interfere in their court. Abu Ja`far's mother was a Greek slave, as was Caliph Mu'tadid's mother. Abu Abd Allah's was Byzantine (i.e. also Greek), and the mother of Abbu al-Abbas was a Slav.[71] In addition to the demand for women, the institution of the harem also created a massive need for trustworthy guards, a need that was filled by eunuchs.[72] Because they could come and go in the harem, eunuchs were also the teachers of women and children, girls as well as boys, and even military instructors. They often cared for the children as well as instructed them.[73] Eunuchs under the Abbasids were the chief bureaucrats of the caliphate. Some guarded major holy sites, and later (in Cairo) freed eunuchs were tomb guardians for the wealthy.[74] Many worked for private individuals,

[68] Murray Gordon, *Slavery in the Arab World* (New York: New Amsterdam Books, 1989), p. 56.

[69] Ibn Buṭlān, 'On Buying Slaves', in *Islam: From the Prophet Muhammad to the Capture of Consantinople*, vol. 2: *Religion and Society*, ed. and trans. Bernard Lewis (New York: Walker and Company, 1974), pp. 243–51.

[70] Nadia Maria El-Cheikh, 'Servants at the Gate: Eunuchs at the Court of Al-Muqtadir', *Journal of the Economic and Social History of the Orient*, 48.2 (2005): 234–52 at p. 236.

[71] Mas'udi, *Meadows of Gold: The Abbasids*, trans. Paul Lunde and Caroline Stone (London: Kegan Paul International, 1989), pp. 267, 329, 299, 281, 317–18, 277.

[72] El-Cheikh, 'Servants at the Gate', p. 236.

[73] Ayalon, *Eunuchs, Caliphs and Sultans*, pp. 39–41.

[74] Shaun Marmon, *Eunuchs and Sacred Boundaries in Islamic Society* (Oxford: Oxford University Press, 1995), pp. 21–6.

striving to earn a place in their local palace.[75] In the end, the expanding uses for slaves during the time of the early Abbasids, including the need for large numbers of enslaved eunuchs, drove much of the slave trade around the Mediterranean basin. The Viking raids, which began barely a generation after the Abbasid dynasty seized the caliphate, met part of that need.

Thus it was within the Muslim world, and especially within the caliphate, that eunuchs were the most prevalent and valued and in the most demand. All slaves sold for less in Europe than Byzantium, and in both Christian domains they were less valuable than in the Muslim world. Once castrated, European males carried a greatly added value within the caliphate.[76] According to the 'Tale of the First Eunuch and the Second' from *1001 Nights*, one eunuch describes in detail how he was made a 'clean eunuch, with nothing left', when he was nine or ten years old. His value increased immediately and he was sold; eventually he earned a place in the palace.[77] So the potential for profit in selling eunuchs was greatest by far in the caliphate. The number of women alone who lived within the caliph's harem was staggering: the caliph's mother (if she was alive), his wives and concubines, all of their children and any other female relatives who were dependent on him. There were more women to serve the caliph's female relations, including female slaves owned by individual women who lived in the harem. By the middle of the ninth century, some sources claim there were as many as 12,000 women in the caliph's harem. Management of an establishment of this size required nothing less than an 'army of slaves and eunuchs'.[78] As Nadia Maria El-Cheikh so elegantly puts it, 'It was the Muslim women's unique seclusion which made the employment of eunuchs inevitable'.[79] Eunuchs administered the entire system. Eunuchs guarded the women.[80] Eunuchs educated the children. Owned by some of the women personally, eunuchs served them, ran errands for them, and even spied for them.

The large number of eunuchs at the court of one Caliph, al-Muqtadir (AD 908–32), is recorded in a number of sources. The tenth/eleventh-century writer Hilal al-Sabi' states that 'It is generally believed that in the days of al-Muqtadir bi-allah [...] the residence contained 11,000 eunuchs: 7,000 blacks and 4,000 white Slavs; 4,000 free and slave girls and thousands of chamber servants'.[81] Ibn 'Abd al-Zāhir, a late thirteenth-century writer, claims that when Saladin conquered the Fatamids he found 12,000 people living there, but the only non-

75 Malcom C. Lyons, *The Arabian Nights: Tales of 1,001 Nights*, vol. 1 (New York: Penguin, 2010), pp. 279–84.

76 McCormick, *Origins of the European Economy*, p. 754; see table 25.1 on pp. 756–7.

77 Lyons, *The Arabian Nights*, pp. 279–84.

78 Piotr O. Scholz, *Eunuchs and* Castrati (Princeton, NJ: Markus Wiener Publishers, 2001), p. 203.

79 El-Cheikh, 'Servants at the Gate', p. 236.

80 Ibid., pp. 234–52.

81 Ayalon, *Eunuchs, Caliphs and Sultans*, p. 21.

eunuchs were the Fatimid caliph himself and his immediate relatives. Even without taking these numbers literally, clearly at the caliph's court alone there were thousands of eunuchs. Considering the need for more eunuchs to guard and serve in every harem in the Muslim world the enormous demand for eunuchs – a demand that Viking raiders attempted to supply – crystallizes.[82] It is unfortunate that the primary sources are not clearer about the origins of these men, but the roles they played gives some idea at least of the importance of training and education. As El-Cheikh points out, 'the eunuchs regulated court ceremonial and controlled a complex structure of spatial sanctity that by the fourth/tenth century had come to surround the Abbasid caliph'.[83] That eunuchs also educated the elite youth as well as the slave army strongly suggests that those with the prime posts were highly educated, and that for any eunuch, an education would have increased their value.

But the caliphate had a huge problem filling its need for massive numbers of eunuchs; it had by far the greatest demand, but unlike Byzantium, *no local supply*.[84] Up to and under the Umayyad rulers (until AD 750), castrating any man was punished by law. The Abbasids (from AD 750 onwards) modified the law so that only non-Muslims could be castrated, though castrated eunuchs could convert and were encouraged to do so. Even so, the numbers of eunuchs who came from within the borders of the caliphate were apparently quite small, so the vast majority were boys and young men who had been castrated before ever entering the caliphate.[85] A tenth-century source describing Cordoba (the capital of Muslim Spain) states that eunuchs in Cordoba were Slavs, as well as Galicians, Franks, Lombards, and many others.[86]

Given the increasing demand for eunuchs, especially literate and educated eunuchs, in the Byzantine and especially Arab world from the ninth century onwards, Viking raids on western monasteries must be seen in a new light. Monasteries were indeed repositories of great treasure, and men and women could and were captured and sold to Iceland and Scandinavia. But the only way to explain the massive drive for captives is to understand the economics of the long-distance slave trade of the Viking Age. The added value of young, literate boys and teens and the fact that Venice castration houses needed a near endless supply of exactly such captives fill in another piece of the puzzle of the economics of the Northern Arc of the slave trade. As long as there was a demand for castrated young boys and teens, whether from Slavic or western European lands, whether pagan or Christian, there would be a supply.

82 Ibid.

83 El-Cheikh, 'Servants at the Gate', pp. 234–52 at p. 240.

84 Ayalon, *Eunuchs, Caliphs and Sultans*, p. 75.

85 Ibid., p. 31.

86 Reinhart Dozy, *Spanish Islam: A History of the Muslims in Spain*, trans. Francis Griffin Stokes (London: Chatto & Windus, 1913), p. 430.

CHAPTER 9

'He took a stone away': Castration and Cruelty in the Old Norse Sturlunga saga

Anthony Adams

We are not so wretched as we are vile.
Michel de Montaigne, 'Démocritus et Héraclitus'

maður er manns gaman ('man is the joy of man')
Hávamal 47

Toward the end of *Íslendinga saga*, the long and bloody narrative that comprises the largest portion of the Old Norse compilation of texts known as *Sturlunga saga*, Gizurr Þorvaldsson, a man who has been deeply implicated in the ongoing violence, arranges a meeting with Hrafn Oddsson for the purpose of mutilating him. Gizurr (like most of the men and women in the saga) has suffered great personal loss, living on after his wife Gróa is burned alive in their home along with their three sons. The poem he composes after their murder ends with the grim vow that 'brjótr lifir sjá við sútir / sverðs, nema hefndir verði' [the sword-breaker will live with grief until vengeance has occurred] (1:496).[1] Ostensibly to arrange a truce, Gizurr goes to meet his enemy with forty of his companions, not the agreed-upon eleven: in other words, a raiding party rather than a band of peaceful apostles. His purpose becomes clear to all present, and Gizurr's voice and visage become angrier the longer they speak; yet somehow, the apparently inevitable conflict is unexpectedly averted:

> [...] ok var Gizurr þess at harðari í talinu, er þeir höfðu lengr talat. Þá gékk at Hrafni Teitr Álason ok mælti við hann eintal, bað hann öllu því játa, er Gizurr beiddi hann, – kvað honum eigi annat duga mundu, þar sem þá var komit. Ok svá gerði Hrafn. Sór Hrafn þá Gizuri eiða, at hann skyldi aldri

[1] *Sturlunga saga*, ed. Jón Jóhannesson, Magnús Finnbogason, and Kristján Eldjárn, 2 vols. (Reykjavík: Sturlunguútgáfan, 1946). Translation mine. Volume and page numbers are given in parentheses in the text.

> honum í móti vera ok aldri veita brennu-mönnum í mót honum. Skilðu þeir við þat. … Gizurr sagði svá sjálfr síðan, at hann kvaðst eigi vita, hvat Hrafni hafði hlíft á þeim fundi, því at hann kvaðst einráðit hafa áðr fyrir sér at meiða hann at nökkuru, blinda eða gelda. (1:502)
>
> […] and the longer they talked the more severe Gizurr became. Then Teit Álason went to Hrafn and spoke with him privately; he asked him to agree to everything Gizurr demanded of him; he said nothing else would help him, considering the way things had gone so far. Hrafn agrees to this; he swore oaths to Gizurr that he would never attack him or even help the burners against him. With that they parted. […] Gizurr himself said later that he did not know what had protected Hrafn at that meeting, for he had earlier been determined to injure him in some way, either to blind him or to castrate him.[2]

Hrafn avoids losing either his eyes or his genitals through a series of submissive and supplicant verbal gestures. Instead of negotiating as if he and Gizurr were equals (men both capable of and prone to violence), Hrafn voluntarily surrenders his right then and in the future to partake in any violence against Gizurr, nor will he assist any who might attempt to do him harm.[3] He does not argue; he does not fight. In the larger sense, Hrafn surrenders his power of volition, his ability to do his will and impose it upon Gizurr. In a culture such as the medieval north, where masculinity was in large part defined by the power and potential of volition, Hrafn surrenders his manhood, offering up a symbolic castration and a virtual blinding for the real ones intended by Gizurr. Overt commentary on Hrafn's words and actions would be contrary to the laconic style typical of saga narratives, but Gizurr's reaction to them makes clear that they are unusual, and even baffling: he implies that there was some unseen force protecting Hrafn from him. Hrafn's own passivity, his voluntary forswearing of violence and the masculine code that such violence represents, offer a glimpse of the masculine aggression that enables a terrible economy of cruelty; a masculinity marked by a code of self-identification that is impulsive, sexually polarizing, and relentless.

2 *Sturlunga Saga*, trans. Julia H. McGrew, 2 vols. (New York: Twayne, 1970), 1:412. I have adapted McGrew's translation slightly from the original here and elsewhere in this chapter, unless otherwise indicated.

3 This is not the only occasion on which Hrafn Oddsson avoids conflict through politics or rhetoric. When a slightly younger man, Hrafn talks his way out of accompanying Þórðr *kakali* Sighvatsson on a raiding expedition, insincerely claiming that he is too young and 'eigi vita, hvárt hann myndi harðnaðr vera nökkut, þar er hann var lítt kominn af barnsaldri' ['I don't know that I'd be strong enough, since I've only just stopped being a child']. Hrafn later becomes the most powerful Icelander following Gizurr's death in 1268. See Nic Percivall, 'Teenage Angst: The Structures and Boundaries of Adolescence in Twelfth- and Thirteenth-Century Iceland', in *Youth and Age in the Medieval North*, ed. Shannon Lewis-Simpson (Leiden: Brill, 2008), pp. 127–49.

Men such as Hrafn are rare in the twelfth/thirteenth-century *Sturlunga saga*; violent confrontations such as the one Gizurr first envisages are far more common. Violence is a form of communication between men, just as surely as Hrafn's persuading words are. Unlike speech acts, however, acts of violence aim at disrupting connections between man and man, man and land, or man and wife, and they are presented suddenly and with shocking bluntness. Lois Bragg observes that in this text 'we confront disfigurement, disability, and dis-integrity of body and soul run wild'.[4] The genital mutilation and blinding (by his own cousin) of Órækja Snorrason, the illegitimate son of one of the most powerful Icelanders of his era, is indeed one of the most memorable sequences in *Sturlunga saga*, but it is not unrepresentative. Perhaps it appears to be only one particularly graphic scene of butchery in a saga filled with them, suggesting that there is little to be gained by prolonged analysis of the scene. The mutilation has received frequent glancing treatment, but has not yet been the subject of detailed study.[5] The injuries inflicted upon Órækja fall into a different category than those suffered in the course of feud or combat. Mutilations such as castration and blinding were a particularly vile and cruel form of injury, a species of lingering death and continual torment enacted upon the bodies not of fellow men and warriors, but of deviants. Through their survival and their scars, those wounded in war might construct an intellectual prosthesis of pride from the ruins of their body, one that might yet betoken masculinity. The mutilations suffered by Órækja are intended rather to mark him as one removed from the realm of masculine action, one declared unfit for rugged male society who instead properly belongs to a very different sphere that includes the sexually deviant, the bestialists, the homosexuals, the priests, the sickly, the beggarly, the unfit, and the old – all types characterized as unmanly and effeminate, and thus as 'non-men'. The intention to castrate is nothing less than an

4 Lois Bragg, 'Disfigurement, Disability, and Dis-integration in *Sturlunga saga*', *álvissmal* 4 (1995 [for 1994]): 15–32 at p. 19. See also Robert J. Glendinning, 'Saints, Sinners, and the Age of the Sturlungs: Two Dreams from *Íslendinga saga*', *Scandinavian Studies* 38.2 (May 1966): 83–97.

5 In addition to Bragg, 'Disfigurement, Disability, and Dis-integration', see Marlene Ciklamini, 'Biographical Reflections in *Islendinga saga*', *Scandinavian Studies* 55.3 (summer 1983): 205–21; David Clark, 'Manslaughter and Misogyny: Women and Revenge in *Sturlunga saga*', *Saga-Book of the Viking Society* 33 (2009): 25–43; Einar Ól. Sveinsson, *The Age of the Sturlungs: Icelandic Civilization in the Thirteenth Century*, trans. Jóhann S. Hannesson (Ithaca, NY: Cornell University Press, 1953); John McKinnell, 'Motivation in Lokasenna', *Saga-Book of the Viking Society* 22 (1986–89): 234–62; Guðrún Nordal, *Ethics and Action in Thirteenth-Century Iceland* (Odense: Odense University Press, 1998), pp. 24, 101, and 180–1; Preben Meulengracht Sørensen, *The Unmanly Man: Concepts of Sexual Defamation in Early Northern Society*, trans. Joan Turville-Petre (Odense: Odense University Press, 1983), pp. 83–4; and Úlfar Bragason, 'The Art of Dying: Three Death Scenes in *Íslendinga saga*', *Scandinavian Studies* 63.4 (autumn 1991): 453–63.

ultimate attempt to effeminize an enemy, and this scene comes close to the heart of a discourse of masculine desire and cruelty that runs through much of *Sturlunga saga*.

The scene with Órækja Snorrason provides insight into an aggressive and violent code of masculinity at its most wantonly cruel. In this world the cruel becomes commonplace and the 'currency' of masculinity becomes debased. Cruelty does not equate to violence in a simple fashion, for certain acts of violence were considered an acceptable and even necessary or desirable response to certain situations. *Njáls saga* presents a stark contrast between manly and unmanly violence in the sequence of events that lead to the deaths of Gunnar and Njál respectively: whereas Gunnarr is slain by men in face-to-face combat, Njál and his family are burned in their home, an act that brings much criticism upon the burners. Such examples of unmanly violence (such as burning, mutilation, and castration) offer a particularly revealing if graphic 'x-ray' of medieval Scandinavian masculinity, exposing a perhaps surprising discomfort at this exhibition of violence, one traumatizing and horrifying in a different way than other scenes of the saga. The subsequent course of the narrative in the aftermath of the mutilation arguably shows the author and the saga's actors attempting in various ways to undo the trauma of the mutual experience of cruelty and its witnessing, suggesting that the experience marks a limit event, a point beyond which it is not possible to make sense of the world.[6] The concept of 'limit event' is central to trauma studies, and indicates an 'extreme or excessive event or experience that transgresses normative limits or suspends constraints and boundaries'.[7] While the term was originally used in reference to significant and large-scale 'historical' events (such as genocide), it can also describe an event that takes an individual to his or her limit point beyond which is oblivion. In *Sturlunga saga*, while mutilation and violence are not themselves frequently moments for such horror, the scene with Órækja does, arguably, present such a scenario to the eyewitnesses. Although the saga authors present the texts as history, the narratives must also be read with an eye on the value and function of their fictionality. *Sturlunga saga*, long mined for historical facts about the period it describes, has been recently read more closely by literary scholars who approach the text with an understanding that the narrative has been shaped by literary tropes as well. A careful, albeit narrow, examination of its grimmest scene provides additional insight about the narrative techniques of medieval Icelandic authors, as well as presenting further evidence of the fascination with, and abhorrence of, the most fundamental unmanning of man – castration.

6 On the concept of 'limit event' and limits in connection with traumatization, see generally the work of Dominick LaCapra, most recently *History and Its Limits: Human, Animal, Violence* (Ithaca, NY: Cornell University Press, 2009).

7 Ibid., p. 7.

Sturlunga saga is the name that has been given to a collection of miscellaneous prose narratives written by various authors and compiled around the year 1300. The title is not actually found in either manuscript source, and dates only from the seventeenth century; neverthless, it remains a fairly accurate description of the subject matter of the compilation's individual texts.[8] As a whole, the texts offer an invaluable overview of the political and social events in Iceland between the years 1117 and 1264, whose later decades are named the Sturlung Age, a troubled era named after the most powerful family of its time, and characterized by increasing violence and rampant feuds which continued up until the eventual breakdown of the Icelandic Free State.[9] Norway brought Iceland under its dominion in 1262, and rule transferred to Denmark in 1380 when the male line of Norway's royal family faltered. The early stages of the Icelandic settlement break with political tradition, but early sagas such as *Egils saga* also demonstrate that the social structures of friendship, honor, poetry, and gift-exchange remained much a part of Icelandic culture. That a 'rupture' and a 'new beginning' occurred when the original Norwegian immigrants settled Iceland after refusing to submit to the king is significant, and the stage is set for the eventual society based around law and feuds like that in *Sturlunga saga*. According to Preben Meulengracht Sørensen,

> The history of the Icelanders during their first four hundred years passed through changes which, in the retrospective literary gaze of the succeeding period, were understood as rupture, loss, and new beginning. The first rupture was the departure. The voyage out and the land-taking were the first generations' most significant experiences. The life they knew up to that point was cut off and a new existence had to be built up, not only in a material sense, but in a cultural and religious sense. The land-taking laid the foundation for the Icelanders as a nation and already in the construction and organization of the new society that had developed a consciousness of themselves as a distinct people.[10]

Sturlunga saga is considered one of the most valuable of the so-called *samtiðarsögur*, the 'same-time' or 'contemporary' sagas of medieval Scandinavia,

[8] *Sturlunga saga*, 2:xiii–xvi. Two manuscript copies of *Sturlunga saga* have survived: *Króksfjarðarbók*, AM 122a fol (written *c.* 1360–70); and *Reykjarfjarðarbók*, AM 122b fol (of uncertain date, but thought to have been written somewhat later than *Króksfjarðarbók*).

[9] Gunnar Karlsson, *The History of Iceland* (Minneapolis: University of Minnesota Press, 2000), pp. 83–6.

[10] Preben Meulengracht Sørensen, 'Social Institutions and Belief Systems of Medieval Iceland (*c.* 870–1400) and the Relations to Literary Production', in *Old Icelandic Literature and Society*, ed. Margaret Clunies Ross (Cambridge: Cambridge University Press, 2000), pp. 8–29 at p. 27.

because of the detailed account it offers of the political intrigues and violent family struggles of the Sturlung Age often related by some of the very men involved, and it remains the most significant biographical work of the era.[11] The saga is filled with relentlessly graphic accounts of the feuds and assaults that took place at that time. There is scarcely a page that does not contain some brief tale of armed conflict, grievous wounding, mutilation, and death. In contrast to the *Íslendinga sögur* ('Sagas of the Icelanders', a specific genre of saga-literature that should not be confused with the single text *Íslendinga saga*), the general impression in many *samtiðarsögur* is that of a country riddled with familial feuds and acts of vengeance, a landscape whose only lasting law is that of the knife, axe, or spear, and one in which even the few peaceable folk are often goaded into acts of murder and maiming by their countrymen, wives, families, or even priests. The violence done to individuals offers a mirror image of the chaos emblematic of the Icelandic community. 'Whereas in *Egils saga*,' according to Bragg,

> readers are filled with awe at the uncanny darkness of this famous skáld, we are simply repulsed by the gratuitous grossness and incommensurate violence of some of his twelfth- and thirteenth-century descendants. Whereas the *Íslendinga sögur* provide a varied array of memorable moments – moments like Gunnarr's fall from his horse as he is leaving his homestead or his first meeting with Hallgerðr at the Alfling, as well as those like Hallgerðr's refusal to give him a strand of her hair – we remember nothing of *Sturlunga saga* so clearly as the blinding and castration of Órækja Snorrason, or the plea of Kristrún, the beggarwoman, during the attack on Sauðafell that she be allowed to keep the salve because "hon sagði ... konu þá, er brjóstin bæði váru af höggvin, yfrit þungt at tekna" [she said ... that woman, both of whose breasts had been cut off, had borne a very great deal].[12]

Bragg alludes to a key difference between the older and the newer sagas: despite the seeming ubiquity in Norse literature of warfare, marauding, dueling, and even home-burnings (see *Njáls saga*, for examples of all these), there is the sense that much of this takes place (in the admittedly artificial world of the *Íslendinga sögur*) within an environment involving heroic action, and a warrior's code. While the death and bloodshed is sometimes heart-breaking, sometimes terrible and senseless, in many of these sagas those guilty of misdeeds are eventually punished to some degree, or they are lionized for other reasons. Legal proceedings and a sense of justice pervades the earlier sagas. Not so with *Sturlunga saga*, in which the 'struggle for power is the

11 Ciklamini, 'Biographical Reflections in *Islendinga saga*', p. 205. See also Stephen Tranter, *Sturlunga saga: The Rôle of the Creative Compiler* (Berne: Peter Lang, 2005).

12 Bragg, 'Disfigurement, Disability, and Dis-integration', p. 19.

dominant mode of life'.[13] This difference has caused more than one critic to blanch, including Icelandic historians who have felt the need to comment (apologetically, perhaps) on the age in which men 'were more grim, treacherous, deceitful, savage, and revengeful. Fair play was not known and men became half-trolls.'[14]

Íslendinga saga, which amounts to approximately 40 percent of the *Sturlunga saga*, is one text in *Sturlunga saga* whose authorship can be assigned to a known personage – Sturla Þórðarson (1214–84), nephew of the famous Icelandic historian and lawman Snorri Sturluson, one of the most powerful men of his time. Sturla painstakingly describes the feuds between Snorri's own family (including his son Órækja) and Snorri's brothers and their sons (including Snorri's other nephew, Sighvatr Sturlasson). Sighvatr Sturlasson carries out the attack upon Snorri's farm in Reykjaholt and is primarily responsible for castrating Órækja. Sturla Þórðarson felt (like Órækja) the social disadvantage of illegitimacy; and he remains somewhat outside the events of the story, gaining confidences of various factions during the long years of feud, and apparently escaping vengeance himself. It is believed that Sturla wrote *Íslendinga saga* within the last years of his life, prior to the capitulation to Norway in 1262, so by the time he commits the narrative to manuscript, he has had considerable time to reflect upon the events described, many of which he saw first-hand.[15]

In many ways the saga centers around questions of legitimacy. Órækja Snorrason is the illegitimate son of Snorri Sturluson. Snorri's wife is Herdís, but as the saga says, Snorri was 'fjöllyndr, ok átti börn við fleirum konum en Herdísi' [loose, and had children with women other than Herdís] (1:212). Snorri is known to modern audiences primarily as a man of letters, outlining much of what we know (or think we know) of pre-Christian Scandinavian mythology in the prose *Edda*, and sketching the raw, early connections between the old homeland of Norway and the nascent state of Iceland in his *Heimskringla*, one of the most important accounts of the Scandinavian kings.[16] He might also have been responsible for one of the most electrifying Icelandic sagas, *Egils saga*, whose main character, the Viking, poet, farmer, and trouble-

[13] Ciklamini, 'Biographical Reflections in *Islendinga saga*', p. 215. Both genders could have the right to representation in a 'Sturlung' theater of cruelty. Indeed, the above scene might well have been seen to function as the female 'equivalent' of male castration.

[14] Boga Th. Melsteð, 'Útanstefnur og erindreka útlendra þjóðhöfðingja á Sturlungaöldinni', *Tímarit* [21] (1900): 57–131 at 126–7; cited in *Sturlunga Saga*, trans. McGrew, 1:24

[15] *Sturlunga saga*, 2:xxxiv.

[16] See Diana Whaley, *Heimskringla: An Introduction* (London: Viking Society for Northern Research, 1991); Jónas Kristjánsson, 'Var Snorri Sturluson upphafsmaður íslendingasagna?' *Andvari* 115 (1990): 85–105; and Vésteinn Ólason, 'Er Snorri höfundur *Egils sögu*?' *Skírnir* 142 (1968): 48–67.

maker Egill Skalla-Grímsson, makes a ghostly cameo in *Sturlunga saga* (1:241–2). Snorri's role in *Sturlunga saga* is considerable, for his family (the Mýramenn), lie at the center of so many of the conflicts and bloodshed in the saga. *Sturlunga saga* reveals a perhaps-unknown side of the antiquarian and historian: an irascible and scheming man of action, who maintains a central position in the violence of the age while also retaining a reflective and respectful persona.[17]

Órækja fully arrives in the saga in chapter 86, after he has built a residence for himself in Deildar-tungu with his kinsman Philipp. His father negotiates an agreement at the Icelandic assembly that summer with another leading Icelander, Kolbeinn *ungi*, one of the Skagfirðings. The agreement includes the marriage of Kolbeinn's sister Arnbjörg to Órækja, along with a good deal of land and a *goðorð* – chieftancy – at Hafliði (*Sturlunga saga*, 1:359). This arrangement displeases other men close to Snorri, who fear that he will now prove to be unreasonable and overbearing. But it is his son who turns out to be a troublemaker instead. Órækja begins a campaign of plundering in Breiðafjörð, making numerous enemies in the process, an outcome that seems to occur to Órækja rather late. He begins to fear for his life after receiving a letter (ostensibly from Odd and Þórdís), detailing a plot against his life. This in turn leads to a pre-emptive attack upon Odd and his men, ending in the rather shameful slaying of Odd while he is already dying (1:367). Meanwhile, Sturla Sighvatsson is in Norway, performing public penance for himself and his father for their part in the cruel treatment of bishop Guðmundr (1:318).[18] For his part Órækja and his men continue to behave cruelly, as they 'fóru óspaklega um sveitir; tóku hesta ok mat þar er þeir þóttusk þurfa' [rambled unpeaceably through the countryside, taking horses and food as they thought necessary]; they 'bjuggu þar óspaklega heyjum ok öðru' [lived there unpeaceably on hay and other stores]; and they 'hjöggu þar oxa níu vetra gamlan er Þórði átti' [slaughtered a nine-year-old ox that Þórði had] (1:373). They ransack large swaths of land in Höfði, and in Bjarnahöfn they capture all the men they can find, slaughtering the lambs for food (1:380–1). Matters worsen before attempts at reconciliation are finally made. Órækja, Sturla Sighvatsson and their men meet at Dýrafjörð, agreeing (in principle) that a temporary peace should be held until Sturla's father Sighvat can come to a decision about compensation that midsummer, but this peace does not last. The two men (with their retainers), and Sturla Þórðarsson, meet at Reykjaholt.

[17] One example would appear to be Snorri's reluctance at one point to acquiesce to an attack during the Christmas season, a decision that seems to have led instead to a defeat for his son Órækja, and the composition of a shameful verse (*Sturlunga saga*, 1:390).

[18] For a synopsis of the story of Guðmundr, see *Sturlunga saga*, 2:cxxii–cxxv and see also Bragg's reading of his (accidental) maiming, 'Disfigurement, Disability, and Disintegration', pp. 23–5.

> Þeir Órækja mötuðust í litlustofu um kveldit. En um morgininn, er þeir gengu frá messu, fóru þeir í stofu. Þá var Órækja kallaðr í litlustofu ok Sturla Þórðarson. Litlu síðar kom Sturla Sighvatsson í stofudyrr, þær er eru frá litluhúsum, ok kallaði Sturlu Þórðarson til sín, ok gengu þeir í loft þat, er þar var. Tók þá Sturla Sighvatsson til orða: 'Þér var kunnigt, nafni, um sætt vára í Dýrafirði. En nú kom faðir minn ekki til. En svá var mælt, at Órækja skyldi hafa Stafaholt ok búa þar, en ek hér. Ok þykkir þat eigi heilligt, at hann siti svá nær við lítit efni, en ek svima í fé Snorra. Er þar nú knefat um annat ráð, at ek ætla, at hann skuli fara norðr til Skagafjörð ok þar útan, ok mun nú skilja yðvart föruneyti.' Tók hann þá til sverðsins Kettlings, er lá hjá þeim, er Sturla Þórðarson hafði í hendi haft. Gengu þeir þá til stofu, ok í durum kómu í móti þeim menn Órækju ok váru þá allir flettir vápnum ok klæðum. Var þeim þá fylgt í loftit ok þar settir menn til gæzlu. (1:395)
>
> Órækja and his men ate in the little room in the evening, but in the morning, when they came from Mass, they went into the sitting-room. Órækja was then summoned into the little room, as was Sturla Þórðarson. A little later Sturla Sighvatsson appeared at the entrance to the sitting-room from the Little House, and called Sturla Þórðarson out to him. They went into a loft there and Sturla Sighvatsson began to speak: 'The agreement made at Dýrafirði was well-known to you, my namesake. But now my father has not come. It was agreed that Órækja was to have Stafaholt and live there, and I here. But it doesn't seem advisable for him to live so near with such slight means while I swim in Snorri's wealth. I have settled on another idea therefore: I think he should go north to Skagafjörð, and from there to Norway, and that your association should now come to an end.' He then reached for the sword Kettlingr which lay near him, and which Sturla Þórðarson had had in his hand. They went to the sittingroom, but Órækja's men came to meet them in the doorway. They were all stripped of their weapons and clothes and led to the loft where man were placed to guard them. (1:298–9)

Sturla's words are filled with irony and nuance; he underscores his continued feelings of ill-will (having been slighted in the past by Snorri) as well as his resentment over Órækja's ongoing harrassment and theft. He reminds Sturla of the name-bond they share with the expression *nafni*, a term used sparingly in the saga indicating an intimate friendship (*vinátta*). Órækja is physically isolated by his cousins, left alone in the living room while they gather to speak privately in the loft of the Little House, away from the main building. The handling of the sword called *Kettlingr* (kitten) carries with it a gesture of authority, and the sword itself proves later to be a desirable weapon.[19]

Órækja's men are symbolically castrated through the stripping off of clothes

[19] In ch. 144, Órækja asks for Kettlingr as compensation (*Sturlunga saga*, 1:445).

and weapons, and the narrative continues with Órækja's forced isolation from the others and from fellowship.

> Sturla reið nú á brott með Órækju upp til jökla ok Svertingr með hónum einn hans manna. Þeir riðu upp á Arnarvatnsheiði, þar til er þeir koma á Hellisfitjar. Þá fara þeir í hellinn Surt ok upp á vígit. Lögðu þeir þá hendr á Órækju, ok kvaddi Sturla til Þorstein langabein at meiða hann. Þeir skoruðu af spjót-skafti ok gerðu af hæl. Bað Sturla hann þar með ljósta út augun. En Þorsteinn lézk eigi við þat kunna. Var þá tekinn knífr, ok vafiðr, ok ætlat af meir en þverfingr. Órækja kallaði á Þorlák biskup sér til hjálpar. Hann söng ok í meiðslunum bænina Sancta Maria, mater Domini nostri, Jesu Christi. Þorsteinn stakk í augun knífinum upp at vafinu. En er því var lokit, bað Sturla hann minnast Arnbjargar ok gelda hann. Tók hann þá brott annat eistat. Eftir þat skipaði Sturla menn til at geyma hans. En Svertingr var þar hjá Órækju.
>
> En þeir Sturla ríða þá í brott ok ofan í Reykjaholt. Lét Sturla þá fara á brott menn Órækju, ok heldu þeir flestum föngum sínum. En hestar Órækju ok vápn váru tekin. (1:395)

> Sturla rode off with Órækja up toward the glacier; alone of his men Svertingr went with him. They rode up along Arnarvatnsheið until they reached Hellisfitjar, where they went into Surt's cave and up to the stronghold. There they seized Órækja, and Sturla ordered Þorstein longbone to maim him. They cut off a piece of a spearshaft and shaped it into a peg, and Sturla bade them strike out his eyes with this. But Þorstein said that he could not make out how to use the instrument. Then they took a knife and wrapped it about as thick as a finger's breadth. Órækja called on bishop Þorlákr to help him; during the maimings[20] he also chanted the prayer *Sancta Maria mater Domini nostri Jesu Christi*. Þorstein stabbed the point of the knife, as far as the wrappings into his eyes. When this was done Sturla bade him think of Arnbjörg, and castrated him. He took then a stone away. After that Sturla arranged for men to guard him. Sverting was still there near Órækja.
>
> Sturla and his companions then rode away, down to Reykjaholt, where Sturla had Órækja's men sent away; most of them kept their belongings, but Órækja's horse and weapons were seized. (1:299)

The initial attempt at the maiming is handed to Þorstein *langabein* (longbone), who is asked to use a makeshift weapon, a broken spearshaft which has pres-

[20] McGrew here translates *meiðslunum* as 'tortures', but lexical evidence indicates that the meaning of *at meiða* is to 'injure in a lasting way', to 'maim' (or 'ruin', if land or other property is the object). See Johan Fritzner s.v. ('beskadige, mishandle noget') and the examples he gives from the law codes and the *Biskupa sögur*, many of which are contemporaneous with *Sturlunga saga*: *Ordbog over det gamle Norske Sprog* (Oslo: Oslo University Press, 1973). In a volume involving so much careful discussion of torture and its legal interpretation, it is probably best to offer a more restrictive translation here.

umably been shaven into a peg or a spike (ON *hæll* can mean both 'peg' and 'pin', and refers to the part of a scythe handle that protrudes from the shaft as a grip or handle). Þorstein refuses to use this crude device, claiming he does not know how to wield it. He settles on a more traditional and perhaps more manly weapon – a knife – but this too is adapted for the unfamiliar procedure to come. Its handle is wrapped in what is probably cloth, a striking inversion of a traditional motif: Weapon handles in Norse sagas are sometimes described as *vafiðr* (wrapped) in metal, such as iron or gold, a gilding treatment that rendered them more precious.[21] The presence of Bishop Þorlákr is notable in this context because this bishop, for whom *Þorláks saga* was written, was considered a saint by the Icelanders and was known for his efforts to strengthen matrimony in Iceland and eliminate adultery.[22] The prayer to the Virgin Órækja desperately utters is an intercessory prayer, a humble request for protection for the body and spirit, for health and for peace. Once the men have blinded Órækja, they set about castrating him. Sturla mocks Órækja during the process, asking him to think about his wife Arnbjörg while his manhood is carved away, this time (it appears) choosing to do the job himself: 'Tók hann þá brott annat eistat' [He took away [*tók … brott*] one stone of the two [*annat eistat*]]. Sturla Þórðarsson takes some pains to clarify that the castration is not complete, that the incident might still leave Órækja some potency – a point that Sturla Þórðarsson returns to shortly. With the worst now accomplished, Órækja is left in the cave while his assailants ride away.

The decision to castrate Órækja rather than kill him suggests that this particular kind of mutilation takes part of its power from the fact that the victim must *live* in that condition. Meulengracht Sørensen has argued that the rationale behind humiliations was to rob enemies of their ability to fight and also to father children who might act as avengers.[23] Castration, he says, is the most serious of these mutilations, the ultimate form of emasculation: yet 'saga writers represent neither this particular injury nor the other disfigurements reserved for captives. Even though they are interested in bodily injuries, they do not explore mutilations that seem to serve no other purpose than to symbolize a man's powerlessness.'[24] It is a punishment that weakens a man physically and socially. This

[21] See the description of Bolli Þorkelsson in *Haralds saga Sigurðarsonar*, in *Heimskringla*, ed. Bjarni Aðalbjarnarson, 3 vols (Reykjavík: Hið íslenzka fornrítafélag, 1941–51), 3:225.

[22] See Kirsten Wolf, 'Pride and Politics in Iceland: Þorlákr Þórhallsson', in *Sanctity in the North: Saints, Lives, and Cults in Medieval Scandinavia*, ed. Thomas A. Dubois (Toronto: University of Toronto Press, 2008), pp. 241–70 at pp. 244–5.

[23] Meulengracht Sørensen, *The Unmanly Man*, p. 81.

[24] For an interesting discussion of castration motifs in the Old Icelandic *Tristram ok Ísodd*, see Karen Anouschka Lurkhur, 'Redefining Gender through the Arena of the Male Body: The Reception of Thomas's *Tristan* in the Old French *Le Chevalier de la Charette* and the Old Icelandic *Saga af Tristram ok Ísodd*' (PhD dissertation, University of Illinois at Urbana-Champaign, 2008).

castration (or partial castration) is a type of mutilation with clearly sexual undertones, combining elements of corporal mutilation and a humiliating sexual assault that could even be read as a type of rape.

Law codes such as the Icelandic *Grágás* offer a legal framework for considering the categorization of blinding and castration to other types of injury. The written evidence in the Scandinavian law codes regarding corporal punishment is somewhat sparse, but this method of criminal punishment appears consistently as one intended for slaves and other unfree members of the society's lowest classes; each incident of punishment delivered lasting markers of humiliation and abjection along with prolonged physical suffering. These restrictions on corporal punishment were eventually loosened and expanded, applying to commoners guilty of petty theft as well. *Grágás* contains a commentary on eleventh-century regulations intended to govern the activities of clerics and laypeople regarding Christian observances; these include 'procedural rules for mounting lawsuits and bringing them before assembly courts, the execution of outlawry penalties, relations between chieftains and followers, and other constitutional matters [...] and with man-slaying and many categories of personal injury'.[25] *Grágás* considers castration a 'major wound' along with 'cutting out a man's tongue, poking out a man's eyes, knocking out a man's teeth, cutting off a man's nose or ears, [... and] striking a shame-stroke across someone's buttocks', the last of which was considered a sort of metaphorical castration, but all of which warranted retribution and payment.[26] Scandinavian law codes did legislate the gelding of men under certain circumstances, such as for men accused of bestiality. Additionally beggars were also considered *úmennzka* (unmanly) and could legally be castrated; *Grágás* clearly stipulates that there would not be a penalty attached to anyone castrating beggars.[27] *Grágás* also mentions that slaves could be mutilated (specifically by the severing of hands and feet) for the murder of their owners or their owners' kin. An apparently singular example of this exists in *Draumr Þorsteins Síðu-Hallssonar* in which Þorsteinn castrates Gilli, an Irish slave.[28] Gilli obtains his

[25] *Laws of Early Iceland: Grágás*, ed. and trans. Andrew Dennis, Peter Foote, and Richard Perkins, 2 vols. (Winnipeg: University of Manitoba Press, 1980), 1:vii.

[26] Ibid., 1:141.

[27] Ibid., 2:219: 'rétt er at gelda göngumenn'.

[28] *Draumr Þorsteins Síðu-Hallssonar*, in *Austfirðinga saga*, ed. Jón Jóhannesson (Reykjavík: Hið íslenzka fornrítafélag, 1950), pp. 321–6. According to John Lindow, this is the only example of a castrated slave found in medieval Icelandic sources: 'Meeting the Other: The Cases of *Draumr Þorsteins Síðu-Hallssonar* and *Kumlbúa þáttr*', in *Myths, Legends and Heroes: Essays on Old Norse and Old English Literature*, ed. Daniel Anlezark (Toronto: University of Toronto Press, 2011), pp. 77–90 at p. 78. However, in this volume, Mary A. Valante explores the Viking practice of castrating slaves who were sold specifically to the Byzantine Empire. See 'Castrating Monks: Vikings, the Slave Trade, and the Value of Eunuchs', pp. 174–86.

revenge at Þorsteinn's home at Svínafell by cutting his throat while he sleeps.[29] After hiding for a while on the property, Gilli is eventually captured and cruelly punished by Þorsteinn's wife, Yngvildr, who sets a metal washbasin of burning coals upon his bare stomach – a method of torture most famous for being used by Óláfr Tryggvason in an attempt to convert the recalcitrant pagan Eyvindr. In Denmark, provincial laws allowed petty theft to be punished with flogging or mutilation, a category that could include the loss of hands, ears, or nose.[30]

The earliest Norwegian laws expand the code to include bestiality as an offense punishable specifically by castration,[31] not unlike the Old Frisian laws examined by Rolf Bremmer in this volume.[32] Later law codes introduce additional gradations of punishment for petty theft, debt, and sex crimes – branding and mutilation are prescribed for repeat offenders. Swedish provincial laws warrant corporal punishment for a wide range of offenses, and such punishment could include the loss of hands, ears, and nose, blinding, or cutting out the tongue.[33] Anne Irene Riisøy notes that efforts to refine the laws were aimed at the *odadafolc*, the transgressors or 'outrageous people' who have defied convention. In one case, she points out that a fourteenth-century decree (of King Hákon Magnusson) stipulates that such *odadafolc* who attempt to return to their communities following banning should be marked by the loss of an ear, and that 'tha skulle the miste ørit oc drage sten aff by' [they should be made to drag stones through the town].[34] All such punishment occurs within a system of shame in which external signs mark out the transgressor from society.

Such pronouncements in the law codes indicate that certain prescribed mutilations were aimed at the least powerful members of society, or at transmuting a more powerful member into an outcast. Physical deformities by themselves did not render someone an outcast. Bragg argues that physical disfigurements, whether purposefully inflicted by another in retaliation for a wrong, incurred by accident in combat or in daily activity, or congenital, were not necessarily considered revolting. Physical disfigurement (such as a harelip),

[29] See discussion of these scenes in William Sayers, 'Clontarf, and the Irish Destinies of Sigurðr digri, Earl of Orkney, and Þorsteinn Síðu-Hallsson', *Scandinavian Studies* 63.2 (spring, 1991): 164–86 at pp. 178–9.

[30] Kari Ellen Gade, 'Crime and Punishment', in *Medieval Scandinavia*, ed. Phillip Pulsiano and Kirsten Wolf (New York and London: Garland Publishing, 1993), pp. 115–17 at p. 116.

[31] *Norges Gamle Love indtil 1387*, ed. Jakob Rudolph Keyser and Peter Andreas Munch (Ghent: Gröndahl and Son, 1849), 1:18 and 2:496.

[32] Rolf H. Bremmer Jr, 'The Children He Never Had; The Husband She Never Served: Castration and Genital Mutilation in Medieval Frisian Law', in this volume, pp. 108–30.

[33] Gade, 'Crime and Punishment', p. 116; and Lizzie Carlsson, 'De medeltida skamstraffen: Ett stycke svensk kulturhistoria', *Rig: Tidskrift utgiven af Föreningen för svensk kulturhistoria* 17.3 (1934): 121–50.

[34] *Norges Gamle Love*, 3:210. See also Riisøy, *Sexuality, Law, and Legal Practice and the Reformation in Norway* (Leiden: Brill, 2009), pp. 99–100; and Carlsson, 'De medeltida skamstraffen', p. 130.

deformities, or handicaps (such as a stammer) were not by themselves cause for rejection; she asserts that a character like Þorgils *skarði* Böðvarsson in *Þorgils saga skarða* would not have automatically been considered ugly because of his harelip.[35] He could still be described, without irony, as *vænn* (handsome) by the saga-author, despite the *skarð*, or cleft, in his lip.[36] On the contrary, he manages to overcome this through a bold, even intractable, manner and through aggression, which King Hákon interprets as manliness; Þorgils is praised, rewarded, and eventually operated upon. The deformity is rendered impotent and finally invisible by virtue of his deeds. Bragg argues, however, that Norse culture did attempt to read physical deformities as what she calls 'metonymy as incarnation', a figure of narrative 'in which the ethical dimension is embodied in the physical'; in other words, they were frequently 'read' by observers as symbolizing a flaw not primarily of the body, but rather of the spirit or character.[37] Thus, certain forced mutilations, such as blinding, would suggest a significant failing or failure of the individual, and these could then cause a loss of prestige, and even concomitant depression. On the one hand, physical wounds, while often debilitating and sometimes fatal, were not in themselves unmanly; to bear great pain and suffering with wit and stoic acceptance was culturally admirable and bestowed masculine virtue. On the other hand, many wounds described in Norse sagas were disabling physically and socially, even if they were not mortal. Losses of legs, hands, feet, eyes, noses, and ears were survivable injuries that *do* often suggest a concurrent loss of manliness in reponse.[38] The opening chapters of *Grettis saga* describe how a brave warrior by the name of Önundr lost his leg below his knee in battle, and was thereafter called Önundr *tréfótr* 'treefoot'. He later attributes his loss of luck to the loss of his leg, and is mocked for it by other men:

> Tröll hafi tréföt allan,
> tröllin steypi þeim öllum!
>
> Let the trolls take you, Treefoot
> Let the trolls take them all!

35 Bragg, 'Disfigurement, Disability, and Dis-integration', pp. 15–18

36 Ian McDougall, however, reads the remark as ironic; see his 'The Third Instrument of Medicine: Some Accounts of Surgery in Medieval Iceland', in *Health, Disease, and Healing in Medieval Culture*, ed. Sheila Campbell, Bert Hall, and David Klausner (Basingstoke: Macmillan, 1992), pp. 57–76. Cited in Bragg, 'Disfigurement, Disability, and Dis-integration', p. 16, n. 4.

37 Bragg, 'Disfigurement, Disability, and Dis-integration', p. 18

38 According to William Ian Miller, the family sagas show only about three instances of torture, but other forms of violence occur much more frequently such as 'handhewing, and leghewing, and occasional geldings': *Bloodtaking and Peacemaking: Feud, Law, and Society in Saga Iceland* (Chicago: University of Chicago Press, 1990), p. 196; see also Theodore M. Andersson and William Ian Miller, *Law and Literature in Medieval Iceland: Ljósvetninga saga and Valla-Ljóts saga* (Stanford, CA: Stanford University Press, 1989), pp. 44–5.

They add that it is a sight seldom seen 'at þeir menn fari til orrustu, er ekki mega sér' [that men go to battle who cannot take care of themselves].[39]

Castration plays a particularly important role in this discourse. Real or imagined, whether a visible mutilation made upon another man's body or a tangible threat, or as an insult of the highest order, castration was the ultimate wound because of its power to effeminize. It was the final, irretrievable means of sending a man from the realm of *hvatr* (keen, hard, manly) to *blauðr* (soft, tender, feminine), rendering the once *magi* (potent) now permanently *úmagi* (impotent), and removing him as a threat from the political and sexual world of real men. It is this effeminization that Sturla Sighvatsson attempts by mutilating Órækja Snorrason in Surtshellir, which Sturla Þórðarson is forced to watch.

Castration is mentioned three times in *Sturlunga* saga – the punishment of Órækja Snorrason and that avoided by Hrafn Oddsson. The third reference to castration is brief, but it demonstrates succinctly the distinction that castration symbolized, the difference between the man of action and a man of passivity:

> Eptir þat hljóp Sturla upp, ok var þá sótt at Áróni, ok stóðu spjót svá þykkt at hónum, at henn fekk trautt fallit, ok varð víða sárr ok þó miðr en þeir ætluðu.
>
> Runnu þá biskupsömenn upp ór fjörunni, en þeir Sturla eftir þeim. En Áron lá þar eftir.
>
> Fóru þeir Sturla þá heim til kirkjugarðs. Váru þar teknir prestar tveir ok geldir, Snorri ok Knútr.
>
> Áron lá í brúkinu, þar til er Eyjólfr Kársson kom til hans ok mælti: 'Hvárt lifir þú, mágr?'
>
> Hann lézk lifa ok leika eigi. (1:291–2)

> After that Sturla leapt up, and an assault was then made on Áron in which so many spears struck at him that he scarcely could fall; he was wounded in many places, yet less than they thought he was.
>
> The bishop's men then ran up from the beach, Sturla and his men after them. But Áron lay behind.
>
> Sturla and his men went on to the churchyard then, and there seized two priests and gelded them; they were Snorri and Knútr.
>
> Áron lay on a pile of seaweed until Eyjólfr Kársson came up to him and said 'Are you alive, kinsman?'
>
> Áron said he was alive, and not playing. (1:187)

The warrior Áron is throughly pierced, yet his status as a man remains unquestioned. His bearing contrasts sharply with that of the two priests who are caught and summarily castrated with none of the lengthy description (and not a drop

[39] *Grettis saga Ásmundarsonar*, ed. Guðni Jonsson (Reykjavík: Hið íslenzka fornritafélag, 1936), p. 6.

of the horror) evident in Órækja's mutilation. That they are mentioned by name only underscores their reality, as well as their real impotence and insignificance in a world of real men. The castration of priests (who are celibate and thus sexually inactive and unthreatening) does not rate an explanation; they might as well have been castrated already. That they cannot, or do not, fight back distinguishes them even more from the figure of Áron, who is penetrated but nevertheless remains a 'kinsman', retaining his voice and perhaps a form of authority. His wounding is severe, yet he manages to outwit his assailants: 'ok varð víða sárr ok þó miðr en þeir ætluðu' [he was wounded in many places, yet less than they thought he was]. He is even allowed the characteristically Norse flourish of a verbal quip before death, the ironic gesture of someone unfazed by their own mortality who refuses to acknowledge vulnerability even for a moment.[40]

In this scene, as in others, penetration is a metaphor for power; the essential divide constituted by Norse masculinity does not come down to one of sex or gender, but to the power symbolized in the act of thrusting or pounding, and the loss of power symbolized by taking a passive sexual role.[41] The importance of this in Norse society is clarified by legal provisions against sodomy which indiscriminately link homosexuality and bestiality and suggest that the passive participant in sodomy is considered less human.[42] Kari Ellen Gade suggests that in some cases, the allusion could be made to taking an active role in penetration without concomitant loss of manliness.[43] What is at stake is obviously not 'homosexuality' *per se* but effeminacy, specifically 'unmanning', or impotence.[44] The true concern for manliness in Norse society was volition – the ability to take free, untrammelled action without impediment. Manly men were one small segment of society that were thus empowered; the sick, the old, the young, the disabled, and most women were not. In the analysis of medieval Scandinavian masculinity offered by Carol Clover, the modern social binary of male and female, masculine and feminine, does not apply to the cultural

40 See Joseph Harris, 'Beowulf's Last Words', *Speculum* 67.1 (Jan. 1992): 1–32, for a full overview of this phenomenon.

41 Paraphrasing Carol J. Clover, 'Regardless of Sex: Men, Women, and Power in Early Northern Europe', *Speculum* 68 (1993): 363–87 at p. 380.

42 In the thirteenth-century *Frostaþingslög*, bestiality was explicitly mentioned and forbidden, with castration prescribed for the man; the animal is to be killed. See Kari Ellen Gade, 'Homosexuality and Rape of Males in Old Norse Law and Literature', *Scandinavian Studies* 58.2 (1986): 124–41; and Jens Rydström, *Sinners and Citizens: Bestiality and Homosexuality in Sweden, 1880–1950* (Chicago: University of Chicago Press, 2003). Cf. Bremmer, 'The Children He Never Had', pp. 114–5.

43 Gade, 'Homosexuality and Rape', p. 132, n. 34.

44 Gade makes this point very clearly in her first footnote: the 'term "homosexuality" in the present discussion refers to sexual acts between two males and is not to be interpreted in light of the institutionalized concept "homosexuality" of the nineteenth and twentieth centuries' ('Homosexuality and Rape', p. 136, n. 1).

community of the sagas.[45] Clover draws upon the arguments made by Thomas Laqueur, concerning the existence of two-sex and one-sex cultures.[46] Modern society, Laqueur explains, from at least the late eighteenth century onward, has seen the world through a lens of two sexes (male and female) and imagined a fairly well-defined (and impermeable) barrier between them. In a two-sex society, the differences between the sexes are well established by virtue of birth itself. These sexes have determined roles, physical and intellectual characteristics, temperaments, environments of influence, and so on. In such a society, it is much more difficult for one sex to become like the other. Just as it would be difficult for a woman to become male, so too would a man be somewhat protected from becoming female. In contrast, in a one-sex society such divisions are confused because all people are simply more or less of one sex – in Old Norse society specifically, more or less male. Masculinity is the single lens through which people are judged, and all people have either more of it or less of it. A girl child might be born with less of the power associated with maleness than her brother, but nevertheless she would be able to 'acquire' it through her life and reputation. Clover cites cases where the saga-author's comments on such 'strong women' describe them in tones neither laudatory nor condemnatory, but neutral. If being female was actually a fairly amorphous and malleable state, then it would not be surprising that 'maleness' is similarly malleable, or even more so. Masculinity is a category or descriptor that indeed seems to be ever at risk; despite the virtue of having been born a man, Norse men were in constant danger of losing their masculinity. A man could also (far more easily) 'lose' his maleness and his attributes of masculinity through his actions or by virtue of his acquired reputation. A lasting image from Clover's

45 Clover, 'Regardless of Sex'. Despite the age of this study, it remains among the most striking and theoretically sophisticated presentations of Norse masculinity; much excellent work has been done in recent decades on women in Old Norse society, but studies of masculinity have been either infrequent, or oblique. See Clark, 'Manslaughter and Misogyny', and also David Ashurst, 'The Transformation of Homosexual *Liebestod* in Sagas Translated from Latin', *Saga-Book of the Viking Society* 26 (2002): 67–96. See also Carol J. Clover, 'Maiden Warriors and Other Sons', *Journal of English and Germanic Philology* 85.1 (Jan. 1986): 35–49. On the subject of women, the resources are far more diverse, from Rolf Heller, *Die literarische Darstellung der Frau in den Isländersagas* (Halle/Saak: M. Niemeyer, 1958), to Jenny Jochens, *Women in Old Norse Society* (Ithaca, NY: Cornell University Press, 1995) and Judith Jesch, *Women in the Viking Age* (Woodbridge: Boydell Press, 1991), both of whom offer some correctives to Clover's assertions about women in the sagas. The collection of essays edited by Sarah M. Anderson and Karen Swenson, *Cold Counsel: Women in Old Norse Literature and Mythology* (New York and London: Routledge: 2002) offers a very useful combination of historical and literary approaches. More recently, see Giselle Gos, 'Women as a Source of *heilræði*, "sound counsel": Social Mediation and Community Integration in *Fóstbræðra saga*', *Journal of English and Germanic Philology* 108.3 (July 2009): 281–300; and Lurkhur, 'Redefining Gender through the Arena of the Male Body'.

46 Thomas Laqueur, *Making Sex: Body and Gender from the Greeks to Freud* (Cambridge, MA: Harvard University Press, 1992).

analysis is the distinction between the Icelandic terms *hvatr* (keen, sharp) and *blauðr* (soft), used not uncommonly in discussions of men and women, and fairly obvious metaphors for male and female genitalia. The terms appear in numerous, non-sexual contexts as well, connected with weakness, age, senility, poverty, and loss.

The slippery field of Norse masculinity featured an ongoing war amongst men for supremacy and survival, and attempts to 'unman' one's enemies through innuendo, slander, and insult are numerous in the sagas and in Eddic poetry. Traditions of men insulting one another include the reciprocal exchange known as the *flyting* (and other examples such as *senna*, *mannjafnaðr*, and *níð*). In addition to insulting claims about cowardice, patriliny, and debauchery, there is a dizzying array of words and phrases for characterizing men as passive rather than active sexual partners (the most offensive are: *ragr*, *stroðinn*, *sorðinn*, all of which can be translated as 'well-fucked'). This last category of insults was so inflammatory that, according to the legal codes, they presented the slandered with an occasion for justifiable homicide. When in *Njál's saga*, Skarpheðinn accuses Flosi of being the recipient of the Svínafell troll's amorous advances, 'ef þú ert brúðr Svínfellsáss, sem sagt er, hverja ina níunda nótt ok geri hann þik at konu' ['If you are the bride of the Svínafell troll, as people say, every ninth night and he uses you as a woman'], or when, in *Gisli's saga*, talk is made of setting up wooden male figures in the act of intercourse with each other, the slanderous allusions can only be resolved through bloodshed.[47] The shame in being accused of playing the role of passive sexual partner was closely connected with castration. The accusation makes its appearance from time to time in poetry, such as in a single strophe from a longer set of vituperative verses spoken by the skaldic poet Örvar-oddr:

> 'Sigurðr, vart eigi,
> er á Sælundi felldak
> bræðr böðharða,
> Brand ok Agnar,
> Ásmund, Ingjald,
> Álfr var inn fimmti;
> en þú heima látt
> í höll konungs,
> skrökmálasamr,
> skauð hernumin.'

> 'Sigurðr, you weren't on Zealand when I felled the battle-hard brothers Brandr and Agnarr, Ásmundr and Ingjaldr, and Álfr was the

[47] *Brennu-Njáls saga*, ed. Einar Ól. Sveinsson (Reykjavík: Hið íslenzka fornritafélag, 1954), p. 314; *Gísla saga Súrssonar*, ed. Björn K. Þórólfsson in *Vestfirðinga sögur* (Reykjavík: Hið íslenzka fornritafélag, 1943), p. 10.

> fifth—while you were lying at home in the king's hall, full of tall stories, a captive gelding.'[48]

The Old Norse translated as 'captive gelding' here is *skauð hernumin*, more literally a 'war-snatched sheath' – the final thrust in an insulting verse implicating the accused in cowardice, castration, impotence, and passivity. In the late Eddic poem *Þrymskviða*, the loss of the hammer Mjöllnir represents a symbolic castration of Þórr; losing his hammer while asleep, in a passive state, is the equivalent of homosexual rape, and by being *sorðinn* in this manner, Þórr has brought shame upon himself and the other gods. Margaret Clunies Ross argues,

> *Þrymskviða* [...] shows how the gods' honour and status depended on Þórr's hammer, the symbol of his virility and the instrument with which he protected them and their women from marauding males and thereby ensured the retention of their domininant social status. The poem postulates what might happen if Þórr lost his hammer and then goes on to represent a successful counter-strategem for its recovery, which involves the god playing out his feminisation by transgressing (very reluctantly) normal gender roles. [...] In *Þrymskviða* the price of humiliation is success and the recovery of honour. By contrast, in Icelandic saga literature and probably in thirteenth-century society, the price of humiliation is usually dishonour.[49]

This poem (while primarily comic) emphasizes the particularly rich field of sexual transgression that links passive homosexuality, bestiality, castration, and violence at the level of symbolic myth. The character of Loki, whose sexually ambiguous presence highlights the comic and transgressive nature of the scenes in *Þrymskviða*, remains particularly polysemic in this regard. Loki represents a type of imprecise, androgynous (or even hermaphroditic), yet still potent sexuality that is entirely at odds with the simpler, overt masculinity of the sagas.[50]

The sense of shame attached to castration and the sort of cultural capital that castration (actual and metaphorical) had in Scandinavian society does not appear to have been radically different than in other medieval societies, as the other essays in this collection attest. What is missing in its treatment in

48 Text edited by Margaret Clunies Ross; trans. Carol Clover, in 'Hárbarðsljóð as Generic Farce', *Scandinavian* Studies 51.2 (spring 1979): 124–45 at p. 128.

49 Margaret Clunies Ross, 'Reading *Þrymskviða*', in *The Poetic Edda: Essays on Old Norse Mythology*, ed. Paul Acker and Carolyne Larrington (New York and London: Routledge, 2002), pp. 177–94 atp. 189.

50 One central scene for any discussion of Loki, sexuality, and castration must be the description in Snorri's *Skáldskaparmál* of how Loki got the giantess Skadi to laugh by tying one end of a rope to his testicles, and the other end to the beard of a she-goat – an animal associated with effeminacy (as in the proverbial expression '*ragr* as a goat'). In *Gylfaginning* we learn that Loki once gave birth, while in the form of a mare, to Sleipnir, Óðinn's eight-legged horse.

Sturlunga saga, however, is the sense of exquisitely cruel pleasure taken by observers of its effects upon the castrated. While the 'caponization' of a man like Abelard draws a parallel between real emasculation and dehumanization[51] (as is implied in the scene between Hrafn and Gizurr), missing in *Sturlunga saga* is any raucous laughter, whether that of *Þrymskviða* or of the Old French tale *De Connebert*, when the blacksmith husband gleefully mocks the freshly castrated priest: 'Vos ne batroiz jamais crepon / Ainz manroiz vie de chapon!' ['You will never again pound the flesh, / but you will henceforth lead the life [or, bear the cock] of a capon!'] (*De Connebert*, vv. 284–5).[52] Given the emphasis by medieval writers upon the 'psychological' effect of cruelty, it would seem possible for a writer to focus on the internal turmoil caused by partaking in an act that is emasculating and dehumanizing for many involved.[53]

Sturla Þórðarson attempts authorial amends almost immediately. In the aftermath of the mutilation, they send for Órækja's wife Arnbjörg. Þórð refuses Sturla Þórðarson absolution for his part in the mutilation, suggesting he will need to seek the higher authority of the bishop in Skálaholt. When Arnbjörg arrives, Sturla tells her (somewhat surprisingly) that her husband still has his sight and is *heill* (healthy or healed). She rides to the cave and finds him already recovered enough to have ridden south. By the time the entire group meets in Skálaholt, he is described as *hressasti* (restored), and Bishop Magnús proceeds to *leysti þá misskunnsamliga* [absolve them mercifully] (1:396). At the bishop's suggestion, Órækja and others travel abroad with Magnús and Bishop Kygri-Björn, while his wife travels north with her brother Kolbeinn *ungi*.[54] Órækja meets King Valdimar the Old in Denmark, and makes a verse in his honor (1:396–7). There are several elements of this little narrative that remain unclear, but what is most evident is that Sturla stresses that the damage to Órækja is minimal (despite certain evidence to the contrary), including the reactions of

51 For more on the castration of Abelard and his construction of it as martyrdom, see Larissa Tracy's article in this volume, '"Al defouleden is holie bodi": Castration, the Sexualization of Torture, and Anxieties of Identity in the *South English Legendary*, pp. 87–107.

52 Translated (and emended) by Laura Kendrick, in *Chaucerian Play: Comedy and Control in the Canterbury Tales* (Berkeley: University of California Press, 1988), p. 66. See also Mary E. Leech, 'The Castrating of the Shrew: The Performance of Masculinity and Masculine Order in *La dame escolliee*' in this volume, pp. 210–28, and Larissa Tracy, 'The Uses of Torture and Violence in the Fabliaux: When Comedy Crosses the Line', *Florilegium* 23.2 (2006): 143–68, and *Torture and Brutality in Medieval Literature: Negotiations of National Identity* (Cambridge: D. S. Brewer, 2012).

53 Daniel Baraz has outlined the major writers in the medieval discourse on cruelty as Seneca, Augustine, Bernard of Clairvaux, and Thomas Aquinas, in 'Seneca, Ethics, and the Body: The Treatment of Cruelty in Medieval Thought', *Journal of the History of Ideas* 59.2 (April 1998): 195–215.

54 This was distinguished company; Kygri-Björn was an accomplished and learned bishop, and traditionally is considered the author of the thirteenth-century *Maríu saga*.

other Icelanders when the mutilation is known, not to mention the description of the acts themselves. It is also suggested (although not certain) that after this incident, Órækja and Arnbjörg no longer live together as husband and wife, suggesting some permanent damage had been done to Órækja despite Sturla's initial protests to the contrary. Any reading that takes the author's claim of Órækja's health at face value must willfully disregard the evidence suggesting that the scene as described offered primal and traumatic cruelty to the eyewitnesses. Jenny Jochens argues that Sturla's original reference to Órækja being 'hale' could imply mere optimism, although in her note to this passage she also voices doubt that the recovery was as complete as Sturla suggests.[55] Gade posits that this event is fictitious, and this is a reading that is closer to the truth – Sturla has been shaken by the event, and has attempted to make amends (or to atone) through imagining at least temporarily a 'happy ending'.[56] But the healing (if it has occurred) does not lead to an immediate resolution for the husband and wife. Instead Órækja's companions in the weeks following the assault are bishops, and through their presence and his own reported prayers and religious sentiments expressed under the most intense duress and terror, Sturla grants his agonies a religious significance. His tribulations might seem analogous to those of Guðmundr, the bishop of Hólar, who suffers a crippling injury to his right foot during a shipwreck, bears the burden humbly, and is miraculously cured.[57] But Órækja's life does not follow the peaceful course of the bishop's; he returns to the saga in chapter 143 to initiate a sequence of revenge (which ends poorly for him), and by chapter 157 he is exiled to Norway and is out of the saga. During these activities, the mutilation is referred to on a few occasions, but there is no suggestion that Órækja Snorrason is changed irrevocably by that visit to Surtshellir. Perhaps that is because Sturla exaggerated the mutilation, or perhaps he obscured its painful after-effects; more important to him, it would seem, were its effects upon the eyewitnesses, including himself as author.

The sadistic attempt to effeminize another man rates among the lasting images of *Sturlunga saga*. Despite the presence of castration as a punishment in the law codes, and in spite of its popularity as a motif when males insult one another, actual castration was rare in Icelandic literature. Contemporary sagas such as *Sturlunga saga* are an exception to the rule, and the mutilation of Órækja thus offers a unique opportunity to see how actors within the saga react to extreme cases of real violation. Even for Icelanders accustomed to violence and brutality, the scene in Surtshellir would seem to have gone beyond acceptable standards of aggression and punishment, and seems to have

55 Jochens, *Women in Old Norse Society*, p. 66.

56 In '1236: Órækja meiddr ok heill gerr', *Griplá* 9 (1995): 115–32.

57 See *Prestssaga Guðmundar góða*, in *Sturlunga saga*, 1:128–35.

had a traumatizing effect upon the viewers as well as the victim. This sadistic turn is also meaningful and beneficial because it prefigures, in its lingering mélange of cruelty and cold comfort, some element of the modern fascination with horror that is to come. To cite a well-worn quotation from film theorist Kaja Silverman:

> I will hazard the generalization that it is always the victim – the figure who occupies the passive position – who is really the focus of attention, and whose subjugation the subject [whether male or female] experiences as a pleasurable repetition from his/her own history. Indeed, I would go so far as to say that the fascination of the sadistic point of view is merely that it provides the best vantage point from which to watch the masochistic story unfold.[58]

Against this critical background, the violation of Órækja Snorrason suggests itself as an early, perhaps pioneering, moment in scrutinized sadism and horror. The wrapped knife, the gouged eyes, the lost 'stone' – all exist as elements of a 'limit event' in a sadistic ritual that reveals a small rotten core within the code of Icelandic masculinity. The disfigurement and disability wrought in Surtshellir are evocative of the worst extremes of the model of sexuality taken for granted in medieval Scandinavia, one that, at its extreme, still held the capacity to shock by making overt the essential link between violence, cruelty, and manhood. The nebulous and fragile quality of Norse masculinity, one ever at risk of penetration, mutilation, and abjection, was perhaps in this way an early species of contemporary sexuality, which understands that the experience of pleasure, like cruelty, depends a great deal upon one's capacity for pain.

[58] Kaja Silverman, 'Masochism and Subjectivity', *Framework* 12 (1980): 2–9 at p. 5. See also the seminal article by Carol Clover, 'Her Body, Himself: Gender in the Slasher Film', *Representations* 20 (autumn, 1987): 187–228.

CHAPTER 10

The Castrating of the Shrew: The Performance of Masculinity and Masculine Identity in La dame escolliee[1]

Mary E. Leech

Seemingly rooted in the shrew-taming tradition, the Old French fabliau *La dame escolliee* (*The Gelded Lady*) defies the rules of any genre in which it is placed. As a fabliau, the setting, characters and the disturbingly graphic violence diverge from the usually light-hearted comedy typical of the fabliaux. As a shrew-taming tale, the story breaks several of the genre's conventions, which generally work to confirm the accepted social order of male dominance and female submission in a marital relationship. In its graphic depiction of a fake castration performed on a woman, *La dame escolliee* does not restore masculine order and dominance, but transforms a female body into a male one through a violent performance, challenging the very concept of what masculinity is. The husband of the castrated woman is not the one who punishes her. His passivity makes him more feminine than masculine in many ways. The man who performs the false castration (the woman's son-in-law) presents a harsh and exaggerated form of masculinity that insists on a narrow construct of maleness that destabilizes the very structures it seemingly tries to preserve. By undermining his father-in-law and transforming his mother-in-law, the supposed shrew-tamer reveals inherent problems with such a limited view of masculinity. The use of a false castration on a woman changes the purpose of the performance and moves the dynamic of the tale from a tale about the proper role of women to a cautionary tale for men and masculine identity.

Castration in medieval literature across cultures works figuratively to verify or enforce a specific concept of masculinity through actions perpetrated on a male body. From perhaps the best-known medieval castration, that of Abelard,

[1] Parts of this essay were originally published as 'That's Not Funny: Comic Forms, Didactic Purpose, and Physical Injury in Medieval Comic Tales', *LATCH: A Journal for the Study of the Literary Artifact in Theory, Culture or History*, 1 (2008): 105–27. The thesis and focus of this essay have been substantially revised for inclusion in this volume.

to comical presentations, such as the fabliau *Le prestre crucefie* (*The Crucified Priest*), castration is enacted on the male body by those attempting to control that body and assert their dominant masculinity.[2] Such masculinities in literature are performative in that they demonstrate accepted male behavior, the consequences of challenging that behavior, and the boundaries of masculine action. Female castration in medieval tales is virtually non-existent.[3] The imposition on sexuality and feminine pleasure, which is the purpose of modern female castration (or genital mutilation),[4] was unknown in medieval Europe. Control over female sexuality, and more importantly female social roles, was usually played out through tales of marriage and marriage dynamics, such as the traditional shrew-taming tale. Castration is a punishment reserved for men – specifically men who have committed sexual transgressions, as several articles in this collection point out.[5] It was not a common, or even accepted, punishment for women or for adultery.[6]

2 Foucault's discussion on how such punishments are used as a means to control a body is often cited as a theoretical hallmark for this concept. Foucault states: 'Discipline increases the forces on the body (in economic terms of utility) and diminishes these same forces (in political terms of obedience). In short, it dissociates power from the body; on the one hand, it turns it into an "aptitude", a "capacity", which it seeks to increase; on the other hand, it reverses the course of energy, the power that might result from it, and turns it into a relation of strict subjugation.' Michel Foucault, *Discipline and Punish: The Birth of the Prison*, trans. Alan Sheridan (New York: Vintage, 1995), p. 138.

3 Only *La dame escolliee*. There is an instance of female genital mutilation (but not castration) in *Trubert*, which is arguably a fabliau. In this tale, Trubert kills a woman and mutilates her, presenting her genitalia to his victim, the duke, as 'proof' of his victory over the duke's enemy. Norris Lacy gives the best and fullest account of this 3,000-line tale in 'Trickery, Trubertage, and the Limits of Laughter', in *The Old French Fabliaux: Essays on Comedy and Context*, ed. Kristin L. Burr and Norris J. Lacy (Jefferson, NC: McFarland & Co., 2007), pp. 82–92. The text of *Trubert* appears in *Nouveau recueil complet des fabliaux*, ed. Willem Noomen and Nico van den Boogaard (Assen: Van Gorcum, 1983–98), Vol. 10 pp. 143–262. See also Larissa Tracy, *Torture and Brutality in Medieval Literature: Negotiations of National Identity* (Cambridge: D. S. Brewer, 2012), p. 216, n. 94.

4 Female castration and circumcision are often referred to as 'female genital mutilation', and have been a central topic for modern human rights. Many pieces have been published on this topic, some medical, and others editorial. See Linda Burstyn, 'Female Circumcision Comes to America', *Atlantic Monthly*, 276.4 (October 1995): 28; J. M. Abu Daia, 'Female Circumcision', *Saudi Medical Journal*, 21.10 (October 2000): 921; P. Brisson, H. Patel, and N. Feins, 'Female Circumcision', *Journal of Pediatric Surgery*, 36.7 (July 2001): 1068–9.

5 Castration was a possible punishment for treason and for rape, according to Norman law, which adopted several of its punishments from Scandinavian tradition. Occasionally it was the prescribed punishment for sodomy. For an analysis of castration in law texts, either as punishment or in reference to compensation for genital wounds, see, in this volume, Rolf H. Bremmer Jr, 'The Children He Never Had; The Husband She Never Served: Castration and Genital Mutilation in Medieval Frisian Law', pp. 108–30; Jay Paul Gates, 'The *Fulmannod* Society: Social Valuing of the (Male) Legal Subject', pp. 131–48; Charlene M. Eska, '"Imbrued in their owne bloud": Castration in Early Welsh and Irish Sources', pp. 149–73.

6 In her article 'The Uses of Torture and Violence in the Fabliaux: When Comedy Crosses the Line', *Florilegium* 23.2 (2006): 143–68, Larissa Tracy cites the following example from

In literature, metaphoric castrations are also signs of sexual impropriety. The female transgressors are often mistreated and physically punished for their part in the sexual act, but they are not mutilated like the men.[7] Concepts of the role of the female body in a patriarchal society contribute to the lack of female mutilation; literary presentations of punishments for women do not normally penetrate the woman's body because penetration carried sexual overtones of illicit intercourse.[8] The dangers of open female bodies are imagined in tales of the loathly lady, in which the bodies of these women are open in their misshapen

the Spanish *Libro de los fueros de Castiella*, which is not a law but a judicial decision called a *fazana*, which established a legal precedent. As Tracy writes, 'While there seem to be no references to castration in French customary law, according to a collection of judicial precedents from thirteenth-century Spain, punishing the offending wife was acceptable, but the lover was protected by the law' (p. 153, n. 31): 'A knight of Ciudad Rodrigo castrated another knight whom he caught sleeping with his wife. The relatives of the other man complained to the king. [...] The decision of the court was that the husband ought to hang, because [...] if the husband wanted to kill anyone, he could kill his wife with no penalties; [...] but since [he] had not killed his wife, he had taken the law into his own hands [and] had also dishonored his victim', *Libro de los fueros de Castiella*, ed. Sanchez, pp. 58–9, titulo 116. See Theresa Vann, 'Private Murders and Public Retribution', in *Proceedings of the Tenth International Congress of Medieval Canon Law*, ed. Kenneth Pennington, et al. *Monumenta Iuris Canonici*, Vol. 11 (Vatican City: Biblioteca Apostolica Vaticana, 2001), p. 812. In French customary law, 'The *Costuma d'Agen* lists public humiliation for both the wife and her lover as the appropriate punishment. According to this thirteenth-century statute, the two offenders, having been caught and *witnessed* in the sexual act by a judge appointed after the initial accusation and two council members, would be bound together naked and led through the town preceded by trumpeters. The audience of assembled villagers could then gawk and even beat the two with clubs': Tracy, 'The Uses of Torture', p. 153. A fourteenth-century customal of Toulouse in MS Paris, BN, lat. 9187, includes an illustration of castration. See Daron Lee Burrows, *The Stereotype of the Priest in the Old French Fabliaux: Anticlerical Satire and Lay Identity* (Oxford: Peter Lang, 2005), pp. 178–9. See also Agen, France, Archives départementales de Lot-et-Garonne, MS 42, fol. 42v., trans. in F. R. P. Akehurst, 'Good Name, Reputation, and Notoriety in French Customary Law', in *Fama: The Politics of Talk and Reputation in Medieval Europe*, ed. Thelma Fenster and Daniel Lord Smail (Ithaca, NY: Cornell University Press, 2003), pp. 75–94, p. 89.

7 The wife in *Bisclavret* has her nose torn off by her wronged wolf/husband, and her descendants are said to have the same deformity. Though she is unfaithful once she learns her husband is a werewolf, her punishment is not so much for sexual transgressions as for betraying her husband's trust. When she confesses, her crimes are the betrayal of her husband and her work to keep him in wolf form, not her remarriage. Her punishment is related to her vanity, as her face is mutilated. Also, she is not portrayed as shrewish. Though she takes advantage of another man's love for her, she is not punished to change her behavior, but to get at the truth. At the end of the tale, she leaves with the second husband and has children with him. She does not return to her original husband, nor does he seek to have her submit to his authority.

8 Marina Warner comments on the sexualized nature of torture performed on female saints: 'In Christian hagiography, the sadomasochistic content of the paeans to male and female martyrs is startling. [...] But the particular focus on women's torn and broken flesh reveals the psychological obsession of the religion with sexual sin, and the tortures that pile up one upon the other with pornographic repetitiousness underline the identification of the female with the perils of sexual contact': *Alone of All Her Sex: The Myth and the Cult of the Virgin Mary* (New York: Vintage, 1976), p. 71.

forms. Hags such as Dame Ragnell or the malformed women of *Kempy Kay* and *The Tale of Florent* appear in the woods, outside of society. It is their ability to enter the culture that is threatening, and it is only in their transformation to the conventions of femininity that the threat is presumably erased.[9] The openness of the female body must be closed before comfort is restored. In other romances, when there is even a thought of illicit sexuality by women, their bodies are often locked away.[10] Penetrating the female body exposes unregulated female power and the threat that power represents to a patriarchal culture.

Castration then, is an issue of the masculine body and trangressive masculine behavior, in both the reason for the castration, as well as the castration itself. Though literary castrations may be largely symbolic, as in Guigemar's wound to the thigh in Marie de France's *lai*, the implications are the same. Sexual transgression by males results in the loss (either literally or figuratively) of male sexuality. However, by punishing a transgression with another transgression, castration confuses masculine roles and behavior more than it reaffirms any sense of authority.[11] In this volume, Jed Chandler explains that castrations, both literal and figurative, are inscriptions of masculine virginity in the Grail cycles – that loss prevents sexual spoiling and allows the final achievement of the Grail.[12] By performing castration on a female body, the sense of masculine authority is further confused, as the female body must first be transformed into a male body. She must be empowered as a man before she can be controlled through castration. The faux castration performed in *La*

9 There are several very good essays on this topic in the volume *The English Loathly Lady Tales: Boundaries, Traditions, Motifs*, ed. S. Elizabeth Passmore and Susan Carter (Kalamazoo, MI: Medieval Institute Publications, 2008). In particular, Susan Carter's essay, 'A Hymenation of Hags', pp. 83–99, addresses the issue of gender power politics in *The Wife of Bath's Tale*. Often, the misshapen and leaking body of the loathly lady is associated with uncontrolled sexuality, which is put back in its proper place with the marriage and transformation of the loathly lady into a beautiful woman. Carter addresses this issue and the issue of sovereignty, normally the central point of power in these tales. Carter argues that 'allegorizing ideas about masculine power through the vehicle of female flesh places sovereignty in the realm of gender power politics. Virginity or its absence ought to be crucial in an allegory that involves an active female sexuality, but curiously it matters less than it might [...]. The Loathly Lady motif consistently makes chastity less of an issue than female control': 'A Hymenation of Hags', p. 83.

10 There are many examples of this motif. Often, the woman is young and the husband is older, so it is the *threat* of infidelity rather than the *actual* infidelity that motivates the husband to lock away his young wife. The young wife in Marie de France's *Yonec* and May in *The Merchant's Tale* are perhaps two of the best-known examples.

11 The fact that those who mutilated Abelard are also mutilated and blinded shows that the very attempt to control Abelard's body and masculine role actually results in the loss of masculinity rather than the role of dominance that was sought in the act of castration. See Larissa Tracy '"Al defouleden is holie bodie": Castration, the Sexualization of Torture, and Anxieties of Identity in the *South English Legendary*', in this volume, pp. 87–107, and Introduction.

12 Jed Chandler, 'Eunuchs of the Grail', in this volume, pp. 229–54.

dame escolliee is an anomaly: the transgression is not sexual, the punisher is not correcting a wrong done to him, and most importantly, the performance is not enacted on a male body.

La dame escolliee begins with a count who goes out hunting near the home of a nobleman, intent on seeking the nobleman's daughter whose beauty is renowned. The count asks the nobleman for hospitality, but the nobleman hesitates for fear of his wife's response. To get around his wife, the nobleman orders exactly the opposite of what he (the nobleman) really wants, and thus the count gets to stay, have a sumptuous meal, and marry the nobleman's daughter. Before the girl leaves with her new husband, her mother advises her not to be mild, but instead to take control over her new husband. The count suspects that his wife may prove troublesome, so he makes an example of two greyhounds given as a wedding gift from the nobleman. When the hounds do not catch a rabbit fast enough for him, the count cuts off their heads in front of his wife. He also beheads a palfrey (another wedding gift from the nobleman) that stumbles after he commands it not to trip. Once installed in her new home, the new wife deliberately orders the cook to over-season the count's food with garlic, against his express wishes. When he finds out, the count first mutilates the cook and then beats his wife with a thorn branch so badly that it takes her three months to recover: 'Iluec jut ele bien .iii. mois / qu'ele ne pot seoir as dois' [There she lay well three months that she could not sit at table] (363–4).[13] The emphasis is not just on the length of time, but also on how long she is unable to fulfill her social duties as wife.

When the nobleman and his wife come to visit, the count sends the nobleman out hunting, and while he is gone the count tells his servants to castrate a bull and bring him the balls. He then tells the mother that her pride is in her testicles, which he will now remove: '"Vos avez coilles comme nos, / s'en est vostre cuers orgueillous / Ge vos i vueil faire taster; s'il i sont, ses ferai oster"' ['You have testicles like us. It is the means of your proud heart. I will feel for them there; if they are there, I will remove them'] (461–4). Holding the mother down, a servant slices a six-inch gash in one buttock, shoves in one of the bull testicles with his fist, and pulls the fist back out. He does the same for the other side, while the mother screams: 'cele se pasme qui fu mue' [she faints letting out a wail] (488). When she recovers, the count says that if she does not do as she is told, he will burn out the roots of her testicles with a hot iron coulter. She then swears that she will obey her husband:

[13] All quotes from *La Dame escolliee* are from *Nouveau recueil complet des fabliaux*, ed. Noomen and van den Boogaard, 8:1–125. Line numbers are given in parentheses in the text. All translations in the footnotes are mine. I chose to have literal translations that are less elegant rather than more polished ones, in order to get across, as much as possible, the exact structure and meaning of the language. I am deeply indebted to Dr Ellen Friedrich for her invaluable help with the translations.

'certes lealment vos affi
& sor sanz le vos jurerai
que mon seignor ne desdirai;
servirai le si com ge doi.'
(498–501)

'I surely give loyalty to you and by the saints I will swear to you that I will not disobey my lord; I will serve him as I should.'

The count shows his wife what he has done to her mother, and says he will do the same to her if she is disobedient. The wife swears she is more like her father than her mother:

'Ge ne sui pas de la nature
ma mere, qui est fiere & dure;
ge retrai plus, sire, a mon pere
que ge ne faz voir a ma mere.'
(517–20)

'I am not of the nature of my mother, who is fierce and proud; I take after more, sir, of my father than I resemble my mother.'

She promises to obey him from now on. When the nobleman returns, he is told the same story, and shown the pail with the bloody balls in it. He acts convinced:

Cil quide que trestot voir soit
por les coillons que iluec voit;
por la dame qu'il voit navree,
cuide qu'ele soit amendee.
(551–4).

This he believes that he has heard because of the testicles he sees; because the lady that he sees wounded, he believes that she will make amends.

After the mother swears to obey her husband, her wounds are treated and she recovers. The tale ends with a moral praising the count's actions and calling for shame on men who are ruled by their wives and on women who would dominate their husbands: 'Honi soient, & il si ierent, / cil qui lour fames trop dangierent!' (May they be shamed they go thus, they whom their wives dominate!) (567–8).

From the start, *Le dame escolliee* departs from the shrew-taming conventions.[14] The basics of the shrew-taming story include a shrewish older sister

[14] The origins of shrew-taming as a comedic form cannot truly be traced. Part of a long oral tradition, the shrew-taming structure is outlined in number 901 of Francis James Childs's *The English and Scottish Popular Ballads* (New York, Dover Publications, 1965). The folktales listed here are referenced in Child's volume by motif number, rather than page numbers.

who must marry before her mild younger sister, a suitor who marries the shrew and then vows to tame her, the killing of animals as an example to the new wife, punishment through deprivation, and a wager to prove the wife's submissiveness.[15] The emphasis is not on the suffering of the wife (which is underplayed), but rather the comedy of her change in attitude – her humiliation – as a result of the punishment inflicted on her.[16] The overall threat of female dominance is played out in the comedy of the violence against the woman and the eventual triumph of the man. Shrew-taming tales were meant to reinforce the proper role of women. These tales are not about sexual transgression, but rather social transgression. In *La dame escolliee*, the punishment is not one of masculine control over a female body, but masculine control over a male body. The female body is transformed into a male body through the enactment of the false castration. The conflict in this tale changes from one of a man asserting control over a woman to a man asserting control over another man.

First of all, the central female character is the mother-in-law, not the wife of the count. Next, the count's wife is not really the problem in the tale, nor does she need to be married off to secure a match for a younger and more compliant sibling. Though she is foolish for following her mother's advice, the impetus for her actions is not her own shrewishness, but rather her mother's. The false castration is particularly gruesome, both in concept and in description in the tale. The presentation of the wife's mutilated mother is really unnecessary in terms of convincing the wife to obey her husband because she has already been beaten into submission. Also, the father-in-law is an unusual

[15] If these tropes sound like the plot of Shakespeare's *The Taming of the Shrew*, it may be due to the influence of oral folklore on Shakespeare. Folklorist Jan Harold Brunvand explores these possible influences in his article 'The Folktale Origin of *The Taming of the Shrew*', in *The Taming of the Shrew: An Authoritative Text, Sources and Contexts, Criticism, Rewritings and Appropriations*, ed. Dymphna Callaghan (New York: W. W. Norton & Co., 2009), pp. 266–279.

[16] Variations on the story, such as the sixteenth-century ballad *A Merry Jeste of a Shrewd and Curst Wife*, include more extreme physical punishments. In this ballad, the wife is beaten and wrapped in a salted horsehide until she swears to behave. While she is wrapped in the skin, the emphasis is on her thoughts of how she has wronged her husband, not her physical pain. The ballad reads: 'Within a while, she did reuiue, / Through the grose salte that did her smarte / She though she should neuer haue gone on lieu, / Out of Morels skin so sore is her harte.' When she berates her husband for his cruelty, he says that he will keep her there to 'wayle and weepe', The song then says: 'With that her moode began to sinke, / And sayd deare husband for grace I call: / For I shall neuer sleepe nor winke, / Till I get your loue whatso befall'. The implication here is that the physical pain does not change her ways as much as the idea that she is not loved by her husband. Any mention of pain is minimal, and she seems to be no worse for wear once she is taken out of the salted hide. Other stories, listed by both Child and the Aarne-Thompson-Uther type 900, include: 'Pride Punished' (Italy), 'The Crumb in the Beard' (Italy), 'Greyfoot' (Denmark). From Child, *The English and Scottish Popular Ballads*.

male character in the tale. Rather than controlling his domineering wife, he has found a way to manipulate her into giving him what he wants. He has control over his house to a degree, but only in execution, not in appearance. The count's actions demand that the appearance of masculine control and feminine obedience be upheld. It is not enough that the nobleman is able to circumvent his wife's will; his wife must accept her subservient place and show public obedience to her husband.

Shrew-taming tales normally place blame on the woman and her desire to dominate. The husband's failing may be implied, but this fault is corrected by his taming of his wife. *La dame escolliee* puts the blame squarely on the husband who allows her to rule him: 'Mais tant avoit amé s'osser / Que desor lui l'avoit levee / & segnorie abandonee' [Because he loved his wife so much he let her be raised up and abandoned his authority] (28–30). In the typical shrew-taming tale, the husband is desperate to find some way of controlling his wife. This is not the case with the nobleman in *La dame escolliee.* He seems perfectly happy with his solution. The count is the one who is upset by the wife's behavior and the nobleman's lack of direct authority over her. The husband's response to his wife's castration is passive as well. In fact, given the violence performed on his wife, the husband's reaction is rather mild. He takes the count at his word, and accepts that his wife's behavior will change. He demands no proof of her obedience, nor is any obedience demonstrated, as is typical in other shrew-taming tales. Throughout the entire tale, the nobleman never aggressively seeks control over his wife. In contrast to the exaggerated masculinity of the count, the nobleman's passivity is more feminine than masculine.

From the contemporary moral standpoint, the nobleman's solution would be troubling. Men were supposed to be the moral center for women, and husbands were morally responsible for their wives. Admonitions about a husband's responsibility for his wife's spiritual well-being as well as his dominance over her can be found in the epistles of Paul: 'Wives, submit yourselves to your own husbands as you do to the Lord. For the husband is the head of the wife as Christ is the head of the church, his body, of which he is the Savior. Now as the church submits to Christ, so also wives should submit to their husbands in everything' (Ephesians 5:22–4). Other theological figures of the early Christian world, particularly Augustine, expressed similar sentiments, arguing that the man gave a child its soul, while the woman gave the child its imperfect flesh, which followed the philosophy of the ancient Greeks.[17] Since the nobleman only rules his wife through subversion, he does not appear to

[17] Aristotle states: 'the male and female principles may be put down first and foremost as the origins of generation, the former as containing the efficient cause of generation, the latter the material of it': 'On the Generation of Animals' 2.716a 5–7, trans. Arthur Platt, in *Great Books of the Western World*, vol. 8: *Aristotle II*, ed. Mortimer J. Adler, 2nd edn (Chicago: Encyclopaedia Britannica, 1990).

fulfill his moral duty as a husband. The tale even states that the authority is hers, not his, when the nobleman says to the count, 'si l'a apris, / sel vorra maintenir toz dis' [So she has taken [authority/control] and will want to continue it] (105–6). The threat to masculinity is in the behavior of the man, not the woman – another man corrects the problem, but has no right to do so.

The passive actions of the nobleman in the tale, then, are a greater threat to the construct of male authority in the tale than his wife and daughter ever are. Jo Ann McNamara asks 'If a person does not act like a man, is he a man? And what does it mean to "act like a man" except to dominate women?'[18] His passivity is traditionally feminine,[19] and he does not uphold the moral or social standards that are expected of him. He is ruled by his emotions, especially love.[20] The wife has control over running the estate, and contradicts him to show her disdain for him. Rather than confronting his wife or asserting his authority as a man, the nobleman develops an underhanded method for tricking his wife into doing what he wants. Trickery and deception, along with passivity, were associated primarily with women.[21] Starting with Eve, women were viewed as weak-willed creatures who were easily deceived.[22] When the nobleman explains the situation to the count, the count laughs and tells him,

[18] Jo Ann McNamara, 'The *Herrenfrage:* The Restructuring of the Gender System, 1050–1150', in *Medieval Masculinities: Regarding Men in the Middle Ages*, ed. Clare A. Lees, Thelma Fenster, and Jo Ann McNamara (Minneapolis: University of Minnesota Press, 1994), pp. 3–29 at p. 5. McNamara's point is primarily about celibacy, but the issue of defining manhood according to dominant relationships with women is applicable here.

[19] This belief was widespread throughout the ancient and medieval eras. The following statement by Aristotle, on the male and female roles in generation, is typical of the belief: 'But the female, as female, is passive, and male, as male, is active': 'On the Generation of Animals', p. 269. For a detailed look at the construct of gender perceptions, particularly the association of masculinity with activity and femininity with passivity, see Joyce E. Salisbury, 'Gendered Sexuality', in *Handbook of Medieval Sexuality*, ed. Vern L. Bullough and James A. Brundage (New York: Garland, 1996), pp. 83–6.

[20] Excess of emotion, particularly love, was seen as a weakness in men. For a more detailed discussion on the concept of lovesickness and its associated effects on masculinity, see Vern L. Bullough, 'On Being Male in the Middle Ages', in *Handbook of Medieval Sexuality*, ed. Bullough and Brundage, pp. 38–40.

[21] In the courtly love tradition, the wives often use tricks to keep their husbands from finding out about their lovers. When a disguised Tristan carries Isolde across a creek on his back, she is able to swear to King Mark that she has had no man between her legs other than the king and the beggar who carried her across the creek. In *The Merchant's Tale*, May convinces January not to trust his newly regained eyesight when he sees her with Damian.

[22] In *The City of God*, Augustine argues that the serpent 'first tried his deceit upon the woman, making his assault upon the weaker part of that human alliance, that he might gradually gain the whole, and not supposing that the man would readily give ear to him, or be deceived, but that he might yield to the error of the woman. [...] we cannot believe that Adam was deceived, and supposed the devil's word to be truth, and therefore transgressed God's law, but that he by the drawings of kindred yielded to the woman': (book XIV ch. 11).

"'Se fussiez preuz, pas nel feïst"' ['If you were strong, she would not do this'] (104). Despite this chiding, the nobleman responds that nothing will change, "'Se Dieux de moi n'en merci"' ['unless God gives to me mercy'] (107). Though the nobleman may have control behind the scenes, his actions do not conform to the ruthless domination performed by the count, nor do the nobleman's actions demonstrate a socially recognized form of masculinity. The nobleman's remedy is not an active solution, or one that asserts authority over his wife. Rather, the nobleman has usurped authority, in the figure of his wife, much as Eve did when she tempted Adam. Since the nobleman is unwilling to take direct action, the count steps in and takes action for him.

But the count's actions are also extreme. In choosing a mock castration, the count violates a host of other social and genre taboos, besides disciplining another man's wife and effectively emasculating him in the process. Castration in the fabliaux is uncommon. It only appears in two other tales, and in each case the punishment is enacted on men – adulterous priests at that. In these stories, castration is a method of exerting masculine authority over a transgressive masculine body. In *Le prestre crucifie* (*The Crucified Priest*) a priest engages in an affair with a crucifix sculptor's wife. When the sculptor arrives home early, the priest, who had merely been dining with the wife, hides in the workshop among the life-sized half-finished crucifixes. The priest strips and climbs up on a cross, but the sculptor is not fooled. Seeing the priest, the sculptor feigns horror at having carved genitals on the figure of Christ and cuts them off. The priest escapes after being castrated, but is caught by two other men, beaten and forced to pay a high ransom. In *Le prestre ki perdi les colles* (*The Priest Who Lost His Balls*), also known as *De Connebert*, a smith takes revenge on a priest having an affair with his wife by nailing the priest's scrotum to the workbench, giving him a razor, and setting the workshop on fire. The priest must slice off his testicles to escape, which he does. After a long convalescence, the priest seeks retribution in the courts, but the court rules against him. The final image of the fabliau is of two dogs fighting over the roasted testicles in the ruins of the blacksmith's shop.

Both of these tales have an underlying theme of justified revenge, with the wronged husbands exacting a punishment that appears to fit the crime. Though the punishments are extreme, and castration as an actual practice was not widely condoned, the audience can take a certain amount of satisfaction in the idea of the priests being humiliated for their transgressions. The transgressive masculinity of the priest is removed by the proper masculine authority and accepted masculine identity. The social reinforcement of the punishment allows a sense of justice to triumph in the tales that may not happen in reality.[23]

[23] William Ian Miller, 'In Defense of Revenge', in *Medieval Crime and Social Control: Medieval Cultures*, vol. 16, ed. Barbara A. Hanawalt and David Wallace (Minneapolis:

In this way, the masculine performance of the married man is reaffirmed by the control he takes over the masculinity of the priests who have usurped the married man's role in his household. The extreme aspect of the punishment is downplayed by social acceptance. The public knowledge of the castration causes no outrage, and the priests' humiliations are continued publicly through the beating of one priest and the failed lawsuit of the other. In terms of masculinity, the priests in these tales violate the philosophy behind clerical celibacy,[24] and usurp the masculine control of feminine sexuality that marriage is supposed to bring to women.[25] Clerical celibacy was not merely an exercise in sexual control. Church fathers, particularly Augustine, believed that sex was a distraction to the true connection between a man and a woman.[26] Abelard attempted to restructure his masculine identity after his castration as intellectual, and not physical or sexual.[27] Chastity (or lack of sexual activity) was meant to elevate the cleric beyond mere physical desire and move him towards a more intellectual and spiritual life. Through their sexual misconduct, the fabliaux priests have undermined a higher concept of masculinity, and threatened the masculine control of sexuality that marriage was supposed to provide.

Male power in these fabliaux is directly connected to control over male genital performance. Masculinity, male identity, and the male body cannot be neatly separated in the medieval world view in which the male body was both metaphorically and philosophically the focus. Women's roles and women's

University of Minnesota Press, 1999), pp. 70–89, contrasts revenge motifs in Icelandic sagas to the modern appeal of revenge. Miller writes that despite 'the antihonor discourse and pretense that revenge is inimical to a just legal order, we still feel at some visceral level that the world of honor and revenge is nobler than ours, and it still remains for us grand and frightfully alluring' (p. 72). Later in the essay, Miller discusses the reality of revenge in Norse culture with the sagas (pp. 77–8). His point as it relates here is that the avenger in fiction can act without shame or repercussions in a way that does not and cannot happen in reality. I would argue that this concept of revenge applies to the castration fabliaux discussed here.

24 McNamara discusses the social implications of priestly celibacy and the fears it brought to concepts of masculinity: 'If men who repudiated connection with women not only remained men, but even claimed to be superior to other men, what did this mean to the self-image of men in the secular world?' 'The *Herrenfrage*' (p. 5). The fear of rampant female sexuality because of clerical celibacy is ridiculed in tales about priests who have affairs with or seduce women, which is part of what these particular priest castration tales may be addressing. See McNamara, 'The *Herrenfrage*', pp. 6–12.

25 Georges Duby discusses how marriage in medieval society was a method of controlling female behavior, both sexually and socially: *Love and Marriage in the Middle Ages*, trans. Jane Dunnett (Chicago: University of Chicago Press, 1994), pp. 4–5 and 11.

26 Augustine, *De bono coniugali*. Quoted in Bonnie Wheeler, 'Origenary Fantasies: Abelard's Castration and Confession', in *Becoming Male in the Middle Ages*, ed. Jeffrey Jerome Cohen and Bonnie Wheeler (New York: Garland, 1997), pp. 107–28 at p. 108.

27 For further discussion on Abelard's castration and its function in shaping medieval discourse of holiness and sanctity, see Tracy "Introduction", pp. 15–18 in this volume.

bodies were part of the male-centric view of the world. In *Making Sex: The Body and Gender from the Greeks to Freud*, Thomas Laqueur explains: 'Instead of being divided by their reproductive anatomies, the sexes are linked by a common one. Women, in other words, are inverted, and hence, less perfect men. They have exactly the same organs, but in exactly the wrong places.'[28] Just as physical differences distinguish men and women, their social roles are necessarily an extension of that natural and cosmological difference. As Laqueur contends, 'both the division of labor and the specific assignment of roles are natural [based on the physical differences of the sexes]'.[29] Therefore, it was through understanding the body (the male body in particular) that the world and the cosmos could be understood. According to William D. Sharpe, Isidore of Seville

> held the traditional philosophical notion that each individual human being is a microcosm within himself, paralleling the universe, the macrocosm, on a miniature scale. [...] Man forms the central link in the great chain of being: this anthropocentricity does not infer that the universe exists for the sake of man but that man in the key to the whole cosmic riddle, and that insight into human nature will provide insight into that of the universe.[30]

Isidore, like most other learned men, believed that only by understanding the universe and having some knowledge of it could man be included in it.[31] In other words, the male body becomes the model for the largest concepts (such as the universe), and more common ones (like the social structure of a culture). In an article on the importance of the male body to the medieval world view, D. Vance Smith explains that '[t]he bodies of man and of the world do not just happen to be similar: man, in fact, produces the body of the world. [...] The natural world in which the male body must labor, in other words, cannot be represented without the intervention of the male body.'[32]

Because the male body was so important to conceptions of the world at large, that body and its behavior had to be specifically defined by a culture in order to preserve the culture's identity. As Michael Uebel asserts, '[m]edieval men, despite the repeated assertion of their superiority and transcendence in learned texts [...] nevertheless were, like women, subject to categorical assump-

[28] Thomas Laqueur, *Making Sex: Body and Gender from the Greeks to Freud* (Cambridge, MA: Harvard University Press, 1992), p. 26.

[29] Ibid., p. 29.

[30] Isidore of Seville, 'On Medicine', in *Isidore of Seville: The Medical Writings*, trans. William D. Sharpe (Philadelphia: American Philosophical Society, 1964), p. 25.

[31] Ibid., p. 26

[32] D. Vance Smith, 'Body Doubles: Producing the Masculine Corpus', in *Becoming Male in the Middle Ages*, ed. Cohen and Wheeler, pp. 3–19 at p. 15.

tions constraining the range of their corporeal activities'.[33] Though in a comic sense the castration of sexual transgressors may fit in with a perverse sense of comic justice, the reality of castration was inherently threatening to masculine identity because male identity was directly connected to the masculine performance of power. In tales that relate to concepts of masculine power, the shape of masculine identity is presented along with the confirmation of a patriarchal world view.[34] Such tales normally work to reinforce these notions, which are culturally produced so that the culture can maintain stability.[35] Comic literature often presents images of underlying fear in order to make the fear ridiculous or absurd.[36] *La dame escolliee* does not appear to do any of these things. Like many fabliaux, it challenges the social structure, but the oddities of this tale do more to contest the existing masculine structure rather than reinforce the cultural norms. The creation of a non-gendered body, one that is overtly female but transformed into male, produces a figure that is neither truly male nor truly female, undermining the very fabric of gender construction. McNamara conceives of the problem in connection with male celibacy and the creation of the ungendered male body: 'the whole male effort would collapse if women also became ungendered'.[37]

From the beginning of *La dame escolliee*, the count exerts his view of masculinity, starting with the hunt,[38] both for prey and for a wife. The count does all he can to undermine the noblewoman's power. Upon entering the nobleman's home, the count addresses the husband first in his greeting. The proposal of marriage is first addressed to the nobleman, not the wife. When

33 Michael Uebel, 'On Becoming Male', in *Becoming Male in the Middle Ages*, ed. Cohen and Wheeler, pp. 367–84 at p. 371. See also Kathleen Biddick, 'Genders, Bodies, Borders: Technologies of the Visible', *Speculum* 68.2 (1995): 389–418.

34 There are more examples of such tales than can be listed. Chivalric tales that set standards of masculine behavior for knights are seen in the tales of Crétién de Troyes. The masculine courtly lovers in the *lais* of Marie de France are perhaps some of the best-known examples. Epics such as *Le chanson de Roland* also establish the ideals of masculine power and masculine behavior.

35 James Clifford challenges how one can understand gender historically. He writes that the conception of culture is 'a coherent *body* that lives and dies. Culture is enduring, traditional, structural (rather than contingent, syncretic, historical). Culture is a process of ordering, not of disruption': *The Predicament of Culture: Twentieth-Century Ethnography, Literature and Art*. (Cambridge, MA: Harvard University Press, 1988), p. 235.

36 The standard for this argument is generally considered to be Mikhail Bakhtin, *Rabelais and His World*, trans. Hélène Iswolsky (Bloomington: University of Indiana Press, 1984).

37 McNamara, '*The Herrenfrage*', p. 5.

38 There are numerous examples of hunting as reflective of honorable masculine behavior. The best-known is the hunting game in *Sir Gawain and the Green Knight*, in which the honor of Gawain is juxtaposed with the spoils of the Green Knight's hunt. John Cummins compares the sport of hunting to preparation for war as well as a reclamation of lost aspects of manhood: 'Introduction', in *The Art of Medieval Hunting: The Hound and the Hawk* (London: Phoenix Press, 1988), pp. 3–4.

the nobleman's wife offers the count a generous dowry, he refuses, saying, "'Molt a qui bone feme prant; / qui male prant, ne prant nïent"' ['More he has whose wife is good. Who has a bad wife, he has nothing'] (215–16). He does, however, accept the hounds and palfrey as gifts from the nobleman, rectifying what he perceives as proper gender roles through his own masculine behavior. The count thus attempts to restore the nobleman to the same position of authority the count enjoys.

Once away from the nobleman's home, the count's actions become excessively aggressive. With thoughts of his mother-in-law in mind, he kills the hounds and palfrey when they disobey his orders. When the new wife comments on the insult to her and her father, the count replies, "'Por seul itant / que trespasserent mon commant"' ['The only reason was that they trespassed my command'] (267–8). Though the main purpose here is to warn the young bride not to imitate her mother, the mention of the father implies a masculine confrontation, challenging the behavior of the nobleman as well as setting up the proper behavior for a wife. The implied confrontation comes up again when the young wife disobeys her husband. He asks her who encouraged her disobedience. While she first takes the blame herself, the count insists she is not acting on her own, and eventually gets her to admit she is following the advice her mother gave her before she left home:

> 'Pranes essample a vostre mere,
> qui toz jors desdit vostre pere:
> ainz ne dist riens ne desdeïst
> ne commenda c'on feïst.'
> (227–30)

> 'Take the example of your mother, who always disobeyed your father. Before he said anything, I did not obey, I did not follow his commands.'

While the punishment of the wife shows a rejection of misplaced pride in a woman, the role of the mother has been set in part by her husband. The punishment of the countess foreshadows the confrontation between the count and the noblewoman; however, because the noblewoman's behavior is a result of an ineffective masculine performance by her husband, the count's actions are a direct challenge to the masculinity of the nobleman and the nobleman's authority within his own marriage.

Because it was the husband's role to keep the wife virtuous (not just sexually, but morally and socially as well), the nobleman has failed in his role as a husband. Since his daughter takes her mother's advice over her father's, the nobleman has failed in his duty as a father as well by continuing the pattern of improper feminine behavior. The daughter does not understand that her mother is being manipulated, and so her intentions to dominate her husband are a direct challenge to masculine authority. In terms of masculine performance, the nobleman has not performed acceptably, and his failure to perform properly threatens the social construction of patriarchal dominance. The count (observing the failures of the nobleman) takes it upon himself to restore the proper masculine roles, even if that restoration is outside the scope of his own authority. Through this attempt to restore masculine control, the count undermines the role of the nobleman as a husband, again threatening the very masculine performance he is attempting to reinstate.

Once the count's wife is subdued, his duty is done. It is clear that the young wife has learned her lesson. When her parents visit, she does everything her husband tells her to, even if it is against her inclinations. When the nobleman and his wife arrive, the tale describes the daughter's reaction:

> La contesse issi de la chanbre,
> qui vers sa mere ot le cuer tendre
> & nequedent le conte crient
> por le baston dont li sovient.
> Primes, son pere salua.
> (393–7)

> The Countess comes out of the bedroom. She who towards her mother has a tender heart, but gesturing the count cries out for the cane which she recalls [she remembers the beating]. First she greets her father.

The focus of the tale shifts away from the countess to the interaction between the count and his in-laws. Throughout the visit, the count enforces the proper feminine roles upon the mother-in-law, and in turn, on the nobleman. The count forces his wife to sit, as the lady of the house, next to her father and not her mother. The count serves the nobleman the best food and wine, while the mother-in-law, seated away from the main table, has less sumptuous food. There can be no question that this performance is for the nobleman and the nobleman's wife. The count's wife is obviously subdued, as she ignores her own inclinations out of fear of her husband's reprisal, and acts in accordance to his expectations.

Before the count chastises the mother-in-law, he sends the nobleman out hunting. Once the nobleman is gone, the count executes his plan to tame his mother-in-law. Not only does the count usurp the nobleman's role of husbandly authority, he makes sure that the nobleman is gone when he punishes the wife. Unlike his other attempts at masculinizing the nobleman, the count does not perform for the nobleman directly. The masculine confrontation has been redirected to one between the count and the nobleman's wife. Even before the false castration, the count has already begun moving the placement of the struggle for masculine identity from the nobleman to the nobleman's wife.

When the nobleman returns, 'assez a prise venoison' [he took a lot of game]

(536). The nobleman, by hunting successfully, has demonstrated a degree of masculine performance that he has not shown before. However, the nobleman's generally passive nature has not really changed. Upon hearing the count's explanation of why he castrated the nobleman's wife, the nobleman accepts at face value the purpose of the castration as well as his wife's change of heart. The outer appearance of masculine dominance has seemingly been demonstrated and accepted, and so the tale ends with the typical praising of the shrew-tamer's actions and a reassertion of the place of women. This ending also includes a justification for the count's extreme actions: 'il otroit mal & contraire / a ramposneuse de put aire' [He should act bad and contrary to the insulting woman of nasty nature] (571–2). While this ending is typical of a shrew-taming tale, the count's actions have not truly been directed at a woman. He has challenged the authority of the nobleman, and created a performance that identifies the nobleman's wife as a castrated male.

The domestic performance of masculine dominance and feminine submission has had no impact on the nobleman's wife. The mother-in-law is still described as *fiere* (haughty). The count's mind is not on her behavior, though; it is on the plight of the nobleman. The tale notes that: 'La nuit se'n va, li jors apert, / li quens lieve, qui dolenz ert / se son seignor, qui feme a male' [the night goes away, the day opened. The count rises he who is pained about his lord who has a bad wife] (419–21). The countess's behavior and the focus of the count's thoughts on the nobleman both point to the necessity (in the count's mind) of showing the nobleman more forcefully how to control a wife. The pointed examples of the count's own behavior do not seem to have any effect on the nobleman. In the count's mind, the nobleman's masculine performance needs more direct interference, which is what the count does.

Questions remain about the veracity of these changes. While the nobleman seemingly accepts his wife's change of heart, he does so with his usual passivity. He does not question her conversion, nor does he question the rather brutal method by which this conversion was achieved. In this sense, the nobleman has not been reinstated into a masculine role, but rather feminized again through the dominant actions of the count. More troubling in terms of masculine performance here are the actions of the count. Besides overstepping the authority of his father-in-law, he gives his mother-in-law a masculine identity in his attempt to tame her. Through the faux castration, the mother-in-law's body is transformed into that of a man. The absence of the nobleman further marginalizes him as a masculine power, and so the fight for masculine dominance takes place between the count and the mother-in-law. Every dynamic of the false castration is one of male/male, not male/female.

Through his assumption of the nobleman's role, the count further destroys his father-in-law's masculinity rather than reinscribing it. By first killing the nobleman's wedding gifts, the count symbolically emasculates him.[39] The count's treatment of the mother-in-law when the nobleman visits is meant as an example of how a wife should be treated, just as the young wife's fear of her husband's retaliation is meant to show that willfulness can be controlled. As with his own wife, the count moves to more violent and excessive actions against his mother-in-law when the subtler hints at proper behavior are ignored. While the count is concerned about the nobleman's situation, the ultimate confrontation is with the mother-in-law.[40] The count takes direct action to modify her behavior, not her husband's. Her unfeminine behavior, which she tries to pass along to her daughter, is compared to that of a man, particularly when the count gives his reasons for the false castration – her manly pride comes from her testicles. More significantly, the count attempts to control her as a man, not a woman.

Nothing about the count's punishment of his mother-in-law presents her in a feminine role. Her body, now made masculine, is not the body of a woman but rather the body of an emasculated man – a eunuch. Nancy F. Partner, in her article 'No Sex, No Gender', makes the point that the social role of the eunuch 'could establish a gender identity strong enough to persist through disabling alteration of the genitals'.[41] She goes on to discuss the relationship of such gender identity to women, saying '[o]nly the most temperate of feminist criticism was necessary to recognize that biological femaleness did not automatically or "naturally" entail femininity when "Feminine" turned out to be every society's catchall for transparent male fears'.[42] If the female represents masculine fear, then the castration of the nobleman's wife becomes a performance of the male working to subdue what is frightening in the male, a loss of masculine identity and power, not a fear of female dominance. Rather than controlling the woman's body and behavior, the false castration performed on the female body redirects that body into a male sphere. The mother-in-law's body is made male by the count, but her castration cannot return the body to that of a female. In performing a castration on his mother-in-law, the count

[39] Most hunting manuals, according to Cummins, list the greyhound as a particularly prized animal in hunting, mainly for its speed, obedience, and ability in catching a variety of quarry (*The Art of Medieval Hunting*, pp. 12–15). The beheading of the nobleman's gifts by the count can be interpreted as a type of castration, which further feminizes the nobleman. Though the destruction of dogs and horses are a part of the shrew-taming tradition, the performance here is directly linked to the nobleman rather than as just an example for the new wife.

[40] The phrase *feme a male* is used throughout this tale. Though the phrase is an indictment of the mother-in-law's character, the phrase is also used to mark the identity of the nobleman (*son seignor, qui feme a male*) as a victim. The focus becomes a man who is identified through his wife, not a man who should control her behavior.

[41] Nancy F. Partner, 'No Sex, No Gender', *Speculum* 68.2 (1993): 419–43 at pp. 422–3.

[42] Ibid., p. 423.

emasculates another male; he is not taming or subduing a female. His actions have undermined the very concepts of masculine order and identity he has been trying to reinstate.

The castrated body of Abelard again offers an insight into the performance and perception of masculinity in this fabliau. Martin Irvine discusses implications raised by Fulk (the prior of Deuil), in a letter where he hints that Abelard's only sexual identity is possibly homosexual in nature. Irvine concludes that for Fulk, 'it is not simply the fact of castration that unmans Abelard: the lack of genitals is a sign of a deeper lack, a deficiency or erasure of *virtus*, which alone allows the true performance of masculinity. And it was this that Abelard sought to perform through his books [...] a re-identification with symbolic power.'[43] Fulk implies that without genitals, Abelard must function as a woman, not a man; that somehow he has lost his essential masculinity. Abelard challenges this assumption, and changes the nature of the discussion from the physical to the philosophical.

Abelard's castration does not destroy his masculine performance, but rather changes the focus of it. The loss of his genitals does not change his sexuality or his role as a man. Bonnie Wheeler argues that in 'resistance to and independent of his castration, Abelard asserts a fixed masculinity that inspires unending feminine desire and the relentless envy of other men.'[44] The male body is fixed; the male body is not dependent on genitalia, but rather on how the body is perceived by others. Wheeler goes on to say that Abelard challenges the conception of his own masculinity, and through his conflict with authorities, establishes a public construction of masculine identity for himself that becomes the 'marks of a masculine reputation founded on mastery, creation, and unbreakable endurance.'[45] In Abelard's case, then, castration is not the end of masculine power, but the reforging of it. His castration makes him more masculine, not less. Castration, therefore, is a male-to-male performance which empowers the victim rather than the castrator.

In the same way, the stage of the mother-in-law's body becomes a stage for masculine competition and masculine identity. Since the nobleman has not controlled his wife through an accepted performance, the count forces the issue in the fake castration. This performance takes place without the nobleman's presence or consent. Afterwards the nobleman appears to go along with the new performance, but this is also similar to his behavior at the start of the tale. In accepting the count's new structure for his marriage, the nobleman can be

43 Martin Irvine, 'Abelard and (Re)Writing the Male Body: Castration, Identity, and Remasculination', in *Becoming Male in the Middle Ages*, ed. Cohen and Wheeler, pp. 87–106 at p. 94.

44 Wheeler, 'Origenary Fantasies', p. 108. McNamara discusses similar concepts of masculinity and its association with sexuality in 'The *Herrenfrage*'.

45 Wheeler, 'Origenary Fantasies', p. 107.

seen as agreeing with the count much in the same way as he appeared to acquiesce to his wife when he tricked her to get his way. At the end of the tale, the surface has changed, but the underlying implications of masculine identity have not. By creating a masculine body from a feminine one, the count has also created a competition not between himself and his father-in-law, but between himself and his mother-in-law. This competition is not one of a man exerting proper authority over a woman, as she is not his wife, but rather the dominance of one man over another. Rather than taming the wife and reestablishing the desired masculine role in the nobleman, the count creates an alternate masculinity to compete with the weaker masculinity of the nobleman and the overly aggressive masculinity in himself. The mother-in-law's submission does not change her new masculine role; she is now in a position to attain a higher level of masculinity (as Abelard does) than the nobleman, who has not shown any ability to perform as a proper man. Likewise, the dominating performance of the count has not removed the threat to masculine authority, but created a new threat.

The imagery of the female castration suggests fundamental challenges to the perceived masculine world order. The castration, set up as a corrective for improper female behavior, actually works to create a new masculine identity through the newly masculinized body of the mother-in-law. The nobleman's performance, which from the start is more feminine than masculine, does not really change. In many ways, the count reinforces the feminine role of the nobleman under the pretense of moving him into a more masculine performance. Though the mother-in-law's performance at home may change, the nobleman has not changed, implying that there will be no masculine role performed in that household. Rather than preserving a masculine dominance, the count has created a masculine vacuum. His use of an unacceptable and extreme punishment points to an excess in his masculine performance that undermines the very concepts he is so desperate to uphold.

La dame escolliee challenges its audience to reconceive the accepted philosophy of masculine roles and gender identity that it superficially appears to support. The female body here is a stage, but not one that asserts masculine dominance or feminine subordination. Rather, this stage enacts a male/male performance that transforms gender and blurs the lines of gender dynamics. Masculine roles and masculine identity, even the male body, are not stable entities. This fluctuation of masculinity and gender roles creates more fears than it relieves, which offers a unique challenge to the concepts of medieval masculine authority and social identity.

CHAPTER 11

Eunuchs of the Grail

Jed Chandler

The medieval quest for the Holy Grail could only be achieved by a very special man. He should be a virgin, utterly pure, and, according to certain of the early versions of the Grail legend, have a rather unusual gender profile: he may (in short) be castrated. The contextual correspondence between the representations of Perceval's 'virgin gender' in the early Grail cycles and the 'spiritual eunuchs' of the early Christian ascetic movement coalesce in sexual wounds. In both of these social contexts, perfect purity is valorized as a transformative grace which renders humans angelic; in both contexts the cultivation of purity represents direct action by the individual to mitigate the effects of the fall and loss of Eden which precipitated humanity into sexual desire.[1] The literary milieu in which the Grail cycles took shape was infused with the idealization of virginity which characterized early Christian society, and immersed in hagiographic narratives which extolled the virtues of virgins. But one particularly pertinent dynamic linked the two environments: both dissect masculinity, teasing out a type of manhood in which sexual purity could be expressed. In medieval Europe, the eleventh-century Gregorian reforms required celibacy of the priesthood, and saw the development of the concept of virginity as a philosophical ideal as well as a religious principle.[2] Both of these factors prompted a renewed interest in conceptualizing a 'non-sexual' man. In both cases, (late ancient and high medieval) focus falls sharply on the uncoupling of humans from their sexual desires and organs by asceticism and by actual or symbolic castration. The organs under scrutiny here are those of Perceval, in Chrétien de Troyes' *Perceval le Conte du Graal* and the Manessier

[1] According to Augustine, sexual desire was the direct results of the fall, 'an evil added accidentally from the ancient sin'. *Against Julian*, trans. Matthew A. Schumacher (Washington, DC: The Catholic University of America Press, 1957), 13:40, p. 345.

[2] I. P. Bejczy discusses the evolution of virginity from religious to social and philosophical ideal in *Virtue Ethics in the Middle Ages: Commentaries on Aristotle's Nicomachean Ethics, 1200–1500* (Leiden: Brill, 2008), pp. 249–73.

continuation of Chrétien's work the *Perlesvaus*, and Galahad, in the *Queste del Saint Graal* with reference to a parallel text in the Vulgate *Lancelot*.

Writing between 1170 and 1181, Chrétien de Troyes effectively established the genre of the Arthurian romance with the publication of his first four works, *Erec and Enide*, *Cligès*, *Yvain, the Knight of the Lion*, and *Lancelot, the Knight of the Cart*. His works represent a radical departure from earlier French *chansons de geste* with their focus on narrative action; Chrétien's romances flow around the nuances of his characters' interiority, charting their development as they reflect and react to events. Particularly, Chrétien focuses on their development as lovers, since utter commitment to an absolute desire (at once erotic and transcendent) is ennobling. The beloved is the object of the chivalric quest and its justification.

Chrétien introduces castration into *Cligès* as a disqualification from the business of romance. In this text he particularly scrutinizes the meaning of marital fidelity and chastity from a technical perspective: his protagonists stay within the letter of the law, yet their love licenses a degree of moral shiftiness. Cligès, the son of Alexander of Constantinople and Soredamors (Gawain's sister), fulfils his father's wishes for him to be knighted at the court of King Arthur. He falls passionately in love with Fenice, the wife of Alis, his uncle and the regent of Constantinople. She refuses to be unfaithful to her husband, but is open to equivocation. She serves Alis a potion which causes him to confuse dreams with memories so that he takes his dreams of passionate nights with her as actual memories, allowing her to retain her virginity. Subsequently she takes a potion prepared by her old nurse Thessala (a sorcerer) to simulate death, and once pronounced legally dead is free to marry Cligès. The romance concludes with the wry comment that because Cligès trusts Fenice he never places her under surveillance, but subsequent Byzantine rulers keep their wives closely confined in their quarters, visible to no other men except eunuchs castrated at birth. The coda adds a retrospective commentary on Alis's performance: sexually active only in his dreams, he is in effect another eunuch in the bedroom.

However, Chrétien's final, unfinished work effectively subverts this paradigm of erotic and platonic desire and its resolution by demonizing desire and valorizing purity. For in *Perceval, le Conte du Graal* he introduces into the literary corpus an enigmatic tale which inspired numerous successive elaborations and exigeses. In *Perceval*, the quest for realization through heterosexual erotic and platonic love is replaced by a quest for virginal purity and spiritual perfection, and throughout the copious Grail narratives that followed Chrétien's work, the sexual realm remains anathema to the Grail questors. They undertake a battle waged against the exigencies of the body; their quest is for union with God rather than a union with the lady. The conventions of romance tales where the man proves his masculinity through battle, through protecting vulnerable women, and through heterosexual sexual union are forced out of shape. The

Grail knight remains embattled, but he is concerned above all with self-defence against threats to his own vulnerable chastity. Chrétien returns to the figure of the eunuch: rather than surrender to lust, and with it to the loss of his sexual purity, the Grail knight undertakes metaphorical or literal castration. Where castration disqualifies a man from winning the lady, it can qualify him for winning the Grail.

Although this conversion in his heroes' orientation from adventures directed towards fulfilment of sexual desire to a quest for its negation represents a radical change of direction in Chrétien's work, it has analogues in earlier Christian cultural and literary texts. The resonances become more distinct as the Grail legend is 'Christianized'. The quest for utter purity assumes even greater significance in the versions of the Grail legend which follow Robert de Boron's redaction (*c.* 1191–1202), which frames the narrative in Christian theology by establishing a provenance for the Grail as the chalice of the Last Supper and the vessel in which Christ's blood was caught when his side was pierced during his crucifixion. There is an intercontextual relationship between such a third 'virgin gender' in the Grail cycles, the congregation of groin wounds and queered gender in the families closely associated with the Grail, and the *tertium genus* of literal and metaphorical eunuchs in early Eastern Christianity.[3] The quest for *apatheia*, a permanent stilling of sexual desire, is in both contexts linked to male attainment of the cross-gendered virtue of absolute, intact chastity and to transcendence of the male body. The stilled male body is not fully, and not exactly, a male body but not a fully feminine one either.

Neither vulnerability to genital wounds nor celibacy were themselves necessarily regarded as feminizing in medieval literary texts. Indeed, male chastity was (on occasion) associated with military prowess in historical combat. In the thirteenth-century *Song of Lewes*, the success of Simon de Montfort's troops at the Battle of Lewes in 1264 is attributed in part to their clean living, contrasted with the degeneracy of King Henry III's troops who '[e]sse ne victoria digni debuerunt, Qui carnis luxuria foeda sorduerunt' [defiled by foul carnal debauchery ought not be worthy of victory].[4] Descriptions of battle and individual combat are integral to chivalric narratives, and injuries inevitably happen in battle. Kenneth Hodges, anxious to

3 In this volume, Shaun Tougher analyzes the classical attitudes towards eunuchs and their reception in the Roman Empire, as well as the indeterminate 'third gender'. See 'The Aesthetics of Castration: The Beauty of Roman Eunuchs', pp. 48–72.

4 Thomas Wright, *Political Songs of England: From the Reign of John to that of Edward II* (London: Printed for the Camden Society by J. B. Nichols and Son, 1839), cited text from *The Battle of Lewes*, lines 164–5, p. 80. When de Montfort was defeated and killed at the Battle of Evesham in 1265, his body was mutilated and castrated. Cf. Larissa Tracy, '"Al defouleden is holie bodi": Castration, the Sexualization of Torture, and Anxieties of Identity the *South English Legendary*', in this volume, pp. 87–107.

counter the overinterpretation of male vulnerability and male weakness which he characterizes as a vogue in gender studies, has written a timely article rearticulating precisely those positive aspects of heroic wounding explicit in medieval accounts.[5] Willingness to suffer wounding in battle demonstrates a knight's commitment and his courage, and one's fighting technique is honed by the painful results of errors. These honourable wounds (particularly those to the groin) are translated into the means of spiritual progress in the Grail cycles, where a wound may function as punishment for sin, prompting repentance and transformation or spiritual insight. In both temporal and spiritual chivalry, wounds can prove and validate the man.

But not all wounds are manly. Peggy McCracken discerns a distinct contrast in the connotations of male blood and female blood.[6] Women's blood is their own business, connected intimately to the body, and its shedding is generally a closeted, private event; men's blood is more often shed publicly and instrumentally to prove or implement or win something – often, in the romances, to win a woman. Moreover, menstrual blood and the blood of parturition were regarded as polluting (the legacy of Eve's primal sin and God's consequent curse), and both stem from woman's perceived imperfection. Castration is, by its nature, unmanning: the body which results is qualitatively different. It is an act of transition, of a radical alteration of status, of genre – a man becomes a eunuch.

This transformation of man is enacted in the early Grail cycles, and particularly in the Vulgate Cycle, as a battle against sexuality itself, against male embodiment and its concomitant desires. The Grail which the questors seek may therefore be handled safely by the female, virginal Grail maidens or by anomalous men. The fisher king, custodian of the Grail, is the castrated and powerless son of a maimed father; the knight who will achieve the quest is foretold and heralded as a creature of compound species and genders with intersexed anatomy. The Grail quest is both a profoundly holy and a prodigiously queer undertaking; it is a quest to become perfectly, asexually pure. The Grail knight faces temptation everywhere, and sin lies within his body, in its sexual responses which assert his earthiness and undermine his purity. The adventures of Perceval, in particular, probe and deconstruct the *qualia* and the qualities of masculinity revealing a compromised, salvaged male embodiment – the Grail virgin who is essentially different from the natural man.

The male groin is a particularly vulnerable area in the Grail cycles. It is vulnerable to wounds in battle, to sexual temptation and assault, and (amongst the chaste questors) to a literary or (almost) literal ablation as the hero under-

5 Kenneth Hodges, 'Wounded Masculinity: Injury and Gender in Sir Thomas Malory's *Le Morte Darthur*', *Studies in Philology* 106.1 (2009): 14–31.

6 Peggy McCracken, *The Curse of Eve, the Wound of the Hero: Blood, Gender, and Medieval Literature* (Philadelphia: University of Pennsylvania Press, 2003).

takes a process of *ascesis* intended to produce the total sexual *apatheia* which alone will permit him to win the Grail. There is a lack of ease with the male body in its entirety reflected in the fragmented, itemized descriptions of Perceval and later Galahad, and their representation as unhuman beings or beasts. Both knights achieve the Grail quest primarily through their virginity, and they are creatures of incongruous parts – Perceval and Galahad are prophetically accorded male and female viscera.[7] While the Grail maiden can hold and minister from the Grail without any injury or danger to herself, men must be wounded and shaped in the female-gendered discipline of virginity – in effect, castrated, because the Grail will damage whole men. King Mordrain, who rescues Joseph of Arimathea from imprisonment, is struck down because he tries to gaze upon the Grail (now identified as the cup in which Christ's blood was caught at his crucifixion) without being worthy.[8] Blinded, sustained indefinitely in pain, he can die only in the arms of a true and sinless knight – Galahad.

The emasculation of the Grail virgins sets them outside the frame of nature, creating an abstract ideal of purity unattainable in the flesh. In the Old French *Perlesvaus*, written between 1198 and 1240, Perceval forces his way into the 'turning castle', a structure Vergil constructed at a time when philosophers were seeking an earthy paradise and which was inhabited by people who followed the 'old law'. This castle is destined to spin unceasingly until the arrival of a knight 'qui averiot le chief d'ore et regart de lion et cuer d'acier et nonbril de virge pucele et teches sanz vilenie et valeur d'ome et de foi et creance de Dieu' [who would have a head of gold, the gaze of a lion, a heart of steel, the navel of a virgin girl free from all villainy, the valour of a man, and faith and belief in God] (250).[9] The advent of the 'good knight' will save their souls and win them

7 Kathleen Coyne Kelly discusses Galahad's femininity in Malory's *Morte Darthur*, finding that in this later redaction of the Grail legend he remains outside the homosocial society of Arthur's knights and represents the 'threatening feminine' which the knights sought to disown in themselves. He was inviolate, 'unscathed by sword or temptation' and 'more feminine than the feminine itself in his invoilateness': 'Menaced Masculinity and Imperiled Virginity in Malory's *Morte Darthur*', in *Menacing Virgins: Representing Virginity in the Middle Ages and Renaissance*, ed. Kathleen Coyne Kelly and Marina Leslie (Newark: University of Delaware Press, 1999), pp. 97–114 at p. 113. Unlike Perceval, Galahad is never naked, and unlike Perceval he never bleeds; he is sanitized, purified femininity.

8 The story of King Mordrain, previously known as King Evalach of the Saracens before his conversion to Christianity, is recounted in Gerbert de Montreuil's *Continuation* of Chrétien's *Perceval*, and in the Vulgate *Estoire del Saint Graal*, which contains the account of his healing and death in the arms of Sir Galahad. *Gerbert de Montreuil. La Continuation de Perceval*, vol. 2, ed. Mary Williams (Paris: Champion, 1925), lines 10450–556, pp. 109–13; *The Vulgate Version of the Arthurian Romances*, vol. 6: *Les aventures ou la queste del Saint Graal. La mort le Roi Artus*, ed. H. Oskar Sommer (Washington, DC: Carnegie Institution of Washington, 1913), pp. 62, 184–5.

9 William A. Nitze and T. Atkin Jenkinson, eds., *Le haut livre du Graal, Perlesvaus: Text, Variants, and Glossary*, vol. 1 (Chicago: University of Chicago Press, 1932). Page numbers are given in parentheses in the text.

respite from death because they can receive baptism and embrace Christianity immediately upon his arrival. Earlier in the text, Perceval's sister describes him in almost identical terms while searching for him: 'Il a le chief d'or e regart de lion e no[m]blil de virge pucele e cuer de valeur e teches sanz vilenie' [He has the head of gold, the gaze of a lion and the navel of a virgin girl. And a valorous heart free from all villainy] (61). Neither of those she approaches (Sir Gawain and a hermit who serves the fisher king) need any further identifying description, they recognize him from this amorphous blend of emblems; Perceval is the unhuman virgin knight.[10]

In the Vulgate *Lancelot*, Merlin prophesies that a beast 'de diuerse manière sor toutes autres bestes' [distinct from all other types of beast] (27),[11] with transgenic and cross-gendered parts, will fulfil the quest for the Grail. The foreordained Grail beast is (in this case) Galahad, and Master Elias reveals the prophecy to Galehaut, close friend and companion of Lancelot. This beast is fleshed out with the 'head and face of a lion and the body and legs of an elephant [...] the kidneys and navel of an untouched maiden, and a heart of hard, dense steel that will be proof against swaying or softening, and it will have the speech of a serious woman and the will to make right judgements'.[12] This hybrid beast is charged with symbolism. Both the lion and the elephant were familiar allegorical images, described and depicted in Latin bestiaries, a genre which flourished in the twelfth and thirteenth centuries in northern Europe and which combined the functions of natural description with supernatural interpretation and didactic moral allegory.[13] The lion (then as now) was titled 'king of the beasts' and symbolized human power and authority, with specific reference to Christ as the Lion of Judah. According to the bestiary preserved in Harley MS 3244, the elephant (an image of might) could not bear evil and

[10] A very similar formula for Perceval also appears in the *Livre d'Artus* continuation of the Vulgate Cycle, As noted by J. Douglas Bruce, 'Pelles, Pellinor, and Pellean in the Old French Arthurian Romances: I', *Modern Philology* 16.3 (1918): 113–28 at p. 118 n.1. Bruce traces the genealogy of this description of the hybrid Grail hero from its first appearance in the *Perlesvaus.*

[11] *The Vulgate Version of the Arthurian Romances*, Vol. 2: *Le livre de Lancelot del Lac*, ed. Heinrich Oskar Sommer (Washington, DC: The Carnegie Institution, 1911). Page numbers are given in parentheses in the text.

[12] There is some variation in the precise anatomical graftings comprising the beast in the various manuscripts of the *Lancelot*, but all agree that it will have the kidneys and navel of an untouched virgin maiden: 'si aura rains & nombril de pucele denterine uirginite' and the discourse of a serious woman. The translation here is that in Lacy's edition of the post-Vulgate Lancelot: Norris J. Lacy, gen. ed., *Lancelot-Grail:* Part 3, *Lancelot* Parts I and II, new edn (Cambridge: D. S. Brewer, 2010). Textual references are taken from Sommers's edition of the British Museum manuscripts.

[13] Ellen Lorraine Friedrich examines medieval bestiaries and their portrayal of beavers as mammals who castrate themselves in her essay in this volume, 'Insinuating Indeterminate Gender: A Castration Motif in Guillaume de Lorris's *Romans de la rose*', pp. 255–79.

so crushed it under its feet.[14] As well as signifying size and strength, the elephant was also associated with purity; they were believed to be naturally chaste animals having, 'no desire for sexual intercourse',[15] living as platonic partners for life and mating only once whereupon the female conceived a single calf.[16] A further allegorical interpretation of a characteristic ascribed to elephants is particularly relevant to the Grail knight in his salvific role. Once fallen, the elephant was believed to be too heavy to get to its feet again, and could be saved only by a smaller elephant which would help it to rise. The fallen elephant represented the Jewish nation and the smaller elephant anagogically represented Christ, who brought salvation to the fallen and the new covenant to the Jewish people.[17] Perceval exists outside the frame of the mundane because he is known through prophecy and recognized through allegory. His liberation of the imprisoned followers of the old law establishes him as a Christ-like figure, the Messiah of Old Testament prophecies who (through the harrowing of Hell) liberated the prophets and pious Jews.[18] He is inscribed into a genealogy of gender variance and metaphorical castration which has shadowed representations of Christian purity since the Pauline epistles.

The description of the compound beast that will achieve the Grail appears again in a somewhat expanded form in the *Tristan en prose* (*c.*1230–42), the latter part of which incorporates much material from the Vulgate Cycle *Queste del Saint Graal.* The account of the Grail beast 'de toutes bestes la plus diverse' [the most diverse of all beasts] (§85. 4)[19] provides a particularly succinct expla-

14 George C. Druce supplies the translation of the relevant part of this manuscript together with other manuscript sources of elephant lore contained in medieval bestiaries, natural scientific and heraldic texts: 'The Elephant in Medieval Legend and Art', *Journal of the Royal Archaeological Institute* 76 (1919): 1–70 at pp. 5–7.

15 This reputation for chastity was elaborated on in devotional literature where elephants were depicted iconographically in pairs and deployed to represent Adam and Eve in the Garden of Eden. In a recapitulation of the biblical narrative of the fall, the female elephant bore the responsibility for their loss of paradise. Like Eve she ate and plied the male with food – in this case the mandrake – which weakened their resistance to carnal desire. The pair retired to an earthly paradise in the east after their mating. Ibid. p. 6. Translation from British Library MS. Harley 3244.

16 D. F. Lach, *Asia in the Making of Europe*, vol. 2: *A Century of Wonder*. Book 1: *The Visual Arts* (Chicago: University of Chicago Press, 1994), p. 129 and refs.

17 Willene B. Clark, ed., *A Medieval Book of Beasts: The Second-Family Bestiary. Commentary, Art, Text and Translation* (Woodbridge: Boydell Press, 2006) p. 128; Christa Grössinge, 'The Unicorn on English Misericords', in *Medieval Art: Recent Perspectives: A Memorial Tribute to C. R. Dodwell*, ed. Gale R. Owen-Crocker and Timothy Graham (Manchester: Manchester University Press, 1998), pp. 142–58 at p. 155.

18 A very similar description of Perceval appears in the *Livre d'Artus* continuation of the Vulgate Cycle, as noted by Bruce, 'Pelles, Pellinor, and Pellean', p. 118, n.1. Bruce traces the genealogy of this description of the hybrid Grail hero from its first appearance in the *Perlesvaus*.

19 Emmanuelle Baumgartner, ed., *Le* Roman de Tristan *en prose*, vol. 6: *Du séjour des amants à la Joyeuse Garde jusquaux premières aventures de la 'queste du Graal'* (Geneva: Librarie Droz, 1993), p. 224. Text and line numbers will be given in parentheses.

nation of the exact effect of the female kidneys and navel: 'par ce qu'il avra rains et nombril de pucele virge et enterine, dont sera il virges et castes' [since it will have the kidneys and navel of an intact virgin maiden, then it will be a chaste and celibate] (§85. 26–8). To the medieval mind, the kidneys were dangerous to the preservation of chastity (particularly male chastity) since they were instrumental in channelling the precursors of semen to the testicles and in triggering its ejaculation. The kidneys are, according to Nemesius of Emesa:

> purgers of the blood and exciters of sexual desire. For the veins which empty into the testicles [...] pass directly through the kidneys, deriving thence a certain pungency provocative of lust, after the same manner that some pungent juice under the skin causes an itch. And inasmuch as the flesh of the testicles is more delicate than skin, they are the more stung by this pungency and cause an unreasoning desire to emit semen.[20]

In this outline of renal function, Nemesius follows the physiological conjectures of Hippocrates and Galen, whose texts on human anatomy and physiology, together with the selected texts translated from the Arabic medical corpora, effectively constituted the Western medieval medical curricula. Received medical consensus held that healthy kidney function was essential for phallic erection and the emission of semen.[21]

The kidneys were believed also to have a role in determining moral behaviour and in cognition, a belief derived from references to them in the Old Testament where the kidneys represent a person's innermost essence, the touchstone of integrity: 'I will bless the Lord, who hath given me understanding: moreover my reins [i.e. kidneys] also have corrected me even till night' (Psalm 16:7), and the essential nature that God will judge: 'I am the Lord who search the heart and prove the reins: who give to every one according to his way, and according to the fruit of his devices' (Jeremiah. 17:10). According to Isidore of Seville, the navel is the source of female sexuality and sensuality. After a brief and delicately worded resumé of the role of the kidneys in the production of semen, with the loins (*lumbus*) as the locus of 'the cause of bodily pleasure in males', he adds 'just as in women it is the navel' (*umbilicus*).[22] He appends a gloss of biblical exigesis to the theory by referring to Job 38:3: 'Gird up your loins like a man'. This is a reminder, he claims, of vigilance against lust. In Pseudo-Athanasius' *On Virginity*, a late ancient treatise falsely accredited to

[20] William Telfer, ed., *Cyril of Jerusalem and Nemesius of Emesa* (Westminster: John Knox Press, 2006), p. 38.

[21] Eustace Dockray Philips outlines early Greek medical thinking about the function of the kidney as regulator of semen in *Aspects of Greek Medicine* (Philadelphia: Charles Press, 1987), pp. 25, 46.

[22] S. A. Barney, ed., *The Etymologies of Isidore of Seville* (Cambridge: Cambridge University Press, 2006), XI.i.89, p. 237.

Saint Athanasius of Alexandria and preserved in two Syriac manuscripts dated between the fifth and ninth centuries, the author provides biblical grounds for distinguishing between the male and female loci of sexuality citing Job 40: 16:

> His strength is in his loins and at the navel. And surely it was in the beauty of chastity that Job spoke, saying 'loins' to mean the man and 'navel' the beautiful form of the woman. Thus, let the man's loins be girded, and let the company of women put on precious chastity.[23]

The Grail beast's virginity, then, has a specifically female type of purity, with female physiology of sexual regulation. It is a compound of virtuous parts, its sexuality indeterminate. The sexual ambiguity of the Grail beast at once reinforces and destabilizes the medieval traditional gender binary. That it should have 'the valour of a man' is a conventional descriptor in perfect accordance with the attributes traditionally accorded to the male. That it should have the navel of a woman, and 'the speech of a serious woman' – the gender associated with garrulousness and levity – goes entirely against the ingrained bias of medieval gender stereotypes. Woman's speech (it was believed) was dangerous talk, loose and licentious, and her place in medieval society was often defined by curtailment and containment. Women had little voice in matters of religion, where Paul's authority was definitive: 'Let women keep silence in the churches: for it is not permitted them to speak but to be subject, as also the law saith. But if they would learn anything, let them ask their husbands at home. For it is a shame for a woman to speak in the church' (1 Corinthians, 14.34). The injunction was taken up and elaborated enthusiastically by the Church fathers. According to Tertullian, woman was 'the devil's gateway' since her speech 'unsealed' the tree of knowledge by persuading Adam to eat its fruit.[24] In the *Ancrene Wisse*, Eve's loquacity teaches the serpent exactly how to get her to eat from the tree of knowledge: 'Eve heold i parais long tale with the neddre, talde him al the lesceun thet Godd hefde i-red hire ant Adam of the eappel, ant swa the feond thurh hire word understod anan-riht hire wacnesse ant i-fond wei toward hire of hire forlorenesse' [Eve had a long talk with the snake in paradise, and told him all the lesson God had taught her and Adam about the apple, and thus the devil understood at once her weakness from her words, and found out the way to destroy her] (216–18).[25] Moreover, unguarded speech is dangerous to a woman's chastity. Writing to an anchoress, the

23 David Brakke, ed., *Pseudo-Athanasius on Virginity*, vol. 2 (Louvain: Peeters, 2002), p. 12 §33.

24 Tertullion, 'On the Apparel of Women', in *The Ante-Nicene Fathers IV*, ed. Alexander Roberts and James Donaldson, trans. S. Thelwall (New York: Christian Literature Publishing, 1885), p. 14.

25 *Ancrene Wisse*, part 2, ed. R. Hasenfratz (Kalamazoo: Western Michigan University Medieval Institute, 2000), p. 111.

twelfth-century Cistercian abbot, Ælred of Rievaulx, cautions that she must be utterly preoccupied with chastity:

> [i]n food and drink, in sleep, in speech let her always be on her guard against a threat to her chastity, lest by allowing the flesh more than its due she may increase the enemy's strength and nourish the hidden foe. [...] Let her always be afraid of hearing something which might cast even the least cloud over the clear skies of her chastity; let not doubt that she will be abandoned by grace if she utters a single word against purity.[26]

A serious woman is a quiet woman, a woman who is constantly vigilant against the temptations of lust and the serpent: and it is precisely in those respects that Perceval (the Grail beast) falls down and is – almost – abandoned by grace because his desire invokes the devil. In a trope familiar to a medieval audience from its frequent occurrence in the *vitae* of holy ascetics, Perceval is assayed and almost lost to the quest by a demon in the form of a woman.

It is precisely in this context of sexual desire that the groins of the Grail virgins are at risk from physical wounds as well as from literary attenuation. A cluster of literal wounds afflict the immediate family of the fisher king, custodian of the Grail. A fisher king is central to the Grail cycles from his first appearance between 1181 and 1190 in Chrétien de Troyes' *Perceval*. He starts his literary career as something of an enigma: there are two kings of the Grail Castle which Perceval visits, a father (the Grail king) and a son (known as the *roi pêcheur*, the fisher king) whose attributes merge. Neither functions as a king; both are maimed, both passive and circumscribed. The fisher king is introduced into the narrative as a fisherman who offers Perceval lodging. He is revealed as the king of a wasted land, himself disabled (*mehaigné* [maimed]), through a wound sustained in battle. He is pierced with a spear through the thighs 'par mi les hanches amedos' [between or through both hips] (A text, v. 3499); 'Parmi les cuisses ambesdeus' [between or through both thighs] (T text, v. 3513).[27] The suggestion here, that the wound may be interpreted as castration, was not lost on early redactors of the Grail cycle. As noted by Anne Wilson, Wolfram von Eschenbach certainly interpreted it that way: his fisher king in the *Parzival* is 'durch die heidruose sîn' [pierced through the testicles] (479.12).[28] The fisher

26 Ælred of Rievaulx, *A Rule of Life for a Recluse*, trans., Mary Paul Macpherson OCSO, in *The Works of Aelred of Rievaulx*, vol. 1: *Treatises* (Collegeville, MN: Cistercian Publications c/o Liturgical Press, 1971), pp. 41–102 at p. 64,

27 I am indebted to Anne Wilson for both of the Perceval citations here – the A text, edited by Lecoy, and the T text, edited by William Roach. A. Wilson, *The Magical Quest: The Use of Magic in Arthurian Romance* (Manchester: Manchester University Press, 1990), p. 118.

28 Wolfram von Eschenbach, *Parzival*, ed. and trans. Peter Knecht as *Parzival: Studienausgabe. Mittelhochdeutscher Text nach der sechsten Ausgabe von Karl Lachmann. Mit Einführung zum Text eer Lachmannschen Ausgabe und in Probleme der Parzival-Interpretation: 2 Auflage.* (Berlin: De Gruyter, 2003), p. 483. The phrase 'par mi les hanches amedos' was a

king presides over a sumptuous feast during which a procession passes through the hall. At its head a youth carries a bleeding lance, at its centre a girl carries a 'grail' – a shallow serving dish – accompanied by radiant lights. After it has been carried in procession through the hall, the Grail is taken into a further chamber and Perceval, restrained and passive, watches in silence. As Helen Adolf remarks, 'a bleeding lance, which is carried around, reminds those who are present of the bleeding warrior',[29] and although Perceval is unaware of the aetiology of the fisher king's wound at this point, the association between weapon and wound relates to his disabled father as well as to the fisher king.[30] The bleeding spear is identified in the First Continuation of the *Conte del Graal* as the spear of Longinus, the soldier named in the Gospel of Nicodemus as the man who pierced the heart of the crucified Christ, but in Chrétien's work it remains an enigma. The last that is heard of the fisher king or Grail king in the *Perceval* is that they disappear (with the castle and all its inhabitants) the morning after Perceval fails to ask any pertinent questions about the bleeding lance or whom the Grail might serve. Later it is revealed that the Grail king has lived entirely within his chamber for twelve years, sustained only by the Host which is brought in the Grail. Since he is so spiritual, he needs nothing else. The author does not reveal whether he is immobilized in the chamber through injury or through choice, nor is it clear whether the fisher king is also fed from the Grail. Other questions relating to Perceval's presence at the Grail castle also remain temporarily unresolved. Why is Perceval invited to the castle? And does the fisher king recognize this strange, mute, awkward youth at his table? For (unknown to the reader at this stage in the story, and unknown to himself) Perceval is cousin to the fisher king and nephew to the Grail king. He learns this from another relative, a hermit whom he visits and who also turns out to be his uncle – the brother of the Grail king and Perceval's mother. Perceval's silence is the speech of a serious woman – a silent witness to a mystery; like a woman silent in a church service he has, as yet, no identity.

Perceval has had to piece himself together from the start. At the beginning of the story, he knows nothing about himself, he even lacks a name. Perceval is set apart from his society, raised in ignorance of his culture and his family and away from other human contact. He is secluded from the world (particularly from male company), confined with his mother in a woodland castle – a

common enough euphemism for the genitals: See Clovis Brunel, 'Les hanches du roi pécheur (Chrétien De Troyes, "Percevalz" 3513)', *Romania* 81 (1960): 37–43.

29 Helen Adolf, 'Studies in Chrétien's *Conte del Graal*', *Modern Language Quarterly* 8.1 (March 1947): 3–19.

30 David C. Fowler suggests that '[t]he lance is to be identified with the hero's father, or the fisher king, and the Grail, containing the sacramental wafer (oiste), with his mother, whose influence has helped determine the form of the entire apparition which we are examining'. *Prowess and Charity in the* Perceval *of Chrétien de Troyes* (Seattle: University of Washington Press, 1959), p. 32.

controlled environment more fitting for a medieval girl than a boy, a cloistered, interior, feminized space. The forest in which the castle is set has returned to nature: it is known as the Gaste Forêt or Waste Forest, desolate territory laid waste by warfare, raped and abandoned by all but the defenceless. But one day Perceval wanders beyond this space and sees men for the first time – armed men, a company of knights riding through the forest. He focuses his gaze on their magnificent armour. He tries to understand them in his mother's Catholic paradigm, rapidly dismissing the possibility they may be demons; these beings are, he marvels, '[p]lus bel … que Dex ne que si enge tuit' [more beautiful than God or all his angels] (417–18).[31] He throws himself on the ground before them to worship them, as his mother had told him to worship God. When one of the knights approaches him, thinking he is cowering in fear, Perceval asks him if he is God, and when they tell him they are knights and explain the function of the lance, shield, and armour, he aspires to become one of these prodigies himself. His mother tries to discourage him by revealing why they live hidden from the world. Her husband met with disaster in battle where he was disabled and lost his lands and riches: '[Il]fu parmi les janbes navrez si que il mahaigna del cors' [He was wounded between the legs, so that he was maimed] (A: 434–5). Their two elder sons were later killed in battle and Perceval's father died of grief. The knights seemed to Perceval to be angels, and he is entranced by the gloss and glamour of their armour, but he is deluded. Battle, seen from the perspective of the Gaste Forêt, destroys men rather than ennobling them. Perceval is unmoved by her words and impervious to her fear for him. He leaves his mother who faints on the threshold of the house. His first autonomous undertaking is to sever himself from maternal control, follow in his father's footsteps and seek his place among knights at the court of King Arthur. However, since his sole model for social interaction is his mother, Perceval lacks any insight into the androcentric culture of chivalry. He is a blank slate, a man without a name, without a male role model, and without any understanding of the world beyond his forest enclosure. He awaits gender confirmation.

The groin wound which Perceval's father sustains receives further attention in the third continuation of Chrétien's *Perceval*, by an author who identifies himself as Manessier, It was written between 1210 and 1230, considerably later than the other continuations and the composition of the Vulgate Grail cycle which follows Robert de Boron's Christianized Grail redaction, from which Manessier borrowed extensively. The work conveys its message through violence rather than finesse: the fisher king mutilates himself in a paroxysm of grief and his healing is effected through revenge. Where Chrétien simply explains the fisher king's mutilation as a battle wound, Manessier provides a more detailed aetiology. The fisher king and his brother, Goon Desert (an invention of

[31] Chrétien de Troyes, *Le Conte du Graal (Perceval)*, ed. F. Lecoy (Paris: Champion, 1975). Line numbers are given in parentheses in the text.

Manessier's), engage in a battle against two giants, Espinogre and Partinal. Goon Desert kills Espinogre, and is killed by Partinal in revenge; Partinal's sword breaks with the stroke. Goon Desert's body and the broken sword are brought back to the Grail king, who injures himself on the shards. His wound cannot be healed until Goon Desert is avenged. There is a critical debate whether this wound is self-inflicted deliberately or the result of clumsiness, but the king's insistence on taking the broken blade, on acting in haste, on the precise line of incision confirm his objective – the fisher king castrates himself:[32]

> Et je ...
> Pris les pieces que me randi
> Ne onques plus n'iatendi,
> Parmi les cuises an travers
> M'anferi, siquetoz les ners
> An tranchai.
> (32910–14)[33]

> I took the pieces [of the blade] which had been returned to me and without any delay I cut along between my thighs so that all the nerves were severed.

[32] Writing in 1888, Alfred Nutt settled on the accidental hypothesis, pronouncing that 'taking up the fragments incautiously [the fisher king] was pierced through the thigh': *Studies on the Legend of the Holy Grail* (Whitefish, MT: Kessinger Publishing, 2003), p. 20. In a similar vein, Jean-Claude Lozac'hmeur insists that 'chez Manessier, le Roi-Pêcheur déclare qu'il s'est blessé en maniant *maladroitement les fragments de l'épée*' (according to Manessier, the fisher king declares that he injured himself while handling the fragments of the sword carelessly). 'De la tête de Bran à l'hostie du Graal', in *Arthurian Tapestry. Essays in Memory of Lewis Thorpe*, ed. Kenneth Varty (Glasgow: British Branch of the International Arthurian Society at the French Department of the University of Glasgow, 1981), 275–86 at p. 285. The fisher king injured himself deliberately, grief-stricken at the death of his brother and notes a correspondence with Perceval's self-harm later in the text (p. 587). Marie-Colombe LeBlanc refers to 'l'automutilation du Roi Pêcheur: fou de chagrin, le Roi Pêcheur, recevant les pièces de l'épée, se blessa entre les cuisses: il se trancha les nerfs, ce qui le rendit impotent' [the self-mutilation of the fisher king: maddened by grief, the fisher king, on receiving the pieces of the sword, injured himself between the thighs: he severed the nerves, which rendered him impotent] (vv. 32910–15), observing that '[l]a répétition des pronoms de la première personne insiste sur la proper responsabilité du roi dans cet acte' [the repetition of first person pronouns stresses the king's personal responsibility for this action]: 'Perceval quêteur du Graal chez les continuateurs' (PhD dissertation, Université Jean Moulin Lyon 3, 2008), p. 231. Hélène Bouget raises his mutilation as a question, an enigma: 'Pourquoi le Roi Pêcheur porte-t-il atteinte à son intégrité physique, en se heurtant les cuisses du tronçon de l'épée qui s'est brisée contre son frère? Le chagrin n'explique pas tout, et encore moins le lien specialist en magique entre la soudure, la vengeance et la guérison' [Why does the fisher king compromise his physical integrity, striking the fragment of the blade which broke which was broken against his brother into his thighs? Grief does not explain it, still less the particular magical relationship between re-forging [the broken sword], vengeance and healing]. 'Enquerre et deviner: poétique de l'énigme dans les romans arthuriens français (fin du XIIe–premier tiers du XIIIe siècle)', (PhD dissertation, Université de Rennes II–Haute Bretagne, 2007), p. 223.

[33] Manessier, *The Continuations of the Old French Perceval of Chrétien De Troyes: The Third Continuation*, ed. W. Roach and R. H. Ivy (Philadelphia: University of Pennsylvania Press, 1949), pp. 11–12.

One day (it is foretold), a knight will repair the sword and avenge Goon Desert. This focus upon revenge effectively transfers Perceval's sphere of action to a temporal arena in keeping with the overarching revenge structure of this continuation, and the fisher king is restored to health and vigour when Perceval brings the head of Partinal to his castle. Perceval (the nephew of both the fisher king and of Goon Desert) eventually succeeds the fisher king as Grail king. The fisher king's self-mutilation in Manessier's continuation seems completely irrational. Autocastration is, at least, a highly eccentric expression of grief. Manessier's rationale for the wound, set as it is in a revenge narrative, seems primarily to demonstrate strong feeling compellingly and serve as a convenient (if implausible) plot device to further the action.

In both the Grail cycles and in early Eastern religious texts, whether the metaphorical 'spiritual castration' of the late ancient ascetic or a wound to the groin of the romance questor, castration generally follows lust. For the ascetics it is a blessing, a divine grace, for those who overindulge in sex it is a punishment; and for Perceval it is penance. But in all these cases it is the consequence of sexual desire. There is an unambiguous instance of punitive castration in Wolfram's *Parzival*, where the evil magician (Clinschor) is unambiguously unmanned for committing adultery with Iblis, the wife of King Ibert of Sicily:

> Clinschor slief an ir arme,
> lager dä iht warme,
> daz muoser sus verpfenden:
> er war mit küneges henden
> zwischenn beinn gemachet sieht.
> (657, 217–21)

> Clinschor slept in her arms; if he had slept warm there he had to pay a penalty for it: he was rendered smooth between his legs by the king's own hand.

In the fifteenth-century *Morte Darthur*, Thomas Malory has the sexually prolific Sir Gareth inflicted with a wound readily interpreted as symbolic castration. He is in bed with Lyonesse and the pair are interrupted by an armed knight who stabs Sir Gareth 'thorow the thycke of the thygh' before being himself killed.[34]

In the *Queste del Saint Graal* spiritual chivalry is valorized and virginity is privileged above other virtues as an expression of holiness.[35] According to

[34] Sir Thomas Malory, *The Works of Sir Thomas Malory*, ed. Eugène Vinaver, 3rd edn, revised. P. J. C. Field (Oxford: Clarendon Press, 1990), p. 333. On the interpretation of this wound, see Karen Cherewatuk, *Marriage, Adultery and Inheritance in Malory's* Morte Darthur (Cambridge: D. S. Brewer, 2006), pp. 14–17. Roger Dalrymple notes the suggestion of homoeroticism between the two knights in this scene: *Middle English Literature: A Guide to Criticism* (Oxford: Wiley-Blackwell, 2004), p. 197.

[35] Albert Pauphilet, ed., *La queste del Saint Graal: Roman du 13e siècle* (Paris: Champion, 1923).

Albert Pauphilet, '[l]a pensée dominante de la *Queste*, qui a dicté le plan d'ensemble, inspiré maint épisode et qui est attestée par quelques phrases catégoriques, c'est que la vie morale est tout entière résumée par l'antithèse de la luxure et de la virginité' [The dominant concept of the *Queste*, which has dictated the overall plan, inspired each episode and which is borne out by particular key phrases, is that a moral life is totally defined as the antithesis to lust and by virginity.][36] The perfect knight in this fully Christianized redaction of the Grail narrative is Galahad, who replaces Perceval as the Grail beast and as paragon, and in whose company Perceval attains the Grail as a privileged witness. Galahad's purity is absolute and is undertaken for the purest of reasons – unreserved love for and commitment to God without any personal desires or interests: 'La figure qui domine tout le tableau de la vie chrétienne, en qui s'incarne la perfection, Galaad, a pour première qualité d'être vierge' [The image which dominates the entire representation of Christian life, in whom its perfection is embodied, Galahad, has as his foremost quality virginity.][37] In the *Queste*, Perceval is tested against this ideal of holiness rather than in the temporal revenge framework of Manessier's continuation and he is found wanting. He is earthly, male, and hormonal. In both the *Queste* and the Manessier continuation, a demon assays Perceval's chastity in the form of a woman. In the *Queste* the test and penance are gritty, graphic, and corporal; assaulted by the devil in female form, Perceval takes direct action against his groin, the source of his imperfection.[38]

Perceval is marooned on an island, and as he scans the horizon he sees a ship with black sails approaching. On board is a woman of extraordinary beauty, who deceitfully plies him with food and wine until he is (for the first and only time in his life) so overcome by sexual desire that he reneges on his commitment to chastity and pleads for her love. She agrees, asking only that he pledge himself to her. In his haste Perceval neglects his duty of prayer as well, until he notices the cross engraved on the handle of his sword and crosses himself. At this the devil reverts to its natural form and (palled in smoke and stinking) it flees from the island into the sea, which roils in flames. As a result of this metamorphosis, Perceval savagely pierces his thigh with his blade, and the blood spurts out to cover him. 'Lors trest s'espee dou fuerre et s'en fiert si durement qu'il l'embat en sa senestre cuisse, et li sans en saut de toutes parz. Et quant il voit ce, si dist: "Biax sire Diex, ce est en amende de ce que je me sui meffet vers vos"' [Then he unsheathes his sword from its scabbard and strikes himself so hard that he embeds it in his left thigh and the blood spurts out

36 Albert Pauphilet, *Études sur* La queste del Saint Graal *attribuée à Gautier Map* (Paris: Champion, 1921), p. 38.

37 Ibid..

38 This is similar to hagiographic accounts of penitential autocastration in *The South English Legendary*. See Tracy, 'Al defouleden is holie bodi', pp. 98–9 in this volume.

everywhere. And when he sees this, he says 'Lord God, this is my reparation for my misdeed against you'] (110.23). Perceval takes stock of himself. He is confronted by an image of unstable gender identity. His clothes lie scattered off to one side, his armor lies discarded on the other; he is naked, pierced, and bleeding, reminiscent of female defloration and of castration. Moreover, the creature he took for a woman was a demon, gendered male.[39] In Manessier's version of this attempted seduction narrative the demon takes the form of Perceval's beloved, Blanchefleur. It is a particularly perverse temptation. Who exactly (or indeed *what* exactly) he desires is equivocal, since on seeing his sword: 'Se seigna, et par ce deçut / Le deable a qui son delit / Volloit faire dedanz le lit' [He crossed himself, and so deceived the devil with which he had wanted to enjoy himself in bed] (38146–8). Perceval sees his sword and is reminded to cross himself only as he joins the Blanchefleur double in bed, at which sign she changes form beneath him and flees: 'Li diables qui soz lui jut / Saut sus, que plus n'i aresta; / Paveillon et lit am porta' [The devil which was lying beneath him immediately jumped up without any delay] (38156–8). The scene in Manessier's continuation turns upon Perceval's vulnerability to the seduction of sin and his escape from metaphorically and literally coupling with the devil. In the *Queste*, where the highest virtue is virginity, it revolves around his vulnerability to, and renunciation of, lust – it is all about his groin.

Perceval has all the signs of strength, all the accoutrements of chivalry. As a knight, Perceval receives his own armor and the entitlement to wear it as an outward expression of a code of masculinity which rigidly prescribes the conduct and attitudes of a social elite. Armor was an intact, impenetrable sealed shell, encasing the male body. Perceval embodies the kind of rigid control of which the armor is emblematic; he is always contained and controlled, first by his mother in the forest castle and later by the patriarchal code of chivalry. Casting aside his performance of chivalric masculinity, Perceval has indeed let his guard down. He jettisons his armor and dispenses with his spiritual discipline by omitting to pray. He has, instead of protecting women, rendered himself passive and vulnerable before a seeming woman (who is in fact gendered male), and who has (almost) mastered him. He is utterly undone, unmanned through castration or effeminizing penetration; both responses enact Perceval's psychic emasculation. Kathleen Coyne Kelly, in her consideration of this act of self-harm as it is recounted by Malory, notes that the thigh is a 'common enough euphemism for the genitals' to read this as castration.[40] Perceval may alterna-

[39] Anna Roberts discusses castration as a 'thematic site' where it is linked to non-heteronormative sexuality, particularly male homoeroticism. Anna Roberts, 'Queer Fisher King: Castration as a Site of Queer Representation (*Perceval*, *Stabat Mater*, the *City of God*)', *Arthuriana* 11.3 (2001): 49–88.

[40] Kelly, 'Menaced Masculinity', p. 111.

tively, she suggests, be both perpetrator and victim of an emblematic rape. Perceval enacts on his own body what an Other (a demon lover) would have done. As both penetrator and penetrated, Perceval is at once a compound of sexes and a negation of both. McCracken sees in the tryst between Perceval and the demon a juxtaposition of 'the chaste body and the body whose gender is indeterminate'.[41] It is also a juxtaposition of two compound, transitional bodies which do not conform to either male or female binaries. Both gender-shifting demon and Grail beast are outside the frame of nature; both manifest and conform to the qualities of both sexes and neither sex.

Raised in isolation in the Gaste Forêt, Perceval lacks any male exemplars. As a consequence, he learns manhood through his mother's cautionary tales of death and of wounds. He reads the knights in the forest as demons first, then as God or as angels, and it is to this status that he aspires. He becomes the Grail beast – a perfected, spiritualized man who is able to attain to the Grail with impunity. Significantly, it is in Manessier's continuation that Perceval most fully achieves the Grail quest, becoming the Grail king and on his death bearing the Grail to heaven with him. In this version of the story he enacts the most profound ablation of his sexuality. Through self-wounding he achieves what the Grail maiden is able to perform naturally – intact, unspotted virginity. In the *Perlevaus*, he attains the Grail as the transgendered Grail beast, becoming the 'virgin gender', a man 'without villainy' and with the *nombril de pucele* – the sexual restraint of an intact virgin girl. He transcends gender, becoming something other than a man.[42]

The subversion and transcendence of gender (and its association with virtue), exemplified in the Grail cycles in the motif of the hybrid beast and the autocastration associated with the Grail virgins, finds its counterpart in late ancient Christian conceptualizations of purity. A concept of gender as a transient, malleable human characteristic and a desire for the status of spiritual eunuch – the 'virgin gender' – is a trope running through early Christian liter-

[41] Peggy McCracken, 'Chaste Subjects: Gender, Heroism, and Desire in the Grail Quest', in *Queering the Middle Ages*, ed. Glenn Burger and Steven F. Kruger (Minneapolis: University of Minnesota Press, 2001), pp. 123–42 at p. 132.

[42] In a tantalising verbal parallel, and as another expression of the subversion and transcendence of gender, the Vulgate *Merlin* relates the story of Grisandole, a female-bodied knight who passes muster as the best knight at the court of King Arthur. Nothing differentiates Grisandole from a male-bodied man, save that he lacks one masculine quality, villainy: 'Si se demena en toutes les maneres k'escuier se demaine, sans vilonie. N'ainc ne fu ravisee por femme.' From Ms. Paris, Bibliothèque Nationale de France 24394 fol. 214r, which constitutes the base text of Merlin: *Roman du XIIIe siècle*, ed. Alexandre Micha. (Geneva: Droz, 1979). Text cited by Laura Jane Campbell, 'Translation and Réécriture in the Middle Ages: Rewriting *Merlin* in the French and Italian Vernacular Traditions' (PhD dissertation, Durham University, 2011), p. 229. I follow the practice of the author of the *Roman de Merlin* in using the male personal pronoun for Grisandole while he presents socially as a man.

ature, particularly the literature of Eastern Christianity. The case for an Eastern Christian origin for, or Eastern influence upon, the Grail narratives has been posited and revived periodically over the past 150 years of scholarship, and attention has been drawn to the role of Byzantium in the cross-fertilization of literary strands which passed through its cosmopolitan cultural centres. An early hypothesis held that the Grail romances derive from Eastern Christian Mass rituals in which a knife was used to cut the bread or to pierce the Host, and where the juxtaposition of knife (masculine) and chalice (feminine) suggested the central motifs of lance and grail in the Grail narratives.[43] William A. Nitze links the Grail procession which Perceval witnessed to the 'great entry' in the Byzantine Mass of St John Chrysostom, noting moreover that the purported lance of Longinus (found in Antioch in 1098) was incorporated into this order of the Mass and was used to pierce the Host.[44] Pierre Gallais argues that Robert de Boron's *Estoire dou Graal* was actually written in Cyprus, and that Robert 'certainly lived in a milieu wide open to Byzantine and Syriac influences' and several scholars have noted the imprint of Eastern intertextuality in the *Estoire*.[45] Robert de Boron was well placed to come into contact with

[43] Wolfgang Golther, *Parzival und der Gral, in Deutscher Sage des Mittelalters und der Neuzeit* (Munich: G. D. W. Callwey, 1908); Rose J. Peebles, *The Legend of Longinus* (Baltimore: J.H. Furst, 1911), pp. 195–221. See also E. Anitchkof, 'Le Saint Graal et les rites eucharistiques', *Romania* 55 (1929): 174–94. This is also found in the symbiotic relationship of the masculine and feminine divine in Kabbalah (*c.* 1200) in the *Zohar*, embodied in the Serfiriot Tree.

[44] William A Nitze, *Perceval and the Holy Grail: An Essay on the Romance of Chrétien De Troyes* (Berkeley: University of California Press, 1949), pp. 307–9.

[45] Pierre Gallais, 'Robert de Boron en Orient', in *Mélanges de langue et de littérature du Moyen Age et de la Renaissance offerts à Jean Frappier*, ed. Jean Charles Payen and Claude Régnier (Geneva: Droz, 1970). Krijna Ciggaar has, in collaboration with Byzantinists and other orientalist scholars, sought to corroborate his hypothesis, finding that '[t]he Grail literature and iconography are impregnated with Eastern elements of which the legend of Joseph of Arimathea is just one': K. N. Ciggaar, 'Joseph of Arimathea in the Service of Pilate', *Romanische Philologie* 3 (1995): 417–21 at p. 421. See also K. N. Ciggaar, 'Robert de Boron en Outremer? Le culte de Joseph d'Arimathie dans le monde byzantin et en Outremer', in *Polyphonia Byzantina: Studies in Honour of Willem J. Aerts*, ed. H. Hokwerda, E. R. Smits, and M. M. Woesthuis (Groningen: Egbert Forsten, 1993), pp. 145–59. Ciggaar's studies of various episodes in the works of Chrétien de Troyes detail his incorporation of Byzantine current affairs into his narratives. K. N. Ciggaar, 'Chrétien de Troyes et la "matière byzantine": Les demoiselles du Château de Pesme Aventure', *Cahiers de civilisation médiévale* 32 (1989): 325–31; K. N. Ciggaar, 'Encore une fois Chrétien de Troyes et la "matière byzantine": La révolution des femmes au palais de Constantinople', *Cahiers de civilisation médiévale* 38 (1995): 267–74; for the historical background of cultural and literary exchanges between north and west Europe and Byzanium, see K. N. Ciggaar, 'Visitors from North-Western Europe to Byzantium: Vernacular Sources: Problems and Perspectives', *Proceedings of the British Academy* 132 (2007): 123–55; K. N. Ciggaar, *Western Travellers to Constantinople: The West and Byzantium, 962–1204: Cultural and Political Relations* (Leiden: Brill, 1996), pp. 186–7; K. N. Ciggaar, A. Davids, and H. G. B. Teule, 'Manuscripts as Intermediaries: The Crusader

Eastern Christianity since he was in the employ of Gautier de Montbeliard, who embarked on the Fourth Crusade in 1202, married Burgundia (daughter of King Amalric of Cyprus and Jerusalem), and after the death of his father-in-law, acted as regent on behalf of his brother-in-law, Hugh of Lasignan.

The argument that the crusades and the influx of holy relics to the west exerted a formative influence on the Christianized Grail legend is compelling. In this context, Helen Nicholson considers the representations of the military orders in romance and epic, investigating the appearance of the Knights Templars in Wolfram's *Parzival*, the connections between the Grail and the Holy Land and the emerging concept of the ideal knight.[46] Krijna Nelly Ciggaar's observation that Byzantine literature and ritual became known to the educated West through the presence of Greek monks in western European religious houses in an environment of peaceful co-operation also suggests a route for the transmission of particularly religious motifs included in the Grail cycles.[47] In one example, John Cassian travelled to Palestine and then to Egypt to live and study the monastic life around the turn of the fourth century, later setting up an Egyptian-style double monastery in Gaul which became the model for later monastic communities in the West. His works were recommended reading in Benedictine monasteries.[48] Some aspects of the earliest Eastern traditions of Christianity were undoubtedly transmitted to the West. The profound anxiety about sexuality and the privileging of virginity had their origins in the early waves of asceticism and the earliest developments of monasticism in Eastern Christianity. The Pauline epistle to the Galatians includes a text which effectively undermines the structure of society, heralding an end to hierarchies: 'For you are all the children of God, by faith in Christ Jesus. For as many of you as have been baptized in Christ have put on Christ. There is neither Jew nor Greek: there is neither bond nor free: there is neither male nor female. For you are all one in Christ Jesus' (Galatians 3:26–8). Every baptized Christian should put off the social prescriptions of gender and 'put on Christ'.

But rather than moderating entrenched status differences between women and men, the Church fathers interpreted this as a loophole for women to tran-

States and Literary Cross-Fertilization', in *East and West in the Crusader States: Context, Contacts, Confrontations: Acta of the Congress Held at Hernen Castle in May 1993*, ed. Krijna Nelly Ciggaar and Herman G. B. Teule, vol. 1 (Leuven: Peeters, 1996), pp. 133–5.

46 Helen Nicholson, *Love, War, and the Grail* (Leiden: Brill, 2001), pp. 102–86.

47 Ciggaar, *Western Travellers to Constantinople*, pp. 336–48.

48 See E. C. Butler, *Benedictine Monachism: Studies in Benedictine Life and Rule* (London: Longmans, Green, 1919), 'Cassian we know was St Benedict's spiritual book of predilection. In two places in the *Rule* he tells his monks to read Cassian, and […] the references to Cassian are more numerous, and also more considerable, than to any other author; and if the references be examined, it will appear that St Benedict was familiar with Cassian's writings, and was saturated with their thought and language, in a greater measure than with any other, save only the Holy Scriptures' (p. 25).

scend their limitations in a culture which regarded the female as anchored in the flesh and the male as allied with the spiritual.[49] They argued that women started with a decided disadvantage since their flesh and their given role in life were particularly unhallowed; the male was crafted in *imago dei*, the female was either a defective copy of the man, or the image of God insofar as she shared anatomy or characteristics with the male.[50] To become at least spiritually male, a woman had to demonstrate the intellectual and spiritual discernment to accept Christianity.[51] Ambrose implies that faith alone induces a modification of gender, writing that '[s]he who does not believe is a woman and should be designated by the name of her sex, whereas she who believes progresses to perfect manhood, to the measure of the adulthood of Christ. She then dispenses with the name of her sex, the seductiveness of youth, the garrulousness of old age.'[52] But faith needed cast-iron reinforcement; she had to renounce her sexuality and her sanctioned social role as wife and mother, as St Jerome teaches: '[a]s long as woman serves for birth and children, she is different from man, as body is from soul. But if she wishes to serve Christ more than the world, then she will cease to be woman and will be called man.'[53] Clement of Alexandria expounded a similar doctrine in the second century in his discussion of celibate 'spiritual' marriage: 'For souls, themselves by themselves, are equal. Souls are neither male nor female, when they no longer marry nor are given in marriage. And is not woman translated into man, when she

49 Augustinian patristic theology infused Christian doctrine on gender with Platonic dualism, and Augustine justified female subordination to male through associating man with spirit and woman with body: woman's deference to the male is, then, a matter of natural law. Through her association with the body, woman was allied with the flesh, the material world, the sexual, and the transitory, and so with death. Cf. Kari Elisabeth Borresen, *Subordination and Equivalence: The Nature and Role of Woman in Augustine and Thomas Aquinas* (Kampen: Kok Pharos, 1995), pp. 26–9; Genevieve Lloyd, *The Man of Reason: 'Male' and 'Female' in Western Philosophy* (Minneapolis: University of Minnesota Press, 1984), pp. 27–37.

50 Augustine of Hippo writes that '[t]he woman together with the man is the image of God, so that the whole substance is one image. But when she is assigned as a helpmate, which pertains to her alone, she is not the image of God: however, in what pertains to man alone, is the image of God just as fully and completely as he is joined with the woman into one' (*De Trinitate*, 12.7.10). On the interpretation of this, see Mathew S. Kuefler, *The Manly Eunuch: Masculinity, Gender Ambiguity, and Christian Ideology in Late Antiquity* (Chicago: University of Chicago Press, 2001), pp. 234–5.

51 Some holy women effected this transformation through cross-dressing and living as men in male monastic communities. See Larissa Tracy, *Women of the Gilte Legende: A Selection of Middle English Saints' Lives* (Cambridge: D. S. Brewer, 2003) and Valerie Hotchkiss, *Clothes Make the Man: Female Cross Dressing in Medieval Europe* (New York: Garland, 1996).

52 Ambrose, *Expositio Evangelii Secundum Lucam Libri X, 161* (1539), *Patrologia Latina*, ed. J.P. Migne (Paris: Garnier, 1844–55), cited by Vern L. Bullough, *Sexual Variance in Society and History* (Chicago: University of Chicago Press, 1976), p. 365.

53 Jerome, *Commentarli in Epistolam ad Ephesios, Libri III, Patrologia Latina* 26, ed. J.P. Migne (Paris: Garnier, 1844–55), col. 533.

has become equally unfeminine, and manly, and perfect?'[54] The sexes will be merged, but the female will be subsumed into the male, a reflection of the stance adopted by Valentinian Gnosticism which sought the reintegration of the male and female elements of a primordial unity through sublimation of the female and its eventual dissolution. But this vocation to transcend the flesh – and particularly the reproductive flesh – was not the sole preserve of female-bodied people. The male flesh carried its own corruption and its singular miasma: original sin was transmitted through the male line by sexual intercourse and every individual is fatally flawed from conception. Augustine of Hippo locates the source of this contagion in Adam's fallen testicles; all men sinned with Adam, as 'all men are understood to have sinned in that first "man" because all men were with him when he sinned'.[55] Elsewhere Augustine clarifies his exact meaning: 'by the hidden corruption of his own carnal lust all those coming from his stock rotted in him'.[56] The male body, polluted and polluting, stands between man and God, anathematized.

A man immersed in this anathematized contamination of the flesh cannot access the Grail, and Perceval must be something more than and something distinct from a man to pursue his quest. Perceval must become the Grail beast, an unhuman and unsexed emblem of human virtue incorporating the virtues traditionally associated with masculine and feminine, and before he can transcend human failings he needs to be aware of them. He has to acknowledge and be vigilant against both female and male components of human inadequacy. As the Grail beast, he has the stereotypically masculine 'heart of hard, dense steel that will be proof against swaying or softening',[57] and he has unmitigated, remorseless steeliness of purpose in his initial pursuit of chivalry. His first autonomous action as a male is to leave his mother unconscious on the doorstep when he leaves home to become a knight. Later he learns from his hermit uncle that she dies of sorrow at his departure and for the first time feels guilt, aware of his hard-hearted callousness. His attention is drawn to the 'feminine' quality of garrulousness (to which Ambrose refers) in a formative

54 Clement of Alexandria, *Stromata*, in Alexander Roberts, James Donaldson, and A. Cleveland Coxe, eds., *The Ante-Nicene Fathers: Fathers of the Second Century – Hermas, Tatian, Theophilus, Athenagoras, Clement of Alexandria*, vol. 2: *The Writings of the Fathers down to AD 325* (Buffalo, NY: Christian Literature Company, 1885), pp. 299–367, 6.12.503.

55 Augustine's version of the mechanics of sin propagation derives from Romans 5:12: 'Therefore, just as sin entered the world through one man, and death through sin, and in this way death came to all men, because all sinned.' The sexual reference Augustine introduces represents his inference drawn from the use of the verb *intrare* in the translation he used. See Martha Ellen Stortz, '"Where or When Was Your Servant Innocent?" Augustine on Childhood', in *The Child in Christian Thought*, ed. Marcia Bunge (Grand Rapids, MI: W. B. Eerdmans Publishing Company, 2001), pp. 78–102 at pp. 92–4.

56 Augustine, *De peccatorum meritis et remissione*, *Patrologia Latina*, ed. J.P.Migne (Paris: Garnier, 1844–55), 1.9.10.

57 *Lancelot-Grail*, ed. Lacy, p. 26.

event in his chivalric career when Gornemant de Goort instructs him in chivalry and knights him. He admonishes Perceval to be sparing of speech and never to repeat his mother's advice to anyone again or admit that she taught him anything (1675–84). Loquacity (his mother's legacy) must be put aside; silence is the discourse of a serious woman which characterizes the Grail beast who incorporates and renounces the feminine. And yet this silence, in mute obedience to the rules of men, stops Perceval from asking the questions which would have healed the fisher king and his land. He is only aware of this failure when the hermit tells him of it. Perceval lacks interiority, depending on other people to supply his human feelings and directing his resolve – spiritual advisors for his moral development, knights for his career development. The spiritual path privileged by the early Church required a further annulment of embodiment. The goal was transcendence of the sexual passions, the attainment of spiritual virginity. There grew up a perception of virgins as a genus apart, based on the text in Matthew 23:30: 'For in the resurrection they shall neither marry nor be married; but shall be as the angels of God in heaven', and celibacy on earth was seen to permit people some share in the purity of heaven. This virginal gender characterized ancient and Eastern Christian traditions and destabilized the categories of male and female. Behaviour and commitment could determine gender. Then (as now) it was a performative iteration. The virgin gender in the Grail cycles is the sex which can handle the Grail unscathed.

However, male virginity, insofar as such a concept could be conceived (let alone validated), was a nebulous construct. The penis was a constant reminder of the conflict between ascetic aspiration and anatomy. Its apparent autonomy, together with the evidence of nocturnal emissions, compromised male purity.[58] The only measure of male purity was the degree to which a man could suppress his sexual thoughts and reflexes. As Maud Burnett McInerney observes, 'if non-ejaculation is the criterion, male virgins must have been as rare as hen's teeth'.[59] But where male virginity was a nebulous and experiential quality, female virginity was a well-elaborated theological and social construct, as Larissa Tracy explains in terms of hagiography.[60] The female virgin body, believed to be

58 Cf. Basil of Caesarea's acknowledgement of his blemished purity: 'I do not know woman, but I am not a virgin.' John Cassian, *The Institutes* 19, trans. Boniface Ramsay (New York: Newman, 2000), p. 161, cited by David Brakke, 'The Lady Appears: Materializations of "Woman" in Early Monastic Literature', *Journal of Medieval and Early Modern Studies*, 33.3 (2003): 387–402 at p. 388. Cf. also Brakke's article discussing Cassian's equation of the absence of nocturnal emissions with intact physical virginity in the female. 'The Problematization of Nocturnal Emissions in Early Christian Syria, Egypt and Gaul', *Journal of Early Christian Studies* 3 (1995): 419–60.

59 Maud Burnett McInerney, 'Rhetoric, Power, and Integrity in the Passion of the Virgin Martyr', in *Menacing Virgins: Representing Virginity in the Middle Ages and Renaissance*, ed. Kathleen Coyne Kelly and Marina Leslie (Newark: University of Delaware Press, 1999) 50–70 at p. 58.

60 Tracy, 'Al defouleden is holie bodi', pp. 99, 101.

hermetically sealed by the intact hymen, was a fit and quantifiable exemplar of sexual purity. A woman could more easily transcend her body than a man could transcend the effect of her body on him, let alone transcend his own body. McInerney writes that in 'the face of such uncertainty about the possibility of maintaining virginity, or of even approximating it, in a male body, the body of the female virgin was an object of admiration to male ascetics and, inevitably, of envy'.[61] Yet measures could be taken in the quest to attain to male virginity. Men committed themselves to celibacy and fierce ascetic practice to flense away the desires of the flesh, and particularly the phallic flesh. They sought spiritual castration, to become eunuchs of the spirit, retreating from the established faith to form radical Christian communities. The earliest of these ascetic communities crystallized in the deserts of Egypt in the third and fourth centuries BC. But still nervousness and vigilance peppered their lives: 'Do not sleep in a place where there is a woman', cautions the desert father Abba Theodore of Pherme, while Abba Daniel advises 'never put your hand in the dish with a woman, and never eat with her; thus you will escape a little from the demon of fornication'.[62] For in her supposed absence, woman was everywhere haunting the male ascetic.[63] Devils in the form of women assaulted men in dreams and in diabolical visions, just as they do in the Grail narratives. The male body (it seems) manifests the apparitions of women, as indeed does Percival's, drawing the demon to him when he is shipwrecked. The male body – the genitals – becomes the devil's gateway. Without extraordinary grace, man cannot escape from the exigence of the body, yet amongst the most pious and rigorously ascetic in the desert, these graces are bestowed.

John Cassian describes such an instance of supernatural aid in stilling desire. Describing six progressive stages of purity to the monks of his Egyptian-style monastic foundation, the Abbey of St Victor of Marseilles (founded *c.* AD 415), he illustrates the final stage of complete nocturnal continence with an account from his days in Egypt. Abba Serenus who 'pleaded night and day for internal chastity of the heart and soul' underwent a spiritual surgical procedure which had the effect of permanently eliminating lust. He saw a vision of an angel one night, who removed his viscera, excised a 'fiery tumour' from his abdomen, replaced his intestines, and explained he had removed his fleshly desires to endow him with the permanent purity he had sought.[64] The location

61 Maud Burnett McInerney, *Eloquent Virgins from Thecla to Joan of Arc* (New York: Palgrave Macmillan, 2003), p. 63.

62 Cited by Susanna Elm, '*Virgins of God': The Making of Asceticism in Late Antiquity* (Oxford: Oxford University Press, 1994), p. 257.

63 David Brakke, *Demons and the Making of the Monk: Spiritual Combat in Early Christianity* (Cambridge, MA: Harvard University Press, 2006).

64 Cassian, *The Conferences*, trans. Boniface Ramsey (New York: Paulist Press, 1997), pp. 267–8.

of the tumour is unknown, but describing the six stages of purity Cassian recommends covering the kidneys with lead plates placed over the abdomen like armor as this will suppress the formation of 'obscene humours'.[65] This practice of stilling the kidney function with iron (instead of lead) was described by Pliny and Galen and employed as late as the sixteenth century to prevent nocturnal emissions.[66] Another desert father gifted with spiritual emasculation was Abba Elias. Out of charity he gathered some 300 wandering ascetic virgins into a monastery, and to still the infighting which broke out among them he lived alongside them as a pastoral adviser. But he was overwhelmed by desire and in his anguish he left the monastery. He dreamed that three angels offered him the opportunity to be free from desire if he would return. He consented willingly, and the angels used a razor to perform a spiritual castration in his dream. He too was released from sexual desire for the remainder of his life.[67]

It was in Byzantium, which Chrétien associated with eunuchs in the coda to *Cligès*, that eunuchs occupied responsible positions in secular and religious hierarchies, and where the eunuch became (in hagiographic contexts) a double for an angel – an image of purity.[68] Byzantine artists from the fourth century began to draw upon representations of the court eunuchs in their depictions of angels.[69] The archangel Michael, for example, appeared as his hierarchical equivalent in the imperial court, 'dressed in the robe of a praepositus' appearing as 'a fearful man as out of the heaven, with a rush descending on horseback on a white and terrible steed' to one Marcianus, a chandler.[70] Indeed, confusion between angels and eunuchs and cases of mistaken identity are remarkably common in Byzantine hagiographic sources.[71] There are other

65 Cited by Dyan Elliott, *Fallen Bodies: Pollution, Sexuality, and Demonology in the Middle Ages* (Philadelphia: University of Pennsylvania Press, 1999), p. 16.

66 Concetta Pennuto, ed., *Girolamo Mercuriale: De arte gymnastica* (Florence: L. S. Olschki, 2008), p. 194. Pennuto suggests that St Paul had this practice in mind when he wrote 'Runners in a race abstain from all these things to obtain a mortal crown, but we do so in order to receive an immortal one' (p. 195).

67 Palladius, *The Lausiac History*, 29A, trans. Robert Meyer (Westminster: The Newman Press, 1965), pp. 89–90.

68 See Shaun Tougher's essay in this volume, 'The Aesthetics of Castration', pp. 48–72.

69 Kathryn A. Ringrose makes her case for this assimilation compellingly in 'Transcending the Material World: Eunuchs and Angels', in *The Perfect Servant: Eunuchs and the Social Construction of Gender in Byzantium* (Chicago: University of Chicago Press, 2003), pp. 142–62. See also Amelia R. Brown, 'Painting the Bodiless: Angels and Eunuchs in Byzantine Art and Culture', Sexualities: Bodies, Desires, Practices, paper presented at Salzburg, Austria, 2007. <http://inter-disciplinary.net/ci/transformations/sexualities/s4/brown%20paper.pdf.

70 This account appears in a *vita* of Saint Michael by the late ninth- to early tenth-century Pantaleon. Cf. G. Peers, 'Apprehending the Archangel Michael: Hagiographic Method', *Byzantine and Modern Greek Studies* 20 (1996): 100–21 at p. 115.

71 Ringrose, *The Perfect Servant*, p. 153.

obvious points of similarity between the two besides the visual iconography: both serve as intermediaries (eunuchs between women and men, angels between humans and God); both are messengers; eunuchs castrated before puberty remain morphologically distinct from the sexually mature, and angels are commonly depicted as prepubescent;[72] while the eunuch is without any role in a family as an adult, angels neither marry nor engage in sexual activity. Both represent a different type of embodiment outside the gendered binary, a being designated other, a *tertium genus*.[73] And in their Otherness and their equivocality, they recall the knights Perceval saw in the forest, shining, on 'terrible steeds', whom he mistakes for angels, who inspire his quest and engender the pure Grail beast.

The collocation of eunuchs and angels represents an intriguing intercontextual commonality between two settings: one, late ancient eastern Christian communities, and the other, high medieval Europe. The angel, the Grail beast, and the Grail virgin belong to a genus beyond binary classifications, occupying a literary locus similar to sexual Otherness, similar to that occupied by eunuchs in late ancient society, and to the sexually neutered virgins of Christ or spiritually virilized women. For these, as for the Grail beast, sex and gender traits could be ephemeral, could be modified, and could be annulled. As the eunuchs of Byzantium stood in for angels iconographically and were believed to have particular access to the supernatural, so the Grail beast and the Grail virgins have unique access to the Holy Grail. For it is in this common ground of gender variance and attenuated gender that the Grail custodians are forged, one remove from humanity. Virgin knights encased in armor, the eunuch appearing before the chandler, and the 'angels' whom Perceval meets in the Gaste Forêt, are the avatars of a purity inconceivable in the flesh. Compounds of male and female perfection, the Grail beasts (hybrids 'without villainy') define themselves through their experiences and articulate their identities through their actions.

Perceval's story is the fullest account in the Grail cycles of this process. The stories of the fisher king, the Grail king, and Perceval's father all represent truncated versions of gender metamorphosis and renunciation. While Galahad lacks the initial flaws to relinquish, Perceval is constantly in flux, undertaking parallel quests for the Grail, for his mother, and for his identity. He assumes provisional identities as he encounters events and characters. Under the tutelage of Goremant he replaces his mother's teachings with the codes of

[72] Ibid.

[73] Terry Wilfong, describing this grouping, discerns a distinct 'third sex' for which there was 'a fairly clear and standard category in the discourse of late antiquity: the idea of a separate gender consisting of eunuchs and others who do not exhibit primary or secondary sexual characteristics of men or women but give off mixed signals or none at all': *Women of Jeme: Lives in a Coptic Town in Late Antique Egypt* (Ann Arbor: University of Michigan Press, 2002), pp. 35–6.

chivalry, the voice of the (lost) father, and under the tutelage of his uncle (the hermit) he understands piety and penitence. In Chrétien's *Perceval*, however, his development is truncated through this lack of a stable identity. At the Grail castle, in servile silence and obedience to Goremant's *parole* of the father, he fails to ask the questions which would heal the king and the land. He lacks the quality accorded him in prophecy – the 'discourse of a serious woman' – and the female-gendered qualities of curiosity and empathy for the king. Along the path to spiritual perfection, in the defence of his contested virginity, in his negation of desire, in his flight from the feminine which costs his mother's life, Perceval fails to learn humanity.

CHAPTER 12

Insinuating Indeterminate Gender: A Castration Motif in Guillaume de Lorris's Romans de la rose

Ellen Lorraine Friedrich

'Castration is a motif running through the *Rose*' asserts Sylvia Huot in *The Romance of the Rose and Its Medieval Readers.*[1] The thirteenth-century Old French *Romans de la rose* that Huot examines, one of the most popular works of the European Middle Ages, occurs in two parts. The original text, an approximately 4,000-line first-person verse allegory composed by Guillaume de Lorris around 1230, recounts the dream vision quest of the young narrator for the rose he seeks. The continuation, written a generation later by Jean de Meun (*c.* 1270), amounts to an encyclopedic 17,000-line, often satiric gloss on Guillaume's *Rose* that retells, amplifies, and at times diverges from the young lover's story.[2] The four primary examples that Huot presents of the mutilation motif in the *Rose* all appear in Jean's poem. David F. Hult, in 'Language and Dismemberment: Abelard, Origen, and the *Romance of the Rose*', arrives at a rather extreme assessment of Jean's work, finding that the author exhibits an 'unrelenting fascination with castration'.[3] Jean presents the four castration

1 Sylvia Huot, *The* Romance of the Rose *and Its Medieval Readers: Interpretation, Reception, Manuscript Transmission* (Cambridge: Cambridge University Press, 1993), p. 277.

2 I use the Old French nominative form of *roman* – *romans* – as a reminder that the work is the product of a language other than modern French, as well as of another time, the thirteenth century. I cite the edition by Daniel Poirion: Guillaume de Lorris and Jean de Meun, *Le Roman de la Rose*, (Paris: Garnier-Flammarion, 1974), and provide the verse numbers from this edition. All translations are my own, unless otherwise indicated. I use the date 1230 for Guillaume's *Rose*, from Daniel Poirion, ed., *Précis de littérature française du Moyen Âge* (Paris: Presses Universitaires de France, 1983), p. 390. See also Poirion, ed. *Roman*, 'Chronologie' (pp. 5–6) for the suggested dates 1230–45. Heather M. Arden, *The* Romance of the Rose: *An Annotated Bibliography* (New York and London: Garland, 1993) estimates the composition of Guillaume's part as between 1225 and 1230, and Jean's part from 1270 to 1276 or earlier (p. xvi).

3 David F. Hult, 'Language and Dismemberment: Abelard, Origen, and the *Romance of the Rose*', in *Rethinking the* Romance of the Rose: *Text, Image, Reception*, ed. Kevin Brownlee and Sylvia Huot (Philadelphia: University of Pennsylvania Press, 1992) 101–30 at p. 115.

FIGURE 12.1 Opening page of the *Romans de la Rose*, British Library, MS Stowe 947 (f.1) depicting (on the left) the dreamer in bed surrounded by roses, and (on the right), Oiseuse, encircled by rosebushes and holding a mirror and a comb. © The British Library Board, MS Stowe 947.

FIGURE 12.2 Detail of self-castrating beaver in the lower right-hand marginalia of the opening page of British Library, MS Stowe 947 (fl.1). © The British Library Board, MS Stowe 947.

commentaries – on Saturn's dismemberment by his son Jupiter, on Abelard's by the henchmen of his wife's uncle, on Genius's exhortation against it, and on Origen's self castration – as generally negative, even if Jean, as author, identifies some positive results from such violent actions.

Hult limits his study of linguistic and literal dismemberment to Jean's *Rose*, and thus does not consider the issue of castration in Guillaume's original narrative. Huot, however, notices unusual marginalia at the bottom of the opening page of the copy of Guillaume's composition in British Library MS Stowe 947 that 'surely' (she maintains) intended to comment on castration thematics in the poem,[4] noting that 'marginal images often did provide a visual gloss on the text'.[5] At the top of the first page of the *Rose* manuscript, a two-part, double-framed miniature portrays (on the left) the dreamer in bed surrounded by roses, and (on the right), encircled by rosebushes and holding a mirror and a comb, Oiseuse – the character who eventually admits the dreaming youth to the *vergiers* (orchard) to which he seeks entrance (Figure 12.1).[6] *Rose* bibliographer Heather Arden remarks that the female gatekeeper figure Oiseuse 'may be a key to understanding Guillaume's conception of love'.[7] Directly under the depiction of Oiseuse, in the lower margin, the viewer can discern a beaver castrating itself (Figure 12.2).[8] While Huot understands the

4 Huot, *The* Romance of the Rose *and Its Medieval Readers*, pp. 275, 277.

5 Ibid., p. 275, n. 4.

6 Some of the discussion on Oiseuse and other pertinent subjects in the *Romans de la rose* may be found in Ellen Lorraine Friedrich, 'Oiseuse: An Introduction to a Homoerotic Reading of Guillaume de Lorris's *Romans de la rose*' (PhD dissertation, University of North Carolina-Chapel Hill, 1999).

7 Arden, *The* Romance of the Rose, p. xxi.

8 The opening page, fol. 1r of British Library MS Stowe 947, is reproduced in Huot, *The* Romance of the Rose *and Its Medieval Readers*, p. 276.

self-injuring beaver as participating in the castration thematics by suggesting that the lover practice continence, or resist temptation,[9] the drawing, by highlighting the animal's eunuch-like body under the image of Oiseuse, also implies a castration motif in Guillaume's *Rose* that involves Oiseuse, intimating that the emasculated beaver somehow relates to her. Michael Camille, writing on thirteenth-century marginalia in *Images on the Edge: The Margins of Medieval Art*, affirms that things 'drawn in the margins add an extra dimension, a supplement, that is able to gloss ... the text's authority'.[10] Therefore, the image of a beaver biting off its own testicles invites inquiry both into what commentary the castrating animal offers on the character of Oiseuse, and into how the mutilation motif functions in Guillaume's *Rose*. Arden's assertion regarding Oiseuse as a key to understanding Guillaume's idea of love suggests that love (or erotic desire) may include castrates, and, as a consequence, represent a more comprehensive conception of love than previously thought. Moreover, the presence of a castration motif in the original *Rose* confirms that castration is not simply an obsession of Jean's, but a thread that weaves itself throughout both works.

Images on the first page of a *Romans de la rose* manuscript normally consist of a singular illustration of the dreamer in bed,[11] or of the dreaming lover along with a representation of another episode from the narrative, usually the dreamer beholding the images on the exterior of the wall that encloses the *vergiers*/orchard.[12] The relatively uncommon placement of a miniature of Oiseuse (as well as the beaver below her) on the initial page of a *Rose* manuscript[13] calls attention to her importance in the work, and closely associates her with both the lover and his quest. Huot recognizes the intimacy of the relationships among the dreaming lover, the rose, and Oiseuse: 'The conflation of the rose, object of desire, with the sensuality and self-absorption of Oiseuse –

9 Ibid., pp. 275, 277.

10 Michael Camille, *Images on the Edge: The Margins of Medieval Art* (Cambridge, MA: Harvard University Press, 1992) p. 10.

11 Alfred Kuhn, in 'Die Illustration der Handschriften des *Rosenromans*', *Jahrbuch der Kunsthistorischen Sammlungen des allerhöchsten Kaiserhauses* 31.1 (1912): 1–66, notes that the earliest images, i.e. those from the earliest manuscripts, represent the dreamer in bed. Kuhn maintains that those miniatures recreate the Nativity scene, a notion to which Huot, *The* Romance of the Rose *and Its Medieval Readers*, 275, n. 6, does not seem to subscribe, and one I too reject. Charles Dahlberg, in 'Love and the *Roman de la Rose*', *Speculum* 44 (1969): 568–84 at pp. 578–81, develops the argument regarding the Nativity scene.

12 Alcuin Blamires and Gail C. Holian, *The* Romance of the Rose *Illuminated: Manuscripts of the National Library of Wales, Aberystwyth* (Tempe: Arizona Center for Medieval and Renaissance Studies, 2002), survey the iconographical studies of the romance in ch. 1 (see especially p. 1 for mention of Kuhn's analysis of incipit miniatures in 'Die Illustration'), and discuss manuscript illuminations in ch. 2 (see especially p. 41 for comments on the opening scenes). Huot, as well as Blamires and Holian, makes use of the study of opening page illuminations by Alfred Kuhn, 'Die Illustration'.

13 Blamires and Holian, *The* Romance of the Rose *Illuminated*, pp. 1–2.

a feminine figuration of Narcissus, in whose mirror the rose is first glimpsed – tells us that the dream is inspired by and focused upon erotic love.'[14] Significantly, Huot's identification of Oiseuse with Narcissus, who (as Guillaume recounts) fell in love with a beautiful young man like himself,[15] links Oiseuse – and perhaps the animal associated with her – with a hint of homoeroticism in the *Rose* narrative and implies that the type of love story portrayed in the text may not be straightforward, or indeed 'straight'.

Although the allegory is traditionally seen as the youth's quest for a lady 'rose',[16] scholars in the late twentieth century began to question the nature of the erotic love portrayed in the romance – at times specifically in Guillaume's poem – focusing on the autoerotic and masturbatory,[17] narcissistic, homosocial, and homoerotic tensions in the *Rose*. Marta Powell Harley decides that through the use of classical myths like those of Narcissus, Hermaphroditus, and Attis, Guillaume is 'conscientiously flirting with sexual ambiguity and homosexuality'.[18] Unlike Jean, who, in the *Rose* continuation, uses the mythical castration of Saturn to establish the birth of heterosexual desire embodied by Venus, Guillaume chooses other myths for his own purposes, apparently homoerotic ones. Harley's argument, employing both the story of Hermaphroditus who lost his full masculinity, thereby becoming half a man (*semivir*)[19] – and thus symbolically or actually castrated – and the account of Attis who castrated himself, becoming 'nec femina nec vir' [neither woman nor man] according to Ovid,[20] supports her reading of gender and erotic anomaly in Guillaume's romance. Therefore, Guillaume's use of the Hermaphroditus and Attis myths sustains the

14 Huot, *The* Romance of the Rose *and Its Medieval Readers*, p. 275. However, I note that it is the rose*bud* (not the rose) that is glimpsed. The young lover looks into the spring of Narcissus – referred to in the *Rose* text as a mirror – where he sees two crystals that reflect the rose garden and its bushes; from one of those bushes he selects a rose*bud*. See Poirion, ed., *Le Roman*, vv. 1536–8, 1549ff, 1560–1, 1615–16; 1655–6.

15 Poirion, ed., *Le Roman*, vv. 1487 ff.

16 Poirion, for example, in his 'Préface' to *Le Roman*, refers to the object of the young lover's quest as 'une jeune fille pudique' (a modest young girl) (p. 12). For a more general assessment, see also Dahlberg's 'Love and the *Roman de la Rose*': 'Whether or not the rose represents a specific young lady, it certainly represents the object of a desire that controls the Lover's actions throughout the poem' (p. 569).

17 Dolores Warwick Frese, *An* Ars Legendi *for Chaucer's* Canterbury Tales*: Re-constructive Reading* (Gainesville: University of Florida Press, 1991). See especially chs 1 and 2 for Frese's analysis of the opening scenes in Guillaume's romance as autoerotic and masturbatory.

18 Marta Powell Harley, 'Narcissus, Hermaphroditus, and Attis: Ovidian Lovers at the Fontaine d'Amors in Guillaume de Lorris's *Roman de la rose*', *PMLA* 101 (1986): 324–37 at p. 333.

19 Ovid, *Metamorphoses* books I–VIII, trans. Franck Justus Miller, rev. G. P. Gould (Cambridge, MA: Harvard University Press, 1977; rpt. 1984, 1994), p. 204.

20 Ovid, *Ibis*, in *The Art of Love and Other Poems*, vol. 2, trans. J. H. Mozley, 2nd edn rev. G. P. Gould (Cambridge, MA: Harvard University Press, 1979; rpt 1985), p. 455.

notion that the emasculation motif, albeit differently conceptualized, runs as strongly through his original text as through Jean's.[21]

Gender ambiguity also exists in the character of Bel Acuel,[22] as Simon Gaunt has remarked.[23] The handsome youth offers his service to the lover narrator, and welcomes the latter to the orchard and through the hedges into the rose garden, where the lover eventually chooses a rosebud as the object of his desire. Even if Bel Acuel has a grammatically masculine name, manuscript illuminators at times portray him as feminine, evidently aware of his – or her – role as the amenable aspect of the beloved (purportedly feminine) rose that the lover seeks. In his study on the *Rose*, Douglas Kelly, although primarily commenting on Jean's continuation, similarly identifies Bel Acuel as the 'receptive agent in the rose complex', and links the lover to sodomites, to castrates, and to effeminates.[24]

Gaunt and Kelly's recognition of Bel Acuel as sexually ambiguous and Kelly's similar association of the lover with non-normative erotic activities that imply non-normative gender, recall the categories of sexual indeterminacy that medieval scholars have identified as confused and conflated with homosexuality. In a like manner, Robert L.A. Clark, in this volume, analyzes the troubled category of eunuchs as not-exactly-male in two works, the thirteenth-century Latin *De Vetula* and its fourteenth-century French translation, Jean Le Fèvre's *La Vieille*.[25] Monica E. McAlpine writes on another ambiguously gendered medieval character, Chaucer's Pardoner from *The Canterbury Tales*, and finds that allusions to the three 'sexual phenomena with which homosexuality was often confused – effeminacy, hermaphroditism, and eunuchry' equal references to homosexuality itself.[26] Her statement brings to mind Guillaume's flirtation (in his *Rose*) with sexual ambiguity and homosexuality. Since the last type (eunuchry) of the three phenomena confused with homosexuality represents a castrated state, all the categories could describe the *Rose* author's use of both the Hermaphroditus and the Attis myth.

21 Hermaphroditus' and Attis' resultant castrated states also recall Jean's textual use of the calamitous castration of Abelard, and the self-mutilation carried out by Origen, discussed below in this essay.

22 I use the old French spelling 'Bel Acuel' throughout, though many scholars use 'Bel Acueil'.

23 Simon Gaunt, 'Bel Acueil and the Improper Allegory of the *Romance of the Rose*', in *New Medieval Literatures*, II, ed. and intro., Rita Copeland, David Lawton, and Wendy Scase (Oxford: Clarendon Press, 1998), pp. 65–93. Although Gaunt, like many scholars, focuses on Jean's *Rose*, he does not neglect Guillaume's composition. Nevertheless, Gaunt – as many, if not most, critics – generally treats the two texts as if they comprised one whole work, whereas Harley and a few others (as do I) concentrate on the original poem by Guillaume.

24 Douglas Kelly, *Internal Difference and Meanings in the* Roman de la Rose (Madison: University of Wisconsin Press, 1995), especially pp. 114–16 at p. 115.

25 Robert L. A. Clark, 'Culture Loves a Void: Eunuchry in *De Vetula* and Jean Le Fèvre's *La Vieille*', in this volume, pp. 280–94.

26 Monica E. McAlpine, 'The Pardoner's Homosexuality and How It Matters', *PMLA* 95 (1980): 8–22 at p. 13.

In Chaucer's work, McAlpine points out the narrator's comment in the General Prologue comparing the Pardoner to two animals, or rather two forms of the same animal: that he is a 'geldyng or a mare'.[27] A gelding, of course, refers to any castrated male animal, usually a horse, and archaically to a eunuch.[28] The narrator effectively calls the Pardoner castrated.[29] Already in the fourth century BC, Aristotle had summed up the standard view of a castrate or eunuch when he remarked that a 'castrated male … assumed pretty well the form of a female'.[30] The twelfth and thirteenth centuries saw similar characterizations of castrates. In the first quarter of the twelfth century, letters attacking the castrated cleric Abelard characterize him as a feminized eunuch with a dual-sexed identity,[31] and in Jean's late thirteenth-century *Rose*, Genius criticizes castrated men as having *meurs feminins* (feminine ways) and as resembling women.[32] Both characterizations recall McAlpine's first category of indirect allusions to homosexuality: effeminacy. So calling the Pardoner a gelding (a castrated male horse) or a mare (a female horse) not surprisingly references the male character's effeminate characteristics, his possible lack of male genitals, and his resulting feminized form deficient in male hormones. The use of such animal analogies for the Pardoner's apparently castrated male (gelding)/female (mare) body blurs the gender line into androgyny or hermaphroditism,[33] and brings to mind the castrating beaver in the *Rose* manuscript as well as Guillaume's use of the self-castrated 'neither woman nor man' Attis and 'half man' Hermaphroditus myths in the *Rose*. Harley locates the use of the two myths in the episode at the fontaine d'amors, the fountain of Narcissus. In the

[27] Geoffrey Chaucer, *The Riverside Chaucer*, 3rd edn, ed. Larry D. Benson (Boston: Houghton Mifflin, 1987) p, 34, v. 691. The note to line 691 glosses the expression as 'a eunuch or a homosexual'.

[28] *Webster's Ninth New Collegiate Dictionary* (Springfield, MA: Merriam-Webster, 1990): 509. Moreover, the noun 'gelding' and the verb 'to geld' are related to the Greek term *gallos* which refers to a eunuch priest of Cybele.

[29] As Lee Patterson points out, this may simply be a form of insult and may not be meant literally. Several scholars, including McAlpine, have translated 'mare' as 'homosexual', but Patterson maintains that there is no textual evidence for this use of 'mare'. See 'Chaucer's Pardoner on the Couch: Psyche and Clio in Medieval Literary Studies,' *Speculum* 76.3 (July 2001): 638–80.

[30] Cited in Thomas Laqueur, *Making Sex: Body and Gender from the Greeks to Freud* (Cambridge, MA: Harvard University Press, 1990), p. 31, from Aristotle's *Generation of Animals* 1.2.716b5–12.

[31] Martin Irvine, 'Abelard and (Re)writing the Male Body: Castration, Identity, and Remasculinization', in *Becoming Male in the Middle Ages*, ed. Jeffrey Jerome Cohen and Bonnie Wheeler (New York and London: Garland, 2000), pp. 87–106, pp. 91–4. See also Larissa Tracy, '"Al defouleden is holie bodi": Castration, the Sexualization of Torture, and Anxieties of Identity in the *South English Legendary*', in this volume, pp. 87–107.

[32] Poirion, ed., *Le Roman*, vv. 20058–60; 20065–7.

[33] Jed Chandler discusses the same kind of gender ambiguity in the Grail narratives with their 'self-wounded' virginal Grail knights in 'Eunuchs of the Grail', in this volume, pp. 229–54.

waters of the fountain, whose self-absorbed owner Huot connects to Oiseuse, the lover sees reflected rosebushes. Drawn to the bushes with the straight-stemmed, plump, ready-to-burst rosebuds upon them, the lover essentially falls in love with one of the bigger vermilion buds, finding it so beautiful that none of the others attracts him at all.[34] Surprisingly, the lover has not fallen for a seemingly feminine object of desire (a rose) as suggested by the title of the work, but rather for the stiff-stemmed, bulbous rose*bud* that Harley and others identify as phallic.[35]

The ambiguously gendered Bel Acuel controls access to the roses, and thus also to the masculine bud 'li boutons' (v. 1666) chosen by the lover. The male–male, or indefinitely gendered desire, begins of course as a longing for the rose. However, even the rose has been interpreted as a masculine object of desire, the entry to which lies with, or through, Bel Acuel. Philological analyses suggest that the rose represents the anus, the lover's first object of desire, found in his beloved Bel Acuel who is eventually imprisoned for their transgressive relationship.[36] Jean's obsession in his later *Rose* with condemning corrupt love, promoting procreation (through Genius), and cautioning about the catastrophe caused by castration, confirms the gravity of ignoring nature and practicing 'unnatural love'.[37] Guillaume, too, demonstrates his awareness of 'amors contre nature' when he has the God of Love caution against it in his speech to the young lover.[38] Generally speaking, medieval audiences[39] understood unnatural love – or love 'contre nature' – as sexual practices that did not produce progeny. Since castration results in sterility, a castrated state therefore permits non-procreative sex acts on the part of the resulting eunuch, typified by the self-mutilating beaver, which, as Huot points out, participates in the castration thematics found in the *Rose*. Consequently, the animal suggests that the character Oiseuse repre-

34 Poirion, ed., *Le Roman*, 'un si tres bel … nus des autres riens ne prisé' [one (masculine 'li boutons') so very beautiful … none of the others did I prize at all] (vv. 1656–7).

35 Harley seems to have been the first – in 'Narcissus, Hermaphroditus, and Attis' – to describe the bud as a 'phallic image' (p. 334). Karl D. Uitti, in '"Cele [qui] doit estre Rose clamee" (*Rose*, vv. 40–44): Guillaume's Intentionality', in *Rethinking the* Romance of the Rose, ed. Brownlee and Huot, pp. 39–64, refers to the closed flower as the 'phallic rose' (p. 40). For a philological analysis, see also Ellen Lorraine Friedrich, 'When a Rose Is not a Rose: Homoerotic Emblems in the *Roman de la Rose*', in *Gender Transgressions: Crossing the Normative Barrier in Old French Literature*, ed. Karen J. Taylor (New York and London: Garland, 1998), pp. 22–43.

36 Friedrich, 'When a Rose'.

37 Genius's warning occurs in Poirion, ed. *Le roman*, vv. 19505 ff. Summary comments on the anal symbolism of the rose, and Jean's obsession with condemning certain types of love and castration come from Ellen Friedrich, '*Romance of the Rose*', in *Encyclopedia of Sex and Gender*, ed. Fedwa Malti-Douglas, 4 vols (Detroit: Thomas Gale, 2007) 4:1269–71 at p. 1271.

38 Poirion, ed. *Le roman*, vv. 2169–74.

39 I understand 'audience' as any person receiving a text, whether by personal reading, hearing the text read, or seeing it performed.

sents some sort of eunuch-like being, and that Guillaume begins his allusions to missing members through her and, indirectly, through the beaver.

The missing masculine organs in Guillaume's *Rose* are not immediately apparent. Toward the end of Guillaume's *Rose*, the character Reason counsels the young lover about the extreme danger in consorting with Oiseuse who carries the key ('porte / la clef'; vv. 3003–4) to the *vergiers*: 'S'acointance est trop perilleuse' [Her acquaintance (acquaintance with her) is too perilous] (v. 3006). Oiseuse's key, never visibly used in the tale, but said to have opened the door to the orchard, is reminiscent of another key that plays a considerable role in the *Rose*. Harley understands as clearly phallic the *clef* – key – that the Diex d'Amors (God of Love) possesses and uses to penetrate the Lover (vv. 2008–10), an action to which the Lover willingly submits in a homoerotically charged scene.[40] Imagine the sexual implication in the positioning of the relatively long and hard 'key' that Amors says he holds over his 'jewels':[41] 'Sous ceste clef sont mi joiau' [under this key are my jewels] (v. 2004). In fact, in order to penetrate the Lover, the God of Love takes his *clef* out of his *aumouniere* 'purse / sack': 'Lors a de s'aumoniere traite / Une petite clef bien faite' [Then from his purse he drew out / A little key well-made] (vv. 1999–2000). In Jean's *Rose*, Genius uses the word *aumoniere* twice (vv. 19667; 19670) to refer to the testicular sac (scrotum) in the character's diatribe against homosexuals. Genius rails against those who will not use their testicles and penises for the right purpose of procreation, and he wishes their testicles torn out and their penises taken away (vv. 19671–3).[42] In this way, in his *Rose*, Jean (through his character Genius) calls for castration as punishment.

In Guillaume's *Rose* it seems that the Diex d'Amors has used his 'key' (whether fully attached to his body or not) for a non-normative sex act with the lover. Amors thus participates in an activity that merits castration (if he is not already in that state). In a parallel way, Oiseuse carries a key that suggests a separation of the phallic-like object from her body, bringing into question the type of body she exhibits. Likewise, the beaver pictured under the character's representation in the Stowe manuscript is separating its genitals from its body. The

40 Harley, 'Narcissus, Hermaphroditus, and Attis', p. 333. See also Ellen Lorraine Friedrich, 'The Mentorship of the Lover by the Diex d'Amors in Guillaume de Lorris's *Romans de la rose*', *Medieval Perspectives* 26 (2011 [2012]): 89–103.

41 OF *Joiau*, 'joiel, joel' (jewel, plaything) derives from Latin *jocalem* 'pleasant' or 'plaything'. It may also refer to 'Le sexe de la femme' (see Algirdas Julien Greimas, *Dictionnaire de l'ancien français* [Paris: Larousse, 1980], p. 347), and, by extension and linguistic evidence in modern French, English, and other languages' slang, to a man's (family) 'jewels', 'balls', or 'testicles'. Medieval Latin *jocale* is attested by 1204, as 'jewel, precious object', and OF *joel, joal* (1175) is regularly derivable from *jocale*. http://sci.tech-archive.net/Archive/sci.lang/2008-05/msg01781.html. (accessed Dec. 30, 2012).

42 Historical records and literary references do not always distinguish between the removal of the penis (a penectomy) and castration, normally the removal of the testicles. Castration can also refer to the removal of the genitalia in general.

animal has a long philological, folkloric, cultural, literary, and even medicinal and economic history that contributes to how medieval readers and listeners understood its presence in a manuscript, and therefore its comment on the character to which it refers, and on the work itself.[43] Similarly, classical and medieval accounts of the beaver influence the interpretation of the castrated animal in the *Rose* manuscript, the understanding of its relationship to Oiseuse, and finally the perception of how Oiseuse also exists in a castrated state.

The sixth-century BC series of animal tales commonly known as Aesop's Fables, although based at least partially on earlier Egyptian material,[44] may offer the earliest observations in the Western world on beavers: they live in pools, and they know hunters pursue them for their genital organs that can cure ailments. When chased, beavers will run, and seeing they cannot escape, chew off their own testicles, and throw them to their pursuers, hence enabling their getaway.[45] In his fifth-century BC *History*, Herodotus mentions that the beaver is hunted for its testicles which are useful for preparing cures.[46] In the fourth century BC, Hippocrates often included *castoreum*, the aromatic substance made from the beaver's testicles and the secretions thereof, in remedies.[47] In a 2002 *Smithsonian Zoogoer* article, Amy Himes summarizes the importance of the beaver in ancient and medieval societies: Although its fur 'could cost up to five times more than the fur of other animals [...] many people hunted beavers for another reason, one originally considered far more valuable than fur'.[48] Both Europeans and others used the *castoreum* for a variety of aches and pains, suggesting that earlier cultures were quite familiar with the animal.[49]

Other facets of the animal's lore may hold even more appeal for ancient and medieval peoples, as Himes explains:

43 The *Romans de la rose* has traditionally been assumed to be a 'book' that was read. Recently Evelyn Birge Vitz has considered its performability: '*Le Roman de la Rose*, Performed', abstract for paper, Fordham University conference, 'Think Romance!' March 31–April 1, 2012. Online at http://www.fordham.edu/mvst/conference12/Romance/Vitz.pdf, accessed March 5, 2012.

44 Ebenezer Cobham Brewer, 'Aesop', in *Brewer's Dictionary of Phrase and Fable*, ed. Ivor H. Evans, 14th edn (London: Cassell, 1991), p. 14.

45 Aesop, *The Complete Fables*, trans. Olivia and Robert Temple; intro. Robert Temple (London: Penguin, 1998); # 153, 'The Beaver', pp. 113–14 at p. 113.

46 Herodotus, *The Histories of Herodotus*, trans. Henry Cary (New York: D. Appleton, 1904), book IV 109.2.

47 Hippocrates, *Coan Prenotions: Anatomical and Minor Clinical Writings*, trans. Paul Potter (Cambridge, MA: Harvard University Press, 2010), e.g. p. 345.

48 Amy Himes, 'At the Zoo: Busy Beavers', *Smithsonian Zoogoer* 31.2 (2002); online at http://nationalzoo.si.edu/Publications/ZooGoer/2002/2/busybeavers.cfm, accessed March 5, 2012.

49 The *castoreum* undoubtedly had some actual medicinal powers since researchers have found that it contains, as Himes points out, 'small amounts of salicylic acid ... found in the bark of one of the beaver's favorite trees, the willow. Salicylic acid is the active ingredient in aspirin' (Himes, 'At the Zoo').

> Castoreum was once thought to enhance sexual energies – an erroneous connection between the oil and beavers' sexual activity. Indeed, beaver sexual function fascinated early cultures because, unlike most mammals, beavers have no external difference in sexual organs that may distinguish one sex from the other. In many males, the external sexual organs look almost exactly like the female's. The penis and testicles are hidden inside the urogenital passage that opens into the cloaca. Some males even have a non-functioning uterus. Because of the absence of external sex organs, ancient Egyptians as well as European writers until the 1600s believed beavers would castrate themselves if threatened with capture.[50]

Even Himes's explanation, taking into account earlier Egyptian and European understandings of the animal's biology, seems contradictory regarding the appearance of gender markers on or in the beaver's body.

A study of the animal's history in Persian- and Arabic-speaking lands elucidates:

> castoreum is a musk-like strong-smelling resinous matter secreted by a pair of bulky glandular pouches united by a common excretory duct and located side by side under the abdominal skin in the urogenital region of both male and female beavers. [...] The fact that she-beavers also possess these musk glands (though less developed than in males) must have passed unnoticed by classical authors [...] hence the confusion of these pouches with he-beavers' testicles.[51]

Thus, ancient and medieval peoples undoubtedly found beavers' genitalia, or the apparent – or actual – lack of them, as well as the substance supposedly derived from it, a source of speculation and fascination.[52]

Given the popularity of beaver fur, and the importance of *castoreum* to cure various ailments, along with the belief that the substance can increase erotic vigor, societies remained well acquainted with the animal and its economic, medicinal, and folkloric values. In addition, viewing or hearing of the beaver's apparently non-gendered body contributed to the fact that earlier cultures believed beavers chose castration over capture, suggesting at the same time that ancient and medieval peoples maintained an interest in emasculated bodies.

50 Himes, 'At the Zoo'.

51 'Beaver', *Encyclopaedia Iranica*; online at http://www.iranicaonline.org/articles/beaver-castor-fiber-l, accessed March 5, 2012.

52 To clarify from a modern biological perspective, according to a standard volume on animals, zoologists must either dissect dead beavers or have experience palpating live ones to be able to determine their sex: Theodore Bookhout, ed., *Research and Management Techniques for Wildlife and Habitats* (Bethesda, MD: Wildlife Society, 1980). See pp. 204–5 for palpation instructions and illustrations of the male and female beavers' vestibular cavity. I thank my colleague, J. Mitchell Lockhart, Department of Biology, Valdosta State University, for sharing the text with me.

For example, in the Byzantine Empire, eunuchs held a special place, and they were valued for their service and for their voices throughout Europe.[53] As Shaun Tougher argues in this volume, Roman eunuchs were objects of beauty and were often sexually desirable.[54] As a result, the medieval audience likely recognized the ramifications of marginal drawings of the castrating (or castrated) and valuable animal and could apply that knowledge to the interpretation of the character Oiseuse, well known for her beauty (vv. 525 ff; 1251).

In fact, people had long conceived of animals in human terms. Aristotle, writing around 350 BC, explains:

> In the great majority of animals there are traces of psychical qualities or attitudes, which qualities are more markedly differentiated in the case of human beings. [...] Some of these qualities in man [...] differ only quantitatively: that is to say, a man has more or less of this quality, and an animal has more or less of some other.[55]

Clearly, the beaver's supposed cognizance of the hunter's objective and the animal's apparent decision to castrate itself depend on the conception of beasts as having at least 'proto-human' qualities, an idea not only common in the ancient and medieval worlds, but one that continued up until the eighteenth century.[56] A related quality of the beaver, that of making choices to sacrifice part of its body for the greater good of saving its life, appears in texts at the turn of the first millennium in Ovid,[57] and in the first century AD in Pliny the Elder's *Natural History*.[58]

Examining the tradition of the beaver as a sexually symbolic animal in the Middle Ages, Michael J. Curley notes that around the turn of the second century AD, Juvenal (in *Satire* 12.34) uses the example of the beaver 'qui se / Eunuchum

53 See Mary A. Valante, 'Castrating Monks: Vikings, the Slave Trade, and the Value of Eunuchs', pp. 174–86 and Kathryn Reusch, 'Raised Voices: The Archaeology of Castration', pp. 29–47, in this volume.

54 Shaun Tougher, 'The Aesthetics of Castration: The Beauty of Roman Eunuchs', in this volume, pp. 48–72.

55 Aristotle, *The History of Animals*, book 8, part 1, trans. D'Arcy Wentworth Thompson, online at http://classics.mit.edu/Aristotle/history_anim.8.viii.html, accessed November 15, 2011.

56 Willene B. Clark and Meradith T. McMunn, 'Introduction', in *Beasts and Birds of the Middle Ages: The Bestiary and Its Legacy* (Philadelphia: University of Pennsylvania Press, 1989), p. 1.

57 Ovid, *The Art of Love and Other Poems*, trans. J. H. Mozley, 2nd edn rev. G. P. Gould (Cambridge, MA: Harvard University Press, 1979; rpt. 1985); *Nux*, line 304. In his poem *Nux* (The Walnut Tree), Ovid refers to the parts imperiling the beaver that, once removed, leave the animal everything else, implying the possibility of a choice eventually understood morally as a sacrifice for a greater good.

58 Pliny the Elder, *The Natural History of Pliny*, trans. John Bostock and H. T. Riley (London: George Bell & Sons, 1890), 8.47.109. Pliny, a source for many later writers, explains that beavers around the Black Sea know hunters seek them for the oil (*castoreum*) produced by an organ that they self-amputate when chased.

ipse facit' [who / makes itself a eunuch] by cutting off its own testicles.[59] By using the term *eunuchum*, Juvenal may have made the first formal connection of the castrated beaver to eunuchs, although Aristotle had earlier described both the assimilation of animals to human (see passage quoted above) and the intersex state of castrated animals in general:

> In the case of all these animals their nature appears in some kind of a way to have got warped, just as some male animals get to resemble the female, and some female animals the male. The fact is that animals, if they be subjected to a modification in minute organs, are liable to immense modifications in their general configuration. This phenomenon may be observed in the case of gelded animals: only a minute organ of the animal is mutilated, and the creature passes from the male to the female form. We may infer, then, that if in the primary conformation of the embryo an infinitesimally minute but absolutely essential organ sustain a change of magnitude one way or the other, the animal will in one case turn to male and in the other to female; and also that, if the said organ be obliterated altogether, the animal will be of neither one sex nor the other.[60]

Aristotle's placing of gelded animals – castrated males – into the category of female or of neither sex recalls not only the sort-of-man Hermaphroditus and *nec femina nec vir* Attis, but the 'geldyng or a mare' Pardoner as well (and any other character in between genders), whether human or animal, since the qualities of both were attributed to each other. Curley also remarks that Apuleius' second-century AD *The Golden Ass* identifies a special punishment enacted for unfaithful lovers that transforms them into self-castrating beavers.[61] Thus, both Juvenal's association of the castrated animal with human eunuchs and Apuleius' linking of faithless lovers with emasculated beavers confirm (not surprisingly) that society, as Aristotle pointed out, conceived of castrated creatures in human terms and vice versa. Therefore, placing a drawing of a self-mutilating beaver below the depiction of the character Oiseuse in a *Rose* manuscript illustration reinforces the idea that the viewer should understand the key-carrying gatekeeper as some sort of castrate/eunuch.

By the beginning of the third century AD, in the *De natura animalium* (*On the Nature of Animals*) 6.34, Claudius Aelianus (Aelian) specifies that the beaver understands why hunters come after it, so it puts its head down, chews off its own testicles, and throws the organs down in front of the men in pursuit. Aelian adds the new information that if the animal has already saved its life by self-castration, and hunters still chase it, that it stands up and shows the pursuers

59 Michael J. Curley, 'A Note on Bertilak's Beard', *Modern Philology: A Journal Devoted to Research in Medieval and Modern Literature* 73.1 (1975): 69–73 at p. 70.

60 Aristotle, *History of Animals*, book 7, part 2, trans. Thompson.

61 Curley, 'A Note on Bertilak's Beard', p. 69.

that its testicles are no longer there so the men will abandon their chase.[62] More importantly perhaps, Aelian writes that beavers escaping with their testicles intact draw them into their bodies,[63] demonstrating yet another understanding both of the apparently deliberate actions of the animals, and of the seemingly indeterminately gendered bodies of beavers. As a result, hunters may believe that the animals do not have what they in fact capably conceal. Consequently, whether by castration or concealment, beavers demonstrate a eunuch-like, ambiguously gendered body, either lacking testicles or seeming to lack them. Their intersex bodies suggest provocative possibilities for interpreting the animal's significance for a text such as the *Rose*, prompting the reader of the work to focus not only on the castrating action of the beaver, but also on its eunuchoid body. That Aelian often took the behavior of animals as a model of human conduct[64] again intriguingly implies that the beaver's body may mirror Oiseuse's or vice versa, i.e. that the *Rose* character possesses the 'keyless' castrated body of a eunuch.

Another influential work, the anonymous Greek *Physiologus*, a relatively compact compendium of animal, non-animate, and plant allegories that subsumed and built upon the earlier traditions of Pliny, Aelian, and others, may have appeared as early as the first part of the second century[65] or as late as the fourth.[66] Translations of the allegories in the *Physiologus* begin to appear almost immediately in Latin and then in European vernacular languages, and the work became one of the most widely read texts during the Middle Ages. Directly, and through its derivations, the *Physiologus* turned into a source for medieval iconography, poetry, preaching manuals, and religious textbooks.[67] The Latin versions generally repeat the information found in Pliny, and most of that in Aelian. The different versions of the *Physiologus* include the description of each animal, often followed by a moral and a meaning. In the case of the beaver, the description generally notes that the beaver's genitals serve as medicine, and that its behavior includes the first two of the self-saving actions. First, the animal bites off its genitals and throws them towards the hunter, and then, if another man pursues it later, it lies down on its back (or stands up, or lifts its leg) to show its lack of genitals.

The next step in the evolution of the beaver lore occurs when the Iberian

62 Michael J. Curley, trans. *Physiologus* (Chicago: University of Chicago Press, 1979; 2009), p. xxiii.

63 William Barker, Mark Feltham, and Jean Guthrie, 'Commentary on Emblem 153' of Alciato's *Book of Emblems* (1531), Department of English, Memorial University of Newfoundland, online at http://www.mun.ca/alciato/c153.html, accessed September 15, 2011.

64 Ibid.

65 Curley, trans. *Physiologus*, pp. xvii–xviii.

66 Ibid., p. xviii.

67 Ibid., pp. ix–x.

scholar Isidore of Seville, in his seventh-century *Etymologies* (book 12, 2:21), establishes the popular etymology of the beaver's name – *Castor fiber* – explaining that the *castor* was so named from its *castrando* 'castrating' action.[68] Isidore does not fully explain his etymologies; instead, he makes references (writing in Latin) that his learned audience would understand. Old French *castor/castre* 'beaver' comes from Latin *castor*, which in turn derives from Greek *Kastōr*, the name of Castor, one of the Gemini twins, the Dioscuri (from *Dios*, genitive of Zeus + *kouroi*, plural of *kouros*, boy),[69] sons of Zeus. Significantly, Zeus castrated his own father, Kronus, who, in turn, had earlier castrated his father, Uranus. Zeus was therefore both the son and grandson (and Castor the grandson and great-grandson) of castrated gods, as well as the father of a number of 'sexually impaired' children, one an androgyne changed into a woman, another two castrated, and still another produced from cast-off genitals.[70] Naming Zeus' son Castor, in addition to referencing the youth's castrated family, may well evoke the latter's absent double, his brother Pollux so loved by Hermes,[71] the Greek god whose name became part of the nomenclature of his emasculated, yet hermaphroditic offspring. The bi-formed boy, Hermaphroditus, re/created both as male (like his father Hermes), and as female (like his mother Aphrodite), serves as an example of Guillaume's allusions to homosexuality and sexual ambiguity in the *Rose*, and fits the second of McAlpine's phenomena with which homosexuality was confused – that of hermaphroditism. A medieval audience would understand a reference to a castrated *castor* as a direct reference to Castor (he of the castrates), and as a veiled reference to Castor's twin Pollux, beloved of Hermes who also loved other males (and rarely females),[72] and who produced a eunuch-like son, Hermaphroditus. The latter's name – as well as that of the *castor*/Castor – precedes Isidore's interest in etymologies, yet highlights the importance of understanding the significance of names (including that of the *Rose* gatekeeper Oiseuse) from antiquity through medieval times, and up until the modern period. Camille explains: 'In the medieval love of etymological thinking, words really were things, and if two words sounded alike it meant that what they designated must also be similar.'[73] Thus a philological examination of Oiseuse's name can substantiate an indeterminate gender identity for her just as the

[68] Isidore of Seville, *Etymologies*, 12.2:21; Robert Bartlett explains that Isidore had himself derived the etymology from the fourth-century grammarian Servius. See Robert Bartlett, *Gerald of Wales, 1146–1223* (Oxford: Clarendon Press, 1982), p. 144.

[69] *Webster's Ninth New Collegiate Dictionary*, p. 357.

[70] Piotr O. Scholz, *Eunuchs and* Castrati: *A Cultural History*, trans. John A. Broadwin and Shelley L. Frisch (Princeton, NJ: Markus Wiener Publishers, 2001), pp. 48–50.

[71] *Encyclopedia of Queer Myth, Symbol and Spirit*, ed. Randy P. Luncunas Conner, David Hatfield Sparks, and Mariya Sparks (London and New York: Cassell, 1997), p. 269.

[72] Ibid., p. 176.

[73] Camille, *Image on the Edge*, p. 40.

extraordinary significance of the names of both the *castor* and the hermaphroditic youth indicate their ambiguous genders.

Isidore's assertion that beavers have a name related to the fact that they often castrate themselves necessarily refers to the Latin infinitive *castrare* (to castrate) which eventually provided Old French *castrer*/*chastrer*. Audiences would associate these words phonologically, from folklore and from ancient and medieval sources with the *castor*/beaver. Authors and translators in the *Physiologus* tradition knew and incorporated Isidore's etymology into their texts. At this point, with the addition of interpolated material from Isidore and other sources, the *Physiologus* texts begin to transform into bestiaries. One form of the work, the *Theobaldus-Physiologus* derived from the *Dicta Chrysostomi*,[74] arises in the eleventh century.[75] Commonly used as a schoolbook, it moves the animal lore into the education and the common consciousness of the learned classes. The considerable *Physiologus* tradition thus contributed to the twelfth-century phenomenon of bestiaries that absorbed the animal legends along with their accompanying lessons.[76] The promulgation of such information in the bestiaries, along with the iconography, poetry, preaching manuals, and religious textbook traditions of animal lore, all provided society with a general awareness of the beaver, of the potential danger to its testicles, and of its resultant (whether in fact, or simulated by the beaver concealing its genitals) castrated ambiguously gendered body.

In particular, the period from 1125 through 1225 – the latter the approximate date of the composition of Guillaume's *Rose* – saw at least four French bestiaries appear. Any or all of them could have further contributed to the medieval marginalia artist's perception of the beaver and the decision to position the drawing under the miniature of Oiseuse as a commentary on her body and her being. The margins provide a comfortable space for the indeterminately gendered body of the beaver, as anthropologist Arnold Van Gennep suggests when he notes that 'the attributes of liminality are necessarily ambiguous'.[77] A comment by Camille on human gender also relates to the character of Oiseuse reflected in the intersex body of the beaver when he asserts 'The margins [...] represent things excluded from official discourse'[78]

[74] Frances McCulloch, in *Medieval Latin and French Bestiaries* (Chapel Hill: University of North Carolina Press, 1962), studies the *Physiologus* and its derivatives. See ch. 2, and especially p. 55.

[75] Curley, trans. *Physiologus*, pp. xviii; xxxiv n. 3.

[76] Ibid., p. xxx. In general, the bestiary tradition elaborated the moral lesson about the beaver's sacrificing its possessions to a hunter into a warning for man to cast aside vices and throw them to the devil. The increase in references to man casting off vices as the beaver does its testicles suggests an association of the parts of generation with evil, an intriguing area for investigation, but one beyond the purview of the present essay.

[77] Quoted by Camille in *Image on the Edge*, p. 9.

[78] Ibid., p. 126.

since depictions of androgynous or genderless characters in medieval romance rarely, if ever, occur.

Frances McCulloch points out that the beaver, 'in both its text and illustrations is one of the most unvarying of all those [animals] in the *Physiologus*'.[79] Her summary recognizes the beaver as 'a very gentle animal'[80] whose testicles contain a valuable medicine for maladies, and her synopsis repeats the series of behaviors previously noted. McCulloch observes that the identical information appears 'in all French bestiaries'.[81] Nevertheless, one may observe some slight differences in the four authors writing close to the time Guillaume de Lorris wrote his *Rose* (*c.* 1230). For example, the earliest, that of the Anglo-Norman poet Philippe de Thaon (or Thaün), probably written between 1121 and 1135,[82] gives the two alternate names, *castor* and *bievre*, and notes that the animal is named for its castrated state: 'chastre sei de sun gré, / pur ço est si numé' [castrated itself by its will, / for that is it so named], and that it signifies the man who abandons *luxure*,[83] a sin that may suggest sodomy.[84] A beaver signifying a sinning man in the *Rose* margin offers an intriguing link to non-normative erotic activities if the reader connects the animal to the nearby Oiseuse who has already been linked to hermaphrodites who are in turn linked to same-sex activity that would likely include sodomy. In the beginning of the thirteenth century, the second French bestiary author, Gervaise, writing in his rhymed *Bestiaire* about the *castor*/*beivre* startlingly states: 'Une beste est d'autre nature' [One beast is of another nature].[85] That nature, of course, consists of neither masculine nor feminine, but something in between, a gender that presents itself as indeterminate. The author explains that 'L'on fait des coillons medicine / meudre que de nule racine' [One makes from the [animal's] testicles a medicine / better than any root].[86] Gervaise describes typical beaver behavior concluding with how the beaver *auce la cuisse* (raises its leg)[87] to show the hunter its castrated state. The longest rhymed French bestiary, the very popular *Bestiaire divin* composed around 1210 or 1211 by the third author, Guillaume le Clerc

79 McCulloch, *Medieval Latin and French Bestiaries*, p. 95.

80 Ibid.; See also the *castor* described as 'mansuetus' (gentle) in the Latin 'Fisiologo, version Bis' in Luigina Morini, *Bestiari Medievali* (Turin: Giulio Einardi Editore, 1996), p. 42; and, as Curley points out, 'the animal's mildness (innocentissimum valde et quietum)', *Physiologus*, p. xxiii.

81 McCulloch, *Medieval Latin and French Bestiaries*, p. 95.

82 McCulloch provides the likely date as *c.* 1121 (ibid., p. 48). Emmanuel Walberg, in *Le bestiare de Philippe de Thaün* (Lund: H. J. Müller), offers the span from 1121 to 1135 as possible dates of composition in his introduction, p. xviii.

83 Walberg, *Le bestiare*, pp. 42–3; vv. 1137–8, 1155.

84 Mark D. Jordan, *The Invention of Sodomy in Christian Theology* (Chicago: University of Chicago Press, 1997); see especially chs 4–7.

85 Morini, *Bestiari*, p. 326, v. 685.

86 Ibid., p. 326, vv. 689–90.

87 Ibid., p. 326, v. 704.

(also called Guillaume le Normand), calls the *castor* quite intelligent and of great wisdom, and recounts the typical steps the animal takes to avoid capture, including how it lies down with its feet in the air to show its castrated body.[88] The fourth author, Pierre de Beauvais, writing his bestiaries – a short version and a long one – before 1217 or 1218,[89] describes the *castor* as a very peaceful beast.[90] McCulloch's summary comment about the beaver's gentleness and Pierre's assessment of it as peaceful suggest qualities that belie the desperate action it finds itself forced to take. The last three writers – Gervaise, Guillaume le Clerc, and Pierre – attribute cognitive behavior typical of humans to the beaver, and facilitate the animal's association with Oiseuse. The last two authors, Guillaume le Clerc and Pierre (in particular), add moral lessons for man to please God and to cast aside evils, or throw their sins to the devil, further linking transgressive behavior to the beaver and to humankind, and through both, indicating that Oiseuse somehow transgresses normative barriers.

Finally, a different sort of bestiary, no longer fully in the tradition of the *Physiologus*, the popular prose *Bestiaire d'Amours* written by Richard de Fournival, appeared sometime before the author's death in 1260.[91] The artist drawing the beaver under Oiseuse in British Library MS Stowe 947 may have known the work.[92] The *Bestiaire d'Amours* recounts the same story of the animal's escapades as the other sources, but, in the context of attempting to convince the author's beloved to give up her heart as easily as the beaver does its testicles, the text also reminds the reader of the willingness of the animal to disfigure itself.

Interest in the beaver's disfigurement may have reflected medieval mutilation concerns.[93] Jacqueline Murray maintains that men experienced a real fear of castration and that it 'occupied a central place in theological, legal, and popular discourses'.[94] Outlining a sort of history of the issue in the Christian West, Murray names the same main moral examples (in their respective historical contexts) of castration provided by Huot and Hult in their discussion of the *Rose*. Murray begins with the well-known quote from Matthew 19:12 regarding eunuchs thus born, those made by men, and those who make them-

88 Gabriel Bianciotto, trans. *Bestiaires du Moyen Âge* (Paris: Stock, 1980; 1992), pp. 92–3.
89 Morini, *Bestiari*, xviii; McCulloch, *Medieval Latin and French Bestiaries*, p. 68.
90 Bianciotto, trans., *Bestiaires*, p. 37.
91 *Dictionnaire des lettres françaises: Le Moyen Âge*, revised edn (Paris: Fayard, 1992), p. 1266. The Latin poem *De Vetula* is attributed to Richard de Fournival and is discussed by Clark, 'Culture Loves a Void', in this volume.
92 Although Guillaume de Lorris wrote his section of the *Rose* around 1230, and Jean de Meun wrote the continuation around 1270, the Stowe manuscript dates to the fourteenth century.
93 Jacqueline Murray, 'Sexual Mutilation and Castration Anxiety: A Medieval Perspective', in Mathew S. Kuefler, ed., *The Boswell Thesis: Essays on Christianity, Social Tolerance, and Homosexuality* (Chicago: University of Chicago Press, 2006) 254–72.
94 Ibid., p. 255.

selves so for the kingdom of heaven. While many, including Church fathers Augustine and Jerome, understood the third category metaphorically to mean choosing the way of the spiritual eunuch (i.e. chastity), at least a few, such as Origen in the third century, took it literally.[95] Jean's *Rose* sets out how Origen cut off his own testicles so he could serve religious women without the suspicion that he might lie with them.[96] While Guillaume does not mention the example of Origen, the author likely knew of the story, and the beaver sketch that appears in the margin of the text of Guillaume's poem sets up the motif of purposeful self-emasculation in the original *Rose*.

Spiritual or mystical castration occurring in the dreams of holy men eventually found itself included in the lives of historical figures, thus keeping castration in the consciousness of medieval culture.[97] Secular law codes, like those examined by Rolf Bremmer, Charlene Eska, and Jay Gates in this volume,[98] also set out castration penalties for sins against nature and for some heterosexual crimes. Formal courts, and, on occasion, informal justice, as in the *c.* 1117–18 case[99] of Abelard, carried out punishments. Abelard, as Jean relates in his *Rose*, had his testicles taken from him at night while he was lying in bed.[100] As Abelard himself communicates in his *Ad amicum suum consolatoria* (*Consolation to his friend*), also known as the *Historia calamitatum*, two of the men who had attacked him were soon caught and in turn emasculated.[101] Similar to Murray's study of cases of medieval castration, Martin Irvine identifies mutilation narratives in accounts of revenge, war, and the crusades, as well as in a number of the French fabliaux that treat male genital removal. Irvine asserts that the twelfth and thirteenth centuries comprise 'an era of heightened anxiety about the body and its sexuality'.[102] R. Howard Bloch details

95 Ibid.. See also Scholz, *Eunuchs and* Castrati, especially the chapter entitled '"Chastity of the Angels?" Sexuality in Early Christianity.'

96 Poirion, ed. *Le Roman*, vv. 17052–8 at vv. 17,052–3: 'Origenés, qui ses coillons / Se copa' [Origen, who his testicles / Cut off]. For more about Origen's autocastrataion, see Jack Collins, 'Appropriation and Development of Castration as Symbol and Practice in Early Christianity', in this volume, pp. 73–86.

97 Murray, 'Sexual Mutilation and Castration Anxiety', pp. 255–6.

98 Rolf H. Bremmer Jr, 'The Children He Never Had; The Husband She Never Served: Castration and Genital Mutilation in Medieval Frisian Law', pp. 108–30; Charlene M. Eska, '"Imbrued in their owne bloud": Castration in Early Welsh and Irish Sources', pp. 149–73; Jay Paul Gates, 'The *Fulmannod* Society: Social Valuing of the (Male) Legal Subject', pp. 131–48, in this volume.

99 Dates come from 'Repères chronologiques' and Jean-Yves Tilliette, 'Introduction', in Éric Hicks and Thérèse Moreau, ed. and trans., *Lettres d'Abélard et Héloïse* (Paris: Librairie Générale Française, 2007), pp. 36–7 at p. 36.

100 Poirion, ed., *Le Roman*, vv. 8759 ff. Jean de Meun was especially familiar with the story as he translated the letters of Abelard and Heloise. See Betty Radice, 'Introduction' to *The Letters of Abelard and Heloise*, trans. Betty Radice (London: Penguin, 1974), p. 47.

101 *Lettres d'Abélard et Héloïse*, ed. Hicks and Moreau; Latin p. 74; French, p. 75.

102 Irvine, 'Abelard and (Re)writing the Male Body', p. 87.

the subject of detached sexual organs in the fabliaux in *The Scandal of the Fabliaux*.[103] In the chapter entitled 'The Body and its Parts', Bloch discusses a series of the comedic and satirical narratives that concern castrated organs, including ones that a person can purchase at market, even if only in one's dreams.[104] To medieval audiences, to Harley, and to others, the possibility of choosing phalluses may recall the phallic rosebuds in the bushes reflected in the fountain of Narcissus in Guillaume's *Rose*.[105] From among these disembodied phallic buds, the young dreaming lover chooses one.

Genitals presented as separated from their corresponding bodies thus continued to appear in medieval society in a number of different contexts, both literary and historical.[106] Many of the well-documented cases of castration, as well as literary descriptions of castrated bodies and unattached or detachable genitals, are contemporary with the two parts of the *Rose*. Therefore, the last two categories of eunuchs from Matthew 19:12 – those made so by other men, as happened to Abelard (and numerous others), and those who make themselves so for the kingdom of heaven, like Origen (and some others) – formed part of the theological, legal, and popular discourses of the Middle Ages.

Intriguingly, the beaver's body actually comprises the three categories of eunuchs listed in Matthew 19:12: those naturally born so,[107] those castrated by

103 R. Howard Bloch, *The Scandal of the Fabliaux* (Chicago: University of Chicago Press, 1986).

104 Ibid., pp. 59–100; see especially pp. 61–5. See also Larissa Tracy, 'The Uses of Torture and Violence in the Fabliaux: When Comedy Crosses the Line', *Florilegium* 23.2 (2006): 143–68; and the related essay by Mary E. Leech on the fabliau *La dame escolliee* in this volume, 'The Castrating of the Shrew: The Performance of Masculinity and Masculine Identity in *La dame escolliee*', pp. 210–28.

105 See footnote 35.

106 Murray, 'Sexual Mutilation and Castration Anxiety', see especially pp. 256–9.

107 Commenting on the first category of Matthew, regarding eunuchs thus born, remains a bit beyond the scope of the present essay, but contemporaneous reports of such would only serve to keep the subject of undifferentiated bodies in front of medieval audiences. Valeria Finucci, in *The Manly Masquerade: Masculinity, Paternity, and Castration in the Italian Renaissance* (Durham, NC: Duke University Press, 2003), and Thomas Laqueur, in *Making Sex* document cases of girls or young men 'born without any visible signs of those parts which are taken out in castration' (Finucci, p. 242), who, around the age of puberty sprout penises (Finucci, p. 243; and Laqueur, pp. 7, 128–9; both relate the case of Marie [later called Germain] and others.). Such incidences probably represent, as Finucci points out, cases of an endocrine disorder recognized even in antiquity, perhaps Reifenstein's syndrome that causes undescended testicles (Finucci, p. 243, and n. 51), or, as Laqueur explains, androgen-dihydrostestoserone deficiency, a genetic disorder known as 'penis at twelve' condition, an inherited type of male pseudo-hermaphroditism (Laqueur, pp. 7, 247, n. 22). In fact, in a modern estimation, the occurrence in the United States of undescended testicles in boy babies is one in three hundred (Finucci, p. 243, n. 51). Vern L. Bulloch discusses 'intersex' children and transgendered individuals in 'Eunuchs in History and Society', in *Eunuchs in Antiquity and Beyond*, ed. Shaun Tougher (London: Classical Press of Wales and Duckworth, 2002), pp. 1–17. So, while no representations of the third category of eunuchs may seem to appear in either Guillaume's or

others, and the self-emasculated. As an animal with no externally visible genitalia, the beaver resembles eunuchs thus born; when castrated by hunters, those made eunuchs by men; and when the beavers purportedly bite off their own testicles, they make themselves eunuch-like. Therefore, the drawing of the beaver placed below the illustration of Oiseuse, serves as a three-fold example *par excellence* of a eunuch or castrate, one whose very name *castor* suggests both its *chastré* nature and the genitally challenged and homoerotically inclined family of Castor (the Gemini twin of Pollux).

Numerous cases of wordplay involving castration and the terms for testicles exist in Jean's *Rose*. The puns cross linguistic boundaries between Latin and French, usually dismembering and re-membering the terms in question.[108] As a result, concomitant with awareness of the significance of the beaver's name and its seemingly de- or un-gendered state, medieval people, looking above the beaver to the miniature of Oiseuse, would seek to appreciate the ramifications of her name and personage. Guillaume, according to E. K. Rand, 'knew his Ovid' intimately.[109] Guillaume de Lorris, well versed in Latin and in its literary tradition, chose a curious name with significant etymology in Latin and in French for his character Oiseuse, whose name has a variety of meanings, although translators often render it as 'Idleness' in English. Hult, calling attention to the form of the word, notices that 'the character is called "Oiseuse" and not "Oisiveté" as might be expected'.[110] Jean Batany comments the odd origin of the character's name: 'L'adjectif *oiseus* est normalement péjoratif, et il en va de même pour ce nom abstrait [*oiseuse*] bizarrement tiré de son féminin par 'dérivation impropre' (par ellipse de *vie-*, *chose-*, *parole-*?), a moins qu'il ne vienne du neutre pluriel latin *otiosa*' [The adjective *oiseus* is normally pejorative, and the same goes for the abstract noun [*oiseuse*] bizarrely taken from its [i.e. the masculine adjective's] feminine [form] by 'improper derivation' [through ellipsis from -life, -thing, -speech] unless it comes from the Latin neuter plural *otiosa*].[111]

The strange name of Oiseuse is an abstract feminine noun, derived improperly from an originally masculine adjective in Old French, which is in turn derived from the Latin masculine adjective *otiosus*, or perhaps from the

Jean's *Rose*, antiquity, the Middle Ages, and modern society all recognize the existence of such 'natural eunuchs'. (The term 'natural eunuchs' occurs in Finucci, *The Manly Masquerade*, p. 249.)

108 Hult, 'Language and Dismemberment', especially 110 ff. See footnote 3 above, and its corresponding text.

109 E. K. Rand, 'The Metamorphosis of Ovid in *Le roman de la rose*', in *Studies in the History of Culture*, ed. Percy W. Long (Freeport, NY: Books for Libraries, 1969), pp. 103–21 at p. 116.

110 David F. Hult, 'The Allegorical Fountain: Narcissus in the *Roman de la rose*', *Romanic Review* 72 (1981): 125–48 at p. 127, n. 8.

111 Jean Batany, 'Miniature, allégorie, idéologie: "Oiseuse" et la mystique monacale récupérée par la "classe de loisir"', in *Études sur le* Roman de la rose *de Guillaume de Lorris*, ed. Jean Dufournet (Paris: Honoré Champion, 1984), pp. 7–36 at p. 19.

Latin neuter plural form, *otiosa*. In the first case, a masculine form turns into a feminine word, recalling the feminizing effects of castration, and in the second case, a feminine word comes from a neuter form, bringing to mind the effeminate appearance of a neutered being. *Oiseuse* may also have originated from the adverb *otiose*, a grammatical form with (of course) no gender at all. All the original Latin or Old French masculine, neuter, or genderless forms would have had to undergo a feminizing transformation, (essentially a linguistic castration), a possibility suggested by Hult's study on language and dismemberment, followed by a change in gender markers to provide the eventual Old French feminine noun. A feminine form resulting from a masculine or neuter one presents a pregnant possibility for understanding Oiseuse as a character who has a name with an ambiguous gender history, much as the beaver's name purportedly conveys its castration and resultant eunuch-like state. Oiseuse's name thus suggests that she has undergone a change in gender, or apparent gender: that she was once masculine, had something removed, and now appears feminine.

The meanings of the Latin and French forms of Oiseuse's name provide additional support for a reading linking the castrated beaver to the indeterminately gendered origin of *oiseuse*, and thus to the character's body, as well as to the mutilation motif in Guillaume's *Rose*. The Old French noun *oiseuse* (or *oisose*) has two main meanings as given in most dictionaries. Both definitions refer to a lack of activity, the first also to types of speech and to other acts. For example, in the standard Tobler and Lommatzsch *Altfranzösisches Wörterbuch*, the first meaning, 'idleness, futility, pointlessness, otioseness/otiosity; invalidity, void(ness), trifle, trivia/triviality, vanity, emptiness', corresponds to one interpretation of the character's significance; the second, 'idleness [idling]; idleness, passivity, dormancy,' reflects the common translation of Oiseuse's name, 'Idleness'.[112] In Latin, as in Old French, the adjective *otiosus, -a, -um* (Old French *oiseuse*) means 'at leisure, without occupation [...] esp. free from public duties or occupied in literary work only [...] [by transference: of persons] calm, quiet [...] in a struggle, indifferent, neutral'.[113] The concept of 'neutral' also approaches the notion of 'neuter'. The term *otiosus* has broad meanings and uses, but basically, the Latin word conveys senses of being inactive or of lacking productive activity, and it therefore sometimes describes states of leisurely activity, including love acts; of uselessness or superfluousness; of being peaceable, undisturbed,

112 Adolf Tobler and Erhardt Lommatzsch, *Altfranzösisches Wörterbuch* (Berlin: Wiedmann; Wiesbaden: Steinen, 1925–) VI Pt. 2:1055–7. *Müßiges*, *Nichtiges*, and *Müßiggang*, *Untätigkeit* are the German definitions given. Translators and scholars often refer to the character as 'Idleness'. See Charles Dahlberg, trans., *The Romance of the Rose* (Hanover, NH: University Press of New England, 1971, 1983); and Frances Horgan, trans., *The Romance of the Rose* (Oxford: Oxford University Press, 1994).

113 For Latin definitions, see *Cassell's Latin Dictionary* (New York: Macmillan, 1959, 1962, 1964, 1966, 1968), p. 418.

unoccupied, vacant, idle, or *sterile*.[114] The word may describe persons, parts of the body, mental states, and things. It may even refer to an idle penis.[115] The sense of sterility, apart from its status as a legitimate meaning, is contained or suggested in other definitions of *oiseuse* such as 'lacking productive activity' or 'uselessness'. 'Sterile' passed into Old and Modern French as a sense of the word *oiseuse*,[116] yet *Rose* scholars seem to have ignored this particular definition that can convey something very important about the figure seen as ambiguous, usually either as a positive aspect of courtly love or as a negative aspect of cupidinous love. Critics instead concentrate on her name and figure as referencing the history of literary leisure, the goddess Venus or the useless idleness of Oiseuse, and only rarely on the form of her name or on the alternate meanings of it.[117] The connotation of sterility – or that of neutrality – in Oiseuse's name recalls Chaucer's Pardoner (called a gelding), understood as neutered or castrated, as eunuch, as infertile as the castrating beaver placed below the illustration of Oiseuse in the manuscript marginalia. The indeterminately gendered animal with a name that points to its dismembered state indicates that Oiseuse could be understood as equally ambiguously gendered through her name, a moniker improperly formed by linguistic dismemberment. While audiences know that a castrated beaver will be sterile, in case there remain any doubt about Oiseuse, Guillaume chooses a name for her that signifies the resultant sterile state of her transformed body. The gatekeeper embodies castration.

Therefore, in Guillaume's original *Rose*, a castrated state amounts to an indicator of indeterminate gender. And if Oiseuse and the Diex d'Amors with their 'Keys', and the disembodied stiff rosebud the lover desires (as well as the latter's relationship with Bel Acuel) serve as examples, being differently gendered also offers the possibility of non-normative sexual activity.[118] Above the beaver's

114 Ibid. Emphasis mine.

115 *Oxford Latin Dictionary* (Oxford: Clarendon Press, 1968), p. 1277; *Thesaurus Linguae Latinae* 10 vols. + (Leipzig: Teubner, 1980), pp. 1165–74.

116 *Le (Nouveau) Petit Robert* (Paris: Dictionnaires Le Robert, 1993, 1996), p. 1527; implied in Frédéric Godefroy, *Dictionnaire de l'ancienne langue française et de tous ses dialectes du IXe au XVe siècle*, 10 vols (Paris: Vieweg, Bouillon, 1881–1902), 5.588–9.

117 See Carlos Alvar, 'Oiseuse, Vénus, Luxure: trois dames et un miroir', *Romania* 106 (1985): 108–17; Batany, 'Miniature, allégorie, idéologie'; John Fleming, 'Further Reflections on Oiseuse's Mirror', *Zeitschrift für romanische Philologie* 100 (1984): 26–40; Herbert Kolb, 'Oiseuse, die Dame mit dem Spiegel', *Germanisch-Romanische Monatschrift* n.s. 15 [46] (1965): 139–49; Earl Jeffrey Richards, 'Reflections on Oiseuse's Mirror: Iconographic Tradition, Luxuria and the *Roman de la rose*', *Zeitschrift für romanische Philologie* 98 (1982): 296–311; and 'The Tradition of "otium litteratum" and Oiseuse in *Le roman de la rose*', *Studi francesi* 32 (1988): 271–3.

118 In addition to Harley, 'Narcissus, Hermaphroditus, and Attis', and Jordan, *The Invention of Sodomy*, John Boswell also discusses categories of sexual phenomena conflated and confused with homosexuality. For example, Boswell states outright: 'Hermaphroditus often signified "homosexual" in the Middle Ages': *Christianity, Social Tolerance, and Homosexuality* (Chicago: University of Chicago Press, 1980), p. 185, n. 58.

depiction, Oiseuse, the first character whom the young lover meets, takes her place. Harley makes a cogent argument for Oiseuse, not just as a feminine figuration of Narcissus as Huot maintains,[119] but also as a reflection of the Hermaphroditus story, thereby equating her with the youth who was unmanned by the waters of the pool. Oiseuse's improperly formed and grammatically ambiguous name signifies sterility, a corollary to the *castre castré*. The suggestion that Oiseuse carries a phallic *clef*, like the one the beaver cuts off or keeps hidden, and the 'key' the Diex d'Amors uses in the homoerotic submission ceremony with the young lover, evoke the eunuch Pardoner who carries his *relikes* (relics)[120] around in a pouch as Amors does his jewels. The next gender-ambivalent character the lover encounters after Oiseuse is Bel Acuel (Kelly's 'receptive agent' in the rose complex), and the lover's male object of desire. At the fountain of Narcissus – the young man who fell in love with a masculine image like himself and who is linked to both Hermaphroditus and Oiseuse – the plump rosebuds on the rosebushes' stiff stalks reflected therein stand as disembodied phallic symbols. As symbols of masculine same-sex desire, the buds offer the lover a choice. Once the youth chooses a manly bud, he submits himself to the God of Love in a ceremony portrayed as nothing short of sodomitic.[121] Eventually the young lover obtains a 'kiss' from Bel Acuel,[122] after which the latter finds himself in prison, punished for the improper relation, blamed at least partially on Oiseuse who initially admitted the lover to the *vergiers*.

In the circular story of castration and non-normative gender states alluding to same-sex desire recounted in Guillaume de Lorris's *Romans de la rose*, Oiseuse plays a crucial part, especially at the beginning of the tale. Both her name (with its gender ambiguity and irregular form) and her personage (perhaps with an unattached phallus) participate in a medieval topos of grammatical abnormality as a comment on irregular sexuality.[123] In the next essay in this volume, Robert L. A. Clark considers the cultural categories of the sterile eunuch, a *demi homme* 'half-man' or *semi-viros* 'sort-of-man', evocative of Ovid's Hermaphroditus as *semivir*, and thus of Oiseuse as semi-something, but as fully part of, indeed the entrée to, the society in the *Rose*. The sterile eunuch is reminiscent of Oiseuse through the derivation and meaning of her name. Clark's difficult-to-categorize character offers a parallel to the ambiguity scholars find in Oiseuse's persona in Guillaume's original *Rose*.

[119] See footnote 14 and the corresponding quote.

[120] Chaucer, *The Riverside Chaucer*, ed. Benson, p. 34, v. 701. Jean uses the same term, 'reliques' as a slang term for testicles (vv. 7111–12).

[121] Friedrich, 'The Mentorship'. See footnote 40 and its accompanying text.

[122] Friedrich, 'When a Rose', pp. 32–3. Through philological analyses, I demonstrate that the 'baisier' scene (e.g. vv. 3769 ff.) recounts an act of sodomy.

[123] For the topos of grammatical irregularity, see Boswell, *Christianity*, pp. 258–9; and Clark, 'Culture Loves a Void', in this volume.

The castration motif in the first *Rose*, couched in words and images like Oiseuse and the beaver, is not always easy for the modern reader to interpret. However, unlike the generally negative and violent cases of castration – Saturn, Abelard, and Origen – in Jean's *Rose*, Guillaume's differently gendered beings participate in a broader culture, one permitting and describing desire among those who fit the categories identified by Harley and others as alluding to homosexuality. Castration therefore serves as a metaphor for Oiseuse (or vice versa) and for the differences in and varieties of bodies and desires in the *vergiers* portrayed in Guillaume de Lorris's *Romans de la rose*.

CHAPTER 13

Culture Loves a Void: Eunuchry in De Vetula *and Jean Le Fèvre's* La Vieille

Robert L. A. Clark

In James Brundage's compendious *Law, Sex and Christian Society in Medieval Europe*, there are only two references to eunuchs, although there are considerably more references to the primary way that one becomes a eunuch, that is, castration.[1] In AD 558 Justinian prohibited 'castration and the making of eunuchs, an oriental practice that had begun to fall into disfavor in the Empire'.[2] At the opposite end of Christendom and of the medieval period, Brundage reports that on March 9, 1350, an Augsburg judge ruled against nullification of a marriage because the husband, a eunuch (the word used in the text is *spado*), had been able to consummate the marriage.[3] Perhaps it is not surprising that in western Christendom, the focus of Brundage's study, the texts should say so little about the condition of being a eunuch, for eunuchs, almost by definition, occupy an ambiguous position with regard to 'law, sex, and society', the three terms of Brundage's title. In so far as the law itself was concerned, this ambiguity is clear considering that, despite Justinian's prohibition, castration was at various times and places the punishment for males who had sex with males; for males who had sex with non-Christian women (the woman's offense was to have her nose cut off); or for rape.[4] Regarding sex, the eunuch's ambiguity might seem a given. Yet it was precisely due to this ambiguity that decre-

[1] James A. Brundage, *Law, Sex, and Christian Society in Medieval Europe* (Chicago: University of Chicago Press, 1987), pp. 122, 512.

[2] Ibid., p. 122.

[3] Ibid., p. 512.

[4] In Visigothic Spain, as punishment for men found guilty of having sex with other men (ibid., p. 149); in the Levant, for men having sex with non-Christian women (ibid., p. 207); for cases of rape, see citations in ibid., p. 471, n. 278. Legal penalties for castration and other genital injuries are discussed in detail by Rolf H. Bremmer Jr, Jay Paul Gates, and Charlene M. Eska in this volume. See Bremmer, 'The Children He Never Had; The Husband She Never Served: Castration and Genital Mutilation in Medieval Frisian Law', 108–30; Gates, 'The *Fulmannod* Society: Social Valuing of the (Male) Legal Subject', pp. 131–48 and Eska, '"Imbrued in their owne bloud": Castration in Early Welsh and Irish Sources', pp. 149–73.

talists, theologians, and jurists struggled with eunuchry for centuries, especially where marriage was concerned. Could a eunuch contract a legitimate marriage, as was the question in the Augsburg case cited by Brundage? Could a legitimate marriage be nullified if the husband became a eunuch? Finally, regarding society, perhaps one can best evoke the endlessly fascinating case of Peter Abelard, whose first reaction to his castration was a shamed retreat from society – and from his marriage – into the monastery.[5]

But what of culture? Here there can be no doubt that in the cultural imaginary of western Europe, the sterile eunuch, because of his ambiguity, was a paradoxically pregnant figure for thinking about culture. As a provocative 'third term', the eunuch (as Marjorie Garber has argued for the cross-dresser) troubles both cultural binaries *and* unity. Is the castrated male still a male? Is he to be assimilated to the category of 'not male' or 'other than male'? Can he be thought of as an 'unmanly male', to use a term that borrows from the registers of biological sex and gender construction? Or is he more properly a liminal figure, caught somewhere in between male and maleness's various others? Regarding the 'third term', Garber writes: 'The "third" is a mode of articulation, a way of describing a space of possibility. Three puts in question the idea of one: of identity, self-sufficiency, self-knowledge.'[6] For Garber, the cross-dresser provokes a 'category crisis' resulting in what she terms the 'transvestite effect'.[7] She writes, 'the transvestite makes culture possible [...] there can be no culture without the transvestite because the transvestite marks the entrance into the Symbolic.'[8] The cultural work accomplished by the figure of the transvestite is not limited to but belongs above all to the realm of representation, as evidenced by the myriad phenomena of cross-dressing as performance in the theater and beyond. The eunuch is, if anything, even more profoundly disturbing to the cultural categories evoked by Garber. For the eunuch belongs not only to the realm of the symbolic but also to that of physical reality, although ultimately it is through representation and especially through discourse that the eunuch serves to trouble those categories.

For the medieval period, the thousand-year history of Byzantium has provided an especially rich vein for thinking about the place of eunuchs in the social construction of gender. Citing Garber's notion of 'category crisis' at the beginning of his study, *The Manly Eunuch*, Mathew S. Kuefler writes: 'This is precisely the role that I argue was played by the eunuch in the later Roman

5 For a fuller discussion of Abelard's castration, and his response to that punishment in hagiographical terms, see Larissa Tracy, '"Al defouleden is holie bodi": Castration, the Sexualization of Torture, and Anxieties of Identity in the *South English Legendary*', in this volume, pp. 87–107.

6 Marjorie Garber *Vested Interests: Cross-Dressing and Cultural Anxiety* (New York and London: Routledge, 1992), p. 11.

7 Ibid., p. 17.

8 Ibid., p. 34.

culture, revealing the anxieties around sexual differentiation and at the same time questioning its foundation, and bringing to the surface all of the uncertainties of masculine identity in public and private life, and in particular, the tension between manliness and unmanliness.'[9] In her work on eunuchs in Byzantium, Kathryn Ringrose has (like Garber) advanced the notion of a third gender and even a third sex, stating that the '"thirdness" of the eunuch is an important part of his gender construct'.[10] Ringrose notes that 'after Late Antiquity there is little indication that eunuchs were believed to constitute a "third sex"'.[11] In her book and in a shorter article, however, she develops the idea that in Byzantine society eunuchs *did* constitute a distinct third gender, a socially recognized (and recognizable) category that possessed a high degree of liminality. Ironically, eunuchs were a critical element of Byzantine culture precisely because their liminality allowed them to serve as intermediaries between social groups that were rigidly separated: the court and the world outside, men and women, even, in their role as care-givers, between the living and the dead.[12]

Things were altogether different in the Christian West, which did not have a centuries-old presence of eunuchs in so many walks of life with the attendant social and cultural schemes of categorization. A particularly rich source for understanding what, after Garber, can be termed the 'eunuch effect' (the profound unsettling of categories) is provided by a pair of two relatively little studied texts, the thirteenth-century *De Vetula* and its fourteenth-century French translation, Jean Le Fèvre's *La Vieille*. The Pseudo-Ovidian Latin poem *De Vetula* is commonly (if problematically) attributed to Richard de Fournival, the author of the *Bestiaire d'Amours*.[13] The Latin poem is extant in some thirty-nine manuscripts, and excerpts and fragments of it survive in many others. *De*

[9] Mathew S. Kuefler, *The Manly Eunuch: Masculinity, Gender Ambiguity, and Christian Ideology in Late Antiquity* (Chicago and London: University of Chicago Press, 2001), p. 14. Shaun Tougher, however, argues that eunuchs were not always figures of anxiety in Roman society, that there is evidence that some were loved and admired – and specifically made eunuchs to preserve their beauty. See 'The Aesthetics of Castration: The Beauty of Roman Eunuchs', in this volume, p. 48–72.

[10] Kathryn M. Ringrose, *The Perfect Servant: Eunuchs and the Social Construction of Gender in Byzantium* (Chicago: University of Chicago Press, 2003), p. 7. In this volume, Jed Chandler explores the virgin 'third gender' of Grail eunuchs. See 'Eunuchs of the Grail', pp. 229–54.

[11] Ringrose, *Perfect Servant*, p. 4.

[12] Ibid., pp. 5–6; Kathryn M. Ringrose, 'Living in the Shadows: Eunuchs and Gender in Byzantium', in *Third Sex, Third Gender: Beyond Sexual Dimorphism in Culture and History*, ed. Gilbert Herdt (New York: Zone, 1996), pp. 85–109 at pp. 94–8. Mary A. Valante discusses the importance of Byzantine eunuchs and how the need for them was fed by the Viking slave trade. 'Castrating Monks: Vikings, the Slave Trade, and the Value of Eunuchs', pp. 174–86.

[13] On the issue of the poem's attribution to Richard, see *Pseudo-Ovidius* De Vetula*: Untersuchungen und Text*, ed. Paul Klopsch (Leiden: Brill, 1967), pp. 78–99; and *The Pseudo-Ovidian Vetula*, ed. Dorothy M. Robathan (Amsterdam: Adolf M. Hakkert, 1968), pp. 6–10.

Vetula's popularity continued into the age of the printing press: There are two incunabula (*c.* 1475 and 1479), as well as one fifteenth- and two sixteenth-century printings. The text's popularity is also attested to by the fourteenth-century translation by Jean Le Fèvre (*c.* 1320–after 1380), sometimes referred to as Jean Le Fèvre de Ressons to distinguish him from another author with the same name. Jean Le Fèvre is best known as the author of the *Respit de la mort* and the *Livre de leesce*. In addition to these two original texts, he also made several translations, the most famous of which is the *Lamentations de Matheolus*. His translation of *De Vetula* appears to have remained as obscure in his own day as it is now. *La Vieille, ou les dernières amours d'Ovide* is extant in only two manuscripts, fr. 881 and fr. 2327 of the Bibliothèque nationale de France.[14] There is only one modern edition that dates from a century and a half ago.[15] The editor, Hippolyte Cocheris, who holds Jean's text in low regard, remarks that *La Vieille* is as much an 'imitation' as it is a translation of his source due to Jean's propensity to amplify certain passages.[16] He does allow, however, that Jean's recourse to *amplificatio*, a hallmark of the medieval translator's art, bears results that are not devoid of interest. He also condemns the salaciousness of both source and translation, although Jean's poetic verve is often most evident in such passages.[17]

De Vetula's success may be likened to that of the *Romans de la Rose*, discussed by Ellen Friedrich in this volume, a text that it resembles on more than one count.[18] Like the *Rose* (especially Jean de Meun's continuation of Guillaume de Lorris's poem), *De Vetula* incorporates into a loose narrative structure a wide range of material, including Ovidian motifs, tips about

14 For a succinct philological presentation of the *La Vieille* and its source, see G. H. [Geneviève Hasenohr], 'Jean Le Fèvre', in *Dictionnaire des lettres françaises: Le Moyen Âge* (Paris: Fayard, 1992), pp. 802–4.

15 Jean Lefevre [*sic*], *La Vieille, ou les dernières amours d'Ovide*, ed. Hippolyte Cocheris (Paris: Aubry, 1861). Cocheris bases his edition on BnF, fr. 881 (formerly ms 7235), a fine copy on vellum dating from the fifteenth century. On the title page of *La Vieille* a miniature represents the author standing before a male figure, perhaps a cleric, who, seated on a high-backed chair, leafs through the pages of the book. *La Vieille* (fols 1–48v) is followed by a glossed translation of Ovid's *Ars Amatoria* (fols 49r–96v), followed in turn by a selection of poetry by Guillaume de Machaut, incomplete at the end (fols 97r–112v). A digitized copy of fr. 881 is available at http://gallica.bnf.fr/ark:/12148/btv1b8449041w. Fr. 2327 is a paper manuscript of the fifteenth century.

16 *La Vieille*, ed. Cocheris, pp. xxxviii–xxxix.

17 Ibid., pp. xiii, xlix.

18 Karen Pratt shows that Jean de Meun's continuation of the *Roman de la Rose* is the main intertext in Jean Le Fèvre's translation of the *Lamentationes Matheoluli* in which Jean de Meun is invoked or quoted either to supplement or to replace the *auctores* in the source text, making the French text more misogynistic in the process. See 'Translating Misogamy: The Authority of the Intertext in the *Lamentationes Matheoluli* and Its Middle French Translation by Jean LeFèvre', *Forum for Modern Language Studies* 35.4 (1999): 421–35. Also see Ellen Lorraine Friedrich, 'Insinuating Indeterminate Gender: A Castration Motif in Guillaume de Lorris's *Romans de la rose*', in this volume, pp. 255–79.

grooming, and theological and scientific matter. And, like the *Rose*, it is a literary text with encyclopedic pretensions. It is the latter element, especially its third book, an astrological treatise with philosophical and theological preoccupations, which doubtless assured its success with generations of readers that included such luminaries as Robert Grosseteste and Roger Bacon.[19] Finally, as in the *Rose*, the narrative itself occupies only a small part of *De Vetula*. The poem's first book, with its long digressions about gaming, hunting, and fishing, deals with the pastimes of Ovida, a typical noble youth of the thirteenth century. Only the second book is devoted in the main to recounting Ovida's final loves, the 'dernières amours' of Jean Le Fèvre's title. As with the *Rose*, the fierce misogyny of *De Vetula* must also have played a role in its success, and in both *De Vetula* and *La Vieille* the *Eunuchenparodie*[20] is a key feature of a masculinist discourse on gender in which misogyny serves as a springboard for a highly elaborate attack on eunuchs. The passage's rigorous scholastic organization does more than provide a coherent structure for the satirical diatribe. Emanating from a position of clerical privilege, the authors position themselves against the threats posed by enemies from without and within, Others perceived as threatening the primacy and plenitude of the clerical class. Women were by definition excluded from the ranks of the clergy, but in the two poems eunuchs are the enemy within, or at least represented as such. The texts anxiously seek to exclude them even as they fill the void embodied by the eunuch's lack, the monstrous breach in nature that he is held to represent. What fills that void is the power wielded by the clerical pen.

In *De Vetula* and *La Vieille* the passage on eunuchry at the beginning of book 2 introduces the Ovidian narrative proper. The title character is the guardian of the poet's love object, who promises to introduce him into the bed of his *amie*. Instead, she takes her mistress's place for a night of blissful lovemaking before the full horror of the poet's situation is revealed to him at dawn. In both *La Vieille* and its source, the section on eunuchs represents less than 8 percent of the text, about 180 out of nearly 2,400 lines in *De Vetula* (2.21–201) and some 470 lines out of almost 6,000 lines in *La Vieille* (2087–2556).[21] The transitions leading into the passage and, at its conclusion, back into the narrative offer only the thinnest of arguments for its inclusion. In the opening of book 2, 'Ovid' says that the games described in the first book did not succeed in freeing him from the cares of love: 'solum felicem super omnes esse putebam / Qui, quotiens vellet, cognoscere posset amicam' [I considered to be happy only he who could 'know' his lady friend whenever he wanted]

[19] Hasenohr, 'Jean Le Fèvre', p. 803.

[20] *De Vetula*, ed. Klopsch, p. 93.

[21] In the discussion below, I treat the two texts together, noting certain elements in Jean's poem that represent departures from or additions to his source.

(*Vet.* 2.4–5).[22] Now that he knows better (or so he says), he is forced to sing the praises of those who can do without women, the *semiviros, demi homes*, 'half men' (*LV* 2087). He will return to this idea at the conclusion of the long digression lambasting eunuchs, saying that he must 'praise' them, even though it may not be proper to do so, because they are able to live a life free from women: 'Talia monstra modo laudo, quia vivere possunt / Feminosque carere, quamvisque solerem / Felices solos coitu reputare potentes, / Felices solos reputo cessare coactos' [Such monsters must I now praise because they can live without women; although I was accustomed to consider only those capable of intercourse to be happy, I now consider to be happy those who have been compelled to cease] (*Vet.* 2.196–9). Jean renders this passage faithfully but then goes on to embellish it with more colorful language, a trait that is typical of his rendering into French: 'Ne puent habiter ne joindre, / Ne de l'instrument charnel poindre' [They cannot copulate nor unite with a woman, nor prick with a member of their flesh] (*LV* 2541–2).[23] The narrator's irony here is, of course, patent and disingenuous, but the author of *La Vetula* and his translator both gloss over what was in fact one of the vexed points in the discourse of the Church regarding eunuchry – that is, whether there was any merit to a eunuch's chastity since it was achieved through no effort of his own but through the mechanics of castration. Though the reader is doubtless not taken in by the ironic narrator and his supposed 'envy' of eunuchs, it is easy to miss the fact that his smirk and wink refer to the thornier issue of 'true chastity' as it was constructed by male clerics: either the complete life-long abstention from sexual relations or the renouncement thereof by men and women who were capable of engaging in them.[24]

The *Vetula* poet is clearly well acquainted with a broad range of discourses about eunuchs, including biblical and theological, medical and the literary

22 Citations from *De Vetula* are from Robathan's edition. All translations from *De Vetula* and *La Vieille* are my own, abbreviated as *Vet.* and *LV*, respectively.

23 In her article on Jean's translation of the *Lamentationes Matheoluli*, Pratt characterizes him as a careful translator who 'is able to preserve and elaborate on many of Matthew's stylistic flourishes, including enumeration and punning' ('Translating Misogamy', p. 427).

24 While virginity was most highly valued, one could be chaste without being a virgin, as in the case of chaste or spiritual marriage. See Dyan Elliott, *Spiritual Marriage: Sexual Abstinence in Medieval Wedlock* (Princeton, NJ: Princeton University Press, 1993). Women's place in society was most often determined by the sole criterion of chastity according to the archaic and static triadic model of Christian society as consisting of virgins, the chaste, and married people. Women were accordingly classified as either virgins, widows (and other chaste women), or wives, and their relative spiritual merit determined as one-hundred-fold for virgins, sixty for widows, and thirty for married women. See Geneviève Hasenohr, 'La vie quotidienne de la femme vue par l'Eglise: L'enseignement des "journées chrétiennes" de la fin du Moyen-Age', *Frau und spätmittelalterlicher Alltag (Internationaler Kongress, Krems an der Donau, 2. bis 5. Oktober 1984)* (Vienna: Verlag der Österreichischen Akademie der Wissenschaften, 1986), pp. 19–101 at pp. 21–3.

heritage of Latin antiquity. For example, he opens his digression on eunuchs by citing the different ways of becoming a eunuch: one can be, through an act of nature, born a eunuch; suffer a violent castration at the hands of a jealous husband (perhaps an evocation of Abelard's unhappy plight); or undergo a medical castration where there is the danger of peritonitis due to a hernia (*Vet.* 2.10–20). The ur-text behind this discourse in the western Christian tradition is the passage in Matthew 19:12 in which Christ says to the disciples: 'sunt enim eunuchi qui de matris utero sic nati sunt, et sunt eunuchi qui facti sunt ab hominibus et sunt eunuchi qui se ipsos castraverunt proptor regnum caelorum' [There are eunuchs born that way from their mother's womb, there are eunuchs made so by men and there are eunuchs who have made themselves that way for the sake of the kingdom of heaven].[25] The *Vetula* poet excises Jesus' cryptic reference to 'eunuchs for the sake of the kingdom of heaven', perhaps because he did not consider it appropriate subject matter for his post-Ovidian poem. But he also may have wished to sidestep the millennial debate over Jesus' words, which were taken literally by some exegetes as recommending self-castration. Brundage states that in the very early Christian era, the Stoic Sextus saw in castration a cure for lust, and St Justin Martyr praised a young man who requested it.[26] As noted earlier in this volume, Origen of Alexandria was the most famous self-castrator, although his act was represented as misguided by Eusebius and other commentators (including Abelard). The matter was serious enough to be prohibited by the Council of Nicaea in 325, and the allegorical reading of Jesus' pronouncement became the standard interpretation.[27]

It is especially interesting that in the *Vetula* poet's formulation, spiritual eunuchry (i.e., self-castration) has been replaced by scientific discourse on the surgical treatment of hernias. Scientific knowledge is certainly deployed here to lend authority to the text but, through the replacement of the positive, spiritual valence of eunuchry, the poet deftly shifts the focus to the supposedly neutral ground of science. And while the attribution of *De Vetula* to Richard de Fournival is questionable, he had in fact been granted a papal dispensation to practice surgery and was thus particularly well placed to possess this kind of knowledge.[28] There is little reason to believe, however, that the *Vetula* poet actually practiced surgery as his knowledge could well have come from surgical manuals. The marshaling of science in the text serves rather to justify his highly

25 *Biblia sacra vulgata*, 3rd rev. edn (Stuttgart: Deutsche Bibelgesellschaft, 1983); trans. *Jerusalem Bible: Reader's Edition* (Garden City, NY: Doubleday, 1968). Jack Collins discusses the original Greek text in the context of rabbinic views on castration. See 'Appropriation and Development of Castration as Symbol and Practice in Early Christianity', in this volume, pp. 73–86.

26 Brundage, *Law, Sex, and Christian Society*, p. 65.

27 Ibid., p. 87.

28 F. F. H. [Françoise Féry-Hue], 'Richard de Fournival', in *Dictionnaire des lettres françaises: Le Moyen Âge* (Paris: Fayard, 1992), p. 1266.

critical attitude toward castration, which he qualifies as a cruel and *reprobabilis usus* 'reprehensible practice' (*Vet.* 2:20). Perhaps the poet knew that the survival rate for certain types of castration was very low and that certain law codes called for death by castration. He may well have been aware that the practice was condemned by Roman law. But Jean Le Fèvre also seems to possess at least a layman's knowledge of what castration involves, for he adds details to his translation that are not in his source, as if to reinforce its authority. After the testicles are ablated, he says, one must sew up the wound, apply a bandage, and then apply a poultice made from eggs and *estoupes* (stuffing) (*LV* 2123–4).[29] As is typical of Jean's more truculent style, and perhaps needing a rhyme for *estoupes*, he finishes off his translation of this passage with a breezy: 'Jamais ne batera les croupes' [Never will he pound rumps] (*LV* 2125). The surgical process for making a eunuch is not, however, what really interests either poet. It is the resulting 'monster' (called *spado* or *eunuchus* in the Latin poem, *spadon* or *eunuche* in Jean) that will exercise their considerable poetic and rhetorical powers in the remainder of the eunuch satire. The rational explanation of how eunuchs are made through the surgeons' handiwork seems little more than a pretext that calls forth the poets' condemnation of the formers' manipulation of nature, which (they have noted) does not need men's help to create eunuchs. Surgery is positioned here as a lower, mechanical practice, as opposed to the higher realms of knowledge from which, through the apparatus of scholasticism, the poets will derive the remainder of their discussion of eunuchry.

What, the *Vetula* poet continues, are these half men, these *semiviros*? He states that he does not know whether he should designate them as *illos* (the masculine accusative pronoun for the third-person plural), whether the eunuch is an *iste* or an *ista* (respectively, the masculine and feminine nominative demonstrative pronouns for the third-person singular) (*Vet.* 2.21–2). It is not an *ista*, he reasons, because it does not have a vulva, a remark that Jean does not translate. He concludes that it must then be neuter. But, he continues, one has never seen an animal that did not have a sex, so it must not be an animal. But if it's not an animal, he pursues, and yet is alive, it must be a plant. But even plants have seed and fruit and, furthermore, never lack a root. But since the eunuch lacks seed, fruit, and testes, which correspond in this analogy to the root in plants, the plant will never flower. His bare face signifies the inability to engender, either due to excessive cold (*frigidus*) or a lack of semen-producing testes.[30] So, if it is not a man, nor a woman, nor an animal, nor a plant: 'quid est? / Non est sine vita. / Ergo quid esse potest? Nichil esse potest nisi monstrum'

[29] Paul of Aegina's seventh-century *Epitome of Medicine*, describes two methods of castration, one by compression and the other by excision that are fairly similar to this. See Shaun Tougher, 'The Aesthetics of Castration', p. 48. It is possible that Jean Le Fèvre had access to a copy of this text, or one very much like it.

[30] Here, one sees the Galenic theory of the humors at work.

[what is it? It is not lifeless, therefore what can it be? It can be nothing but a monster] (*Vet.* 2.43–4). Having reached this conclusion through a series of syllogisms, the poet will proceed to support it by bringing to bear the full force of his scholastic training in the *trivium* (grammar, dialectic, rhetoric) and the *quadrivium*, ('matheses', an amalgam of the mathematical and scientific arts).

Remaining in the grammatical register, the poet turns, naturally enough, from gender to declension in order to demonstrate that the eunuch is a monster of grammar. 'Nullus sibi congruit articulorum' [No article can be joined to it] (*Vet.* 2.46). In Jean's formulation, the eunuch is a *cas non declinable*, a 'case with no declension' (*LV* 2183) to which no article can be joined 'soit devant ou derriere' [neither before or behind] (*LV* 2185). This is Jean's somewhat clumsy effort to gloss over the fact that Old French, with its rudimentary case system, did not use endings as the primary markers of grammatical inflection for nouns and pronouns, although it does allow him to make a pun rich in sexual innuendo. Since the eunuch has no genitive, the *Vetula* poet continues, he cannot join his possessions to him. On the other hand, he *does* have a marked preference for the ablative, a pun on the etymological meaning of *aufero*, to carry away or remove. Since one can only take away from the eunuch and not add to him, the other cases are inoperative; and since all grammatical constructions are closed to him (there is not even a 'relative' that can comfort him), he is denied recourse to speech: 'non est oratio que sit / Huic cum parti totum, sed pars est est sine toto' [there is no speech that can be his as part of a whole, for he is a part without wholeness] (*Vet.* 2.33–4). In an interesting twist on the stereotype of the eunuch as possessing a high, shrill voice, the *Vetula* poet denies him the very possibility of constituting himself through speech, cut off as he is from the copulative functions of grammar. His inability to perform sexually as a male is in a sense replicated by the loss of his tongue, the member that through speech would allow him to join in social intercourse. The poets are particularly anxious to exclude eunuchs from the clerical class to which they belong. By identifying the male member so closely with the phallic pen, eunuchs are (by definition) denied access to the higher functions of the word.

The poets' punning evocation of grammatical monstrosity bears a striking similarity to the *De planctu naturae* (*Plaint of Nature*) by his twelfth-century predecessor, Alan of Lille, where unnatural grammatical couplings are used to evoke the 'sin against nature'. But the *Vetula* poet's discourse is, in fact, almost the negative image of Alan's in that the former denies the possibility of any kind of coupling, even monstrous or unnatural. Surprisingly, there does not seem to be any evocation of sodomy in either *De Vetula* or *La Vieille*, and Alan's poem is, conversely, all but silent on the question of eunuchs. In one passage, Alan does make a parenthetical remark to the effect that 'quidam homines depauperati signaculo, juxta meam opinionem, possent neutri generis designatione censeri' [some men, deprived of a sign of sex, could, in my opinion, be classified as of neuter gender].[31] This reflection of Alan's, which he himself does not pursue, raises an interesting question. Since Latin possesses a neuter gender in which neuter nouns function quite happily, why could this not be the grammatical paradigm applied to eunuchs? Neither the *Vetula* poet nor his translator raises this point, perhaps because the overarching discourse of the diatribe against eunuchs is that of natural philosophy and not the more specific discursive parameters of the different liberal arts, in this instance, grammar. It is more likely, however, that they simply did not want to open the door to any positive or neutral valences of eunuchry, as with the exclusion of any mention of spiritual eunuchry.

Having shown that the eunuch is monster of grammar, the *Vetula* poet moves on to dialectic (i.e., logic) and then to rhetoric. Eunuchs are a hopeless case for the dialectician because they do not fall into one species or genus. One does not know how to divide their flesh, presumably because it has already been divided. Punning on the terms of dialectic, the poet states that they are neither a *species speciosa*, a 'beautiful species', nor a *genus generosum*, a 'generous genus' (*espece specieuse* and *genre genereus* in the French); rather, as a class they constitute a *monstrum individuum*, an 'indivisible monster' (*monstre indivisable*) that defies logic (*Vet.* 2.62–6; *LV* 2207–15). With rhetorical art, there is appropriately a shift in rhetorical strategy. Here, the *Vetula* poet imagines the eunuch as judge, the better to judge and condemn him in turn. With another cutting pun, rendered by Le Fèvre as 'le theume tranché lui puet nuire' [cutting to the heart of the matter can hurt him], the poet argues that the eunuch will be unable to hear a case fairly and will thus be a cruel and uncomprehending judge. Whatever *facundia*, or eloquence, he might bring will remain sterile in its effects; his *science* will issue in *infecondité*, or sterility (*Vet.* 2.67–73; *LV* 2221–30).

Having dispatched the *trivium*, the *Vetula* poet turns to the *quadrivium*, to which he devotes a single passage, one of the most difficult in the poem. He uses the argument that in every *demonstratio* or scientific proof there must properly be four components: number, measure, movement, and sound. Regarding number, 'deficiente sibi numero pare' [he is lacking an even number] (*Vet.* 2:83), that is, he quite literally does not have a 'pair', and thus measurement is impossible and movement abhorrent, although why this should be is not made clear. As for sound, the poet concludes with the remark: 'quem si temptarit, tandem lira murmurat ani,' which Jean renders as 's'il y tempte par adventure / La harpe du cul lui murmure' [if he should try it [i.e., movement], his ass's harp murmurs] (*Vet.* 2.85; *LV* 2258–9). Although it is far from clear

31 Alanus de Insulis, *Liber de planctu naturae*, ed. J.P. Migne, *Patrologia latina* (Paris: Garnier, 1844–55) 210: col. 457; Alan of Lille, *Plaint of Nature*, trans. James J. Sheridan (Toronto: Pontifical Institute of Medieval Studies, 1970), p. 157.

what the eunuch's murmuring ass is supposed to denote, this colorful image undercuts the argument being made – there *is* movement and sound. As for the 'music' emanating from his lower body, in the logic of the text, it can be only yet another sign of his imperfection. The passage in *De Vetula* includes the adverb *tandem*, 'in the end', which is not rendered in Jean's translation. It suggests a loss of control over the body, in keeping with the eunuch's loss of manliness, his hopeless incapacity and ineptitude. His efforts at movement can issue only in foul winds.

After establishing the eunuch's monstrosity according to the liberal arts, the *Vetula* poet turns to another scheme to prove that the eunuch is, by turns, a monster of nature, a moral monster, a metaphysical monster, and, finally, a *monstrum fastorum*, in Jean's rendering, a *monstre de destinées*, or 'monster of destinies'. In the first of these four sections, where the poet returns to the discourse of natural philosophy, he remarks that, paradoxically, nature can find either a *vacuum*, a 'void', or an *infinitum*, an 'infinity' in the eunuch, depending on the form of his neutering (*Vet.* 2.90–1). If his *folles* (*fueilles* in Jean, i.e., 'bags') have been ablated, she will find them empty, *bourses vuides*, as Jean puts it (*LV* 2275). If, on the other hand, his testicles were crushed, she will find an abnormal enlargement due to the mutilation. Here, Jean introduces into his translation a distinction that is not in his source: if the *couillons*, or 'balls', have been removed, the term *eunuche* should be used; in the other case, the term *spadon* is more appropriate (*LV* 2271–80). Jean himself is not consistent in his use of these terms, nor is the Latin poet. But this confusion over terms and definitions is in fact emblematic of the medieval discourse on eunuchry, which embraced a variety of conditions. Castration could be achieved, as Kuefler observes in his overview of eunuchry in the *Medieval Handbook of Sexuality*, by removing or crushing the testicles, or by the much rarer and more dangerous practice of removing the penis.[32] In other cases, the terms 'eunuch' or 'spadon' might designate men born with genital abnormalities, men who became impotent because of disease or injury, or castrated men. In some cases there might be overlap between or among these categories.[33] The *Vetula* poet sidesteps these difficulties – after all, what can be unnatural about a congenital condition? – which is consistent with his practice of avoiding anything that might naturalize or spiritualize eunuchry. Yet despite the impression of plenitude and completeness that both poets seek to convey, the gaps and omissions in their texts belie their agenda of defining a certain idea of clerical privilege, one where eunuchs are marked as outsiders.

Sticking to a more specifically scientific and medical discourse, the *Vetula*

32 Mathew S. Kuefler, 'Castration and Eunuchism in the Middle Ages', in *Handbook of Medieval Sexuality*, ed. Vern L. Bullough and James A. Brundage (New York and London: Garland, 1996), pp. 279–306 at pp. 285–6.

33 Ibid.

poet says that eunuchs are either healthy or diseased, but he insists that in any case medicine offers no cure or remedy for his condition. Indeed, since the eunuch offers no recognizable *complexio* 'constitution or temperament', other than lacking one, he remains a conundrum to which the discourses of natural philosophy and medicine cannot be applied (*Vet.* 2.93–9). Just as the two texts had sought to deny to the eunuch any possibility of self-representation through speech, they now seek to push him even further from the realm of signification. He can be neither the subject nor the object of discourse.

The poet now moves onto the eunuch as *monstre moral*. This section is little more than a list of all the traits that are 'naturally' those of a eunuch. Since eunuchs are physically sterile, it inevitably follows that they are morally so as well: envious, lazy, fearful, thieving, and wretched. Their supposed physiological coldness, a condition that they share with women, makes them naturally covetous. Their wrinkled faces – Jean says, 'Com vieille qui mangue frommaige' [like that of an old woman eating cheese] (*LV* 2332)[34] – are the mark of their moral shame. Finally, the text returns to the vexed issue of chastity, rejecting out of hand the notion that eunuchs are truly chaste. Eunuchs who have to struggle to be chaste are vainglorious; those who do not have to struggle are simply insensitive to carnal desire. The issue of chastity with regard to eunuchs was indeed a constant in medieval discourse. It is, for example, at the heart of a twelfth-century Greek text that it is doubtful that the *Vetula* poet knew, the *Defense of Eunuchs* by Theophylaktos, a text analyzed by Kathryn Ringrose.[35] The text takes the form of a debate between a testiculated man and a eunuch in which the latter marshals a number of arguments to support his contention that eunuchs can indeed achieve chastity. Why, he asks, should voluntary celibates be less evil than eunuchs, who were given no choice in the matter? Why should ascetics who destroy their bodies through their extreme practices be considered more holy than eunuchs? Why should the loss of testes be considered an evil when their presence can impede one's progress toward spiritual good? And, most interestingly, why should eunuchs be considered unnatural when it is impossible to say what is 'natural'? The *Defense of Eunuchs* shows that the *Vetula* poet's text is but one voice in a medieval dialogue in which both sides could argue the same points using the same terms. Furthermore, the learned arsenal and scholastic trappings deployed by the *Vetula* poet in his eunuch satire are, in fact, doubly satirical: the passage is as much a parody of the scholastic method as it is a satire against eunuchs. Despite its many self-authorizing gestures, it does not (and doubtless was not intended to) bear the weight of the ecclesiastical, legal, or indeed scientific discourse

34 A variant in BNF, fr 2327, has 'Comme vieille qui vent frommage' (Like an old woman who sells cheese).

35 Ringrose, *Perfect Servant*, pp. 194–202; Ringrose, *Living in the Shadows*, pp. 103–7.

from which it borrows. It is a second-hand discourse got up in scholastic 'drag'. In this, it is not unlike Jean de Meun's *Romans de la Rose*, another *bricolage*, or patchwork, to which medieval readers, especially male clerics, readily granted the status of authority.

The *Vetula* poet opens his attack against eunuchs by echoing Jesus' words. In the last sections of the anti-eunuch satire, the Old Testament is pressed into service. The language echoes Jewish condemnation of eunuchs to support the poet's portrait of the eunuch as metaphysical monster.[36] In a development not present in his source, Jean returns to the issue of gender in language. If an *escouillé* – literally, a man whose testes have been removed – becomes a priest, is he a *prestre* or a *prestresse* (*LV* 2388–9)?[37] Without offering an answer, the poet wonders how God can allow this hideous, filthy, deformed creature into his temple, where he *affemine*, 'feminizes', the Lord's altars (*LV* 2397). The final section on the eunuch as *monstrum fastorum*, a *monstre de destinées* (monster of destinies) is a retelling of the Jacob and Esau story (*Vet.* 2.170–85; *LV* 2467–98). Although Jacob was not a eunuch (the poet assures us), he had the eunuch's high voice and hairless body. Through his machinations, he tricks Isaac in order to gain his father's benediction and Esau's rightful heritage, perverting the destinies that were to be theirs. So will the eunuch, the poet argues, go to any lengths to become a prelate, to achieve domination, to sit in high estate, and to seize the possessions he covets. In these sections of the eunuch diatribe that follow the deployment of the liberal arts scheme, the context is quite clearly and specifically clerical. Indeed, the rubric of the final section on eunuchs in *La Vieille* is 'Comment Ovide dit qui feist sa volounté jamais home spadon ou escouillé ne fust en prelature' [How Ovid says that, if one were to do his will, a man with crushed or ablated testicles will never enter the priesthood] (*LV*, after 2526). Here, the example of Moses is cited, who fortunately did not allow Aaron to wear priestly vestments with his *vultuque Maria* (*visaige de Marie* in Jean) 'Mary's face' (*Vet.* 2.191–5, *LV* 2931–6).

Although Klopsch grants that one cannot attribute *De Vetula* to Richard de Fournival with any degree of certainly, he speculates that, were Richard the author, through the eunuch satire he might have been attacking his nemesis in the cathedral chapter at Amiens, Gérard de Conchy. The latter had sought to deprive Richard of his chancellorship on the grounds that he practiced surgery as a deacon and subdeacon.[38] Klopsch admits that this is pure speculation, and indeed, one would have to assume that Gérard was an effeminate, eunuch-like

[36] Cf. Collins, 'Appropriation and Development', pp. 73–86.

[37] Mary E. Leech explores the manning and unmanning of men and women in the Old French fabliaux in her analysis of *La dame escolliee* in this volume. See 'The Castrating of the Shrew: The Performance of Masculinity and Masculine Identity in *La dame escolliee*', pp. 210–28.

[38] *De Vetula*,, ed. Klopsch, pp. 87–8.

cleric. Klopsch's speculation does, however, have the merit of raising the question of just who these eunuchs *were* that the *Vetula* poet claims were scheming to attain high positions in the Church. As noted above, there is not a single reference to sodomy in *De Vetula* and *La Vieille* – especially surprising since charges of passive sodomy were often directed at eunuchs – but the nascent medieval discourse on sodomy offers striking parallels with the rhetorical strategies and ambiguities of these two poems.

The *Vetula* poet's attack on eunuchs shares many features with condemnation of sodomy in Alan of Lille's *De planctu naturae* and Peter Damian's *Liber Gomorrhianus*.[39] In his study of *De planctu naturae*, William Burgwinkle proposes five possible readings, allowing that there may be some degree of truth in all of them. Two are especially relevant to the discussion here: Alan's text may be read primarily as an attack on sodomy, or it may be 'a true Menippean satire which emphasizes form over philosophy, humor over moralism.'[40] The same formulation, with 'eunuch' in the place of 'sodomy', can apply equally well to *De Vetula* and *La Vieille*, of which form and humor are major constituents. Cary Howie notes that Peter Damian's text, in which the author rails against the legions of clerics who supposedly were practicing the sin against nature, is permeated with anxiety over the Church's integrity, the supposed breach opened up by the presence of sodomites within its clerical ranks: 'What is fascinating about this contention is not only its staging of anxieties not that different from those of contemporary culture's heteronormative custody of the so-called back door, but the fact that Damian must insist upon the sodomites' inability to achieve their aim.'[41] And, as Mark Jordan observes: 'The Sodomite is unfit for full membership in the Church, especially in its ministerial orders, and yet Peter fears that Sodomites have taken over the Church, constituting a shadow hierarchy with its own means of recognition and recruitment.'[42] Like Peter Damian, the poets of *De Vetula* and *La Vieille* loudly and anxiously proclaim the impossibility of eunuchs carrying out clerical functions even as their texts implicitly allow that their vilified objects are doing precisely that.

Medieval anti-Semitic and misogynist discourses of the Other also offer useful parallels for the understanding of *De Vetula* and *La Vieille*. Sylvia Tomasch has advanced the term 'virtual Jew' in the context of anti-Jewish

39 Alanus de Insulis, *Liber de planctu naturae*; Peter Damian, *Liber Gomorrhianus*. There is an abundant literature that queers these two authors and their preoccupation with sodomy. Among the most important titles: Mark D. Jordan, *The Invention of Sodomy in Christian Theology* (Chicago: University of Chicago Press, 1997); William Burgwinkle, *Sodomy, Masculinity, and Law in Medieval Literature: France and England, 1050–1230* (Cambridge: Cambridge University Press, 2004); Cary Howie, *Claustrophilia: The Erotics of Enclosure in Medieval Literature* (New York: Palgrave Macmillan, 2007).

40 Burgwinkle, *Sodomy*, p. 192.

41 Howie, *Claustrophilia*, p. 75.

42 Jordan, *Invention of Sodomy*, pp. 161–2.

discourse in post-expulsion England. That is, the anti-Semitic fury of texts like the Croxton *Play of the Sacrament* is no less real for its lack of a real Jewish presence, let alone a Jewish 'threat'.[43] Such texts are clearly not mere rhetorical exercises but rather are doing cultural work in the service of forming a community of orthodox believers. Similarly, Étienne de Fougères' estates poem, the *Livres des manières*, includes women as one of Christian society's six estates, all the better to tax them for their role in the social ills he sees as threatening social stability and the primacy of the Church: the rise of the merchant class and the ideology of *fin'amors*. But he cannot resist exercising his satirical verve in a violent diatribe against women who have sex with other women.[44] It would be a mistake to view the eunuch satire in *De Vetula* and *La Vieille*, in many regards a variant on misogynist discourse in texts such as Etienne's, as simply an extended rhetorical exercise, a *tour de force* demonstration of how to do something new with the scholastic method, although its tongue-in-cheek style might lead to that conclusion. By attacking virtual eunuchs, *De Vetula* is also doing cultural work, most obviously in the area of gender regulation in the Church and the society at large. 'Quid est?' the poet asks with regard to his hapless eunuch, usually in order to say what it is not, or, more interestingly, to say at times both what it is and is not. But the more pertinent question is not 'What is it?' but 'What does it do?' The answer is clearly: a great deal indeed. The sterile eunuch is, if not father or mother or lover, the midwife of culture.

[43] Sylvia Tomasch, 'Postcolonial Chaucer and the Virtual Jew', in *The Postcolonial Middle Ages*, ed. Jeffrey Jerome Cohen (New York: St Martin's Press, 2000), pp. 243–60. For an argument similar to Tomasch's, see Robert L.A. Clark and Claire Sponsler, 'Othered Bodies: Racial Crossdressing in the *Mistere de la Sainte Hostie* and the *Croxton Play of the Sacrament*', *Journal of Medieval and Early Modern Studies* 29.1 (1999): 61–87.

[44] See Robert L.A. Clark, 'Jousting without a Lance: The Condemnation of Female Homoeroticism in the *Livre des manières*', in *Same Sex Love and Desire among Women in the Middle Ages*, ed. Francesca Canadé Sautman and Pamela Sheingorn (New York: St Martin's Press, 2001) 143–77.

CHAPTER 14

The Dismemberment of Will: Early Modern Fear of Castration

Karin Sellberg and Lena Wånggren

The soldier's pole is fall'n: young boys and girls
Are equal bow with men: the odds are gone,
And there is nothing left remarkable
Beneath the visiting moon.
Shakespeare, *Antony and Cleopatra*, 4.15.67–70[1]

The works of William Shakespeare often look back from the early modern period upon the sensibilities of the medieval world, illuminating similar anxieties about culture, identity, ethnicity, and gender. In his plays, taboo subjects of medieval literature and history are given centre stage, acted out for an early modern audience coming to grips with its own fraught place in history. Shakespeare's dramas (*Antony and Cleopatra* perhaps more explicitly and completely than any other) feature numerous instances of emasculation, yet these are seldom considered in corporeal terms. Recent scholarship on early modern castration shares a number of curious features: the majority of the discussion takes place in relation to a very select number of Shakespearean sources, and the references are invariably contextualized through psychoanalytic theories of phallic lack. Through the new historicist and cultural materialist turn of late twentieth- and early twenty-first-century academia, Shakespeare has become recognized as the spokesperson for Western sensibility in general, not just a historical time and place in particular – and the deep-seated fear of effeminization or castration that is extracted from his work does indeed often appear more modern than early modern. The anachronistic moves that have been made in these studies can be conceptualized through three specific types of 'cuts': a temporal cut that removes Shakespeare's plays

1 William Shakespeare, *Antony and Cleopatra*, ed. John Wilders (London: Routledge, 1995), 4.15.65–9. Act, scene and line numbers are given in parentheses throughout, after the initial reference.

from their contemporary contexts; a textual cut that removes drama from its social functions; and finally an often horrifying and graphically illustrated corporeal cut found in early modern medical compendia.

From within these dismemberments of contemporary Shakespearean criticism emerges an early modern fear of castration which is both a historical relic and a modern projection. The cultural and social constructions surrounding castration take form both within and without the framework of the anachronistic scholarship that surrounds them, both embracing and challenging the historical differentiation between past and present castration. There was an undisputed unease about the idea of castration in the early modern period that in many ways is reminiscent of contemporary popular fears. To some extent this unease must be conceptualized in reference to contemporary discourses of emasculation and gender differentiation, but it also has its source in a more visceral concern about the relationship of body and soul and the decline of the spirit in any act of bodily fragmentation, harking back to medieval spirituality and humorous science. The early modern fear of castration is thus a fear of incompleteness and imbalance as much as a loss of manly embodiment.

Thomas Laqueur argues, in *Making Sex*, that the early modern idea of embodiment, gender, and sexuality is so different from any modern understanding of these concepts, that it is practically impossible for a modern reader to comprehend it. According to Laqueur, this was a time before sexual difference, since 'no image, verbal or visual, of "the facts of sexual difference" exists independently of prior claims about the meanings of such'[2] and the common beliefs employed in order to define what makes a man, or something masculine, 'are so farfetched to the modern scientific imagination that it takes a strenuous effort to understand how reasonable people could ever have held them'.[3] According to the first volume of Michel Foucault's *The History of Sexuality*, the seventeenth century was the scene for the first of two crucial 'ruptures' in the social imaginary surrounding sexual practice and embodiment that enabled the development of what is nowadays considered in terms of sexuality and sexual difference.[4] The sexual and gendered past of Western culture has thus been drastically dislocated from its present form. There is a temporal rift established between early modern and contemporary discourses of sexuality that is even more pronounced in modern discussions of the *medieval* body explored throughout this volume. There is a tendency to approach medieval and early modern narratives of castration through a theoretical lens, applying psychoanalytic, Freudian or Foucauldian paradigms to

[2] Thomas Laqueur, *Making Sex: Body and Gender from the Greeks to Freud* (Cambridge, MA: Harvard University Press, 1990), p. 66.

[3] Ibid., p. 70.

[4] Michel Foucault, *The History of Sexuality*, vol. 1: *The Will to Knowledge*, trans. Robert Hurley (London: Penguin Books, 1998), p. 115.

texts and laws, rather than examining the literal acts of castration within their social and temporal context.

This anachronistic 'cut' is continually reiterated in late twentieth- and early twenty-first-century studies of Shakepearean gender and sexuality (which themselves, of course, are anachronistic terms). The body of sexual thought has, itself, been brutally castrated and any study into the history of gendered embodiment is an attempt to recover an earlier sense of completeness. Laqueur argues that Sigmund Freud and psychoanalytic theories of gender and sexuality provide the most definitive division (or 'cut'), between early modern and modern sexual thought.[5] Despite his active participation in this divide, Freud is prevalent in a great deal of critical writing on early modern sexuality, which is practically invariably read through a psychoanalytic lens. The Freudian concept of castration especially is so imbued in the modern sense of the term (and the modern conception of sexuality in general) that it seems almost impossible for modern interpreters of medieval or early modern sexuality to leave it behind, although the modern Freudian framework attributes meanings to medieval and early modern conceptions of castration that in many cases do not make much sense. Contemporary readings of medieval and early modern castration (including Laqueur's, which claims to be aware of its anachronistic position) invariably tend to express a sense of confusion or 'lack' of understanding, which says more about the theorists' symbolic fear of some type of temporal castration than their subjects' actual experience of the practice.

As Gary Taylor acknowledges in *Castration: An Abbreviated History of Western Manhood*, the fact that Freud is reiterated in historical as well as contemporary studies of sexuality is because he has not merely become castration's 'most famous modern theorist',[6] but one of its few modern interpreters. Freud formulates the castration complex (*Kastrationskomplex*) in his 1908 paper 'On the Sexual Theories of Children', which became the basis for a psychoanalytic concept about the origins of sexual difference to which many literary critics and scholars of the history of sexuality subscribe. Freud claims that the first sexual inclination in children consists in '*attributing to everyone, including females, the possession of a penis*',[7] leading to the formulation of the castration complex.[8] According to this complex, men will suffer from an eternal threat of castration, and female genitalia are regarded as 'a mutilated organ'.[9]

5 Laqueur, *Making Sex*, p. 20.

6 Gary Taylor, *Castration: An Abbreviated History of Western Manhood* (New York and London: Routledge, 2002), p. 15.

7 Sigmund Freud, 'On the Sexual Theories of Children', in *The Standard Edition of the Complete Psychological Works of Sigmund Freud*, vol. 7, ed. James Strachey (London: Hogarth Press and the Institute of Psycho-Analysis, 1953), pp. 207–26 at p. 215. Italics in original.

8 Ibid., p. 217.

9 Ibid.

Women – feeling themselves unfairly treated – suffer from penis envy.[10] For Freud, castration is a genital loss that all women believe that they have suffered and that all men fear to suffer. According to this illogical logic, a woman is a mutilated man, and castration (for Freud castration always signifies penile castration) must for the man involve effeminization.

Freud in this way treats castration (*Kastration*) as a synonym for unmanning (*Entmannung*), as feminizing, and psychoanalytical literary critics have followed this reading. A number of prolific late twentieth-century works on early modern drama, including Stephen Orgel's *Impersonations*, Laura Levine's *Men in Women's Clothing* and Dympna Callaghan's *Shakespeare without Women*, argue that the all-male early modern stage was generated in a culture imbued with 'fear of effeminisation'.[11] For these scholars, Shakespeare's works are full of metaphorical castrations signifying effeminization. Janet Adelman, in *Suffocating Mothers* (and elsewhere), associates 'wounds with castration and hence effeminisation [...] displayed wounds and mouths both seem to me to function as the sign of the female'.[12] Coppélia Kahn, in *Man's Estate*, also equates castration with 'losing masculine identity'.[13] As Anthony Adams, Mary Leech, and Larissa Tracy point out in this volume, the question of 'unmanning' and the loss of masculine identity was a prevalent, and literal, concern for medieval audiences as well.[14] For many Shakespeare scholars, Shakespeare's plays contain the imagery that Freud's subsequent theories of sexual development formulate as castration anxiety. Lee Edelman unquestioningly accepts Freud's assertion that a child sees the mother as a castrated man in his readings of Shakespeare, while Orgel and Levine read early modern femininity in general in terms of phallic lack, and Callaghan considers early modern effeminization to be a form of castration.[15] Shakespeare's dramas have thus been used as examples (or before-the-fact templates) for

[10] Ibid., p. 218. See also Freud's 'Three Essays on Sexuality' (1905), in *The Standard Edition*, vol. 7, ed. Strachey, pp. 135–243 at p. 195.

[11] Stephen Orgel, *Impersonations: The Performance of Gender in Shakespeare's England* (Cambridge: Cambridge University Press, 1996); Laura Levine, *Men in Women's Clothing: Anti-Theatricality and Effeminization 1579–1642* (Cambridge: Cambridge University Press, 1994), quote at p. 134; Dympna Callaghan, *Shakespeare without Women: Representing Gender and Race on the Renaissance Stage* (New York and London: Routledge, 2000).

[12] Janet Adelman, *Suffocating Mothers: Fantasies of Maternal Origin in Shakespeare's Plays,* Hamlet *to* The Tempest (New York and London: Routledge, 1992), p. 327, n. 61.

[13] Coppélia Kahn, *Man's Estate: Masculine Identity in Shakespeare* (Berkeley: University of California Press, 1981), p. 43; cf. p. 132 and passim on 'psychosocial castration'.

[14] See in this volume Anthony Adams, '"He took a stone away": Castration and Cruelty in the Old Norse *Sturlunga saga*', pp. 188–209; Mary E. Leech, 'The Castrating of the Shrew: The Performance of Masculinity and Masculine Identity in *La dame escolliee*', pp. 210–28; and Larissa Tracy, '"Al defouleden is holie bodi": Castration, the Sexualization of Torture, and Anxieties of Identity in the *South English Legendary*', pp. 87–107.

[15] See Lee Edelman, *Essays in Gay Literary and Cultural Theory* (New York and London: Routledge, 1994), pp. 2–10; Orgel, *Impersonations*, pp. 103–5; Levine, *Men in Women's Clothing*, pp. 134–5; Callaghan, *Shakespeare without Women*, pp. 36–8.

contemporary psychoanalytic conceptions of self,[16] a fact that entirely obscures more historically sensitive pre-Freudian readings of Shakespearean castration.

Readings of Shakespeare's *King Lear* (1608) are a case in point for this kind of criticism. Several critics have read the blinding of Gloucester in this play as a figurative castration.[17] Gloucester's simultaneous loss of sight and socio-political influence signifies a symbolic loss of psychosexual phallic power. However, there are less anachronistic connections between castration and blinding. The medieval punishment for rape required the rapist to lose his eyes as well as his testicles because the eye was held responsible for inspiring uncontrolled sexual desire.[18] Charlene Eska explains that William the Conqueror supplemented the death penalty in England as punishment for treason with castration and blinding. She writes that 'The Anglo-Saxon codes already had elements of this practice in place, thus making the addition of judicial blinding and castration to the legal system seem more of a point on a continuum rather than a wholesale new practice'.[19] So there is a pervasive link between castration and blinding that dates back to the law texts of the early Middle Ages. At the end of the play, Lear himself is also, in a sense, 'blinded' (castrated) by his loss.[20]

This ahistorical reading of castration is problematic. Freud (and many of his followers) ignores historical context, but instead assumes that the meaning of castration is always the same; for psychoanalysis, the castration complex shapes the psychological character of every individual throughout history. As Taylor states: 'If Freud is right, there is no real reason to read a text about castration from 1624, because any text about castration, or any other aspect of human sexuality, should be telling the same story.'[21] But the historical context needs to be considered, rather than trying to fit texts into an essentialist and ahistorical system. Castration existed both before and after psychoanalysis, but Freud

16 Even Freud himself uses Shakespeare as an example of his theories; see for example his famous use of *Hamlet* in his explanation of the Oedipus complex in *The Interpretation of Dreams*, trans. James Strachey, ed. Angela Richards (London: Penguin, 1991) e.g. pp. 164, 247–9, 418.

17 Adelman, *Suffocating Mothers*, p. 107; Hillary M. Nunn, *Staging Anatomies: Dissection and Spectacle in Early Stuart Tragedy* (Aldershot: Ashgate, 2005), p. 173.

18 Nunn, *Staging Anatomies*, p. 172.

19 Charlene M. Eska, '"Imbrued in their owne bloud": Castration in Early Welsh and Irish Sources', in this volume, p. 157.

20 Callaghan points to the phallic imagery in Lear's lamentation over his dead daughters, using words such as 'stones', 'eyes', and 'tongues' (*Shakespeare without Women*, pp. 91–2). Another play that has come to feature heavily in studies of figurative castration is *Twelfth Night*. Scholars like Callaghan and Orgel repeatedly discuss the unfortunate character Malvolio's spelling out of the letters C, U, and T (which Callaghan takes the liberty to read in a Freudian light: interchangeably as CUT and CUNT) and consider this in terms of the subsequent social castration that the character experiences as a punishment for coveting and making advances towards a woman above his social status (Callaghan, *Shakespeare without Women*, pp. 36–47; Orgel, *Impersonations*, pp. 53–4).

21 Taylor, *Castration*, p. 31.

ignored what castration had meant for millennia and 'substituted a radical new meaning of his own'.[22] Taylor writes: 'In twentieth-century psychoanalysis, castration means loss, unequivocal loss, the epitome of loss. In the world before Freud, castration could produce a powerful voice, a powerful general, a powerful intimate of women and emperors, and powerful spirituality.'[23] Eunuchs throughout history have often occupied important positions in society. Kathryn Reusch provides burial evidence of modern *castrati* graves, arguing that their physical state affected their social acceptance, even in death.[24] As Shaun Tougher explains, 'eunuchs remained a desirable commodity into the later Roman Empire, when they became an institutional feature of the imperial court, serving primarily in the capacity of chamberlains (*cubicularii*)'.[25] But, as Robert Clark argues, 'there can be no doubt that in the cultural imaginary of western Europe, the sterile eunuch, because of his ambiguity, was a paradoxically pregnant figure for thinking about culture'.[26] The laws examined by Rolf Bremmer, Jay Gates, and Charlene Eska reveal cultural concerns about the loss of potency, the inability to procreate, inherent in castration or genital wounding. Mary Valante explains the financial value placed on castrated clerics sold into slavery in Byzantium.[27] But there were other cultural considerations at play, especially in the discourse of virginity and bodily purity.[28] Castration did not mean *one* thing in the Middle Ages, nor did the cultural implications diminish in the early modern period. Taylor argues that there are *two entire cultural traditions at war in this argumentation*: early modern drama and Freud's psychoanalysis 'represent two rival systems of theories, experiences, and memories about what castration means'.[29]

Importantly, Freud equates castration with penile loss, since for him this 'essential constituent' is the basis of the whole human sexual imaginary.[30] But castration does not necessarily revolve around the penis; it usually signifies the removal of the testicles. The first extant medical description of castration, by the seventh-century Byzantine physician Paul of Aegina, makes clear that the operation concerns the testicles only,[31] and early modern physicians often care-

22 Ibid., p. 43.

23 Ibid.

24 Kathryn Reusch, 'Raised Voices: The Archaeology of Castration', in this volume, pp. 29–47.

25 Shaun Tougher, 'The Aesthetics of Castration: The Beauty of Roman Eunuchs', in this volume, pp. 48–9.

26 Robert L. A. Clark, 'Culture Loves a Void: Eunuchry in *De Vetula* and Jean Le Fèvre's *La Vieille*', in this volume, p. 281.

27 Mary A. Valante, 'Castrating Monks: Vikings, the Slave Trade, and the Value of Eunuchs', in this volume, pp. 174–86.

28 See Jack Collins, 'Appropriation and Development of Castration as Symbol and Practice in Early Christianity', in this volume, pp. 73–86.

29 Taylor, *Castration*, p. 46.

30 Freud, 'On the Sexual Theories of Children', p. 216.

31 Taylor, *Castration*, p. 53; and Tougher, 'The Aesthetics of Castration', p. 48.

fully elaborate this point. Poets, playwrights, and philosophers in the early modern period, Taylor argues, knew this as well as physicians.[32] Not until the sixteenth and seventeenth centuries did surgical operations on diseased or injured penises become more common (because of the recent syphilis epidemic), as a last resort to save the patient from death.[33] So by the seventeenth century, Europeans knew of medical castration, genital war wounds as well as disciplinary dismemberment of all the genitalia (to humiliate a criminal) – but they had known for millennia about castration of the scrotum, and the differences between these operations.[34] Freud completely disregards this difference: anachronistically, he 'reduced castration to a single meaning and reduced sexuality to a single organ', thus 'erect[ing] a penis-shaped model of the mind'.[35]

Despite the absence of a Freudian castration complex, there is still evidence of a certain amount of early modern anxiety regarding the emasculating effects of castration, as Callaghan explains in *Shakespeare without Women*. In his *Anthropometamorphosis: Man Transform'd* (1653), the early modern English physician John Bulwer states that it is 'manifestly against the Law of Nature to tamper with the witness of mans virility', which makes men 'not current for men'.[36] He makes it clear that there is a distinct difference between penile and testicular castration, however:

> Two waies there are of this unnatural dilapidation of the body, one is performed by contusion, the other by excision, the last being more approved of; for they who have suffered the contusion of the Testicles, may now and then affect to play the man.[37]

Bulwer implies that castrated men exist in a differently gendered space, but that some who have only suffered 'contusion' (that is the bruising or rupture of the testicles) can still behave as men. Freudian conceptions of castration disregard this difference and contemporary Shakespearean critics thus often express confusion and disbelief when confronted with references to castrated men. Shakespeare's *Twelfth Night* simultaneously refers to figurative castration in comical and berating terms, and embraces a character who takes on the appearance of a eunuch. Considering the difference between penile and testicular castration at the time, and the social positions that followed these proceedings, this is not surprising. When *Twelfth Night*'s heroine Viola

32 Taylor, *Castration*, pp. 52–3.

33 Ibid., p. 57.

34 Ibid., pp. 57–8.

35 Ibid., pp. 60–1.

36 John Bulwer, *Anthropometamorphosis: Man transform'd; or, The artificiall changling historically presented, in the mad and cruell gallantry, foolish bravery, ridiculous beauty, filthy finenesse, and loathsome loveliness of most nations, fashioning and altering their bodies from the mould intended by natvre …* (London: 1653), p. 362.

37 Ibid., p. 359.

announces to the captain that 'thou shalt present me as an eunuch' (1.2.55),[38] this does not invoke any type of negative reaction, because eunuchs are not considered in a negative light. Viola's eunuch alter-ego Cesario takes up a socially recognized position, which makes her/him the possessor of such a degree of masculinity that she/he is considered fit to stir the emotions of the play's most eligible woman, Lady Olivia. Castrated men had an important role to play in early modern English as well as European society – especially one that was associated with the stage. As Marjorie Garber acknowledges in *Vested Interests*, *castrati* were common on the stages of Italy and France and they were occasionally seen in the courts of Elizabethan and Jacobean England.[39] Although they may not have been a frequent sight on the London streets, their presence was thus an acceptable, and to some extent expected, part of early modern upper-class entertainment and drama, lending them a hint of the exotic and spectacular, but in the case of the ordinary man, often unattainable.

The figure of the eunuch, if considered in relation to this connotation, becomes an embodiment of spectacle itself. Callaghan thus interprets the eunuch as a person who, despite his genital incompleteness, becomes respectable because of the completion granted him through his art. She compares a set of penile prostheses invented in 1634 by French surgeon Ambroise Paré in order to overcome the physical obstacles arising in connection to urination by patients who had to undergo penile castration due to syphilis,[40] and the voices ('pipes') and musical instruments used by *castrati* performers. According to Callaghan, the music or art of the eunuch becomes his phallus, and as such makes him something close enough to a man to be accepted in early modern society.[41] Although the idea that a specific social role gives early modern eunuchs a place in society is credible, the interpretation of music or expression as a replacement phallus is of course once more entirely reliant on a Freudian, figurative, and distinctly penile idea of castration. Where Callaghan attempts to recover the masculinity of her subjects through an anachronistic and anatomically incorrect phallic replacement, what the eunuchs truly gained was a specific space, where they could develop a reasonably respectable role *despite* their exclusion from the ordinary gender

38 William Shakespeare, *Twelfth Night*, ed. J.M. Lothian and T.W. Craik (London: Routledge, 1988), 1.2.55.

39 Marjorie Garber, *Vested Interests: Cross-Dressing and Cultural Anxiety* (New York and London: Routledge, 1992), p. 130.

40 Ambroise Paré, *The Workes of that famous chirurgion Ambrose Parey translated out of Latine and compared with the French. by Th: Johnson* (London: Th. Cotes & R. Young, 1634), p. 583. Paré explains that 'Those that have their yards cut off close to their bellies, are greatly troubled in making of urine, so that they are constrained to sit down like women, for their eas. I have devised this pipe or conduit, having an hole through it as big as one finger, which may be made of wood, or rather of latin' (p. 583).

41 Callaghan, *Shakespeare without Women*, pp. 62–9.

dynamic. As the description of Viola/Cesario in *Twelfth Night* attests, eunuchs resided both inside and outside the gender binary:

> they shall yet belie thy happy years,
> That say thou art a man: Diana's lip
> Is not more smooth and rubious; thy small pipe
> Is as the maiden's organ, shrill and sound –
> And all is semblative of a woman's part.
> (1.4.25–9)

Although eunuchs undeniably were men, they were thus often considered more feminine than masculine. As Kathryn Ringrose recognises in *The Perfect Servant*, eunuchs were not thought to have the humorous balance that a man was meant to display. Balance was a pivotal element in early modern medicine. Since Hippocrates, European medical writing stressed the importance of harmony and control and both the rivalling camps of Aristotelian and Galenic followers among the medical and scientific profession believed that this was maintained through the moderation of animating spirit and heat. A body that was moderately and harmoniously heated was a healthy body, and nothing should be allowed to disturb 'the perfect balance that became the hallmark of the ideal masculine body'.[42] Such balance was considered *exclusively* masculine; however, 'the sense of control, balance, and harmony was generally contrasted with women's lack of control – the assumption that women became upset and cried easily, proving that they were emotionally unstable'.[43] Quoting Aristotle, Bulwer states that the reason for this effect is that 'the Heart is stretched by the Testicles, and therefore relaxed when they are cut away'.[44] Despite their masculine position in general, eunuchs were thus also thought to harbour distinctly 'unmanly' traits: 'Like women, they were assumed to be unable to maintain the focus of either the mind or the body. They lacked balance and harmony in body, mind, and behaviour. As a result eunuchs, like women, were believed to be unable to control their desires for food, drink, and physical pleasure.'[45] To have the testicles removed meant relinquishing manly self-control.

The eunuch is thus a man that has something 'lack[ing] of a man' (*Twelfth Night*, 3.4.308), but this 'thing' cannot simply be translated into a figurative phallus like Callaghan, Orgel, and Levine would have it. *Twelfth Night*'s eunuch, Cesario, has the appearance and social manners of a man, but he lacks a man's strength and humorous balance. This is why he is particularly useless with a sword. Viola/Cesario's lack of manliness is only openly ridiculed at one point

42 Kathryn Ringrose, *The Perfect Servant: Eunuchs and the Social Construction of Gender in Byzantium* (Chicago: University of Chicago Press, 1996), p. 52.

43 Ibid., p. 52.

44 Bulwer, *Anthropometamorphosis*, p. 356.

45 Ringrose, *The Perfect Servant*, p. 52.

in the play, and that is in her/his fight with another unbalanced character, Sir Andrew Aguecheek.[46] As the early modern Jesuit and scholar Thomas Wright states in *The Passions of the Mind in General*, manly composure is of the utmost importance on the battlefield, where humorous balance, precision, and level-headedness are crucial, which is why only mature and fully developed men should be deployed in war.[47] Viola/Cesario and Sir Andrew are not fully masculine, and they are thus not warriors. They have to be urged by the other characters to fight and their duel ends up a veritable debacle, because neither is balanced or focused enough to bring it to a conclusion.

The loss of this perfect warrior masculine balance is arguably also what brings Mark Antony to his tragic end in Shakespeare's *Antony and Cleopatra*. Although he is the most powerful warrior in the Roman Empire at the start of the play, 'the greatest soldier of the world' (1.3.37), he loses all his public thrust when he falls in love with Egypt's forceful queen Cleopatra, whose demands and desires eventually 'rob [him] of [his] sword' (4.14.24), as well as his masculine power. With sooted eyes, dressed like the actor of a continuous court drama (and surrounded primarily by women and eunuchs), Antony himself becomes a form of eunuch, powerless even to end his own life with his sword like a soldier. He is ridiculed throughout the world outside of Egyptian court spectacle, for although eunuchs were accepted on stage and in court performances, they were also restricted from many important social, political, and religious gatherings in early modern English society. King James's Bible of 1611 states that 'He that is wounded in the stones, or hath his privy member cut off, shall not enter into the congregation of the LORD' (Deuteronomy 23:1). The social exclusion that followed as a result of castration was possibly one of the reasons why the character of the castrated man fascinated early modern theatre-goers: the noun *eunuch(s)* appears at least 240 times in at least seventy-eight different English plays written between 1580 and the closing of the theatres in 1642; early modern synonyms for the verb *castrate* appear more than 150 times in the plays of those decades.[48] There are actual eunuchs as speaking characters in twenty-five dramatic texts written between 1600 and 1640.[49] Eunuchs abound on the stage, because like so many of the great Renaissance tragedies and tragi-comedies, they come to communicate a loss of self and social position.

The consequences of castration are thus conceptualized primarily in social

[46] See Gail Kern Paster's discussion of Sir Andrew Aguecheek as a man who suffers from a character-defining deficiency of blood and spirit in 'Nervous Tension', in *The Body in Parts: Fantasies of Corporeality in Early Modern Europe*, ed. David Hillman and Carla Mazzio (New York and London: Routledge, 1997), pp. 107–25.

[47] Thomas Wright, *The Passions of the Mind in General*, 2nd edn (London: Valentine Simmes, 1604), F6.

[48] Taylor, *Castration*, p. 30.

[49] Ibid.

psycho-chemical terms. The actual surgical 'cut' is neither commonly described in medical texts nor directly portrayed on the early modern stage. Shakespeare never uses the words 'castrate', 'castration', 'emasculation', or 'evirate' in his texts, although 'geld' and its derivatives appear thirteen times.[50] The only known early modern play that sports an explicit 'castration plot' is John Middleton's *A Game at Chess* (1624). Nevertheless, the threat of dismemberment and bodily mutilation with more or less direct references to castration is not uncommon in Shakespearean drama. There is a reference to literal castration in Westmorland's speech to King Henry in Shakespeare's *I Henry IV*, in which he relates the barbarous actions of the Welsh women who do unspeakable things to the corpses of dead Englishmen. As Eska notes, Shakespeare immortalizes the lie found in his source, Raphael Holinshed's *Chronicles* (since there is no historical evidence for this),[51] but it reveals a profound concern with castration and emasculation within early modern society, one that was equally prevalent in medieval society before it. The most famous Shakespearean castration episode is possibly Shylock the Jew's demand of 'a pound of flesh' off Antonio's body in retribution for Antonio's failure to comply with the terms of their 'bond' in *The Merchant of Venice.* As Suzanna Penuel argues in 'Castrating the Creditor in *The Merchant of Venice*' this could possibly echo medieval disciplinary castration in response to adultery, punning on the multiple meanings of the word 'bond',[52] but the episode can also be seen as a form of mercenary–marital fulfilment. No scenes in the play are portrayed in as meaningful, yet gruesomely precise, terms as when Shylock prepares to consummate his and Antonio's legal agreement in front of the duke and all the 'Magnificoes' of Venice.

Although Shylock's demand for flesh is portrayed in grisly terms, it is strikingly similar to the other mercenary marriage transactions in the play. Indeed, Antonio originally agrees to Shylock's bond so that his beloved Bassanio may have the funds to procure himself a rich heiress. Shylock becomes the character who makes these hidden concerns of the play visible. He verbalizes the juxtaposition of the mercenary and the marital: when his daughter elopes his pain is expressed through interchangeable exclamations of 'My daughter! O my ducats! O my daughter! Fled with a Christian! O my Christian ducats! Justice! the law! my ducats, and my daughter!' (2.3.15–17). The threat of Shylock's cut in the climactic court scene becomes the final testimony of the inhumanity of

50 Ibid., p. 12.

51 Eska, '"Imbrued in their owne bloud"', p. 150.

52 Suzanna Penuel, 'Castrating the Creditor in *The Merchant of Venice*', in *Studies in English Literature, 1500–1900* 44. 2 (2004): 255–75. As Larissa Tracy points out in *Torture and Brutality in Medieval Literature* (Cambridge: D. S. Brewer, 2012), ch. 5, castration was rarely, if ever actually, a punishment for adultery, however. There are only a couple references to it, and those may be anecdotal rather than historical. See also Leech, 'The Castrating of the Shrew' in this volume, pp. 210–28.

arranged marriage. The fear and horror that the possibility of castration produces is so powerful that it comes to function as a useful metaphor for other social injustices.

The carnality of the simultaneously public and personal proceedings in the court scene of *The Merchant of Venice* is reminiscent of the official marriage act, as well as the following consummation. It also evokes emerging medical discourses and the public operating theatres in early modern London. Castration, like many early modern surgical procedures, was a bloody affair. Surgery itself was a relatively new specialization which was only properly reconceived as a profession through the merger of the Surgeons' Guild and the Barbers' Company under the leadership of the English physician Thomas Vicary in 1540. This official act ensured that only barber surgeons were allowed to perform surgical procedures and that they were educated sufficiently in the art.[53] It also gave rise to the first sets of official praxes in relation to medical incision. The translation of Paré's *Workes* recommends that the patient be bound and that:

> it is fit to have four strong men at hand; that is, two to hold his arms, and other two who may so firmly and straightly hold the knee with one hand, and the foot with the other, that hee may neither move his lims, nor stir his buttocks, but bee forced to keep in the same posture with his whole bodie.[54]

Medical castrations were performed with the help of tools as varied as a hot gridiron, bone and steel scalpels[55] or a pair of scissors. If a mere removal of the patient's testicles was required, the procedure was relatively simple and had been perfected through centuries of farmyard geldings throughout Europe. If, on the other hand, a full penis had to be removed, the procedure was both complicated and dangerous. The English physician Richard Wiseman describes a number of more and less successful ventures in his *Eight Chirurgical Treatises* (1696) all of which present equally gruesome scenarios:

> A young fellow came to me with the Prepuce inflamed, and a mortification on the upper part of it, which had spread the compass of a broad Shilling on that part of the Glans. In scarifying the Eschar I found it had penetrated through: upon which consideration I made the separation of the Prepuce with a pair of Scissors cutting it off round.[56]

[53] Jonathan Sawday, *The Body Emblazoned: Dissection and the Human Body in Renaissance Culture* (New York and London: Routledge, 1995), p. 22.

[54] Paré, *The Workes*, p. 427.

[55] Ambroise Paré includes pictures of his various invented surgical instruments in the section on the 'Treatment of Wounds' in his *Workes*, including elaborate bone and steel scalpels.

[56] Richard Wiseman, *Eight Chirurgical Treatises on these following heads, viz. I. Of tumours. II. Of ulcers. III. Of diseases of the anus. IV. Of the kings-evil. V. Of wounds. VI. Of gun-shot wounds. VII. Of fractures and luxations. VIII. Of the lues venerea* (London: Benj. Took and Luke Meredith, 1696), p. 506. http://eebo.chadwyck.com.ezproxy.webfeat.lib.ed.ac.uk/search/full_rec?SOURCE=pgimages.cfg?ACTION=By10§ID=V137217.

Wiseman adds that 'In making the extirpation of the Prepuce I had permitted him to bleed freely',[57] drawing attention to the common connection made between venery, venereal disease, and blood at the time. As Robert Burton states, excessive venery and appetites were thought to be connected to overly heated and 'corrupted' blood,[58] and venereal disease becomes an embodied manifestation of this.

An important, although often ignored, detail about the means by which the legal conflict in Shakespeare's *The Merchant of Venice* is resolved, is that Portia releases Antonio from his bond to the bloodthirsty Shylock by pointing out the difference between a demand for flesh and a spilling of blood:

> This bond doth give thee here no jot of blood;
> The words expressly are 'a pound of flesh':
> Take then thy bond, take thou thy pound of flesh;
> But, in the cutting it, if thou dost shed
> One drop of Christian blood, thy lands and goods
> Are, by the laws of Venice, confiscate
> Unto the state of Venice.
>
> (4.1.297–303)

A pound of flesh is a lifeless substance – an object that can be requested in exchange for a sum of money, whereas blood is something more transient and simultaneously more fundamental to the subject. The loss of flesh results in the loss of a part of Antonio, but the spilling of the blood that runs through this flesh means that a substantial part of Antonio's character and being (and in this instance most probably his life, considering that Shylock wants to claim the flesh closest to Antonio's heart) is forfeit. Even Shylock himself acknowledges that Antonio is generally considered 'a good man' (1.3.12), and thus such a thing must not be allowed to happen. The piece of flesh that is removed from Wiseman's patient, on the other hand, is an emblem of his unrestrained lifestyle, and in order to cure such a condition it is appropriate that some of the blood of the character was discharged with the excised penis.

Early modern anatomists (who based many of their assumptions on medieval medical treatises) were not entirely agreed on the precise connection between blood, life, and sex, but most of them subscribed to the idea that there was a definite connection. An overactive sex drive and hotheadedness were commonly explained through excess of blood and heat flowing through the body. The racing pulse that is often associated with physical attraction and the

[57] Ibid.

[58] Robert Burton, *The Anatomy of Melancholy: What it is, vvith all the kindes, cavses, symptomes, prognosticks, and seuerall cvres of it: in three maine partitions, with their seuerall sections, members, and subsections: philosophically, medicinally, historically opened and cut up* (Oxford: J. Lichfield & J. Short, 1624), p. 248.

simultaneous flow of seminal fluids and blood to the penis during coitus suggest that the two are not unrelated. The English physician Helkiah Crooke goes as far as to suggest that blood turns into semen if the conditions are right and sufficient amount of heat is produced.[59] This theory should be contextualized by Crooke's specific conception of the flows of energy or 'spirits' in the body: 'Vnder the name of vessels we vnderstand three kinds, Veines, Arteries and Sinewes, because out of these as out of riuers, doe flow into all the parts of the body Blood, Heate, Spirits, Life, Motion and Sense.'[60] Blood, like semen, not merely enables life – blood *is* a stream of sensuality, spirituality, and life. As Gail Kern Paster argues in her essay 'Nervous Tension', blood thus becomes one of the means through which early modern conceptions of the body and the soul are united: '"Blood" becomes related integrally to "sense", and blood vessels become, in effect, sites of production and dissemination for the lower reaches of somatic consciousness.'[61] Blood is thus not merely integral to life: blood *is* life, energy, or life spirit. Whereas the body in general is a material vessel, detachable from the more eternal soul, blood for Crooke becomes almost indistinguishable from and incorporates this soul.

According to Crooke, who wrote his influential *Microkosmographia* in 1615, more than ten years before William Harvey lay the foundation for a modern conception of the circulation of the blood in 1628, the primary function of blood is to transport energy or spirit to the otherwise dull and lifeless flesh: 'Hauing wrought our way through the darke and shady groue of the Muscels [...] the vessels like so many brookes do water and refresh this pleasant Paradise or model of heauen and earth; I mean the body of man.'[62] Spirits, on the other hand, 'are the Instruments of the Soul'[63] in its tripartite incarnations; 'Naturall, Vitall and Animall',[64] and as such their properties completely condition the character of both body and mind. A pound of Antonio's flesh in *The Merchant of Venice* is of no particular consequence without its concomitant blood. It is what makes flesh alive, and the removal of blood results in the loss of a section of the soul. Similarly, castration is primarily horrific because of the concurrent letting of genital blood and its hotter and more spirited form – the sperm.[65] This carries the part of the soul in which masculine heat is generated and, as

59 Helkiah Crooke, *Mikrokosmographia: A description of the body of man; together with the controversies and figures thereto belonging*, 2nd edn (London: Th. Cotes & R. Young, 1631). Crooke also argues that breast milk is a particularly hot and 'spirited' incarnation of blood. Paré reversely argues that menstrual blood is a 'corruption of the seede' (*The Workes*, p. 939).

60 Crooke, *Mikrokosmographia*, p. 825.

61 Paster, 'Nervous Tension', p. 113.

62 Crooke, *Mikrokosmographia*, p. 825.

63 Ibid., p. 58.

64 Ibid., p. 824.

65 Ibid., p. 58.

Bulwer establishes, the loss of such spirits results in the ultimate loss of masculinity. A castrated man, whether he has undergone penile or testicular castration, can thus never truly be a man because the seat of masculinity, his manly soul, is mutilated with the removal of the male genitalia.

Crooke's theories rely on what to some extent can be considered a fully embodied circulation of soul and spirits. Such a corporeal philosophy should inspire a medical methodology the very opposite of what emerged in early modern Europe. As David Hillman and Carla Mazzio acknowledge in their introduction to *The Body in Parts*, not merely was early modern dissection an act of cutting, but the anatomy compendia that were produced in response to this practice are complicated exercises of division.[66] As Thomas Vicary puts it, anatomy is an art 'touching a part of every member particularly'[67] and as Burton acknowledges in *The Anatomy of Melancholy*, anatomy is a space where concepts are divided into 'Sections, Members, and Subsections – Philosophically, Medicinally, Historically opened and cut up'.[68] In *Staging Anatomies* Hillary Nunn argues that there are significant connections between the emerging public interest in medical dissection and the increase of threatened or actual dismemberment portrayed on the Jacobean playhouse stage.[69] Shakespeare's *Titus Andronicus* is possibly one of the best examples of this. It builds a full catalogue of dismembered body parts and corporeal cuts.

Titus Andronicus is without doubt Shakespeare's most graphically violent play, featuring on-stage rape and repeated bodily mutilation. As such, it embodies the early modern fear of corporeal division; that bodily mutilation which would, by removing any part of the body, disarrange the entire humorous balance. There are two key scenes in particular that demonstrate this embodied mutiny: the aftermath of Lavinia's mutilation and rape (act 2, scene 3), and the cutting off of Titus's hand (act 3, scene 1). While the first act of cutting (that of Lavinia's mutilation and rape) is not depicted on stage, its results are given in the stage directions: '*Enter the empress' sons, with* LAVINIA, *her hands cut off, and her tongue cut out, and ravish'd*' (2.4).[70] Chiron and Demetrius, the empress's sons who have just mutilated Lavinia, exit the stage

66 David Hillman and Carla Mazzio, eds., 'Introduction' in *The Body in Parts: Fantasies of Corporeality in Early Modern Europe* (New York and London: Routledge, 1997), pp. xi–xxix at pp. xiv–xv.

67 Thomas Vicary, *The English-man's Treasvre. With the true anatomie of mans body: compiled by Mr. Thomas Vicary* (London: 1633), p. 1.

68 Burton, *The Anatomy of Melancholy*, p. 1.

69 This was by no means the first time an interest in dissection arose in Europe since ancient times. As Carolyn Walker Bynum shows in her book *Fragmentation and Redemption: Essays on Gender and the Human Body in Mediaeval Religion* (Cambridge, MA: MIT Press, 1991) there was an increased interest in dissection in the thirteenth century, which made church officials highly uncomfortable.

70 William Shakespeare, *Titus Andronicus*, ed. J.C. Maxwell (London: Methuen, 1985), 2.4.

after taunting their victim. Marcus enters, noticing his niece's state, and in a forty-seven-line monologue laments Lavinia's bleeding wounds and lost beauty:

> Alas, a crimson river of warm blood,
> Like to a bubbling fountain stirr'd with wind,
> Doth rise and fall between thy rosed lips,
> Coming and going with thy honey breath.
> …
> Ah, now thou turns't away thy face for shame,
> And, notwithstanding all this loss of blood,
> As from conduit with three issuing spouts,
> Yet do thy cheeks look red as Titan's face
> Blushing to be encount'red with a cloud.
> (2.4.22–32)

For Pascale Aebischer, Marcus's imagery of 'bubbling' blood and 'conduit' images, are 'attempts to render her wounds "speakable" through metaphoric distancing'.[71] But as Mariangela Tempera points out, Marcus's monologue carries Galenic allusions. Shakespeare in this soliloquy pays homage to early modern beliefs about the 'one-directional flow of blood through veins and arteries by referring to the "river" and the "conduit" of Lavinia's blood'.[72] The colourful descriptions of Lavina's mutilation are indeed more reminiscent of a fountain of life than a fountain of death. The warmth of the 'bubbling' and 'stirr'd' blood that 'rise[s] and fall[s]' expressly speaks of Lavinia's vitality; what Crooke would term her heat and spirit.

Indeed, there are recurring references throughout the play to Galenic notions of heat and humours; depicting heat/cold, and blood – and the mutinous role that chopping and cutting, dividing bodies, has in these unsettlements. Demetrius shows a dangerous imbalance in heat and humours, needing to 'find the stream / To cool this heat, a charm to calm these fits' (2.1.133–4). Together with his brother, Demetrius rapes Lavinia in order to 'cool' his 'heat'. When Lavinia has been mutilated, Titus wants to 'chop off my hands too / … Now all the service I require of them / Is that the one will help to cut the other' (3.1.72–9). He goes on later, lamenting and not knowing what to do: 'Or shall we cut away our hands like thine? / Or shall we bite our tongues, and in dumb shows / Pass the remainder of our hateful days?' (3.1.130–2). There is even more hand-chopping when Titus, Lucius, and Marcus debate who will have the honour of offering their cut hand in exchange for Titus's two captured sons (3.1.160–87).

71 Pascale Aebischer, *Shakespeare's Violated Bodies: Stage and Screen Performance* (Cambridge: Cambridge University Press, 2004), p. 28.

72 Mariangela Tempera, '*Titus Andronicus*: Staging the Mutilated Body', in *Questioning Bodies in Shakespeare's Rome*, ed. Maria del Sapio Garbero, Nancy Isenberg, and Maddalena Pennacchia (Goettingen: V&R Unipress, 2010), 109–19 at p. 111.

The sight of the sons' chopped heads, Titus's cut-off hand (returned with the heads), and the mangled Lavinia, strikes Lucius 'pale and bloodless' and Marcus himself 'Even like a stony image, cold and numb' (3.1.257–8). The purely corporeal cutting and unbalancing of characters leave Lucius and Marcus unbalanced too – bloodless, without heat. Titus has now seemingly gone mad with sorrow, for which his friends are asked to 'attend him carefully, / And feed his humour kindly as we may, / Till time beget some careful remedy' (4.3.28–30). The use of 'humour' here carries a double significance: imbalanced temper and imbalanced bodily humours. Tamora, mother of the two rapists, says to herself: 'But, Titus, I have touch'd thee to the quick; / Thy life-blood [is] out' (4.4.36–7). She tells her sons, regarding Titus's supposed madness, to uphold and maintain in their speeches whatever she forges 'to feed his brain-sick humours' (5.2.70–2).

Throughout *Titus Andronicus*, the rivers of blood flow freely and almost uncontrollably. The play portrays a leaky or haemophiliac body politic, the stability and continence of which can only be restored through a final act of bloodletting. With the help of Lavinia, Titus bleeds Tamora's sons to death, before making pies of them: 'Hark, wretches, how I mean to martyr you. / This one hand yet is left to cut your throats, / Whiles that Lavinia 'tween her stumps doth hold / The basin that receives your guilty blood' (5.2.180–3). Lavinia, in a final act of revenge, with her stumped arms collects the blood, the loss of which finally incapacitates the two rapist brothers. Once the over-heated lustful and 'guilty' blood of the state has been discharged, and the 'corrupted' substances have been removed, Lucius enters as a physician of the state, 'To heal Rome's harms, and wipe away her woe' (5.3.148), offering a new beginning and a virtuous future. This is the desired end of a successful surgical intervention: purification through evacuation.

In Shakespeare's *Titus Andronicus*, corporeal cuts thus disable and destroy the harmony of the state, finally escalating in a cathartic bleeding out of over-active sexual spirits.[73] In *Antony and Cleopatra*, a final balance of the state is also restored through a slowly draining sword cut. Mark Antony comes to stand for the image of the emasculated man not merely in Shakespearean drama, but in Western cultural history in general. Cleopatra provides him excess of food, drink, and sensual pleasures, 'tie[ing] up the libertine in a field of feasts' (2.1.23) and 'makes hungry where most she satisfies' (2.2.242–3), and when he is powerlessly inebriated she literally robs him of his masculine attire: 'Ere the ninth hour I drunk him to his bed; / Then put my tires and mantles on him, whilst / I bore his sword Philippan' (2.5.21–3). The relationship is the onset of a thoroughly disabling love-sickness which exclusively 'with a wound … must be cured' (4.14.79). Antony and Cleopatra's 'heated blood' and 'monstrous feasts'

[73] See Tracy, *Torture and Brutality*, ch. 6.

are an infection on the Roman state; 'launch[ing] Diseases in our bodies' (5.1.36–7) and although Antony's loyal followers mourn the 'gap in nature' (2.2.223) that his death causes, for 'never shall there be such a man' (4.14.83), he is a part the Roman public corpus that needs to be removed through a 'vent of blood' (5.2.344).

Similarly, the surgical castrations that took place in early modern London were considered necessary evils, the results of immoderate living and humorous corruption, which the barber surgeon's scalpel and the flow of blood and heated spirits to an extent could cure. As Wiseman and Paré both point out, castration is never a desirable solution to venereal disease, however.[74] Regardless of whether a man had to undergo a penile or a testicular castration, neither his position in society nor his soul would remain the same. He would lose his masculine forcefulness as well as his humorous balance. Castration may thus alleviate an acutely serious condition (and calm the blood for the moment), but it does not necessarily have an effect on the original cause of the problem: the carnal lusts. If anything, the loss of masculine ability to control the appetites would have made the situation worse. As the eunuch Mardian in *Antony and Cleopatra* sorrowfully points out, his condition only disables him from partaking in venery 'in deed': 'for I can do nothing / But what is honest to be done; / Yet have I fierce affections, and think / What Venus did with Mars' (1.2.17–18). The art of cutting a virtuous balance is not something that can be surgically introduced to a body. It has to be taught spiritually.

In the medieval and early modern imaginations castration is a prevalent concern, especially in the construction of masculinity. The eunuchs of antiquity, noted for their beauty and desirability, emerge as figures on the early modern stage, giving voice to anxieties of maleness and femaleness that evolved continuously over the course of more than one thousand years. Shaped in some sense by Abelard's rehearsal of his own calamitous wounding in the *Historia calamitatum*, medieval ideas of castration carry over into the early modern period and into modern discourse. From late antiquity, when eunuchs could achieve great power and prominence, to the fraught relationship between male genitalia and Christian purity in early Church discourse, to the legal proscriptions for and prohibitions against castration and the literary constructions of masculine identity, Western society has struggled to define itself in relation to the male body in all its permutations and all its paradoxes. The history of castration and of how societies dealt with its physical ramifications is a history of calamities that tells a story of loss, of love, of law, of sacrifice, of punishment, of wounding, and of healing. This is (perhaps) where the importance of early modern drama becomes most expressly apparent. Although Mardian and the other twenty-four eunuchs

[74] Wiseman, *Eight Chirurgical Treatises*, p. 505; Paré, *The Workes*, p. 421.

who express themselves on the early modern stage may never develop into balanced and virtuous men themselves, their examples furnish the theatre-going public with a means to do so. As Aristotle decrees in his *Poetics*, drama – and tragedy in particular – has the ability to cathartically restore the mental balance of its audience.[75] Plays such as *Titus Andronicus* and *Antony and Cleopatra* may not present very happy outcomes for their protagonists, but they have the ability to cleanse the many perturbed spirits that suffer with them. The literal flows of blood on stage result in a figurative release of spirits among the audience. The various embodiments of fear and unease evoked by references to castration and castrated men on the early modern stage may thus be more than a mere precautionary example. They are a figurative cure.

75 Aristotle, *Poetics*, in *Rhetorics and Poetics of Aristotle*, ed. Friedrich Solmsen (New York: Random House, 1954).

Select Bibliography

Unpublished Manuscript Sources

Cambridge, Corpus Christi College MS 454
Bodorgan MS, the property of Sir George Meyrick
British Library, MS Cotton Cleopatra A.XIV
British Library, MS Cotton Cleopatra BV
British Library, MS Harleian 4353
National Library of Wales, MS Peniarth 37
National Library of Wales, MS Peniarth 259

Printed Primary Sources

Abelard, Peter. *Historia calamitatum*, ed. Jacques Monfrin. Paris: Vrin, 1962. English translation: *The Story of Abelard's Adversities*, trans. J. T. Muckle. Toronto: Pontifical Institute of Mediaeval Studies, 1964.

Adams, Francis, ed. *The Seven Books of Paulus Aegineta*, vol. 2. London: The Sydenham Society, 1846.

Adomnán, *Vita Sancti Columbae*, in *Adomnán's Life of Columba*, ed. and trans. Alan Orr Anderson and Marjorie Ogilvie Anderson. 2nd edn. Oxford: Oxford University Press, 1991.

Aesop. *The Complete Fables*, trans. Olivia and Robert Temple. London: Penguin, 1998.

Alanus de Insulis. *Liber de planctu naturae*. In *Patrologia Latina*, ed. Jacques-Paul Migne. Paris: Garnier, 1844–92: 210; col. 457.

Alan of Lille. *Plaint of Nature*, trans. James J. Sheridan. Toronto: Pontifical Institute of Medieval Studies, 1970.

al Djahiz, *A Clear Look*, trans. Michael McCormick. In *Origins of the European Economy: Communications and Commerce AD 300–900*. Cambridge: Cambridge University Press, 2001, p. 761.

Ambrose. *Expositio Evangelii Secundum Lucam Libri X, 161*. In *Patrologia Latina*, ed. Jacques-Paul Migne. Paris: Garnier, 1844–55 Vol. 15: 1527–1850.

Ancient Laws of Ireland, ed. and trans. W. N. Hancock *et al.* 6 vols. Dublin: A Thom, 1865–1901.

d'Ancillon, Charles. *Eunuchism Display'd. Describing All the Different Sorts of Eunuchs;. Written by a Person of Honour*, trans. Robert Samber. London: E. Curll, 1718.

d'Anghiera, Pietro Martyr. *De orbe novo: Petri Martyris Anglerii decades octo, diligenti temporum observatione et utilissimis annotationibus illustratae, suoque nitori restitutae, labore et industria*, ed. Richard Hakluyt. Paris: G. Auvray, 1587.

Anglo-Saxon Laws of Alfred, trans. Oliver J. Thatcher. The Library of Original Sources 4: The Early Medieval World. Milwaukee: University Research Extension Co., 1901, pp. 211–39.

Annála as Breifne, ed. Éamonn De hÓir. *Breifne* 4.13 (1970): 59–86.

Annála Connacht. The Annals of Connacht (AD 1224–1544), ed and trans. A. Martin Freeman. Dublin: Dublin Institute for Advanced Studies, 1996.

Annala Uladh. The Annals of Ulster, otherwise Annala Senait, Annals of Senait; A Chronicle of Irish Affairs from AD 431 to AD 1540, ed and trans. W. M. Hennessy and B. MacCarthy. Dublin: A. Thom, 1887–1901.

Annales Cambriae, ed. John Williams ab Ithel. Rolls Series 20. London: Longman, Green, Longman, and Roberts, 1860.

'Annales Ricardi Secundi et Henrici Quarti'. In *Johannis de Trokelowe et Anon Chronica et Annales*, ed. H. T. Riley. Rolls Series. London: Longmans, Green, Reader, and Dyer, 1866.

The Annals of Clonmacnoise, being Annals of Ireland from the earliest period to AD 1408 translated into English AD 1627 by Conell Mageoghagan, ed. Denis Murphy. Dublin: Royal Society of Antiquaries of Ireland, 1896, repr. Felinfach, 1993.

Annals of the Four Masters, ed. and trans. John O'Donovan. Dublin: Hodges, Smith, and Co., 1854.

The Annals of Inisfallen, ed. and trans. Seán Mac Airt. Dublin: Dublin Institute for Advanced Studies, 1988.

The Annals of Loch Cé, ed. and trans. William M. Hennessy. London: Longman and Co., 1871.

The Annals of Tigernach, ed. and trans. Whitley Stokes. Felinfach: Llanerch Publishers, reprint 1993.

The Annals of Ulster (to AD 1131), ed. and trans. Seán Mac Airt and Gearóid Mac Niocaill. Dublin: Dublin Institute for Advanced Studies, 1983.

The Arabian Nights: Tales of 1,001 Nights, trans. Malcom C. Lyons. 3 vols. New York: Penguin, 2010.

Aristotle. 'On the Generation of Animals', trans. Arthur Platt in *Great Books of the Western World*, vol. 8: *Aristotle II*, 2nd edn, ed. Mortimer J. Adler. Chicago: Encyclopaedia Britannica, 1990.

———. *The History of Animals*, book 7 part 1, trans. D'Arcy Wentworth Thompson. Online at http://classics.mit.edu/Aristotle/history_anim.8.viii.html, accessed May 20, 2012.

Ashburner, Walter, ed. 'The Farmer's Law (Continued)'. *Journal of Hellenic Studies* 32 (1912): 68–95.

Augustine of Hippo. *Against Julian*, trans. Matthew A. Schumacher. Washington DC: Catholic University of America Press, 1957.

———. 'De peccatorum meritis et remissione 1.9.10'. In *Patrologia Latina*, ed. Jacques-Paul Migne. Paris: Garnier, 1844–92 (1865): 44: 115.

———. *The City of God*, vol. 2, trans. Marcus Dods. Edinburgh: T&T Clarke, 1888.

Barney, S. A., ed. *The Etymologies of Isidore of Seville*. Cambridge University Press, 2006.

Barsby, John, ed. *Terence*, vol. 1. Cambridge, MA: Harvard University Press, 2001.

Baumgartner, Emmanuelle, ed. *Le Roman de Tristan en Prose*, vol. 6: *Du séjour des amants à la Joyeuse Garde jusquaux premières aventures de la 'Queste du Graal'*. Geneva: Droz, 1993.

Bernard. 'Itinerarium', ed. Titus Tobler and August Molinier. *Itinera hierosolymitana et descriptiones terrae sanctae bellis sacris anteriora* 1.2 (Geneva, 1880): 311.

Bianciotto, Gabriel, trans. *Bestiaires du Moyen Âge*. Paris: Stock, 1980, 1992.

Bird, H. W., ed. *Aurelius Victor:* De Caesaribus. Liverpool: Liverpool University Press, 1994.

Bostock, John, and H. T. Tiley, trans. *The Natural History of Pliny*. London: George Bell & Sons, 1890.

de Bracton, Henry. *De legibus et consuetudinibus Angliæ*, ed. George E. Woodbine. New Haven, CT: Yale University Press, 1915–42.

———. *On the Laws and Customs of England*, trans. Samuel E. Thorne. Cambridge, MA: Harvard University Press, 1968.

Brakke, D., ed. *Pseudo-Athanasius on Virginity*, vol. 2. Corpus Scriptorum Christianorum Orientalium. Louvain: Peeters, 2002.

Brenhinedd y Saesson, ed. and trans. Thomas Jones. Cardiff: University of Wales Press, 1971.

Bretha Crólige, ed. D. A. Binchy. *Ériu* 12 (1934–1938): 1–77.

Brothers, A. J., ed. *Terence,* The Eunuch. Warminster: Aris & Philips Ltd, 2000.

Browne, Thomas Sir. *Pseudodoxia epidemica: or, enquiries into very many received tenents, and commonly presumed truths*. London: T. H[arper] for Edward Dod, 1646.

Brut y Tywysogyon: Peniarth MS. 20, ed. Thomas Jones. Cardiff: University of Wales Press, 1941.

Brut y Tywysogyon: Peniarth MS. 20, trans. Thomas Jones. Cardiff: University of Wales Press, 1952.

Brut y Tywysogyon: Red Book of Hergest Version, ed. and trans. Thomas Jones. Cardiff: University of Wales Press, 1955.

Bulwer, John. *Anthropometamorphosis: Man transform'd; or, The artificiall changling historically presented, in the mad and cruell gallantry, foolish bravery, ridiculous beauty, filthy finenesse, and loathsome loveliness of most nations, fashioning and altering their bodies from the mould intended by natvre*. London: 1653.

Buma, Wybren Jan and Wilhelm Ebel, eds. *Das Fivelgoer Recht*, Altfriesische Rechtsquellen 5. Göttingen: Vandenhoeck & Ruprecht, 1972.

——. *Das Hunsigoer Recht*. Altfriesische Rechtsquellen 4. Göttingen: Vandenhoeck & Ruprecht, 1967.

——. *Das Emsiger Recht*. Altfriesische Rechtsquellen 3. Göttingen: Vandenhoeck & Ruprecht, 1965.

Buma, Wybren Jan and Wilhelm Ebel, with Martina Tragter-Schubert, eds. *Westerlauwerssches Recht I. Jus municipale Frisonum*, 2 vols. Altfriesische Rechtsquellen 6/1–2. Göttingen: Vandenhoeck & Ruprecht, 1977.

Burton, Robert. *The Anatomy of Melancholy: What it is, vvith all the kindes, cavses, symptomes, prognosticks, and seuerall cvres of it: in three maine partitions, with their seuerall sections, members, and subsections: philosophically, medicinally, historically opened and cut up*. Oxford: J. Lichfield & J. Short, 1624.

Butler, H. E., ed. *The* Institutio Oratoria *of Quintilian*. vol. 2. Cambridge MA and London: Harvard University Press and Heinemann, 1960.

Cáin Lánamna, ed. and trans. Charlene M. Eska. In *Medieval Law and Its Practice*, Series 5. Leiden: Brill, 2010.

'Canones Hibernensis IV'. In *The Irish Penitentials*, ed. and trans. Ludwig Bieler. Scriptores Latini Hiberniae 5. Dublin: Dublin Institute for Advanced Studies, 1975, pp. 170–171.

Cary, Ernest, ed. *Dio's* Roman History. vol. 8. London and Cambridge MA: Heinemann and Harvard University Press, 1925.

Cary, Henry, trans. *The Histories of Herodotus*. New York: D. Appleton, 1904.

Cassell's Latin Dictionary. New York: Macmillan, 1959, 1962, 1964, 1966, 1968.

Cassian, John. *The Conferences*, ed. B. Ramsey. Mahwah, NJ: Paulist Press, 1997.

Champlin, Edward, ed. *Nero*. Cambridge, MA: The Belknap Press of Harvard University Press, 2003.

Chaucer, Geoffrey. *The Riverside Chaucer*. 3rd edn, ed. Larry D. Benson. Boston: Houghton Mifflin, 1987.

Child, Francis James, ed. *The English and Scottish Popular Ballads*. New York: Dover Publications, 1965.

Chrétien de Troyes. *Le conte du Graal (Perceval)*, ed. Félix Lecoy. 2 vols. Paris: Champion, 1975.

Chronica de Mailros, ed. Joseph Stevenson. Edinburgh: Bannatyne Club, 1835.

Chronicum Scottorum: A chronicle of Irish affairs from the earliest times to AD 1135, with a supplement containing the events from 1141–1150, ed. and trans. William M. Hennessy. Rolls Series 46. London: Her Majesty's Stationery Office, 1866.

Clark, Willene B., ed. *A Medieval Book of Beasts: The Second-Family Bestiary. Commentary, Art, Text and Translation*. Woodbridge: Boydell Press, 2006.

Clement of Alexandria. *Stomata*. In *The Ante-Nicene Fathers: Fathers of the Second Century – Hermas, Tatian, Theophilus, Athenagoras, Clement of Alexandria*, vol. 2:

The Writings of the Fathers Down to AD *325*, ed. Alexander Roberts, James Donaldson, and A. Cleveland Coxe. Buffalo: Christian Literature Company, 1885, pp. 299–367.

Cogadh Gaedhel re Gallaib, ed. and trans. James H. Todd. Rolls Series 48. London: Her Majesty's Stationery Office, 1867.

Cohoon, J. W., ed. *Dio Chrysostom*. vol. 2. London and Cambridge, MA: Heinemann and Harvard University Press, 1939.

Cornish, F. W., ed. *Catullus*. London and Cambridge, MA: Heinemann and Harvard University Press, 1962.

Corpus Iuris Hibernici, ed. D. A. Binchy. 6 vols. Dublin: Dublin Institute for Advanced Studies, 1979.

Críth Gablach, ed. D. A. Binchy. Medieval and Modern Irish Series 11. Dublin: Stationery Office, 1941.

Crooke, Helkiah. *Mikrokosmographia: A description of the body of man; together with the controversies and figures thereto belonging*. 1615. 2nd edn. London: Th. Cotes & R. Young, 1631.

Curley, Michael J., trans. *Physiologus*. Chicago: University of Chicago Press, 1979; 2009.

La dame escolliee. In *Nouveau recueil complet des fabliaux*, ed. Willem Noomen and Nico van den Boogaard. 10 vols. Assen: Van Gorcum, 1983–98: 8: 1–125.

Douglas, David C. and George W. Greenway, eds. *English Historical Documents 1042–1189*. 2nd edn. London: Eyre & Spottiswoode, 1968.

Domesday Book: A Complete Translation, ed. and trans. Ann Williams and G. H. Martin. London: Penguin, 2002.

Dumville, David N., ed. *Annales Cambriae,* AD *682–954: Texts A–C in Parallel*. Basic Texts for Brittonic History 1. Cambridge: Department of Anglo-Saxon, Norse and Celtic, 2002.

Earle, John, ed. *Two of the Saxon Chronicles Parallel*. Oxford: Clarendon Press, 1865.

The Early South-English Legendary or Lives of Saints, MS Laud 108 in the Bodleian Library, ed. Carl Horstmann. EETS, os 87. Oxford: Oxford University Press, 1887; rpt 2000.

Eckhardt, Karl August and Albrecht Eckhardt, eds. *Lex Frisionum*, Monumenta Germaniae Historica, Fontes Iuris Germanici Antiqui 12. Hanover: Hahn, 1982.

Edwards, Catherine, ed. *Suetonius,* Lives of the Caesars. Oxford: Oxford University Press, 2000.

Emanuel, Hywel D., ed. *The Latin Texts of the Welsh Laws*. Cardiff: University of Wales Press, 1967.

Encyclopedia of Queer Myth, Symbol and Spirit, ed. Randy P. Luncunas Conner, David Hatfield Sparks, and Mariya Sparks. London and New York: Cassell, 1997.

The Etablissements de Saint Louis: Thirteenth-Century Law Texts from Tours, Orléans, and Paris, trans. F. R. P Akehurst. Philadelphia: University of Pennsylvania Press, 1996.

Eusebius. *The Ecclesiastical History*, trans. J. E. L. Oulton. Loeb Classical Library. Cambridge, MA: Harvard University Press, 1932.

Fletcher, Ian F., trans. *Latin A Redaction of the Law of Hywel*. Pamphlets on Welsh Law. Aberystwyth: Center for Advanced Welsh and Celtic Studies, University of Wales, 1986.

Fragmentary Annals of Ireland, ed. and trans. Joan Newlon Radner. Dublin: Dublin Institute for Advanced Studies, 1978.

Frazer, J. G., ed. *Ovid's* Fasti. London: and Cambridge MA: Heinemann and Harvard University Press, 1967.

Gerbert de Montreuil. *La continuation de Perceval*, ed. Mary Williams. 2 vols. Paris: Champion, 1925.

Die Gesetze der Angelsachsen, ed. and trans. F. Liebermann. Halle: M. Niemeyer, 1898–1912.

Godden, Malcolm and Susan Irvine, eds. *The Old English Boethius: An Edition of the Old English Versions of Boethius's* De consolatione philosophiae, 2 vols. Oxford: Oxford University Press, 2009.

Gratian, *The Treatise on Laws: (Decretum DD. 1–20)*, trans. Augustine Thompson, with *The Ordinary Gloss*, trans. James Gordley, and intro. Katherine Christensen. Washington DC: The Catholic University of America Press, 1993.

Guibert of Nogent. *The Deeds of God through the Franks*, trans. Robert Levine. Woodbridge: Boydell Press, 1997.

Guillaume de Lorris and Jean de Meun. *The Romance of the Rose*, trans. Charles Dahlberg. Hanover, NH: University Press of New England, 1971, 1983.

———. *Le roman de la Rose*, ed. Daniel Poirion. Paris: Garnier-Flammarion, 1974.

———. *The Romance of the Rose*, trans. Frances Horgan. Oxford: Oxford University Press, 1994.

Herodotus. *The Histories of Herodotus*, trans. Henry Cary. New York: D. Appleton, 1904.

Hicks, Éric, and Thérèse Moreau, ed. and trans. *Lettres d'Abélard et Héloïse*. Paris: Librairie Générale Française, 2007.

Hippocrates. *Coan Prenotions. Anatomical and Minor Clinical Writings*. vol. 9, trans. Paul Potter. Loeb Classical Library. Cambridge, MA: Harvard University Press, 2010.

Historia Langobardorum, ed. Ludwig Bethmann and Georg Waitz. Monumenta Germaniae Historica, Scriptores rerum langobardicarum et Italicarum. Hanover: Hahnian, 1878.

Holinshed, Raphael. *The Chronicles of England, Scotland and Ireland.* London: John Harison, George Bishop, Rafe Newberie, Henrie Denham, and Thomas Woodcocke, 1587.

Ibn Buṭlān. 'On Buying Slaves'. In *Islam: From the Prophet Muhammad to the Capture of Constantinople*, vol. 2: *Religion and Society*, ed. and trans. Bernard Lewis. New York: Walker and Company, 1974, pp. 243–51.

'The "Iorwerth" Text', ed. and trans. T. M. Charles-Edwards. In *The Welsh Law of Women*, ed. Dafydd Jenkins and Morfydd E. Owen. Cardiff: University of Wales Press, 1980, pp. 161–179.

Isidore of Seville. 'On Medicine'. In *Isidore of Seville: The Medical Writings*, trans. William D. Sharpe. Philadelphia: American Philosophical Society, 1964.

Jackson, John, ed. *Tacitus*. vol. 3. London and Cambridge, MA: Heinemann and Harvard University Press, 1951.

Jenkins, Dafydd, ed. 'The "Cyfnerth" Text'. In *The Welsh Law of Women*, ed. Dafydd Jenkins and Morfydd E. Owen. Cardiff: University of Wales Press, 1980, pp. 132–45.

Jerome. *Commentarius in Epistolam ad Ephesios*. In *Patrologia Latina*, ed. Jacques-Paul Migne. Paris: Garnier, 1844–92: 26.

Lacy, Norris J., gen. ed. *Lancelot-Grail 3. Lancelot Part I and II*, trans. S. N. Rosenberg and R. L. Krueger. New edn. Cambridge: D. S. Brewer, 2010.

The Law of Hywel Dda: Law Texts from Medieval Wales, ed. and trans. Dafydd Jenkins. Llandysul: Gomer Press, 1986.

The Laws of the Earliest English Kings, ed. and trans. F. L. Attenborough. Cambridge: Cambridge University Press, 1922; rpt Clark, NJ: The Lawbook Exchange, 2006.

Laws of Early Iceland: Grágás, ed. and trans. Andrew Dennis, Peter Foote, and Richard Perkins. Winnipeg: University of Manitoba Press, 1980.

Laxdœla Saga: Halldórs Þættir Snorrasonor Stúfs Þáttr, ed. Einar ól Sveonsson. Íslenzk Fornrit 5. Rekjavik: Hid Islenzka Fornritafelag, 1934.

Laxdœla Saga, trans. Magnus Magnusson and Hermann Pálsson. New York: Penguin, 1995.

Lefevre, Jean, *La Vieille, ou les dernières amours d'Ovide*, ed. Hippolyte Cocheris. Paris: Aubry, 1861. Bibliothèque nationale de France, ms. fr. 881. http://gallica.bnf.fr/ark:/12148/btv1b8449041w.

The Letters of Abelard and Heloise, ed. Betty Radice. London: Penguin Books, 1974.

The Life of Saint George. In *The Early South-English Legendary or Lives of Saints, MS Laud 108 in the Bodleian Library*, ed. Carl Horstmann. EETS, os 87. Oxford: Oxford University Press, 1887; rpt 2000, pp. 294–6.

The Life of Saint James the Great. In *The Early South-English Legendary or Lives of Saints, MS Laud 108 in the Bodleian Library*, ed. Carl Horstmann. EETS, os 87. Oxford: Oxford University Press, 1887; rpt 2000, pp. 33–45.

The Life of Saint Laurence. In *The Early South-English Legendary or Lives of Saints, MS Laud 108 in the Bodleian Library*, ed. Carl Horstmann. EETS, os 87. Oxford: Oxford University Press, 1887; rpt 2000, pp. 340–5.

The Life of Saint Wulfstan. In *The Early South-English Legendary or Lives of Saints, MS Laud 108 in the Bodleian Library*, ed. Carl Horstmann. EETS, os 87. Oxford: Oxford University Press, 1887; rpt 2000, pp. 70–7.

Llawysgrif Pomffred: An Edition and Study of Peniarth MS 259B, ed. and trans. Sara Elin Roberts. Medieval Law and Its Practice Series 10. Leiden: Brill, 2011.

Llyfr Blegywryd, ed. Stephen J. Williams and J. Enoch Powell, 2nd edn. Cardiff: University of Wales Press, 1961.

Lucian. *The Syrian Goddess: Being a Translation of Lucian's 'De Dea Syria': with a Life of Lucian*, trans. Herbert A. Strong. London: Constable, 1913.

Manessier. *The Continuations of the Old French Perceval of Chrétien de Troyes: The Third Continuation*, ed. W. Roach and R. H. Ivy. Philadelphia: University of Pennsylvania Press, 1949.

Mas'udi. *Meadows of Gold: The Abbasids*, trans. Paul Lunde and Caroline Stone. London: Kegan Paul International, 1989.

Merlin: Roman du XIIIe siècle, ed. Alexandre Micha. Geneva: Droz, 1979.

de Meun, Jean. *Roman de la Rose*, trans. Charles Dahlberg. Princeton, NJ: Princeton University Press, 1971.

Miscellaneous Irish Annals (AD 1114–1437), ed. and trans. Séamus Ó hInnse. Dublin: Dublin Institute for Advanced Studies, 1947.

Moore, Frank Gardner, ed. *Livy*. vol. 8. London and Cambridge, MA: Heinemann and Harvard University Press, 1949.

Morini, Luigina. *Bestiari Medievali*. Turin: Giulio Einardi Editore, 1996.

Ní Dhonnchadha, Máirín. 'The Law of Adomnán: A Translation'. In *Adomnán at Birr, AD 697*, ed. Thomas O'Loughlin. Dublin: Four Courts Press, 2001, pp. 53–68.

Nitze, William A. and T. Atkin Jenkinson, eds. *Le haut livre du Graal, Perlesvaus*, vol. 1: *Text, Variants, and Glossary*. Chicago: University of Chicago Press, 1932.

O'Donovan, John, ed. and trans. *The Genealogies, Tribes, and Customs of Hy-Fiachrach: Commonly Called O'Dowda's Country*. Dublin: The Irish Archaeological Society, 1844.

Ovid. *The Art of Love and Other Poems* vol. 2. trans. J. H. Mozley. 2nd edn rev. G. P. Gould. Loeb Classical Library. Cambridge, MA: Harvard University Press, 1979; rprt. 1985.

———. *Metamorphoses* books I–VIII, trans. Franck Justus Miller, rev. G. P. Gould. Loeb Classical Library. Cambridge, MA: Harvard University Press, 1977; rprt. 1984, 1994.

Palladius. *The Lausiac History, 29A*, trans. Robert Meyer. Long Prairie, MN: The Newman Press, 1965.

Paré, Ambroise. *The Workes of that famous chirurgion Ambrose Parey translated out of Latin and compared with the French. by Th: Johnson*. London: Th. Cotes & R. Young, 1634.

Paul of Aegina. *Surgery*, ed. J. L. Heiberg. In *Paulus Aegineta*. 2 vols. Corpus Medicorum Graecorum 9. Leipzig: Teubner, 1921–24.

Paul the Deacon. *History of the Lombards*, trans. William Dudley Foulke. Philadelphia: University of Pennsylvania Press, 1974.

de Pizan, Christine. *The Book of the City of Ladies*, trans. Earl Jeffrey Richards. New York: Persea Books, 1998.
Platnauer, Maurice, ed. *Claudian*. vol. 1. London and Cambridge, MA: Heinemann and Harvard University Press, 1963.
Pliny the Elder. *The Natural History of Pliny*, trans. John Bostock and H. T. Riley. London: George Bell & Sons, 1890.
Potter, Paul, trans. *Hippocrates, Coan Prenotions. Anatomical and Minor Clinical Writings*. vol. 9. Loeb Classical Library. Cambridge, MA: Harvard University Press, 2010.
Procopius. *History of the Wars*, trans. H. B. Dewing. Loeb Classical Library, No. 217. London: Hutchinson, 1928.
——. *The Secret History: with Related Texts*, trans. Anthony Kaldellis. Indianapolis, IN: Hackett Publishing Company, 2010.
The Pseudo-Ovidian Vetula, ed. Dorothy M. Robathan. Amsterdam: Adolf M. Hakkert, 1968.
Pseudo-Ovidius De Vetula*: Untersuchungen und Text*, ed. Paul Klopsch. Leiden: Brill, 1967.
Quintus Curtius Rufus, *The History of Alexander*, ed. and trans. John Yardley. London: Penguin Books, 2004.
Richards, Melville, trans. *The Laws of Hywel Dda (The Book of Blegywryd)*. Liverpool: Liverpool University Press, 1954.
Rígsþula, trans. R. I. Page. In *Chronicles of the Vikings, Records, Memorials and Myths*. London: British Museum Press, 1996, pp. 150–1.
Robertson, A.J., ed. *The Laws of the Kings of England from Edmond to Henry I*. Cambridge: Cambridge University Press, 1925.
'Rule of the Céli Dé', ed. and trans. Edward Gwynn. In *The Rule of Tallaght*. Hermathena 44, second supplemental volume. Dublin: Hodges, Figgis, 1927, pp.64–89.
Russell, Paul. *Welsh Law in Medieval Anglesey: British Library Harleian MS 1796 (Latin C)*. Texts and Studies in Medieval Welsh Law 2. Cambridge: Seminar Cyfraith Hywel, 2011.
Shackleton Bailey, D. R., ed.*Statius,* Silvae. Cambridge, MA: Harvard University Press, 2003.
——. ed. *Valerius Maximus,* Memorable Doings and Sayings. 2 vols. Cambridge, MA: Harvard University Press, 2000.
——. *Martial,* Epigrams. 3 vols. Cambridge, MA: Harvard University Press, 1993.
Shakespeare, William, *I Henry IV*, in *The Norton Shakespeare*, gen. ed. Stephen Greenblatt. New York: W. W. Norton & Company, 1997.
——. *Antony and Cleopatra*. 1607, ed. John Wilders. Arden Shakespeare. London: Routledge, 1995.
——. *King Lear*. 1608, ed. R.A. Foakes. Arden Shakespeare. London: Thomson Learning, 2001.
——. *Titus Andronicus*. 1594, ed. J.C. Maxwell. Arden Shakespeare. London: Routledge, 1989.
——. *Twelfth Night*. 1601, ed. J.M. Lothian and T.W. Craik. Arden Shakespeare. London: Routledge, 1988.
——. *The Merchant of Venice*. 1596, ed. John Russell Brown. Arden Shakespeare. London: Thomson Learning, 1964.
The South English Legendary Corpus Christi College Cambridge MS 145 and British Museum MS Harley 2277, vol. 1, ed. Charlotte d'Evelyn and Anna J. Mill. EETS os 235. Oxford: Oxford University Press, 1956, rpt. 1967.
Sweet, Henry, ed. *King Alfred's West-Saxon Version of Gregory's Pastoral Care*, 2 vols. EETS os 45, 50. Oxford: Oxford University Press, 1871–72; rpt 1958.
Telfer, William, ed. *Cyril of Jerusalem and Nemesius of Emesa*. The Library of Christian Classics. Louisville, KY:Westminster John Knox Press, 2006.

Vicary, Thomas. *The English-man's Treasvre. With the true anatomie of mans body: compiled by Mr. Thomas Vicary*. 1586. London, 1633.

Vita Rimberti, ed. Georg Waitz. Monumenta Germaniae Historica, Scriptores Rerum Merovingicarum. Hanover: Hahnian, 1884.

The Vulgate Version of the Arthurian Romances, vol. 6: *Les aventures ou la queste del Saint Graal. La mort le roi Artus*, ed. Heinrich Oskar Sommer. Washington DC: Carnegie Institution of Washington, 1913.

The Vulgate Version of the Arthurian Romances, vol. 2: *Le livre de Lancelot del Lac*, ed. Heinrich Oskar Sommer. Washington DC: The Carnegie Institution, 1911.

Walberg, Emmanuel, ed. *Le bestiare de Philippe de Thaün*. Lund and Paris: H. J. Müller and H. Welter, 1900.

Whitelock, Dorothy. ed. *Sermo Lupi ad Anglos*. Exeter: University of Exeter Press, 1977.

——, trans. *The Anglo-Saxon Chronicle*. New Brunswick, NJ: Rutgers University Press, 1961.

Whitelock, Dorothy, M. Brett, and C. N. L. Brooke, eds. *Councils and Synods with Other Documents Relating to the English Church*, vol. 1: *AD 871–1204*, part 1, *871–1066*. Oxford: Clarendon Press, 1981.

William of Malmesbury. *Vita Wulfstani*, ed. R. R. Darlington. Camden Society Third Series 40. London: Royal Historical Society, 1928.

William of Newburgh. *The History of English Affairs: Book I*, trans. P. G. Walsh and M. J. Kennedy. Warminster: Aris & Phillips, 1988.

Wiseman, Richard. *Eight Chirurgical Treatises: on these following heads, viz. I. Of tumours. II. Of ulcers. III. Of diseases of the anus. IV.Of the kings-evil. V. Of wounds. VI. Of gun-shot wounds. VII. Of fractures and luxations. VIII. Of the lues venerea*. London: Benj. Took and Luke Meredith, 1696.

Wolfram von Eschenbach. *Parzival*, trans. André Lefevere. New York: Continuum, 1991.

Wright, Thomas. *The Passions of the Mind in General*. 2nd edn. London: Valentine Simmes, 1604.

——. *Political Songs of England: From the Reign of John to that of Edward II* London: Printed for the Camden Society, by J. B. Nichols and Son, 1839.

Secondary Sources

Adelman, Janet. *Suffocating Mothers: Fantasies of Maternal Origin in Shakespeare's Plays,* Hamlet *to* The Tempest. New York and London: Routledge, 1992.

Aebischer, Pascale. *Shakespeare's Violated Bodies: Stage and Screen Performance*. Cambridge: Cambridge University Press, 2004.

Agrawal, Anuja. 'Gendered Bodies: The Case of the "Third Gender" in India'. *Contributions to Indian Sociology* 31.2 (1997): 273–97.

Algra, Nikolaas E. 'The *Lex Frisionum*: The Beginnings of a Legalized Life'. In *The Law's Beginnings*, ed. Ferdinand J. M. Feldbrugge. Leiden: Brill, 2003, pp. 77–92.

Alterthum, Ernst. 'Folgezustände nach Castration'. *Beiträge zur Geburtshülfe und Gynäkologie* 2 (1899): 13.

Alvar, Carlos. 'Oiseuse, Vénus, Luxure: trois dames et un miroir'. *Romania* 106 (1985): 108–17.

von Amira, Karl. *Die germanischen Todesstrafen. Untersuchungen zur Rechts- und Religionsgeschichte*. Abhandlungen der Bayerischen Akademie der Wissenschaften. Philosophisch-philologische und historische Klasse 31.3. Munich: Verlag Bayerischen Akademie der Wissenschaften, 1922.

Anderson, Mary M. *Hidden Power: The Palace Eunuchs of Imperial China*. Buffalo, NY: Prometheus Books, 1990.

André, Naomi Adele. *Voicing Gender:* Castrati, *Travesti, and the Second Woman in Early Nineteenth-century Italian Opera*. Bloomington: Indiana University Press, 2006.

Andrews, Edmund. 'The Oriental Eunuchs'. *JAMA: Journal of the American Medical Association* 30.4 (January 22, 1898): 173–7.

Anitchkof, E. 'Le Saint Graal et les rites eucharistiques', *Romania*, 55 (1929): 174–94.

Arden, Heather M. *The* Romance of the Rose: *An Annotated Bibliography*. New York and London: Garland, 1993.

Aucoin, Michael William, and Richard Joel Wassersug. 'The Sexuality and Social Performance of Androgen-Deprived (Castrated) Men throughout History: Implications for Modern Day Cancer Patients'. *Social Science and Medicine (1982)* 63.12 (2006): 3162–73.

Ayalon, David. *Eunuchs, Caliphs and Sultans: A Study in Power Relationships*. Jerusalem: The Magnes Press, The Hebrew University, 1999.

——. *Outsiders in the Lands of Islam: Mamluks, Mongols, and Eunuchs*. London: Variorum Reprints, 1988.

Bakhtin, Mikhail. *Rabelais and His World*, trans. Hélène Iswolsky. Bloomington: University of Indiana Press, 1984.

Baldwin, John W. *The Language of Sex: Five Voices from Northern France around 1200*. Chicago: University of Chicago Press, 1994.

Barbier, Patrick. *The World of the* Castrati*: The History of an Extraordinary Operatic Phenomenon*. New edn. London: Souvenir Press, 1998.

Bartlett, Anne Clark. *Male Authors, Female Readers: Representations and Subjectivity in Middle English Devotional Literature*. Ithaca, NY: Cornell University Press, 1995.

Bartlett, Robert. *Gerald of Wales, 1146–1223*. Oxford: Clarendon Press, 1982.

Batany, Jean. 'Miniature, allégorie, idéologie: "Oiseuse" et la mystique monacale récupérée par la "classe de loisir"'. In *Études sur le* Roman de la rose *de Guillaume de Lorris*, ed. Jean Dufournet. Paris: Honoré Champion, 1984, pp. 7–36.

von Bayern, Rupprecht. *Reiseerinnerungen aus dem süd-osten Europas und dem Orient*. Munich: Kösel & Pustet, 1923.

Baynham, Elizabeth. *Alexander the Great: The Unique History of Quintus Curtius*. Ann Arbor: University of Michigan Press, 1998.

Beard, Mary. 'The Roman and the Foreign: The Cult of the "Great Mother" in Imperial Rome'. In *Shamanism, History, and the State*, ed. Nicholas Thomas and Caroline Humphrey. Ann Arbor: University of Michigan Press, 1994, pp. 164–90.

Becker, Philipp. *Der männliche Castrat mit besonderer Berücksichtigung seines Knochensystems*. Freiburg im Breisgau: Kuttruff, 1898.

——. 'Über das Knochensystem eines Castraten'. *Archiv für Anatomie und Physiologie [anat. Abth.]* 1 and 2 (1899): 83.

Beime, Piers. *Confronting Animal Abuse: Law, Criminology, and Human–Animal Relationships*. Lanham, MD: Rowman & Littlefield, 2009.

Bejczy, I. P. *Virtue Ethics in the Middle Ages: Commentaries on Aristotle's* Nicomachean Ethics, *1200–1500*. Leiden: Brill, 2008.

Belcastro, Maria Giovanna, Antonio Todero, Gino Fornaciari, and Valentina Mariotti. 'Hyperostosis Frontalis Interna (HFI) and Castration: The Case of the Famous Singer Farinelli (1705–1782)'. *Journal of Anatomy* 219.5 (2011): 632–7.

Bell, Kimberly K. '"Holie mannes liues": England and Its Saints in Oxford, Bodleian Library, MS Laud Misc. 108's *King Horn* and *South English Legendary*'. In *The Texts and Contexts of Oxford, Bodleian Library, MS Laud Misc. 108: The Shaping of English Vernacular Narrative*, ed. Kimberly K. Bell and Julie Nelson Couch. Medieval and Renaissance Authors and Texts 6. Leiden: Brill, 2011, pp. 251–74.

Berdolt, K. 'Kastration', *Reallexikon des germanischen Altertums* 16 (2000): 326–7.

Bergmann, Frédéric-Guillaume. *Origine, signification et histoire de la castration, de l'eunuchisme et de la circoncision*. Palermo: L. Pedone Lauriel, 1883.

Berman, Harold J. *Law and Revolution: The Formation of the Western Legal Tradition*. Cambridge, MA: Harvard University Press, 1983.

Bernau, Anke. 'Gender and Sexuality'. In *A Companion to Middle English Hagiography*, ed. Sarah Salih. Cambridge: D. S. Brewer, 2006:, pp. 104–21.

Biddick, Karen. 'Genders, Bodies, Borders: Technologies of the Visible'. *Speculum* 68 (1993): 389–418.

Biggs, Frederick M. 'The Politics of Succession in *Beowulf* and Anglo-Saxon England'. *Speculum* 80 (2005): 709–41

Binchy, D. A. *Celtic and Anglo-Saxon Kingship*. Oxford: Oxford University Press, 1970.

Bitel, Lisa M. *Land of Women: Tales of Sex and Gender from Early Ireland*. Ithaca, NY: Cornell University Press, 1996.

Blamires, Alcuin, and Gail C. Holian. *The* Romance of the Rose *Illuminated: Manuscripts of the National Library of Wales, Aberystwyth*. Tempe: Arizona Center for Medieval and Renaissance Studies, 2002.

Bloch, R. Howard. *The Scandal of the Fabliaux*. Chicago: University of Chicago Press, 1986.

Bookhout, Theodore, ed. *Research and Management Techniques for Wildlife and Habitats*. Bethesda, MD: Wildlife Society, 1980.

Borresen, Kari Elisabeth. *Subordination and Equivalence: The Nature and Role of Woman in Augustine and Thomas Aquinas*. Kampen: Kok Pharos, 1995.

Boswell, John, *Christianity, Social Tolerance, and Homosexuality*. Chicago: University of Chicago Press, 1980.

Bouget, Hélène. 'Enquerre et deviner: poétique de l'énigme dans les romans arthuriens français (fin du XIIe–premier tiers du XIIIe siècle)'. Doctoral thesis, Université de Rennes II– Haute Bretagne, 2007.

Bowden, Hugh. *Mystery Cults in the Ancient World*. London: Thames & Hudson, 2010.

Boyle, Elizabeth. 'A Welsh Record of an Anglo-Saxon Political Mutilation'. *Anglo-Saxon England* 35 (2006): 245–9.

Brakke, D. *Demons and the Making of the Monk: Spiritual Combat in Early Christianity* Cambridge, MA: Harvard University Press, 2006.

——. 'The Lady Appears: Materializations of "Woman" in Early Monastic Literature'. *Journal of Medieval and Early Modern Studies* 33.3 (2003): 387–402.

——. 'The Problematization of Nocturnal Emissions in Early Christian Syria, Egypt and Gaul'. *Journal of Early Christian Studies* 3 (1995): 419–60.

Braund, Susanna Morton. *Juvenal and Persius*. Cambridge, MA: Harvard University Press, 2004.

Breatnach, Liam. *A Companion to the* Corpus Iuris Hibernici. Early Irish Law Series 5. Dublin: Dublin Institute for Advanced Studies, 2005.

Bremmer, Jan N. *Greek Religion and Culture, the Bible and the Ancient Near East*. Leiden: Brill, 2008.

——. 'Myth and Ritual in Greek Human Sacrifice: Lykaon, Polyxena and the Case of the Rhodian Criminal'. In *The Strange World of Human Sacrifice*, ed. J. N. Bremmer. Studies in the History of Religion and Anthropology 1. Leuven: Peeters, 2007, pp. 55–80.

Bremmer Jr, Rolf H. 'Dealing Dooms: Alliteration in the Old Frisian Laws'. In *Alliteration in Culture*, ed. Jonathan Roper. Basingstoke: Palgrave Macmillan, 2011, pp. 74–92.

——. *Introduction to Old Frisian: History, Grammar, Reader, Glossary*. Amsterdam and Philadelphia: John Benjamins, 2009; corrected rpr. 2011.

Brett, Caroline. 'The Prefaces of Two Late Thirteenth-Century Welsh Latin Chronicles'. *Bulletin of the Board of Celtic Studies* 35 (1988): 63–73.

Brower, Gary Robert. 'Ambivalent Bodies: Making Christian Eunuchs'. PhD dissertation. Durham, NC: Duke University, 1996.

Brown, Amelia R. 'Painting the Bodiless: Angels and Eunuchs in Byzantine Art and Culture'. Paper presented at Sex and Desire across Boundaries. Persons and Sexuality

4th Global Conference, Salzburg, Austria, 2007. http://inter-disciplinary.net/ci/transformations/sexualities/s4/brown%20paper.pdf.

Brown, Peter Robert Lamont. *The Body and Society: Men, Women, and Sexual Renunciation in Early Christianity*. New York: Columbia University Press, 1988.

Bruce, J. Douglas. 'Pelles, Pellinor, and Pellean in the Old French Arthurian Romances: 1'. *Modern Philology*, 16.3 (1918): 113–28.

Brundage, James A. *Medieval Canon Law*. London: Longman, 1994.

——. *Law, Sex, and Christian Society in Medieval Europe*. Chicago: University of Chicago Press, 1987.

Brunel, Clovis. 'Les hanches du roi pécheur (Chrétien de Troyes, "Perceval" 3513)'. *Romania* 81 (1960): 37–43.

Brunvand, Jan Harold. 'The Folktale Origin of *The Taming of the Shrew*.' In *The Taming of the Shrew: An Authoritative Text, Sources and Contexts, Criticism, Rewritings and Appropriations*, ed. Dymphna Callaghan. New York: W. W. Norton & Co., 2009, pp. 266–279.

Buikstra, Jane E., and Douglas H. Ubelaker. *Standards for Data Collection from Human Skeletal Remains: Proceedings of a Seminar at the Field Museum of Natural History*, ed. Jane E. Buikstra. Fayetteville: Arkansas Archeological Survey, 1994.

Bullough, Vern L. 'Eunuchs in History and Society'. In *Eunuchs in Antiquity and Beyond*, ed. Shaun Tougher. London: Classical Press of Wales and Duckworth, 2002, pp. 1–17.

——. 'On Being Male in the Middle Ages.' In *Medieval Masculinities: Regarding Men in the Middle Ages*, ed. Clare A. Lees. Medieval Cultures 7. Minneapolis: University of Minnesota Press, 1994, pp. 31–45.

——. *Sexual Variance in Society and History*. Chicago: University of Chicago Press, 1976.

Buma, Wybren Jan. *Vollständiges Wörterbuch zum westerlauwerschen Jus Municipale Frisonum*. Leeuwarden: Fryske Akademy, 1996.

Burgwinkle, William. *Sodomy, Masculinity, and Law in Medieval Literature: France and England, 1050–1230*. Cambridge: Cambridge University Press, 2004.

Burrows, Daron Lee. *The Stereotype of the Priest in the Old French Fabliaux: Anticlerical Satire and Lay Identity*. Oxford: Peter Lang, 2005.

Butler, E. C. *Benedictine Monachism: Studies in Benedictine Life and Rule*. London: Longmans, Green, 1919.

Bynum, Caroline Walker. *Christian Materiality: An Essay on Religion in Late Medieval Europe*. New York: Zone Books, 2011.

——. *The Resurrection of the Body in Western Christianity, 200–1336*. New York: Columbia University Press, 1995.

——. 'Why All the Fuss about the Body? A Medievalist's Perspective'. *Critical Inquiry* 22 (1995): 1–33.

——. *Fragmentation and Redemption: Essays on Gender and the Human Body in Medieval Religion*. New York: Zone Books, 1992.

Cadden, Joan. *Meanings of Sex Difference in the Middle Ages: Medicine, Science, and Culture*. Cambridge: Cambridge University Press, 1993.

Calbi, Maurizio. *Approximate Bodies: Gender and Power in Early Modern Drama and Anatomy*. New York and London: Routledge, 2005.

Callaghan, Dympna. *Shakespeare without Women: Representing Gender and Race on the Renaissance Stage*. New York and London: Routledge, 2000.

——. *Woman and Gender in Renaissance Tragedy: A Study of* King Lear, Othello, The Duchess of Malfi *and* The White Devil. New York and London: Harvester Wheatsheaf, 1989.

Camille, Michael. *Images on the Edge: The Margins of Medieval Art*. Cambridge, MA: Harvard University Press, 1992.

Caner, Daniel F. 'The Practice and Prohibition of Self-Castration in Early Christianity'. *Vigiliae Christianae* 51.4 (1997): 396–415.

Carter, Susan. 'A Hymenation of Hags.' In *The English Loathly Lady Tales: Boundaries, Traditions, Motifs*, ed. S. Elizabeth Passmore and Susan Carter. Studies in Medieval Culture 48. Kalamazoo, MI: Medieval Institute Publications, 2008, pp. 83–99.

Charles-Edwards, T. M. *Early Irish and Welsh Kinship*. Oxford: Oxford University Press, 1993.

———. *The Welsh Laws*. The Writers of Wales. Cardiff: University of Wales Press, 1989.

Ciggaar, K. N. 'Visitors from North-western Europe to Byzantium. Vernacular Sources: Problems and Perspectives'. *Proceedings of the British Academy* 132 (2007): 123–55.

———. *Western Travellers to Constantinople: The West and Byzantium, 62–1204: Cultural and Political Relations*. Medieval Mediterranean 10. Leiden: Brill, 1996.

———. 'Encore une fois Chrétien de Troyes et la "matière byzantine": la révolution des femmes au palais de Constantinople'. *Cahiers de civilisation médiévale* 38 (1995): 267–74.

———. 'Joseph of Arimathea in the service of Pilate'. *Romanische Philologie*, 3 (1995): 417–21.

———. 'Robert de Boron en Outremer? Le culte de Joseph d'Arimathie dans le monde byzantin et en Outremer'. In *Polyphonia Byzantina. Studies in Honour of Willem J. Aerts*, ed. H. Hokwerda, E. R. Smits, and M. M. Woesthuis. Mediaevalia Groningana. Groningen: Egbert Forsten, 1993, pp. 145–59.

———. 'Chrétien de Troyes et la "matière byzantine": les demoiselles du Château de Pesme Aventure'. *Cahiers de civilisation médiévale* 32 (1989): 325–31.

Ciggaar, K. N., A. Davids and H.G.B Teule. 'Manuscripts as Intermediaries: The Crusader States and Literary Cross-fertilization'. In *East and West in the Crusader States: Context, Contacts, Confrontations. Acta of the Congress held at Hernen Castle in May 1993*. vol. 1. Orientalia Lovaniensia Analecta 75. Leuven: Peeters, 1996, pp. 113–51.

Clapton, Nicholas. *Moreschi: The Last Castrato*. London: Haus, 2004.

Clark, Robert L.A. 'Jousting without a Lance: The Condemnation of Female Homoeroticism in the *Livre des manières*.' In *Same Sex Love and Desire among Women in the Middle Ages*, ed. Francesca Canadé Sautman and Pamela Sheingorn. New York: St Martin's Press, 2001. pp. 143–77.

Clark, Robert L.A. and Claire Sponsler. 'Othered Bodies: Racial Crossdressing in the *Mistere de la Sainte Hostie* and the *Croxton Play of the Sacrament*'. *Journal of Medieval and Early Modern Studies* 29.1 (1999): 61–87.

Clark, Willene B., and Meradith T. McMunn. *Beasts and Birds of the Middle Ages: The Bestiary and Its Legacy*. Philadelphia: University of Pennsylvania Press, 1989.

Clifford, James. *The Predicament of Culture: Twentieth Century Ethnography, Literature, and Art*. Cambridge, MA: Harvard University Press, 1988.

Coatsworth, Elizabeth, and Gale R. Owen-Crocker. *Medieval Textiles of the British Isles* AD *450–1100*. British Archaeological Reports British Series 445. Oxford: Archaeopress, 2007.

Coleman, Julie. 'Rape in Anglo-Saxon England'. In *Violence and Society in the Early Medieval West*, ed. Guy Halsall. Woodbridge: Boydell Press, 1998, pp. 193–204.

Constable, Olivia Remie. *Trade and Traders in Muslim Spain: The Commercial Realignment of the Iberian Penninsula, 900–1500*. Cambridge: Cambridge University Press, 1996.

Corley, Corin. 'Manessier's Continuation of Perceval and the Prose "Lancelot" Cycle', *Modern Language Review* 81.3 (1986): 574–91.

Cosgrove, Art. 'Marriage in Medieval Ireland'. In *Marriage in Ireland*, ed. Art Cosgrove. Dublin: College Press, Ltd., 1985, pp. 25–50.

Corner, George W. *Anatomical Texts of the Earlier Middle Ages: A Study in the Transmission of Culture, with a Revised Latin Text of* Anatomia Cophonis *and Translations of Four Texts*. Washington, DC: Carnegie Institution, 1927.

Crachiolo, Beth. 'Female and Male Martyrs in the *South English Legendary*'. In *'A Great*

Effusion of Blood'? Interpreting Medieval Violence, ed. Mark D. Meyerson, Daniel Thiery, and Oren Falk. Toronto: University of Toronto Press, 2004, pp. 147–63.

Crawford, Sally. *Childhood in Anglo-Saxon England.* Stroud: Sutton, 1999.

Crompton, Louis. *Homosexuality and Civilization.* Cambridge, MA: Harvard University Press, 2003.

Cummins, John. *The Art of Medieval Hunting: The Hound and the Hawk.* London: Phoenix Press, 1988.

Curley, Michael J. 'A Note on Bertilak's Beard'. *Modern Philology: A Journal Devoted to Research in Medieval and Modern Literature* 73.1 (1975): 69–73.

Dahlberg, Charles. 'Love and the *Roman de la Rose*', *Speculum* 44 (1969): 568–84.

Davidson, H. R. Ellis. 'The Sword at the Wedding', *Folkore* 71 (1960): 1–18.

Davies, R. R. *The Revolt of Owain Glyn Dŵr.* Oxford: Oxford University Press, 1995.

Davis, Kathleen. 'National Writing in the Ninth Century: A Reminder for Postcolonial Thinking about the Nation'. *Journal of Medieval and Early Modern Studies* 28 (1998): 611–37.

Davis, Simon J. M. 'The Effect of Castration and Age on the Development of the Shetland Sheep Skeleton and a Metric Comparison Between Bones of Males, Females and Castrates'. *Journal of Archaeological Science* 27.5 (2000): 373–90.

Dechow, Jon Frederick. *Dogma and Mysticism in Early Christianity: Epiphanius of Cyprus and the Legacy of Origen*. Macon, GA: Mercer University Press, 1988.

DeMarco, Laura E. 'The Fact of the *Castrato* and the Myth of the Countertenor'. *Musical Quarterly* 86.1 (2002): 174–85.

Dozy, Reinhart. *Spanish Islam: A History of the Muslims in Spain*, trans. Francis Griffin Stokes. London: Chatto & Windus, 1913.

Drout, Michael D. C. 'Blood and Deeds: The Inheritance Systems in *Beowulf*'. *Studies in Philology* 104 (2007): 199–226.

Druce, George C. 'The Elephant in Medieval Legend and Art', *Journal of the Royal Archaeological Institute* 76 (1919): 1–70.

Duby, Georges. *Love and Marriage in the Middle Ages*, trans. Jane Dunnett. Chicago: University of Chicago Press, 1994.

Dunlap, James E. 'The Office of Grand Chamberlain in the Later Roman and Byzantine Empires'. In *Two Studies in Later Roman and Byzantine Administration*, ed. Arthur E. R. Boak and James E. Dunlap. New York and London: Macmillan, 1924, pp. 161–324.

Easton, Martha. 'Pain, Torture and Death in the Huntington Library *Legenda aurea*'. In *Gender and Holiness: Men, Women and Saints in Late Medieval Europe*, ed. Samantha J. E. Riches and Sarah Salih. Routledge Studies in Medieval Religion and Culture. New York and London: Routledge, 2002, pp. 49–64.

Ecker, Alexander. *Zur Kenntniss des Körperbaues schwarzer Eunuchen: Ein Beitrag zur Ethnographie Afrika's*. Frankfurt am Main, 1865.

Edelman, Lee. *Homographesis: Essays in Gay Literary and Cultural Theory*. New York and London: Routledge, 1994.

van Eickels, Klaus. 'Gendered Violence: Castration and Blinding as Punishment for Treason in Normandy and Anglo-Norman England'. In *Violence, Vulnerability, and Embodiment: Gender and History*, ed. Shani D'Cruze and Anupama Rao. Oxford: Blackwell, 2005, pp. 94–108.

——. 'Gendered Violence: Castration and Blinding as Punishment for Treason in Normandy and Anglo-Norman England'. *Gender and History* 16 (2004): 588–602.

Elam, Keir. 'The Fertile Eunuch: *Twelfth Night*, Early Modern Intercourse, and the Fruits of Castration'. *Shakespeare Quarterly* 47.1 (1996): 1–36.

El-Cheikh, Nadia Maria. 'Servants at the Gate: Eunuchs at the Court of Al-Muqtadir'. *Journal of the Economic and Social History of the Orient* 48.2 (2005): 234–52.

Elliott, Dyan. *Fallen Bodies: Pollution, Sexuality, and Demonology in the Middle Ages* Philadelphia: University of Pennsylvania Press, 1999.

———. *Spiritual Marriage: Sexual Abstinence in Medieval Wedlock*. Princeton, NJ: Princeton University Press, 1993.

Elm, Susanna. *'Virgins of God': The Making of Asceticism in Late Antiquity*. Oxford: Oxford University Press, 1994.

Elsakkers, Marianne. '*Her anda neylar*: An Intriguing Criterion for Abortion in Old Frisian Law'. *Scientiarum Historia* 30 (2004): 107–54.

———. 'Inflicting Serious Bodily Harm: The Visigothic *Antiquae* on Violence and Abortion'. *Tijdschrift voor Rechtsgeschiedenis-Legal History Review* 71 (2003): 55–63.

Eng, J. T., Q. Zhang, and H. Zhu. 'Skeletal Effects of Castration on Two Eunuchs of Ming China'. *Anthropological Science* 118 (2010): 107–16.

Engelstein, Laura. *Castration and the Heavenly Kingdom: A Russian Folktale*. Ithaca, NY: Cornell University Press, 1999.

Enlow, Donald H., and Seong Bang. 'Growth and Remodeling of the Human Maxilla'. *American Journal of Orthodontics* 51.6 (1965): 446–64.

Eska, Charlene M. 'Women and Slavery in the Early Irish Laws'. *Studia Celtica Fennica* 8 (2011): 29–39.

Fauber, Lawrence Herbert. *Narses, Hammer of the Goths: The Life and Times of Narses the Eunuch*. New York: St Martin's Press, 1990.

Félix, Charles-Emile. *Recherches sur l'excision des organes génitaux externes chez l'homme*. Lyon: L. Dec et F. Demaison, 1883.

Fichera, Gaetano. 'Sur l'hypertrophie de la glande pituitaire consecutive a la castration'. *Archives italiennes de biologie* 43 (1905): 405–26.

Field, Rosalind. 'The King Over the Water: Exile-and-Return Revisited'. In *Cultural Encounters in the Romance of Medieval England*, ed. Corinne Saunders. Studies in Medieval Romance. Cambridge: D. S. Brewer, 2005, pp. 41–53.

Finucci, Valeria. *The Manly Masquerade: Masculinity, Paternity, and Castration in the Italian Renaissance*. Durham, NC: Duke University Press, 2003.

Fisher, Will. 'Queer Money'. *ELH: English Literary History* 66.1 (1999): 1–23.

Fleming, John. 'Further Reflections on Oiseuse's Mirror'. *Zeitschrift für romanische Philologie* 100 (1984): 26–40.

Foucault, Michel. *Discipline and Punish: The Birth of the Prison*, trans. Alan Sheridan. New York: Vintage, 1995.

———. *The History of Sexuality*, vol. 1: *The Will to Knowledge*, trans. Robert Hurley. London: Penguin, 1984.

Fowler, David C. *Prowess and Charity in the* Perceval *of Chrétien De Troyes*. Seattle: University of Washington Press, 1959.

Francis, Alfred G. 'On a Romano-British Castration Clamp Used in the Rights of Cybele'. *Proceedings of the Royal Society of Medicine* 19 (1926): 95–110.

Frantzen, Allen J. 'The Form and Function of the Preface in the Poetry and Prose of Alfred's Reign'. In *Alfred the Great*, ed. Timothy Reuter. Aldershot: Ashgate, 2003, pp. 121–36.

———. *Before the Closet: Same-sex from* Beowulf *to* Angels in America. Chicago: University of Chicago Press, 2000.

———. *King Alfred*. Boston, MA: Twayne, 1986.

Frederick, Jill. 'The *South English Legendary*: Anglo-Saxon Saints and National Identity'. In *Literary Appropriations of the Anglo-Saxons from the Thirteenth to the Twentieth Century*, ed. Donald Scragg and Carole Weinberg. Cambridge Studies in Anglo-Saxon England. Cambridge: Cambridge University Press, 2000, pp. 57–73

Freitas, Roger. 'The Eroticism of Emasculation: Confronting the Baroque Body of the *Castrato*'. *Journal of Musicology* 20.2 (2003): 196–249.

Frese, Dolores Warwick. *An* Ars Legendi *for Chaucer's* Canterbury Tales: *Re-constructive Reading*. Gainesville: University of Florida Press, 1991.

Freud, Sigmund. 'On the Sexual Theories of Children' (1908). In *Standard Edition of the Complete Psychological Works of Sigmund Freud*, vol. 9, ed. James Strachey. London: Hogarth Press and the Institute of Psycho-Analysis, 1959, pp. 205–26.

Friedrich, Ellen Lorraine. 'The Mentorship of the Lover by the Diex d'Amors in Guillaume de Lorris's *Romans de la rose*'. *Medieval Perspectives*, 26 (2011 [2012]): 89–103.

———. '*Romance of the Rose*'. In *Encyclopedia of Sex and Gender*, ed. Fedwa Malti-Douglas. Detroit: Thomas Gale, 2007.

———. 'When a Rose Is not a Rose: Homoerotic Emblems in the *Roman de la Rose*'. In *Gender Transgressions: Crossing the Normative Barrier in Old French Literature*, ed. Karen J. Taylor. New York and London: Garland, 1998, pp. 22–43.

———. 'Oiseuse: An Introduction to a Homoerotic Reading of Guillaume de Lorris's *Romans de la rose*'. PhD dissertation, University of North Carolina-Chapel Hill, 1999.

Funk, Robert Walter, and Roy W. Hoover, eds. *The Five Gospels: The Search for the Authentic Words of Jesus*. New York: Macmillan, 1993.

Gade, Kari Ellen. 'Homosexuality and Rape of Males in Old Norse Law and Literature'. *Scandinavian Studies* 58 (1986): 124–41.

Gallais, Pierre. 'Robert de Boron en Orient'. In *Mélanges de langue et de littérature du Moyen Age et de la Renaissance offerts à Jean Frappier*, ed. Jean Charles Payen and Claude Régnier. Publications romanes et françaises 112.1. Geneva: Droz, 1970, pp. 313–19.

Garber, Marjorie. *Vested Interest: Cross-Dressing and Cultural Anxiety*. New York and London: Routledge, 1992.

Garthwaite, John. 'Statius, *Silvae* 3.4: On the Fate of Earinus'. *Aufstieg und Niedergang der römischen Welt* II.32.1 (1984): 111–24.

Gaunt, Simon. 'Bel Acueil and the Improper Allegory of the *Romance of the Rose*'. In *New Medieval Literatures*, II, ed. and intro., Rita Copeland, David Lawton, and Wendy Scase. Oxford: Clarendon Press, 1998, pp. 65–93.

Gerbino, Giuseppe. 'The Quest for the Soprano Voice: *Castrati* in Renaissance Italy'. *Studi Musicali* 33 (2004): 303–57.

Gil Harris, Jonathan. *Foreign Bodies and the Body Politic: Discourses of Social Pathology in Early Modern England*. Cambridge: Cambridge University Press, 1998.

Gilchrist, Roberta. *Gender and Archaeology: Contesting the Past*. New York and London: Routledge, 1999.

Giles, Ryan D. 'The Miracle of Gerald the Pilgrim: Hagiographic Visions of Castration in the *Liber Sancti Jacobi* and *Milagros de Nuestra Senora*'. *Neophilologus* 94 (2010): 439–50.

Gillingham, John. 'Killing and Mutilating Political Enemies in the British Isles from the Late Twelfth to the Early Fourteenth Century: A Comparative Study'. In *Britain and Ireland 900–1300*, ed. Brendan Smith. Cambridge: Cambridge University Press, 1999, pp. 114–34.

Gilson, Etienne. *The Christian Philosophy of St Thomas Aquinas*, trans. Edward Bullough. Salem, NH: Ayer, 1983.

Girsch, Elizabeth Stevens. 'Metaphorical Usage, Sexual Exploitation, and Divergence in the Old English Terminology for Male and Female Slaves'. In *The Work of Work: Servitude, Slavery, and Labor in Medieval England*, ed. Allen J. Frantzen and Douglas Moffat. Glasgow: Cruithne Press, 1994, pp. 30–54.

Gleissner, Reinhard. *Die 'zweideutigen' altenglischen Rätsel des Exeter Book in ihrem zeitgenössischen Kontext*. Frankfurt: P. Lang, 1984.

Godden, Malcolm. 'Did King Alfred Write Anything?' *Medium Aevum* 76 (2007): 1–23.

Golther, Wolfgang. *Parzival und der Gral, in Deutscher Sage des Mittelalters und der Neuzeit*. Munich: G. D. W Callwey, 1908.

Gordon, Murray. *Slavery in the Arab World*. New York: New Amsterdam Books, 1989.

Gray, Ross E., Richard J. Wassersug, Christina Sinding, Angela M. Barbara, Christine Trosztmer, and Neil Fleshner. 'The Experiences of Men Receiving Androgen Deprivation Treatment for Prostate Cancer: A Qualitative Study'. *Canadian Journal of Urology* 12.4 (2005): 2755–63.

Green, Monica H. 'The *De genecia* Attributed to Constantinus the African'. *Speculum* 62 (1987): 299–323.

Grigg, Erik. '"Mole Rain" and Other Natural Phenomena in the Welsh Annals: Can *Mirabilia* Unravel the Textual History of the *Annales Cambriae*?' *Welsh History Review* 24.4 (2009): 1–40.

Groebner, Valentin. 'Das Gesicht wahren: Abgeschnittene Nasen, abgeschnittene Ehre in der spätmittelalterlichen Stadt'. In *Verletzte Ehre: Ehrkonflikte in Gesellschaften des Mittelalters und der frühen Neuzeit*, ed. Klaus Schreiner and Gerd Schwerhoff. Cologne: Böhlau, 1995, pp. 361–80.

Grössinge, Christa. 'The Unicorn on English Misericords'. In *Medieval Art: Recent Perspectives, a Memorial Tribute to C. R. Dodwell*, ed. Gale R. Owen-Crocker and Timothy Graham. Manchester: Manchester University Press, 1998, pp. 142–58.

Grumbach, Melvin M., and Richard J. Auchus. 'Estrogen: Consequences and Implications of Human Mutations in Synthesis and Action'. *Journal of Clinical Endocrinology and Metabolism* 84.12 (1999): 4677–94.

Guilland, Rodolphe. 'Les eunuques dans l'empire byzantin: Étude de titulature et de prosopographie byzantines'. *Études Byzantines* 1 (1943): 197–238.

Guyot, Peter. *Eunuchen als Sklaven und Freigelassene in der griechisch-römischen Antike*. Stuttgart: Klett-Cotta, 1980.

Hamelinck, Renee. 'St Kenhelm and the Legends of the *South English Legendary*'. In *Companion to Early Middle English Literature*, ed. N. H. G. E. Veldhoen and H. Aertsen. Amsterdam: V. U. University Press, 1995, pp. 19–28.

Hanson, R.P.C. 'A Note on Origen's Self-Mutilation.' *Vigiliae Christianae* 20.2 (June 1966): 81–2.

Harley, Marta Powell. 'Narcissus, Hermaphroditus, and Attis: Ovidian Lovers at the Fontaine d'Amors in Guillaume de Lorris's *Roman de la rose*'. *PMLA* 101 (1986): 324–37.

Harrington, Christina. *Women in a Celtic Church: Ireland 450–1150*. Oxford: Oxford University Press, 2002.

Harrison, Julian. 'A Note on Gerald of Wales and *Annales Cambriae*'. *Welsh History Review* 17 (1994): 252–5.

Harvey, A. E. 'Eunuchs for the Sake of the Kingdom'. Paper presented at the Ethel M. Wood Lecture. London, March 15, 1995.

Hasenohr, Genevieve. 'Religious Reading amonst the Laity in France in the Fifteenth Century'. In *Heresy and Literacy, 1000–1530*, ed. Peter Biller and Anne Hudson. Cambridge: Cambridge University Press, 1994, pp. 205–21.

———. 'Jean Le Fèvre.' In *Dictionnaire des lettres françaises: Le Moyen Âge*. Paris: Fayard, 1992, pp. 802–4.

———. 'La vie quotidienne de la femme vue par l'Eglise: L'enseignement des "journées chrétiennes" de la fin du Moyen-Age'. In *Frau und spätmittelalterlicher Alltag (Internationaler Kongress, Krems an der Donau, 2. bis 5. Oktober 1984)*. Österreichische Akademie der Wissenschaften, Philosophisch-Historische Klasse, Sitzungsberichte 473. Veröffentlichungen des Instituts für mittelalterliche Realienkunde Österreichs 9. Vienna: Verlag der Österreichischen Akademie der Wissenschaften, 1986, pp. 19–101.

Hastrup, Kristen. *Culture and History in Medieval Iceland: An Anthropological Analysis of Structure and Change*. Oxford: Oxford University Press, 1985.

Hathaway, Jane. *Beshir Agha*. Oxford: Oneworld, 2005.

Hatzaki, Myrto. *Beauty and the Male Body in Byzantium: Perceptions and Representations in Art and Text.* Basingstoke: Palgrave Macmillan, 2009.

Heeren, Stijn. 'New Views on the Forfex of Virilis the Veterinarian: Shears, Emasculator or Twitch?' *Journal of Archaeology in the Low Countries* 1 (2009): 87–95.

Heim, Nikolaus, and Carolyn J. Hursch. 'Castration for Sex Offenders: Treatment or Punishment? A Review and Critique of Recent European Literature'. *Archives of Sexual Behavior* 8.3 (1979): 281–304.

van Helten, Willem L. 'Zur Lexicologie und Grammatik des Altwestfriesischen'. *Beiträge zur Geschichte der deutschen Sprache und Literatur* 19 (1894): 345–440.

Henriksén, Christer. 'Earinus: An Imperial Eunuch in the Light of the Poems of Martial and Statius'. *Mnemosyne* 50 (1997): 281–94.

Henstra, Dirk Jan. 'Het probleem van de geldbedragen in de *Lex Frisionum*'. In *'Fon jelde': Opstellen van D. J. Henstra over middeleeuws Frisia*, ed. Anne T. Popkema. Groningen: Barkhuis, 2010, pp. 47–70.

Hester, J. D. 'Eunuchs and the Postgender Jesus: Matthew 19.12 and Transgressive Sexualities'. *Journal for the Study of the New Testament* 28.1 (2005): 13.

Hickmet, A., and Félix Régnault. 'Les eunuques de Constantinople'. *Bulletins de la Société d'anthropologie de Paris* 2.1 (1901): 234–40.

Higley, Sarah L. 'The Wanton Hand: Reading and Reaching into Grammars and Bodies in Old English Riddle 12'. In *Naked Before God: Uncovering the Body in Anglo-Saxon England*, ed. Benjamin C. Withers and Jonathan Wilcox. Morgantown: West Virginia University Press, 2003, pp. 29–59.

Hill, John M. 'The Sacrificial Synecdoche of Hands, Heads, and Arms in Anglo-Saxon Heroic Story'. In *Naked Before God: Uncovering the Body in Anglo-Saxon England*, ed. Benjamin C. Withers and Jonathan Wilcox. Morgantown: West Virginia University Press, 2003, pp. 116–37.

Hillman, David, and Carla Mazzio. 'Introduction'. In *The Body in Parts: Fantasies of Corporeality in Early Modern Europe*, ed. David Hillman and Carla Mazzio. New York and London: Routledge, 1997, pp. xi–xxix.

Himes, Amy. 'At the Zoo: Busy Beavers'. *Smithsonian Zoogoer* 31.2 (2002).Online at http://nationalzoo.si.edu/Publications/ZooGoer/2002/2/busybeavers.cfm, accessed May 20, 2012.

Hiort, Olaf. 'Androgens and Puberty'. *Best Practice and Research Clinical Endocrinology and Metabolism* 16.1 (March 2002): 31–41.

His, Rudolf. *Das Strafrecht des deutschen Mittelalters. II: Die einzelnen Verbrechen.* Weimar: Hermann Böhlaus, 1935.

———. *Das Strafrecht der Friesen.* Leipzig: Dieters'che Verlagbuchhandlung, 1901.

Hodges, Kenneth. 'Wounded Masculinity: Injury and Gender in Sir Thomas Malory's *Le Morte Darthur*'. *Studies in Philology* 106.1 (2009): 14–31.

Hopkins, Keith. *Conquerors and Slaves.* Cambridge: Cambridge University Press, 1978.

Horner, Shari. 'The Language of Rape in Old English Literature and Law: Views from the Anglo-Saxon(ist)s'. In *Sex and Sexuality in Anglo-Saxon England*, ed. Carol Braun Pasternack and Lisa M. C. Weston. Tempe: Arizona Center for Medieval and Renaissance Studies, 2004, pp. 149–181.

Hosley, Richard, ed. *Shakespeare's Holinshed.* New York: G. P. Putnam's Sons, 1968.

Hough, Carole. 'Two Kentish Laws Concerning Women: A New Reading of Æthelberht 73 and 74'. *Anglia* 119 (2001): 554–78.

———. 'Alfred's *Domboc* and the Language of Rape: A Reconsideration of Alfred ch.11'. *Medium Ævum* 66 (1997): 1–27.

Howie, Cary. *Claustrophilia: The Erotics of Enclosure in Medieval Literature.* New York: Palgrave Macmillan, 2007.

Hsun-tžu. *Xunzi: A Translation and Study of the Complete Works*, trans. John Knoblock. Stanford, CA: Stanford University Press, 1988.

Huang, Martin W. *Negotiating Masculinities in Late Imperial China*. Honolulu: University of Hawai'i Press, 2006.

Huang, Ray. *1587, A Year of No Significance: The Ming Dynasty in Decline*. New Haven, CT: Yale University Press, 1981.

Hughes, Kathleen. 'The Welsh Latin Chronicles: *Annales Cambriae* and Related Texts'. *Proceedings of the British Academy* 59 (1973): 233–58.

———. *Celtic Britain in the Early Middle Ages*, ed. David Dumville. Studies in Scottish and Welsh Sources 2. Woodbridge: Boydell Press, 1980.

Hull, Vernam. 'Two Anecdotes Concerning St Moling'. *Zeitschrift für celtische Philologie* 18 (1930): 90–9.

Hult, David F. 'Language and Dismemberment: Abelard, Origen, and the *Romance of the Rose*'. In *Rethinking the* Romance of the Rose: *Text, Image, Reception*, ed. Kevin Brownlee and Sylvia Huot. Philadelphia: University of Pennsylvania Press, 1992, pp. 101–30.

———. 'The Allegorical Fountain: Narcissus in the *Roman de la rose*'. *Romanic Review* 72 (1981): 125–48.

Hunwick, John O., and Eve Troutt Powell. *The African Diaspora in the Mediterranean Lands of Islam*. Princeton, NJ: Markus Wiener Publishers, 2002.

Huot, Sylvia. *The* Romance of the Rose *and Its Medieval Readers: Interpretation, Reception, Manuscript Transmission*. Cambridge: Cambridge University Press, 1993.

Huws, Daniel. *Medieval Welsh Manuscripts*. Aberystwyth: University of Wales Press and The National Library of Wales, 2000.

Hyams, Paul R. *Rancor and Reconciliation in Medieval England*. Ithaca, NY: Cornell University Press, 2003.

Irvine, Martin. 'Abelard and (Re)writing the Male Body: Castration, Identity, and Remasculinization'. In *Becoming Male in the Middle Ages*, ed. Jeffrey Jerome Cohen and Bonnie Wheeler. The New Middle Ages 4. New York: Garland Publishing, 2000, pp. 87–106.

Jaffrey, Zia. *The Invisibles: A Tale of the Eunuchs of India*. New York: Pantheon Books, 1996.

James, Elizabeth, ed. *Women, Men and Eunuchs: Gender in Byzantium*. New York and London: Routledge, 1997.

Jankofsky, Klaus P. 'National Characteristics in the Portrayal of English Saints in the *South English Legendary*'. In *Images of Sainthood in Medieval Europe*, ed. Renate Blumenfeld-Kosinski and Timea Szell. Ithaca, NY: Cornell University Press, 1991, pp. 81–93

Jay, Jennifer W. 'Another Side of Chinese Eunuch History: Castration, Marriage, Adoption, and Burial'. *Canadian Journal of History/Annales canadiennes d'histoire* 28.3 (1993): 459–78.

Jenkins, John S. 'The Voice of the *Castrato*'. *Lancet* 351.9119 (1998): 1877–80.

Jesch, Judith. *Women in the Viking Age*. Woodbridge: Boydell Press, 1991.

Jia, Yinghua. *The Last Eunuch of China: The Life of Sun Yaoting*, trans. Sun Haichan. Beijing: China Intercontinental Press, 2008.

Jochens, Jenny. *Women in Old Norse Society*. Ithaca, NY: Cornell University Press, 1998.

Johnson, Lizabeth. 'Mutilation as Cultural Commerce and Criticism: The Transmission, Practice, and Meaning of Castration and Blinding in Medieval Wales'. *Istoria* 1 (2008): 1–23.

Johnson, Richard W. *Going Outside the Camp: The Sociological Function of the Levitical Critique in the Epistle to the Hebrews*. Sheffield: Sheffield Academic Press, 2001.

Johnson, Thomas W., Richard J. Auchus, Lesley F. Roberts, Michelle Brett Sutherland, and Michael B. First. 'Desire for Castration Is not a Body Integrity Identity Disorder (BIID): A Response'. *Journal of Sexual Medicine* 7.2 part 1 (2010): 853–5.

Jones, Thomas. 'Historical Writing in Medieval Welsh'. *Scottish Studies* 12 (1968): 15–27.

Jordan, Mark D. *The Invention of Sodomy in Christian Theology.* Chicago: University of Chicago Press, 1997.

Jurasinski, Stefan. 'Germanism, Slapping and the Cultural Contexts of Æthelberht's Code: A Reconsideration of Chapters 56–58'. *Haskins Society Journal* 18 (2006): 51–71.

Kahn, Coppélia. *Man's Estate: Masculine Identity in Shakespeare.* Berkeley and Los Angeles: University of California Press, 1981.

Karkov, Catherine E. 'Exiles from the Kingdom: The Naked and the Damned in Anglo-Saxon Art'. In *Naked Before God: Uncovering the Body in Anglo-Saxon England*, ed. Benjamin C. Withers and Jonathan Wilcox. Morgantown: West Virginia University Press, 2003, pp. 181–220.

Karras, Ruth Mazo. *Sexuality in Medieval Europe: Doing unto Others.* New York and London: Routledge, 2005.

———. *Slavery and Society in Medieval Scandinavia.* New Haven, CT: Yale University Press, 1998.

———. 'Desire, Descendants, and Dominance: Slavery, the Exchange of Women, and Masculine Power'. In *The Work of Work: Servitude, Slavery, and Labor in Medieval England*, ed. Allen J. Frantzen and Douglas Moffat. Glasgow: Cruithne Press, 1994, pp. 16–29.

Kelch, Robert P., M. R. Jenner, Richard L. Weinstein, Selna L. Kaplan, and Melvin M. Grumbach. 'Estradiol and Testosterone Secretion by Human, Simian, and Canine Testes, in Males with Hypogonadism and in Male Pseudohermaphrodites with the Feminizing Testes Syndrome'. *Journal of Clinical Investigation* 51.4 (1972): 824–30.

Kelly, Douglas. *Internal Difference and Meanings in the* Roman de la Rose. Madison: University of Wisconsin Press, 1995.

Kelly, Fergus. 'Texts and Transmissions: The Law-Texts'. In *Ireland and Europe in the Early Middle Ages: Texts and Transmission/Irland und Europa im früheren Mittelalter: Texte und Überlieferung*, ed. Próinséas Ní Chatháin and Michael Richter. Dublin: Four Courts Press, 2002, pp. 230–42.

———. *Early Irish Farming.* Early Irish Law Series 4. Dublin: Dublin Institute for Advanced Studies, 1998.

———. *A Guide to Early Irish Law.* Early Irish Law Series 3. Dublin: Dublin Institute for Advanced Studies, 1988.

Kelly, Kathleen Coyne. 'Menaced Masculinity and Imperiled Virginity in Malory's *Morte Darthur*'. In *Menacing Virgins: Representing Virginity in the Middle Ages and Renaissance*, ed. Kathleen Coyne Kelly and Marina Leslie. Newark: University of Delaware Press, 1999, pp. 97–114.

Kenny, Anne M., and Lawrence G. Raisz. 'Androgens and Bone'. In *Androgens in Health and Disease*, ed. Carrie J. Bagatell and William J. Bremner. Totowa, NJ: Humana Press, 2003, pp. 221–32.

Kenny, Gillian. *Anglo-Irish and Gaelic Women in Ireland* c. *1170–1540.* Dublin: Four Courts Press, 2007.

Kern Paster, Gail. *Humoring the Body: Emotions and the Shakespearean Stage.* Chicago: University of Chicago Press, 2004.

———. 'Nervous Tension'. In *The Body in Parts: Fantasies of Corporeality in Early Modern Europe*, ed. David Hillman and Carla Mazzio. New York and London: Routledge, 1997, pp. 106–25.

Kittel, Ruth. 'Rape in Thirteenth-Century England: A Study of the Common-Law Courts'. In *Women and the Law*, vol. 2, ed. D. Kelly Weisberg. Cambridge, MA: Schenkman Publishing, 1982: 101–15.

Kolb, Herbert. 'Oiseuse, die Dame mit dem Spiegel'. *Germanisch-romanische Monatschrift.* n.s. 15 [46] (1965): 139–49.

Kolling, Alfons. 'Römische Kastrierzangen'. *Archäologisches Korrespondensblatt* 3 (1973): 353–7.

Krimmer, Elisabeth. '"Eviva Il Coltello"? The *Castrato* Singer in Eighteenth-Century German Literature and Culture'. *PMLA* 120.5 (2005): 1543–59.

Kuefler, Mathew S. *The Manly Eunuch: Masculinity, Gender Ambiguity, and Christian Ideology in Late Antiquity*. Chicago: University of Chicago Press, 2001.

———. 'Castration and Eunuchism in the Middle Ages.' In *The Handbook of Medieval Sexuality*, ed. Vern L. Bullough and James A. Brundage. Garland Reference Library of the Humanities 1696. New York: Garland, 1996, pp. 279–306.

———. '"A Wryed Existence": Attitudes toward Children in Anglo-Saxon England'. *Journal of Social History* 24 (1991): 823–34.

Kuhn, Alfred. 'Die Illustration der Handschriften des *Rosenromans*'. *Jahrbuch der Kunsthistorischen Sammlungen des allerhöchsten Kaiserhauses* 31.1 (1912): 1–66.

Lach, Donald F. *Asia in the Making of Europe*, vol. 2: *A Century of Wonder*. Book 1: *The Visual Arts*. Chicago: University of Chicago Press, 1994.

Lacy, Norris. 'Trickery, Trubertage, and the Limits of Laughter.' In *The Old French Fabliaux: Essays on Comedy and Context*, ed. Kristin L. Burr and Norris J. Lacy. Jefferson, NC: McFarland & Co., 2007.

Lang, Johannes. *Clinical Anatomy of the Nose, Nasal Cavity, and Paranasal Sinuses*, trans. Philip M. Stell. New York: Thieme-Stratton Corp, 1989.

Lapidge, Michael, John Blair, Simon Keynes, and Donald Scragg, eds. *The Blackwell Encyclopaedia of Anglo-Saxon England*. Oxford: Blackwell, 1999.

Lacqueur, Thomas. *Making Sex: Body and Gender from the Greeks to Freud*. Cambridge, MA: Harvard University Press, 1990.

Latimer, Paul. 'Henry II's Campaign against the Welsh in 1165'. *Welsh Historical Review* 14.4 (1989): 523–52.

LeBlanc, Marie-Colombe. 'Perceval quêteur du Graal chez les continuateurs'. PhD dissertation, Université Jean Moulin Lyon 3, 2008.

Lee, Christina. 'Body Talks: Disease and Disability in Anglo-Saxon England'. In *Anglo-Saxon Traces*, ed. Jane Roberts and Leslie Webster. Tempe: Arizona Center for Medieval and Renaissance Studies, 2011, pp. 145–64.

Lees, Clare A. 'Engendering Religious Desire: Sex, Knowledge, and Christian Identity in Anglo- Saxon England'. *Journal of Mediaeval and Early Modern Studies* 27 (1997): 17–45.

Levine, Laura. *Men in Women's Clothing: Anti-Theatricality and Effeminization 1579–1642*. Cambridge: Cambridge University Press, 1994.

Lewis, Katherine J. 'Gender and Sanctity in the Middle Ages'. In *Gendering the Middle Ages*, ed. Pauline Stafford and Anneke B. Mulder-Bakker. Oxford: Blackwell, 2001, pp. 205–14.

Lewis, Suzanne. 'Medieval Bodies Then and Now: Negotiating Problems of Ambivalence and Paradox'. In *Naked Before God: Uncovering the Body in Anglo-Saxon England*, ed. Benjamin C. Withers and Jonathan Wilcox. Morgantown: West Virginia University Press, 2003, pp. 15–28.

Liebermann, Felix. *Die Gesetze der Angelsachsen: Text und Übersetzung*, 3 vols. Halle: Max Niemeyer, 1903.

Llewellyn-Jones, Lloyd. 'Eunuchs and the Royal Harem in Achaemenid Persia (599–331 BC)'. In *Eunuchs in Antiquity and Beyond*, ed. Shaun Tougher. London: Classical Press of Wales and Duckworth, 2002, pp. 19–49.

Lloyd, Genevieve. *The Man of Reason: 'Male' and 'Female' in Western Philosophy*. Minneapolis: University of Minnesota Press, 1984.

Lloyd, John Edward. 'The Welsh Chronicles', *Proceedings of the British Academy* 14 (1928): 369–91.

Long, Jacqueline. *Claudian's* In Eutropium: *Or, How, When, and Why to Slander a Eunuch*. Chapel Hill, NC: University of North Carolina Press, 1996.

Lopez, Robert Sabatino. 'The Dollar of the Middle Ages'. *Journal of Economic History* 11.3 (1951): 209–34.

Lortet, Louis-Charles. 'Allongement des membres inférieurs du a la castration'. *Archives d'Anthropologie Criminelle* 64 (1896): 361–4.

Lozac'hmeur, Jean-Claude. 'De la tête de Bran à l'hostie du Graal'. In *Arthurian Tapestry. Essays in Memory of Lewis Thorpe*, ed. Kenneth Varty. Glasgow: Published on behalf of the British Branch of the International Arthurian Society at the French Department of the University of Glasgow, 1981, pp. 275–86.

Lück, Heiner. 'Der wilde Osten: Fränkische Herrschaftsstrukturen im Geltungsbereich der *Lex Saxonum* und *Lex Turingorum* um 800'. In *Von den* leges barbarorum *bis zum* ius barbarum *des Nationalsozialismus: Festschrift für Hermann Nehlsen zum 70. Geburtstag*, ed. Thomas Gutmann, Hans-Georg Hermann, Joachim Rückert, Mathias Schmoeckel, and Harald Siems. Cologne: Böhlau, 2007, pp. 118–31.

Lüthje, Hugo. 'Über die Castration und ihre Folgen'. *Archiv für experimentelle Pathologie und Pharmakologie* 48.3 (1902): 184–222.

Luz, Ulrich. *Matthew: A Commentary*, trans. Wilhelm C. Linss. Hermeneia. Minneapolis, MN: Augsburg Fortress, 1989.

MacLeod, Catriona. 'The "Third Sex" in an Age of Difference: Androgyny and Homosexuality in Winckelmann, Friedrich Schlegel, and Kleist'. In *Outing Goethe and His Age*, ed. Alice A. Kuzniar. Stanford, CA: Stanford University Press, 1996, pp. 194–214.

Magennis, Hugh. 'No Sex Please, We're Anglo-Saxons: Attitudes to Sexuality in Old English Prose and Poetry'. *Leeds Studies in English* 26 (1995): 1–27.

Maier, B. 'Gotteslästerung'. *Reallexikon des germanischen Altertums* 12 (2001): 483–5.

Maresh, Marion M. 'Paranasal Sinuses from Birth to Late Adolescence: I. Size of the Paranasal Sinuses as Observed in Routine Posteroanterior Roentgenograms'. *American Journal of Diseases of Children* 60.1 (1940): 55–78.

Markschies, Christoph. 'Kastration und Magenprobleme? Einige neue Blicke auf das asketische Leben des Origenes'. In *Origenes und sein Erbe: Gesammelte Studien*. Texte und Untersuchungen zur Geschichte der Altchristlichen Literatur 160. Berlin: Walter de Gruyter, 2007, pp. 15–34.

Marmon, Shaun Elizabeth. *Eunuchs and Sacred Boundaries in Islamic Society*. Oxford: Oxford University Press, 1995.

Marshall, William A. *Human Growth and Its Disorders*. New York: Academic Press, 1977.

Matignon, Jean-Jacques. 'La castration industrielle en Chine'. *Gazette hebdomadaire des sciences médicales de Bordeaux* 17 (1896): 403.

Mazzio, Carla. 'Sins of the Tongue'. In *The Body in Parts: Fantasies of Corporeality in Early Modern Europe*, ed. David Hillman and Carla Mazzio. New York and London: Routledge, 1997, pp. 52–79.

McAlpine, Monica E. 'The Pardoner's Homosexuality and How It Matters'. *PMLA* 95 (1980): 8–22.

McCormick, Michael. *Origins of the European Economy: Communications and Commerce* AD *300–900*. Cambridge: Cambridge University Press, 2001.

McCracken, Peggy. *The Curse of Eve, The Wound of the Hero: Blood, Gender, and Medieval Literature*. Philadelphia: University of Pennsylvania Press, 2003.

——. 'Chaste Subjects: Gender, Heroism, and Desire in the Grail Quest'. In *Queering the Middle Age*, ed. Glenn Burger and Steven F Kruger. Medieval Cultures. Minneapolis: University of Minnesota Press, 2001, pp. 123–42.

McCulloch, Frances. *Medieval Latin and French Bestiaries*. Chapel Hill: University of North Carolina Press, 1962.

McInerney, Maud Burnett. *Eloquent Virgins from Thecla to Joan of Arc*. The New Middle Ages. New York: Palgrave Macmillan, 2003.

——. 'Rhetoric, Power, and Integrity in the Passion of the Virgin Martyr'. In *Menacing*

Virgins: Representing Virginity in the Middle Ages and Renaissance, ed. Kathleen Coyne Kelly and Marina Leslie. Newark: University of Delaware Press, 1999, pp. 50–70.

McLaughlin, Roisin. *Early Irish Satire*. Dublin: Dublin Institute for Advanced Studies, 2008.

McNamara, Jo Ann. 'The *Herrenfrage*: The Restructuring of the Gender System, 1050–1150'. In *Medieval Masculinities: Regarding Men in the Middle Ages*, ed. Clare A. Lees. Medieval Cultures 7. Minneapolis: University of Minnesota Press, 1994, pp. 3–29.

McNeill, John T., and Helena M. Gamer, eds. *Medieval Handbooks of Penance*. New York: Columbia University Press, 1990.

Meens, Rob. *Het tripartite boeteboek: overlevering en betekenis van vroegmiddeleeuwse biechtvoorschriften*. Hilversum: Verloren, 1994.

Mews, Constant J., ed. *The Lost Love Letters of Heloise and Abelard: Perceptions of Dialogue in Twelfth-Century France*. 2nd edn. New York: Palgrave Macmillan, 2008.

Millant, Richard. *Castration criminelle et maniaque (étude historique et médico-légale)*. Paris: Jules Rousset: 1902.

Miller, William Ian. *Eye for an Eye*. Cambridge: Cambridge University Press, 2006.

———. 'In Defense of Revenge'. In *Medieval Crime and Social Control*, ed. Barbara A. Hanawalt and David Wallace. Medieval Cultures 16. Minneapolis: University of Minnesota, 1999, pp. 70–89.

Mills, Robert. 'Violence, Community and the Materialisation of Belief'. In *A Companion to Middle English Hagiography*, ed. Sarah Salih. Cambridge: D. S. Brewer, 2006, pp. 87–103.

———. *Suspended Animation: Pain, Pleasure, and Punishment in Medieval Culture*. London: Reaktion Books, 2005.

———. '"Whatever You Do Is a Delight to Me": Masculinity, Masochism, and Queer Play in Representations of Male Martyrdom'. *Exemplaria* 13.1 (2001): 1–37

Milner, Anthony. 'The Sacred Capons'. *Musical Times* 114.1561 (1973): 250–2.

Mitamura, Taisuke. *Chinese Eunuchs: The Structure of Intimate Politics*. Rutland, VT: C. E. Tuttle Co, 1970.

Mitchell, Bruce. *Old English Syntax*, 2 vols. Oxford: Clarendon Press, 1985.

Mitchell, Sarah. 'Kings, Constitution and Crisis: "Robert of Gloucester" and the Anglo-Saxon Remedy'. In *Literary Appropriations of the Anglo-Saxons from the Thirteenth to the Twentieth Century*, ed. Donald Scragg and Carole Weinberg. Cambridge Studies in Anglo-Saxon England. Cambridge: Cambridge University Press, 2000, pp. 39–56.

Mol, Johannes A. 'Gallows in Late Medieval Frisia'. In *Advances in Old Frisian Philology*, ed. Rolf H. Bremmer Jr, Stephen Laker, and Oebele Vries. Amsterdamer Beiträge zur älteren Germanistik 64. Amsterdam and New York: Rodopi, 2007, pp. 263–99.

Mooney, Catherine M., ed. *Gendered Voices: Medieval Saints and Their Interpreters*. Philadelphia: University of Pennsylvania Press, 1999.

Moran, Neil. 'Byzantine *Castrati*'. *Plainsong and Medieval Music* 11.2 (2002): 99–112.

Muir, Bernard, ed. *The Exeter Anthology of Old English Poetry*, 2nd edn, 2 vols. Exeter: University of Exeter Press, 2000.

Mukherjee, J. B. 'Castration – A Means of Induction into the *Hijirah* Group of the Eunuch Community in India'. *American Journal of Forensic Medicine and Pathology* 1.1 (1980): 61–5.

Murison, Charles Leslie. *Rebellion and Reconstruction: Galba to Domitian. An Historical Commentary on Cassius Dio's* Roman History *Books 64–67 (AD 68–96)*. Atlanta, GA: Scholars Press, 1999.

Murphy, Patrick J. *Unriddling the Exeter Riddles*. University Park: Pennsylvania State University Press, 2011.

Murray, Jacqueline. 'Sexual Mutilation and Castration Anxiety: A Medieval Perspective'.

In *The Boswell Thesis: Essays on Christianity, Social Tolerance, and Homosexuality*, ed. Matthew S. Kuefler. Chicago: University of Chicago Press, 2006, pp. 254–72.

———. '"The law of sin that is in my members": The Problem of Male Embodiment'. In *Gender and Holiness: Men, Women and Saints in Late Medieval Europe*, ed. Samantha J. E. Riches and Sarah Salih. Routledge Studies in Medieval Religion and Culture. New York and London: Routledge, 2002, pp. 9–22.

———. 'Mystical Castration: Some Reflections on Peter Abelard, Hugh of Lincoln and Sexual Control'. In *Conflicted Identities and Multiple Masculinities: Men in the Medieval West*, ed. Jacqueline Murray. Garland Medieval Casebooks 25. Garland Reference Library of the Humanities 2078. New York: Garland Publishing, 1999, pp. 73–91.

———. 'Hiding Behind the Universal Man: Male Sexuality in the Middle Ages'. In *The Handbook of Medieval Sexuality*, ed. Vern L. Bullough and James A. Brundage. Garland Reference Library of the Humanities 1696. New York: Garland Publishing, 1996, rpt. 2000, pp. 123–52.

Musson, Anthony. *Boundaries of the Law: Geography, Gender and Jurisdiction in Medieval and Early Modern Europe*. Aldershot: Ashgate, 2005.

———. *Medieval Law in Context: The Growth of Legal Consciousness from Magna Carta to the Peasants' Revolt*. Manchester: Manchester University Press, 2001.

Muth, Robert. 'Kastration'. In *Reallexikon für Antike und Christentum. Sachwörterbuch zur Auseinandersetzung des Christentums mit der antiken Welt*, ed. Georg Schöllgen *et al.* vols. 1–24 (in progress). Stuttgart: Anton Hierschmann, 2004, vol. 20, cols. 285–342.

Nachtigal, Gustav. *Sahara and Sudan: Wadai and Darfur*, trans. Allan G. B. Fisher and Humphrey J. Fisher. London: C. Hurst, 1971.

Nanda, Serena. *Neither Man Nor Woman: The* Hijras *of India*. Belmont, CA: Wadsworth Publishing Co., 1999.

———. '*Hijras*: An Alternative Sex and Gender Role in India'. In *Third Sex, Third Gender: Beyond Sexual Dimorphism in Culture and History*, ed. Gilbert Herdt. New York: Zone Books, 1994, pp. 373–417.

Nelson, Marie. 'The Rhetoric of the Exeter Book Riddles'. *Speculum* 49 (1974): 421–40.

Newlands, Carole E. *Statius'* Silvae *and the Poetics of Empire*. Cambridge: Cambridge University Press, 2002.

Nicholson, Helen. *Love, War, and the Grail*. Leiden: Brill, 2001.

Ní Chonaill, Brónagh. 'Impotence, Disclosure and Outcome: Some Medieval Irish Legal Comment'. Online at http://www.arts.gla.ac.uk/scottishstudies/earticles/LegalConcern.pdf. Accessed October 18, 2011.

Niederhellmann, Annette. *Arzt und Heilkunde in den frühmittelalterlichen Leges*. Arbeiten zur Frühmittelalterforschung 12. Berlin and New York: Walter de Gruyter, 1983.

Niles, John D. *Old English Enigmatic Poems and the Play of the Texts*. Turnhout: Brepols, 2006.

Nijdam, Han. *Lichaam, eer en recht in middeleeuws Friesland. Een studie naar de Oudfriese boeteregisters*. Hilversum: Verloren, 2008.

Nitze, William A. *Perceval and the Holy Grail: An Essay on the Romance of Chrétien de Troyes*. Berkeley and Los Angeles: University of California Press, 1949.

Noomen, Paul N. 'De Friese vetemaatschappij: sociale structuur en machtsbases'. In *Fryslân, staat en macht 1450–1650*, ed. Johan Frieswijk, Arend H. Huussen Jr, and Y. B. Kuiper. Hilversum: Verloren, 1999, pp. 43–64.

Nunn, Hillary M. *Staging Anatomies: Dissection and Spectacle in Early Stuart Tragedy*. Literary and Scientific Cultures and Early Modernity. Aldershot: Ashgate, 2005.

Nutt, A. *Studies on the Legend of the Holy Grail with Especial References to the Hypothesis of Its Celtic Origin*. London: Harrison and Sons, Printers, 1888. Rpt Whitefish, MT: Kessinger Publishing, 2003.

O'Brien O'Keeffe, Katherine. 'Body and Law in Late Anglo-Saxon England'. *Anglo-Saxon England* 27 (1998): 209–32.

Ó Cróinín, Dáibhí. *Early Medieval Ireland: 400–1200*. New York: Longman, 1995.
Oliver, Lisi. *The Body Legal in Barbarian Law*. Toronto: University of Toronto Press, 2011.
———. *The Beginnings of English Law*. Toronto: University of Toronto Press, 2002.
———. 'Forced and Unforced Rape in Early Irish Law'. *Proceedings of the Harvard Celtic Colloquium* 13 (1993): 93–105.
Olson, Todd P. '"Long Live the Knife": Andrea Sacchi's Portrait of Marcantonio Pasqualini'. *Art History* 27.5 (2004): 697–722.
Orgel, Stephen. *Impersonations: The Performance of Gender in Shakespeare's England*. Cambridge: Cambridge University Press, 1996.
Owen, Morfydd E. 'The *Excerpta de Libris Romanorum et Francorum* and *Cyfraith Hywel*'. In *Tair Colofn Cyfraith, The Three Columns of Law in Medieval Wales: Homicide, Theft and Fire*, ed. T. M. Charles-Edwards and Paul Russell. Welsh Legal History Society 5. Bangor: Welsh Legal History Society, 2005, pp. 171–95.
Partner, Nancy F. 'No Sex, No Gender'. *Speculum* 68.2 (1993): 419–43.
Patterson, Lee. 'Chaucer's Pardoner on the Couch: Psyche and Clio in Medieval Literary Studies'. *Speculum* 76.3 (2001): 638–80.
Patterson, Orlando. 'The Ultimate Slave'. In *Slavery and Social Death: A Comparative Study*. Cambridge, MA: Harvard University Press, 1982, pp. 299–333.
Pauphilet, A. *Études sur la queste del Saint Graal attribuée à Gautier Map*. Paris: Champion, 1921.
Payer, Pierre J. *Sex and the Penitentials: The Development of a Sexual Code, 550–1150*. Toronto: University of Toronto Press, 1984.
Peers, G. 'Apprehending the Archangel Michael: Hagiographic Method'. *Byzantine and Modern Greek Studies* 20 (1996): 100–21.
Pelikan, Eugen. *Gerichtlich-medicinische Untersuchungen über das Skopzenthum in Russland*, with historical notes by E. Pelikan, trans. from Russian into German by N. Iwanoff. Giessen: J. Ricker, 1876.
Pelteret, David A. E. *Slavery in Early Medieval England: From the Reign of Alfred until the Twelfth Century*. Woodbridge: Boydell Press, 1995.
Penuel, Suzanne. 'Castrating the Creditor in *The Merchant of Venice*'. *Studies in English Literature, 1500–1900* 44.2: Tudor and Stuart Drama (2004): 255–75.
Pequigney, Joseph. 'The Two Antonios and Same Sex Love in *Twelfth Night* and *The Merchant of Venice*'. In *Shakespeare and Gender: A History*, ed. Deborah E. Barker and Ivo Kamps. London: Verso, 1995, pp. 178–95.
Pittard, Eugène. *La castration chez l'homme et les modifications morphologiques qu'elle entraîne. Recherches sur les adeptes d'une secte d'eunuques mystiques: Les Skoptzy*. Paris: Masson et Cie, 1934.
Plymate, Stephen. 'Hypogonadism in Men: An Overview'. In *Androgens in Health and Disease*, ed. Carrie J. Bagatell and William J. Bremner. Totowa, NJ: Humana Press, 2003, pp. 45–76.
Poirion, Daniel, ed. *Précis de littérature française du Moyen Âge*. Paris: Presses Universitaires de France, 1983.
Pollock, Sir Frederick, and Frederic William Maitland. *The History of English Law before the Time of Edward I*, 2nd edn. Cambridge: Cambridge University Press, 1898. Rpt Indianapolis, IN: Liberty Fund, 2009.
Porter, Roy. 'History of the Body Reconsidered'. In *New Perspectives on Historical Writing*, 2nd edn, ed. Peter Burke. University Park: Pennsylvania State University Press, 2001, pp. 233–60.
Potter, John. 'The Tenor-*Castrato* Connection, 1760–1860'. *Early Music* 35.1 (2007): 97–112.
Powell, Timothy E. 'The "Three Orders" of Society in Anglo-Saxon England', *Anglo-Saxon England* 23 (1994): 103–32.
Pratt, Karen. 'Translating Misogamy: The Authority of the Intertext in the

Lamentationes Matheoluli and Its Middle French Translation by Jean LeFèvre.' *Forum for Modern Language Studies* 35.4 (1999): 421–35.
Preston, Laurence W. 'A Right to Exist: Eunuchs and the State in Nineteenth-Century India'. *Modern Asian Studies* 21.2 (1987): 371–87.
Prioreschi, Plinio. *A History of Medicine*, vol. 5: *Medieval Medicine*. Omaha, NE: Horatius Press, 2003.
Prochownick, Ludwig. *Beiträge zur Castrationsfrage: Nach einem am 6. April 1886 im ärztlichen Vereine zu Hamburg gehaltenen Vortrage*. Leipzig: A. Th. Engelhardt, 1886.
Rabin, Andrew. 'The Wolf's Testimony to the English: Law and the Witness in the *Sermo Lupi ad Anglos*'. *JEGP* 105 (2006): 388–414.
Rand, E. K. 'The Metamorphosis of Ovid in *Le roman de la rose*'. In *Studies in the History of Culture*, ed. Percy W. Long, 1942. Rpt Freeport, NY: Books for Libraries, 1969. 103–21.
Renault, Mary, *The Persian Boy* (London: Longman, 1972)
Retief, F.P., J.F.G. Cilliers, and S. Riekert. 'Eunuchs in the Bible'. *Acta Theologica* 26.2 (2010): 247–58.
Richards, Earl Jeffrey. 'The Tradition of "otium litteratum" and Oiseuse in *Le roman de la rose*'. *Studi francesi* 32 (1988): 71–3.
———. 'Reflections on Oiseuse's Mirror: Iconographic Tradition, Luxuria and the *Roman de la rose*'. *Zeitschrift für romanische Philologie* 98 (1982): 296–311.
Richards, Mary. 'The Body as Text in Early Anglo-Saxon Law'. In *Naked Before God: Uncovering the Body in Anglo-Saxon England*, ed. Benjamin C. Withers and Jonathan Wilcox. Morgantown: West Virginia University Press, 2003, pp. 97–115.
Riches, Samantha J. E., and Sarah Salih, eds. *Gender and Holiness: Men, Women and Saints in Late Medieval Europe*. Routledge Studies in Medieval Religion and Culture. New York and London: Routledge, 2002.
———. 'St George as a Male Virgin Martyr'. In *Gender and Holiness: Men, Women and Saints in Late Medieval Europe*, ed. Samantha J. E. Riches and Sarah Salih. Routledge Studies in Medieval Religion and Culture. New York and London: Routledge, 2002, pp. 65–85
Richlin, Amy. 'Invective against Women in Roman Satire'. In *Latin Verse Satire: An Anthology and Critical Reader*, ed. Paul Allen Miller. New York and London: Routledge, 2005, pp. 377–89.
Rieger, Conrad. *Die Castration in rechtlicher, socialer und vitaler Hinsicht*. Jena: Fischer, 1900.
Riisøy, Anne Irene. *Sexuality, Law and Legal Practice and the Reformation in Norway*. Leiden and Boston: Brill, 2009.
Ringrose, Kathryn M. *The Perfect Servant: Eunuchs and the Social Construction of Gender in Byzantium*. Chicago: University of Chicago Press, 2003.
———. 'Passing the Test of Sanctity: Denial of Sexuality and Involuntary Castration'. In *Desire and Denial in Byzantium*, ed. Liz James. Aldershot: Ashgate, 1999, pp. 123–37.
———. 'Living in the Shadows: Eunuchs and Gender in Byzantium.' In *Third Sex, Third Gender: Beyond Sexual Dimorphism in Culture and History*, ed. Gilbert Herdt. New York: Zone, 1996.
Roberts, Alexander, and James. Donaldson, eds. *The Ante-Nicene Fathers*. 10 vols. Peabody, MA: Hendrickson, 1995.
Roberts, Anna. 'Queer Fisher King: Castration as a Site of Queer Representation (*Perceval, Stabat Mater, The City of God*)'. *Arthuriana*, 11.3 (2001): 49–88.
Roberts, Brynley. 'Geoffrey of Monmouth and Welsh Historical Tradition'. *Nottingham Medieval Studies* 20 (1976): 29–40.
Roberts, Lesley F., Michelle A. Brett, Thomas W. Johnson, and Richard J. Wassersug. 'A Passion for Castration: Characterizing Men who Are Fascinated with Castration, but Have not Been Castrated'. *Journal of Sexual Medicine* 5.7 (2008): 1669–80.

Roller, Lynn E. *In Search of God the Mother: The Cult of Anatolian Cybele.* Berkeley and Los Angeles: University of California Press, 1999.

Rollinger, Robert. 'Extreme Gewalt und Strafgericht. Ktesias und Herodot als Zeugnisse für den Achaimenidenhof'. In *Der Achämenidenhof*, ed. Bruno Jacobs and Robert Rollinger. Wiesbaden: Harrassowitz, 2010, pp. 559–666.

Rosselli, John. 'The *Castrati* as a Professional Group and a Social Phenomenon, 1550–1850'. *Acta Musicologica* 60.2 (1988): 143–79.

Rouyer, Jules. 'Des eunuques'. *Gazette medicale de Paris* 14 (1859): 601–2, 606, 609.

Rubin, Miri. 'The Person in the Form: Medieval Challenges to Bodily Order'. In *Framing Medieval Bodies*, ed. Sarah Kay and Miri Rubin. Manchester: Manchester University Press, 1994, pp. 100–22.

Rubin, Stanley. 'The *Bot*, or Composition in Anglo-Saxon Law: A Reassessment'. *Legal History* 17 (1996): 144–54.

Salih, Sarah. *Versions of Virginity in Late Medieval England.* Cambridge: D. S. Brewer, 2001.

Salisbury, Joyce E. *The Beast Within: Animals in the Middle Ages.* New York and London: Routledge, 2011.

———. 'Gendered Sexuality.' In *Handbook of Medieval Sexuality*, ed. Vern L. Bullough and James A. Brundage. New York: Garland, 1996, pp. 81–102.

———. 'Bestiality in the Middle Ages'. In *Sex in the Middle Ages: A Book of Essays*, ed. J. E. Salisbury. New York: Garland, 1991, pp. 173–86.

Salvador, Mercedes. 'The Key to the Body: Unlocking Riddles 42–46'. In *Naked Before God: Uncovering the Body in Anglo-Saxon England*, ed. Benjamin C. Withers and Jonathan Wilcox. Morgantown: West Virginia University Press, 2003, pp. 60–96.

Sanderlin, Sarah. 'The Manuscripts of the Annals of Clonmacnoise'. *Proceedings of the Royal Irish Academy* 82C (1982): 111–23.

Sanock, Catherine. *Her Life Historical: Exemplarity and Female Saints' Lives in Late Medieval England.* The Middle Ages Series. Philadelphia: University of Pennsylvania Press, 2007.

Saunders, Corinne. *Rape and Ravishment in the Literature of Medieval England.* Cambridge: D. S. Brewer, 2001.

Sawday, Jonathan. *The Body Emblazoned: Dissection and the Human Body in Renaissance Culture.* New York and London: Routledge, 1995.

Schaff, Philip, ed. *The Nicene and Post-Nicene Fathers.* 14 vols. Series 2. Peabody, MA: Hendrickson, 1999.

Schild, Wolfgang. 'Der gequählte und entehrte Körper. Spekulative Vorbemerkungen zu einer noch zu schreibenden Geschichte des Strafrecht'. In *Gepeinigt, begehrt, vergessen. Symbolik und Sozialbezug des Körpers im späteren Mittelalter und in der frühen Neuzeit*, ed. Klaus Schreiner and Norbert Schnitzler. Munich: Wilhelm Fink, 1992, pp. 147–68.

Schmidt-Wiegand, Ruth. 'Spuren paganer Religiosität in den frühmittelalterlichen Leges'. In Iconologia sacra*: Mythos, Bildkunst und Dichtung in der Religions- und Sozialgeschichte Alteuropas*, ed. Hagen Keller and Nikolaus Staubach. Berlin and New York: Walter de Gruyter, 1994.

Scholten, Helga. *Der Eunuch in Kaisernähe: zur politischen und sozialen Bedeutung des* praepositus sacri cubiculi *im 4. und 5. Jahrhundert n. Chr.* Frankfurt and New York: Peter Lang, 1995.

Scholz, Piotr O. *Eunuchs and* Castrati*: A Cultural History*, trans. John A. Broadwin and Shelley L. Frisch. Princeton, NJ: Markus Wiener Publishers, 2001.

Schrader, Richard J. 'Succession and Glory in *Beowulf*. *JEGP* 90 (1991): 491–504.

Schubert, Ernst. 'Vom Wergeld zur Strafe: die übersehene Bedeutung der friesischen Rechtsquellen zur Interpretation eines epochalen mittelalterlichen Wandels'. In *Tota Frisia in Teilansichten: Hajo van Lengen zum 65. Geburtstag*, ed. Heinrich Schmidt,

Wolfgang Schwarz and Martin Tielke. Aurich: Ostfriesische Landschaft, 2005, pp. 97–120.

Schulz, F. N., and O. Falk. 'Phosphorsäureausscheidung nach Castration'. *Zeitschrift für Physiologische Chemie* 27.3 (1899): 250–4.

Schumacher, Gert-Horst. 'Principles of Skeletal Growth'. In *Fundamentals of Craniofacial Growth*, ed. Andrew D. Dixon, David A. N. Hoyte, and Ollie Ronning. New York: CRC Press, 1997, pp. 1–21.

Segal, Ronald. *Islam's Black Slaves: The Other Black Diaspora*. New York: Farrar, Straus and Giroux, 2001.

Sellheim, Hugo. 'Castration und Knochenwachsthum'. *Beiträge zur Geburtshülfe und Gynäkologie* 2 (1899).

Siems, Harald. *Studien zur* Lex Frisionum. Abhandlungen zur rechtswissenschaftlichen Grundlagenforschung 42. Ebelsbach: Rolf Gremer, 1980.

Simms, Katharine. *Medieval Gaelic Sources*. Maynooth Research Guides for Irish Local History 14. Dublin: Four Courts Press, 2009.

——. *From Kings to Warlords*. Studies in Celtic History 7. Woodbridge: Boydell Press, 1987.

Skinner, Marilyn B. '*Ego mulier*: The Construction of Male Sexuality in Catullus'. *Helios* 20 (1993): 107–30.

Smith, D. Vance. 'Body Doubles: Producing the Masculine Corpus.' In *Becoming Male in the Middle Ages*, ed. Jeffrey Jerome Cohen and Bonnie Wheeler. The New Middle Ages 4. New York: Garland, 1997, pp. 3–19.

Smith, J. Beverley. *The Sense of History in Medieval Wales*. Aberystwyth: University College of Wales, 1991.

Smith, James O. 'The High Priests of the Temple of Artemis in Ephesus'. In *Cybele, Attis and Related Cults*, ed. Eugene N. Lane. Leiden: Brill, 1996, pp. 323–35.

Sørenson, Preben Meulengracht. *The Unmanly Man: Concepts of Sexual Defamation in Early Northern Society*. Odense: Odense University Press, 1983.

Speed, Diane. 'The Construction of the Nation in Medieval English Romance'. In *Readings in Medieval English Romance*, ed. Carol M. Meale. Cambridge: D. S. Brewer, 1994, pp. 135–57.

Spencer, Diana. *The Roman Alexander: Reading a Cultural Myth*. Exeter: University of Exeter Press, 2002.

Spreitzer, Birgitte. *Die stumme Sünde: Homosexualität im Mittelalter*. Göppingen: Kümmerle, 1988.

Stacey, Robin Chapman. *Dark Speech: The Performance of Law in Early Ireland*. Philadelphia: University of Pennsylvania Press, 2007.

——. *The Road to Judgment: From Custom to Court in Medieval Ireland and Wales*. Philadelphia: University of Pennsylvania Press, 1994.

Stafford, Pauline. 'Succession and Inheritance: A Gendered Perspective on Alfred's Family History'. In *Alfred the Great: Papers from the Eleventh-Centenary Conference*, ed. Timothy Reuter. Aldershot: Ashgate, 2003, pp. 251–64.

Stent, Carter G. 'Chinese Eunuchs'. *Journal of the North China Branch of the Royal Asiatic Society* new series 11 (1876): 143–84.

Stevenson, Walter. 'Eunuchs and Early Christianity.' In *Eunuchs in Antiquity and Beyond*, ed. Shaun Tougher. London: Classical Press of Wales and Duckworth, 2002, pp. 123–42.

——. 'The Rise of Eunuchs in Greco-Roman Antiquity.' *Journal of the History of Sexuality* 5.4 (1995): 495–511.

Stokes, Whitley. 'The Annals of Ulster'. *Revue celtique* 18 (1897): 74–86.

Stortz, Martha Ellen. '"Where or When Was Your Servant Innocent?": Augustine on Childhood'. In *The Child in Christian Thought*, ed. Marcia Bunge. Grand Rapids, MI: W. B. Eerdmans Publishing Company, 2001, pp. 78–102.

Stratakis, Constantine A., Alessandra Vottero, Angela Brodie, Lawrence S. Kirschner, David DeAtkine, Qing Lu, *et al.* 'The Aromatase Excess Syndrome Is Associated with Feminization of Both Sexes and Autosomal Dominant Transmission of Aberrant P450 Aromatase Gene Transcription'. *Journal of Clinical Endocrinology and Metabolism* 83.4 (1998): 1348–57.

Suppe, Frederick. 'The Cultural Significance of Decapitation in High Medieval Wales and the Marches'. *Bulletin of the Board of Celtic Studies* 36 (1989): 146–60.

Tabuteau, Emily Zack. 'Punishments in Eleventh-Century Normandy'. In *Conflict in Medieval Europe: Changing Perspectives on Society and Culture*, ed. Warren C. Brown and Piotr Górecki. Aldershot: Ashgate, 2003, pp. 131–49.

Talbott, Rick Franklin. 'Imagining the Matthean Eunuch Community: Kyriarchy on the Chopping Block'. *Journal of Feminist Studies in Religion* 22.1 (2006): 21–43.

Tandler, Julius, and Siegfried Grosz. 'Über den Einfluss eer Kastration auf den Organismus I. Beschreibung eines Eunuchen Skeletes'. *Archiv für Entwicklungsmechanik der Organismen* 27 (1909): 35–45.

———. 'Über den Einfluss eer Kastration auf den Organismus II. Die Skopzen'. *Archiv für Entwicklungsmechanik der Organismen* 28 (1910): 236–53.

———. 'Über den Einfluss eer Kastration auf den Organismus III. Die Eunuchoide'. *Archiv für Entwicklungsmechanik der Organismen* 29 (1910): 290–324.

Taylor, Gary. *Castration: An Abbreviated History of Western Manhood.* New York and London: Routledge, 2002.

Tempera, Mariangela. '*Titus Andronicus*: Staging the Mutilated Body'. In *Questioning Bodies in Shakespeare's Rome*, ed. Maria del Sapio Garbero, Nancy Isenberg, and Maddalena Pennacchia. Goettingen: V&R Unipress, 2010, pp. 109–19.

Thurneysen, Rudolf. 'Die Bürgschaft im irischen Recht'. *Forschungen und Fortschritte* 4.18 (1928): 183.

———. 'Irische Recht'. II. Zu den unteren Ständen in Irland: *Abhandlungen der preussischen Akademie der Wissenschaften, Philosophisch-historische* 2. Berlin: Verlag der Akademie der Wissenschaften, 1931, pp. 60–87.

Tilliette, Jean-Yves. 'Repères chronologiques' and introduction. In *Lettres d'Abélard et Héloïse*, ed. and trans. Éric Hicks and Thérèse Moreau. Paris: Librairie Générale Française, 2007, pp. 36–7.

Tomasch, Sylvia. 'Postcolonial Chaucer and the Virtual Jew'. In *The Postcolonial Middle Ages*, ed. Jeffrey Jerome Cohen. New York: St Martin's Press, 2000, pp. 243–60.

Tompkins, Peter. *The Eunuch and the Virgin: A Study of Curious Customs.* New York: C. N. Potter, 1962.

Tougher, Shaun. *The Roman* Castrati*: Eunuchs of the Roman Empire* (forthcoming).

———. *The Eunuch in Byzantine History and Society.* London and New York: Routledge, 2008.

———. 'The Renault Bagoas: The Treatment of Alexander the Great's Eunuch in Mary Renault's *The Persian Boy*'. *New Voices in Classical Reception Studies* 3 (2008): 77–89.

———. 'Social Transformation, Gender Transformation? The Court Eunuch, 300–900'. In *Gender in the Early Medieval World: East and West, 300–900*, ed. Leslie Brubaker and Julia M. H. Smith. Cambridge: Cambridge University Press, 2004, pp. 70–82.

———. ed. *Eunuchs in Antiquity and Beyond.* London: Classical Press of Wales and Duckworth, 2002.

———. 'Images of Effeminate Men: The Case of the Byzantine Eunuchs'. In *Masculinity in Medieval Europe*, ed. Dawn M. Hadley. London: Longman, 1999, pp. 89–100.

———.'Byzantine Eunuchs: An Overview, with Special Reference to Their Creation and Origin'. In *Men, Women and Eunuchs: Gender in Byzantium*, ed. Liz James. New York and London: Routledge, 1997, pp. 168–84.

Tournés, G. *La liberté par l'humanité Les eunuques en Égypte. Extrait des notes sur l'Égypte (inédit).* Geneva: Vaney, 1869.

Tracy, Larissa. *Torture and Brutality in Medieval Literature: Negotiations of National Identity*. Cambridge: D. S. Brewer, 2012.

———. 'The Uses of Torture and Violence in the Fabliaux: When Comedy Crosses the Line'. *Florilegium* 23.2 (2006): 143–68.

———. *Women of the Gilte Legende: A Selection of Female Saints' Lives*. Cambridge: D. S. Brewer, 2003.

Treschow, Michael. 'The Prologue to Alfred's Law Code: Instruction in the Spirit of Mercy'. *Florilegium* 13 (1994): 79–110

Tsai, Shih-shan Henry. *The Eunuchs in the Ming Dynasty*. Albany, NY: SUNY Press, 1996.

Tuchel, Susan. *Kastration im Mittelalter*. Studia Humaniora 30. Düsseldorf: Droste, 1998.

Turcan, Robert. *The Cults of the Roman Empire*, trans. Antonia Nevill. Oxford: Blackwell, 1996.

Turner, Bryan S. *The Body and Society: Explorations in Social Theory*, 2nd edn. London: Sage Publications, 1996.

Uebel, Michael. 'On Becoming Male.' In *Becoming Male in the Middle Ages*, ed. Jeffrey Jerome Cohen and Bonnie Wheeler. The New Middle Ages 4. New York: Garland, 2000, pp. 367–84.

Uitti, Karl D. '"Cele [qui] doit estre Rose clamee" *Rose*, vv. 40–44: Guillaume's Intentionality'. In *Rethinking the* Romance of the Rose: *Text, Image, Reception*, ed. Kevin Brownlee and Sylvia Huot. Philadelphia: University of Pennsylvania Press, 1992, pp. 39–64.

Valante, Mary A. *The Vikings in Ireland: Settlement, Trade and Urbanization*. Dublin: Four Courts Press, 2008.

Vanderschueren, Dirk, Steven Boonen, and Roger Bouillon. 'Action of Androgens versus Estrogens in Male Skeletal Homeostasis'. *Bone* 23.5 (1998): 391–4.

Vickers, Nancy J. 'Members Only: Marot's Anatomical Blazons'. In *The Body in Parts: Fantasies of Corporeality in Early Modern Europe*, ed. David Hillman and Carla Mazzio. New York and London: Routledge, 1997, pp. 2–21.

Vitz, Evelyn Birge. '*Le Roman de la Rose*, Performed'. Abstract for a paper presented at Fordham University conference 'Think Romance!' March 31–April 1, 2012. Online at http://www.fordham.edu/mvst/conference12/Romance/Vitz.pdf, accessed May 20, 2012.

Vout, Caroline. *Power and Eroticism in Imperial Rome*. Cambridge: Cambridge University Press, 2007.

Wagenseil, Ferdinand. 'Beiträge zur Kenntnis der Kastrationsfolgen und des Eunchoidismus beim Mann'. *Zeitschrift für Morphologie und Anthropologie* 26.2 (1927): 264–304.

———. 'Chinesische Eunuchen. (Zugleich ein Beitrag zur Kenntnis der Kastrationsfolgen und der rassialen und körperbaulichen Bedeutung der anthropologischen Merkmale)'. *Zeitschrift für Morphologie und Anthropologie* 32.3 (1933): 415–68.

Warner, Marina. *Alone of All Her Sex: The Myth and the Cult of the Virgin Mary*. New York: Vintage, 1976.

Weinstein, Richard L., Robert P. Kelch, M. R. Jenner, Selna L. Kaplan, and Melvin M. Grumbach. 'Secretion of Unconjugated Androgens and Estrogens by the Normal and Abnormal Human Testis Before and After Human Chorionic Gonadotropin'. *Journal of Clinical Investigation* 53.1 (1974): 1–6.

Wheeler, Bonnie. 'Origenary Fantasties: Abelard's Castration and Confession'. In *Becoming Male in the Middle Ages*, ed. Jeffrey Jerome Cohen and Bonnie Wheeler. The New Middle Ages 4. New York: Garland Publishing, 2000, pp. 107–28.

Whitelock, Dorothy. *The Beginnings of English Society*. London: Penguin, 1954.

Whitman, James Q. *The Origins of Reasonable Doubt: Theological Roots of the Criminal Trial*. New Haven, CT: Yale University Press, 2008.

Wilfong, Terry G. *Women of Jeme: Lives in a Coptic Town in Late Antique Egypt*. Ann Arbor: University of Michigan Press, 2002.

Williams, Craig A. *Roman Homosexuality*. 2nd edn. New York: Oxford University Press, 2010.

Wilson, Anne. *The Magical Quest: The Use of Magic in Arthurian Romance*. Manchester: Manchester University Press, 1990.

Wilson, Jean D., and Claus Roehrborn. 'Long-Term Consequences of Castration in Men: Lessons from the Skoptzy and the Eunuchs of the Chinese and Ottoman Courts'. *Journal of Clinical Endocrinology and Metabolism* 84.12 (1999): 4324–31.

Winstead, Karen, ed. *Chaste Passions: Medieval English Virgin Martyr Legends*. Ithaca, NY: Cornell University Press, 2000.

———. *Virgin Martyrs: Legends of Sainthood in Late Medieval England*. Ithaca, NY: Cornell University Press, 1997.

Winters, Stephen J., and Barbara J. Clark. 'Testosterone Synthesis, Transport and Metabolism'. In *Androgens in Health and Disease*, ed. Carrie J. Bagatell and William J. Bremner. Totowa, NJ: Humana Press, 2003, pp. 3–22.

Wogan-Browne, Jocelyn. 'Chaste Bodies: Frames and Experiences'. In *Framing Medieval Bodies*, ed. Sarah Kay and Miri Rubin. Manchester: Manchester University Press, 1994, pp. 24–42.

———. *Saints' Lives and Women's Literary Culture c. 1150–1300: Virginity and Its Authorisations*. Oxford: Oxford University Press, 2001.

Wolf, Gerhard K., Wolfgang Anderhuber, and Frank Kuhn. 'Development of the Paranasal Sinuses in Children: Implications for Paranasal Sinus Surgery'. *Annals of Otology, Rhinology and Laryngology* 102 (1993): 705–11.

Woods, David. 'Nero and Sporus'. *Latomus* 68 (2009): 73–82.

Wormald, Patrick. 'The *Leges Barbarorum*: Law and Ethnicity in the Medieval West'. In Regna *and* Gentes*: The Relationship between Late Antique and Early Medieval Peoples and Kingdoms in the Transformation of the Roman World*, ed. Hans-Werner Goetz, Jörg Jarnut, and Walter Pohl. Leiden and Boston: Brill, 2003, pp. 21–53.

———. *The Making of English Law: King Alfred to the Twelfth Century*, vol. 1: *Legislation and Its Limits*. Oxford: Blackwell, 2001.

———. *The Making of English Law: King Alfred to the Twelfth Century*. Oxford: Blackwell, 1999.

———. '*Lex Scripta* and *Verbum Regis*: Legislation and Germanic Kingship, from Euric to Cnut'. In *Early Medieval Kingship*, ed. P. H. Sawyer and I. N. Wood. Leeds: University of Leeds, 1977, pp. 105–38.

Wu, Chieh Ping, and Fang-Liu Gu. 'The Prostate in Eunuchs'. *EORTC Genitourinary Group Monograph* 10 (1991): 249–55.

Wyatt, David R. *Slaves and Warriors in Medieval Britain and Ireland, 800–1200*. Leiden: Brill, 2009.

Zhu, Xie. *Zheng He*. Beijing: Sheng huo, du shu, xin zhi san lian shu dian, 1956.

Index

www.ingramcontent.com/pod-product-compliance
Lightning Source LLC
LaVergne TN
LVHW020504100826
845148LV00003B/695

9781843845249